Islam and Rationality

Islamic Philosophy, Theology and Science

TEXTS AND STUDIES

Edited by

Hans Daiber
Anna Akasoy
Emilie Savage-Smith

VOLUME 98

The titles published in this series are listed at *brill.com/ipts*

Islam and Rationality

The Impact of al-Ghazālī. Papers Collected on His 900th Anniversary. Vol. 2

Edited by

Frank Griffel

BRILL

LEIDEN | BOSTON

Cover illustration: Colored reproduction of a water-painting, probably lost, by the artist André Sevruguin (also: Sevrugian, 1894–1996) from Ernst Diez' *Die Kunst der islamischen Völker* (Berlin Akademische Verlagsgesellschaft Athenaion 1915). It shows the ruins of a building that we think is the mausoleum of al-Ghazali in his hometown Tabaran-Tus in Iran. For more information on the building see p. 173 of this book.

This publication has been typeset in the multilingual "Brill" typeface. With over 5,100 characters covering Latin, IPA, Greek, and Cyrillic, this typeface is especially suitable for use in the humanities.
For more information, please see www.brill.com/brill-typeface.

ISSN 0169-8729
ISBN 978-90-04-30695-0 (hardback)
ISBN 978-90-04-30749-0 (e-book)

Contents

Preface VII
List of Figures and Tables XVI
List of Contributors XVII
Keys and Conventions XX

PART I
Al-Ghazālī's Works and His Thought

1 **Al-Ghazālī on Error** 3
Taneli Kukkonen

2 **Al-Ghazālī's Concept of Philosophy** 32
Ulrich Rudolph

3 **Problems in al-Ghazālī's Perfect World**
Objections and Counter-Objections to His Best Possible World Thesis 54
Stephen R. Ogden

4 **Al-Ghazālī's Teleology and the Galenic Tradition**
***Reading* The Wisdom in God's Creations (al-Ḥikma fī makhlūqāt Allah)** 90
Ahmed El Shamsy

5 **Al-Ghazālī and *Kalām***
The Conundrum of His Body-Soul Dualism 113
Ayman Shihadeh

6 **Al-Ghazālī's Veil Section**
Comparative Religion before Religionswissenschaft? 142
Anna Ayşe Akasoy

7 **Is There an Autograph of al-Ghazālī in MS Yale, Landberg 318?** 168
Frank Griffel

PART II
Al-Ghazālī's Influence

8 Intuition, Intellection, and Mystical Knowledge
Delineating Fakhr al-Dīn al-Rāzī's Cognitive Theories 189
Damien Janos

9 Fakhr al-Dīn al-Rāzī's Use of al-Ghazālī's *Mishkāt* in His Commentary on the Light Verse (Q 24:35) 229
Jules Janssens

10 Ottoman Perceptions of al-Ghazālī's Works and Discussions on His Historical Role in Its Late Period 253
M. Sait Özervarlı

11 Al-Ghazālī's "Demarcation of Science"
A Commonplace Apology in the Muslim Reception of Modern Science—and Its Limitations 283
Martin Riexinger

12 The Revival of the Religious Sciences in the Twenty-First Century
Su'ād al-Ḥakīm's Adaptation of al-Ghazālī's Revival 310
Kenneth Garden

Indices

General Index of Names and Subjects 335
Index of Passages in Works by al-Ghazālī 340
Index of Verses in the Qur'an 344

Preface

> One of the conditions of being a servile follower of other people's views (*muqallid*) is that one does not realize that one is a *muqallid*. Once one finds this out, the glass of servile following (*taqlīd*) is shattered; an irreparable rift and disorder that cannot be pieced together or reassembled (…).
>
> AL-GHAZĀLĪ, *al-Munqidh min al-ḍalāl*, 15.

∴

On 14 Jumāda II 505 / 18 December 1111, al-Ghazālī died, approximately 56 years old, in his birthplace Ṭābarān in the district of Ṭūs in northeastern Iran. Almost 800 years later, in 1908, the Indian Muslim reformer Shiblī Nuʿmānī (1857–1914) addressed his followers in India and spoke about the merits of this great master and what the Islamic scholars (*ʿulamāʾ*) of the modern age could learn from his example. Nuʿmānī was a teacher and educational reformer at the turn of the 20th century. He began his distinguished career as a professor of Arabic and Persian at the Muhammadan Anglo-Oriental College in Aligarh, the cradle of Muslim modernist thinking on the South-Asian Subcontinent. In 1892, Nuʿmānī was a founding member of the Nadwatul Ulamāʾ, the association of reformist Muslim scholars in India, and four years later one of the driving forces when the organization founded its own school, the Dārul ʿUlūm Nadwatul ʿUlamāʾ in Lucknow in northern India. In his vision for this reformed school, Nuʿmānī was inspired by the example of Sayyid Aḥmad Khan (1817–98), the founder of the Aligarh College, yet in comparison to him he had a more traditionalist agenda. One of the objectives of the new Dārul ʿUlūm in Lucknow was to teach the traditional discipline of *kalām* – rationalist Muslim theology and philosophy – in accord with the traditional *madrasa* curriculum in India. This curriculum, the so-called *Dars-i Niẓāmī*, was created in the early 18th century and included books on Qur'anic studies, *ḥadīth* studies, Muslim

* The author is grateful to Waleed Ziad who helped him with the Urdu texts used in this preface and translated Urdu passages into English.

jurisprudence (*fiqh*), theology, philosophy and many other Muslim sciences.[1] Nuʿmānī and his colleagues at the Dārul ʿUlūm Nadwatul ʿUlamāʾ believed in the merits of this two-hundred year old course of study. However, they updated it with new texts covering advancements in the natural sciences. The goal was for students to develop skills that would be in harmony with traditional Muslim education in India and could at the same time answer to the religious challenges of the modern era and its sciences.[2]

For Shiblī Nuʿmānī, being a Muslim in India at the early 20th century meant, first of all, being confronted with modern sciences that were developed in Europe and that were introduced into India through translations from English. He, however, did not think that this situation was particularly new for Muslims. Centuries before, Islam had already been challenged by a potent force of ideas that came from outside. In the era following the Abbasid revolution of 750 CE, the "Greek sciences" and Greek philosophy were introduced to Arabic literature and Muslim culture. The intellectual leader who, according to Shiblī Nuʿmānī, responded most productively to the challenges coming from the tradition of Greek philosophy and who created a reconciliation between Islam and these set of ideas was al-Ghazālī.

Al-Ghazālī, according to Nuʿmānī, was the outstanding model of a successful joining of old and new, of the coming together of Islam's traditions with Greek science and with philosophy (*falsafa*).[3] In his Urdu address of 1908, Nuʿmānī describes al-Ghazālī as the scholar who should be credited that the Greek sciences and Greek wisdom took root in Islam. "For Shiblī," writes Christian Troll, "the past personification and his ideal for today is Imām al-Ghazālī (d. 1111 CE). He is the outstanding model of (...) the joining of Islam (...) with Greek science and philosophy as it had been propagated in his time by the *falāsifa*."[4] In his address of 1908, Shiblī said that al-Ghazālī's must be credited for the fact that

> the Greek sciences became Muslim sciences, with the result that today no scholar (*ʿālim*) is considered one as long he is not an expert, not only in *ḥadīth* and *fiqh* but also in the Greek sciences, i. e. in logic and *falsafa*. Similarly, today the *ʿulamāʾ* must acquire together with the *ʿulūm-i*

1 Robinson, "Ottoman-Safavids-Mughals: Shared Knowledge and Connective Systems," 181–84.

2 Hashmi, *Muslim Response to Western Education*, 117–46.

3 Troll, "Muhammad Shiblī Nuʿmānī (1857–1914) and the Reform of Muslim Religious Education," 155.

4 Ibid.

> *ʿarabiyya* the *ʿulūm-i gharbiyya* (the sciences of the West) and make a special effort to establish a correspondence between the religious (*madhhabī*) and the modern scientific questions. (…) I am convinced that as long as the *ʿulamāʾ* do not make them their own and defend the new sciences, these will continue to be loathed and opposed by the Muslims and will fail to take root in our community (*qawm*).[5]

Shiblī Nuʿmānī's view of al-Ghazālī in his 1908-address is reminiscent of a notion about the relationship between the Greek sciences and Islam that in Western scholarship was introduced many years after the speech, in the 1980s. Two important articles were published in 1987, Richard M. Frank's (1927–2009) "Al-Ghazālī's Use of Avicenna's Philosophy" – based on a paper given at a conference at Château de Morigny near Étampes (France) in November 1986 – and Abdelhamid I. Sabra's (1924–2013) "The Appropriation and Subsequent Naturalization of Greek Sciences in Medieval Islam." Sabra was one of the first scholars writing in a Western language who suggested that – in the words of Shiblī Nuʿmānī – "the Greek sciences had become Muslim sciences." For Sabra this happened in a two-step development of first appropriating Greek sciences in a process of translation and adaptation to a new cultural context, characterized by the use of the Arabic language and a Muslim majority culture, and secondly naturalizing them so that the Greek origins of these sciences were no longer visible. Although he did not work with Sabra's categories, Frank's article of 1987 can easily be corresponded to Sabra's suggestions. Whereas Avicenna's (Ibn Sīnā, d. 428/1037) philosophy is an expression of the process of appropriation where the Greek origins of many of his teachings are clearly visible and even stressed, al-Ghazālī, who adopts many of Avicenna's teachings, obscures their origins and thus contributes to – or maybe even initiates – the process of naturalization. Frank's article of 1987 launched a whole new direction of research on al-Ghazālī. Earlier Western contributions on him highlighted his critical attitude towards the teachings of al-Fārābī and Ibn Sīnā. After Frank's contributions in 1987 and 1992,[6] however, books and articles appeared that would investigate what al-Ghazālī adopted from *falsafa*. A second subject also became important – again initiated by Richard M. Frank in a monograph that came out in 1994[7] – and this was al-Ghazālī's conflict with the intellectual

---

5 Shiblī Nuʿmānī, *Khuṭbāt-i Shiblī*, 90. English translation taken from Troll, "Muhammad Shiblī Nuʿmānī (1857–1914) and the Reform," 155.

6 Frank, *Creation and the Cosmic System. Al-Ghazâlî & Avicenna.*

7 Frank, *Al-Ghazālī and the Ashʿarite School.*

environment that he grew up in, most importantly the clash with his fellow Ashʿarites in Khurasan.

Today, scholars in the field of Ghazali-studies are well aware that this great thinker did not destroy philosophy in Islam. Rather, we know that he was an initiator and an important instigator of the process of naturalization that Sabra described in 1987. Sabra did not think of al-Ghazālī when he wrote his article and he nowhere mentions him. Since his suggestion of the appropriation and naturalization of the Greek sciences in Islam came out, however, it became clear that *kalām* together with Sufism were the most important vehicles in the latter process of naturalizing the Greek science into Islam. Today we readily use words like "integration" and "fusion" when we describe what *kalām* did to philosophy in the Islamic world and talk of a continuation of the Greek philosophical tradition within *kalām*. Muslim theologians such as al-Ghazālī or Fakhr al-Dīn al-Rāzī (d. 606/1210) were experts not only in fields of knowledge that were identified as "Arabic" and "Muslim" but also in *falsafa* and in the so-called *ʿulūm al-awāʾil* ("the sciences of those who began"), meaning the Greek sciences. For Shiblī Nuʿmānī they were role models of 20th century Muslim scholars who must acquaint themselves with the "Arabic Sciences" (*ʿulūm-i ʿarabiyya*) as well as those of the West (*ʿulūm-i gharbiyya*).

When Shiblī gave this speech in 1908, his contemporaries at universities in the West had a very different impression of al-Ghazālī and his role in Muslim intellectual history. Throughout the 19th and early 20th centuries, Western scholarship on al-Ghazālī followed the influential French scholar Ernest Renan (1823–98), who had characterized al-Ghazālī as an opponent of reasonable inquiry in Islam, responsible for its destruction. For Renan, al-Ghazālī was a skeptic, "who undertook to prove the radical incapacity of reason."[8] In his 1852 book *Averroès et l'averroisme*, Renan introduces al-Ghazālī as "an enemy of philosophy" who was behind the persecution of philosophers and "the war against philosophy at the end of the 12th century."[9] Renan compared this war with the almost two centuries of civil strife and warfare that followed the Protestant Reformation in the early 16th century. According to Renan, Averroes (Ibn Rushd, d. 595/1198) was the last exponent of philosophy in the Islamic world. "When he died in 1198," Renan wrote, "Arab philosophy had lost its last representative and the triumph of the Qur'an over free-thinking was assured for at least six-hundred years."[10] What relieved the Islamic world from the

8 Renan, *Averroès et l'averroisme*, 29.

9 Ibid. 29.

10 Ibid., 2.

"triumph of the Qur'an" was, according to Renan, the French invasion of Egypt in 1798.

One scholar who followed Renan was the Dutch historian of philosophy Tjitze J. de Boer (1866–1942). He published the first textbook on the history of philosophy in Islam in 1901 that would remain influential for many decades and was still used as textbook when both Sabra's and Frank's articles came out. For Boer, al-Ghazālī "abandoned the attempt to understand this world" and devoted himself to "the religious problem," which he comprehended much more profoundly than the philosophers of his time. In his history of philosophy in Islam – a book that would represent the height of Western knowledge when Shiblī Nuʿmānī gave his speech – Boer reduces al-Ghazālī to a Sufi, "who feels bound to battle with [Aristotelianism], as from a catholic standpoint."[11] After al-Ghazālī, there were only "epitomists" in the Eastern Islamic world. Philosophers they were, Boer acknowledges, but of a philosophy that was in decline and, "in no department did they pass the mark which had been reached of old: Minds were now too weak to accomplish such a feat. (...) Ethical and religious doctrine had ended in Mysticism; and the same was the case with Philosophy (...)."[12]

The notion of a decline of Islam in its post-classical period was a powerful idea in all of Islamic studies during the 19th and 20th centuries. It prevented Western scholars to assess al-Ghazālī's role in the history of Islamic thought in similar terms as Shiblī Nuʿmānī did. He, however, was not a lone voice in appreciating al-Ghazālī's role as an integrator of Greek philosophy into Islam. Once we understand Nuʿmānī's position on al-Ghazālī we can also better understand comments that Sayyid Aḥmad Khān made more than twenty years earlier, in 1884, in an Urdu address to a newly founded modernist organization in Lahore.[13] Sayyid Aḥmad Khān was, of course, much more influential than Shiblī Nuʿmānī. He is the most important founding figure of modernist Islam and thus one of the most influential Muslim thinkers of the past two centuries.[14] In his speech of 1884 Aḥmad Khān never mentions al-Ghazālī.[15] Knowing how Shiblī Nuʿmānī thought about al-Ghazālī, however, helps us understand

11 Boer, *The History of Philosophy in Islam*, 158–59.

12 Ibid., 169–70.

13 "Association for the Support of Islam" (*Anjuman-i Ḥimāyat-i Islām*).

14 If in his home countries India and Pakistan he is today not given due credit as the founder of one of their most important intellectual movements, a movement that, in fact, led to the creation of Pakistan, it is largely because his memory is tainted by his close cooperation (or even collaboration) with the British colonial rulers.

15 Khān, *Mukammal majmūʿah*, 238–57. The address is translated in Troll, *Sayyid Ahmad* Khan, 307–32, from where I take the English text quoted here.

the role that his example played in Aḥmān Khān's vision of what a modern Muslim must do.

Many Muslims of his time, so Aḥmad Khān describes in his 1884 speech, had an education in the "modern sciences" (*ʿulūm-i jadīdah*) or had at least heard what these new sciences teach. They looked at the scholars of Islam and expected from them, "philosophical arguments, that the doubts of their hearts be removed so that their hearts may find satisfaction."[16] Aḥmad Khān compared the situation in his days to that during the Abbasid caliphate, when "Greek philosophy and natural science had gained popularity among the Muslims." In those days the leading scholars (*ʿulamaʾ*) of Islam took up the challenge and they responded in three ways:

> The first was to prove that those tenets of Greek wisdom and philosophy (*yūnānī ḥikmat o-falsafa*) which were against Islamic teachings were wrong. The second was to formulate such objections to the propositions of [Greek] wisdom and philosophy by which these tenets would themselves become doubtful. Third, to harmonize (*taṭbīq karnā*) between the tenets of Islam and the tenets of wisdom and philosophy.[17]

Talking to an audience of laypeople, Aḥmad Khān does not identify the Muslim scholars who devised this strategy but simply says that this was accomplished in *ʿilm-i kalām*. There can be hardly any doubt, I think – and if there were, Shiblī Nuʿmānī's later comments lay them to rest – that Aḥmad Khān here talks about a whole range of scholars the first of whom was al-Ghazālī. His *Tahāfut al-falāsifa* (*The Incoherence of the Philosophers*) – a work of *kalām* literature – can be seen as making the first as well as the second steps. The book aims to prove that at least three teachings in *falsafa* that violate widespread convictions among Muslim theologians are wrong. In addition, it raises doubt about many other teachings of *falsafa*. This aspect of al-Ghazālī's oeuvre had been known for long among Western scholars. The third step of harmonizing (*taṭbīq karnā*) between the teachings of *falsafa* and that of Muslim theology has been however, only recently appreciated among Westerns scholars of al-Ghazālī. Yet that al-Ghazālī did precisely these three things described by Aḥmad Khān in 1884 is now – with a delay of more than a hundred years – almost universally acknowledged among those who work on him in the West.

For Sayyid Aḥmad Khān, the *ʿilm al-kalām* of al-Ghazālī should be a model for the young Muslims of his day, whom he asks to develop, "a modern *ʿilm*

---

16 Khān, *Mukammal majmūʿah*, 240; English trans., 310.

17 Ibid., 241; English trans., 311.

al-kalām (*jadīd ʿilm-i kalām*), by which we either render false (*bāṭil*) and incorrect (*mushtabā*) the teachings of the modern sciences, or bring them into harmony with the doctrines of Islam."[18] Aḥmad Khān was well aware that the first part of this task was much more difficult than it had been historically. The teachings of *falsafa* that the *mutakallimūn* of old addressed were based on "rational and analogical arguments" (*ʿaqlī awr qiyāsī dalīlōñ par*) and not upon experiment (*tajribah*) and observation (*mushahādah*). Refuting them was possible when their rational and philosophical arguments failed to be entirely convincing. The modern sciences, so Aḥmad Khān pointed out, are different since they establish "natural phenomena through experimentations that happen before our eyes."[19]

The example of the adaptation of al-Ghazālī's strategy toward *falsafa* among modernist thinkers in India proves that a proper understanding of his teachings must precede any attempt to investigate his influence in Islamic intellectual history. Had Tjitze J. de Boer heard or read Shiblī Nuʿmānī's speech of 1908, he would most probably have rejected and even ridiculed the latter's suggestion that modern Muslims should walk in the footsteps of al-Ghazālī. What's more, no Western expert of al-Ghazālī in the generations before 1987 thought of him when he or she read Aḥmad Khān's characterization of the accomplishments of *kalām*. Earlier Western scholars would have concluded that Shiblī Nuʿmānī created a wrong picture of al-Ghazālī's accomplishment and that Aḥmad Khān grossly mischaracterized *kalām*'s relationship to the Greek sciences. Only now, after almost thirty years of a new kind of Ghazali-studies can we appreciate and truly understand the remarks of these two Indian scholars. Only now can we truly begin to understand which impact al-Ghazālī had on later Muslim scholars.

This volume assembles five contributions that explore al-Ghazālī's influence on later Islamic thinking together with seven chapters that further explain aspects of his teachings and his works. With our change of view on al-Ghazālī comes a change of view of his influence; but the example discussed here in this preface shows that the latter cannot be done without the former. The contributions to this volume are therefore devoted to two subjects: first, continuing

18 Ibid., 242; adapted from Troll's English trans., 313.

19 *Ab maṣā'il tabʿī tajribah say ṣābit kīyay jātay haiñ awr voh ham ko dikhlā dīyay jātay haiñ*, ibid. 241. Troll , *Sayyid Ahmad Khan*, 312, translates this sentence: "Today doctrines are established by natural experiments [i.e. experiments in natural science] and they are demonstrated before our eyes."

the ongoing reassessment of al-Ghazālī's thought and, second, exploring al-Ghazālī's influence.

Al-Ghazālī death on 14 Jumāda II 505 / 18 December 1111 had its 900th anniversary in December 2011. Several conferences and meetings were held on that occasion. This volume brings together papers that were delivered at a workshop on December 9–10, 2011 at Yale University in New Haven, USA. Two papers, namely those of Stephen Ogden and Damien Janos, were not delivered at that conference and were added later. As organizer of the workshop and editor of this volume I would like to thank Lora LeMosy and Amaar Al-Hayder – the staff of Yale's Council on Middle East Studies – for making the workshop possible. I thank the participants in the workshop and my students and colleagues at Yale for their contributions. Special thanks go to Alyssa Bernstein, Grace Brody, and Rona Johnston Gordon, as well as the editorial staff at Brill Publishers for their help in improving chapters of this book. I am grateful to the editors of "Islamic Philosophy, Theology and Science. Texts and Studies" for inclusion in the series.

Frank Griffel

Bibliography

Boer, Tjitze J. de. *Geschichte der Philosophie im Islam*. Stuttgart: Frommanns Verlag, 1901.

———. *The History of Philosophy in Islam*. Translated by E. R. Jones. London: Luzac & Co., 1903.

Frank, Richard M. "Al-Ghazālī's Use of Avicenna's Philosophy." *Revue des études islamiques* 55–57 (1987–89): 271–85. Reprinted in idem, *Philosophy, Theology, and Mysticism in Medieval Islam*. Edited by Dimitri Gutas. Aldershot (Hampshire, UK): Ashgate, 2005. Text xi.

———. *Creation and the Cosmic System. Al-Ghazâlî & Avicenna*. Heidelberg: Carl Winter, 1992.

———. *Al-Ghazālī and the Ashʿarite School*. Durham: Duke University Press, 1994.

al-Ghazālī, Muḥammad ibn Muḥammad. *al-Munqidh min al-ḍalāl / Erreur et délivrance*. Edition and French translation by Farid Jabre. 3rd edition. Beirut: Commission libanaise pour la traduction des chefs-d'œuvre, 1969.

———. *Tahāfut al-falāsifa / The Incoherence of the Philosophers*. A parallel English-Arabic text. Edited and translated by Michael E. Marmura. 2nd. edition. Provo (Utah): Brigham Young University Press, 2000.

Hashmi, M. A. A. *Muslim Response to Western Education (A Study of Four Pioneer Institutions)*. New Delhi: Commonwealth Publishers, 1989.

Robinson, Francis. "Ottoman-Safavids-Mughals: Shared Knowledge and Connective Systems." *Journal of Islamic Studies* 8 (1997): 151–184.

Shiblī Nuʿmānī, *Khuṭbāt-i Shiblī*, Edited by M.-ʿA. Ṣ. Nadvī. Azamgarh: Maṭbūʿat-i Maʿārif, 1360/1941.

Khān, Sayyid Aḥmad. *Mukammal majmūʿah lakcarz va-ispīciz (1863–1898)*. Edited by M. Imām ul-Dīn Ṣāhib Gujrātī. Lahore: Malik Fażl al-Dīn *et alii*, Tājirān-i Kutub, n. d. [1909?].

Renan, Ernest. *Averroès et l'averroisme*. 3rd. ed. Paris: Michel Levy, 1866.

Sabra, Abdelhamid I. "The Appropriation and Subsequent Naturalization of Greek Sciences in Medieval Islam: A Preliminary Statement." *History of Science* 25 (1987): 223–43.

Troll, Christian W. *Sayyid Ahmad Khan: A Reinterpretation of Muslim Theology*. Delhi: Vikas Publishing House, 1978.

———. "Muhammad Shiblī Nuʿmānī (1857–1914) and the Reform of Muslim Religious Education." In: *Madrasa: La transmission du savoir dans le monde musulman*. Edited by N. Grandin and M. Gaborieau. Paris: Éditions Arguments, 1997. 145–57.

List of Figures and Tables

Figures

4.1 Al-Ghazālī's empiricist teleology in law 93
4.2 Channels of transmission of Galen's teleology 107
7.1 Beinecke Rare Book and Manuscript Library, Yale University, MS Landberg 318, fol. 1a 183
7.2 Beinecke Rare Book and Manuscript Library, Yale University, MS Landberg 318, fol. 230a 184
7.3 Beinecke Rare Book and Manuscript Library, Yale University, MS Landberg 318, fol. 230b 185

Tables

4.1 A comparison of corresponding sections in *al-Ḥikma fī makhlūqāt Allāh* and *Bayān kayfiyyat al-tafakkur fī khalq Allāh* in al-Ghazālī's *Iḥyāʾ ʿulūm al-dīn* 95
4.2 Occurrences of teleological terms in al-Ghazālī's *Ḥikma* 98
4.3 A comparison of corresponding sections in *al-Ḥikma fī makhlūqāt Allāh, al-Dalāʾil wa-l-iʿtibār*, and *al-ʿIbar wa-l-iʿtibār* 105
5.1 Synoptic table analysing the argument described in each of ¶¶ 2 and 3 119

List of Contributors

Anna Ayşe Akasoy
teaches Islamic intellectual history at the City University of New York (Hunter College and Graduate Center). Her research interests include the relationship between mysticism and rationalism, particularly in the Muslim West, and contacts between the Islamic world and other cultures. Her current research project deals with Alexander the Great as a religious figure in the Middle East and Asia.

Ahmed El Shamsy
is Assistant Professor of Islamic Thought at the University of Chicago. He studies the intellectual history of Islam, focusing on the classical Islamic disciplines and their interplay with the media of orality, literacy, and print. His book *The Canonization of Early Islamic Law: A Social and Intellectual History* (Cambridge University Press 2013) traces the transformation of Islamic law from a primarily oral tradition to a systematic written discipline. His current research investigates the reinvention of the Islamic scholarly tradition and its textual canon via the printing press in the early twentieth century.

Kenneth Garden
is Associate Professor at Tufts University in Massachusetts. He received his PhD in Near Eastern Languages and Civilizations from the University of Chicago and is the author of *The First Islamic Reviver: Abū Ḥāmid al-Ghazālī and his Revival of the Religious Sciences* (Oxford University Press 2014).

Frank Griffel
is Professor of Islamic Studies at Yale University, New Haven, USA. He is the author of numerous articles on Islamic theology and philosophy, on al-Ghazālī, and on Fakhr al-Dīn al-Rāzī. In 2009 he published *Al-Ghazālī's Philosophical Theology* (Oxford University Press) and in 2000 *Apostasie und Toleranz im Islam* (Leiden: Brill). He is a translator of al-Ghazālī and Averroes and the editor of two other collective volumes.

Jules Janssens
is researcher at the De Wulf-Mansioncentrum of the Katholieke Universiteit Leuven, Belgium, and an associated researcher at the CNRS, Paris (Centre Jean Pépin, UMR 8320). He is a specialist in medieval Islamic philosophy, especially in Avicenna, dealing not only with the latter's own thought, but also with its reception in both the Islamic world and the Latin West. Commissioned by the

Académie Royale de Belgique, he currently edits the Latin translation of Avicenna's *Physics*.

Damien Janos
received his PhD at McGill University in 2009 and has worked for several years as a postdoctoral researcher in Germany and Canada. His research focuses mainly on the cosmology and metaphysics of al-Fārābī and Avicenna, with a secondary interest in the history of Arabic science and the reception of Greek learning in Islam. He is currently preparing a monograph on Avicenna's theories of intelligible unity and multiplicity.

Taneli Kukkonen
is Professor of Philosophy at New York University Abu Dhabi. He works on Arabic philosophy and the Aristotelian commentary tradition. He is the author of *Ibn Tufayl. Living the Life of Reason* (Oxford: Oneworld 2014) and of over thirty articles and book chapters on a range of topics including logic, cosmology, metaphysics, and cognitive and moral psychology. At present he is putting the finishing touches to a monograph study of al-Ghazālī's thought.

Stephen R. Ogden
earned his PhD in Philosophy and Religious Studies at Yale University in the spring of 2015, completing his dissertation "Receiving and Making Aristotle's Intellect: A New Assessment of Averroes and Aquinas." He is currently on a Mellon postdoctoral fellowship at Johns Hopkins University.

M. Sait Özervarlı
is Professor at Yıldız Technical University, Department of Humanities and Social Sciences. He works mainly on Ottoman intellectual history, Islamic philosophical thought, East-West scholarly interactions, and alternative modernizations. Among his publications are *Kelâmda yenilik arayışları—19. yüzyıl sonu–20. yüzyıl başı* (Aspects of Ottoman Intellectual History in the Late 19th and Early 20th Centuries) (Istanbul: İSAM, 2008) and the critical edition of ʿAlāʾ al-Dīn al-Usmandī's (d. 552/1157–58) *Lubāb al-kalām* (Istanbul: İSAM, 2005). He also contributes to the *Grundriss der Geschichte der Philosophie* (*Ueberweg*). *Philosophie in der islamischen Welt* (edited by Ulrich Ruldoph, Basel: Schwabe Verlag).

Martin Riexinger
is Associate Professor for Arabic and Islamic Studies at Aarhus University, Denmark. He received his PhD at University Freiburg, Germany, and his Habilitation at Göttingen. In his research he focuses on the modern intellectual

history of Islam, in particular the reception of modern science and puritan movements, on the basis of sources in Arabic, Urdu, and Turkish.

Ulrich Rudolph
is Professor of Islamic Studies at Zurich University, Switzerland, and the editor of *Grundriss der Geschichte der Philosophie* (*Ueberweg*). *Philosophie in der islamischen Welt*, to be published in four volumes, the first of which appeared with Schwabe Verlag in Basel 2012. He has published extensively on Islamic philosophy and theology. His recent works include *Al-Māturīdī and the Development of Sunnī Theology in Samarqand* (Leiden: Brill 2015) as well as the short introduction *La philosophie islamique. Des commencements à nos jours* (Paris: Vrin, 2014).

Ayman Shihadeh
is based at SOAS, University of London. He has his DPhil from Oxford University and has published widely on the history of medieval Arabic philosophy and rational Islamic theology, including *Doubts on Avicenna: A Study and Edition of Sharaf al-Dīn al-Masʿūdī's Commentary on the Ishārāt* (Leiden: Brill, 2015) and *The Teleological Ethics of Fakhr al-Dīn al-Rāzī* (Leiden: Brill, 2006). He serves as the Section Editor for Philosophy and Theology at the *Encyclopaedia of Islam THREE* (Leiden: Brill).

Keys and Conventions

This book uses the transliteration system for Arabic, Persian, and Turkish established by the *International Journal of Middle East Studies* (IJMES) with the exception that it employs *-ah* in Persian for the *tāʾ marbūṭa* instead of *-ih*. Unlike in *IJMES* we use full diacritical marks in names and titles of books and articles. Dates before 1800 CE appear in the dual format of AH/CE; dates after 1800 only in CE.

An attempt has been made to establish a canonic body of editions of works by al-Ghazālī that will be referred to throughout the field of Ghazali-studies. All authors in this volume quote the same editions of works by al-Ghazālī. For instance, when referring to *Iḥyāʾ ʿulūm al-dīn* all authors use the 16-part edition of the Lajnat Nashr al-Thaqāfa al-Islāmiyya in Cairo, 1937–39. This edition is, for instance, currently available at http://www.ghazali.org/site/ihya.htm. In addition to the listed bibliography at the end of each contribution, the editions of works by al-Ghazālī used in this volume are also identified in the index of passages at the end of the book. These are the most reliable editions available, established on the basis of manuscript readings. The recent 10-volume edition of *Iḥyāʾ ʿulūm al-dīn*, published by Dār al-Minhāj in Jeddah, Saudi Arabia, came too late to be used by all authors in this volume. It is included, however, in the index of passages of works by al-Ghazālī.

PART 1

Al-Ghazālī's Works and His Thought

CHAPTER 1

Al-Ghazālī on Error

Taneli Kukkonen

Given that God is omnipotent and supremely good and that He has decreed that our true happiness should lie in the contemplation of reality as it truly is, how and why do humans ever go wrong in their beliefs or stray from the path of true religion? Al-Ghazālī's answer to this question has attracted little commentary in modern scholarship,[1] which is surprising given the prominence of the concept of error in the very title of his best-known work in the West—the quasi-autobiographical *al-Munqidh min al-ḍalāl* (*Deliverer from Error*)—and the amount of attention lavished on the related issue of skepticism in al-Ghazālī. This study aims at filling a minor lacuna in the scholarship.

A suitable starting point is found in the *Mishkāt al-anwār* (*Niche of Lights*), where al-Ghazālī states categorically that as the light of the heavens and earth, God by His own light is the most manifest of all things. Consequently, people are only ever held back from the divine light, "either by their human attributes; or by sensation, imagination, and faulty reasoning (*muqāyisat al-ʿaql*); or else by sheer light."[2] For all that it is extremely brief, al-Ghazālī's remark reads practically like a programmatic run-through of the sources of error when it comes to religious matters. What is more, al-Ghazālī's exposition here can be mapped on to things he says elsewhere in his authorship in a reasonably tidy manner.

It turns out that underlying al-Ghazālī's occasional remarks there is a fairly well-developed theory, one that amounts to a kind of psychology of error. The fact that al-Ghazālī's account starts from, and essentially ends with, the familiar notion that it is our passions (our "human attributes") that lead us astray should not dissuade us from digging deeper, for there is a fair bit more to establish about error and its sources. In fact, the problem about mistaken beliefs and misplaced evaluations is a useful prism through which to view much of what al-Ghazālī has to say about the acquisition, retention, and loss of faith. At the same time, the generic nature of much of al-Ghazālī's analysis—what goes for

1 A corresponding lacuna exists in the study of Arabic philosophy in general. For a Latin scholastic parallel that is helpful in pointing out the kind of work that needs to be done see Evans, *Getting It Wrong*.

2 al-Ghazālī, *Mishkāt al-anwār*, 185.18–19; cf. *Iḥyāʾ* 8:1359.17–19 (XXI, *bayān* 4).

 | DOI 10.1163/9789004307490_002

errant religious belief goes for belief-formation in general—allows for a wider application of the results.

1 Innate Nature Incomplete

Let us begin from the well-worn saying attributed to the Prophet according to which every person is born with an innate nature (*fiṭra*), whereafter one's parents then make one into a Jew, a Christian, or a Magi. Although al-Ghazālī cites this *ḥadīth* in a number of permutations, often in elliptical form and sometimes in paraphrase, and although he applies it across a number of argumentative contexts, he is nonetheless reasonably consistent in what he means for it to say.

Perhaps the most famous evocation of *fiṭra* occurs in the well-known account concerning al-Ghazālī's own formative years in the *Deliverer from Error* (*al-Munqidh min al-ḍalāl*):

> Since my first years and all the way to maturity, the thirst to perceive the real natures of things (*darak ḥaqā'iq al-umūr*) was my custom and habit: it was an innate disposition and nature (*gharīza wa-fiṭra*) placed in me by God, not something I would have chosen and cultivated for myself. The shackles of authoritarianism (*taqlīd*) therefore fell from me and inherited beliefs fell to pieces in my sight even while I was still a youth: this happened when I saw how the children of Christians never grew up to embrace anything other than Christianity, or the children of Jews anything other than Judaism, or the children of Muslims anything other than Islam. I also heard the Tradition according to which the Messenger of God said: "Every newborn is born with an innate nature (*fiṭra*): then his parents make him into a Jew, a Christian, or a Magi." Through this my inner being was moved into researching the reality of that original innate nature (*ḥaqīqat al-fiṭra al-aṣliyya*) as well as the true nature of those accidental beliefs that [come about] by authoritative adherence to parents and instructors.[3]

We would do well to notice first of all how the whole passage is a deliberate literary construct. Instead of describing actual events in al-Ghazālī's youth, the author seeks to set the stage—in effect, to justify the discussion that is to follow concerning the four groups of truth-seekers. Al-Ghazālī's primary aim is to

3 al-Ghazālī, *al-Munqidh*, 10.21–11.6.

paint a picture where his own searching inquiries into the domains of philosophy, Isma'ili doctrine, and Sufism—activities which were sure to raise questions if not outright suspicion—can be seen as the manifestations of an innate disposition handed down by God Himself, lying within a spectrum of natural potentiality (albeit at the far end of it) that in principle encompasses all humankind.[4]

The positive side of the inborn *fiṭra* tradition is thus that all people (in principle at least) are born receptive to the message of Islam, being predisposed towards loving God and desiring to know reality in its essential aspects. This, we may note, is at once more and less than what other thinkers have said on the basis of Q 30:30. In light of that Qur'anic passage, having a *fiṭra* could effectively be taken to mean that everyone is born the functional equivalent of a Muslim, as for instance Abraham was (Abraham being the paradigmatic *ḥanīf* or righteous man). Al-Ghazālī by contrast holds that all true religious knowledge, crucially including knowledge of right and wrong, is of the acquired sort, which already opens up the space for things to go wrong as well as right in the process of our faculties maturing.[5] Even non-believers when pressed on the point might be forced to acknowledge and testify to God's creation of the world,[6] but the fact remains that each and every person needs to be awakened to this fact and that this kind of recollection can just as soon fail to manifest. The first book in al-Ghazālī's *Iḥyā' ʿulūm al-Dīn* (*The Revival of the Religious Sciences*), *Kitāb al-ʿIlm* (*Book of Knowledge*) introduces this principle in the context of explicating the true meaning of the term "intellect" (*ʿaql*); it is noticeable just how finely al-Ghazālī threads the needle of at once establishing that all humans are capable of and indeed disposed towards recognizing the reality of God, while at the same time acknowledging that not everybody develops this capacity.

> God Most High has said: "If you were to ask them, 'who created the heavens and earth?' they would say, 'God'." The meaning of this is that if they were to reflect on their states, their souls and their innermost being would testify to this—that is, "the disposition (*fiṭra*) with which God has

---

4 The immediate context for this apologetic work is that al-Ghazāli's return to state-sponsored teaching in 499/1105 was met with considerable opposition and that an active libel campaign sought to associate his *Iḥyā' ʿulūm al-dīn* with philosophy and Isma'ili esotericism: see Garden, "Coming Down from the Mountaintop."

5 al-Ghazālī, *Iḥyā'*, 8:1369.9–15 (XXI, *bayān* 6, *sabab* 5); for this Ash'arite element in al-Ghazālī's epistemology see Frank, "Knowledge and *Taqlīd*;" for important points of dissent, Frank, "Al-Ghazālī on *taqlīd*."

6 al-Ghazālī, *Mīzān al-ʿamal*, 110; cf. *Iḥyā'*, 1:182.14–183.3 (II, *faṣl* 3, *rukn* 1).

> endowed them" (Q 43:87). All this is to say that all humans are predisposed towards believing in God, indeed towards an understanding of things according to what they are in themselves (*maʿrifa al-ashyāʾ ʿalā mā hiya ʿalayhī*): I mean that human beings stand in ready proximity, as it were, for the receptivity of such a perception. Belief having been instilled in souls by way of innate disposition, people divide into two groups: those who have turned away and forgotten [about their faith], these being the apostates and infidels (*kuffār*), and those who have taken heed and remembered. [The latter] resemble one who has borne witness to something, [then] forgotten about it through neglect, then finally come to remember it. Because of this He has said: "Perhaps they will remember" (Q 30:29) (…).[7]

Al-Ghazālī goes on to underline how labelling this kind of cognitive awakening remembrance (*tadhakkur*) does not signal a strong innatism of any kind. It is not as though a form had yet been actually present in the heart, rather, what one intends is a potentiality waiting to be kindled in one's innate disposition.[8] All this points in the direction of treating humanity's innate disposition for veridical knowledge in al-Ghazālī as the rough equivalent to the Avicennian material intellect.[9]

Further to expand on the epistemological as well as ontological implications of the Prophetic saying, al-Ghazālī in many places uses the tradition regarding our innate *fiṭra* in order to ground in unassailably Islamic materials the Sufi notion of a natural desire deep within us to meet with God and to contemplate His countenance. This unabashedly teleological and rationalist conception of humanity allows al-Ghazālī to state, e.g., that service to God and obedience to Him has only been decreed so that the soul may be purified and illumined.[10] But it also transposes the whole *fiṭra* tradition, taking it far beyond questions of responsibility for our religious beliefs and into deep ontological

---

7 al-Ghazālī, *Iḥyāʾ*, 1:148.6–14 (I, *bāb* 7, *bayān* 2).

8 Frank in "Al-Ghazālī on *taqlīd*," 225, n. 24 already astutely notes that al-Ghazālī's choice of terminology is studiedly cautious: it is *as if* the forms were already lying dormant in the intellect, etc. The overall effect is to underline the need for the actual forms to be imprinted from without.

9 See Kukkonen, "Receptive to Reality;" Griffel, "Al-Ghazālī's Use of 'Original Human Disposition' (*Fiṭra*)" has more materials and a somewhat different interpretation.

10 See, e.g., al-Ghazālī, *Iḥyāʾ*, 8:1370.14–15 (XXI, *bayān* 6, *sabab* 5); ibid., 8:1450.10 (XXII, *bayān* 4, *wajh* 2); cf. *Iḥyāʾ*, 13:2358.17 (XXXIII, *shaṭr* 2, *bayān* 5), where it is said that both knowledge and works aim solely at acquaintance (*maʿrifa*) with God.

waters when it comes to the isomorphic nature of divine reality and our human powers of cognition.

With this, we may take our leave of al-Ghazālī's noetics and cognitive psychology, which is a topic treated more comprehensively elsewhere.[11] It is clear already that the outline of al-Ghazālī's understanding of true knowledge is Avicennian, and that since its element of innatism is sufficiently diluted, there is ample room for things to go wrong as well as right. Once we delve into the question of where things actively go askew, the question of Avicennianism in al-Ghazālī becomes more pronounced.

2 The Passions Entrenched

For al-Ghazālī, it is predominantly the darkness of our sins or transgressions (pl. *dhunūb*) that comes between our innate nature, which is sound originally, and its natural desire to attain to the proximity of the Lord.[12] As to what such sins are and where they originate, al-Ghazālī's basic answer is simple: it is our passions (singl. *hawā* in Qur'anic parlance) that lead us astray, more specifically our proclivity towards prioritizing the enjoyment of the objects of our passions over everything else, including the love of God and doing His will. When the heart grows to desire something more than it desires the proximity of God, it is overcome by a kind of darkness that represents a fundamental sickness of the soul. This will not only occlude the heart's power of insight, but lead to a fundamental turning away from God.[13]

I have examined the basic framework for al-Ghazālī's account of the passions in another study that effectively forms a companion piece to this one. Here, I will only summarize the results.[14] For al-Ghazālī, the passions are seated in the appetitive and spirited parts of the soul (*shahwa, ghaḍab*) and are outward expressions of their natural dynamics. Appetite and spirit are described in Platonic fashion as representing the animal side of our existence: they are sub-rational responses to our natural environment which include an affective component. In and of themselves, appetite and spirit are rooted in indispensable facets of our embodied life, meaning that they should not be uprooted

11 See Kukkonen, "Receptive to Reality" and more at length Treiger, *Inspired Knowledge*.

12 See, e.g., al-Ghazālī, *Iḥyā'*, 11:2096.17–19 and what follows (XXXI, *rukn* 1, *bayān* 5).

13 al-Ghazālī, *Iḥyā'*, 12:2215.15–18 (XXXII, *shaṭr* 2, *rukn* 1, *bayān* 2, *aṣl* 2); ibid., 14:2611.3–6 (XXXVI, *bayān* 5); *Mīzān*, 14–15, 93–94; *al-Maqṣad*, 44.

14 For full documentation of the following claims see Kukkonen, "Al-Ghazālī on the Emotions;" in the first volume of this work. cf. also Sherif, *Ghazali's Theory of Virtue*.

(any attempt to do so would only be foolish): but in the case of humans, appetite and spirit should be made to submit to the rule of reason, in which case justice results as the proper and orderly harmony of the soul's various functions and orientations. The trouble according to al-Ghazālī is that appetite is entrenched from birth, while the spirited part of the soul is awakened at the age of seven. Both thus have ample time to assume dominance before the intellect reaches maturity (this begins at fourteen and continues all the way until a person reaches forty years of age). Overall, notwithstanding intellect's natural dominance in accordance with the order originally imposed by God, al-Ghazālī considers it at least as likely that people become ensnared by their passions. This is what is meant by the dreaded "love of the world" to which many fall prey.[15]

In the context of providing a taxonomy of offences against God—what we would normally term sins—and their psychological and natural basis (noticeably, the word *fiṭra* is evoked here), al-Ghazālī says that these come in stages. At first our bestial character assumes precedence, leading to our appetites becoming oversized; after this, our predatory side comes to the fore, which leads to aggressive and at worst murderous behaviour. It is in what follows that al-Ghazālī elucidates his understanding of how things begin to go wrong in earnest. Al-Ghazālī says that when the beastly and the predatory faculties join forces, they may twist the intellect to do the work of deceit, wiliness, and duplicity, all of which are satanic qualities. Following this, the worst kind of sin and sinner may emerge, that which assumes a "lordly" character (*al-ṣifa al-rubūbiyya*). While the wrongful actions of the lordly kind may take many forms (e.g., seeking fame, power, or praise; seeking to extend one's life at all costs), the underlying fallacy is that of self-worship, which bespeaks a fundamental ignorance of God's Lordship and therefore constitutes an affront against true religion.[16]

In general, habituation for al-Ghazālī forms the key both to the formation of character and to the pleasures one learns to appreciate. This cuts both ways: by enumerating the weird and wonderful ways in which things oftentimes go wrong, al-Ghazālī can simultaneously establish how the correct kind of acculturation will lead to the more exalted habits becoming second nature, indeed an indispensable part of life, despite the fact that the rewards they offer are at first far from immediate. I resort to a lengthy citation from the 22nd book in

15 See *Kitāb Dhamm al-dunyā* (*Book of Condemning this World*), the 26th book in al-Ghazālī, *Iḥyā'*, 9:1708–58.

16 al-Ghazālī, *Iḥyā'*, 11:2101.19–2102.4 (XXXI, *rukn* 2, *bayān* 1).

Iḥyāʾ ʿulūm al-dīn, Riyāḍat al-nafs (*On Disciplining the Soul*) and avail myself of Tim J. Winter's excellent translation because both capture the flavour of al-Ghazālī's thought so well:

> It is wrong to deem it unlikely that one's delight might be in prayer and that one's worship might become delectable, for everyday life draws even more wondrous things from the soul:
>
> (1) We see kings and the voluptuous rich in constant misery, and the bankrupt gambler so overcome with delight and joy during his gambling that one might well discount the possibility of [that] person's gaining any pleasure without this practice, even after it had taken away his wealth, ruined his home and left him quite penniless, for he will still love and enjoy it by reason of his soul's long familiarity with it.
>
> (2) Similarly with the man whose hobby is pigeons, who may stand all day in the hot sun without feeling and pain due to the pleasure he takes in his birds, and their movement, flight and soaring around in the sky.
>
> (3) Then there is the criminal who boasts of the blows and stabs he receives, and of his steadfastness under the whip, and who goes up to the cross or the gibbet bragging about his endurance of these [punishments] (...) because of his joy at what he considers to be his courage and virility. Despite the torment provided by his circumstances, he takes delight in these things and finds in them a source of pride.
>
> (4) And there is no condition more ugly and despicable than that of an effeminate man who imitates women by plucking out his hair, tattooing his face and keeping their company, so that you see him rejoicing in his state and boasting of the perfection of his effeminacy to other such men. Even the cupper and sweepers can be seen boasting to one another just as much as the kings and the scholars. All of this is the result of habit (*ʿāda*) and persisting in one course for a long period and seeing the same thing in one's acquaintances.
>
> Since the soul commonly takes pleasure even in vain things and inclines towards ugliness, how could it not take pleasure in the Truth were it to be restored to it for a while and made to persevere therein? The soul's inclination to these disgusting things is unnatural, and resembles an inclination to the eating of mud; yet even this may gain control over some people and become a habit. As for the inclination to wisdom and the love, knowledge and worship of God, this resembles the inclination towards food and drink. It is the expression of the heart's nature, and is a

> divine command, while an inclination to the demands of one's desires is in itself something strange, and is not part of its nature.[17]

Notice how in the cases of the convicted criminal, the effeminate man, the cupper, and the sweeper, an appeal is made to the reinforcing mechanisms provided by the approval of others.[18] It is this that allows one to continue to find pleasure in things that by rights should, and normally would, be considered abhorrent and unpleasant by nature. It is also the same mutually supportive mechanism of affirming the passions and their object that lies at the heart of idol worship, as the following passage from the *Book of Knowledge*, the first book in the *Iḥyāʾ*, spells out:

> Falling outside the pale of monotheism are those who follow their passion (*hawā*), for anyone who follows his passion makes this into that which he worships. God said, "Have you seen the one makes his passion his god," (Q 45:23) and the Messenger of God likewise said: "Of the earthly things worshipped as god, the thing most hated by God is passion." In actual fact, upon consideration one comes to understand that the idol-worshipper does not worship the idol, instead, he worships his passion, since his soul inclines (*māʾila*) towards the religion of his fathers and he follows this inclination, and the soul's inclination towards familiar things is one of the meanings that the expression "passion" denotes.[19]

Notice, furthermore how the two passages just cited accord with the tenor of the *Deliverer from Error* (*al-Munqidh min al-ḍalāl*). There is a contingent element to ordinary belief-formation that has to do as much with the socialization process as it does with divine instruction, to say nothing of formal argument

17 Ibid., 8:1450.17–1451.18 (XXII, *bayān* 4, *wajh* 2); transl. by Winter in al-Ghazālī, *On Disciplining the Soul*, 33–34, lightly modified.

18 By contrast the pigeon-fancier is presented in a fairly innocuous light—al-Ghazālī only seems to want to reiterate how somebody can manifestly do themselves harm while pursuing their pleasure—and the element of socialization is absent. Bird-watching is comparable to other frivolous pastimes such as lute-playing, backgammon, and chess (*Iḥyāʾ*, 8:1527.12–14 [XXIII, *al-qawl fī shahwat al-farj*]). Interestingly, when it comes to the latter, al-Ghazālī hints at the possibility of analyzing any oversized investment in some particular art in terms of a misplaced intellectualism. An expert chess player will revel in the minutiae of the art, which, even though it finds satisfaction in a gross triviality, still reflects a primitive admiration for, and delight in, knowledge. See *Iḥyāʾ*, 14:2603.14–18 (XXXVI, *bayān* 4).

19 al-Ghazālī, *Iḥyāʾ*, 1:57.1–5 (I, *bāb* 3, *bayān* 2, *lafẓ* 3); cf. also ibid., 8:1393.20–21 (XXI, *bayān* 11).

and proof. This has been picked up earlier by both Richard M. Frank and Hermann Landolt: the latter postulated on the basis of the passage from the *Deliverer* that al-Ghazālī would have presumed true religion to be established in people's minds much the same way as false ones are.[20] While I think it would be too much to say on the basis of either the *Deliverer* or the *Niche of Lights* that al-Ghazālī approached empirical religions in a way that would have been *religionswissenschaftlich* in any strong sense, the second book of the *Revival*, entitled *Qawāʾid al-ʿaqāʾid* (*The Rules on What-To-Believe*), proves a more promising text on the basis of which to extrapolate. Here, al-Ghazālī affirms without hesitation that fixity and firmness in faith, whether Jewish, heretical, or Sunni Muslim, arises as a rule out of habit, experience, and custom, as established through a lifetime of practice. The insulating cocoon provided by a like-minded community furthermore acts as the layperson's shelter from doubt and serves to deflect stray thoughts (*khawāṭir:* see below) that might otherwise lead the individual on a different path.[21]

Taking into account the testimony of the *Revival*, then, we may affirm that al-Ghazālī is indeed willing to concede that the mechanisms by which the majority of Muslims come to their beliefs and hold firm to them are just as mundane and contingent as the ones by which heretics and unbelievers stand by theirs. And, of course, since the wrong kinds of value systems often do speak to people's immediate wants and desires more directly than does the true interpretation of Islam (which has an ultimately otherworldly orientation) they may very well grow to exercise a powerful hold on many, so that even a clear and persuasive presentation of the correct path will not have the desired effect. As an illustration, in speaking of guidance in matters of good and evil, al-Ghazālī avers that the books and the messengers and people's intellectual insight should generally suffice in bringing about righteous behaviour. These sources of insight can, however, become obscured by envy, pride, love of the present world and, "those causes that blind hearts even where eyesight is unaffected." Al-Ghazālī lists among the latter kinds of causes convention, custom, and the love of both of these: these in turn he illustrates with a trio of Qur'anic citations. The citations in question are more illuminating than usual, as they all have to do with the unwillingness of people to relinquish their established religion or to accept Muḥammad's mission, given that it comes from an unusual

20 Landolt, "Al-Ghazālī and 'Religionswissenschaft;'" Frank, "Al-Ghazālī on *taqlīd*."

21 al-Ghazālī, *Iḥyāʾ*, 2:211.10–212.5 (II, *faṣl* 4, *masʾala* 2, *q.* 2, *iṭlāq* 1); cf. also ibid., 1:162.4–13 (II, *faṣl* 2).

source (Q 43:22, 43:31, 54:24). Blindness, we may conclude, often issues from *taqlīd*, even if al-Ghazālī does not use that particular term in this instance.[22]

3 Reason Gone Wrong

Al-Ghazālī points out in *Mīzān al-ʿamal* (*The Scale of Action*) how many of those who are deluded or devious nonetheless teach, preach, and hold religious office. They claim to serve religion but in reality serve only their own passions, in the manner of those who have made their passion their God.[23] The devious part we may now understand as arising out of a wicked disposition. But what about delusion? How do false beliefs arise in human beings, as opposed to a misguided orientation?

From al-Ḥārith al-Muḥāsibī (d. 243/857) al-Ghazālī will have learned that it is the soul's passions that lie at the heart of all erroneous opinions and heretical innovations.[24] For a more technical account, he will have found resources in the Galenic tradition, as mediated by writers such as Miskawayh (d. 421/1030) and Avicenna (Ibn Sīnā, d. 428/1037). Al-Ghazālī plainly differentiates between the immediate passionate responses that we have towards our environment and actual erroneous opinions: only the latter take a propositional form. At the same time, the psychophysical account of cognition from which both the medical and the Peripatetic traditions work allows for a feedback mechanism that can have the passions contribute to belief formation. This explanatory model is in evidence in two Galenic treatises which we know were available in Arabic literature: a treatise on the *Passions and Errors of the Soul* and another called *On Morals.* Tim J. Winter and Yasien Mohamed have sufficiently established that the latter work had a marked impact on al-Ghazālī's conception of moral psychology through the mediating offices of Miskawayh and al-Rāghib al-Iṣfahānī (d. 422/1031).[25] Whether the first work also did is uncertain, but possible.[26]

---

22 Ibid., 12:2256.13–19 (XXXII, *shaṭr* 2, *rukn* 2, *hidāya* 1); cf. ibid., 8:1365.1–10 (XXI, *bayān* 5). Al-Ghazālī presents the philosophical tradition as resting on largely authoritarian grounds as well, blinding its followers from obvious truths: see Frank, "Al-Ghazālī on *taqlīd*," 244–46 and Griffel, "*Taqlīd* of the Philosophers."

23 al-Ghazālī, *Mīzān al-ʿamal*, 48–49, evoking the Qur'anic passage 45:23 once again.

24 See Picken, *Spiritual Purification in Islam*, 175, n. 49.

25 See Winter, "Introduction," in al-Ghazālī, *On Disciplining the Soul*; Mohamed, "The Ethical Philosophy of al-Rāghib al-Iṣfahānī;" Mohamed, "Knowledge and Purification of the Soul."

26 Ḥunayn Ibn Isḥāq lists the treatise on the *Passions and Errors of the Soul* as being available in Arabic: see §123 in Bergsträsser, "Ḥunain ibn Isḥāq über die syrischen und arabischen

Before we delve into the whys and the wherefores, a word is in order regarding the evaluative judgement that al-Ghazālī passes on any instance where our emotions are allowed to determine the directionality of our reasoning. According to al-Ghazālī it is always a reversion of the natural order to have our reasoning faculty receive its impetus from the passions, yet this is what happens, e.g., when the sexual appetites are allowed to run amok. In such a case we will frequently find a person making constant excuses for his or her behaviour, in effect putting one's powers of reasoning in the service of one's desires.[27] In the 32nd book of the *Revival*, the *Book of Patience and Thankfulness* (*Kitāb al-Ṣabr wa-l-shukr*), al-Ghazālī further expands on the notion that in a disordered soul reason is made into a slave of the passions. As a Muslim should naturally rule over the unbeliever, so also reason should rule over the passions: however, where the passions suppress the religious impulse (*bāʿith al-dīn*), "the intellect of such a miserable person has become a slave to his appetite, so that he does not use his intellect for anything except for crafting subtle plans as the means to satisfy his appetites." This is a grave misdeed, tantamount to the sins of those who would enslave Muslims and sell them to unbelievers.[28] But while al-Ghazālī's choice of example is inventive and his language affecting, it is the underlying point that is important here. What happens in the disordered soul is that reason is concretely made to serve the passions: the power of reasoning—understood here in the sense of our ability to argue and reason discursively—is not extinguished altogether, but is instead twisted to corrupt ends.

When it comes to how experience can misguide us and how the senses and the appetites work together, an interesting point is made in the 36th book of the *Revival*, the *Kitāb al-Maḥabba wa-l-shawq wa-l-uns wa-l-riḍā* (*Book of Love, Longing, Intimacy, and Contentment*). Al-Ghazālī explains that those perceptions that directly bear witness to God are frequently experienced in childhood, before the onset of the intellect: unfortunately, as the disposition of intellect (*gharīza al-ʿaql*) gradually attains maturity, so also do the appetites achieve dominance. As one "becomes accustomed to one's perceptions and sensations," the senses become dulled and one's experience of the world trivialized to the point that only a truly extraordinary event—in effect, a miracle—can shake the soul out of its stupor anymore.

Galen-Übersetzungen." A recent edition and French translation is available in Galen, *L'âme et ses passions*.

27 al-Ghazālī, Iḥyāʾ, 9:1527.5–11 (XXIII, *qawl fī shahwat al-faraj*); cf. idem, *al-Maqṣad*, 74.

28 Ibid., 12:2188.9–2189.10 (XXXII, *shaṭr* 1, *bayān* 5, *ḥāla* 2); see also ibid., 8:1363.18–22 (XXI, *bayān* 5); and cf. Miskawayh, *Tahdhīb al-akhlāq*, 53.

This to al-Ghazālī's eyes is ludicrous in a sense. In truth, everything in creation testifies equally to God's creative activity and His benevolent governance, so that in principle there should be no difference between a natural and a supernatural occurrence. Both are equally works of God.[29] But there is a reason for this disenchantment with the world and for the degradation of our sense of wonder, and it is quite illuminating. In the course of our lives, al-Ghazālī suggests, our very perceptions and experiences serve to frame our understanding of the world, so that most of us end up viewing it in more and more mundane terms. This is because the sensory world and our personal experience of it is for most of us all that we have time for, all that we have to go by; an easy familiarity with our daily surroundings leads to jurists dreaming only of jurisprudence and traders only of trade, and in general for each of us to perceive in the world only that to which their attention is customarily drawn.[30]

This is because specific activities are accompanied not only by primitive pleasures and pains, but also by representations in the animal soul of those things as being good and bad or beneficial and harmful.[31] This allows the inner senses to form memory imprints of such events, imprints which are reinforced through repetition so that eventually they influence even the heart.[32] Experience and custom thus gradually build up a network of gut-level assessments of what to pursue and what to avoid in this world. And if our conception of what life holds for us is limited to the satisfaction of our bodily needs, then this can effectively obscure from our sights the very existence of higher things and higher pleasures: we become unable any longer even to see reality for what it is.[33]

Al-Ghazālī presents the idea of incipient beliefs being filtered through one's predilections in the dress of occurrent notions (*khawāṭir*, singl. *khāṭir*). These passing fancies, which according to al-Ghazālī affect us all throughout our embodied life, can tilt our thoughts and actions either in a good or an ill direction, all according to whether they are of an angelic or a demonic provenance. (Upon closer reading, it becomes apparent that both in the end derive from God.[34]) The principal thing to notice is that occurrent notions primarily act as a spur towards practical rather than theoretical reasoning: their endpoint is

29 Ibid., 14:2627.17–2628.6 (XXXVI, *bayān* 8).

30 Ibid., 13:2377.15–17 (XXXIII, *shaṭr* 2, *bayān* 7).

31 Ibid., 13:2377.19–22 (XXXIII, *shaṭr* 2, *bayān* 7).

32 Ibid., 8:1390.21–1391.4 (XXI, *bayān* 11).

33 Ibid., 8:1367.12–16 (XXI, *bayān* 6, *sabab* 2).

34 See Ibid., 8:1390.16–1392.9 (XXI, *bayān* 11); 12:2238.10–2239.10 (XXXII, *shaṭr* 2, *rukn* 1, *bayān* 4). Similarly, al-Ghazālī explains "devilish temptations" or "devilish whisperings" (*wasāwis*, singl. *waswās*) as coming from the same source as the (angelic) inspirations (singl. *ilhām*),

action rather than belief, disobedience rather than heresy. They thus correspond rather closely to the *logismoi* one finds in Patristic authors such as Evagrius of Pontus and Gregory the Great.[35] But because there is a representational aspect to these *khawāṭir*—they make things appear pleasant or unpleasant in our eyes, desirable or undesirable—they occupy the curious position of having at once a cognitive and a motive function.

A further way in which the passions can end up feeding false and pernicious beliefs is delineated in the second book of the *Revival*. Here, al-Ghazālī avers that the grave sinner (*al-fāsiq*) is apt to stray from the correct understanding of religion at the slightest instigation, which is one reason why nobody who is in the thrall of their appetites should be let near *kalām*. Such a person, after all, will not wish to dispel doubts when it comes to the interpretation of religion, instead, the appetitive soul will simply seize those doubts by the horns in order to justify by their means an abrogation of religious duty (*taklīf*).[36] Thus does enslavement to the passions lead to error, which in turn will lead only to worse laxity in religious observance and the consequent further erosion of one's moral fibre. The criticism can usefully be compared with al-Ghazālī's account of the excuses Avicenna had given for his indulgence in drinking wine. There, as here, the impression is that of clever rationalizations being made to serve morally degraded ends.[37]

Al-Ghazālī famously takes a dim view of both law and theology in the form that the two disciplines were practiced in his day.[38] Here we may begin to glimpse how al-Ghazālī would explain the way these two worldly, but nonetheless utmost necessary, sciences could have gone wrong so dramatically. It is because the practitioners of *fiqh* and *kalām* became addicted to fame, to the riches that a position of repute brings, and to the very pleasures of disputation itself that they managed to lose sight of the important but limited function that their efforts originally enjoyed.[39] At the same time, practitioners of these mundane sciences (*ʿulūm al-dunyā*) had become actively disdainful of those

---

namely a celestial intellect, see Griffel, "Al-Ghazālī at His Most Rationalist: *The Universal Rule for Allegorically Interpreting Revelation* (*al-Qānūn al-kullī fī l-taʾwīl*)."

35 See Corrigan, *Evagrius and Gregory*, 73–101.

36 al-Ghazālī, *Iḥyāʾ*, 1:171.3–6 (II, *faṣl* 2, *masʾala* 1).

37 See al-Ghazālī, *al-Munqidh*, 47.17–48.10.

38 See, e.g., al-Ghazālī, *Iḥyāʾ*, 1:36.21–39.16 (I, *bāb* 2, *bayān* 1); Gianotti, "Beyond Both Law and Theology."

39 Al-Junayd's (d. 298/910) treatise, addressed to an otherwise unknown ʿAmr ibn ʿUthmān al-Makkī, anticipates this line of argument, crucially including the notion that errors multiply with the desire for glory: see al-Junayd, *Life, Personality, and Writings*, 12–13 (English translation 132–34).

who would aim higher and take the other world as their goal, going as far as to belittle the achievements of the genuinely pious and cast aspersions on their motives. In a passage in *Jawāhir al-Qurʾān* (*The Jewels of the Qurʾan*), al-Ghazālī effectively underlines how it is largely on the level of sub-rational passions that such malignant forces take hold. Normally, witnessing the piety of the pious will serve to strengthen the belief of the believers, however, when it comes to those wayward souls that see religion only in the light of worldly fame and material gain, the only thing likely to result from witnessing such magnificence is an increase in the observer's own arrogance and error. First the outward aspects of revelation become a muddle of confusion (*tashawwush*); then objections occur to one; then one begins to imagine (*takhāyala*) the opposite of the articles of faith. In this way the foundation for one's belief in religion becomes null and void and the bridles of the fear of God (*taqwā*) and the bonds of piety (*waraʿ*) both come loose, after which all manner of reprehensible behaviour follows all too easily.[40]

> All this [came to pass] because the speculation of their intellects was limited to the forms of things and their imaginative appearance (*ṣuwar al-ashyāʾ wa-qawālibuhā al-khayāliyya*)[41] instead of attaining to their spiritual aspects and their real natures (*arwāḥuhā wa ḥaqāʾiquhā*). Such people did not perceive the correspondence between the manifest world and the world of dominion: then when they failed to perceive this, and what was apparent regarding the questions perplexed them, they lapsed into error and led [others] into error as well.[42]

Characteristic of what al-Ghazālī calls the specifically pectoral offences against God is that in the manner just outlined, they have a religious as well as intellectual dimension—they include unbelief, heretical innovation, hypocrisy, and malicious designs on other people.[43] The story is made the more compelling by al-Ghazālī's frank admission that he himself once numbered among

40 al-Ghazālī, *Jawāhir*, 95–96.

41 The exact same dual expression ("forms and appearances") is used in *Mishkāt al-anwār*, 124.8, in relation to what the power of eyesight is able to perceive.. It is clear from the context that the term 'form' here does not refer to the Aristotelian hylomorphic essence—in al-Ghazālī's recasting of Avicennian terminology, that would be the *ḥaqīqa* of a particular existent—but simply as a shorthand for the thing's outward shape, *shakl*, as perceived by the outer senses and abstracted to some degree by the inner senses. Cf. similarly Ibn Ṭufayl, *Ḥayy Ibn Yaqẓān*, 46 and for comments Kukkonen, "No Man Is an Island," 194–195.

42 al-Ghazālī, *Jawāhir*, 96.7–9.

43 al-Ghazālī, *Iḥyāʾ*, 11:2102.9–16 (XXXI, *rukn* 2, *bayān* 1).

such benighted souls.[44] Though we may wish to write off the description as a mere polemical construct, it is still useful to consider the light in which the story paints al-Ghazālī's own activity up to the second half of 488/1095. Without the benefit of the light of insight (*nūr al-baṣīra*) the examination of religious questions will necessarily be both confused and confusing, even to the trained professional and proficient dialectician. It is because of the lack of such insight that the scholars (*ʿulamāʾ*), by whom al-Ghazālī plainly means the *kalām* theologians, had in the main proved unable to rise above corporeal models for explaining God's mode of being and His influence in the world. The veil of familiar notions had fatally impacted the theologians' ability to begin their speculation from sound notions.[45]

The underlying reason, as we have just read, is that the person—any person—who attempts to reason her or his own way to the truth in matters of religion only has the facts of this world to go by and only the mundane shapes of things on which to draw. This is not necessarily a doomed process in and of itself, because there is indeed a subtle correspondence between this world and the next due to the fact that God is the maker of both worlds. The crucial question is that of directionality. Isolated facts concerning creation will only reveal any of the deeper divine mysteries if they are examined in the light of divine guidance, and this in turn can only come from the inside, following the heart's purification and its awakening to the infusion of divine purpose in everything.[46] By contrast, any attempt to build a system of thought from the ground up that is unenlightened—in the sense of not being conducted in the light of divine disclosure—can only end up in failure, both because of our tendency to let our baser motives skew the results and because the information conveyed by our senses only has limited utility when it comes to construing the rules that govern the supernal realm.

More than the testimony of the senses themselves, this has to do with the intransigence of the faculty of estimation (*wahm*)—a faculty that is unable to rise above the unshakeable convictions it has of the physical world—and the unruliness of the compositive imagination (*khayāl*), which is prone to flights of fancy.[47] Al-Ghazālī most fully exploits what he perceives as the weaknesses of

44 al-Ghazālī, *Jawāhir*, 96.12–14.

45 al-Ghazālī, *Iḥyāʾ*, 8:1368.9–15 (XXI, *bayān* 6, *sabab* 4).

46 For details see Kukkonen, "Receptive to Reality;" idem, "Al-Ghazālī on the Signification of Names;" idem, "Al-Ghazālī on Accidental Identity and the Attributes."

47 See Kukkonen, "Al-Ghazālī's Skepticism Revisited," 44–51; for a telling reference to imagination and estimation, see *Fayṣal*, 50.12–51.2. For the epistemological limitations of *wahm* see also Griffel, "Al-Ghazālī's Use of 'Original Human Disposition' (*fiṭra*)," 19–24.

the judgements reached by the estimative and the imaginative faculties in *Tahāfut al-falāsifa* (*The Incoherence of the Philosophers*), where wide swathes of his argumentation rely on pointing out how the mere inability to picture a given scenario does not yet mean that it is impossible. To al-Ghazālī, to say that it does only serves to reveal a thinker's overt reliance on the inner senses, which are still tied to the material world in important ways, instead of aspiring to pure intellectual judgement.[48] A similar analysis had been offered earlier by Avicenna in conjunction with his presentation of estimative premises (*wahmiyyāt*); in Avicenna, too, the problem is that the rules we are accustomed to in physical reality need not apply in the immaterial domain, but that our estimative faculty refuses to make the leap from one to the other.[49] As Frank Griffel has shown, al-Ghazālī replicates this facet of Avicenna's technical exposition both in his two textbooks on logic, *Miḥakk al-naẓar* (*Touchstone of Reasoning*) and *Miʿyār al-ʿilm* (*The Standard of Knowledge*) and in his late work on the principles of jurisprudence.[50]

As with wrongful attitudes, so with false beliefs the problem is that habituation and familiarity ultimately lead to the heart becoming so hardened that reality has hardly any chance of piercing through the veil of error. Consistent with this, al-Ghazālī in the 31st book of the *Revival*, *Kitāb al-Tawba* (*The Book of Repentance*), equates ignorance and error with unbelief and describes the two in terms of a veil coming between God and the human being. Ignorance and error, too, lead to a distance opening up between God and us, and they therefore count as sins, possibly mortal ones.[51] By way of illustration, we may turn to *Kitāb al-Khawf wa-l-rajāʾ* (*The Book of Fear and Hope*), the 33rd in the *Revival*, where al-Ghazālī describes the dreaded evil of the seal (*sūʾ al-khātima*), the kind of doubt or ignorance (*shakk aw-juḥūd*) that so consumes the heart at the moment of death that the human individual becomes altogether unable to receive salvation. Al-Ghazālī presents two ways in which the seal can be imprinted on the human heart: one is the love of the world, which is to say the desire for something other than God, and this we have already seen skews a

48 al-Ghazālī, *Tahāfut*, 32.14–33.18, 35.1–36.6; for comments, Kukkonen, "Mind and Modal Judgement," 122–126.

49 See Black, "Estimation," 228–32; Kukkonen, "Ibn Sīnā and the Early History of Thought Experiments."

50 See al-Ghazālī, *Miḥakk*, 52–55; on estimative premises also al-Ghazālī, *al-Mustaṣfā*, 1:145–50, and for an example of estimation refusing to extend the ambit of the term "bad," see *al-Mustaṣfā*, 1:153.12–13; Griffel, "Al-Ghazālī's Use of 'Original Human Disposition' (*Fiṭra*)," 7.

51 al-Ghazālī, *Iḥyāʾ*, 11:2108.9–17 (XXXI, *rukn* 2, *bayān* 1, *qisma* 3, *martaba* 1).

person's entire orientation in life in a way that can only lead to perdition.[52] The second cause for the seal is in some ways more disconcerting, and therefore more liable to strike fear in the heart of the believer, since it can afflict even those who are righteous and sound of action (*ṣalāḥ fī l-aʿmāl*). A seriously misbegotten way of conceiving of God, His attributes, and His works—in short, heretical innovation or *bidʿa*—can serve to obscure one's understanding of reality so profoundly that at death, when the scales fall off our eyes and the World of Dominion (*ʿālam al-mulk*) dawns upon us, we may have become altogether unable to see it for what it is and become so blinded to God's truth that we turn away from him, rather than towards Him. Our own skewed beliefs, in other words, may deny us the bliss of the divine countenance for all eternity.[53]

With this, our catalogue of the sources of error in al-Ghazāli is largely complete. It remains to be said that al-Ghazālī also expends a good amount of energy on the art of correct inference; moreover, it is the philosophical tradition of syllogistic, especially the Aristotelian ideal of demonstration, that he wishes to promote, although he is everywhere careful to underline that this is an authentically Islamic tradition of reasoning and that there is nothing in Peripatetic logic that would not have been sanctioned by the Prophet as well. This topic has been ably covered by many scholars and there is no need to repeat that side of the story here.[54] Suffice it to say that al-Ghazālī distinguishes between the matter and form of syllogisms,[55] and that while the present article concentrates the way in which premises are arrived at—how one obtains the materials from which one reasons—al-Ghazālī holds that the reasoning process itself is vulnerable in another sense: specifically, argumentative techniques and supposed proofs, too, can be picked up in a manner that is imitative and subservient to authority rather than independently affirmed.[56] This is the reason why the careful study of the correct rules of inference is sanctioned and even mandated for those drawn to the subject, and why the insertion of textbook Avicennian logic serves a useful purpose in warding off familiar but unsound forms of argument. After all, the "criterion of knowledge" (*miʿyār al-ʿilm*) remains the best tool when it comes to the difficult task of separating truth from falsehood.

---

52 Ibid., 13:2371.17–2372.9 and 13: 2375.23–2376.22 (XXXIII, *shaṭr* 2, *bayān* 7).

53 Ibid., 13:2373.11–2374.12 (XXXIII, *shaṭr* 2, *bayān* 7). The same basic distinction between passions and errors is presented in al-Ghazālī's *al-Maqṣad al-asnā*, 43, though the statement there is rendered opaque by its lack of context or explanation..

54 See, e.g., Marmura, "Al-Ghazālī and Demonstrative Science;" Rudolph, "Die Neubewertung der Logik durch al-Gazālī."

55 See Lagerlund, "Al-Ghazālī on the Form and Matter of the Syllogisms."

56 al-Ghazālī, *Iḥyāʾ*, 1:162.22 (II, *faṣl* 2).

It is to *al-Qisṭās al-mustaqīm* (*The Straight Balance*) that al-Ghazālī directs the reader who wants to study the correct and indubitable forms of inference.[57] Perhaps tellingly, and in any case intriguingly, there is to my knowledge no corresponding exposé of incorrect inferences in al-Ghazālī's authorship, no analogue to the *Sophistical Refutations* that is to say. Al-Ghazālī has many clever analyses to offer when it comes to specific instances of faulty reasoning put forward by philosophers, theologians, traditionalists, and Bāṭinites, but he has no developed view of faulty reasoning as such, in the mechanical sense. Overall, al-Ghazālī seems more interested in the psychology of error than he is in the theory of fallacies. This is entirely in keeping with his overall moralizing project.

4 Veils upon Veils

With an interpretive framework in place, we may now turn to the "Veils Section" in the *Mishkāt al-anwār* (*Niche of Lights*). The overall context is determined by the Qur'an's celebrated Light Verse (24:35) and its interpretation. Following what was by then established tradition, al-Ghazālī in the *Niche of Lights* makes use of this poetical and highly allusive passage in order to defend the possibility on the part of the religious aspirant to gain authentic experience of the supernal domain (*al-malakūt*). But while al-Ghazālī's exegesis of the Light verse is devoted to discussing the different levels of religious enlightenment, in the final section of the book he moves adroitly to a different verse in the same portion of revelation (Q 24:40) in an effort to show how *that* verse effectively captures the different levels of benightedness to which people also fall prey. The latter verse speaks of waves, clouds, and darknesses, all of which al-Ghazālī finds remarkably apt metaphors for what happens when the human's sights are turned to that which is other than God.[58] To recapitulate these in brief terms:[59]

---

57 See, e.g., al-Ghazālī, *Mīzān*, 49–50; idem, *Fayṣal*, 49–50.

58 Q 24:40 says about the acts of the unbelievers, mentioned in Q 24:39: "Or, they are like darkness in a vast deep sea, which is covered by a wave (*mawj*) over which is [another] wave, and over that one clouds (*saḥāb*)—one darkness above the other. If one stretches one's hand out one can hardly see it. Whom God does not give light, he has no light [at all]."

59 The analysis offered here is not meant to surpass but to supplement Landolt's in "Al-Ghazālī and 'Religionswissenschaft'." Landolt in his article ably maps out the taxonomy of al-Ghazālī's heresiography, while I choose to explore the psychological underpinnings of the various emergent heresies.

a. The fathomless sea which according to the Qur'anic verse envelopes the wayward soul is to al-Ghazālī a representation of the sensible world itself, that murky realm which stands at the opposite end of God in the hierarchy of being—nothingness to God's being, transitoriness to His permanence, imperfection to His majesty and beauty. Accordingly, al-Ghazālī interprets the consecutive "waves" (singl. *mawj*) that swell above this sea as the impulses that arise from the appetitive and spirited parts of the soul, engulfing the soul in that world even as it struggles to break free. Appetite is straightforwardly preoccupied with simple sensory pleasures, and since the latter exist solely in the present world, love for such things will necessarily make one blind and deaf to any higher reality. As for the spirited part of the soul, this ignites harmful impulses related to the societal domain, its vices ranging from anger and malice to vanity and arrogance. Al-Ghazālī makes note of the fact that the spirit's demands are typically stronger than those of the appetite; he even calls the soul's spirited part the ghoul of the intellect (*ghūl al-ʿaql*). This signals an especial ability on the part of *thumos* to twist reason to its purposes, something we have already seen. In each case, the appellation darkness (*ẓulma*) is richly deserved, as these impulses represent a comprehensive turning away from the divine light.[60]

b. In discussing those who follow their desires al-Ghazālī singles out a group that somewhat transcends the gross materialism of the people led by appetite and the sheer aggression of those whose predatory nature overwhelms them. These people, al-Ghazālī avers, make a show of ratiocination (*taʿāqul*). In reality, what they desire is fame and reputation, followers and influence. As an example of reasoning going wrong in this manner, al-Ghazālī points to how a vain person may go hungry rather than compromise in his choice of clothing.[61] Characteristic of such people is that none of them believe in the next world "at all" (*aṣlan*), any more than do the rank materialists who seek the causes of things only in the natures of bodies.[62] If the people who are thus benighted do profess the confession of faith, it is only with their tongues, and with some worldly end in mind, like the fear of persecution or the urge to

60 al-Ghazālī, *Mishkāt al-anwār*, 172.5–173.3 (cf. *Iḥyāʾ*, 8:1400.12ff. [XXI, *bayān* 12]); similarly *Mishkāt*, 177.9–178.10. In the latter context al-Ghazālī additionally mentions those who become entangled in an unending desire of possessions, and gives what amounts to an Aristotelian critique: possessions and money are only instrumental to happiness, and whosoever does not recognize their instrumental nature and put them to use in pursuit of higher-order desires is severely misguided. *Mishkāt*, 178.11–179.3 and cf. Aristotle, *Eth. nic.*, 1.5, 1096a6–8.

61 al-Ghazālī, *Mishkāt al-anwār*, 179.4–9.

62 Ibid., 177.2–3.

defend the school of thought of one's forefathers (*madhhab al-ābāʾ*). The proof for this is that if religious belief (*īmān*) had genuinely set upon their hearts, this would be reflected in their deeds.[63]

c. By comparison with the afore-mentioned waves of passion, the clouds (*saḥāb*), which in al-Ghazālī's curious literally-minded exegesis of metaphorical devices reside somewhere above the sea and the waves, do in fact rise up in the direction of the heavens, while nonetheless having the practical effect of drawing a veil in front of the sun's true light. For al-Ghazālī, real illumination comes from the direction of the Qur'an and from the intellect, and these two jointly point towards the truth (or the Truth, as the case may be). Consequently and correspondingly, the clouds that obscure the truth will be of the nature of "wicked beliefs, false opinions, and corrupt imaginings."[64] This leads al-Ghazālī into a fully-fledged exposition of the different kinds of errors people fall into when engaging in God-talk. While this is not the place to discuss the various sects to which al-Ghazālī alludes—Hermann Landolt and Frank Griffel have made good progress on this[65]—a brief look at how he classifies the various sorts of errors is useful for our purposes insofar as it illustrates the way in which al-Ghazālī maps them onto the framework of Avicenna's cognitive psychology.

(i) The first group of errant religionists al-Ghazālī introduces is incapable of rising above the level of sensation, and therefore thinks that God and His attributes must also have an existence like that disclosed by the senses. Accordingly, idolatry, understood literally as the crafting and worship of idols, takes the shape that it does because the idolater wants to honour the false god in the most exalted form he or she knows—statues made out of precious material substances. Even if misguided, the effort still represents an attempt to translate into terms of worship such inklings as the errant believer has about the fundamental divine attributes of glory and beauty (*ʿizza wa-jamāl*).[66]

A slightly higher form of worship according to al-Ghazālī is the worship of a particularly beauteous creature, whether tree or horse or human. This is a worship of beauty as such (*al-jamāl al-muṭlaq*), in addition to which it is the worship of natural rather than artificial beauty (*al-jamāl al-maṭbūʿ lā al-maṣnūʿ*).[67] These remarks sound Platonic and Plotinian, respectively,

63 Ibid., 179.13–14.

64 See ibid., 173.4–9.

65 See Landolt, "Al-Ghazālī and 'Religionswissenschaft'," and Griffel, "Al-Ghazālī's Cosmology."

66 al-Ghazālī, *Mishkāt al-anwār*, 180.8–15.

67 Ibid., 181.2.

although it is not immediately clear where al-Ghazālī could have come by his knowledge of Neo-Platonic aesthetics.[68] Yet another way of getting caught up in sensory notions is to fixate on the qualities of visible light: this leads to the worship of fire, stars, sun, and absolute light (*al-nūr al-muṭlaq*) in an ascending order of abstraction. But because visible light is set up against darkness in this world, such a sensual understanding of the meaning of light will necessarily result in dualism all the same.[69]

(ii) The second group acknowledges the existence of something beyond mere sensibles (*al-maḥsūsāt*), yet gets tripped up by the workings of the imagination (*al-khayāl*). Al-Ghazālī deliberately abstains from elaborating on the resulting claims and schools of thought, which in a sense is a curious omission: all he says is that the *mujassima* ("corporealists") and the Karrāmiyya are examples of such people, and that the directionality of "upwards" (*fawqa*) is the final thing one must let go off when getting rid of such vain imaginings, since such a letting-go represents the first step when it comes to the degrees by which the intelligibles transcend any relation to directionality.[70] Al-Ghazālī's example is revealing in the way that it plays up the imagination's limits in going beyond what it knows of corporeal existence. Al-Ghazālī claims that both the *mujassima* and the Karrāmiyya had proved themselves unable to understand the Throne on which God sits in anything other than in literal terms: this had led to an affirmation of God's corporeality willy-nilly.[71] On the opposing end of the scale, sincere thinkers had managed to extricate from their understanding of God every trace of anthropomorphism—every trace, that is, expect for their continued insistence that there be some real sense in which God resides above (*fawqa*) creation. But then, such a directionality of "above," understood in physical terms, is enough to bring in all of the unacceptable implications of corporealizing God.

What is interesting about this passage is how al-Ghazālī implicitly recognizes that the reviled corporealists and likeners (of God to some creature: *mushabbihūn*) had not really set out to be anything of the sort. As Binyamin Abrahamov has noted, no faction in Islamic theology ever self-identified as

68 Ibid., 181.13–13; see Kukkonen, "The Good, the Beautiful, and the True," 93–95.

69 al-Ghazālī, *Mishkāt al-anwār*, 181.3–182.3.

70 (...) *anna awwal darajāt al-ma'qūlāt tajāwazu l-nisba ilā l-jihāt*: see al-Ghazālī, *Mishkāt al-anwār*, 182.4–13.

71 To these labels we may add the *ḥashwiyya* (the bull-headedly literal-minded traditionalists) on the basis of al-Ghazālī, *al-Maqṣad*, 115–18. For the Ash'arite heresiography regarding the issue of assigning a body to God (*tajsīm*) see, e.g., al-Ash'arī, *Maqālāt*, 207ff.; on the Karrāmiyya being so described, al-Baghdādī, *al-Farq*, 177–84; but on the suspect nature of these designations, e.g., van Ess, *Der Eine und das Andere*, 1:706–8 and 2:1347–48.

corporealist. Rather, the derogatory designation seems to have been arrived at through someone—perhaps the proponent of a literal understanding of the Throne, say, or perhaps more plausibly its opponent—finding that a likening of God to creatures is what such a position amounts to. Assuming we are right to map this degree of error to the workings of the inner senses, more especially the faculty of estimation (*wahm*), then al-Ghazālī's account captures compactly some of the underlying themes in Avicenna. Purely on the level of an allegorical reading of the Qur'an, al-Ghazālī also manages the neat trick of embracing what the Peripatetic tradition has to say about mist, clouds, and the like (see Aristotle, *Meteor.* 1.8–9). As rarefied and vaporized water, these phenomena, too, reflect their source in earthbound elements and will consequently never rise up to the heavens.

(iii) A third class of errors arises from "intellectual ratiocinations" (*muqāyisāt ʿaqliyya*) that are corrupt and benighted (*fāsida, muẓlima*). The example al-Ghazālī gives is the faulty analogy that some people draw between our attributes and the divine attributes: the likening of God's will to our will, His intentions to ours, or His seeing, hearing, and living to the way that we ourselves see, hear, or are alive.[72] This specific form of inference, from the seen to the unseen, constitutes one form of analogical reasoning (*qiyās*), a procedure that comes under heavy criticism in *al-Qisṭās al-mustaqīm* (*The Straight Balance*), a work in which al-Ghazālī purports to reveal the true Qur'anic forms of inference and to set them apart from the false counterparts that have led only to needless confusion.[73] In *The Straight Balance* analogical reasoning is set out essentially as an instance of incomplete induction,[74] and while this may not be a fair representation of the *kalām* tradition, it at least allows us to uncover some of the reasons al-Ghazālī may have had for differentiating between the judgements of the inner senses and actual faulty inferences. What the inner senses produce are instantaneous impressions; what is at stake in false ratiocination may be the disingenuous justification of such shaky premises, but it need not be.

All of the above confirms for us that al-Ghazālī's actual exposition in the "veils section" of the *Niche of Lights* precisely mirrors his programmatic statement at its end. The appetite and the spirit (our "human attributes") provide the first and most primal reason for our straying from the straight path, since it

72 al-Ghazālī, *Mishkāt al-anwār*, 182.14–183.5.

73 On al-Ghazālī's *al-Qisṭās al-mustaqīm*, see Kleinknecht, "Al-Qisṭās al-Mustaqīm."

74 See al-Ghazālī, *Qisṭās*, 95.20ff.; a much lengthier and more balanced assessment of *qiyās* is given in *al-Mustaṣfā*, 3:479–747, but it should be noted that this is *qiyās* in the realm of jurisprudence.

is these that actually incline us away from God and in the direction of the world; on the cognitive side, the senses, the imagination, and the estimative faculty each provide their own opportunities for our understanding of things to go wrong. The intellect, meanwhile, when considered in itself, will never err about its proper objects—objects which, we should notice, encompass everything in the sensible as well as the intelligible realm.[75] However, because it is so very difficult for the intellect to detach (*tajarrada*) itself fully from the workings of the estimative and the imaginative faculties that threaten to throw a cover over it (*ghiṭāʾ*: see Q 50:22), it is in fact exceedingly rare to find anybody operating at the requisite level of abstraction (*tajrīd*).[76]

In connection with this, and by way of closing, it is perhaps appropriate to address at least in passing the final veil mentioned in the *Niche of Lights*. This we may pass over briefly, even though the point is central to al-Ghazālī's overall concerns and those of the *Niche of Lights* taken as a whole: sheer light frustrates our attempts to view it just as the divine essence in the final end resists every attempt at conceptualization and commensuration, even while the divine attributes exercise a fundamental fascination upon us as so many modes of divine perfection.[77] To say that the very brightness of sheer light can serve to obscure our senses is equivalent to saying that the divine essence due to its very ontological superiority is fundamentally inaccessible to every human experience, cognition, and descriptive effort, at the same time that God's omnipresence makes it impossible to distinguish Him by what He is not.[78] Among other things, this means that even God's saints may come up with misleading or mistaken descriptions of what they have experienced once the throes of their ecstasy are past.[79] Here the experience itself is not at fault; rather, it is the yawning chasm between this and our mundane existence that leads to an improper interpretation being imposed on it. Al-Ghazālī explicitly identifies this as a mistaken rationalization, a factual claim that is impossible and that can be demonstrated to be such. Indeed, the very propositionality of these mistaken claims ("I am He," "There is nothing in this robe but God") betrays their nature as after-the-fact reconstructions of what occurred, rather than straightforward accounts of the experience itself.

---

75 al-Ghazālī, *Mishkāt al-anwār*, 123.5–8.

76 Ibid., 127.10–128.7.

77 For comments see Kukkonen, "Al-Ghazālī on Accidental Identity," 671–674; Kukkonen, "Al-Ghazālī on the Signification of Names," 70–71; also Shehadi, *Al-Ghazālī's Unique Unknowable God*, though Shehadi's apophaticism is exaggerated.

78 See, e.g., al-Ghazālī, *Mishkāt al-anwār*, 148.1–15; likewise *al-Maqṣad*, 147–49, and *Iḥyāʾ*, 14:2625.3–2627.8 (xxxvi, *bayān* 8).

79 al-Ghazālī, *al-Maqṣad*, 165–71.

5 Stumbling through the Dark

It is time to draw some conclusions from our discussion of al-Ghazālī on the sources of error. Richard M. Frank has already noted how in the *Niche of Lights* wicked beliefs, false opinions, and corrupt imaginings are juxtaposed with proper religious belief (*īmān*), knowledge of the truth, and the illumination of the sun of the Qur'an and the intellect.[80] The *Kitāb al-Ṣabr wa-l-shukr* (*The Book of Patience and Thankfulness*), which is the 32nd book in the *Revival*, adds some needed context. Here, al-Ghazālī says that the righteous fix their sights on the real natures of things first, and their meanings, and that they do so by the aid of the divine light: aided by such insight, they then venture to view creation. The unbelievers go astray precisely because they try to reverse this proper order, attempting to reason their own way from the mundane world to the supernal, or from effects to causes. The gulf between the two being what it is, however, it is a foregone conclusion that the inquirer will stumble at some point.[81] Consequently, as the *Revival's* first book, the *Book of Knowledge* (*Kitāb al-ʿIlm*) puts it, when it comes to the inner meaning of the verses of Scripture,

> These realities (*haqāʾiq*) are evident to one who reflects with the light of insight (*nāẓir bi-nūr al-baṣīra*) but become obscured from the one who relies on hearsay and authority (*al-samāʿ wa-l-taqlīd*) without [the benefit of] unveiling and personal insight (*al-kashf wa-l-ʿiyān*). Because of this you will see [the one without insight] snared by verses such as those [we mentioned earlier]. He will attempt to interpret remembrance as some kind of affirmation of the soul and end up imagining that the *ḥadīth*-reports (*akhbār*) and Qur'anic verses (*āyāt*) are thick with contradictions. Perhaps this [tendency] will become so overpowering for him that he will end up viewing [revelation] with a denigrating eye, seeing in it actual incoherence (*tahāfut*). An apt simile for this is the blind person who enters a house, knocks over some jars and then proclaims: "Why were these jars not taken out of the way and put where they belong?" Such a person will consequently be told: "[The jars] are in their places and the fault lies with your [faculty of] sight."[82]

The image is quite lovely, but it conceals a sharply honed point. One who lives in error suffers from a serious misalignment, insofar as such a person's putative

80 Frank, "Al-Ghazālī on *taqlīd*," 243–44.

81 al-Ghazālī, *Iḥyāʾ*, 12:2187.14–19 (XXXII, *shaṭr* 1, *bayān* 4).

82 Ibid., 1:148.16–21 (I, *bāb* 7, *bayān* 2).

"knowledge" is fundamentally at odds with reality as it actually is. And what holds true for the interpretation of scripture (theoretical knowledge) also holds true for the choices one makes in life (practical reasoning), and the two moreover meet in the way that the science of the hereafter encompasses both, so that proceeding by anything other than the light of divine guidance can in the end only lead to innumerable bruises, scrapes, and ultimate (indeed eternal) frustration. Yet the fact that one has become accustomed to a certain way of seeing and judging things means that the necessary readjustment may not occur easily.

All this may help to explain why for al-Ghazālī theological inquiries concerning the proclamation of divine unity are among the whisperings of Satan (*wasāwis*, singl. *waswās*).[83] Al-Ghazālī's desire to have those whose faith is solid and undisturbed be left alone is well documented and frequently emphasized in the literature.[84] Across a wide range of texts, from the early *al-Iqtiṣād fī l-iʿtiqād* (*The Balanced Book on What-To-Believe*) to the very late treatise *Iljām al-ʿawāmm ʿan ʿilm al-kalām* (*Restraining the Ordinary People from the Science of Kalam*), al-Ghazālī consistently maintains that there is no call to stir up doubts in the minds of the great majority who have not come across them on their own. In fact, to do so would be decidedly counterproductive, seeing as doubt is detrimental to the simple faith of the commoners and a simple faith is correct and conducive to salvation as far as it goes.[85] But what is also evident to al-Ghazālī is that the very practice of theological inquiry can serve to shape a person's mind in all the wrong ways. In the *Qawāʿid al-ʿaqāʾid* (*Rules on What-To-Believe*), the second book in the *Revival*, al-Ghazālī illustrates this through the example of the putative student of theology whose upbringing has occurred in a town in which disputation and partisanship (*jadal wa-taʿaṣṣub*) are rife. In such a case, even the combined efforts of the first and the last—that is to say, the ancient and the moderns—will not be able to uproot the innovation from his inmost being. Rather, passion (*hawā*), partisanship, and the resentment of one's disputational opponents and divergent sects so consume the theologian's heart as to prevent him from perceiving the truth, to the point that if someone were to ask him: "Do you wish for God to lift from you the veil and the cover, so that He may grant you in person the understanding that the truth lies with your opponent?" He would shun the opportunity, for fear that a public about-face might delight his opponent. For al-Ghazālī, this astonishing state of affairs is representative of a standing ailment that has spread throughout the

83 Ibid., 8:1484.2–5 (XXII, *bayān* 11); cf. *Iḥyāʾ*, 9:1638.16–1639.6 (XXIV, *āfa* 20).

84 The defining treatment remains Frank, "Al-Ghazālī on *taqlīd*."

85 al-Ghazālī, *Iḥyāʾ*, 13:2374.13–20 (XXXIII, *shaṭr* 2, *bayān* 7).

countries and peoples. It is a kind of corruption (*fasād*) resulting from partisan disputes.[86]

Many of the concerns brought up in this passage are the same ones to which al-Ghazālī draws attention in his writings on the formation of wrongful values and erroneous beliefs. Above everything else, the excesses of appetite and spirit are liable to distort one's engagement in the search for the truth concerning God and His creation, to the extent that the truth is no longer what is sought at all, only victory in disputation for oneself or one's own preferred party. This observation lends some added weight to al-Ghazālī's famous adaptation of Caliph 'Alī's words in the *Deliverer from Error* to the effect that a man's authority should be judged by the truth that he speaks rather than judging the truth by the authority that their speakers boast;[87] but it still leaves open the question of what the road to the truth might be. The answer to that remains as simple as it is beguiling. It is the light of divine guidance, under the twin guises of the pure unadulterated intellect and the Prophet's *sunna*, that provides us with a reliable access to the deeper truths underlying all things. Elsewhere I have commented on al-Ghazālī's conviction that this is the case;[88] for now, it is enough to underline how without such guidance, al-Ghazālī thinks we are condemned to stumble in the dark, forever mistaking elephants for stretches of rope.[89]

Bibliography

al-Akiti, M. Afifi. "Index to Divisions of al-Ghazālī's Often-Cited Published Works." *Muslim World* 102 (2012): 70–200.

al-Ash'arī, 'Alī ibn Ismā'īl. *Maqālāt al-islāmiyyīn.* Edited by H. Ritter. 2nd ed. Wiesbaden: Franz Steiner Verlag, 1963.

al-Baghdādī, 'Abd al-Qāhir ibn Ṭāhir. *al-Farq bayna l-firaq.* Edited by N. Ḥ. Zarzūr. Beirut: al-Maktaba al-'Aṣriyya, 2009.

86 Ibid., 1:167.24–168.6 (II, *faṣl* 2, *mas'ala* 1).

87 al-Ghazālī, *al-Munqidh*, 25.14–17.

88 See Kukkonen, "Al-Ghazālī on Accidental Identity and the Attributes."

89 For the page references to the *Iḥyā'* in this article I have relied on Mohammed Hozien's reconstruction of the 1356–1357 (1937–1938) printing of the work; my warmest thanks are due to Mr. Hozien for his efforts. I have strived to identify chapters in accordance with M. Afifi al-Akiti's recently published "Index to Divisions of al-Ghazālī's Often-Cited Published Works." The preparatory work for this article was made possible by European Research Council SIRG grant 201767 (project acronym SSALT).

Bergsträsser, Gotthelf. *Ḥunain ibn Isḥāq über die syrischen und arabischen Galen-Übersetzungen. Abhandlungen für die Kunde des Morgenlandes* 17, no. 2 (1925).

Black, Deborah L. "Estimation (*Wahm*) in Avicenna: The Logical and Psychological Dimensions." *Dialogue* 32 (1993): 219–58.

Corrigan, Kevin. *Evagrius and Gregory. Mind, Soul and Body in the 4th Century.* Farnham: Ashgate, 2009.

Evans, Gillian R. *Getting It Wrong. The Medieval Epistemology of Error.* Leiden: Brill, 1998.

Frank, Richard M. "Al-Ghazālī on *taqlīd.* Scholars, theologians, and philosophers." *Zeitschrift für Geschichte der Arabisch-Islamischen Wissenschaften* 7 (1991–92): 207–52.

———. "Knowledge and *Taqlīd.*" *Journal of the American Oriental Society* 109 (1989): 37–62.

Galen of Pergamon (Galien). *L'âme et ses passions.* Paris: Les Belles Lettres, 1995.

Garden, Kenneth. "Coming Down from the Mountaintop: Al-Ghazālī's Autobiographical Writings in Context." *Muslim World* 101 (2011): 581–96.

al-Ghazālī, Muḥammad ibn Muḥammad. *Fayṣal al-tafriqa bayna l-Islām wa-l-zandaqa.* Edited by M. Bījū. Damascus: Maḥmūd Bījū, 1993.

———. *Iḥyāʾ ʿulūm al-dīn.* 16 vols. Cairo: Lajnat Nashr al-Thaqāfa al-Islāmiyya, 1356–1357 [1937–1938].

———. *The Incoherence of the Philosophers / Tahāfut al-falāsifa.* Edited and transl. by M. E. Marmura. 2nd ed. Provo: Brigham Young University Press, 2000.

———. *Jawāhir al-Qurʾān wa-duraruhu [wa-Kitāb al-Arbaʿīn fī uṣūl al-dīn].* Edited by Kh. M. Kāmil and ʿI. al-Sharqāwī. Cairo: Maṭbaʿat Dār al-Kutub wa-l-Wathāʾiq al-Qawmiyya, 1432/2011.

———. *al-Maqṣad al-asnā fī sharḥ maʿānī asmāʾ Allāh al-ḥusnā,* Edited by F. Shehadi. 2nd. ed. Beirut: Imprimerie Catholique, 1982.

———. *Miḥakk al-naẓar fī l-manṭiq.* Edited by M. B. al-Naʿsānī and M. al-Qabbānī. Cairo: al-Maṭbaʿa al-Adabiyya, w.d. [1925].

———. *Mīzān al-ʿamal.* Edited by Muḥyī al-Dīn Ṣabrī al-Kurdī. Cairo: al-Maṭbaʿa al-ʿArabiyya, 1342 [1923].

———. *al-Munqidh min al-ḍalāl / Erreur et délivrance.* Edition (following J. Ṣalībā and K. ʿAyyād) and French transl. by F. Jabre. Beirut: Commission libanaise pour la traduction des chefs-d'œuvre, 1969

———. *al-Mustaṣfā min ʿilm al-uṣūl.* Edited by Ḥ. ibn Z. Ḥāfiẓ. 4 vols. Medina (Saudi Arabia): al-Jāmiʿa al-Islāmiyya—Kulliyyat al-Sharīʿa, 1413 [1992–93].

———. *Mishkāt al-anwār wa-miṣfāt al-asrār.* Edited by ʿAbd al-ʿAzīz ʿIzz al-Dīn al-Sayrawān. Beirut: ʿĀlam al-Kutub, 1407/1986.

———. *On Disciplining the Soul. Kitāb Riyāḍāt al-nafs. And On Breaking the Two Desires. Kitāb Kasr al-shahwatayn. Books XXII and XXIII of the Revival of the Religious Sciences. Iḥtāʾ ʿulūm al-dīn.* Transl. by T. J. Winter. Cambridge: The Islamic Text Society, 1995.

———. *al-Qisṭās al-mustaqīm*. Edited by V. Chelhot. Beirut: Dār al-Mashriq, 1986.

Gianotti, Timothy J. "Beyond Both Law and Theology: An Introduction to al-Ghazālī's 'Science of the Way of the Afterlife' in *Reviving Religious Knowledge* (*Iḥyā' 'Ulūm al-Dīn*)." *Muslim World* 101 (2011): 597–613.

Griffel, Frank. "Al-Ghazālī at His Most Rationalist: *The Universal Rule for Allegorically Interpreting Revelation* (*al-Qānūn al-kullī fī l-ta'wīl*)." In *Islam and Rationality. The Impact of al-Ghazālī*. Vol. 1. Edited by G. Tamer. Leiden: Brill, 2015. 89–120.

———. "Al-Ghazālī's Cosmology in the Veil Section of His *Mishkāt al-Anwār*," in *Avicenna and His Heritage. A Golden Age of Science and Philosophy*. Edited by Y. T. Langermann. Turnhout: Brepols, 2009. 27–49.

———. "Al-Ghazālī's Use of 'Original Human Disposition' (*Fiṭra*) and Its Background in the Teachings of al-Fārābi and Avicenna." *Muslim World* 102.1 (2012): 1–32.

———. "Taqlīd of the Philosophers. Al-Ghazālī's Initial Accusation In the *Tahāfut*." In *Ideas, Images, and Methods of Portrayal. Insights into Arabic Literature and Islam*. Edited by S. Günther. Leiden: Brill. 2005. 273–96.

Ibn Ṭufayl, Muḥammad ibn 'Abd al-Malik. *Ḥayy ibn Yaqẓān*. Edited by L. Gauthier. 2nd. ed. Beirut: Imprimerie Catholique, 1936.

al-Junayd, Abū l-Qāṣim ibn Muḥammad. *The Life, Personality, and Writings of al-Junayd*. Edited and translated by A. H. Abdel-Kader. London: Luzac, 1962.

Kleinknecht, Angelika. "Al-Qisṭās Al-Mustaqīm: Eine Ableitung der Logik aus dem Koran." In *Islamic Philosophy and the Classical Tradition*. Edited by S. M. Stern et al. Columbia: University of South Carolina Press, 1972. 159–87.

Kukkonen, Taneli. "Al-Ghazālī on Accidental Identity and the Attributes." *Muslim World* 100 (2011): 658–79.

———. "Al-Ghazālī on the Emotions." In *Islam and Rationality. The Impact of al-Ghazālī*. Vol. 1. Edited by G. Tamer. Leiden: Brill, 2015. 138–64.

———. "Al-Ghazālī on the Signification of Names." *Vivarium* 48 (2010): 55–74.

———. "Al-Ghazālī's Skepticism Revisited." In *Rethinking the History of Skepticism. The Missing Medieval Period*. Edited by H. Lagerlund. Leiden: Brill, 2010. 29–59.

———. "Mind and Modal Judgement: Al-Ghazālī and Ibn Rushd on Conceivability and Possibility." In *Mind and Modality. Studies in the History of Philosophy in Honour of Simo Knuuttila*. Edited by. V. Hirvonen et al. Leiden: Brill, 2006. 121–139.

———. "No Man Is an Island: Nature and Neo-Platonic Ethics in Ḥayy Ibn Yaqẓān." *Journal of the History of Philosophy* 46 (2008): 187–204.

———. "Receptive to Reality: Al-Ghazālī on the Structure of the Soul." *Muslim World* 102 (2012): 541–561.

———. "The Good, the Beautiful, and the True. Aesthetical Issues in Islamic Philosophy." *Studia Orientalia* 111 (2011): 87–103.

———. "Ibn Sīnā and the Early History of Thought Experiments." *Journal of the History of Philosophy*, 52 (2004): 433–59.

Lagerlund, Henrik. "Al-Ghazālī on the Form and Matter of the Syllogisms." *Vivarium* 48 (2010): 193–214.

Landolt, Hermann. "Ghazālī and 'Religionswissenschaft': Some Notes on the Mishkāt al-Anwār for Professor Charles J. Adams." *Asiatische Studien* (Zurich) 45 (1991): 19–72.

Marmura, Michael E. "Ghazali and Demonstrative Science." *Journal of the History of Philosophy* 3 (1965): 183–204.

Miskawayh, Aḥmad ibn Muḥammad. *Tahdhīb al-akhlāq*. Edited by C. K. Zurayk. Beirut: American University of Beirut, 1966–67.

Mohamed, Yasien. "The Ethical Philosophy of al-Rāghib al-Iṣfahānī." *Journal of Islamic Studies* 6 (1995): 51–75.

———. "Knowledge and Purification of the Soul. An Annotated Translation with Introduction of Iṣfahānī's *Kitāb al-dharīʿa ilā makārim al-sharīʿa (58–76; 89–92)*." *Journal of Islamic Studies* 9 (1998): 1–34.

Picken, Gavin. *Spiritual Purification in Islam*. New York: Routledge, 2011.

Rudolph, Ulrich. "Die Neubewertung der Logik durch al-Ġazālī." In *Logik und Theologie. Das Organon im arabischen und lateinischen Mittelalter*. Edited by D. Perler and U. Rudolph. Leiden: Brill, 2005. 73–97

Shehadi, Fadlou. *Al-Ghazālī's Unique Unknowable God*. Leiden: E. J. Brill, 1964.

Sherif, Mohamed A. *Ghazali's Theory of Virtue*. Albany (N.Y.): State University of New York Press, 1975.

Treiger, Alexander. *Inspired Knowledge in Islamic Thought. Al-Ghazālī's Theory of Mystical Cognition and its Avicennian Foundation*. London: Routledge, 2011.

van Ess, Josef. *Der Eine und das Andere. Beobachtungen an islamischen häresiographischen Texten*. 2 vols. Berlin and New York: Walter de Gruyter, 2011.

CHAPTER 2

Al-Ghazālī's Concept of Philosophy

Ulrich Rudolph

I

It is well known that al-Ghazālī's attitude towards philosophy is rather conflicted and unclear. On the one hand, he composed *Tahāfut al-falāsifa* (*The Incoherence of the Philosophers*), considered by most of its readers the harshest refutation of Arabic philosophy ever written. On the other, he shares quite a number of positions with the philosophers and made ample use of their writings in order to express his own ideas.

This ambivalence is puzzling and has led to much debate. Numerous scholars have tried to find a key to understanding al-Ghazālī's relationship with philosophy and an explanation as to why he reacted to philosophical reasoning in such a mystifying variety of ways. The explanations vary, but on the whole can be reduced to four interpretations, namely: (1) Al-Ghazālī's comments on philosophy changed as his attitude towards philosophy evolved over his lifetime, so that his later works reflect a position different from the earlier. (2) Al-Ghazālī's statements about philosophy depend on his audience, for he practised a kind of multi-level writing in order to speak to each audience in a way they understood and were willing to accept. (3) His comments depend on the subject, accepting philosophical concepts in some fields, but not in others, so that his approach to philosophy is selective, if not actually inconsistent. (4) He has a kind of master plan concerning philosophy, and all his comments, the critical as well as the affirmative, were parts of the same strategy and were meant to attain the same goal, though they may seem to diverge from one another upon first reading.[1]

---

* A first draft of this paper has been presented at the Dies Academicus II of the Accademia Ambrosiana (Milan, November 7, 2011) and has been published in the proceedings of the Dies; cf. Rudolph, "How did al-Ġazālī conceptualize philosophy?"

1 Some of these interpretations can be traced back to older publications such as Obermann, *Subjektivismus*, Wensinck, *La pensée*, Abd-El-Jalil, "Autour de la sincérité," Jabre, *La notion de certitude*, idem, *La notion de la maʿrifa*, and Watt, *Muslim Intellectual*, which are still worth reading. The state of discussion, however, has considerably shifted since Richard M. Frank published, in the early 1990s, his article "Al-Ghazālī's Use of Avicenna's Philosophy" and two monographs, *Creation and the Cosmic System* and *Al-Ghazālī and the Ashʿarite School*. Several

 | DOI 10.1163/9789004307490_003

All these explanations are based on viable arguments and deserve further discussion. It may well be that al-Ghazālī's attitude towards philosophy is complex and multifarious, and we need a complex set of interpretations to adequately describe it. Given this assumption, however, our considerations should not be confined to the level of individual philosophical doctrines and arguments. We should also take into account how al-Ghazālī argues on a deeper, conceptual level. Therefore, I plan to ask what philosophy really is, according to al-Ghazālī. How does he conceptualize and define philosophy, or at least, how does he describe its different parts and its place among the sciences?

While evaluating these problems, I will argue that al-Ghazālī's concept of philosophy draws heavily on earlier models. This does not mean that his ideas about philosophy are not original, which goes without saying. It seems to me, however, that they rely at least partly on earlier ideas, the origin of which can still be discerned. In order to show this, my paper will be divided into three parts. In the first part, I will summarize three concepts of philosophy that were developed in the centuries before al-Ghazālī. Strictly speaking, I will outline (1) the concept developed by Abū Naṣr al-Fārābī (d. 339/950) and followed—with considerable modification—by Avicenna (Ibn Sīnā, d. 428/1037); (2) the concept of the Islamic theologians (*mutakallimūn*), and (3) the concept shared by authors who can be assigned to the philosophical tradition of Abū Isḥāq al-Kindī (d. 246/861–251/866), such as Abū l-Ḥasan al-ʿĀmirī (d. 381/992), Miskawayh (d. 421/1030), Abū Sulaymān as-Sijistānī (d. ca. 377/987), and al-Rāghib al-Iṣfahānī (d. 422/1031). In the second part of this paper, I will connect these models with al-Ghazālī's own idea of philosophy as he expressed it in the *Tahāfut al-falāsifa* and in particular in *al-Munqidh min al-ḍalāl* (*The Deliverer from Error*). In this manner, I will try to evaluate in which sense and to what extent they may have influenced al-Ghazālī. This evaluation will eventually lead us to some general considerations about al-Ghazālī's position in the intellectual history of Islam and about the way in which his position is viewed and analysed today. Far from exhaustive, these considerations will merely touch on

scholars heavily criticized Frank's suggestion to interpret al-Ghazālī along Avicennian lines, among them Marmura, "Ghazālian Causes and Intermediaries" (cf. idem, "Ghazali and Ashʿarism Revisited"), Mayer in his review of Frank, *Al-Ghazālī and the Ashʿarite School*, and Dallal, "Al-Ghazālī and the Perils of Interpretation." Notwithstanding this criticism, however, Frank's work led to a serious reconsideration of al-Ghazālī's attitude towards philosophy that proved on the whole promising and is still dominating the research agenda nowadays. For a short account of the vicissitudes of research on al-Ghazālī see Treiger, *Inspired Knowledge in Islamic Thought*, 1–4, and Griffel, *Al-Ghazālī's Philosophical Theology*, 179–82.

some points which seem to me striking in the current debate about al-Ghazālī and which deserve more thorough reflection.

II

(1) The first concept to be mentioned is the one by al-Fārābī. His thought can be characterized as a further development of the Aristotelian notion of philosophy. According to al-Fārābī, philosophy is more or less synonymous with universal science.[2] It comprises all cognitive activities that rely on true premises and valuable syllogisms, whose results must be accepted by all who understand them.[3] This idea was expressed in several of his writings, including *The Enumeration of the Sciences* (*Iḥṣāʾ al-ʿulūm*). As al-Fārābī explains, we must distinguish between two kinds of sciences. First are disciplines that are limited in their scope and are based on arguments that do not necessarily have to be shared by all people. This category includes Arabic grammar and Islamic theology. Islamic theology, for instance, is only relevant for persons who accept Qur'anic revelation, meant to defend revealed knowledge by dialectical arguments that may be convincing for Muslim believers but never attain the epistemological status of demonstrative proofs (singl. *burhān*). The second category of sciences is based on premises that are true and universally recognized; their arguments are indisputable because they consist of demonstrative syllogisms as described by Aristotle in *Posterior Analytics*. This category includes logic, mathematics, natural sciences, metaphysics, ethics and politics, constituting together the universal sciences, called "philosophy."[4]

Philosophy as conceived in this manner is independent of any other kind of knowledge. In particular, it is independent of prophecy, which is not located in the realm of universally recognized premises and Aristotelian epistemological rules. Nevertheless, al-Fārābī accepted the existence of prophecy. According to him, prophets—like philosophers—have access to the Active Intellect and are thereby able to receive knowledge about things that were hitherto unknown. The crucial point is, however, that the knowledge they receive is not of the

---

2 For a general introduction into al-Fārābī's philosophy, his life and his works see now Rudolph, "Abū Naṣr al-Fārābī."

3 Endress, "The Defense of Reason," 16–23.

4 For a detailed analysis of al-Fārābī's classification of sciences as expressed in his *Iḥṣāʾ al-ʿulūm* see Mahdi, "Science, Philosophy, and Religion in al-Fārābī's Enumeration of the Sciences," and Schramm, "Theoretische und praktische Disziplin bei al-Fārābī." The text was also influential in the Latin tradition; cf. al-Fārābī, *Über die Wissenschaften/De scientiis. Nach der lateinischen Übersetzung Gerhards von Cremona*, and idem, *De scientiis secundum versionem Dominici Gundisalvi/Über die Wissenschaften. Die Version des Dominicus Gundissalinus.*

same kind as the knowledge of philosophers. It is not demonstrative because prophets are neither interested nor in a position to grasp things as they really are. According to al-Fārābī, prophecy is confined rather to the representation of truth on the level of symbols, pictures and parables in order to make (a version of) truth accessible to the great majority of people who are not able to understand it on the philosophical level.[5]

On this, Avicenna disagrees. He is basically willing to accept al-Fārābī's notion of philosophy, which equates philosophy with universal science, and distinguishes it from religious forms of representing the truth. But Avicenna does not accept this notion of philosophy unconditionally. According to him, demonstrative reasoning and revelation are not opposed and exclusive as al-Fārābī suggests. They share at least one common feature, i.e. intuition (*ḥads*), a movement of the mind in its effort to acquire knowledge spontaneously.[6]

In principle, intuition is the apogee of rationality. Avicenna describes it as the ability to grasp the middle term of syllogisms instantly, without mediation and instruction. As such, it constitutes the highest cognitive act and the noblest way to acquire demonstrative, philosophic knowledge. At the same time, however, Avicenna uses the concept of intuition to bridge the gap between philosophy and prophecy. He considers *ḥads* to be a sacred faculty (*quwwa qudsiyya*) that is accessible to prophets too. Prophecy is thus not confined to the representation of truth on the level of symbols, pictures and parables but simultaneously acts on a second level: It enables those who are gifted with it to acquire demonstrative knowledge and to grasp things as they really are.[7]

---

5 For al-Fārābī's theory of prophecy cf. Walzer, "Al-Fārābī's Theory of Prophecy and Divination," and Rahman, *Prophecy in Islam*, 30–31, 36–38, 40–41, 57–61.

6 Gutas, *Avicenna and the Aristotelian Tradition*, 179–201; Hasse, *Avicenna's De anima*, 155 and 163–5; for a detailed discussion of the different views on intuition which Ibn Sīnā developed during his life see Gutas, "Intuition and Thinking: The Evolving Structure of Avicenna's Epistemology."

7 The "classical" outlines of Ibn Sīnā's theory of prophecy are described in Gardet, *La pensée religieuse d'Avicenne*, 109–41, and Rahman, *Prophecy in Islam*, 30–64. Ibn Sīnā's theory has been further investigated by several scholars, among them Elamrani-Jamal, "De la multiplicité des modes de la prophétie chez Ibn Sīnā," and Michot, *La destinée de l'homme chez Avicenne*, 118–53. For a recent analysis of his doctrine of the "three properties of prophethood" see al-Akiti, "The Three Properties of Prophethood in Certain Works of Avicenna and al-Ġazālī," 190–95. Al-Akiti's analysis is mainly based on Ibn Sīnā's *Aḥwāl al-nafs*, 114–126. Cf. also Frank, "The science of *kalām*," 28–29, and Griffel, "Al-Ġazālī's Concept of Prophecy," 114. The fact that Ibn Sīnā did not only accept prophecy in general but in particular acknowledged Muḥammad as a prophet is explicitly stated in his *Risāla fī Ithbāt al-nubuwwāt*, 53.1. The authenticity of this text has been disputed but there are still reasons to attribute it to him.

Consequently, Avicenna pays more attention to the Qur'an than al-Fārābī. He credits the revealed text as a source of real knowledge,[8] in particular on practical matters.[9] Thus, he writes a considerable number of specialised tracts on religious matters, including the exegesis of Qur'anic passage and discussions of prayer, prophecy, and the hereafter.[10]

The fact that Avicenna is responsive to the revealed text, however, did not imply that he abandons the notion of philosophy as universal science. On the contrary, he strengthens philosophy's position, for it is the only way to attain demonstrative knowledge on theoretical and on practical matters—including philosophical analysis of religious doctrines and issues to trace them back to their universal theoretical principles. Avicenna thus subscribes to al-Fārābī's concept of philosophy, and by enlarging it he confirms and stresses its importance. This becomes evident when Avicenna defines philosophy (*ḥikma*) much in Farabian terms as, "the perfection of the human soul through the conception (*taṣawwur*) of things and the acknowledgement (*taṣdīq*, judgement) of the true theoretical and practical realities (*ḥaqāʾiq*) as far as it is humanly possible."[11]

(2) The second concept of philosophy developed in the centuries preceding Ghazālī, propagated by the Islamic theologians called *mutakallimūn*, is in a way the opposite of the ideas that I have just explained. In the opinion of the *mutakallimūn*, philosophy is anything but a universal science; it is simply a doctrine, and what is worse: it is a heretical doctrine concerning improper ideas about God and the world which He created. Hence, the only allowable reaction to philosophy is refutation. So, the *mutakallimūn* usually talk about philosophy when discussing erroneous opinions about God and His creation. They analyze all doubtful arguments (*šubah*) presented by their adversaries, be they Muslim heretics or stubborn infidels—the latter generally including philosophers.[12]

8 See e.g. Ibn Sīnā, *ʿUyūn al-ḥikma*, 17, where he explains that "the principles of the parts of theoretical philosophy are received from the masters of true religion by way of admonishment (*tanbīh*)," and "the principles of the parts of practical philosophy are received from the divine law (*al-sharīʿa l-ilāhiyya*)" (the English translation is taken from Endress, "The Defense of Reason," 31).

9 Janssens, "Ibn Sīnā (Avicenne): un projet 'religieux' de philosophie?"

10 Mahdi, "Avicenna. i. Introductory Note;" Janssens, "Avicenna and the Qur'ān: A Survey of his Qur'ānic Commentaries."

11 Ibn Sīnā, *ʿUyūn al-ḥikma*, 16 (the English translation is taken from Endress, "The Defense of Reason," 31).

12 Frank, "Reason and Revealed Law," 134–35.

This practice can be found in works by authors such as Abū l-Ḥasan al-Aš'arī (d. 323/935), who mentions the philosophers twice in his famous book on the Islamic doctrines (*Maqālāt al-Islāmiyyīn*). In one place, they figure as part of a long list of infidels including the Manicheans, Marcionites, Dualists, Naturalists (*aṣḥāb al-ṭabā'i'*), and Christians. In another, the Mu'tazilites are accused of having developed an erroneous doctrine about God's attributes because they followed the teachings of the philosophers.[13]

Another revealing example of the rejection of philosophy is in *The Book on God's Oneness* (*Kitāb al-Tawḥīd*) by Abū Manṣūr al-Māturīdī (d. 332/944). It contains a long chapter about God's essence, His names, and His attributes, beginning with al-Māturīdī's own teaching and continuing with the refutation of incorrect doctrines. Al-Māturīdī's first target are Muslim heretics, which for him include the Mu'tazilites, the Isma'ilites and the rival Hanafite school of Abū 'Abdallāh al-Najjār (d.*c.* 235/850). Al-Māturīdī then turns to the infidels, which include not only the Skeptics, Manicheans, Marcionites, and Zoroastrians but also the so-called *dahriyya*, a group recorded as having maintained the doctrine of the eternity of the world, whose alleged leader was Aristotle.[14]

The list of *mutakallimūn* who followed the same practice could easily be extended. Many theologians writing in the 3rd/9th, 4th/10th or 5th/11th centuries included long refutations or at least short polemical remarks against philosophy within their expositions of the true doctrine.[15] Obviously, most of them were convinced that the philosophers were nothing but heretics and should be treated as one of a panoply of erroneous groups and sects.[16] We can thus confine ourselves to the two examples that I have just given and proceed to the third concept of philosophy which is relevant to our discussion.

(3) The ideas of the authors who can be characterized as working in the tradition of al-Kindī differ from both approaches to philosophy that I have already mentioned. They conceive of philosophy neither as a unique and absolutely privileged form of science nor as a doctrine which has to be rejected and disapproved. Instead, they try to integrate it into a wider spectrum of disciplines and modes of reflection. In their opinion, philosophy is one of several relevant ways of attaining knowledge that can possibly complement each other.

---

13 van Ess, *Der Eine und das Andere*, 1:460 and 474.

14 Rudolph, *Al-Māturīdī and the Development of Sunnī Theology in Samarqand*, 207, cf. 166–79.

15 For further examples seethe texts translated in van Ess, *Theologie und Gesellschaft*, 5:70, no. 8; 5:229, no 8; 5:285, no. 49, and idem, *Der Eine und das Andere*, 1:711–712.

16 Frank, "The science of *kalām*," 19.

The roots of this concept can be traced back to al-Kindī himself. As he writes in his *Epistle on the Quantity of the Books of Aristotle* (*Risāla fī Kammiyyat kutub Arisṭūṭālīs*), philosophy is not the only way of accessing truth. Prophets, too, have access to knowledge. Indeed, their knowledge is as complete and precise as the knowledge of philosophers, the only difference being that prophets understand everything at once, whereas philosophers need much time and effort in order to find the truth.[17]

Many authors from the 3rd/9th to the 5th/11th centuries share al-Kindī's view. In its general outlines, Aḥmad ibn al-Ṭayyib al-Sarakhsī (d. 286/899),[18] Abū Zayd al-Balkhī (d. 322/934),[19] Abū l-Ḥasan al-ʿĀmirī[20] and Miskawayh[21] follow al-Kindī's philosophy closely. Besides, there are authors who combine al-Kindī's philosophy with ideas from other traditions such as Abū Sulaymān al-Sijistānī and al-Rāghib al-Iṣfahānī. Abū Sulaymān follows al-Kindī in many respects, but he was also a pupil of Yaḥyā ibn ʿĀdī (d. 363/974), who had introduced him to the logical studies of the Baghdādī Aristotelians.[22] Al-Rāghib al-Iṣfahānī, who lived at the turn of the 5th/11th century, connects Kindian Ethics (which he mainly takes from Miskawayh) with Ṣūfī convictions. This is all the more important in our discussion considering that al-Ghazālī draws heavily on al-Rāghib al-Iṣfahānī's teaching in his own ethical writings.[23]

Although all these authors adhere, in principle, to al-Kindī's concept of philosophy, we must pay attention to the fact that they sometimes interpret his idea of multiple pathways to knowledge in different ways. Miskawayh, for example, has no problem combining these multiple pathways in the same argument and on the same level. In his treatises on Ethics he uses philosophical considerations taken from Plato and Aristotle side by side with traditions of

17 al-Kindī, *Risāla fī Kammiyyat kutub Arisṭāṭālīs wa-mā yuḥtāj ilayhi fī taḥṣīl al-falsafa*, 372–76.

18 For Sarakhsī's philosophy, his life and his works see now Biesterfeldt, "Aḥmad ibn aṭ-Ṭaiyib as-Saraḫsī."

19 Biesterfeldt, "Abū Zaid al-Balḫī."

20 Wakelnig, "Abū l-Ḥasan al-ʿĀmirī."

21 Endress, "Antike Ethik-Traditionen für die islamische Gesellschaft: Abū ʿAlī Miskawaih."

22 For a detailed analysis of Abū Sulaymān's philosophical orientation see Endress, "Die Integration philosophischer Traditionen in der islamischen Gesellschaft des 4./10. Jahrhunderts: at-Tauḥīdī and as-Siǧistānī," in particular 201–209.

23 For al-Rāghib al-Iṣfahānī's teaching and his dependence on Miskawayh see Daiber, "Griechische Ethik in islamischem Gewand," Mohamed, "The Ethical Philosophy of al-Rāghib al-Iṣfahānī," idem, "The Concept of Justice in Miskawayh and Iṣfahānī," and idem, "Knowledge and the Purification of the Soul." For his impact on al-Ghazālī see Madelung, "Ar-Rāġib al-Iṣfahānī und die Ethik al-Ġazālīs," and Mohamed, "The Unifying Thread."

religious provenance.[24] Abū l-Ḥasan al-ʿĀmirī is less open-minded. Despite his deep philosophical interests, he insists on subordinating philosophy to religion. According to him, our soul can only profit from the light of intellect if it is guided by the light of religion.[25]

The most interesting case, however, may be Abū Sulaymān al-Sijistānī. He is reported to have said: "… the reason which is the representative of God on this earth …" (*al-ʿaql alladhī huwa khalīfat Allāh fī hādhā l-ʿālam*)[26] what seems to be an unambiguous profession of the importance of rational thinking and thus of philosophy. Yet, at the same time, he is convinced that human beings can only attain their goal if they are also given what he calls "the dress of mercy" (*libās al-raḥma*), i.e. God's guidance.[27] Therefore, al-Sijistānī is very suspicious of people who, to his mind, overrated the importance of philosophy. This becomes evident in a passage where he sharply critiques the intentions of the so-called Brethren of Purity (*Ikhwān al-ṣafāʾ*). As he explains, the *Ikhwān* try to improve religion through philosophy. According to them, religion is soiled by ignorance and can only be cleaned and purified by the enlightening effect of philosophy. However, this is a fatal error in al-Sijistānī's opinion. Philosophy is nothing but human knowledge, whereas religion is perfect wisdom because it has access to revelation as well as to the intelligible world.[28] Consequently, al-Sijistānī emphasizes the priority and the superiority of religion.[29] He is an interesting early example of a Muslim scholar who was engaged in philosophy and even taught philosophy, while at the same time insisting on its limitations.[30]

---

24 For a concise description of his ethical theory see Endress, "Antike Ethiktraditionen," 232–38.

25 Wakelnig, "Abū l-Ḥasan al-ʿĀmirī," 184–85; how al-ʿĀmirī and some other representatives of the Kindian tradition conceived philosophy is also described by Adamson, "The Kindian Tradition: the Structure of Philosophy in Arabic Neoplatonism."

26 al-Tawḥīdī, *al-Muqābasāt*, 119.3; cf. 467.4–5.

27 Ibid., 134.3.

28 al-Tawḥīdī, *al-Imtāʿ wa-l-muʾānasa*, 2:21.10–22.19; cf. 2:5.15–11.2. For a discussion of the whole passage see Endress, "The Limits to Reason: Some Aspects of Islamic Philosophy in the Būyid Period," 122–23, and the recent article by Griffel and Hachmeyer, "Prophets as Physicians of the Soul" which contains a comprehensive English translation of the passage.

29 al-Tawḥīdī, *al-Imtāʿ wa-l-muʾānasa*, 2:10.3; cf. 2:18.8–11.

30 Abū Sulaymān's statements about the relation between philosophy and religion are discussed in detail by Kraemer, *Philosophy in the Renaissance of Islam*, 230–43; cf. Endress, "Die Integration philosophischer Traditionen," 204–5.

III

Let us now turn to our principal subject, al-Ghazālī. He expresses his views on philosophy on several occasions, but it seems appropriate to start our investigation with the famous passage in his autobiographical book *al-Munqidh min al-ḍalāl* where he describes his experiences with different disciplines and modes of reflection that include philosophy, theology, Isma'ili teaching and Sufism.

According to this text, philosophy should not be subject to simple, general judgments. Every part of the philosophical sciences should be evaluated in its own right in order to recognize its characteristics and specific value. The evaluation actually presented in al-Ghazālī's *Munqidh* is quite long but its conclusion can be summarised as follows: First, the mathematical sciences have to be accepted without reservation. As he explains, "(...) nothing in them entails denial or affirmation of religious matters. On the contrary, they concern rigorously demonstrated facts which can in no wise be denied once they are known and understood."[31] The same is true for logic: "There is nothing in this which must be rejected. On the contrary, it is the sort of thing mentioned by the *mutakallimūn* and the partisans of reasoning in connection with the proofs they use (...)" the only difference being that the modes of expression and the methods of proof which the philosophers have learnt to apply are much more refined than those of the *mutakallimūn*.[32] The natural sciences is a more complicated case. In principle it is a useful science, but when studying it the philosophers tend to forget that physical phenomena are not to be explained in and of themselves. As al-Ghazālī puts it: "The basic point regarding all of them is for you to know that nature is totally subject to God Most High: it does not act of itself but is used as an instrument by its Creator."[33] Metaphysics seems to be the crucial point of the whole evaluation for, "it is in the metaphysical sciences that most of the philosopher's errors are found. Owing to the fact that they could not carry out apodictic demonstration according to the conditions they had postulated in logic, they differed a great deal about metaphysical questions."[34] For that reason, the philosophers developed several doctrines which according to al-Ghazālī must be considered either heresy or unbelief. In contrast, the political sciences and the moral sciences are less problematic. In these two fields, the philosophers do not contradict the

31 al-Ghazālī, *al-Munqidh*, 20.20–22; Engl. transl. in McCarthy, *Deliverance From Error*, 63.

32 Ibid., 22.13–14; Engl. transl. in McCarthy, *Deliverance From Error*, 65.

33 Ibid., 23.11–12; Engl. transl. in McCarthy, *Deliverance From Error*, 66.

34 Ibid., 23.14–15; Engl. transl. in McCarthy, *Deliverance From Error*, 66.

teaching of religion but rather depend on it. As far as political ideas are concerned, al-Ghazālī affirms: "They (i.e. the philosophers) simply took these over from the scriptures revealed to the prophets by God Most High and from the maxims handed down from the predecessors of the prophets," and concerning philosophical teachings on ethics and on the soul, its qualities and habits, he hurries to add: "This they simply took over from the sayings of the Sufis."[35]

In sum, we thus have a threefold division. In al-Ghazālī's opinion, logic and mathematics are universally acknowledged sciences, natural sciences, and metaphysics include or tend to include heretical doctrines, and ethics and politics can be considered a valuable means to access to knowledge insofar as they argue in the same manner as prophets and Sufis.

This tripartitioning corresponds, in its general outlines, to the three concepts of philosophy we have already discussed: Al-Ghazālī describes logic and mathematics more or less the way al-Fārābī and Avicenna describe philosophy, natural sciences, and metaphysics like the *mutakallimūn*, and ethics and politics like the followers of al-Kindī. The last point is not even surprising. As we have seen, al-Kindī's followers focus their writings on the fate of the soul and on ethical questions, and al-Ghazālī draws heavily on their teaching when writing his own ethical works.[36]

We should, however, not stop at this stage of our evaluation. Up to now, we have only made the general observation that al-Ghazālī knows these earlier concepts and makes use of them. We have not yet specified in which way he combines them. Thus, we have to reconsider all three concepts in detail in order to see how he applies them and how he describes their respective function and contribution to his own ideas.

With respect to the *mutakallimūn's*, it is quite easy to answer this question. Its purpose was confined to detecting and refuting heretical doctrines (in the realm of the natural sciences and metaphysics), and it was exactly in this sense that al-Ghazālī made use of it. Wherever he treats *kalām* topics and argues as a *kalām* author, he applies the *mutakallimūn*'s insistence on refuting philosophy. This is particularly the case in *al-Iqtiṣād fī l-iʿtiqād* (*The Balanced Book on What-To-Believe*) where he attacks the philosophers just as al-Ashʿarī, al-Māturīdī and many *mutakallimūn* had done before him.[37] Yet, to a lesser degree, he does the same in *Tahāfut al-falāsifa* (*The Incoherence of the Philosophers*), of

35 Ibid., 24.14–15, 24.17–18; Engl. transl. in McCarthy, *Deliverance From Error*, 67.

36 See above p. 38 and in particular n. 23.

37 al-Ghazālī, *al-Iqtiṣād fī l-iʿtiqād*, 1.12; 27.6; 103.12; 129.10; 132.2; 137.8; 250.9.

course a more ambitious work than the *Iqtiṣād* that nonetheless shares some features with *kalām* writings.[38]

The scope of these refutations in *kalām* style is, however, rather limited. As al-Ghazālī himself explains, theological arguments are useful to defend religious teachings but they are not meant to analyze reality and to study the true nature of things. Theology (*kalām*), as he puts it, is an auxiliary discipline which is limited in its range and function: "(…) I found it a science adequate for its own aim, but inadequate for mine."[39] As a consequence, theological arguments can only be a first approach to complicated matters and issues. When it comes to evaluating philosophy, they are particularly provisional and incomplete. In al-Ghazālī's own words: "What the *mutakallimūn* had to say in their books, where they were engaged in refuting the philosophers, was nothing but abstruse, scattered remarks, patently inconsistent and false, which could not conceivably hoodwink an ordinary intelligent person, to say nothing of one familiar with the subtleties of the philosophical sciences."[40]

The *kalām* approach to philosophy thus leaves much to be improved. It must be completed by other approaches. This leads al-Ghazālī to refer to the second concept mentioned above which conceives philosophy as a real science whose results cannot be denied once they are known and understood. At first glance, al-Ghazālī had restricted the application of this concept to mathematics and logic, but closer examination shows that this is only a preliminary judgment. Al-Ghazālī's distinction between the scientific and the doctrinal parts of philosophy is not as evident and absolute as it may have appeared in the sentences from the *Munqidh* quoted earlier.

In the end, al-Ghazālī is willing to accept that philosophy—in all its parts—is able to reveal the true nature of things. For him, philosophy is the only science which is able to study the true nature of things, because all the other ways, namely *kalām*, the Isma'ili doctrine, and Sufism, are either not in a position to find it or are not interested in studying created things at all. There is, however, a very important qualification: According to al-Ghazālī, philosophy is not an autonomous science. It is subject to certain conditions which cannot be defined by the philosophers themselves. This point had often been neglected by the philosophers and, as a consequence, they failed to recognize the

38 See e.g. al-Ghazālī, *The Incoherence of the Philosophers / Tahāfut al-falāsifa*, 1.11–2.21; 4.3–5.4. In the *Tahāfut* the philosophers are conceived as a *firqa*, "sect," (e.g. ibid., 5.5) and their doctrines are sometimes opposed to the doctrines of other *firaq*, "sects," (or religious groups) such as the Muʿtazila, the Karrāmiyya and the Ashʿariyya (e.g. ibid., 50.15–52.17); Shihadeh, "From al-Ghazālī to al-Rāzī", 143; Griffel, *Al-Ghazālī's Philosophical Theology*, 98–99.

39 al-Ghazālī, *al-Munqidh*, 16.3–4; Engl. transl. in McCarthy, *Deliverance From Error*, 59.

40 Ibid., 18.7–9; Engl. transl. in McCarthy, *Deliverance From Error*, 60–61.

limitations of their own science. As we have already seen, al-Ghazālī explained this by saying that the philosophers study the natural phenomena without recognizing the underlying point, namely "that nature is totally subject to God (...): it does not act of itself but is used as an instrument by its Creator."[41]As a result, actual philosophical teachings are a melting pot of divergent doctrines and arguments. To quote al-Ghazālī, they contain "truth" and "error", "gold ... mixed with dirt", "pure gold" and "false and counterfeit coins."[42] If we want to find the true elements in them we must act like a man who is willing to find "honey ... in a cupper's glass."[43] To distinguish truth and error is, however, quite a difficult task. If we want to accomplish it, we cannot confine ourselves to philosophical studies. We rather need the assistance of other disciplines and other sources of knowledge. This is finally the point where the third concept of philosophy, used by al-Kindī's followers, comes into play.

As has been pointed out, al-Kindī's followers tried to combine philosophy with other ways to attain knowledge. In particular, they insist on the fact that every scholar, including the philosophers, has to accept knowledge that has been revealed to the prophets by God. This affirmation corresponds exactly with al-Ghazālī's own conviction. As we are told in the later parts of *al-Munqidh*, prophecy is an indispensable source of wisdom that we must all acknowledge.[44] Philosophers, too, have to respect prophecy as the unquestionable and indispensable fundament of all knowledge. Only when prophetical knowledge is accepted can philosophy become a respectable way to study the true nature of things.

In the end, al-Ghazālī's concept of philosophy is close to the concept held by some authors of 4th/10th and 5th/11th centuries who were working in al-Kindī's tradition. We can even go one step further, for one scholar expressed views on philosophy that were particularly close to al-Ghazālī's ideas, namely Abū Sulaymān al-Sijistānī. This may be surprising at first given the fact that—unlike al-Rāghib al-Iṣfahānī and Miskawayh—al-Sijistānī has not yet been credited as influencing al-Ghazālī in any noteworthy way. However, it seems that his name should be added to the Ghazalian dossier. In some points at least, the parallels between al-Sijistānī's and al-Ghazālī's ideas are striking. This applies to ethics (where both of them ultimately followed al-Kindī's tradition)[45] and logic (where both of them followed al-Fārābī's tradition) as well as their general

41 Ibid., 23.11–12; Engl. transl. in McCarthy, *Deliverance From Error*, 66.

42 Ibid., 25.14–23; Engl. transl. in McCarthy, *Deliverance From Error*, 68.

43 Ibid., 26.17–19; Engl. transl. in McCarthy, *Deliverance From Error*,69.

44 Ibid., 41–44, Engl. transl. in McCarthy, *Deliverance From Error*, 83–87.

45 For al-Sijistānī's views on ethics cf. Endress, "Die Integration philosophischer Traditionen," 206–7.

approach to philosophy. As I pointed out above, al-Sijistānī engaged heavily in philosophy while insisting on its limitations. According to him, it is even dangerous to overrate the importance and the scope of philosophy as the *Ikhwān al-ṣafāʾ* do.[46]

Al-Ghazālī uses the same example. He mentions the *Ikhwān al-ṣafāʾ* three times in his *Munqidh*, and every time they are subject to sharp attacks.[47] This does not mean that al-Ghazālī is only critical of the *Ikhwān*. As in many other cases, his relationship to them seems to have been rather ambivalent, for he sometimes takes passages from their *Rasāʾil* and integrates them into his own writings.[48] In the *Munqidh*, however, his position towards the *Ikhwān* is clear. In his opinion, their way of philosophizing is wrong; it even compromises philosophy as a science. He expresses this, for example, as follows:

> If we were to (…) aim at forgoing every truth which had been first formulated by the mind of one in error, we would have to forgo much of what is true. We would also have to give up a lot of the verses of the Qurʾān and the traditions of the Apostle and the recitals of our pious forebears and the sayings of the sages and the Sufis. For the author of *The Brethren of Purity* cites these in his own work, appealing to their authority and thereby enticing the minds of stupid men to embrace his false doctrine. That would be an invitation to those in error to wrest the truth from our hands by putting it into their own books.[49]

Certainly, the parallel attacks on the *Ikhwān al-Ṣafāʾ* presented by al-Ghazālī and al-Sijistānī might have been pure chance, but this is not likely. Even in that case, it remains obvious that the attitude of both scholars toward philosophy was similar in many respects. We can thus summarize what has been said up to now as follows: When evaluating philosophy, al-Ghazālī draws on several earlier models which he connects skillfully for different purposes. The *kalām* approach serves him in his attack on unacceptable or, as he would perhaps say, anti-prophetical doctrines. The Farabian-Avicennian approach allows him to use the scientific methods and discoveries made by philosophers. Al-Sijistānī's approach, however, seems to be the one which most shaped his own attitude

---

46 Cf. above, n. 28.

47 al-Ghazālī, *al-Munqidh*, 26.14–15, 27.3, 33.21–22; Engl. transl. in McCarthy, *Deliverance From Error*, 69, 70, 77.

48 Landolt, "Al-Ghazālī and 'Religionswissenschaft,'" 23; De Smet, "Die Enzyklopädie der Iḫwān aṣ-Ṣafā,'" 530.

49 al-Ghazālī, *al-Munqidh*, 26.11–17; Engl. transl. in McCarthy, *Deliverance From Error*, 69.

toward philosophy and led him to be deeply engaged in philosophical discussions while, at the same, sharply critiquing them.

IV

Thus far, our discussion has focused on describing how al-Ghazālī conceptualized philosophy. I have tried to evaluate his position by comparing it to different approaches to philosophy developed by earlier authors in the Arabic tradition of which he was probably aware. In addition to these considerations, there is yet another dimension of our topic. It does not concern al-Ghazālī's conception of philosophy as such, but the conclusions we can draw from it. These conclusions deserve our attention too, because they allow us to situate his statements on philosophy in a wider historical context. This will bring us to some general considerations about al-Ghazālī's position in the intellectual history of Islam and about the way in which contemporary research views and analyzes this position.

Considering our discussion, three remarks seem to be appropriate. The first one relates to the observation that al-Ghazālī's concept of philosophy draws on several earlier models. As I have argued, he does not develop a single and unambiguous notion of what philosophy is and whether it is valid. This is revealing in several respects. On the one hand, it demonstrates al-Ghazālī's versatility, his intellectual curiosity and his open-mindedness. On the other hand, it appears that his approach to philosophy is not only shaped by conceptual reflections and theoretical reasons but also by pragmatic considerations. This does not mean that al-Ghazālī has no overarching strategy concerning philosophy. Obviously, he has one which he tried to apply whenever discussing a related topic. Still, this strategy seems to be less based on intrinsic and consistent theoretical reasons than on extrinsic considerations such as, for instance, the compatibility of a doctrine with revealed truth.

In view of this pragmatism, it is not really surprising that al-Ghazālī sometimes argues on different levels. This is even true for logic: As we have seen, he acknowledges logic as a universally recognized science. Consequently, he wrote manuals such as *Miʿyār al-ʿilm* (*Standard of Knowledge*) and *Miḥakk an-naẓar* (*Touchstone of Reasoning*) in order to initiate serious logical studies among his colleagues.[50] Yet, at the same time, he produced *al-Qisṭās al-mustaqīm* (*The Straight Balance*) where he argued that all kinds of syllogisms can be

50 On al-Ghazālī's logic see Street, "Arabic Logic," 555–559, and my "Die Neubewertung der Logik."

derived from the Qur'an, hardly a theoretically based and logically demonstrable statement.[51]

When evaluating al-Ghazālī as a conceptual thinker, we are thus left with an ambiguous impression. There are certainly good reasons to declare: "al-Ghazālī was a very systematic thinker"[52] But in view of al-Ghazālī's "flexibility" and his indecision in conceptual matters it also seems appropriate to say: "His theology appears to be comprehensive in its scope (...). On the other hand, it also appears to be curiously incomplete. Theses are set forth in formally conceptual terms, sometimes at length, with great assurance and even eloquence, but also superficially and inconclusively, as implications are left unclarified and apparent inconsistencies unresolved."[53]

The second remark is in a certain sense connected to the first. It concerns the sources available to al-Ghazālī. Which books and writings did he know? How extensive was the corpus he read? Who were the authors that shaped his ideas on philosophical topics? At first sight, the answer to these questions seems simple. Al-Ghazālī often referred to Avicenna. By following these hints, scholars have for long been able to prove that al-Ghazālī actually studied and discussed his writings. Recent scholarship even goes one step further. As has been shown in articles since the early 1990s, al-Ghazālī's use of Avicenna's writings is much more extensive than previously thought. He even takes up sentences or whole passages from the books of his predecessor when he openly criticizes and contradicts Avicenna; still more often, he makes use of Avicenna's arguments and phrases without mentioning his name at all.[54]

There can thus be no doubt that Avicenna is the principal source (and the principal target) when al-Ghazālī discusses any philosophical topic. But this does not necessarily mean that Avicenna is his only source of information and inspiration in this field. On the contrary: philosophical discourse (as intellectual discourse in general) always has a historical horizon beyond the immediate line of discussion. When Aristotle, for instance, reflected on philosophical topics, his main challenge was without doubt Plato; but this does not mean that Aristotle was not aware of the teachings of Parmenides, Anaxagoras and others who had a considerable impact on him, too.

The same seems to be true for al-Ghazālī. His main challenge was, without any doubt, Avicenna. But this does not prevent him from studying the writings of other philosophical authors whose ideas may have been closer to his own convictions. As far as ethical questions are concerned, this has already been

51 See Kleinknecht, "Al-Qisṭās al-mustaqīm."

52 Griffel, *Al-Ghazālī's Philosophical Theology*, 11.

53 Frank, "Al-Ghazālī's Use of Avicenna's Philosophy," 284.

54 See, in particular the articles by Frank and Janssens.

proven. When considering his overall conception of philosophy, however, one gets the impression that ethics was not an exceptional case. Al-Ghazālī seems to have shared a number of ideas and preoccupations with several authors who were working in the tradition of al-Kindī (e.g. al-Sijistānī, Miskawayh and al-Rāghib al-Iṣfahānī), which suggests that their teaching should be taken more into account in further research about him.

These considerations lead me finally to my third and final remark, which is once again on the relationship between al-Ghazālī and Avicenna. This time, however, the question is not whether or not al-Ghazālī exclusively studied Avicenna's books when he consulted philosophical writings, but whether or to which extent his own teaching can be interpreted in Avicennian lines.

The answers given to this question by scholarship have changed considerably during the last decades. In the past, Ghazālī was commonly assumed to have been a strict adversary of Avicenna. Accordingly, it seemed to be anathema to interpret his own teaching in terms of Avicenna's ideas. Nowadays, however, many scholars tend to the opposite assumption. Having detected that al-Ghazālī made extensive use of Avicenna's writings, they consider him as an author who was in many respects close to Avicenna. Sometimes al-Ghazālī is described as being fascinated by Avicenna's teaching. Sometimes he is even qualified as a kind of crypto-Avicennian. Alternatively, both of them are supposed to pursue basically the same philosophico-religious project continued later by other prominent authors such as Fakhr al-Dīn al-Rāzī or even Ibn Taymiyya.

Many of these ideas are still unfolding. As a matter of fact, one of the most important results of recent scholarship is determining that al-Ghazālī cannot be seriously interpreted without considering Avicenna's impact on him. Yet, this line of interpretation, if exclusively applied, risks creating its own problems. Sometimes one gets the impression that Avicenna's impact on al-Ghazālī is unduly stressed or even fabricated. To search for affinities can be a hermeneutical tool but it can also be suggestive. One risks interpreting al-Ghazālī's writings from an Avicennian view while, at the same time, understanding Avicenna in a Ghazalian way.

It may thus be appropriate to diversify the field of interpretation without fixing it on one perspective. The fact that al-Ghazālī made ample use of Avicenna's writings does not necessarily imply that they both had the same intellectual project.[55] Al-Ghazālī rather seems to have pursued his own goals

---

55 Another example that may fit our context in a certain way: St. Augustine was an enthusiastic reader of Platonic writings but his own intellectual and religious project can hardly be qualified as a Platonic one. See the well-balanced considerations of Flasch, *Augustinus*, 37–41 and 292–299.

by following various sources and different lines of argumentation—a conclusion that can at least be drawn from the way he conceptualized philosophy.

Bibliography

Abd-el-Jalil, J.-M. "Autour de la sincérité d'Al-Ġazzālī." In *Mélanges Louis Massignon*. 3 vols. Damascus: Institut français de Damas, 1956–58. Vol. 1. 57–72.

Adamson, Peter. "The Kindian Tradition: the Structure of Philosophy in Arabic Neoplatonism." In *The Libraries of the Neoplatonists, Proceedings of the Meeting of the European Science Foundation Network: Late Antiquity and Arabic Thought. Patterns in the Constitution of European Culture (Strasbourg, March 12–14, 2004)*. Edited by C. D'Ancona. Leiden: Brill, 2007. 351–70.

Al-Akiti, M. Afifi. "The Good, the Bad, and the Ugly of Falsafa: Al-Ghazālī's Maḍnūn, Tahāfut, and Maqāṣid, With Particular Attention to Their Falsafī Treatments of God's Knowledge of Temporal Events." In *Avicenna and his Legacy: A Golden Age of Science and Philosophy*. Edited by Y. T. Langermann. Turnhout: Brepols, 2009. 51–100.

———. "The Three Properties of Prophethood in Certain Works of Avicenna and al-Ghazālī." In *Interpreting Avicenna: Science and Philosophy in Medieval Islam: Proceedings of the Second Conference of the Avicenna Study Group*. Edited by J. McGinnis. Leiden: Brill, 2004. 189–212.

Biesterfeldt, Hans Hinrich, "Abū Zaid al-Balḫī." In *Philosophie in der islamischen Welt. Bd. 1: 8.–10. Jahrhundert*. Edited by U. Rudolph. Basel: Schwabe Verlag, 2012. 156–167, 244–246.

———. "Aḥmad ibn aṭ-Ṭaiyib as-Saraḫsī." In *Philosophie in der islamischen Welt. Bd. 1: 8.–10. Jahrhundert*. Edited by U. Rudolph. Basel: Schwabe Verlag, 2012. 148–156, 243–244.

Daiber, Hans. "Griechische Ethik in islamischem Gewande. Das Beispiel von Rāġib al-Iṣfahānī (11. Jh.)."In *Historia Philosophiae Medii Aevi: Studien zur Geschichte der Philosophie des Mittelalters*. Edited by B. Mojsisch and O. Pluta. 2 vols. Amsterdam: Grüner, 1991. Vol. 1. 181–192.

Dallal, Ahmad. "Al-Ghazālī and the Perils of Interpretation."*Journal of the American Oriental Society* 122 (2002): 773–87.

De Smet, Daniel. "Die Enzyklopädie der Iḫwān aṣ-Ṣafā'." In *Philosophie in der islamischen Welt. Bd. 1: 8.–10. Jahrhundert*. Edited by U. Rudolph. Basel: Schwabe Verlag, 2012. 531–539, 551–554.

Elamrani-Jamal, Abdelali. "De la multiplicité des modes de la prophétie chez Ibn Sīnā." In *Études sur Avicenne*. Edited by J. Jolivet and R. Rashed. Paris: Les Belles Lettres, 1984. 125–42.

Endress, Gerhard. "Antike Ethiktraditionen für die islamische Gesellschaft: Abū ʿAlī Miskawaih." In *Philosophie in der islamischen Welt. Bd. 1: 8.–10. Jahrhundert*. Edited by U. Rudolph. Basel: Schwabe Verlag, 2012. 210–243, 254–259.

———. "The Defense of Reason: The Plea for Philosophy in the Religious Community." *Zeitschrift für Geschichte der arabisch-islamischen Wissenschaften* 6 (1990): 1–49.

———. "Die Integration philosophischer Traditionen in der islamischen Gesellschaft des 4./10. Jahrhunderts: at-Tauḥīdī und as-Siǧistānī." In *Philosophie in der islamischen Welt. Bd. 1: 8.–10. Jahrhundert*. Edited by U. Rudolph. Basel: Schwabe Verlag, 2012. 185–209, 249–254.

———. "The Limits to Reason: Some Aspects of Islamic Philosophy in the Būyid Period." In *Akten des 7. Kongresses für Arabistik und Islamwissenschaft (Göttingen 1974)*. Edited by A. Dietrich. Göttingen: Vandenhoeck & Ruprecht, 1976. 120–125.

van Ess, Josef. *Der Eine und das Andere. Beobachtungen an islamischen häresiographischen Texten*. 2 vols. Berlin: Walter De Gruyter, 2011.

———. *Theologie und Gesellschaft im 2. und 3. Jahrhundert Hidschra. Eine Geschichte des religiösen Denkens im frühen Islam*. 6 vols. Berlin: Walter De Gruyter, 1991–97.

al-Fārābī, Muḥammad ibn Muḥammad. *Iḥṣāʾ al-ʿulūm*. Edited by ʿU. Amīn. 3rd ed. Cairo: Maktabat al-Anjilū al-Miṣrīyah, 1968.

———. *Über die Wissenschaften/De scientiis. Nach der lateinischen Übersetzung Gerhards von Cremona*. Edition and German transl. by F. Schupp. Hamburg: Felix Meiner, 2005.

———. *De scientiis secundum versionem Dominici Gundisalvi/Über die Wissenschaften. Die Version des Dominicus Gundissalinus*. Edition and German transl. by J. H. J. Schneider. Freiburg: Herder, 2006.

Flasch, Kurt. *Augustinus. Einführung in sein Denken*. Stuttgart: Reclam, 1980.

Frank, Richard M. *Creation and the Cosmic System: Al-Ghazālī and Avicenna*. Heidelberg: Carl Winter, 1992.

———. *Al-Ghazālī and the Ashʿarite School*. Durham: Duke University Press, 1994.

———. "Al-Ghazālī's Use of Avicenna's Philosophy." *Revue des études islamiques* 55–57 (1987–89): 271–85. Reprinted in idem, *Philosophy, Theology and Mysticism in Medieval Islam: Texts and Studies on the Development and History of Kalām*. Edited by D. Gutas. Aldershot (UK): Ashgate 2005. Text XI.

———. "Reason and Revealed Law. A Sample of Parallels and Divergences in kalām and falsafa." In *Recherches d'islamologie. Recueil d'articles offert à Georges C. Anawati et Louis Gardet par leurs collègues et amis*. Louvain and Louvain-la-Neuve: Peeters, 1977. 123–38. Reprinted in idem, *Philosophy, Theology and Mysticism in Medieval Islam: Texts and Studies on the Development and History of Kalām*. Edited by D. Gutas. Aldershot (UK): Ashgate 2005. Text VII.

———. "The Science of Kalām." *Arabic Sciences and Philosophy* 2 (1992): 7–37.

Gardet, Louis. *La pensée religieuse d'Avicenne (Ibn Sīnā)*. Paris: J. Vrin, 1951.

al-Ghazālī, Muḥammad ibn Muḥammad. *al-Iqtiṣād fī l-iʿtiqād*. Edited by I. A. Çubukçu and H. Atay. Ankara: Nur Matbaası, 1962.

———. *al-Munqidh min al-ḍalāl / Erreur et délivrance*. Edition and French transl. by F. Jabre. Beirut: Commission libanaise pour la traduction des chefs-d'œuvre, 1969.

———. *al-Qisṭās al-mustaqīm*. Edited by V. Chelhot. Beirut: Dār al-Mashriq, 1991.

———. *The Incoherence of the Philosophers /Tahāfut al-falāsifa*. Edition and transl. by M. E. Marmura. 2nd ed. Provo: Brigham Young University Press, 2000.

Griffel, Frank. "Al-Ghazālī's Concept of Prophecy: The Introduction of Avicennan Psychology into Ašʿarite Theology." *Arabic Sciences and Philosophy* 14 (2004): 101–44.

———. *Al-Ghazālī's Philosophical Theology*. New York: Oxford University Press, 2009.

———. "The Relationship Between Averroes and al-Ghazālī as It Presents Itself in Averroes' Early Writings, Especially in His Commentary on al-Ghazālī's al-Mustaṣfā." In *Medieval Philosophy and the Classical Tradition, Judaism, and Christianity*. Edited by J. Inglis. Richmond: Curzon Press, 2002. 51–63.

———. "Taqlīd of the Philosophers: al-Ghazālī's Initial Accusation in His Tahāfut." In *Ideas, Images, and Methods of Portrayal: Insights into Classical Arabic Literature and Islam*. Edited by S. Günther. Leiden: Brill, 2005. 273–96.

Griffel, Frank and Hachmeier, Klaus. "Prophets as Physicians of the Soul: A Dispute about the Relationship between Reason and Revelation Reported by al-Tawḥīdī in his *Book of Delightful and Intimate Conversations* (*Kitāb al-Imtāʿ wa-l-muʾānasa*)." *Mélanges de l'Université Saint-Joseph* 63 (2010–11): 222–57.

Gutas, Dimitri. *Avicenna and the Aristotelian Tradition: Introduction to Reading Avicenna's Philosophical Works Including an Inventory of Avicenna's Authentic Works*. 2nd ed. Leiden: Brill, 2014.

———. "Intuition and Thinking: The Evolving Structure of Avicenna's Epistemology." In *Aspects of Avicenna*. Edited by R. Wisnovsky. Princeton: Markus Wiener, 2001. 1–38.

Hasse, Dag Nikolaus. *Avicenna's De Anima in the Latin West: The Formation of a Peripatetic Philosophy of the Soul 1160–1300*. London and Turin: The Warburg Institute and Nino Aragno Editore, 2000.

Ibn Sīnā, al-Ḥusayn ibn ʿAbdallāh. *Aḥwāl al-nafs*. Edited by A. F. al-Ahwānī. Cairo: ʿĪsā al-Bābī al-Ḥalabī, 1371/1952.

———. *Risāla fī Ithbāt al-nubuwwāt* (*Proofs of Prophecies*). Edited by M. E. Marmura. Beirut: Dār al-Nahhār, 1991.

———. *ʿUyūn al-ḥikma*. Edited by ʿA. Badawī. Cairo: Institut Français d'Archéologie Orientale, 1954.

Jabre, Farid. *La notion de certitude selon Ghazālī dans ses origines psychologiques et historiques*. Paris: J. Vrin, 1958.

———. *La notion de la maʿrifa chez Ghazālī*. Beirut: Les Lettres Orientales, 1958.

Janssens, Jules. "Avicenna and the Qur'ān. A Survey of His Qur'ānic Commentaries." *Mélanges d'institut dominicain d'études orientales* 25–26 (2004). 177–92.

———. "Al-Ghazālī, and His Use of Avicennian Texts." In *Problems in Arabic Philosophy*. Edited by M. Maróth. Piliscsaba: The Avicenna Institute of Middle Eastern Studies, 2003. 37–49. Reprinted in idem, *Ibn Sīnā and His Influence on the Arabic and Latin World*. Aldershot (UK): Ashgate, 2006. Text XI.

———. "Al-Ghazālī: The Introduction of Peripatetic Syllogistic in Islamic Law (and Kalām)." *Mélanges d'institut dominicain d'études orientales* 28 (2010): 219–33.

———. "Al-Ghazālī's *Mīzān al-ʿamal*: An Ethical Summa Based on Ibn Sīnā and al-Rāghib al-Iṣfahānī." In *Islamic Thought in the Middle Ages.Studies in Text, Transmission and Translation in Honour of Hans Daiber*. Edited by A. Akasoy and W. Raven. Leiden: Brill, 2008. 123–37.

———. "Al-Ghazzālī's *Miʿyār al-ʿilm fī fann al-manṭiq*: Sources avicenniennes et farabiennes." *Archives d'histoire doctrinale et littéraire du moyen âge* 69 (2002) : 39–66. Reprint in idem, *Ibn Sīnā and His Influence on the Arabic and Latin World*. Aldershot (UK): Ashgate, 2006. Text IX.

———. "Al-Ghazālī's *Tahāfut*: Is It Really a Rejection of Ibn Sīnā's Philosophy?" *Journal of Islamic Studies* 12 (2001): 1–17. Reprinted in idem, *Ibn Sīnā and His Influence on the Arabic and Latin World*. Aldershot (UK): Ashgate, 2006. Text X.

———. "Ibn Sīnā (Avicenne): Un projet 'religieux' de philosophie?" In *Was ist Philosophie im Mittelalter?* Edited by J. A. Aertsen and A. Speer. Berlin: Walter De Gruyter, 1998. 863–70. Reprinted in idem, *Ibn Sīnā and His Influence on the Arabic and Latin World*. Aldershot (UK): Ashgate, 2006. Text V.

Khalidi, Muhammad Ali (ed. and transl.) *Medieval Islamic Philosophical Writings*. Cambridge: Cambridge University Press, 2005.

al-Kindī, Yaʿqūb ibn Isḥāq. *Risāla fī Kammiyyat kutub Arisṭāṭālīs wa-mā yuḥtāj ilayhi fī taḥṣīl al-falsafa*. In *Rasāʾil al-Kindī al-falsafiyya*. Edited by M. ʿA. Abū Rīda. 2 vols. Cairo: Dār al-Fikr al-ʿArabī, 1369–72/1950–53. Vol. 1. 363–384.

Kleinknecht, Angelika. "Al-Qisṭās al-mustaqīm: Eine Ableitung der Logik aus dem Koran." In *Islamic Philosophy and the Classical Tradition. Essays Presented by His Friends and Pupils to Richard Walzer on his Seventieth Birthday*. Edited by S. M. Stern, A. Hourani and V. Brown. Oxford: Cassirer, 1972. 159–187.

Kraemer, Joel L. *Philosophy in the Renaissance of Islam: Abū Sulaymān al-Sijistānī and His Circle*. Leiden: Brill, 1986.

Kukkonen, Taneli. "Al-Ghazālī's Skepticism Revisited." In *Rethinking the History of Skepticism*. Edited by H. Lagerlund. Leiden: Brill, 2009. 29–59.

Landolt, Hermann. "Al-Ghazālī and 'Religionswissenschaft:' Some Notes on the Mishkāt al-Anwār." *Asiatische Studien* (Zurich) 45 (1991): 19–72.

Madelung, Wilferd. "Ar-Rāġib al-Iṣfahānī und die Ethik al-Ġazālīs." In *Islamwissenschaftliche Abhandlungen Fritz Meier zum sechzigsten Geburtstag*. Edited by R. Gramlich. Wiesbaden: Harrassowitz, 1974. 152–163.

Mahdi, Muhsin. ""Avicenna. i. Introductory Note." in *Encyclopaedia Iranica*. Edited by E. Yarshater. London, New York, and Cosa Mesa (Calif.): Routledge & Kegan, Mazda, and Bibliotheca Persica, 1982– . Vol. 3. 66–67.

———. "Science, Philosophy, and Religion in Alfarabi's Enumeration of the Sciences." In *The Cultural Context of Medieval Learning*. Edited by J. E. Murdoch and E. D. Sylla. Dordrecht: Reidel, 1975. 113–47.

Marmura, Michael E. "Ghazali and Ash'arism Revisited." *Arabic Sciences and Philosophy* 12 (2002): 91–110.

———."Ghazālian Causes and Intermediaries." *Journal of the American Oriental Society* 115 (1995): 89–100.

Mayer, Toby. Review of Richard M. Frank, *Al-Ghazālī and the Ashʿarite School*. In *Journal of Qur'anic Studies* 1 (1999): 170–82.

McCarthy, Richard J. *Al-Ghazali: Deliverance from Error. Five Key Texts Including His Spiritual Autobiography, al-Munqidh min al-Dalal*. Louisville (Kenn.): Fons Vitae, 2000.

Michot, Jean R. *La destinée de l'homme selon Avicenne:Le retour à Dieu (maʿad) et l'imagination*. Louvain: Peeters, 1986.

Mohamed, Yasien. "The Concept of Justice in Miskawayh and Iṣfahānī." *Journal for Islamic Studies* (Cape Town)18–19 (1998): 51–111.

———. "The Ethical Philosophy of al-Rāghib al-Iṣfahānī." *Journal of Islamic Studies* (Oxford) 6 (1995): 51–75.

———. "Knowledge and Purification of the Soul. An annotated translation of Iṣfahānī's Kitāb al-Dharīʿa ilā Makārim al-sharīʿa (58–76; 89–92)." *Journal of Islamic Studies* (Oxford) 9 (1998): 1–34.

———. "The Unifying Thread: Intuitive cognition of the intellect in al-Farabi, al-Isfahani and al-Ghazali." *MAAS Journal of Islamic Science* (Aligarh, India)12 (1996): 27–47.

Nagel, Tilman. "Der Textbezüglichkeit entrinnen? Al-Ġazālīs Erneuerung der Lehre vom tauḥīd." *Der Islam* 83 (2008): 417–51.

Obermann, Julian. *Der philosophische und religiöse Subjektivismus Ghazālīs: Ein Beitrag zum Problem der Religion*. Vienna and Leipzig: W. Braunmüller, 1921.

Ormsby, Eric. *Ghazali: The Revival of Islam*. Oxford: Oneworld, 2008.

Rahman, Fazlur. *Prophecy in Islam: Philosophy and Orthodoxy*. London: Allen and Unwin, 1958.

Rudolph, Ulrich. "Abū Naṣr al-Fārābī." In *Philosophie in der islamischen Welt. Bd. 1: 8.–10. Jahrhundert*. Edited by U. Rudolph. Basel: Schwabe Verlag, 2012. 363–457.

———. "How did al-Ġazālī conceptualize Philosophy?" In *Al-Ġazālī (1058–1111). La prima stampa armena. Yehūdāh Ha-Lēvī (1075–1141). La ricezione di Isacco di Ninive*. Edited

by C. Baffioni, R. B. Finazzi, A. P. Dell'Acqua and E. Vergani. Milano: Bulzoni Editore, 2013. 25–35.
———. *Al-Māturīdī and the Development of Sunnī Theology in Samarqand.* Translated by R. Adem. Leiden: Brill, 2015.
———. "Die Neubewertung der Logik durch al-Ġazālī." In *Logik und Theologie. Das Organon im arabischen und im lateinischen Mittelalter*. Edited by D. Perler and U. Rudolph. Leiden: Brill, 2005. 73–97.
Schramm, Matthias. "Theoretische und praktische Disziplin bei al-Fārābī." *Zeitschrift für Geschichte der arabisch-islamischen Wissenschaften* 3 (1986): 1–55.
Shihadeh, Ayman. "From al-Ghazālī to al-Rāzī: 6th/12th Century Developments in Muslim Philosophical Theology." *Arabic Sciences and Philosophy* 15 (2005): 141–79.
Street, Tony. "Arabic Logic." In *Handbook of the History of Logic. Bd. 1: Greek, Indian and Arabic Logic.* Edited by D. M. Gabbay and J. Woods. Amsterdam: Elsevier, 2004. 523–96.
al-Tawḥīdī, Abū Ḥayyān 'Alī ibn Muḥammad. *al-Muqābasāt*. Edited by M. T. Ḥusayn. Baghdad: Maṭba'at al-Iršād, 1970.
———. *al-Imtāʿ wa-l-mu'ānasa*. Edited by A. Amīn and A. al-Zayn. 3 vols. Cairo: Lajnat al-Ta'līf wa-l-Tarjama wa-l-Nashr, 1939–1944.
Treiger, Alexander. *Inspired Knowledge in Islamic Thought: Al-Ghazālī's Theory of Mystical Cognition and Its Avicennian Foundation*. London: Routledge, 2012.
Wakelnig, Elvira. "Abū l-Ḥasan al-'Āmirī." In *Philosophie in der islamischen Welt. Bd. 1: 8.–10. Jahrhundert*. Edited by U. Rudolph. Basel: Schwabe Verlag, 2012. 174–185, 248–249.
Walzer, Richard. "Al-Fārābī's Theory of Prophecy and Divination." *Journal of Hellenic Studies* 77 (1957): 142–148. Reprinted in idem, *Greek into Arabic: Essays on Islamic Philosophy*. Oxford. Bruno Cassirer, 1962. 206–19.
Watt, W. Montgomery. *Muslim Intellectual: A Study of al-Ghazali.* Edinburgh: Edinburgh University Press, 1963.
Wensinck, Arent Jan. *La pensée de Ghazzālī.* Paris: Adrien-Maisonneuve, 1940.

CHAPTER 3

Problems in al-Ghazālī's Perfect World

Objections and Counter-Objections to His Best Possible World Thesis

Stephen R. Ogden

The view of Gottfried Wilhelm Leibniz (1646–1716) and others that this is the best of all possible worlds has been widely studied in Anglophone philosophy, particularly philosophy of religion, over the past forty years. Much work remains to be done, however, on a similar view found in the philosophical theology of Abū Ḥāmid al-Ghazālī. Like Avicenna (Ibn Sīnā, d. 428/1037) before him, al-Ghazālī most certainly held some such view, and this fact incited a protracted and fascinating debate among his successors, even within his own Ashʿarite school of theology. Eric Ormsby has chronicled and discussed much of the contours of that debate in his book *Theodicy in Islamic Thought*. Nevertheless, I think al-Ghazālī's "optimism" (i.e., the view that this is the best of all possible worlds) still presents unexplored and interesting facets, including some problems that stem from his corresponding divine command meta-ethical theory.[1] I am, thus, less interested than Ormsby in a comprehensive view of al-Ghazālī's theodicy and in the historical figures who took up the question after al-Ghazālī. I intend, rather, to focus mainly on a small segment of al-Ghazālī's corpus, Book 35 of *Iḥyāʾ ʿulūm al-dīn* (*Revival of the Religious Sciences*), *Kitāb al-Tawḥīd wa-l-Tawakkul* (*Professing Divine Unity and Having Trust in God*), primarily investigating its philosophical consistency. Al-Ghazālī's optimism is threatened by several problems, especially (A) its affinity to another Muʿtazilite version of optimism that he rejects, and by (B) the suggestion that there simply may not be a best possible world. I will defend al-Ghazālī's position with respect to most of the problems, including (A); however, after considering possible replies to (B), I will argue that his view of the best possible world, in combination with his divine command theory, is philosophically unsatisfactory. Thus, he should abandon (or significantly modify) one of the two theses.

1 Ormsby, *Theodicy*, 32, describes the debate as stretching from al-Ghazālī's coevals until the 19th century.

 | DOI 10.1163/9789004307490_004

1 Al-Ghazālī's Best of Possible Worlds (BPW) and the Problems

Several philosophers, Eastern and Western, have historically held the optimistic thesis:

> (BPW): this world is the best of all possible worlds.[2]

Al-Ghazālī's philosophical predecessor Avicenna argued for BPW; indeed, given Avicenna's inherited Neo-Platonic cosmological view that the world emanates from God in a necessary way , this is not only the *best* possible world, but also the *only* possible world.[3] Richard M. Frank has elucidated the large extent to which al-Ghazālī's BPW is based on that of Avicenna,[4] despite some crucial departures. Notwithstanding those differences, al-Ghazālī is committed to BPW, and this fact is most notoriously proven from a crucial text in Book 35, *Kitāb al-Tawḥīd wa-l-tawakkul* of his *Iḥyāʾ ʿulūm al-dīn*:[5]

> Indeed, of everything which God Most High created in heaven and earth, if human beings would but turn their eyes to it all and prolong their gaze, they would not see diversity or discontinuity in it. For everything which God Most High distributes among His servants: care and an appointed time (*ajal*), happiness and sadness, weakness and power, faith and unbelief, obedience and apostasy—all of it is unqualifiedly just with no injustice in it, true with no wrong infecting it.
>
> Indeed, all this happens according to a necessary and true order (*al-tartīb al-wājib al-ḥaqq*), according to what is appropriate as it is appropriate and in the measure that is proper to it; nor is anything more fitting, more perfect, and more attractive within the realm of possibility. For if [there were something more fitting, etc.] and it was withheld, despite [God's] having the power, and yet God did not graciously deign to do [i.e., create] it, then it would be miserly, contradicting [His] generosity, and

2 For the sake of this paper, I will generally assume contemporary "possible worlds semantics," in which a possible world, *w*, is a maximal state of affairs, a "way the world could be." I do not claim that this way of stating the issues would be immediately natural to al-Ghazālī. Indeed, I will discuss ways in which he might view possibility differently than we. Still, I will also argue for significant overlap in these conceptions of modality such that this understanding of possible worlds will serve the purposes of the paper and will not distort al-Ghazālī's own view.

3 Ibn Sīnā, *The Metaphysics of The Healing / al-Shifāʾ: al-Ilāhiyyāt*, 339–47.

4 Frank, *Creation and the Cosmic System*, esp. 21, 61–77, and 83–86.

5 Al-Ghazālī, *Iḥyāʾ ʿulūm al-dīn*, 13:2490–577. I rely heavily on David B. Burrell's translation of this book of the *Iḥyāʾ*, *Faith In Divine Unity and Trust In Divine Providence*.

> injustice, contradicting [His] justice. And if God were not omnipotent, He would be impotent, thereby contradicting the nature of divinity.[6]

Al-Ghazālī thinks there is nothing in possibility (*al-imkān*) that is better (*aḥsan*), more complete (*atamm*), or more perfect (*akmal*) than our world. Al-Ghazālī repeats this same idea in several other texts,[7] including in *al-Imlāʾ fī ishkālāt al-Iḥyāʾ* (*The Dictation on Difficult Passages in the Revival*): "There is not in possibility anything more wonderful (*abdaʿ*) than the form of this world, or more excellent (*aḥsan*) in order, or more perfect (*akmal*) in workmanship."[8] These particular declarations of al-Ghazālī's BPW were merged into a single lapidary phrase, which became the crux of the future debate in Muslim circles: "There is not in possibility anything more wonderful than what is (*laysa fīʾl-imkān abdaʿ mimmā kān*)."[9] Thus, it seems that we can safely attribute BPW to al-Ghazālī's corpus.

Yet, BPW seems an infelicitous thesis for al-Ghazālī to adopt for multiple reasons. It introduces a subtle but potentially treacherous balance between God's justice and His omnipotence, since BPW is typically offered (as it is above in the *Iḥyāʾ* passage) as a *theodicy*, i.e., a way of defending the compossibility of God's omnipotence, God's justice, and the presence of evil in the world. But BPW can cut in the exact opposite direction (as some of al-Ghazālī's opponents

6 al-Ghazālī, *Iḥyāʾ*, 13:2517.12–18. The English translation is adapted from Burrell's in *Faith In Divine Unity*, 48–49. In the third sentence I depart from Burrell and replace his with my own. Burrell's translation of the sentence in question reads: "For if something were to exist and to remind one of the sheer omnipotence [of God] and not of the good things accomplished by His action, that would utterly contradict [God's] generosity, and be an injustice contrary to the Just One." See also Ormsby, *Theodicy*, 38–41, for another English translation.

7 Cf. Ormsby, *Theodicy*, 38.

8 al-Ghazālī, *al-Imlāʾ fī ishkālāt al-Iḥyāʾ*, 16:3083.18–19. Cf. Ormsby, *Theodicy*, 35–36. Ormsby also notes that the other versions of this basic statement occur in *al-Arbaʿīn fī uṣūl al-dīn* (*Book of Forty*) and in *Maqāṣid al-falāsifa* (*The Doctrines of the Philosophers*), though the latter is simply a compendium of the views of prior philosophers with whom al-Ghazālī was not always in agreement. Al-Ghazālī also seems to confirm BPW in *al-Maqṣad al-asnā fi sharḥ maʿānī asmāʾ Allāh al-ḥusnā* (*The Highest Goal in Explaining the Beautiful Names of God*), 47.12–13: "The specific divine [property] is that God is a being necessarily existing by his essence, from whom there exists everything the existence of which is possible according to the best ways of order and perfection." Cf. Frank, *Creation and the Cosmic System*, 21. This passage, however, is ambiguous. It could be evidence of BPW; however, al-Ghazālī may also mean that for any existing thing that *is* the best possible, we know that God is the creator of it, but that there are still other existents that are not the best possible. For more discussion of the doctrine throughout al-Ghazālī's corpus, see Griffel, *Al-Ghazālī's Philosophical Theology*, 348–49, n. 87.

9 Ormsby, *Theodicy*, 37.

noticed), fueling objections that this is clearly *not* the best possible world due to the amounts of evil observed[10] and/or that God is *impotent* to create a better possible world (if indeed He has created this one and it is the best He can do).[11] Other opponents worried that al-Ghazālī had, in adopting a BPW doctrine similar to that of the philosophers, also committed himself to the heretical opinion that God had no free choice and had to create *necessarily*. I will address two of these problems here, albeit quite briefly since I think al-Ghazālī's responses to them are more straightforward than the other issues I raise below.

Perhaps the most common objection to any BPW theory is that the actual world is most obviously not the best possible since it contains so much evil, pain, and discord. It certainly seems that we can conceive of a better possible world simply by imagining this world without any number of these ills. Al-Ghazālī, however, as we shall see throughout this article, thinks such an objection is shortsighted.

His response is essentially two-pronged. First, he argues quite fervently that if one carefully examines the world, she will realize that the empirical facts confirm BPW:

> If everything that God creates were defective in comparison to another creation that He could have created but didn't create, the deficiency that would infect this existence of His creation would be evident just like it is evident that there are in His [actual] creation particular individuals whom He did create deficient in order to show thereby the perfection of what He creates otherwise.[12]

Here and in the crucial passage confirming BPW in *Iḥyāʾ* quoted above, al-Ghazālī argues that thorough investigation will reveal a "necessary and true order" to the world that makes it the best. And this insistence by al-Ghazālī is

10 In fact, if it is argued that God *must* create the best possible world, and it can be shown that this is *not* the best possible world, then it looks like a simple argument that God does not exist. See, e.g., Cohen, "Creating the Best Possible World," and the conclusion of Steinberg, "Leibniz, Creation, and the Best of All Possible Worlds."

11 Or, to note a different but related contemporary objection, even if God is not impotent strictly speaking, then God is not perfect or morally unsurpassable. Cf. Rowe, "The Problem of Divine Perfection" and a more complete list of such recent arguments in Steinberg, "Leibniz, Creation, and the Best of All Possible Worlds," 125.

12 al-Ghazālī's *Imlāʾ*, quoted and translated by Griffel in *al-Ghazālī's Philosophical Theology*, 231. Griffel, *Al-Ghazālī's Philosophical Theology*, 348, n. 85, notes his use of MS Yale, Landberg 428 here for this passage, citing the corruption in other printed Arabic editions of *Imlāʾ*.

more than a mere contradiction of the objection and a challenge to look more closely at the facts. For, second, he also argues that we must take into account our limited epistemic abilities and consider the ways in which many occurrences that seem prima facie evil are actually factors contributing to the best possible overall order. He does this in many ways, some of which will be highlighted below. The gist of this argument is, as in the quote above, that deficiencies actually serve the greater good of the whole, often by manifesting or contributing to the wellbeing of other more perfect existents in the world. Thus, some evils and harms are not only allowed by God but are in fact necessary for the best possible world. This is another idea that al-Ghazālī's BPW inherits from Avicenna.[13]

This mention of Avicennan influence, however, raises its own objection. How could al-Ghazālī adopt so much of Avicenna's BPW teaching while rejecting its philosophical root—i.e., that creation is *necessary* and that this is, indeed, the *only* possible world? Al-Ghazālī's BPW was subjected continually to this suspicion by later Ashʿarite thinkers.[14] In our own time, Richard M. Frank has argued that al-Ghazālī's BPW was not just influenced by Avicenna, but that al-Ghazālī also ultimately accepted the God of the philosophers who creates out of the necessity of the divine nature.[15]

While I must be brief in addressing this problem as well, I do not think this interpretation is correct. Al-Ghazālī's BPW need not entail Avicennan necessitarianism, nor did al-Ghazālī intend to imply such. First, as I have noted above, al-Ghazālī (unlike Avicenna) never argues for BPW as a consequence of the divine nature.[16] Rather, he chooses to argue for it *empirically*—we see that God has created this world (though there were other possibilities) and this world is the best. Second, al-Ghazālī (unlike Avicenna) considers his BPW not as a consequence of divine knowledge, but of divine *will*. This Ashʿarite spin on BPW will be the subject of further discussion below. Third, al-Ghazālī explicitly and forcefully denies Avicennan necessitarianism in his works, most often by emphasizing our last point—God creates the actual world from among other possibilities by a free choice of his will:

13 For a more thorough discussion of al-Ghazālī's response to this objection and its Avicennan influences, see Griffel, *Philosophical Theology*, 229–230, and Ormsby, *Theodicy*, 78–79 and 257.

14 See Ormsby, *Theodicy*, 182–92.

15 Frank, *Creation and the Cosmic System*, 55–63.

16 Griffel, *Al-Ghazālī's Philosophical Theology*, 230.

> We say: "Agent" is an expression [referring] to one from whom the act proceeds, together with the will to act by way of choice and the knowledge of what is willed. But, according to you [philosophers], the world [proceeds] from God as the effect from the cause, as a necessary consequence, inconceivable for God to prevent, in the way the shadow is the necessary consequence of the individual and the light (...) of the sun. And this does not pertain to action in anything (...).The agent, however, is not called an agent and a maker by simply being a cause, but by being a cause in a special respect—namely, by way of will and choice (*al-irāda wa-l-ikhtiyār*).[17]

In fact, the entire first three discussions of the *Tahāfut al-falāsifa* (*The Incoherence of the Philosophers*) are designed specifically to attack the philosophers' doctrines of the world's necessity and its eternity. Al-Ghazālī insists that there are other possible worlds (other ways the world could be)—for instance, the earth could be larger or smaller.[18] Indeed, God could have willed "the opposite of every work that came into existence through His will" and could have willed not to create at all.[19] Therefore, it seems that al-Ghazālī successfully rebuts the problems of empirical confirmation and of necessitarianism.

There are, however, two more potent challenges to al-Ghazālī's BPW, which concern BPW's consistency with his other philosophical and theological views. First (A), one might think that his BPW commits him to the Muʿtazilite doctrine that God has to do what is best for individuals (known as *al-aṣlaḥ*), a doctrine that al-Ghazālī (like every other major Ashʿarite theologian) rejected. He offers BPW as a theodicy, as an explanation for why God's divine decree (*qadar*) should necessitate good for some and evil for others. If BPW is meant to comfort the reader of *Iḥyāʾ*, must it not claim that God ultimately does what is best for each person? A second and closely-related problem (B) is that al-Ghazālī himself may suggest that BPW is not possible. In sentences that follow just after the central *Iḥyāʾ* passage quoted above, al-Ghazālī seems to describe the afterlife in such a way that the pleasures of the saved are increased proportionately to the punishments of the damned, a scenario which seems to

17 al-Ghazālī, *The Incoherence of the Philosophers / Tahāfut al-falāsifa*, 56; cf. also ibid., 22.

18 Ibid., 38.

19 al-Ghazālī, *al-Risāla al-qudsiyya* (*Letter for Jerusalem*), edited and translated in Tibawi, "Al-Ghazālī's Sojourn in Damascus and Jerusalem," 82, 88–89, 105, 112; see also the same text in *Iḥyāʾ*, 1:188–89, 2:195, and *al-Iqtiṣād fī l-iʿtiqād*, 174. For more discussion on al-Ghazālī's avoidance of Avicennan necessitarianism, see Griffel, *Al-Ghazālī's Philosophical Theology*, 233–234, and Ormsby, *Theodicy*, 196 and 207.

point toward an infinity of further possible (and better) worlds. I argue that his meta-ethical divine command theory (hereafter "DCT") and his interesting view of possibility can resolve this problem. However, that very solution seems to unearth another striking and more general tension between BPW and DCT, forcing al-Ghazālī into either an unsatisfactory theodicy or relinquishing one of the two tenets.

II Problem (A)—al-Ghazālī's *abdaʿ* and the Muʿtazilites' *aṣlaḥ*

The Muʿtazilites argued that *goodness* and *justice* are objective concepts knowable by human reason. In addition, these concepts apply more or less univocally to God and creatures such that we can be assured that God would not do wrong to any individual; God is obligated (just as we are) to do the best or most beneficial (*al-aṣlaḥ*) for each person that He can. The relatively late Muʿtazilite theologian ʿAbd al-Jabbār (d. 415/1025) argues thus: "He does not punish anyone for someone else's sin because that would be morally wrong (*qabih*), [and] God is far removed from such (…). He only causes sickness and illness in order to turn them to advantage (…). And you know that, for their sakes, He does the best for all His creatures."[20]

Certainly not all Muʿtazilites held this exact view. There were disagreements between the Baghdādian and Baṣran schools, as well as between individual thinkers, for example over whether *al-aṣlaḥ* extended to all animals or only human beings.[21] But the majority of secondary literature confirms some such basic position of at least a notable number of Muʿtazilites.[22] However, Josef van Ess, in his magisterial study *Theologie und Gesellschaft*, has argued (i) that the Muʿtazilite view cannot technically be a kind of BPW, since their doctrine is limited to creatures (not the cosmos), and (ii) that at least some Muʿtazilites

20 See the Engl. translation of the Qāḍī ʿAbd al-Jabbār's *Sharḥ al-uṣūl al-khamsa* (mistakenly identified as *Kitāb al-Uṣūl al-khamsa*) in Martin et al. *Defenders of Reason in Islam*, 90–115, 93.

21 Cf., Stone and Wisnovsky, "Philosophy and Theology," 700; Vasalou, *Moral Agents*, 28–29 and 39; Gwynne, "Al-Jubbāʾī, al-Ashʿarī and the Three Brothers," 132 and 135.

22 See the citations in the preceding footnote; Brunschvig "Muʿtazilism et Optimum (*al-aṣlaḥ*);" Ormsby, *Theodicy*, 21 and 217; Abrahamov, "Al-Ḳāsim Ibn Ibrāhīm's Theory," 92, fn. 53; Martin, et al., *Defenders of Reason*, 186; Gilliot, "La théologie musulmane," 152; Ormsby, *Ghazali*, 13. Hourani, *Reason and Tradition*, 105, gives a nuanced view of ʿAbd al-Jabbār, viz., that "although it is logically possible (*yumkin*) it is not admissible to think (*lā yajūz*) that God does less than the best."

(e.g., al-Naẓẓām) did not conceive of *al-aṣlaḥ* as a superlative, i.e., as "the best."[23] Rather, God has a wide range of options for instantiating each person's great benefit, even if there are other very beneficial possibilities that remain unrealized. I cannot here attempt an exhaustive study of *al-aṣlaḥ*. If van Ess is right regarding (i) and (ii) for all (or most) Muʿtazilites, then as a matter of *historical record*, Problem (A) could be solved fairly straightforwardly. If al-Ghazālī's is a true form of optimism and the Muʿtazilites' doctrine is not, Ghazālī's BPW cannot be accused directly of holding a position identical to Muʿtazilism. Perhaps then, many of the Ashʿarites and Muʿtazilites were talking past each other concerning *al-aṣlaḥ*. But even if (i) alone is enough to simply differentiate the exact views of al-Ghazālī and the Muʿtazilites, one might still wonder whether al-Ghazālī's BPW nevertheless somehow implies *al-aṣlaḥ*, which would be sufficient for the *philosophical* Problem (A) to get off the ground. In other words, although al-Ghazālī's BPW has a wider scope than (and is thus different from) *al-aṣlaḥ*, *al-aṣlaḥ* might naturally be thought of as a part of a full BPW picture like al-Ghazālī's. Van Ess, after all, notes the two positions' affinity and that the Muʿtazilite view is clearly some sort of background to al-Ghazālī's own.[24] Moreover, even if both (i) and (ii) are correct for all (or most) Muʿtazilites, the philosophical Problem (A) also still lurks as long as al-Ghazālī himself *thought* that the Muʿtazilites held some such form of BPW and rejected it as such in his writings. Logically, it seems impossible to overrule this latter point, since al-Ghazālī not only states that the Muʿtazilites think God is obligated to do "the best," but also argues against them by conceiving of a *better* possible world than the actual world.[25] Such an argument would only work if he thought the Muʿtazilite opponent held a form of superlative optimism. I quote and further discuss this particular passage below.

The Muʿtazilites also definitively held that human beings have robust libertarian freedom and are responsible for their own acts, for if God compelled their actions, He would not be just in punishing them:

> Thus, if God committed injustice He would be unjust, just as if He acted justly He would be just (...). [These verses] indicate that these ethically bad acts are not created by God but that they are human acts, and on that basis they deserve blame and punishment. How can it be possible for God to create erroneous behavior in them and then punish them (...).

23 van Ess, *Theologie und Gesellschaft*, 4:509–10.

24 Ibid., 4:32.

25 al-Ghazālī, *al-Qisṭās al-mustaqīm*, 94; Engl. transl. in McCarthy, *Deliverance from Error*, 278.

> Isn't that the same as someone commanding his slave to do something, then punishing him for it? And that would clearly be corrupt.[26]

Even the sufferings of children and animals were justified on this system, both supposedly recompensed in the afterlife.[27]

As noted above, Ashʿarite theologians such as al-Ghazālī rejected these positions. Indeed, the legend of the founding of the Ashʿarite school relates al-Ashʿarī's rejection of his teacher's *al-aṣlaḥ* doctrine because of its inability to make sense of a thought experiment involving three brothers in different everlasting abodes in the afterlife.[28] After the infant in a lower rank of Paradise complains to God about having his life curtailed before having the chance to do well and enjoy the higher ranks (like his one blessed brother), the divine response is that God knew he would have done evil and ended up in Hell. To which the final brother in Hell retorts, "Why was I not taken in infancy too, since you knew I would do evil?" In other words, how could everlasting punishment in Hell somehow be in the individual's best interest, and thereby constitute a just act of God? Hence, in contrast to this view, the Ashʿarites' general approach was to deny that God had any obligations to human beings, to argue that justice and goodness are only determined by God's command, and to adopt a more predestinarian view of *kasb* or *iktisāb* (the view that God creates all human actions, while the human somehow *acquires* them and is therefore held responsible):[29]

---

26 ʿAbd al-Jabbār, *Sharḥ uṣūl al-khamsa*, Engl. transl. in Martin et al. *Defenders of Reason in Islam*, 97.

27 Cf. Ormsby, *Theodicy*, 244–245; Watt, *Islamic Philosophy and Theology*, 51; van Ess, *Theologie und Gesellschaft*, 4:32. The views of both Marilyn M. Adams in "Horrendous Evils" and Robert M. Adams in "Must God Create the Best?" display similarities with these Muʿtazilite views, as they hold that, if God is to be counted as morally perfect, he must ensure that each person has enough blessing (on balance with evil suffered) to make one's life "a great good overall" or at least better than if that person had never existed. But of course neither of the Adamses needs to affirm that each person receives the *best* possible life overall.

28 See, e.g., Watt, *Islamic Philosophy and Theology*, 51, and Gwynne, "Al-Jubbāʾī, al-Ashʿarī and the Three Brothers." Al-Ghazālī himself repeats a version of this story to the same end in *al-Qisṭās al-mustaqīm*, 95 (Engl. transl. in McCarthy, *Deliverance from Error*, 279) and in *al-Risāla al-qudsiyya* (ed. and transl. Tibawi, "Al-Ghazālī's Sojourn in Damascus and Jerusalem"), 90, 114–115 (*Iḥyāʾ*, 2:196).

29 Roughly speaking, this would be categorized as a type of compatibilism in the contemporary debate regarding free will and determinism. However, the doctrine is very complex, and al-Ghazālī's version diverges in key respects from al-Ashʿarī's. So, although it is an important piece of al-Ghazālī's overall theodicy, I cannot devote any more space to a discussion of *kasb* in this article.

> The proof that He [*scil.* God] is free to do whatever He does is that He is the Supreme Monarch, subject to no one, with no superior over Him who can permit, or command, or chide, or forbid, or prescribe what He shall do and fix bounds for Him. This being so, nothing can be evil on the part of God….And if He declared it [*scil.* lying] to be good, it would be good; and if He commanded it, no one could gainsay Him.[30]

This was al-Ghazālī's theological milieu, and (for the most part) he accepted these basic precepts against the Muʿtazilite doctrines. In fact, al-Ghazālī explicitly rejects *al-aṣlaḥ* in his writings.[31] He argues against the Muʿtazilite claim by asserting that God has not done the best for each individual:

> I say: "If the best were obligatory on God, He would do it. But it is known that He has not done it; so [that] proves that it is not obligatory—for He does not omit the obligatory (…). Had He done the 'best,' He would have created them in the Garden and left them there—for this would have been better for them; but it is known that He has not done that; so [that] proves that He has not done the best."[32]

Not only are human beings not created immediately in Paradise (which, in this context, al-Ghazālī thinks by itself is proof enough against *al-aṣlaḥ*), but al-Ghazālī (along with most Ashʿarite, Sunnī thinkers) also holds a double-predestination doctrine, i.e., that God specifically assigns believers to their belief (and corresponding fate in Paradise) and unbelievers to their unbelief (and corresponding punishment in Hell):

> He is the cause (*minhu*) of good and evil, benefit and harm, Islam and unbelief, acknowledgement and denial [of God], success and failure, rectitude and error, obedience and rebellion, association of other gods with Him and belief [in Him alone]. There is nothing that can defeat His predetermined purpose (*qaḍāʾ*), and none to question His dominion.[33]

---

30 al-Ashʿarī, *Kitāb al-Lumaʿ*, 71; Engl. transl., 99–100; §§ 170–171. For more on the Ashʿarite view, see Frank, "Moral Obligation," and Hourani, *Reason and Tradition*, 57–66.

31 See, e.g., al-Ghazālī, *al-Risāla al-qudsiyya* (ed. and transl. Tibawi), 90, 114 (*Iḥyāʾ*, 2:196). Ormsby, *Theodicy*, 219, fn. 12, gives a list of references in at least three different works.

32 al-Ghazālī, *al-Qisṭās al-mustaqīm*, 94; Engl. transl. in McCarthy, *Deliverance from Error*, 278.

33 al-Ghazālī, *al-Risāla al-qudsiyya* (ed. and transl. Tibawi), 88.13–15, 111 (*Iḥyāʾ*, 2:194.6–8). Al-Ghazālī immediately includes two important Qurʾānic quotes: "He leads astray whom-

The clear implication of double predestination is also present in the crucial *Iḥyāʾ* BPW passage quoted above and its immediately surrounding context.[34] Again, given that al-Ghazālī holds this doctrine of predestination, it is difficult to see how Hell could possibly be the best for an individual.

How then is al-Ghazālī's "most wonderful" (*al-abdaʿ*) BPW distinguished from the *al-aṣlaḥ* doctrine of the Muʿtazilites? The answer is that his *al-abdaʿ* stance is a *global* BPW, as distinct from the Muʿtazilite *individualistic* BPW.[35] Thus, on al-Ghazālī's view, it is not the case that every individual human being (and certainly not every animal) is guaranteed the best possible existence by God's justice. On the contrary, he employs the idea of "ransom" or "redemption" in which some individuals receive particularly unhappy lots in order to improve the life of some other individual in the whole:

> Just as if one ransoms human lives (*arwāḥ*) with the lives (*bi-arwāḥ*) of animals, having the authority over their slaughter, there is no wrong so also the perfect taking priority over the deficient is the essence (*ʿayn*) of justice.[36]

Ormsby discusses how this concept, for the Ashʿarites, replaced that of animal recompense in *al-aṣlaḥ* and was expanded: "animals reveal the superiority of man by the very fact of their 'lower' level of existence (…) they also serve as sacrifices whereby human souls are ransomed. The same applies to other forms of imperfection: the diseased, the destitute, the damned themselves. All exist solely as sacrifices for the perfect."[37] Thus, al-Ghazālī thinks that no individual part of the whole is promised the best; rather, some parts are subjected to evil in order that the world, on the whole, be balanced with justice and reveal perfection.

---

soever He will, and He guides whomsoever He will" (Q 14:4 and 16:93); and "He shall not be questioned as to what He does, but they shall be questioned" (Q 21:23).

34 Cf. particularly the sentence that "(…) good (*al-khayr*) and bad (*al-sharr*) are determined by it," i.e., the divine decree (*al-qadar*); al-Ghazālī, *Iḥyāʾ*, 13:2518.8, Engl. transl. in *Faith In Divine Unity*, 50.

35 Of course, here regarding the Muʿtazilites, I mean "BPW" in a rough sense since the "world" involved may be limited to *living creatures* and, thus, would not strictly speaking be a *world* at all. Rather, BPW here is used to mean the best possible world *for each individual* person (or living creature), even if not the best in some larger, cosmic sense. Cf. van Ess, *Theologie und Gesellschaft*, 4:509, and the mention of his point (i) above at the beginning of this section.

36 al-Ghazālī, *Iḥyāʾ*, 13:2517.22–23.

37 Ormsby, *Theodicy*, 68.

One might raise several objections here. First, as we saw in Section I above, if al-Ghazālī is presented with counter-evidence to his global BPW, he must reply that much of evil is only "apparent" or "local," serving some greater purpose in the whole.[38] But, in the *Qisṭās*, when he gives his argument that *al-aṣlaḥ* is false because we know it to be false, the hypothetical Muʿtazilite will respond in the same way: "We concede that if it (*al-aṣlaḥ*) were obligatory, He would do it; but we do not concede that He has not done it"[39]—i.e., we might just not be able to tell that God has done the best for each individual. Why is al-Ghazālī's counterexample of a better world for the individual (i.e., immediate creation in Paradise) more persuasive than any counterexample we might imagine for his own global BPW? If he can deflate such counterexamples to his own BPW, his counterexample to *al-aṣlaḥ* should be subject to a similar deflationary move. Indeed, the opponent replies that the problem with instantaneous Paradise is that "then their happiness would not be by their effort and their merit. And consequently the blessing (*minna*) would be [too] great for them, and the blessing would be oppressive."[40] In other words, al-Ghazālī might here be guilty of what Alvin Plantinga terms "Leibniz's Lapse." God may not be able to actualize just any possible world, since it may be that every possible world, if it is to contain important moral good (in the case of the Muʿtazilites, the moral good of freely chosen human actions justly recompensed), must also contain some moral evil; thus, instantaneous Paradise is not a live option.[41] This is an important objection for, although al-Ghazālī glibly dismisses it in this context of *al-Qisṭās al-mustaqīm*,[42] he considers it quite carefully as a counterexample to his own view elsewhere in *Iḥyāʾ*.[43] In the latter work, al-Ghazālī evades the problem by outlining a system of secondary causes and "conditions" such that "[one of God's actions] clears the way for a condition (*sharṭ*) [whose fulfillment is required] for the existence of another of God's actions."[44] Thus, Griffel concludes:

38 See ibid., 255–57.

39 al-Ghazālī, *al-Qisṭās al-mustaqīm*, 94; Engl. transl. in McCarthy, *Deliverance from Error*, 278.

40 Ibid, 95.3–4.

41 See Plantinga, *The Nature of Necessity*, 184.

42 al-Ghazālī, *al-Qisṭās al-mustaqīm*, 95; Engl. transl. in McCarthy, *Deliverance from Error*, 279: "I make it easy for your hearing and my tongue [by refraining] from the report of such discourse and consider them [hearing and tongue] above it [too good for it], to say nothing of replying to it!"

43 al-Ghazālī, *Iḥyāʾ*, 12:2224. On this important argument, see Griffel, *Al-Ghazālī's Philosophical Theology*, 223–225.

44 al-Ghazālī, *Iḥyāʾ*,12:2224.21–22. Translated in Griffel, *Al-Ghazālī's Philosophical Theology*, 224. Cf. *al-Iqtiṣād*, 97–98.

> God cannot simply move humans from their cradle into paradise, because the "conditions" of entering paradise are not yet fulfilled when the human is still in the cradle. Entering paradise has a specific cause. Having a cause means one or more conditions must be fulfilled before the creation of the event can take place (...). Thus God cannot create someone's entry into paradise unless He has earlier created good deeds in the person.[45]

I cannot dwell more on this specific counterexample.[46] Regardless of what he thinks about the specific counterexample, I will simply point out that the general epistemological claims are intuitively more in al-Ghazālī's favor than the Muʿtazilites' when considering defeaters for their respective BPW theories. Perhaps human knowledge is inadequate to make judgments about any apparent evils that might undermine *either* BPW position. Nevertheless, it seems plausible that, if people can recognize clear defeaters at all, it is probably more likely on the level of the *individual* BPW rather than the *global* BPW. The scope of the latter includes so much more that is simply beyond our limited epistemic abilities.[47] Thus, in general, al-Ghazālī's BPW will be able to handle particular defeaters more easily than *al-aṣlaḥ*.

---

45 Griffel, *Al-Ghazālī's Philosophical Theology*, 224; cf. also ibid., 232.

46 The issue is complex for several reasons. First, we see al-Ghazālī arguing against the Muʿtazilite BPW in one book using a counterexample that he rejects as a possibility in relation to his own BPW in a different book. Readers of al-Ghazālī will not be surprised at this for he often makes arguments, the contours of which he does not ultimately accept himself, simply to undermine certain opponents' positions in a particular context. This fact is crucial for understanding his *Tahāfut*, wherein he argues against many positions of the philosophers that he nonetheless holds on the basis of different reasons; see Marmura's introduction to the *Tahāfut*, xxii–xxiii, and Griffel, *Al-Ghazālī's Philosophical Theology*, 98–101. Second, al-Ghazālī's response in the *Iḥyā'* depends on a system of secondary causation and an apparently necessary order of conditions (*shurūṭ*)—a teaching that places him ambiguously between Avicennan necessitarianism and Ashʿarite occasionalism, as Griffel discusses (pp. 225, 231–34). On these questions of secondary causation and whether al-Ghazālī is an occasionalist, see Marmura, "Al-Ghazālī's Second Causal Theory" for a *pro* occasionalist interpretation; Frank, *Creation and the Cosmic System* for the opposite; and McGinnis, "Occasionalism" and Griffel, *Al-Ghazālī's Philosophical Theology*, for two alternative *via media* interpretations. I myself think either McGinnis or Griffel is probably right, but I cannot argue for that here. I discuss the same problem below in fn. 113.

47 The idea here is similar to a strand of "skeptical theism" in contemporary philosophy of religion that demands that CORNEA (the "condition of reasonable epistemic access") be satisfied in order to make epistemic "appears" claims, specifically with respect to seemingly morally unwarranted instances of evil—see Wykstra, "The Humean Obstacle." One

A second objection might be garnered from further apparent instances of *al-aṣlaḥ* in al-Ghazālī's own texts. In the second part of Book 35 of the *Iḥyā'*, he describes one method for not relying on wealth, viz., that a person may, "reconcile himself to the fact that *God only does with him what is best for him* (*ṣalāḥuhu*): that if his wealth be wiped out, that is better for him, since perhaps if it were left to him it would have become a factor corrupting his religion (...)."[48] He urges a similar response if someone's property is stolen.[49] It looks as if al-Ghazālī does, in fact, endorse an *individual* BPW like the Muʿtazilite. However, both of these quotes are taken from the section on trusting in divine providence (*al-tawakkul*), which is applicable only to believing Muslims. In this way, he does not commit himself to an *individual* BPW, except for believers.[50] Furthermore, al-Ghazālī could hold that God may ultimately *in fact* provide the best for each individual, so long as he does not hold (with the Muʿtazilites) that God is *obligated* to do so. Ormsby notes that a later defender of al-Ghazālī's BPW, al-Suyūṭī (d. 911/1505), held that, albeit God is not obligated to do the best for each individual, He nevertheless does so "out of sheer magnanimity."[51] A defender of al-Ghazālī could even explain the predestined reprobate in Hell as receiving the "best," assuming varied levels of punishment in Hell—the Ashʿarite al-Juwaynī (d. 478/1085) suggests that even they, in another possible world, might have committed even graver sins, meriting a lower level (and more severe punishment) in Hell.[52] Al-Ghazālī could affirm all these explanations, and, so long as he only explicitly commits to a global *al-abdaʿ* BPW and refuses to admit that God is obligated to do the best for any one individual, then his position is not plagued by inconsistently holding the Muʿtazilite *al-aṣlaḥ* BPW.

---

should not claim that *p* about cognized situations that would appear exactly the same to the subject (because of epistemic limitations) even if *not-p* were true.

48 al-Ghazālī, *Iḥyā'*, 13:2535.6–8; Engl. transl. in *Faith In Divine* Unity, 85. Emphasis mine, S.O.

49 "(...) if there were no good in it, God Most High would not have taken it away," ibid., 14:2559.11–12; Engl. transl. in *Faith In Divine Unity*, 121.

50 Indeed, such a view dovetails with the above remarks concerning "ransom."

51 Ormsby, *Theodicy*, 250. In fact, al-Ghazālī does not always employ *abdaʿ*; he uses the Muʿtazilite phrase in speaking of God's grace: "God is generous (*mutafaḍḍil*) in creating, in inventing and in imposing obligation,—not out of any necessity (*wujūb*)—and He is lavish in providing favors and 'the optimal' (*al-aṣlaḥ*)—not out of any obligation (*luzūm*)." (*Iḥyā'*, 1:157.16–17, quoted and translated in Ormsby, *Theodicy*, 248). Ormsby, *Theodicy*, 246, also notes that al-Ghazālī leaves this option "open" in the *Qisṭās* when he speaks of the mystery of God's doing the "best" in His divine decree (*al-qadar*). Cf. *al-Qisṭās al-mustaqīm*, 95.16–17; Engl. transl. in McCarthy, *Deliverance from* Error, 279.

52 Ormsby, *Theodicy*, 22.

III Problem (B)—Is BPW Possible?[53]

Aside from indicating obvious instances of evil in the actual world that seem to militate against BPW, many philosophers have questioned whether BPW is true in a different way. BPW is false if it can be shown that there is no *best* among all possible worlds or that there *could not* be any best possible world. This could follow in one of two basic situations: (1) a tie between optimals; or (2) if, for every possible world, there is another which is better.[54] For example, Robert Adams supports (2): "I do not in fact see any good reason to believe that there is a best among possible worlds. Why can't it be that for every possible world there is another that is better?"[55] Note that this strategy can work just as well in defending divine omnipotence. BPW provides a theodicy since, because God created the *best*, logically speaking He could *not* have done any better (so He is not to be blamed for evil in the world).[56] But on (2), it is actually *impossible* for God to do the best, since for any world actualized, He could have done better—thus, God cannot be blamed, at least not for failing to create the best.[57]

---

53 Blumenfeld in his "Is the Best Possible World Possible" argues that BPW is at least possible, and tries to show that, from Leibniz's argument itself, one can argue to the consistency of the concept of BPW. Yet, as discussed above (in Plantinga's notion of Leibniz's Lapse) and as will be discussed below, even if a concept seems *intrinsically* possible (logically consistent), it may prove to be impossible because of some further implication. Furthermore, even if BPW is possible, this problem also concerns whether it is true.

54 Haji, "A Conundrum," 12, lays out the alternatives in this way.

55 R. M. Adams, "Must God Create the Best?" 51. Adams also supports the view in *Finite and Infinite Goods*, 157, stating that he thinks it is "plausible" that the "disparity between finite and infinite goods has among its consequences (…) that there is no best possible set of creatures." However, he relies for a full defense on his earlier article (*Finite and Infinite Goods*, 133, fn. 3, and 157, fn. 12). Others who hold this view include Plantinga, *The Nature of Necessity*, 168; Geach, *Providence and Evil*, 125–126 and *Truth and Hope*, 92–93; and Swinburne (whom I discuss below).

56 This is precisely how al-Ghazālī can answer any purely philosophical worries that his BPW curtails God's omnipotence—inability to do the impossible is, for most in his tradition as the Western one, not strictly speaking a kind of *impotence* at all. Cf. al-Ghazālī, *Incoherence of the Philosophers / Tahāfut al-falāsifa*, 175, §29; *al-Iqtiṣād*, 97.1–2; Ormsby, *Theodicy*, 157–58.

57 Cf. Rowe, "The Problem of Divine Perfection," 230: "There is something forceful and right about this reasoning. If, no matter what world an omnipotent being creates, there is a morally better world that being can create, then, provided that the omnipotent being creates a significantly good world, it cannot be morally at fault for not having created a morally better world."

Now, (2) could be true in broadly two ways: in quantity (more good things—whether creatures or pleasures) or in quality (an increase in beauty or an intensification of excellences).[58] For example, Richard Swinburne argues that joyful conscious beings are a good-making feature of any possible world, and that

> if the enjoyment of the world by each is a valuable thing, surely a world with a few more conscious beings in it would be a yet more valuable world (…). I conclude that it is not, for conceptual reasons, plausible to suppose that there could be a best of possible worlds (…)."[59]

Nor is it only contemporary philosophers who find these potential pitfalls for BPW. Al-Ghazālī's own defenders, e.g., the 13th/19th century author Hamdān ibn ʿUthmān al-Jazāʾirī (d. 1252/1836), could recognize that "the things of which God is capable (*maqdūrāt Allāh*) stop at no limit and end; and that [with respect to, S.O.] the order of this world, even if it is in perfect wisdom and excellent design (…) God is capable of creating one more excellent than it, and one still more excellent than that most excellent *ad infinitum*."[60]

Al-Ghazālī himself seems to envisage just such a (2)-type scenario, similar to what Swinburne and al-Jazāʾirī describe. First, note that al-Ghazālī appears committed to the same basic principle of God's omnipotence:

> One of the precepts concerning [divine power] is that it is related to all objects of power. By "objects of power" I mean all of the infinite possibles. Now everybody knows that the possibles are infinite, and so the objects of power are infinite (…). So [the divine power] is suited to always creating one motion after another, and likewise one color after another, and one substance after another, and so on. That is what we meant by saying that His power (exalted be He!) is related to every possible; for possibility is neither limited in number nor is the relation of that power itself specific to a given number to the exclusion of another.[61]

---

58 Cf. Kraay, "Divine Unsurpassability," 299. Kraay's references are helpful here.

59 Swinburne, *The Existence of God*, 114.

60 al-Jazāʾirī as quoted in Ormsby, *Theodicy*, 33. The author is not related to the more famous ʿAbd al-Qādir al-Jazāʾirī (d. 1300/1883). An earlier historical example for the same criticism is the Mamlūk theologian al-Biqāʿī (d. 885/1480); see Ormsby, *Theodicy*, 45.

61 al-Ghazālī, *al-Iqtiṣād*, 81.10–82.2, and 82.13–83.3; Engl. transl. in McGinnis/Reisman, *Classical Arabic Philosophy*, 255, 256.

Second, in the central *Iḥyā'* passage, he offers a vivid example of the principle of omnipotence coupled with God's balancing justice in the afterlife:

> Indeed, all need and harm in the world, while it represents a deficiency in this world, nonetheless spells an enhancement in the next, and everything which amounts to a deficiency in the next world for one person spells a benefice for another (...). If there were no hell, the inhabitants of paradise would not know the extent of their blessing. (...) Similarly, amplifying blessing on behalf of the inhabitants of Paradise while increasing the punishments of the inhabitants of Hell, so that the price of the people of faith is paid by the people of unbelief, is quite proper to justice.[62]

Here again, we see the concept of "ransoming," the unbelievers for the faithful.[63] But this passage looks as if it gives fodder for an infinity of better possible worlds. If for every number, *n*, of punishments, *P*, inflicted on an unbeliever in Hell there will be a benefice, *B*, to every believer in Paradise—$(P_n \rightarrow B_n)$—then, given the possibility of an infinite number of *P* and *B*, there will be an infinite number of better possible worlds.[64] To adapt al-Ghazālī's point slightly to Swinburne's observation, if the above principle is true, then one way of obtaining a greater number of *P* (and thus *B*) would be to simply create more conscious human beings capable of experiencing *P*s and *B*s—i.e., unbelievers, *U*, to be punished, and faithful, *F*, to be benefitted. Then, $(U_n \rightarrow F_n)$, and *F*s (experiencing *B*s) are a good-making feature of any world. Thus, given the possibility of an infinite number of *U*s and, thereby, of *F*s, there will be an infinite number of better possible worlds. But if al-Ghazālī's observation about the afterlife (although meant as some corroboration of his BPW) is true, and he

62 al-Ghazālī, *Iḥyā'*, 13:2517.18–24; Engl. transl. in *Faith In Divine Unity*, 49.

63 The second ellipse in the quote above marks an omitted passage on animal "ransom," translated and quoted above in Section II at fn. 37.

64 The principle need not be, as I have laid it out, a one-to-one ratio in the numbers of punishments and benefices in Paradise and Hell. Indeed, God might have to work out a balancing act to account for all the additional suffering involved in these increasing possibilities. Although, on al-Ghazālī's view the punishment of the wicked is also itself a good since the punishment is deserved. As noted above in Section I, on his view and Avicenna's, harm is *necessary* for the realization of the best possible world—see *Iḥyā'*, 13:2517; Griffel, *Philosophical Theology*, 229–30; and Ormsby, *Theodicy*, 104. Nevertheless, maybe a more plausible formula to account for these complexities would be: $(P_n \rightarrow B_{n+1})$, such that the goods will always clearly outweigh the suffering. The basic point is, however, that al-Ghazālī is committed to *some sort* of proportional increase of *B* relative to *P*.

also holds that God has power over all the "infinite possibles," then BPW is false—there simply could be no stopping point at a truly *best* possible world, given that each possible world could be made better.

Before trying to defend al-Ghazālī's specific account, we should note that Daniel Cohen and Stephen Grover have recently argued against Swinburne's kind of attack on BPW.[65] They think that Swinburne's idea of increasing the number of happy conscious individuals yields an exemplification of Derek Parfit's *mere addition paradox*.[66] Imagining a world (A) with a billion happy people, they argue that Swinburne's principle will lead us to suppose that another world with another billion people (and equally distributed resources) will be better. But then:

> If Swinburne is right that additional populations of people with lives worth living can only make the world better, then by continually adding additional people to the world (even people with a lower than average well-being), equalizing resources, adding yet new people, and so on, God could only improve the world. Ultimately, we are bound to be led to the repugnant conclusion: the claim that a world (Z) containing, say, 10 trillion people with lives only barely worth living is a better world than the original world (A) of 1 billion happy people.[67]

Therefore, Cohen and Grover argue that Swinburne's objection to BPW should be rejected. Their argument, however, does not succeed, especially as applied to al-Ghazālī, because the mere addition paradox can only issue its repugnant results *assuming* the same limited space and resources. Yet, why should the possible worlds be limited in space and resources even as we imagine them increasing in people? An omnipotent God surely is able to make each successive world bigger and more abundant, thus avoiding the paradox. Indeed, God would be even more free to tweak these conditions in al-Ghazālī's picture of possible worlds including the *afterlife*—arguably Paradise and Hell can also be indefinitely extended, and, on some views of the afterlife, resources and space as we know them may not even exist.[68] I can also see no indication that even

65 Cohen, "Creating the Best Possible World," and Grover, "Mere Addition."

66 Cf. Parfit, *Reasons and Persons*, 419–41.

67 Cohen, "Creating the Best Possible World," 145.

68 Ultimately al-Ghazālī and others might disagree with this statement because of a belief in bodily resurrection, though such a belief need not imply that there will be resources and space as we know them. For a more clear-cut case, however, there seems to be nothing impossible about a view of the afterlife in which non-physical immortal souls are rewarded and punished, without need of resources or space.

al-Ghazālī's "conditions," which might curtail the possibilities that God can realize, would ever include in al-Ghazālī's view anything beyond basic essences of creatures, and, therefore, would in no way limit the numbers of creatures or the quantity of inhabitable space and of resources that God could create.[69]

Seeing that Cohen and Grover's arguments do not succeed in showing that there cannot be an infinite number of better possible worlds, we must investigate whether al-Ghazālī's apparent commitment to both BPW and the (2)-type scenario of infinitely better possible worlds can be defended by some other route, internal to his own thought. First, we can consider the suggestion that *Iḥyāʾ* is primarily a practical work expressing al-Ghazālī's Sufi theology, as opposed to a rigorously coherent work of philosophy.[70] In this case, al-Ghazālī's BPW may fail to be philosophically consistent, but that is not his aim. David Burrell (quoting Ormsby) hints at this approach:

> Yet while it may be "logically correct and permissible to affirm that our world could be different than it is, (…) it is not theologically correct and permissible (…)." Yet the excellence in question is not one which we can assess independently of the fact that it is the product of divine wisdom, so al-Ghazālī is not asserting that ours is the 'best of all possible worlds,' as though there were a set of such worlds (…). Such an assertion would quite miss the point of al-Ghazālī's quest.[71]

There is something right to this suggestion. It would certainly be inappropriate and unfair to treat al-Ghazālī's work as if he were some type of rationalist, proto-contemporary Leibnizian philosopher merely concerned with modality and possible worlds semantics. Al-Ghazālī cannot be understood apart from his theological convictions. Yet, I think this approach is misguided for two reasons. In my view, theological writing should be held to standards of consistency and coherence, even if its *style* and *content* differ from or extend beyond "pure" philosophy. This is a conviction that even if faith reveals truths unknown to reason alone, it will not contradict reason—and al-Ghazālī himself

69 On the "conditions," see above, fn. 47, and below, fn. 113.

70 Ormsby, *Theodicy*, 38, says that al-Ghazālī's theodicy is, "not a systematic or even a closely reasoned proof," but instead, "an exhortation to a specific stage on the Sufi path."

71 Burrell in his introduction to al-Ghazālī, *Faith In Divine Unity*, xix. As in this quote and the footnote above, Ormsby also gestures towards this approach to the issue. Griffel, *Al-Ghazālī's Philosophical Theology*, 334, n. 20, observes that Richard M. Frank accuses Ghazālī of a lack of clarity in writing, in part due to his "traditional language" and religious goals.

held the same perspective.[72] Second, even if he ultimately understands modality in interestingly different ways than contemporary analytic philosophers, al-Ghazālī still shows unmistakable signs that he means to treat BPW *philosophically*. Not only does he clearly draw on philosophical precedent in explaining his view,[73] he also addresses BPW in a treatise among other equally abstruse philosophical topics such as action theory, causation, and the problem of "the one and the many."[74] While it is true that he appeals to a level of Sufi mastery and mystery in these instances, he also defended his BPW thesis as a truth fully accessible to human knowledge and empirical observation, as I argued in Section I.[75] Finally, as I will discuss below, he also does have his own thoroughly philosophical account of modality, so I must conclude that his Sufi-theological goals do not relieve him of the charge of inconsistency regarding BPW.

A second approach to resolving the conflict might involve obtaining a fuller grasp of this view of possibility to which al-Ghazālī subscribes. Ormsby mentions several proposals for clarifying or limiting the notion of possibility at play in BPW, and it will be instructive to consider them. For example, he argues that al-Ghazālī's BPW should be regarded as limited to this specific time: "The world, at this precise instant, cannot be better;"[76] al-Ghazālī "does not mean, for instance, 'there is not in potentiality' (...) or 'there is not in future possibility' (...) anything more wonderful than what is."[77] However, these remarks are confusing. A possible world, other than the actual world, is simply another way the actual world *could be*, at this (or any) instant. If al-Ghazālī meant that the world could not be better generally "in potential" (but only better at some

72 I cannot argue for this claim fully, though I think it is implicit in his Rule of Allegorical Interpretation (*qanūn al-taʾwīl*) and other parts of his thought. See Griffel, *Al-Ghazālī's Philosophical Theology*, 111–22. On this point, I agree with Burrell's position, expressed in his introduction to al-Ghazālī, *Faith In Divine Unity*, xi.

73 Frank, *Creation and the Cosmic System*, 12–22, 61–77, and 83–86. Cf. Ormsby, *Theodicy*, 183–84, 215.

74 See, for example, al-Ghazālī's rationalistic attempt to quell doubts about the "one and the many" in the *Iḥyāʾ*, 13:2496–97; Engl. transl. *Faith In Divine Unity*, 13–14.

75 Cf. Griffel, *Al-Ghazālī's Philosophical Theology*, 228 and 231. In fact, he was also accused of revealing the divine secret of the best of all possible worlds and of attempting "to explain this secret in rationalistic terms, instead of confining himself to an assertion of its ultimate inscrutability" (Ormsby, *Theodicy*, 215). On the balance between the overt evidence for BPW and its treatment as a divine secret, see also Griffel, *Al-Ghazālī's Philosophical Theology*, 231.

76 Ormsby, *Theodicy*, 259.

77 Ibid., 175, cf. also 142–43.

future time), that would amount to just the claim that "the world at this moment cannot *possibly* be anything other than what it *actually* is at this moment," which would certainly be an unsatisfying form of BPW for al-Ghazālī since it would imply necessitarianism. While it is true that most ancient theories of modality did not envisage *synchronic* possible worlds (as analytic philosophy does today) and that John Duns Scotus is typically considered the first to introduce such a concept in the West,[78] Frank Griffel argues convincingly that the synchronic notion of modality is already partially advanced by Avicenna (who separates modality from time and attaches it primarily to mental conceivability) and is fully at work in Ashʿarite theology, both of which inform al-Ghazālī's own view.[79] al-Ghazālī adopts Avicenna's notion of conceivability,[80] but jettisons, *inter alia*, the latter's remaining tie to Aristotelian modality in terms of temporality—i.e., the Avicennan necessitarianism. Therefore, we should see al-Ghazālī's view of modality as sufficiently like the contemporary view in contemplating synchronic possible worlds.

Similarly, I do not think another of Ormsby's responses, i.e., taking temporal succession into our account of infinite possible worlds, will help the problem.[81] It is true that BPW does not commit one to the view that the world does not change, and al-Ghazālī does clarify God's power over the infinite possibles in terms of the sequence of time:

> We mean by "the possibles are infinite"' that the creation of one temporal event after another never reaches a limit beyond which it is impossible for the intellect [to conceive] of some [further] temporal event's coming to be. So possibility is temporally limitless, and the [divine] power extends to all of that.[82]

---

78 Cf. Normore, "Duns Scotus's Modal Theory" and Griffel, *Philosophical Theology*, 169–170.

79 See, e.g., Griffel, *Al-Ghazālī's Philosophical Theology*, 167–173, esp. 170: "The *kalām* concept of preponderance (*tarjīḥ*), however, explicitly discusses the assumption of possible worlds. The preponderator [who is God, S.O.] distinguishes the actual state of being from its possible alternative state of nonbeing (....) each time a future contingency becomes actual, the preponderator decides between an actual world and an alternative world in which that particular contingency is nonexistent."

80 al-Ghazālī, *Incoherence of the Philosophers / Tahāfut al-falāsifa*, 42.1–4. Cf. Griffel, *Al-Ghazālī's Philosophical Theology*, 166.

81 Cf. Ormsby, *Theodicy*, 139–42, where Ormsby discusses the responses from Jalāl al-Dīn al-Suyūṭī (d. 911/1505) and al-Samhūdī (d. 911/1505–06).

82 al-Ghazālī, *al-Iqtiṣād*, 82.2–4; ; Engl. transl. in McGinnis/Reisman, *Classical Arabic Philosophy*, 255. This quote also highlights the above point that al-Ghazālī thinks of modality in terms of conceivability.

However, this does not remove the conflict, for, in conceiving of possible worlds, we can take into account the infinite sequence of time, such that the above counterexample of increasingly more faithful (*F*s) or benefits (*B*s) in the afterlife is not to be construed just as *the same*, yet temporally progressive, possible world. The point is that we can imagine a possible world including the cessation at some finite number, *n*, of *F*s and *B*s in the afterlife, and then can imagine *another* possible world which contains *n*+1 *F*s and *B*s. It is plausible to think that al-Ghazālī must hold that God will not create persons *ad infinitum*,[83] so for any finite number at which the process stops in a world, it looks as if there would be another possible world in which Paradise is sweeter (due to a few more inhabitants in Hell)![84]

IV Al-Ghazālī's Modality as a Solution to Problem (B)

Leaving aside those suggestions, let us turn more directly now to al-Ghazālī's precise view of possibility, which bears great resemblance to that of Avicenna.[85] One concise statement of al-Ghazālī's theory of modality is in *al-Iqtiṣād fī l-iʿtiqād* (*The Balanced Book on What-To-Believe*):

> Thus, there are three ways to consider [a possible world relative to divine omnipotence]. The first is to make the existence of the [divine] will and its relation a condition for it, and so by this consideration it is necessary. The second is to consider the absence of the will, and so by this consideration it is impossible. The third is that we avoid taking into account the

83 al-Ghazālī rejects Ibn Sīnā's consideration of the possibility of an infinite number of human souls in *Incoherence of the Philosophers / Tahāfut al-falāsifa*, 219 (cf. also 19 and 80–81). Ibn Rushd, too, seems to reject this possibility in his responses to al-Ghazālī, see *Tahāfut al-tahāfut* (*The Incoherence of the Incoherence*), 26–27; Engl. transl., *Averroes' Tahāfut al-tahāfut*, 14. For more on this debate, see Marmura, "Avicenna and the Problem of the Infinite Number of Souls." Furthermore, as a faithful Muslim and with reference to Q 18:47–49, al-Ghazālī must believe in a *final* Day of Judgment which would presumably stop the process of the generation of humans.

84 This also addresses al-Samhūdī's point that whatever world God actualizes must be *finite*—see Ormsby, *Theodicy*, 165. If God could actualize another *infinite* (in every respect), that world would be God, which is impossible. But these sensible considerations do not effect the infinity of *possible worlds* in relation to divine omnipotence.

85 Ormsby, *Theodicy*, 177–181 and 260, does seem to settle on a reading of al-Ghazālī's view of modality that is in large agreement with what I delineate. His other comments discussed above may seem obscure primarily because of his more historical approach to the issue.

> will and cause and consider neither its existence nor nonexistence, but isolate the investigation to the world itself, and so by this consideration the third thing remains for it, namely, possibility. We mean by ["possibility"] that it is possible in itself, that is, when we do not impose any conditions other than it itself, then it is possible. From which it is obvious that one thing can be possible and impossible; however, it is possible by considering it itself and impossible by considering another.[86]

Therefore, (i) the world considered in the absence of God's will (to actualize it) is *impossible* ($\sim\Diamond$)—without God as its First Cause, the world could not possibly exist.[87] (ii) On the other hand, considered with the condition of God's will, it is *necessary* ($\Box$)—for whatever God wills (on this view of omnipotence) is necessary and cannot possibly be thwarted. (iii) Finally, abstracted from the condition of God's will altogether (neither affirming nor denying it), the world is in itself *possible* ($\Diamond$).[88] In this sense, the actual world is both *necessary* (in virtue of God's willing it to be, i.e., $\Box_{(ii)}$) and at the same time just another *possible* world (considered in itself apart from God's will, i.e., $\Diamond_{(iii)}$).

Will this modal theory help make sense of Problem (B) and BPW? It seems so. Considering the world as willed by God, modality (ii) above, al-Ghazālī can claim that the actual world is the best possible—since the world (because of God's will) is *necessary*, that means, considered in this way, it is *impossible* that there be some other, better world. However, in response to Problem (B) and the additions to Paradise counterexample, al-Ghazālī can claim that these further and better possible worlds are indeed *possible*, so long as we are considering them (and the actual world) simply as possible *in themselves* and apart from the existence or nonexistence of God's will, i.e., modality (iii) above. As Ormsby summarizes this response (quoting from al-Samhūdī):

> (…) the "impossibility of any addition" (*ʿadam imkān al-zāʾid*) to this present creation (…) is not to be understood as a *per se* impossibility (*istiḥālah li-dhātihi*);[89] it is God's profound "wisdom that renders impossible the

86 al-Ghazālī, *al-Iqtiṣād*, 84.9–85.3; Engl. transl. in McGinnis/Reisman, *Classical Arabic Philosophy*, 257. Cf. also Ibn Sīnā, *The Metaphysics of The Healing / al-Shifāʾ: al-Ilāhiyyāt*, 330: "The effect in itself is possible of existence and, through the First, is necessary of existence."

87 Indeed, this view of modality is the crux of Ibn Sīnā's proof for God's existence.

88 Thus, there are three types of possibility (or necessity) to which we will refer: (i)—possibility explicitly considering the absence of God's will; (ii)—possibility explicitly considering God's will; (iii)—possibility in itself, without considering whether God wills or not.

89 Meaning a logical or metaphysical impossibility. S. O.

> creation (of anything additional)." Hence, it is an impossibility "because of something else" (*li-ghayrihi*), i.e., God's wisdom, will, and power which have, respectively, selected, determined, and realized the best out of all possibilities.[90]

Only *per se* or *li-dhātihī*[91] impossibilities, such as logical impossibilities, are impossible for God to actualize. Every other possible world we can imagine, while possible *in itself*, is rendered impossible *propter aliud* or *li-ghayrihī*.[92] Thus, a better possible world is (without contradiction) both $\Diamond_{(iii)}$ and $\sim\Diamond_{(ii)}$.

V Problem (B) Continued—BPW and DCT

Thus, we have seen a potentially successful solution to the initial counterexample of Problem (B) through al-Ghazālī's philosophy of modality—there is no real inconsistency between the actual world as the best possible and the consideration of other, better possible (*per se*) worlds. By God's will (*propter aliud, li-ghayrihī*) the actual world is rendered the best and the other possible worlds are rendered impossible. Ormsby concudes:

> This "something [else]" which confers existence as well as non-existence on the things of this world, and the world itself, also confers their condition of "most excellentness." That which confers existence and its concomitant insuperable excellence is the divine power, acting in concert with wisdom and will. It is not anything inhering in the world itself.[93]

Note that, *qua* willed by God, in modality (ii), this world is not only the best, but also the *only* possible world. Still, at this point, this does not render BPW totally vacuous, because (as the above quote attests), al-Ghazālī's strong DCT (divine command theory) ensures that God's willing this world also confers *goodness* and *excellence* in a way that is not merely based on the lack of other possible candidates for the best. In this sense, al-Ghazālī's BPW may fare better than other BPW views, such as Leibniz's. On al-Ghazālī's BPW, an infinity of increasingly better possible worlds poses no problem (as it does for Leibniz, since he is committed to the view that God would not create if there were no

90 Ormsby, *Theodicy*, 166.
91 Literally, "on account of its essence."
92 Literally, "on account of something other."
93 Ormsby, *Theodicy*, 179.

absolute best). Indeed, al-Ghazālī's God can simply make a decision about actualizing one among the infinity of good possibles and it, by God's very will, will be rendered genuinely the best. But Leibniz has to argue that "arbitrarily" selecting one among good possibles would violate the principle of sufficient reason and undermine our reason for praising God.[94]

However, this solution via al-Ghazālī's conception of modality presents a further and perhaps deeper difficulty. As Ormsby's quote above explains, the actual world is the best *only* because of God's will and not because of the world's objective intrinsic features.[95] Behind this notion is the Ashʿarite DCT mentioned above, which al-Ghazālī certainly held (at least to some extent). On this view, God has no obligations and "goodness" and "justice" are determined by his command. Ormsby summarizes the Ashʿarite position: "Whatever God wills is good; and since whatever happens cannot happen except as a result of His will, whatever happens is *ipso facto* good."[96] Richard M. Frank quotes al-Kiyāʾ al-Harrāsī (d. 504/1110), a contemporary of al-Ghazālī who was also trained by al-Juwaynī:

> We refuse to say that its [*scil.* the human act's, S.O.] being good or being bad is grounded in any essential property [of the act]. Good and bad are grounded in the very giving of the law (*nafs al-sharʿ*) itself (…). Good and bad are grounded simply in God's command and prohibition.[97]

---

94 Leibniz, "Discourse on Metaphysics," § 3, 37. On the problems of Leibniz's God with respect to practical rationality and creation see Blumenfeld, "Is the Best Possible World Possible" and Haji, "A Conundrum."

95 This is a simplification since al-Ghazālī mentions also God's wisdom and power. I cannot go into a discussion here of the Ashʿarite view of divine attributes, which are somehow considered substantively as additions and not merely identical with one another and the divine essence. Yet, it does seem that, in this discussion, it is God's power which simply effects God's choice; and God's wisdom, having to do with "arranging causes," might ultimately collapse into God's will (especially if al-Ghazālī is an occasionalist). Even if al-Ghazālī is not an occasionalist, there are clear reasons to focus on the will as primary. As we have seen, al-Ghazālī's theory of modality regarding worlds is formulated explicitly with reference to God's will. In Section I, I also argued that al-Ghazālī's focus on the free divine will is what truly separates his view from Avicenna's and ensures that God is a truly creative *agent*. On a closely related point, see also Griffel, *Al-Ghazālī's Philosophical Theology*, 256–57 and 281, for how al-Ghazālī "gives God's 'command' (*amr*) a central position in his cosmology" (281). Thus, I will limit my discussion here to simply speaking of will. On God's wisdom, see Ormsby, *Theodicy*, 196–197.

96 Ormsby, *Theodicy*, 155.

97 Frank, "Moral Obligation," 208–9. The quote is from al-Kiyāʾ al-Harrāsī's unedited *Uṣūl al-dīn*, MS Cairo, Dār al-Kutub, *kalām 295*, fol. 119b. The Arabic text was not available to me.

It seems that al-Ghazālī also holds these positions himself. For example, he argues that, "injustice, which is the disposal of what belongs to others without permission is impossible in God most high, for He encounters no possessions of others besides Him so that His disposal of these possessions could be injustice."[98] Thus, whatever God wills and does is just. In the conclusion to the central *Iḥyāʾ* passage, al-Ghazālī states that "good (*al-khayr*) and evil (*al-sharr*) are determined" by the divine decree (*al-qadar*).[99] Ormsby thus summarizes that al-Ghazālī's "final position is that all is just and right solely because God has willed it. The guaranty of his theodicy is the unassailable fact of the divine predestination."[100] In these discussions of Ashʿarite meta-ethics, including al-Ghazālī's, there is an inexactitude. Contemporary forms of DCT often distinguish between theories of the *right* and (the more robust) theories of the *good*,[101] but I have not found any such explicit distinction in the primary Ashʿarite texts. It suffices for my argument at this point to say that I think the Ashʿarite view and al-Ghazālī's own is some *strong* form of a DCT of the *good*, and not just the right.

Yet this meta-ethic yields a surprising and unsatisfactory conclusion. The best possible world is the best because it is the one willed and created by God. Though in modality (ii) it is the *only* possible world, I stated above that this version of BPW is not vacuous because of the conferring of real excellence by the divine will. But if whatever is willed and created by God is not only good but necessarily the best (*qua* willed by God—i.e., $\Box_{(ii)}$ above), then al-Ghazālī's BPW nonetheless turns out to be virtually trivial *as a theodicy*! In the present case, "best possible world" does not just mean "the world willed by God" (so it is not strictly speaking *trivial*). Yet, that it is willed by God is necessarily coextensive with and the exhaustive cause of the best possible world's being the best.[102] God's *will* fully explains the BPW thesis and makes the best possible world to be what it is. Yet, in a theodicy, we expect God's *goodness* to play some crucial explanatory role.

To use another example, the explanations of ancient physics are not trivial (i.e., relying on meaning equivalence), yet they are unsatisfactory from a modern scientific point of view because they do not utilize the terms and discovered elements that we have come to expect of physical explanations. This deficiency

---

98 al-Ghazālī, *al-Risāla al-qudsiyya* (ed. and transl. Tibawī) 89.24–25, 113 (*Iḥyāʾ*, 2:195.21–23).

99 al-Ghazālī, *Iḥyāʾ*, 13:2518.8; Engl. transl. in *Faith In Divine Unity*, 50.

100 Ormsby, *Theodicy*, 69.

101 For example, see R. M. Adams, *Finite and Infinite Goods*, 231–233, 250.

102 In contemporary philosophy of language, this type of fine-grained distinction between necessarily coextensive descriptions is often called 'hyperintensionality.' Cf. Swoyer and Orilia, "Properties," § 6.

of explanation is not only undesirable in philosophical theodicies generally; it is at odds with al-Ghazālī's own purposes in setting out a genuine response to the problem of evil.[103] In the central *Iḥyāʾ* passage of his theodicy, we have seen that BPW is used as an *explanation* for the apparent evils of this life and the next. Al-Ghazālī's response is that globally speaking, this actual world is the most wonderful (*abdaʿ*)—there is a *reason* for evil in that every evil of some part serves some greater good on the whole. However, this reasons-based explanation for evil seems empty when we learn that the "greater good" which constitutes the best possible world is utterly determined by God's sheer *fiat*. Why explain that the sufferings of the damned add to the pleasures of the saved, if any arrangement of the afterlife would be just if willed by God? In the words of the 18th century commentator on the *Iḥyāʾ* al-Murtaḍā al-Zabīdī (d. 1205/1791)—"if God made all of them enter heaven without prior virtue from them, this would be His right [*kāna lahu*]; and if He sent them all down into hell without any fault from them, this would also be His right."[104] If God had created only perfectly just human beings during their lifetimes and subsequently punished all of them in Hell, by al-Ghazālī's lights, that would still necessarily be the best possible world (in virtue of God's will), despite the myriads of other better possible (*per se*) worlds which God could have actualized. The strong DCT seems to preclude God's having reasons to create one world rather than another—at least reasons concerning each world's integral respective goodness—, thus undermining a rational theodicy: "He has no desire, and any wrong (*qabīḥ*) is inconceivable with respect to Him, and similarly any injustice (*ẓulm*) is inconceivable with respect to Him, since the disposal of pos-

103 Ormsby, *Theodicy*, 252ff, notes that al-Ghazālī is more interested in responding to the problem of evil with a bit more empathic touch than his Ashʿarite tradition.

104 al-Zabīdī *Itḥāf al-sāda*, 2:186.26–28; Engl. transl. modified from Ormsby, *Theodicy*, 229. Al-Zabīdī is commenting on a passage in al-Ghazālī's *al-Risāla al-qudsiyya* (ed. and transl. Tibawi), 90.1, 114–15 (*Iḥyāʾ*, 2:196.7). Al-Zabīdī's comment seems especially fitting with al-Ghazālī's statements concerning the apparent impossibility of any decision God makes regarding humans' eternal destinies being morally unjust, and that God is "all-powerful (*qādir*) to perfect their make according to His will (*irāda*)" (ibid., 90.23, 115; *Iḥyāʾ*, 2:197.4–5). Al-Ghazālī also makes similar points in a passage closeby, where he says that God, "may inflict pain on His creatures or torment them for no previous offence or subsequent reward. (…) For He has absolute control over [His creatures in] His dominion" (ibid., 89.22–23, 113; *Iḥyāʾ*, 2:195.20–21). Ormsby, *Theodicy*, 229, fn. 42 references the same view in al-Ashʿarī, *Kitāb al-Lumaʿ*, 71; Engl. transl., 99: "Whatever God does, He is just (*ʿādil*), though He punish the faithful in hell and reward the faithless in heaven; even so, He is just."

sessions belonging to others is also inconceivable with respect to Him;"[105] "Indeed, He created the whole world without a reason (*lā li-ʿilla*)."[106] These features of his DCT aided al-Ghazālī initially with Problem (B), and they may help him avoid some of the problems related to Leibniz's BPW and the principle of sufficient reason. Yet, it seems that DCT can also prove equally damaging to a philosophical theodicy that utilizes BPW.

Is there some further way out of this predicament for al-Ghazālī's system? Perhaps we can qualify "best" in BPW in some other way that avoids the *moral* implications of DCT. Ormsby discusses just this maneuver regarding al-Ghazālī's term *abdaʿ*:

> The word *aḥsan* (which he had first used) could also mean "best" in the moral sense, as well as "most excellent" and "most beautiful." Thus, it may have seemed too suggestive of Muʿtazilite usages. By contrast, the word *abdaʿ* directed attention to what is amazing, unexpected, and ingenious in the structure of the world; it implied nothing about the creator's moral nature.[107]

Along with al-Samhūdī, Ormsby says al-Ghazālī's *abdaʿ* carries aesthetic, rather than moral force.[108] This suggestion, however, is not consistent with al-Ghazālī's usage—it is not so simple to partition the aesthetic from the moral in al-Ghazālī's corpus beyond the one term *abdaʿ*.[109] In the main *Iḥyāʾ* passage, he clearly includes inferences about God's justice (*ʿadl*), just as in this mirror passage: "Nothing exists except what occurs by God's action and flows from His justice in a most excellent way (*ʿalā aḥsan al-wujūh*), most perfect (*akmaluhā*), most complete (*atammuhā*), and most just (*aʿdaluhā*), for God is wise in His actions, just in His judgments. God's justice is not compared with the justice of His servants."[110] al-Ghazālī is also genuinely interested in constructing a

105 al-Ghazālī, *al-Risāla al-qudsiyya* (ed. and transl. Tibawi), 90.19–20 (*Iḥyāʾ*, 2:197.1–2).

106 al-Ghazālī, *al-Mustaṣfā, min ʿilm al-uṣūl*, 1:208; Engl. transl. in Ḥammād, "Abū Ḥāmid al-Ghazālī's Juristic Doctrine," 349. Cf. Frank, "Moral Obligation," 209, citing various Ashʿarite authors in support: "(…) there can be no reason (*ʿillah*) for His action. He can have no motive or purpose for what He does."

107 Ormsby, *Theodicy*, 232.

108 Ibid., 238.

109 In fact, it is not so clear that *abdaʿ* cannot have moral implications. Lane, *An Arabic-English Lexicon*, 1:167, notes usages of the root for indicating superlative in kind, including in "good and evil."

110 al-Ghazālī, *Iḥyāʾ*, 1:157.9–10. Cf. Ormsby, *Theodicy*, 247. Ormsby (pp. 247–48, fn. 110) himself notes that at least al-Zabīdī sees the "connection" and "glosses the string of elatives in

theodicy to deal with the painful reality of evil in the world, and theodicies are typically responses to the problem of evil, a *moral* challenge to the classical theist conception of God.

While the preceding remarks serve as further evidence that al-Ghazālī's notion of "best" covers a wide range of intimately-related types of goodness including the aesthetic, the moral, and the just, perhaps al-Ghazālī's DCT is not as robust a theory of the *good* as I suppose above. Richard M. Frank has argued that al-Ghazālī departs from the more extreme views of his Ashʿarite forebears on various issues, including that of the definition of *goodness*, in part because of the concepts he adopts from Avicenna.[111] In even conceiving of the idea of possible worlds among which God chooses prior to creation, Frank thinks al-Ghazālī (like Avicenna) has a view of *essences* (in the possibilia) which are ontologically prior to creation. Therefore, God's will

> … is not alone and of itself the sole rule and measure of what is good and what is just …. Since the possibles do not depend on God for their being as possibles but are already there for Him as essences instances of which He can cause to exist, the measure of the good of what God can create and of what He does create does not have its origin in Him, but stands as an independent measure by which His action is to be judged.[112]

One problem with this suggestion is that al-Ghazālī criticized Avicenna's theory of modality in part because of its realism regarding the ontological status of these essences and universals; in turn, al-Ghazālī wanted to adopt a kind of

---

this passage by inserting the single word *abdaʿuhā*, 'most wonderful.'" See al-Zabīdī, *Itḥāf al-sāda*, 2:32.17.

111 Frank, *Creation and the Cosmic System*, 64–70. I think Frank is most likely wrong in at least some of this analysis, particularly, as I argued in Section I, in the argument that al-Ghazālī commits himself to *necessary* creation.

112 Frank, *Creation and the Cosmic System*, 65. Al-Ghazālī, *Iḥyāʾ*, 13:2512.3–2513.8 (Engl. transl. in *Faith In Divine Unity*, 39–41), does speak of certain basic "conditions" which follow upon one another in a logical order in creation, which is quite suggestive of some view of essences. Cf. Griffel, *Al-Ghazālī's Philosophical Theology*, 224–25: "(…) God's creative activity is limited by rather strict conditions (…). Al-Ghazālī leaves open the idea whether God Himself chooses such conditions upon His actions or whether they are requirements beyond God's control with which He must comply." But, as Griffel continues, the latter position would move al-Ghazālī much closer to the necessitarian view of Avicenna, which, at some point, must be untenable—see Section I above. How seriously one takes such passages also impacts the large debate over whether al-Ghazālī is an occasionalist, which I cannot enter into here.

nominalism (or at least conceptualism) which would ensure that the essences do not have real existence outside particulars and the mind (or, we might add, independently of God).[113] Furthermore, Frank admits that there is significant counterevidence in al-Ghazālī's corpus.[114] However, maybe Frank is right. If so, then the DCT is less pronounced. In fact, maybe al-Ghazālī only holds a DCT of the *right*, and not of the good.[115] On such a view, God would still not have moral obligations and whatever he did would be *ipso facto* necessarily right and just,[116] but goodness more broadly would not be determined solely by God's will. Then, however, the original solution to Problem (B) would be weakened, for we have seen that it relies on a notion of necessity and excellence conferred by God's will. If God's will necessitates in modality (ii), then the actual world is the *only* possible world. But, with a strong DCT of the good, al-Ghazālī can additionally insist that at least God's creative will also confers the property of goodness on it in some important way. However, if the *excellence-* or *good-making* feature of God's will is stripped (by weakening the DCT), then we are left with an even thinner and more vacuous picture of BPW where the actual world must be deemed "best" solely by default (and perhaps by some very basic intrinsic goodness in the essences of things). The main work of the "best" in BPW will follow merely as a matter of course in virtue of there being only one possible candidate world for that title.

Notice furthermore that even a DCT of the right will still clash with al-Ghazālī's BPW since he offers BPW as a response to the problem of evil. As mentioned above, BPW theodicies are meant to show at least that God is not *morally culpable* for having created this world. Philosophers of religion often address the

---

113 See al-Ghazālī, *Incoherence of the Philosophers / Tahāfut al-falāsifa*, 42, 199. Cf. Griffel, *Al-Ghazālī's Philosophical Theology*, 166–67, and van den Bergh's introduction and notes to *Averroes' Tahāfut al-tahāfut*, xxxiii, 201–202. Another problem here is that al-Ghazālī's understanding of modality as explicated in *al-Iqtiṣād* seems to deal with *worlds* as possibles while the point of the quote above from Frank would seem to envisage *properties* (specifically normative properties, like goodness, and/or essential properties) as possibles.

114 Frank, *Creation and the Cosmic System*, 66.

115 Frank Griffel suggested in an oral conversation that he thinks this. Alternatively, even if al-Ghazālī did not hold a DCT theory of the right, one might suggest that he *could have* thus altered and improved his DCT position.

116 Cf. R. M. Adams, "A Modified Divine Command Theory," 115: "If we accept a divine command theory of ethical rightness and wrongness, I think we shall have to say that *dutifulness* is a human virtue which, like sexual chastity, is logically inapplicable to God. God cannot either do or fail to do his duty, since he does not have a duty (…). For he is not subject to a moral law not of his own making."

problem of evil by investigating whether God could have a "morally sufficient reason" for allowing evil in the world.[117] Thus, the problem of evil is a *moral* problem for God, and a BPW theodicy must at least claim that God has created the *morally best* or *most just* possible world. Indeed, throughout the original *Iḥyāʾ* passage, al-Ghazālī is concerned to defend God's *justice* (*ʿadl*) in precisely this way.[118] However, on a DCT of the right, whatever God wills is morally right and just. As we have seen, al-Ghazālī's DCT ensures that "injustice (...) is impossible in God"[119] and that God has no moral obligations. This theory paired with al-Ghazālī's theory of modality entails that whatever God creates by His will is necessarily the most just possible arrangement. Therefore, as I argued above, the result is a wholly inadequate theodicy, since God could have willed a world with maximally greater amounts of evil and it would still be the best, morally speaking. Even if al-Ghazālī's theories of the good and the right were so fine-grained that the *morally good* is distinguished from the *morally right*, the most pressure the problem of evil could generate towards a view like al-Ghazālī's is that this world is perhaps morally *bad* or even morally *horrific*.[120] But still there could not be a shred about it that is morally *wrong*, blameworthy,[121] or unjust.[122]

---

117 See, for example, Pike, "Hume on Evil," 40.

118 "(...) all of it is unqualifiedly just with no injustice in it, true with no wrong infecting it." al-Ghazālī, *Iḥyāʾ*, 13:2517.13–15, Engl. transl. in *Faith In Divine Unity*, 48. See the longer quote of the main passage in Section I above.

119 al-Ghazālī, *al-Risāla al-qudsiyya* (ed. and transl. Tibawi), 89, 113 (*Iḥyāʾ*, 2:195).

120 For example, R. M. Adams, *Finite and Infinite Goods*, 104–107, distinguishes moral goodness from moral rightness and, in turn, moral badness or horror from moral wrongness.

121 R. M. Adams (ibid., 235) ties *blame* to moral wrongness: "If an act is morally wrong, then in the absence of sufficient excuse, it is appropriate for the agent to be blamed, by others and by himself."

122 While R. M. Adams (ibid., 254) suggests that *justice* is an excellence that God must have independently of moral obligations rooted in divine commands, he appropriately terms it a "thin theory" of justice according to which "God judges in accordance with the facts, and cares about each person's interests in a way that is good;" God's justice thus lies not in being "dutiful or law-abiding" but rather "responding well to the various claims and interests involved in a situation." We have seen, however, that al-Ghazālī himself argues that it makes no sense to speak about God's possibly being unjust because there simply are no "possessions" (which I think would include for al-Ghazālī "claims and interests") which God must honor other than His own. Duns Scotus similarly holds that "there is no justice in God except that which inclines him to render to his own goodness what is its due (...). But there is nothing in the divine will that inclines it specifically to any secondary object in such a way that it would be impossible for it justly to incline towards its opposite" (*Ordinatio* IV, d. 46, Wadding 10:252; Engl. transl. in Wolter, *Duns Scotus on the Will and Morality*, 187). For Scotus, God can be called "just" only in a qualified sense, namely that

Again, this makes al-Ghazālī's particular theodicy nugatory because any possible arrangement of benefits and suffering would necessarily be the most just, however the proportions were arranged in this and the next life.

VI Conclusion

I have argued that al-Ghazālī successfully defends his BPW against the basic charges of empirical disconfirmation and of Avicennan necessitarianism. Moreover, his BPW can avoid the Muʿtazilite implications of *al-aṣlaḥ* as discussed in Problem (A). However, the difficulties of Problem (B) seem intractable—for the very modal theory which proves a solution to the intuition of other better possible worlds gives rise to an ultimately unsustainable tension between BPW and DCT in his theodicy. Therefore, if I am correct and if al-Ghazālī would prefer to avoid BPW's unsatisfactory consequences, he would have to give up (or significantly modify) either BPW or DCT. We have seen above how an attempt at adapting the latter might go: the product is inconclusive (since it is unclear that al-Ghazālī would want to adopt a modified DCT) and even more unsatisfactory as a theodicy (since it would remove all but the vacuous truth of BPW). DCT in a stronger form, especially in his responses to Muʿtazilism as in Problem (A), seems fundamental for his Ashʿarite theology. On the other hand, there are powerful objections to the concept of BPW, as we have seen, and al-Ghazālī does not seem to need it.[123] Therefore, although we cannot be sure of all his motives, I propose that al-Ghazālī probably should have abandoned BPW. Though it makes some sense given his claims about God's will and the world, it ultimately leads to near triviality, a result which would seem to defeat the entire purpose of a theodicy from the outset. Al-Ghazālī could categorically deny that there is a best possible world. In turn, the actual world, albeit not "the best," might still be altogether very good, and

He chooses to provide creatures what their natures demand "from his generosity (*ex liberalitate*)," i.e., not out of any obligation or necessity (ibid., 10:253;190). Similarly, I do not think al-Ghazālī would want to amend his view of divine justice; he certainly would not want to hold that there is something in human natures or their claims and interests which would obligate God to provide for their ultimate well-being (whether sparing them from any ills in this life or from damnation in the afterlife). God may very well do what is best for each individual, but not from any primordial sense of justice other than God's own generosity or magnanimity. See the end of Section II above.

123 After all, many Ashʿarite theologians and followers of Ghazālī, such as Fakhr al-Dīn al-Rāzī, rejected BPW. See for example his *Tafsīr al-kabīr*, 1:4.2–19, esp. 7–9 (ad Q 1:2) and Setia, "Fakhr al-Dīn al-Rāzī on Physics and the Nature of the Physical World," 176–77.

God could not be blamed (with respect to either his justice or omnipotence) for not actualizing the impossible. Thus, in sacrificing his best possible world, al-Ghazālī might have secured a better overall philosophy. However, I hope I have shown why al-Ghazālī's BPW does not fail for the usual and most prominent traditional reasons—in defending his view, al-Ghazālī proved himself a genius who also possessed admirable pastoral attentiveness. His thought should be instructive for contemporary philosophers and theologians as they continue to ponder Optimism, divine command theories, and the relation between God and the world.[124]

Bibliography

Abrahamov, Binyamin. "Al-Ḳāsim Ibn Ibrāhīm's Theory of the Imamate." *Arabica* 34 (1987): 80–105.

Adams, Marilyn M. "Horrendous Evils and the Goodness of God." In *The Problem of Evil*. Edited by Marilyn M. Adams and Robert Adams, 209–221. Oxford: Oxford University Press, 1990. (Originally published in *Proceedings of the Aristotelian Society*, Suppl. 63 (1989): 297–323).

Adams, Robert M. "Must God Create the Best?" In idem, *The Virtue of Faith and Other Essays in Philosophical Theology*, Oxford: Oxford University Press, 1987. 51–64. (Originally published in *The Philosophical Review* 81 (1972): 317–332).

———. "A Modified Divine Command Theory of Ethical Wrongness." In idem, *The Virtue of Faith and Other Essays in Philosophical Theology*. Oxford: Oxford University Press, 1987. 97–122.

———. *Finite and Infinite Goods*. Oxford: Oxford University Press, 1999.

al-Ashʿarī, ʿAlī ibn Ismāʿīl:. *Kitāb al-Lumaʿ*. In *The Theology of Al-Ashʿarī*. Edited and trans. by Richard J. McCarthy, 5–118. Beirut: Imprimerie Catholique, 1953.

Blumenfeld, David. "Is the Best Possible World Possible?" *The Philosophical Review* 84 (1975): 163–177.

Brunschvig, Robert. "Muʿtazilism et Optimum (al-aṣlaḥ)." *Studia Islamica* 39 (1974): 5–23.

Cohen, Daniel. "Creating the Best Possible World: Some Problems from Parfit." *Sophia* 48 (2009): 143–150.

Duns Scotus, John. *Opera Omnia*. Edited by Luke Wadding. 12 vols. Lyon: Durand, 1639. Reprint. Hildesheim (Germany): Georg Olms, 1968.

124 I wish to thank especially Frank Griffel and John Hare, but also participants in the Yale philosophy of religion colloquium and my commentators and audience at the University of Toronto for very helpful feedback on earlier versions of this paper.

———. *Duns Scotus on the Will and Morality*. Edited by William Frank. Translated by A. Wolter. Washington (D.C.): Catholic University of America Press, 1997.

Frank, Richard M. "Moral Obligation in Classical Muslim Theology." *The Journal of Religious Ethics* 11 (1983): 204–223.

———. *Creation and the Cosmic System: Al-Ghazālī & Avicenna*. Heidelberg: Carl Winter, 1992.

Geach, Peter T. *Providence and Evil: The Stanton Lectures 1971–72*. Cambridge: Cambridge University Press, 1977.

———. *Truth and Hope*. Notre Dame, IN: University of Notre Dame Press, 2001.

al-Ghazālī, Muḥammad ibn Muḥammad. *Faith In Divine Unity and Trust In Divine Providence. Kitāb al-tawḥīd wa-l-tawakkul. Book XXXV of The Revival of the Religious Sciences. Iḥya' ʿulūm al-dīn*. Transl. by David B. Burrell. 2nd. ed. Louisville, (Ky.): Fons Vitae, 2001.

———. *Iḥyā' ʿulūm al-dīn*. 16 vols. Cairo: Lajnat Nashr al-Thaqāfa al-Islāmiyya, 1356–1357 [1937–1938].

———. *al-Imlā' fī ishkālāt al-Iḥyā'*. In: *Iḥyā' ʿulūm al-dīn*. 16 vols. Cairo: Lajnat Nashr al-Thaqāfa al-Islāmiyya, 1356–1357 [1937–1938]. 6:3035–3095.

———. *The Incoherence of the Philosophers / Tahāfut al-falāsifa*. Edited and transl. by M. E. Marmura. 2nd ed. Provo: Brigham Young University Press, 2000.

———. *al-Iqtiṣād fī l-iʿtiqād*. Edited by Ibrahim Agâh Çubukçu and Hüseyin Atay. Ankara: Nur Matbaasi, 1962.

———. *al-Maqṣad al-asnā fī sharḥ maʿānī asmā' Allāh al-ḥusnā*, Edited by F. Shehadi. 2nd. ed. Beirut: Imprimerie Catholique, 1982.

———. *al-Mustaṣfā min ʿilm al-uṣūl*. Edited by Ḥamza ibn Zuhayr Ḥāfiẓ. 4 vols. Medina (Saudi Arabia): al-Jāmiʿa al-Islāmiyya—Kulliyyat al-Sharīʿa, 1413 [1992–93].

———. *al-Qisṭās al-mustaqīm*. Edited by V. Chelhot. Beirut: Dār al-Mashriq, 1986.

Gilliot, Claude. "La théologie musulmane en Asie centrale et au Khorasan." *Arabica* 49 (2002): 153–203.

Griffel, Frank. *Al-Ghazālī's Philosophical Theology*. New York: Oxford University Press, 2009.

Grover, Stephen. "Mere Addition and the Best of All Possible Worlds." *Religious Studies* 35 (1999): 173–190.

Gwynne, Rosalind W. "Al-Jubbā'ī, al-Ashʿarī and the Three Brothers: The Uses of Fiction." *The Muslim World* 75 (1985): 132–161.

Haji, Ishtiyaque. "A Conundrum Concerning Creation." *Sophia* 48 (2009): 1–14.

Ḥammād, Aḥmad Zakī Mansūr, "Abū Ḥāmid al-Ghazālī's Juristic Doctrine in *al-Mustaṣfā min ʿilm al-uṣūl* with a Translation of Volume One of *al-Mustaṣfā min ʿilm al-uṣūl*." Ph.D. dissertation, University of Chicago, 1987.

Hourani, George F. *Reason and Tradition in Islamic Ethics*. Cambridge: Cambridge University Press, 1985.

Ibn Rushd. *Tahāfut al-tahāfut*. Edited by Maurice Bouyges. Beirut: Imprimerie Catholique, 1930.

———. *Averroes' Tahāfut al-tahāfut (The Incoherence of the Incoherence)*. Translated by S. van den Bergh. 2 vols. Cambridge: Gibb Memorial Trust and Cambridge University Press, 1954.

Ibn Sīnā. *The Metaphysics of The Healing / al-Shifāʾ: al-Ilāhiyyāt. A Parallel English-Arabic Text*. Edited and transl. by Michael E. Marmura. Provo (Utah): Brigham Young University Press, 2005.

Kraay, Klaas. "Divine Unsurpassability." *Philosophia* 35 (2007): 293–300.

Lane, Edward William: *Arabic-English Lexicon, Derived From the Best and Most Copious Sources*, 2 books in 4 vols. London and Edinburgh: Williams and Norgate 1863–85. Reprint in 8 vols. Beirut: Librairie du Liban, 1968.

Leibniz, Gottfried Wilhelm. "Discourse on Metaphysics." In *Philosophical Essays*. Transl. by Roger Ariew and Daniel Garber, 35–68. Indianapolis: Hackett, 1989.

———. *Theodicy: Essays on the Goodness of God, the Freedom of Man, and the Origin of Evil.* Edited, with an introduction by Austin Farrer, transl. by E. M. Huggard from C. J. Gerhardt's edition of the Collected philosophical works, 1875–90. 5th ed. La Salle (Il.): Open Court, 1996.

Marmura, Michael E. "Avicenna and the Problem of the Infinite Number of Souls." *Mediaeval Studies* 22 (1960): 232–239.

———. "Al-Ghazālī's Second Causal Theory in the 17th Discussion of His Tahāfut." In *Islamic Philosophy and Mysticism*. Edited by Parviz Morewedge. Delmar (N.Y.): Caravan Books, 1981. 85–112.

Martin, Richard C. Mark R. Woodward u. Dwi S. Atmaja. *Defenders of Reason in Islam: Muʿtazilism from Medieval School to Modern Symbol*. Oxford: Oneworld Publications, 1997.

McCarthy, Richard J. (ed. and transl.) *Deliverance from Error. Five Key Texts Including His Spriritual Autobiography, al-Munqidh min al-Dalal*. Translated and annotated by R. J. McCarthy. Louisville (Ky.): Fons Vitae: 2000.

McGinnis, Jon. "Occasionalism, Natural Causation and Science in al-Ghazālī." In *Arabic Theology, Arabic Philosophy. From the Many to the One: Essays in Celebration of Richard Frank*, edited by James E. Montgomery, 441–463. Leuven: Peeters, 2006.

McGinnis, Jon and David C. Reisman (eds. and transl.) *Classical Arabic Philosophy. An Anthology of Sources*. Transl. with introd., notes and glossary by Jon McGinnes and David C. Reisman. Indianapolis: Hackett, 2007.

Normore, Calvin. "Duns Scotus's Modal Theory." In *The Cambridge Companion to Duns Scotus*. Edited by Thomas Williams. Cambridge: Cambridge University Press, 2003. 129–160.

Ormsby, Eric. *Theodicy in Islamic Thought: The Dispute Over Al-Ghazālī's "Best of All Possible Worlds".* Princeton, NJ: Princeton University Press, 1984.

———. *Ghazali: The Revival of Islam*. Oxford: Oneworld Publications, 2007.

Parfit, Derek. *Reasons and Persons*. Oxford: Oxford University Press, 1987.

Pike, Nelson. "Hume on Evil." In *The Problem of Evil*. Edited by Marilyn Adams and Robert Adams, 38–52. Oxford: Oxford University Press, 1990. Originally in The Philosophical Review 72 (1963): 180–197.

Plantinga, Alvin. *The Nature of Necessity*. Oxford: Clarendon Press, 1974.

al-Rāzī, Fakhr al-Dīn. *Tafsīr al-kabīr / Mafātiḥ al-ghayb*. Edited by Muḥammad Muḥyī al-Dīn ʿAbd al-Ḥamīd. 32 vols. Cairo: al-Maṭbāʿa al-Bahiyya al-Miṣriyya, 1933.

Rowe, William. "The Problem of Divine Perfection and Freedom." In *Reasoned Faith: Essays in Philosophical Theology in Honor of Norman Kretzmann*. Edited by Eleonore Stump. Ithaca, NY: Cornell University Press, 1993. 223–233

Setia, ʿAdī. "Fakhr al-Dīn al-Rāzī on Physics and the Nature of the Physical World: A Preliminary Survey." *Islam and Science* 2 (2004): 161–80.

Steinberg, Jesse. "Leibniz, Creation and the Best of All Possible Worlds." *International Journal for Philosophy of Religion* 62 (2007): 123–133.

Stone, M. W. F. and Robert Wisnovsky. "Philosophy and Theology." In *The Cambridge History of Medieval Philosophy*, Vol. II. Edited by Robert Pasnau and Christina Van Dyke. Cambridge: Cambridge University Press, 2010. 689- 706.

Swinburne, Richard. *The Existence of God*. 2nd, revised edition. Oxford: Clarendon Press, 1991.

Swoyer, Chris and Francesco Orilia. "Properties." In *The Stanford Encyclopedia of Philosophy*. Edited by Edward N. Zalta. Stanford University, 2011. <http://plato.stanford.edu/entries/ properties>.

Tibawi, Abdel Latif. "Al-Ghazālī's Sojourn in Damascus and Jerusalem." *Islamic Quarterly* 9 (1965): 65–122.

van Ess, Josef. Theologie und Gesellschaft im 2. und 3. *Jahrhundert Hidschra. Eine Geschichte des religiösen Denkens im frühen Islam*. 6 vols. Berlin: Walter de Gruyter, 1991–97.

Vasalou, Sophia. *Moral Agents and Their Deserts: The Character of Muʿtazilite Ethics*. Princeton (N.J.): Princeton University Press, 2008.

Watt, W. Montgomery. *Islamic Philosophy and Theology*. 2nd edition. Edinburgh: Edinburgh University Press, 1985.

Wykstra, Stephen. "The Humean Obstacle to Evidential Arguments from Suffering: On Avoiding the Evils of 'Appearance'." In *The Problem of Evil*. Edited by Marilyn M. Adams and Robert M. Adams. Oxford: Oxford University Press, 1990. (Originally published in *International Journal for Philosophy of Religion* 16 (1984): 73–93).

al-Zabīdī, al-Murtaḍā Muḥammad ibn Muḥammad. *Itḥāf al-sāda al-muttaqīn bi-sharḥ Iḥyāʾ ʿulūm al-dīn*. 10 vols. Cairo: al-Maṭbaʿa al-Maymaniyya, 1311 [1894].

CHAPTER 4

Al-Ghazālī's Teleology and the Galenic Tradition

Reading The Wisdom in God's Creations (al-Ḥikma fī makhlūqāt Allah)

Ahmed El Shamsy

Recent studies of al-Ghazālī, including several included in this volume, have emphasized al-Ghazālī's deeply complicated involvement with philosophy. The interest in his philosophical thought marks a welcome departure from previous scholarship, which has tended to take al-Ghazālī's dismissal of the "incoherence of the philosophers" at face value. Most studies have focused on al-Ghazālī's engagement with peripatetic philosophy as mediated and developed by Avicenna (Ibn Sīnā, d. 428/1037).[1] Looking beyond Avicenna, Stephen Menn has pointed out al-Ghazālī's adoption of the autobiographical style of Galen of Pergamon (d. *c.* 200 CE) and the role of its precedent in al-Ghazālī's fashioning of his own intellectual persona in his famous *al-Munqidh min al-ḍalāl* (*The Deliverer from Error*).[2] My aim in this chapter is to pursue the issue of al-Ghazālī's engagement with Galen further by examining his use of the latter's teleological approach as a means of reasoning toward the nature of God as well as of analyzing and elaborating on the divine law. I will argue that al-Ghazālī's thought contains a certain methodological and substantive orientation that owes an identifiable debt to Galen. This orientation can be described as empiricist, in that it bases conclusions on inductive reasoning from empirical observations; and it is fundamentally teleological, in that it assumes the existence of a divine, providential *télos* (Gr. "end, goal, purpose") aimed at perfecting creation for the benefit of its creatures (*maṣlaḥa*). This empiricist teleology is evident in a number of al-Ghazali's writings, especially in his *al-Ḥikma fī makhlūqāt Allāh* (*The Wisdom in God's Creations*), and it is central to his theory of the "aims of the law," *maqāṣid al-sharīʿa*.

I will first outline the teleological principle in al-Ghazālī's legal thought and show how he applies this principle and its accompanying terminology to the much wider issue of learning about God in creation. I will then investigate the sources from which al-Ghazālī is likely to have drawn his teleology. I suggest that his main inspiration was the work of Galen, both directly through its Arabic translation and indirectly through the mediation of Avicenna and a

1 See, e.g., Janssens, "Al-Ghazālī's *Tahāfut*," or Griffel, *Al-Ghazālī's Philosophical Theology*.
2 Menn, "The *Discourse on the Method* and the Tradition of Intellectual Autobiography."

 | DOI 10.1163/9789004307490_005

cluster of texts that entered Arabo-Islamic thought via translations and reworkings of late antique Christian works. I conclude with a brief discussion of the most innovative feature of al-Ghazālī's teleology, namely, its integration of the empirical observation of creation and the study of Qur'anic scripture into a single epistemological framework.

Teleology in Law

The idea that the divine law serves human benefit (*maṣlaḥa*)[3] was historically most fully elaborated by Muʿtazilite thinkers, and it was closely connected to the ethical claim that God is obligated to bring about the optimum in His creation.[4] Abū Bakr al-Qaffāl al-Shāshī (d. 365/976), a Shāfiʿī jurist whose legal thought was deeply influenced by Muʿtazilite ethics, wrote:

> If you affirm that things have a creator who is wise and powerful, then He must intend good for His servants, rendering satisfaction for them according to virtuous governance that is based on seeking their benefit.[5]

For al-Qaffāl as for the Muʿtazilites in general, the beneficiality of the law was the necessary conclusion of a deductive process of reasoning: from the divine attributes of wisdom and power, they deduced that the law issued by the wise and omnipotent Creator must benefit those for whom it is laid down. Arriving at this result is a logical necessity and thus requires no actual observation of the individual points of law.

Al-Ghazālī, as is well known, was at least nominally an Ashʿarite, and he shared his peers' disdain for Muʿtazilism. Why and how, then, did the rationalist concept of *maṣlaḥa* come to play such a central role in his legal thought? An answer is suggested by the following passage in his legal-theoretical work *Shifāʾ al-ghalīl fī bayān al-shabah wa-l-mukhīl* (*The Quenching of Thirst in Explaining Analogy by Similarity and Suggestiveness*). After arguing that observance (*riʿāya*) of humans' good reason is one of the purposes of the lawgiver (singl. *maqṣūd al-shāriʿ*), he comments:

> Although we say that God may to do to His subjects as He wills and that the observance of their good reason is not incumbent upon Him, we do

3 Opwis, *Maṣlaḥa and the Purpose of the Law*, 65–88.

4 Zysow, "Two Theories."

5 al-Qaffāl al-Shāshī, *Maḥāsin al-sharīʿa*, 25.

> not deny that reason indicates what is advantageous and disadvantageous and warns against ruin and urges the attractions of what is of benefit. Nor do we deny that the messengers were sent for the good of creation in religion and worldly matters as a bounty from God, not as a duty obligatory upon Him (…). And we have only made this point lest we be associated with the teachings of the Muʿtazila and lest the nature of the student recoil from what we say for fear of being soiled with a rejected dogma, contempt for which is rooted in the souls of the Ahl al-Sunna.[6]

Al-Ghazālī here makes a point of distancing his position from that of the Muʿtazilites: although he, too, holds that the goal of the law is to promote the benefit of humankind, he does not declare the rendering of benefit to be a moral obligation upon God, as the Muʿtazilites had done. What allows him, rather, to arrive at the same conclusion and to defend the inherent beneficiality of the sacred law is the method of induction. In contrast to the deductive approach of the Muʿtazilites, al-Ghazālī identifies observable human needs on the one hand and patterns within the body of the law on the other and then points out that the latter display the feature of appropriateness (*munāsaba*) in catering to the former. The match between human needs and the rules of the law, he argues, points toward the overall aims (*maqāṣid*) that the divine law, through its individual rules, seeks to secure. One such aim, for example, is that "property is intended (*maqṣūda*) to be preserved for its owners; this is known by the prohibition to infringe on others' rights, and the obligation of liability, and the punishment of the thief."[7]

These aims, once identified, can be used to formulate new legal rules to adjudicate novel scenarios by evaluating potential new rules, and specifically their "legal causes" (*ʿilal*), against the standard of the aims that have been identified inductively from the correlation between human needs and divine laws. Figure 4.1 illustrates this relationship between human needs, legal rules, and overall aims.

This conceptualization of the law can be called empiricist, because it relies on the observation of individual, concrete phenomena—that is, individual human needs and individual rules of the law—not only to propose a fundamental harmony between the two but also to develop a method for analogically extending this harmonious relationship to hitherto undetermined cases. It is also teleological, because it embodies the belief that the divine law, rather than representing an arbitrary set of commands, is structured by identifiable and

6 al-Ghazālī, *Shifāʾ al-ghalīl*, 162–63; the translation is from Zysow, "Economy of Certainty," 345.

7 al-Ghazālī, *Shifāʾ al-ghalīl*, 160.

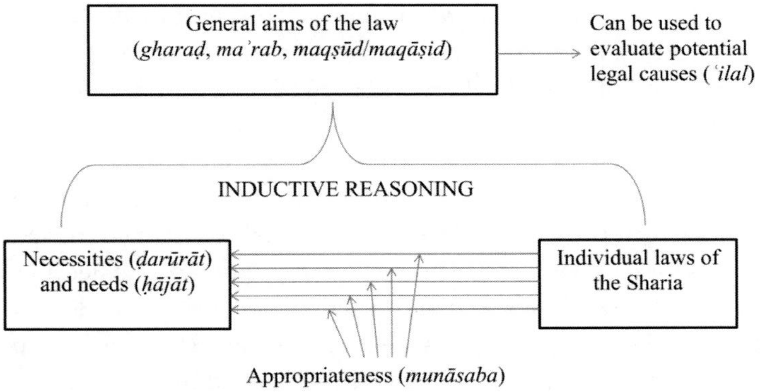

FIGURE 4.1 *Al-Ghazālī's empiricist teleology in law.*

intelligible aims whose overall function is to meet human needs and thus to secure the welfare of humankind.

Nature, Creation, and God

Al-Ghazālī's empiricist teleology was not limited to the realm of the law. His belief in an overall *télos* in divine creation, manifested in and graspable through the latter's details, permeated other aspects of his thought and several of his writings. For example, in *al-Maqṣad al-asnā fī sharḥ maʿānī asmāʾ Allāh al-ḥusnā* (*The Highest Goal in Explaining the Beautiful Names of God*), al-Ghazālī on several occasions directs the reader to

> observe God's attributes in the constitution of the human body. Its parts cooperate to establish an order (*niẓām*) for its purpose (*gharaḍ*) and aim (*maqṣūd*). The cosmos is the macrocosm of the human being.[8]

In other words, by observing phenomena in creation, whether within the human body or in the cosmos as a whole, one can discern an order in which parts cooperate to form a whole that achieves specific, recognizable aims. Al-Ghazālī thus depicts natural phenomena as manifestations of the divine names using the same methodology that allowed him to connect individual, beneficial legal rules to the overall aims of the law. He also produces a Qur'anic proof text for his empiricist methodology, namely, the first half of verse 41:53:

8 al-Ghazālī, *al-Maqṣad al-asnā*, 152, in the section on the divine name *mālik al-mulk*.

"We shall show them Our signs (*āyātunā*) on the horizons and within themselves until it will be clear to them that it is the truth."[9] Elsewhere, however, he makes clear that contemplation of the divine through His creation is inferior to contemplation of God Himself:

> The majority of mankind see everything except God. They seek evidence of Him in that which they see, and they are the ones who are addressed by God's words, "Have they not considered the dominion of the heavens and the earth and what things God hath created?" (Q 7:185). The devout (on the other hand) do not see anything except Him, and thus it is in Him that they seek evidence of Him, and they are the ones addressed by God's words, "Doth not thy Lord suffice, since He is witness over all creation?" (Q 41:53)[10]

In *al-Maqṣad al-asnā*, teleological references are scattered throughout the text. But in a chapter of *Iḥyāʾ ʿulūm al-dīn* (*The Revival of the Religious Sciences*) titled *Bayān kayfiyyat al-tafakkur fī khalq Allāh*, "Explication of How to Reflect on God's Creation" (henceforth *Tafakkur*), al-Ghazālī expands on this theme in a unified discussion of how the contemplation of God's handiwork (*ṣunʿ Allāh*) reveals His wisdom and allows the believer to encounter God's attributes.[11] Although al-Ghazālī admits that the objects of contemplation in creation are for all intents and purposes countless, he proceeds to outline, on about fifteen pages in the printed edition, the wisdom and benefits inherent in the sun, moon, plants, and animals, as well as the organs of the human body.

The same topic forms the subject of an independent treatise by al-Ghazālī, titled *al-Ḥikma fī makhlūqāt Allāh* (*The Wisdom in God's Creations*), which has received very little attention to date. Part of this neglect probably derives from Mourice Bouyges's and, following him, ʿAbd al-Raḥmān Badawī's listing of the work under the rubric of doubtful attributions to al-Ghazālī in their respective bibliographies of al-Ghazālī's writings.[12] Bouyges says that the attribution of *al-Ḥikma* to al-Ghazālī had been discussed among historians of Jewish philosophy. Bouyges himself adds, "we say only that *al-Ḥikma* would be worthy of al-Ghazālī."[13]

---

9 al-Ghazālī, *al-Maqṣad al-asnā*, 107, on *al-ʿadl*.

10 al-Ghazālī, *al-Maqṣad al-asnā*, 139, on *al-ḥaqq*; the translation is from Robert Stade, *Ninety-Nine Names of God in Islam*, 99.

11 al-Ghazālī, *Iḥyāʾ ʿulūm al-dīn*, 15:2822–44.

12 Bouyges, *Essai de chronologie*, 89; Badawī, *Muʾallafāt al-Ghazālī*, 257.

13 "[D]isons simplement que le *Ḥikma* serait digne d'Algazal (…)"; Bouyges, *Essai de chronologie*, 89.

TABLE 4.1 *A comparison of corresponding sections in* al-Ḥikma fī makhlūqāt Allāh *and* Bayān kayfiyyat al-tafakkur fī khalq Allāh *in al-Ghazālī's* Iḥyāʾ ʿulūm al-dīn.

***Ḥikma*, 47**	***Tafakkur*, in *Iḥyāʾ*, 15:2827**
Then consider how He raised the nose in the middle of the face, and made it beautiful, and opened up its two nostrils; and how He placed the sense of smell in it, so as to indicate through the inhaling of smells its food and drink, and to luxuriate in fragrant smells and to avoid what is filthy. And [the nose also allows one] to inhale the spirit/refreshment of life to nourish the heart and to cool the internal heat.	Then [consider how] He raised the nose in the middle of the face, and made it beautiful, and opened up its two nostrils; and how He placed the sense of smell in it, so as to indicate through the inhaling of smells its food and its nourishing qualities. And [the nose also allows one] to inhale through the opening of the nostrils the refreshment of the air to nourish the heart and to cool the internal heat.
ثُمَّ انظر كيف رَفعَ الْأَنْفَ فِي وَسَطِ الْوَجْهِ وَأَحْسَنَ شَكْلَهُ وَفتح مَنْخَرَيْهِ وجعل فيه حاسة الشم ليستدل باستنشاق الروائح على مطاعمه و مشاربه و ليتنعم بالروائح العطرة ويجتنب الخبائث القذرة و ليستنشق ايضا روح الحياة غِذَاءً لِقَلْبِهِ وَتَرْوِيحًا لِحَرَارَةِ بَاطِنِهِ	ثُمَّ رَفعَ الْأَنْفَ مِنْ وَسَطِ الْوَجْهِ وَأَحْسَنَ شَكْلَهُ وَفَتَحَ مَنْخَرَيْهِ وَأَوْدَعَ فيه حاسّه الشمّ ليستدل باستنشاق الروائح على مطاعمه وأغذيته و ليستنشق بِمَنْفَذِ الْمَنْخَرَيْنِ رَوْحَ الْهَوَاءِ غِذَاءً لِقَلْبِهِ وَتَرْوِيحًا لِحَرَارَةِ بَاطِنِهِ

As Bouyges noted, the scholars of Judaism Abraham S. Yahuda and David Neumark had discussed *al-Ḥikma*, and both noted parallels between it and the *Tafakkur* chapter in al-Ghazālī's *Iḥyāʾ*.[14] Neither expressed doubts concerning *al-Ḥikma's* authenticity, although Yahuda seemed to believe that Martin Schreiner had called its attribution to al-Ghazālī into question.[15] Neumark explained the similarities by assuming that al-Ghazālī copied the text of one book into the other, thus acknowledging al-Ghazālī's authorship of both works.[16] A comparison of the two works indeed reveals a close textual resemblance. A discussion of the features of the nose, presented in Table 4.1, provides an example. (Note that since neither text has been critically edited, the textual variation should be viewed with caution.)

14 Yahuda, *Prolegomena*, 11, n. 2; Neumark, *Geschichte der jüdischen Philosophie*, 1:487.

15 Schreiner, review of *Résumé des réflexions*, 124. Schreiner, however, seems to have simply been agnostic regarding the work's authenticity.

16 Neumark, *Geschichte der jüdischen Philosophie*, 1:487.

The reason why historians of Jewish thought such as Yahuda and Neumark discussed the attribution of *al-Ḥikma* to al-Ghazālī lies in a problem of chronology that they thought this attribution would entail. A work by the Jewish mystic Baḥya ibn Paqūda (fl. *c.* 431/1040) displays close parallels to *al-Ḥikma*, suggesting that Baḥya was familiar with the text; but Baḥya lived perhaps half a century before al-Ghazālī in Saragossa in al-Andalus.[17] Yahuda assumed that Baḥya copied from al-Ghazālī and thus must have lived after 1100, yet already Neumark suggested that the similarities might stem from a common source used by both Baḥya and al-Ghazālī.[18] The apparent problem was fully solved in 1938 by David Z. Baneth, who demonstrated that both Baḥya and the author of *al-Ḥikma* drew on an earlier text, *al-Dalāʾil wa-l-iʿtibār* (*Indications and Consideration*), which I will discuss below.[19]

More recently, Eric Ormsby has also voiced doubt regarding the authenticity of *al-Ḥikma*. His conclusion, made in a footnote, is based on the alleged existence of Muʿtazilite elements in the work;[20] however, he does not give details, and I have been unable to find any such elements in the text of *al-Ḥikma*. He also notes that the work is not mentioned in al-Ghazālī's other books nor in classical lists of his writings. However, this argument from silence is particularly weak with respect to a minor work such as *al-Ḥikma*, and in fact a work called *Kitāb Badāʾiʿ ṣunʿ Allāh* (*The Book of God's Marvelous Handiwork*) is named in the list of al-Ghazālī's works compiled by Abū ʿAbdallāh al-Wāsiṭī (d. 776/1374).[21] It seems likely that this is an alternative title for *al-Ḥikma*.[22] Ormsby mentions some parallels between *al-Ḥikma* and passages in the *Iḥyāʾ*, suggesting that these are attributable to shared sources used by the authors—especially Galen. But the parallel passages shown in Table 4.1, for example, are not found in the most likely source texts. The clear correlation, both structural and substantive, between *al-Ḥikma* and *Tafakkur*, together with the universally attested authorship of al-Ghazālī in the extant manuscripts,[23] make al-Ghazālī's authorship of *al-Ḥikma* seem almost certain.

17 Lobel, *Sufi-Jewish Dialogue*, 119.

18 Yahuda, *Prolegomena*, 12; Neumark, *Geschichte der jüdischen Philosophie*, 1:487.

19 Baneth, "Common Teleological Source," 23–30; (Pseudo-)Jāḥiẓ, *al-Dalāʾil wa-l-iʿtibār*.

20 Ormsby, *Theodicy in Islamic Thought*, 48, n. 46.

21 Edited in al-Aʿsam, *al-Faylasūf al-Ghazālī*, 183. Kātib Çelebī (d. 1067/1657), *Kashf al-ẓunūn*, 1:230, lists a work by the title of *Badāʾiʿ ṣanīʿ* by al-Ghazālī. See also Badawī, *Muʾallafāt al-Ghazālī*, 398–99.

22 Yahuda, *Prolegomena*, 11, n. 2, had already pointed to the possibility that the book is identical with *ʿAjāʾib ṣunʿ Allāh*, which appears in the list of al-Ghazālī's works in al-Murtaḍā al-Zabīdī (d. 1205/1791), *Itḥāf al-sāda*, 1:42.6. See also Badawī, *Muʾallafāt al-Ghazālī*, 396, 399. The two titles *ʿAjāʾib* and *Badāʾiʿ ṣunʿ Allāh* are likely variants of one and the same work.

23 Badawī, *Muʾallafāt al-Ghazālī*, 257.

Al-Ḥikma fī makhlūqāt Allāh is structured by the various areas of creation that al-Ghazālī addresses: the heavens, the sun, and the planets (twelve pages in the printed edition); the sea (three pages); water (two pages); air (four pages); fire (four pages); birds (eight pages); beasts of burden (one page); insects and spiders (eight pages); fish (four pages); and the human body (twenty-six pages). Al-Ghazālī introduces each section by quoting a relevant Qurʾanic verse. So, for example, the section on the anatomy of the human body is prefaced by the famous verses on foetal development at the beginning of Sūrat "al-Muʾminūn" (Q 23:12–14).[24] These verses are then followed by accounts of how the various body parts cooperate to serve the overall function of preserving the human body, accompanied by the argument that the way they are constructed is optimal; that is, they could not have been designed better. For al-Ghazālī, the beneficial nature of creation and its perfection serve as signs that point toward God. The most precious of these signs is the human intellect, because it is at the same time a supreme sign of God's marvelous handiwork and capable of deciphering God's other signs.

From the element of design that he sees as ever-present in creation, al-Ghazālī inductively concludes that the goal of creation is to promote benefit and to avoid harm—the very same logic that he proposed for the divine law in his works of legal theory, which derived the purposeful nature of the law from the observed correlation between the law on the one hand and the generation of benefit and fulfillment of needs on the other. For example, a description of the various benefits of water leads to conclusions regarding God's intentions and nature:

> So behold the vastness of this blessing and the ease of accessing it, and yet [our] unawareness of its real value, despite the intensity of the need for it, to the extent that were it to become scarce, life in this world would become miserable. From this, we know that God, by sending it down and making it easy [to procure], wished the world to be inhabited by animals, plants, and minerals, as well as [providing] other benefits [so bountiful] that someone trying to enumerate them will fall short. So praise be to the great dispenser of favors.[25]

A close reading of *al-Ḥikma* reveals that also the work's terminology mirrors that of al-Ghazālī's legal discussions. Table 4.2 presents a summary of the teleological terms used in *al-Ḥikma* and their relative frequency.

24 al-Ghazālī, *al-Ḥikma fī makhlūqāt Allāh*, 43.
25 Ibid., 36–7.

TABLE 4.2 *Occurrences of teleological terms in al-Ghazālī's* Ḥikma.

Root	Terms used	Number of occurrences
Terms denoting the fulfillment of human benefit and needs:		
n-f-ʿ	نفع ,منافع , منفعة	62
ṣ-l-ḥ	مصلحة , أصلح	57
h-w-j	محتاج , حاجة	57
Terms denoting harm and necessity:		
f-s-d	مفاسد , مفسدة	9
ḍ-r-r	ضرورة , ضرر	28
Terms denoting divine *télos*:		
q-ṣ-d	مقاصد , مقصد , قصد	14
ʾ-r-b	مآرب , مأرب	9
Terms denoting suitability and appropriateness:		
l-ʾ-m	يلائم , ملاءمة	2
n-s-b	مناسبة	8
w-f-q	وفاق , موافقة	at least 5

Al-Ghazālī's Sources

What and who inspired al-Ghazālī's teleological approach? Al-Ghazālī's Ashʿarite affiliation cannot sufficiently explain his teleological approach. While al-Ashʿarī himself employed teleological arguments, the Ashʿarī school subsequently sidelined these arguments to emphasize God's sovereign will vis-à-vis the Muʿtazilite claim that God was obligated to create the optimum (*al-aṣlaḥ*) and that the law therefore had to serve humans' best interests.[26] While the idea that the law serves human benefit appears to have been a universal assumption of Islamic jurists, including Ashʿarīs,[27] this purposefulness remained strangely undertheorized in the wider Ashʿarī system, both in law and in theology.[28]

The next obvious source would be Avicenna. As is becoming increasingly evident, Avicenna had a strong influence on al-Ghazālī. Al-Ghazālī's scrapbook of Avicennan quotations, MS London Or 3126, shows that the material he

26 Compare al-Ashʿarī's *al-Lumaʿ*, 17–19, with Abū Bakr al-Bāqillānī's commentary, which is quoted in Ibn Taymiyya, *Darʾ taʿāruḍ al-ʿaql wa-l-naql*, 7:304–6.

27 Zysow, "Economy of Certainty," 347.

28 For al-Ghazālī's teacher al-Juwaynī, see Opwis, *Maṣlaḥa and the Purpose of the Law*, 41–5.

received from Avicenna included texts that affirmed a teleological structure in creation. In this work, al-Ghazālī quotes the metaphysical section of Avicenna's *al-Shifāʾ* (*Healing*), which urges his readers to "contemplate the state of the usefulness of the organs in animals and plants and how each has been created. There is [for this] no natural cause at all, but its principle is necessarily [divine] providence."[29] This passage is immediately followed in the manuscript by another quotation from Avicenna's *al-Shifāʾ* that also invokes a teleological argument. Further, the second quotation makes reference to anatomical details (eyebrows, eyelashes, and the arches of the feet) and uses teleological terminology familiar from al-Ghazālī's *al-Ḥikma*, including the concepts of need (*ḥāja*), benefits (*manāfiʿ*), necessity (*ḍarūra*), and providence (*ʿināya*).

A second indication of the overlap between Avicenna and al-Ghazālī in terms of the teleological approach can be found in Avicenna's *al-Ishārāt wa-l-tanbīhāt* (*Pointers and Reminders*), where Avicenna acknowledges the argument from design even though he discounts it vis-à-vis the "superiority" of metaphysical arguments for God's existence. Contemplating pure being, he claims, is sufficient to establish God's existence and oneness; it is not necessary to consider God's creation, "even though it is an indicator toward Him" (*wa-in kāna dhālika dalīlan ʿalayhī*).[30] (In his commentary on the *Ishārāt*, al-Ṭūsī justifies this bifurcation by arguing that while contemplation of creation yields only probable knowledge, contemplation of God's self leads to certain knowledge.)[31] As Qurʾanic proof text, Avicenna quotes the same verse that al-Ghazālī would also later call upon in his *al-Maqṣad al-asnā*, namely, 41:53. For both Avicenna and al-Ghazālī, empirical reasoning from the design of creation represents a viable, though inferior, path to recognizing God, while the contemplation of God Himself is the high road, reserved for the elect.

Avicenna was familiar with the teleological argument and even, it seems, endorsed it in principle. However, he was a metaphysician, and his use of the argument appears to be limited to the minor instances quoted by al-Ghazālī. Al-Ghazālī's adoption and development of the teleological approach as a prominent feature of his philosophical thought thus clearly goes beyond Avicenna's engagement with teleology, and it suggests that the primary source of al-Ghazālī's engagement lies elsewhere. This primary source, I believe, was the Graeco-Roman physician Galen of Pergamon and his work *De usu partium* (*On the Usefulness of the Body Parts*)—a connection that Ormsby speculatively

29 Ibn Sīnā, *al-Shifāʾ*, *al-Ilāhiyyāt*, 362; cf. MS London Or 3126, fol. 238a.

30 Ibn Sīnā, *al-Ishārāt wa-l-tanbīhāt*, 3:54–5.

31 Ibid.

endorses but does not explore.[32] *De usu partium* is a substantial anatomical work about the various parts of the body, their constitution and function. Although the bulk of the work consists of minute and detailed anatomical descriptions, Galen always concludes his descriptions by emphasizing that the body part or organ under study is perfectly designed to fulfill its function and therefore indicates the existence of a wise creator. Stephen Menn has already argued that al-Ghazālī found in Galen a kindred spirit in his disillusionment with the limitations of the rationalism of the philosophers and that he saw in Galen's stress on proper demonstration and experience a viable corrective to the philosophers' shortcomings. Al-Ghazālī mentions two of Galen's books in his *Munqidh*, one of which is *De usu partium*, in Arabic *Manāfiʿ al-aʿḍāʾ*:

> The second group are the natural philosophers (*al-ṭabīʿiyyūn*): they are a party who devote most of their efforts to investigating the natural world and the wonders of animals and plants and plunge into the science of the anatomy of the parts of animals. And what they see there of the wonders of God's craftsmanship (*ʿajāʾib ṣunʿ Allāh*)[33] and the inventions of His wisdom compels them to acknowledge a wise creator who is aware of the ends and purposes of things (*ghāyat al-umūr wa-maqāṣidihā*). No one can study anatomy and the wonders of the benefits of the parts (*manāfiʿ al-aʿḍāʾ*) without acquiring this necessary knowledge of the perfection of the governance of the constructor in the construction of animals, and especially the construction of human beings.[34]

The "natural philosophers," for al-Ghazālī, represent a group that holds that things are what they are due to the agency of natures: "They believe that the faculty of intelligence in humans follows the mixture [of the four humors]." Their denial of the afterlife makes them unbelievers; however, what distinguishes them from the materialists (*dahriyyūn*), whom al-Ghazālī discusses in a previous paragraph, is the former's recognition that natures or the "four humors" are causal intermediaries that themselves depend on God as their creator.[35] Given that Galen's *De usu partium* was the most prominent work of natural philosophy on anatomy and that al-Ghazālī referenced the title of the

32 Ormsby, *Theodicy in Islamic Thought*, 45–6.

33 Note that this is quite likely the alternative title of the *Ḥikma*.

34 al-Ghazālī, *al-Munqidh min al-dalāl*, 19; the translation follows Menn, "Discourse on the Method," 184, with some modifications.

35 This was, indeed, Galen's position; see Hankinson, *Cause and Explanation in Ancient Greek Thought*, 382–8.

book in his writing, it is clear that al-Ghazālī was familiar with the work, which had been available in a complete Arabic version since Ḥunayn ibn Isḥāq's (d. 260/873) translation in the third/ninth century.[36] An examination of the Arabic translation of the work, which remains unedited, reveals that most of the material in al-Ghazālī's discussion of the human body in *al-Ḥikma* indeed originates from Galen's *De usu partium*. Furthermore, much of the repertoire of teleological terms found in *al-Ḥikma*—including *maqāṣid, ma'ārib, manfaʿa,* and *ʿināya*—is already found in the Arabic version of *De usu partium* as well as in Arabic translations of late antiquity works drawing on it (see below).[37] The only significant Ghazalian term I have not yet encountered in these earlier works is the root n-s-b (*munāsaba, munāsib,* etc.) to denote the appropriateness of the relationship between creation or individual laws on the one hand and God's overall aims on the other. In *Manāfiʿ al-aʿḍāʾ* (as also in places in al-Ghazālī's own writing)[38] the same idea seems to be expressed primarily by the root w-f-q (*muwāfaqa, awfaq,* etc.), as when judging the specific connection between fingers and muscles to be "appropriate to what is needed and beneficial (*muwāfiq li-l-ḥāja wa-l-manfaʿa*), and this is because the Creator (…) did not make this in an idle manner or in jest."[39] However, Ḥunayn uses the term *munāsib* in his description of *De usu partium*, so it is possible that it is also found in the translation itself.[40]

36 For Ḥunayn ibn Isḥāq's inclusion of *De usu partium* in a list of the works of Galen that he translated, see Bergsträsser, "Ḥunain ibn Isḥāq," 27–8 (Arabic text) and 22 (German). At least five manuscript copies of the Arabic text appear to be extant: MS Bibliothèque Nationale de France, Fonds arabe 2853, copied in 682/1283; National Library of Medicine, Bethesda, Maryland, MS A 30.1, undated (*c.* 17th century); Escorial, MS 850, copied in 539/1145; Iraqi National Museum, Baghdad, MS 1378–5, undated (*c.* 16th century); and John Rylands, Manchester, MS 809, undated (*c.* 17th century). See Ullmann, *Die Medizin im Islam*, 41, and Sezgin, *Geschichte des arabischen Schrifttums*, 3:106. Subsequent references to *Manāfiʿ al-aʿḍāʾ* are to the first mentioned manuscript at the BNF Paris, which is complete and well readable.

37 For uses of the root ṣ-l-ḥ see *Manāfiʿ al-aʿḍāʾ*, e.g., fols. 26b, 43b, and 58b; for n-f-ʿ see, e.g., 16a, 40b, and 43a; for *ʿināya* see, e.g., 34b, 55a, 58a, and 60a; for ḥ-w-j see, e.g., 16a, 62b, and 63a; for ʾ-r-b see *al-Dalāʾil wa-l-iʿtibār*, e.g., 2 and 51.

38 For al-Ghazālī's use of the root w-f-q see, e.g., *al-Ḥikma fī makhlūqāt Allāh*, 19, 46, 51, and 70.

39 Galen, *Manāfiʿ al-aʿḍāʾ*, fol. 16a. For additional examples, see fols. 34b, 43b, 58b, 62b, and 63a.

40 Bergsträsser, "Ḥunain ibn Isḥāq," 28 (Arabic text).

Avicenna and Galen

The influence of Galen provides an explanation for a riddle involving the two passages that al-Ghazālī copied from Avicenna's *al-Shifāʾ*. The first of these, quoted above, straightforwardly affirms divine teleology in the structure and functioning of creation. The second, however, veers into the subject of prophecy:

> Reciprocal transactions (*al-muʿāmala*) must have law and justice (*sunna wa-ʿadl*), and law and justice necessarily require a lawgiver and a dispenser of justice (*sānn wa-muʿaddil*). This [lawgiver] must be in a position that enables him to address people and make them adhere to the law. He must, then, be a human being. He must not leave people to their private opinions concerning [the law] so that they disagree, each considering as just what others owe them, unjust what they owe others.
>
> Thus, with respect to the survival and actual existence of the human species, the need (*ḥāja*) of this person is greater than the need for such benefits (*manāfiʿ*) as the growing of hair on the eyebrows [and the pulpebral margins], the concave shaping of the arches of the feet, and many others that are not necessary (*ḍarūra*) for survival but are, at best, useful for it. [Now,] the existence of the righteous man to legislate and to dispense justice is possible, as we have previously remarked. It becomes impossible, therefore, that divine providence (*ʿināya*) should ordain the existence of those [former] benefits (*manāfiʿ*) and not these [latter], which are their bases.[41]

Al-Ghazālī's combination of these passages into a single section in his Avicennan scrapbook may seem puzzling, but it is explained by the likelihood that al-Ghazālī knew that they have a common origin and purpose. It seems that Avicenna, too, was familiar with Galen's thought, and these passages formed part of his response to Galen—who championed the argument from design in favor of a wise creator but who did not believe in prophecy. These ideas coincide in the eleventh book of *De usu partium*, where Galen describes the beneficial design of the eyebrows and the eyelashes, which protect the eye by their existence but do not interfere with its function because they cease to grow at a certain length. In the context of this discussion Galen remarks that

41 Ibn Sīnā, *al-Shifāʾ*, *al-Ilāhiyyāt*, 364–5, Marmura's translation.

> Moses claims that it is sufficient that God wishes to give shape and form to the matter in order to let it take shape and form instantly, and this because he believes that all things are possible with God … We do not accept this, but say: There are things which are impossible in themselves, and these God never wishes to occur, but he wishes only possible things to occur, and among the possible things he only chooses the best and most adequate and excellent (*ajwaduhā wa-awfaquhā wa-afḍaluhā*).[42]

Although Galen does not explicitly address the issue of prophecy, his juxtaposition of the views of Moses and Aristotle and his preference for the latter shows that he did not accord Moses any exceptional status.

Maimonides's rebuttal of Galen's position is well known, but the passages that al-Ghazālī quotes from Avicenna's *al-Shifāʾ* must be considered an even earlier refutation of Galen via an *a fortiori* argument. Avicenna makes implicit reference to Galen's arguments for the teleological nature of the constitution of the human body down to the hairs surrounding the eye, which, like other parts of the body, are designed for the optimal facilitation of human life. He then goes on to argue that the sending of prophets is a necessary corollary of such a teleology, since the existence of prophets is even more necessary for human flourishing than the practical length of eyebrows and lashes.

Al-Ghazālī, Galen, and Intermediaries

Al-Ghazālī also received Galen's ideas through indirect routes. As noted above, Baneth pointed out already in 1938 that al-Ghazālī's *al-Ḥikma* drew on a text titled *al-Dalāʾil wa-l-iʿtibār* (*Indications and Consideration*)[43] which seeks to discredit the positions of atheists and Manicheans by arguing for the visibility of divine providence in the teleological features of creation, from the planets all the way down to the human body, animals, and plants. Although the printed edition is attributed to al-Jāḥiẓ, it now seems likely that the author was in fact his contemporary, the Christian Jibrīl ibn Nūḥ al-Anbārī (fl. 240/850), whose name appears on the manuscript.[44] Jibrīl was the grandson of Abū Nūḥ

42 Schacht and Meyerhof, "Maimonides against Galen," 70–1, quoting Galen's *De usu partium*, translated from Greek to English as *Galen on the Usefulness of the Parts of the Body*, 2:532–3; for the Arabic text, see *Manāfiʿal-aʿḍāʾ*, fol. 203a.

43 In its manuscript the text is called *al-Fikr wa-l-iʿtibār* and will be referred to as such in the footnotes.

44 al-Anbārī, *al-Fikr wa-l-iʿtibār*.

al-Anbārī, who was a *catholicos* of Nusaybin (Nisibis) in the so-called Jazira of Upper Mesopotamia and the translator of Greek texts into Arabic.[45]

A separate, recently edited work with a very similar title, *al-ʿIbar wa al-iʿtibār* (*Examples and Consideration*), has similar content and is likewise attributed to al-Jāḥiẓ. Hamilton A. R. Gibb, who examined the manuscript, seems to have found no reason to doubt its attribution.[46] In the introduction, the author lists a number of works that he draws on. These include *al-Dalāʾil wa-l-iʿtibār* as well as a *Kitāb al-Tadabbur* (*Book of Reflection*) by Diodorus of Tarsus (d. *c.* 390 CE) and *De providentia* (*On Divine Providence*) by Theodoret of Cyrus (d. around 462 CE).[47] Diodorus's work is no longer extant, but the author of *al-ʿIbar* mentions it in the context of Diodorus's opposition to the pagan Emperor Julian the Apostate (reg. 361–363 CE), so it was likely a defense of Christian theology. Theodoret's *De providentia* has been edited and translated. The work provides a defense of divine providence by appealing to, among other things, the beneficial design of the human body.[48] It contains clear, systematic parallels with both *al-Dalāʾil* and *al-ʿIbar*. As but one example, all three works make the argument that the human speech organ is the model for musical instruments made out of bronze.[49] All three likewise follow Galen's *De usu partium* in drawing a teleological inference from the anatomical description of eyelashes and eyebrows.[50]

These texts, in turn, display significant overlap with al-Ghazālī's *al-Ḥikma*. However, a comparison of *al-Ḥikma*, *al-Dalāʾil*, and *al-ʿIbar* reveals that al-Ghazālī drew specifically on *al-Dalāʾil* but not on *al-ʿIbar* in his work. Table 4.3 provides an example. The discussion of memory in *al-ʿIbar* is clearly influenced by *al-Dalāʾil*, as indeed the author of the former admits. However, the source text is used selectively, in altered wording and with some information (e.g., the point about memory's retention of what one has received and given) omitted in the retelling. *Al-Ḥikma*, by contrast, corresponds almost verbatim to *al-Dalāʾil* and reproduces faithfully all of the material absent in *al-ʿIbar*.

While the indebtedness of the two *Iʿtibār* works to Galen's *De usu partium* is evident, it seems likewise clear that their source for the text was not Ḥunayn ibn Isḥāq's translation. This is indicated by a quotation from Hippocrates that

---

45 See van Ess, *Theologie und Gesellschaft*, 2:469, 3:23, and 4:208.

46 Gibb, "Argument from Design." On the relationship between *al-Dalāʾil wa-l-iʿtibār*, *al-Fikr wa-l-iʿtibār*, and *al-ʿIbar wa-l-iʿtibār*, see Daiber, *Das theologisch-philosophische System*, 159–60.

47 Gibb, "Argument from Design," 152–4; Theodoret, *On Divine Providence*.

48 Theodoret, *On Divine Providence*, 4 (introduction) and discourse no. 3.

49 Theodoret, *On Divine Providence*, 27; *al-Dalāʾil wa-l-iʿtibār*, 50; *al-ʿIbar wa-l-iʿtibār*, 86.

50 Theodoret, *On Divine Providence*, 37; *al-Dalāʾil wa-l-iʿtibār*, 52; *al-ʿIbar wa-l-iʿtibār*, 87.

TABLE 4.3 *A comparison of corresponding sections in* al-Ḥikma fī makhlūqāt Allāh*,* al-Dalā'il wa-l-iʿtibār*, and* al-ʿIbar wa-l-iʿtibār.

Ḥikma, 63	*Dalā'il*, 58-9	*ʿIbar*, 94-5
أرأيت لو نقص من الإنسان من هذه الصفات الحفظ وحده كيف كون يكون حاله وكان لا يحفظ ماله وما عليه وما أصدر وما أورد وما أعطي وما أخذ وما رأى وما سمع وما قال وما قيل له ولم يذكر من أحسن إليه ولا من أساء له ولا من نفعه ممن ضَرّه وكان لا يهتدي لطريق لو سلكه ولا لعلم ولو درسه ولا ينتفع بتجّربه ولا يستطيع أن يعتبر بمن مضى. فانظر إلى هذه النعم	أرأيت لو نقص من الإنسان من هذه الخلال الحفظ وحده كيف كانت تكون حاله وكم من خلل كان سيدخل عليه في أموره اذا لم يكن يحفظ ماله وما عليه وما أخذ وما أعطي وما رأى وما سمع وما قال وما قيل له ولم يذكر من أحسن إليه ولا من أساء اليه وما نفعه ما ضَرّه ثم كان لا يهتدي الطريق لو سلكه مرارا لا تحصى ولا يعقل علما ولو درسه عمره ولا ينتفع بتجربة ولا يستطيع أن يعبر شيئاً على ما مضى فانظر إلى هذه النعم	أفرأيت لو نقص الإنسان من هذه الخلال و الحفظ واحد كيف كانت تكون حالته اذا لم يحفظ ماله وما قال وما قيل له ولم يذكر من أحسن إليه و تعدى عليه وما نفعه من و كيف كان يرجع في طريق سلكه الى موضع فارقه و متى كان يعي علما و يبقى عليه معرفة شيء و ينتفع بتجربة ويعتبر شيئا بشيء قد غاب عنه خليقا أن يكون أمره بحبك بل كان ينسلخ من الانسانية فانظر من النعمة على الانسان

is reproduced both in *De usu partium* and in the *I'tibār* works. In the passage, Hippocrates describes saliva as the "vehicle of nutrition." Ḥunayn translates this expression straightfowardly as *markab al-ghadhā'*, while the *Iʿtibār* texts contain the more florid translation *maṭiyyat al-ghadhā'*.[51] The discrepancy supports the contention that the Galenic material in the *Iʿtibār* works made its way into the Islamic discourse through late antique reworkings and via a route of translation that bypassed the node of Ḥunayn.

The third/ninth century thus witnessed an influx into Islamic thought of teleological ideas that had initially been crafted by Christian thinkers to counter Manichean and Greek philosophical objections to the existence of God by demonstrating the presence of a divine *télos* in the design and structure of manifest reality. These works drew on Galen's *De usu partium*, which, though

51 Compare *Galen on the Usefulness of the Parts of the Body*, 1:207, and *Manāfiʿ al-aʿḍā'*, fol. 63b, with (Pseudo-)Jāḥiẓ, *al-Dalā'il wa-l-iʿtibār*, 55, and *al-ʿIbar wa-l-iʿtibār*, 92; see also *al-Fikr wa-l-iʿtibār*, fol. 179a, which also has "*maṭiyyat al-ghadhā'*."

not written by an Abrahamitic monotheist, was intended to serve, the author asserts, as a "true hymn of praise to our Creator" (*tasbīḥ wa-taqdīs khāliṣ li-khāliqinā*).[52]

Nature and Scripture

Al-Ghazālī inherited the teleological discourse from the Greek philosophical thought of Galen via the Christian theology of Jibrīl al-Anbārī (and of Diodorus and Theodoret) as well as the Muslim philosophy of Avicenna; these channels are illustrated schematically in Figure 4.2. The primary innovation that al-Ghazālī contributed to this discourse was its integration with Qur'anic scripture. Galen (obviously) and al-Anbārī (evidently) do not quote the Qur'an or any other sacred texts but rather limit their discussions to observable phenomena in nature. Al-Ghazālī, by contrast, embeds the empirical approach firmly in a scriptural framework by establishing inherent links between the two. He begins *al-Ḥikma* with the verse "Say: Behold what is in the heavens and on earth" (Q 10:101), thereby defining the empirical approach as the execution of a divine command. Further, he introduces each section of the work with a Qur'anic verse that demonstrates the correlation between empirical observation and revelation.

Most interesting, however, are al-Ghazālī's reflections on the nature and potential of empiricism at the end of the *Tafakkur* chapter in the *Iḥyā'*:

> When the natural philosopher (*al-ṭabīʿī*) considers all that we have considered [here], his consideration will be a cause of his misguidance (*ḍalālihi*) and misery. And when the divinely aided person considers it, it will be a cause of his guidance and felicity. There is no speck of dust in heaven or on earth that God does not use to misguide through it whomever He wishes and to guide through it whomever He wishes.[53]

Al-Ghazālī stresses that observation of the same phenomena by an enlightened person (*muwaffaq*) on the one hand and by a natural philosopher on the other can lead the two in diametrically opposed directions: the former to guidance and bliss and the latter to misguidance and misery. (After all, Galen rejected prophecy and professed belief in the eternity of the world in *De usu*

---

52 The English translation is from the Greek, but it also fits the Arabic version. *Galen on the Usefulness of the Parts of the Body*, 189; *Manāfiʿ al-aʿḍā'*, fol. 55b.

53 al-Ghazālī, *Iḥyā' ʿulūm al-dīn*, 15:2844.

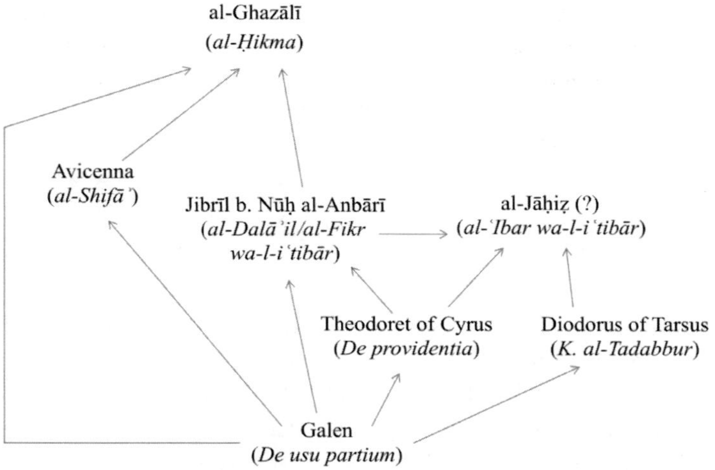

FIGURE 4.2 *Channels of transmission of Galen's teleology.*

partium.) His justification for this conclusion, namely, the statement that every particle in the cosmos can serve as a means of guidance as well as of misguidance, clearly refers to the Qurʾanic verse 2:26, "He guides by it [the Qurʾan] whom He wishes and leads astray (*yuḍillu*) with it whom he wishes, and he misleads no one but the evildoers." Here, then, we have come full circle: observing nature and reading the Qurʾan have been integrated into a single epistemological spectrum. Natural phenomena, in al-Ghazālī's conceptualization, are signs pointing toward God, in precisely the same way that the verses of the Qurʾan are literally signs (*āyāt*). By equating the signs in nature and the signs in scripture, al-Ghazālī is in effect raising the status of empirical observation and justifying the validity of its results, in contrast to the more dismissive attitude displayed by Avicenna toward contemplation of creation as a path to insight.

The Galenic discussions in al-Ghazālī's *al-Maqṣad al-asnā*, *Tafakkur*, and *al-Ḥikma* thus constitute a coherent hermeneutic approach to the cosmos, including humankind, nature, and divine revelation. It is an empiricist and teleological hermeneutics, in the same way that al-Ghazālī's conceptualization of the aims of the law (*maqāṣid al-sharīʿa*) represents an empiricist and teleological ethics: in each area, al-Ghazali begins with individual phenomena and inductively derives from them knowledge of God's commands and nature, respectively. In consequence, both theories suffer from the bane of empirical observation, namely, the inherent uncertainty of the knowledge that inductive reasoning produces. Avicenna still considered this a fatal weakness and dedicated himself to the "high road" of allegedly certain metaphysical enquiry. Al-Ghazālī, on the other hand, appears to have chosen to follow a two-tiered approach, writing on metaphysics for the elite (see, for example, the introduction to his *Mishkāt al-anwār* [*Niche of Lights*])[54] while producing teleological treatises on the wonders of divine providence for non-metaphysicians.

Conclusion

The available evidence clearly suggests that al-Ghazālī was familiar with Galen's *De usu partium*, referencing it in *al-Munqidh* and drawing on it through Ḥunayn's Arabic translation as well as secondhand through Avicenna and through Jibrīl al-Anbārī, whose book, together with a host of similar Christian teleological works, entered Islamic discourse in the third/ninth century. Almost all of al-Ghazālī's teleological vocabulary, enumerated in Table 4.2, can be traced to these earlier works. The influence of this empiricist teleology is evident in al-Ghazālī's writings: he uses Galen's approach to exemplify, derive, and prove divine attributes by pointing at features in nature that create a sense of wonder (*ʿajāʾib*) and thus permit the beholder to follow his or her reason back to the originator of these wondrous features.[55] Al-Ghazālī employs the same teleological approach in the *Shifāʾ al-ghalīl* and in *al-Mustaṣfā*, arguing that divine law, like nature, displays a teleology that allows humans to learn about God (in the case of law, about His commands and His prohibitions) and that can be used fruitfully in the process of legal reasoning. In the realm of law this injection of a teleological methodology marked a breakthrough by providing a coherent and practical basis for the inclusion of considerations of human benefit in legal reasoning.[56]

Taking into account the influence of Galenic teleology on al-Ghazālī's thought helps us make sense of his otherwise perplexing views on creation, which fuse a voluntarist conception of God's activity with the famously cryptic statement that "there is in possibility nothing more wondrous than what is" (*laysa fī al-imkān abdaʿ mimmā kān*).[57] One could read both *Tafakkur* and *al-Ḥikma* as commentaries and defenses of this statement, that is, as empirical investigations into the perfect design that is observable in creation. The

54 al-Ghazālī, *Mishkāt al-anwār*, 1–2.

55 al-Ghazālī, *al-Ḥikma fī makhlūqāt Allāh*, 17–18.

56 See Opwis, *Maṣlaḥa and the Purpose of the Law*, 65, and El Shamsy, "The Wisdom of God's Law."

57 Griffel, *Al-Ghazālī's Philosophical Theology*, 226.

confusion arises from mistakenly seeing al-Ghazālī in conversation either with the theological currents of Ashʿarite voluntarism and Muʿtazilite rationalism or with Avicennan philosophy, in which, as Frank Griffel has noted, "observational or empirical evidence of the perfection of God's creation plays next to no role."[58] In contrast to these, Galenic teleology, with its empirically grounded claim that the world was created with the utmost providence (*bi-l-ʿināya allatī lā ʿināya baʿdahu*),[59] enabled al-Ghazālī to argue for the perfection of creation without limiting divine agency.

What is remarkable is the seamlessness with which al-Ghazālī's manages to fuse Galenic thought with Qurʾanic descriptions of divine providence. Rather than being forced to rely solely on Galenic ideas to introduce teleology into the legal, philosophical, and theological debates of his time, al-Ghazālī appears to recover an element that was already present in the Qurʾan. The cluster of works discussed above shows that teleology, and particularly Galen's ideas, had been a hot topic in late antiquity, and the Qurʾanic discussion could fruitfully be read in the context of and in conversation with this debate. Nor did teleological arguments remain limited to the Qurʾan. Al-Ashʿarī himself was not averse to teleological reasoning,[60] and the famous *ḥadīth*-scholar Abū Ismāʿīl al-Khaṭṭābī (d. 388/998) penned a theological tract that emphasized the empirical dimension of reason and its ability to recognize design in nature.[61] By al-Ghazālī's time, however, teleology had fallen out of the discourses in which he participated, excepting some less rigorous discussions in works of Sufism.[62] Drawing directly and indirectly on Galen but at the same time grounding his approach squarely in scripture, al-Ghazālī succeeded in reintroducing teleology into the discourses of law and theology, which had become formalistic and voluntarist to the extent that they excluded considerations of divine design.

As of yet, there has been no systematic study of teleological thought in Islam that would allow us to judge the influence of al-Ghazālī's embrace of the teleological approach on later thought. However, a tentative survey demonstrates that Galenic teleology remains visible in the work of several major thinkers who followed al-Ghazālī, including Ibn Rushd (d. 595/1198), Ibn al-Nafīs (d. 687/1288), Ibn Taymiyya (d. 728/1328), and Ibn Qayyim al-Jawziyya

58 Ibid.

59 Galen, *Manāfiʿ al-aʿḍāʾ*, fol. 34b.

60 See, e.g., al-Ashʿarī, *Risāla ilā ahl al-thaghr*, 147–56.

61 al-Khaṭṭābī, *al-Ghunya ʿan al-kalām wa-ahlihi*.

62 Griffel, *Al-Ghazālī's Philosophical Theology*, 226.

(d. 751/1351).[63] These appear to have deployed such teleological ideas to counterbalance the increasingly transcendentalizing forms of later Ashʿarism, which posited an unknowable God who created without purpose. The integration of Galenic teleology thus demonstrates that forms of Sunnī thought continued to draw actively, creatively, and explicitly on Greek philosophy in order to critique developments within Sunnī theology.

Bibliography

al-Anbārī, Jibrīl ibn Nūḥ. *al-Fikr wa-l-iʿtibār*. MS Istanbul, Ayasofya 4836, fols. 160a–187b.

al-Aʿsam, ʿAbd al-Amīr. *al-Faylasūf al-Ghazālī: Iʿādat taqwīm li-munḥanā taṭawwurihi al-rūḥī*. 3rd ed. Beirut: Dār al-Andalus, 1981.

al-Ashʿarī, ʿAlī ibn Ismāʿīl. *Risāla ilā ahl al-thaghr*. Edited by ʿA. Sh. M. al-Jundī. Medina: Maktabat al-ʿUlūm wa-l-Ḥikam, 2002.

———. *Kitāb al-Lumaʿ fī l-radd ʿalā ahl al-zaygh wa-l-bidʿa*. Edited by Ḥ. Ghurāba. Cairo: Maṭbaʿat Miṣr, 1955.

Badawī, ʿAbd al-Raḥmān. *Muʾallafāt al-Ghazālī*. Cairo: al-Majlis al-Aʿlā li-Riʿāyat al-Funūn wa-l-Adab, 1961.

Baneth, David Z. "The Common Teleological Source of Baḥya ibn Paqūda and al-Ghazālī" [in Hebrew]. In *Sefer Magnes* (*Magnes Anniversary Book*). Edited by F. Baer et al. Jerusalem: Hebrew University, 1938. 23–30.

Bergsträsser, Gotthelf. "Ḥunain ibn Isḥāq über die syrischen und arabischen Galen-Übersetzungen." *Abhandlungen für die Kunde des Morgenlandes* 17, no. 2 (1925).

Bouyges, Maurice. *Essai de chronologie des oeuvres de al-Ghazali*. Edited by M. Allard. Beirut: Imprimerie Catholique, 1959.

Daiber, Hans. *Das theologisch-philosophische System des Muʿammar ibn ʿAbbād as-Sulamī (gest. 830 n. Chr.)* Wiesbaden: F. Steiner, 1975.

El Shamsy, Ahmed. "The Wisdom of God's Law: Two Theories." In *Islamic Law in Theory: Studies on Jurisprudence in Honor of Bernard Weiss*. Edited by A. Kevin Reinhart and Robert Gleave. Leiden: Brill, 2014. 19–37.

Galen of Pergamon. *Galen on the Usefulness of the Parts of the Body*. Transl. by M. May. 2 vols. Ithaca, NY: Cornell University Press, 1968.

———. *Manāfiʿ al-aʿḍāʾ*. MS Paris, Bibliothèque Nationale de France, Fonds arabe 2853.

Gibb, Hamilton A. R. "The Argument from Design." In *Ignace Goldziher Memorial Volume*. Vol. 1. Edited by S. Löwinger and J. Somogyi. Budapest: w.p., 1948. 150–62.

63 Ibn Rushd, *Manāhij al-adilla*, 122; Ibn Taymiyya, *Bayān talbīs al-jahmiyya*, 1:499; Ibn al-Nafīs, *Sharḥ tashrīḥ al-Qānūn*, 25; Ibn Qayyim, *Miftāḥ dār al-saʿāda*, 2:223–27.

al-Ghazālī, Muḥammad ibn Muḥammad. *al-Ḥikma fī makhlūqāt Allāh ʿazza wa-jalla*. Edited by R. F. ʿAbd al-Muṭṭalib and ʿA. ʿA. Mazīd. Cairo: Maktabat al-Khānjī, 1422/2002.

———. *Iḥyāʾ ʿulūm al-dīn*. 16 parts. Cairo: Lajnat Nashr al-Thaqāfa al-Islāmiyya. Cairo 1356–57 [1937–38].

———. *al-Maqṣad al-asnā fi sharḥ maʿānī asmāʾ Allāh al-ḥusnā*. Edited by F. A. Shehadi. 2nd ed. Beirut: Dār al-Mashriq, 1982.

———. *al-Munqidh min al-ḍalāl / Erreur et deliverance*. Edition and French transl. by F. Jabre. 2nd ed. Beirut: Commission libanaise pour la traduction des chefs-d'œuvre, 1969.

———. *The Niche of Lights / Mishkāt al-anwār*. Edited and transl. by D. Buchman. Provo (Utah): Brigham Young University Press, 1998.

———. *Ninety-Nine Names of God in Islam*. Transl. by R. Stade. Ibadan (Nigeria): Daystar Press, 1970.

———. *Shifāʾ al-ghalīl fī bayān al-shabah wa-l-mukhīl wa-masālik al-taʿlīl*. Edited by Ḥ. al-Kubaysī. Baghdad: Maṭbaʿat al-Irshād, 1971.

Griffel, Frank. *Al-Ghazālī's Philosophical Theology*. Oxford: Oxford University Press, 2009.

Hankinson, R. J. *Cause and Explanation in Ancient Greek Thought*. Oxford: Oxford University Press, 1998.

Ibn al-Nafīs, ʿAlī ibn Abī l-Ḥazm. *Sharḥ tashrīḥ al-Qānūn*. Edited by S. al-Qaṭāya. Cairo: al-Hayʾa al-Miṣriyya al-ʿĀmma li-l-Kutub, 1988.

Ibn Qayyim al-Jawziyya, Muḥammad ibn Abī Bakr. *Miftāḥ dār al-saʿāda*. Edited by ʿA. al-Ḥ. al-Ḥalabī. 3 vols. Khobar (Saudi Arabia): Dār Ibn ʿAffān, 1997.

Ibn Rushd, Muḥammad ibn Aḥmad. *Manāhij al-adilla*. Edited by M. ʿA. al-Jābirī. Beirut: Markaz al-Dirāsāt al-Waḥda al-ʿArabiyya, 1988.

Ibn Sīnā, al-Ḥusayn ibn ʿAbdallāh. *al-Ishārāt wa-l-tanbīhāt*. Edited by S. Dunyā. 4 vols. Cairo: Dār al-Maʿārif, 1960–8.

———. *The Metaphysics of The Healing / al-Shifāʾ: al-Ilāhiyyāt*. Edited and transl. by M. E. Marmura. Provo (Ut.): Brigham Young University Press, 2005.

Ibn Taymiyya, Aḥmad ibn ʿAbd al-Ḥalīm. *Bayān talbīs al-jahmiyya*. Edited by Y. al-Hunaydī. 10 vols. Riyadh (Saudi Arabia): Majmaʿ al-Malik Fahd, 1426/2005.

———. *Darʾ taʿāruḍ al-ʿaql wa-l-naql*. Edited by M. R. Sālim. 2nd ed. 11 vols. Riyadh (Saudi Arabia): Jāmiʿat al-Imām Muḥammad ibn Saʿūd al-Islāmiyya, 1991.

(Pseudo-)Jāḥiẓ. *al-Dalāʾil wa-l-iʿtibār*. Aleppo: Maṭbaʿat al-Ṭabbākh, 1928.

al-Jāḥiẓ (?). *al-ʿIbar wa-l-iʿtibār*. Cairo: al-ʿArabī, 1994.

Janssens, Jules. "Al-Ghazālī's *Tahāfut*: Is It Really a Rejection of Ibn Sīnā's Philosophy?" *Journal of Islamic Studies* 12 (2001): 1–17.

Kātib Çelebī Ḥājjī Khalīfa, Muṣṭafā ibn ʿAbdallāh. *Kashf al-ẓunūn ʿan asāmī l-kutub wa-l-funūn*. Edited by Ş. Yaltkaya and R. Bilge. 2nd ed. 2 vols. Istanbul: Milli Eğitim Basimevi, 1971–72.

al-Khaṭṭābī, Abū Ismāʿīl Ḥamd ibn Muḥammad. *al-Ghunya ʿan al-kalām wa-ahlihi*. Cairo: Dār al-Minhāj, 2004.

Lobel, Diana. *A Sufi-Jewish Dialogue: Philosophy and Mysticism in Baḥya b. Paqūda's "Duties of the Heart."* Philadelphia: University of Pennsylvania Press, 2007.

Menn, Stephen. "The *Discourse on the Method* and the Tradition of Intellectual Autobiography." In *Hellenistic and Early Modern Philosophy*. Edited by J. Miller and B. Inwood. Cambridge: Cambridge University Press, 2003. 141–91.

al-Murtaḍā al-Zabīdī, Muḥammad ibn Muḥammad. *Itḥāf al-sāda al-muttaqīn bi-sharḥ Iḥyāʾ ʿulūm al-dīn*. 10 vols. Cairo: al-Maṭbaʿa al-Maymaniyya, 1311 [1894].

Neumark, David. *Geschichte der jüdischen Philosophie im Mittelalter*. 2 vols. in 3. Berlin: Reimer, 1907–28.

Opwis, Felicitas. *Maṣlaḥa and the Purpose of the Law: Islamic Discourse on Legal Change from the 4th/10th to 8th/14th Century*. Leiden: Brill, 2010.

Ormsby, Eric L. *Theodicy in Islamic Thought: The Dispute over al-Ghazālī's "Best of All Possible Worlds."* Princeton: Princeton University Press, 1984.

al-Qaffāl al-Shāshī, Muḥammad ibn ʿAlī. *Maḥāsin al-sharīʿa*. Edited by A. ʿA. Samak. Beirut: Dār al-Kutub al-ʿIlmiyya, 2007.

Sezgin, Fuat. *Geschichte des arabischen Schrifttums*. 13 vols. Leiden: Brill, 1967–.

Schacht, Joseph, and Max Meyerhof. "Maimonides against Galen on Philosophy and Cosmogony." *Bulletin of the Faculty of Arts, Cairo University*, May 1937: 53–88.

Schreiner, Martin. Review of *Résumé des réflexions sur l'âme de Baḥya ben Joseph ibn Paḳuda*, transl. by Isaac Broydé. *Zeitschrift für Hebräische Bibliographie* 1 (1896–7): 121–28.

Theodoret of Cyrus. *On Divine Providence*. Transl. by T. Halton. New York: Newman Press, 1988.

Ullmann, Manfred. *Die Medizin im Islam*. Leiden: E. J. Brill, 1970.

van Ess, Josef. *Theologie und Gesellschaft im 2. und 3. Jahrhundert Hidschra: Eine Geschichte des religiösen Denkens im frühen Islam*. 6 vols. Berlin: Walter de Gruyter, 1991–97.

Yahuda, Abraham S. *Prolegomena zu einer erstmaligen Herausgabe des Kitāb al-hidāja ʾila farāʾiḍ al-qulūb [ḥovot ha-levavot] von Bachja ibn Josef ibn Paqūda aus dem ʾAndalus nebst einer grösseren Textbeilage*. Frankfurt: J. Kauffmann, 1904.

Zysow, Aron. "The Economy of Certainty: An Introduction to the Typology of Islamic Legal Theory." Ph.D. dissertation, Harvard University, 1984.

———. "Two Theories of the Obligation to Obey God's Commands." In *The Law Applied: Contextualizing the Islamic Shariʿa; A Volume in Honor of Frank E. Vogel*. Edited by P. Bearman et al. London: I. B. Tauris, 2008. 397–421.

CHAPTER 5

Al-Ghazālī and *Kalām*

The Conundrum of His Body-Soul Dualism

Ayman Shihadeh

My aim in this article is twofold. First, I shall interpret two discussions in al-Ghazālī's main *kalām* compendium, *al-Iqtiṣād fī l-iʿtiqād* (*The Balanced Book on What-To-Believe*), which appear discrepant with the substance dualism espoused in some of his other works, and instead seem to coincide with the materialist ontology and anthropology of classical Ashʿarism.[1] Although both discussions have already received a fair amount of attention, the discrepancies have hitherto remained either unresolved or unexplained. The present study shall attempt to resolve an ostensible discrepancy in one discussion and to identify and explain a real and serious discrepancy in the other. By doing so, it will shed light on the main dilemmas and sensitivities that al-Ghazālī's subscription to substance dualism presented him in a *kalām* setting.

Second, I will advocate a more general point, namely that interpreting al-Ghazālī's *kalām* works—including *al-Iqtiṣād* and, to an extent, the more advanced *Tahāfut*—must take account of his views on the objectives and workings of *kalām* in general.[2] It will be argued that his low view of the discipline of *kalām* (low, that is, in comparison both to the earlier Ashʿarī high view thereof and to his view of his own higher theology), affects his choice of doctrines defended and arguments deployed in *al-Iqtiṣād*, as well as aspects of his style of presentation. These in turn will explain the incongruence between his views in this work and positions championed in some of his other works.

1 See Shihadeh, "Classical Ashʿarī Anthropology." On al-Ghazālī's body-soul dualism, see Kukkonen, "Receptive to Reality," Treiger, *Inspired Knowledge in Islamic Thought*, Gianotti, *Al-Ghazālī's Unspeakable Doctrine of the Soul*, Frank, *Al-Ghazālī and the Ashʿarite School*, 48–67, Griffel, "Al-Ġazālī's Concept of Prophecy," idem, "Review," Hennig, "Ghazali on Immaterial Substances," Sīdbī, *Naẓariyyat al-nafs bayna Ibn Sīnā wa-l-Ghazālī*, Abū Saʿda, *al-Āthār al-sīnawiyya fī madhhab al-Ghazālī fī l-nafs al-insāniyya*.

2 This point follows on from my earlier article, "From al-Ghazālī to al-Rāzī." Both the present study and this earlier article concentrate on al-Ghazālī's *kalām* output, rather than his theology in general.

 | DOI 10.1163/9789004307490_006

1 *Iqtiṣād*, Eschatology

Our first problematic passage occurs in the discussion on resurrection (*ḥashr*) in the eschatological part of *al-Iqtiṣād*, the main context in which the ontology and nature of the spirit (*rūḥ*, *nafs*) are normally propounded in a *kalām* source.[3] Resurrection is treated in the section on doctrines characterised as being affirmed by revelation and confirmed as possible by the mind (otherwise known as the *samʿiyyāt*, "matters known through revelation"), which are all eschatological.[4] Al-Ghazālī defines resurrection as God's restoration (*iʿāda*) of the bodies of the dead on the Day of Judgement.[5] He affirms the doctrine on the basis of "unambiguous" scriptural evidence, and argues that the restoration of human bodies is possible on the grounds that God was capable of creating them the first time, and hence must be capable of creating them a second time.[6] This is the standard, Qur'ān-inspired theological argument.[7]

Next, he turns to the ontology of restoration, particularly the manner in which the atoms and accidents of bodies are restored.[8] That some accidents of the human body need to be re-created is obvious. For when the body dies, it immediately loses its animate attributes, such as life, knowledge and volition; and as it decays it loses further accidents, such as composition (*tarkīb*), colour and moisture. Less obvious is whether God causes the atoms of the human body (and all other atoms of the world) to pass away as well, and correspondingly whether resurrection involves the re-creation *ex nihilo* of both the body's atoms and accidents, or the restoring only of its accidents. Both scenarios, al-Ghazālī opines, are rationally possible, and both remain possible since neither is supported by scriptural evidence.[9]

Delineating these models of the ontology of restoration leads to the problem of the identity of the entities "restored" (*al-muʿād*): in particular, whether the individual entity re-created in the resurrected body—be the entity an atom or an accident—would be none other than (*ʿayn*) the individual entity

3 al-Ghazālī, *al-Iqtiṣād*, 213–15. Unless noted otherwise, all references to *al-Iqtiṣād* are to the edition of I. A. Çubukçu and H. Atay published 1962 in Ankara. On earlier Ashʿarite discussions of the spirit, see Shihadeh, "Classical Ashʿarī Anthropology," 436–7, 465–74.

4 Al-Ghazālī uses the standard label *al-samʿiyyāt* in *al-Risāla al-Qudsiyya*, 92–4, 118–22. The text is also part of al-Ghazālī, *Iḥyāʾ ʿulūm al-dīn*, 2:199–202.

5 al-Ghazālī, *al-Iqtiṣād*, 213.

6 Ibid., 213.

7 Cf. Q 7:29, 21:104, 36:79, 36:81, 50:15.

8 al-Ghazālī, *al-Iqtiṣād*, 213–14.

9 The suspension of judgment on this point is a standard classical Ashʿarite position. See, for instance, al-Juwaynī, *al-Irshād*, 374.

that existed in the body before it died, or only a replica (*mithl*) thereof. Al-Ghazālī here defends bodily resurrection against the backdrop of Avicenna's denial thereof, in particular, his view that an entity supposedly "returned" into existence, having gone from prior existence into non-existence, is not the same entity that existed before, but only a replica.[10] In the case of accidents, he explains briefly that this question poses no difficulty for him and his fellow Ashʿarīs, since "in our view" (*ʿinda-nā*) no accident continues to exist (*yabqā*) for more than one moment in the first place, as each accident must be re-created, or "renewed" (*yatajaddadu*), at each moment. Accordingly, the accident "restored" (*iʿāda*) in an atom need not be the very same accident that existed therein prior to the death of the body.[11] In this case, the identity of the individual human being will be preserved in his body, i.e. in the atoms that constitute it. As to the atoms, although they too are susceptible to passing away, if God so wills, the preservation of their identity will be guaranteed through their presence in God's knowledge. An atom, therefore, can pass away and then, properly speaking, be restored, whereas a replica is an entity that comes to be having had no pre-existence.[12]

The discussion of the ontology of resurrection and the identity of the individual restored leads to the passage that concerns us most. Here is a translation of the passage as it appears in the standard edition of *al-Iqtiṣād*:

> [¶1] We have discussed this question (*masʾala*) [i.e. bodily resurrection] at length in the *Tahāfut*.
>
> [¶2] To refute (*ibṭāl*) [the philosophers'] doctrine, we followed [this method]: affirming (*taqrīr*) that the soul, which, according to them, does not occupy space, continues to exist (*baqāʾ*) [after the death of the body]; and postulating (*taqdīr*) that it returns to the governance of a body, whether it be the very same body of the individual or another. This is a forced consequent (*ilzām*) that does not correspond to what we ourselves believe. For that book was written to refute their doctrines, not to affirm true doctrines.
>
> [¶3] Rather, since they considered what a human is, he is with respect to his soul, and that his involvement in the governance of a body is, as it were, accidental to him and the body is an instrument for him, we forced them (*alzamnā-hum*), given their belief that the soul continues to exist, to concede that they must affirm the resurrection (*wujūb al-taṣdīq*

10 Ibn Sīnā, *Shifāʾ*, *Ilāhiyyāt*, 28–29; cf. Marmura, "Bodily Resurrection," 282–3.

11 al-Ghazālī, *al-Iqtiṣād*, 213–14.

12 Ibid., 214–15. On this point, see Marmura, "Bodily Resurrection," 284.

> *bi-l-iʿāda*), which is for the soul to return to the governance of some body or other (*badan min al-abdān*).
>
> [¶4] To discuss this subject further to get to the truth of the matter would lead us to investigate the spirit (*al-rūḥ*), the soul (*al-nafs*), life and the reality (*ḥaqīqa*) of each. However, creedal works (*al-muʿtaqadāt*) are not suited to delving to these great depths in rational subjects (*al-maʿqūlāt*).[13] Accordingly, what we have said suffices for establishing the right balance of belief (*al-iqtiṣād fī l-iʿtiqād*) in order to confirm what is taught in revelation.[14]

This passage has been interpreted as indicating that in *al-Iqtiṣād* al-Ghazālī espouses the materialist anthropology of classical Ashʿarism and opposes the philosophical theory of the rational soul, and that although he appears in the *Tahāfut* to subscribe to the latter theory, he does so only for the sake of argument. Some discussions in the *Tahāfut* indeed suggest that he does subscribe to this philosophical theory, so his above remark that certain views expressed in the *Tahāfut* are not true expressions of his beliefs was taken to refer to the theory as a whole.[15] This reading is represented by Marmura:

> The above statement speaks for itself. Al-Ghazālī's declaration that in the *Tahāfut* he defended a doctrine that acknowledges the immateriality of the human soul simply for the sake of argument is quite explicit. This is not the doctrine he holds to be true. The true doctrine is that of the *kalām* (in one of its versions).[16]

I will argue that this interpretation is erroneous. A slightly different reading is proposed by Richard M. Frank, who finds some ambiguity in the passage:

---

13 That *al-muʿtaqadāt* here refers to relatively basic theological works meant to establish creed (*ʿaqīda*) is confirmed in other occurrences of the expression in *al-Iqtiṣād* (50; 221; 233; 234). Compare this to the sense in which "*ʿaqīda*" refers to a genre.

14 al-Ghazālī, *al-Iqtiṣād*, 215.1–10 (all translations are my own). An important variant will be discussed below. For earlier, partial translations of this passage, see: Frank, *Al-Ghazālī and the Ashʿarite School*, 55; Gianotti, *Unspeakable Doctrine of the Soul*, 74; Marmura, "Bodily Resurrection," 284–5; Nakamura, "Was Ghazālī an Ashʿarite?," 16.

15 For a summary see Marmura, "Bodily Resurrection," 279–82, and Gianotti, *Unspeakable Doctrine of the Soul*, 88 ff.

16 Marmura, "Bodily Resurrection," 285; cf. 273–4; Nakamura, "Was Ghazālī an Ashʿarite?" 16; Gianotti, *Unspeakable Doctrine of the Soul*, 74.

> That is, as the basis of the argument in *Tahāfut*[17] he accepted their theses that (a) the soul does not die, that (b) its relation to the body which it governs does not belong to it essentially but only temporarily, but rather (c) it uses the body as an instrument, in order to show that one must assert that the soul returns to govern a body ... He says that the premises of the argument do not correspond to his own belief concerning what is true. Because of the way the paragraph is cast, however, it is not immediately clear exactly what element or elements of the premises of the argument or its conclusion he may reject or accept.[18]

Nonetheless, Frank too reads the passage as a 'denial of ... something that he manifestly believes', namely 'the immateriality of the soul.'[19] So the problem we are presented with is that, according to one reading, the above passage contradicts views that al-Ghazālī expresses elsewhere, since a materialist conception of humans contradicts the substance dualism championed in the *Iḥyāʾ ʿulūm al-dīn* (*Revival of the Religious Sciences*) and other works, and according to another reading, it is ambiguous. Neither reading attempts to explain the one or two arguments described.

Let us take a closer look at this passage. From the broader context, it is clear that "this topic" (¶ 1) denotes the problem of the restoration of the body, which al-Ghazālī treats in Discussion 20 of the *Tahāfut*. It follows that "their doctrine" (¶ 2)—the philosophical doctrine said to have been refuted—refers precisely to Avicenna's denial of bodily resurrection, which finds expression here in the aforementioned notion that once a thing passes away, it cannot be brought back into existence.

Each of ¶ 2 and ¶ 3 describes, rather ambiguously, an argument through which the refutation is executed. That a specific line of reasoning is being described is confirmed by the expression "we followed a certain method" (*salaknā*), which introduces ¶ 2. The two descriptions could be referring to two distinct arguments, or to one and the same argument. The verbal noun "*ilzām*" (¶ 2) and the verb "*alzama*" (¶ 3) identify the reasoning involved in both cases as an *ad hominem* (*ex concessis*) argument, which is a type of argument prevalent in classical *kalām*.[20] An argument can be classed as *ad hominem* if, in order to refute another party's position, the arguer premises the argument on

17 Referring to al-Ghazālī, *Tahāfut al-falāsifa*, ed. Marmura 218ff., ed. Bouyges 362ff.

18 Frank, *Al-Ghazālī and the Ashʿarite School*, 55–6.

19 Frank, *Al-Ghazālī and the Ashʿarite School*, 56; 65; 91.

20 I render "*ilzām*" as "*ad hominem* argument" in the sense of an argument *ex concessis*, from commitment, rather than in the more popular sense of an attack on a person's character

one or more views held by the other party (the antecedent, or antecedents), and concludes that they must concede another view (the consequent), which is, one way or another, problematic to them. The antecedent (or antecedents) will be granted, and the consequent will be affirmed, both for the sake of argument. So the arguer's own position on the antecedents and the consequent is, in principle, of no immediate bearing on the argument.

Now, as shown in the synoptic table on p. 119 the *ad hominem* argument described in ¶ 3—to start with the least problematic of the two descriptions—seems premised on two antecedents: (a) the notion that "human" (*insān*) properly speaking denotes the immaterial rational soul, and that the body serves only as an instrument for the soul, and (b) the view that the rational soul is indestructible and hence survives the death of the body. According to ¶ 3, the argument somehow proves—we are not told exactly how—that by subscribing to these two Avicennan views, one must then concede a third view, namely that after the death of its original body the soul *must* return to the governance of some body or other, be that the very same original body or an entirely different one. This consequent contradicts Avicenna's views on the soul's immortality.

The argument described in ¶ 2 is harder to decipher. Particularly problematic are the two verbal nouns "affirming" (*taqrīr*) and "postulating" (*taqdīr*), which introduce the doctrines mentioned and link them together. It seems that the argument described here starts by affirming two doctrines: (a) the soul's indestructibility, such that it survives the death of the body, and (b) the soul's immateriality. These are the same two antecedents stated in ¶ 3. The consequent too is the same as in ¶ 3—namely that the soul returns to the governance of the body to which it was originally connected or a different body—except that in ¶ 2 this consequent is only "postulated" (i.e. conceded as possible), whereas in ¶ 3 it is said to be entailed *necessarily* by the antecedents. What is described in ¶ 2 is an unmistakably weaker argument.

Notwithstanding this discrepancy, I believe that ¶ 2 and ¶ 3 are meant to describe one and the same argument, given the correspondence between the antecedents and the consequent in both cases. ¶ 3 appears intended only to clarify the point made at the end of ¶ 2. The discrepancy can be resolved if we make a slight adjustment to the text of ¶ 2, which is to swap the expressions "*taqrīr*" and "*taqdīr*" on the grounds that the two can appear very similar in

---

instead of their views (see Walton, *Ad Hominem Arguments*, 21ff.; 104 ff.; Shihadeh, "The Argument from Ignorance," 196, n. 75).

TABLE 5.1 *Synoptic table analysing the argument described in each of ¶¶ 2 and 3.*

Element	Description	¶ 3	¶ 2
Type of argument	*Ad hominem* argument (*ilzām*).	ألزمناهم	سلكنا في إبطال مذهبهم … وذلك إلزام لا يوافق ما نعتقده
Antecedent I	The human soul is immaterial and separate from the body.	قدروا أن الإنسان هو ما هو باعتبار نفسه، وأن اشتغاله بتدبير البدن كالعارض له والبدن آلة له	هي [= النفس] غير متحيز عندهم
Antecedent II	The soul survives the death of the body.	اعتقادهم بقاء النفس	تقرير بقاء النفس
Consequent	The soul returns to the governance of a body, whether it be its original body or a different body.	وجوب التصديق بالإعادة، وذلك برجوع النفس إلى تدبير بدن من الأبدان	تقدير عود تدبيرها إلى البدن، سواءً كان ذلك البدن هو عين جسم الإنسان أو غيره

some manuscript hands, and that "*taqrīr*" in fact appears as "*taqdīr*" in some manuscript copies.[21] The modified reading would go as follows:

> [¶2] To refute [the philosophers'] doctrine, we followed [this method]: postulating (*taqdīr*) that the soul, which, according to them, does not occupy space, continues to exist [after the death of the body]; and affirming (*taqrīr*) that it returns to the governance of a body, whether it be the very same body of the individual or another.

This reading has the advantage of being consistent with ¶ 3, in that the arguer hypothesises the antecedents and affirms the consequent, forcing the opponent to concede it as necessary (rather than merely as possible). As we shall see, however, the original reading of ¶ 2 is more consonant with the actual

21 As in one manuscript used for the 1962 edition (see *al-Iqtiṣād*, 215.2–3), and in MS Dublin, Chester Beatty, Ar 3372 (ff. 56a–b), which is dated 517/1123. Also, two recent uncritical editions, which use different manuscript copies, read '*taqdīr*' (ed. al-Sharfāwī, 2012, 274; and ed. 'Imrān, 2009, 489). Neither edition, however, is furnished with a critical apparatus.

discussion in the *Tahāfut*. So, having proposed what seems in some respects a compelling modified reading, I must for now suspend judgement on it.

II Correspondences with the *Tahāfut* and Avicennan Texts

The closest match in the *Tahāfut al-falāsifa* (*The Incoherence of the Philosophers*) for the argument described in the above passage from *al-Iqtiṣād* occurs in the 20th discussion, on the philosophers' denial of bodily resurrection, in the course of al-Ghazālī's response to philosophical arguments against this notion.[22] In both content and organisation, the first philosophical argu-

22 al-Ghazālī, *Tahāfut al-falāsifa*, ed. Marmura 218–220, ed. Bouyges 363–6. Another argument that bears resemblance to the description appears in Discussion 19 (*Tahāfut*, 202–5 / 335–9) among objections to Ibn Sīnā's theory that the human soul is incorruptible and everlasting, particularly his argument that since the soul exists independently of the body, which only serves as its instrument, and since it has its own intellectual activity, which is independent of the body, it does not pass away with the death of the body (*Tahāfut*, 201–2/ 333–4). The *ad hominem* argument in question starts from Ibn Sīnā's views (i) that an individual human soul must have a connection (*ʿalāqa*) to an individual human body that particularises (*khaṣṣaṣa*) one to the other, and, as al-Ghazālī puts it, (ii) that the temporal origination of the human body is a condition (*sharṭ*) only for the temporal origination of the human soul, but not for its continued existence (cf. *al-Shifāʾ*, *al-Ṭabīʿiyyāt*, *al-Nafs*, 223–5; 227–31; *al-Najāt*, 378–86; on Ibn Sīnā's views on the soul-body relationship, see Druart, "The Human Soul's Individuation and its Survival after the Body's Death," 259–73). For Ibn Sīnā, since the body is only an accidental cause, rather than an essential cause, for the origination of the soul, it cannot be an essential cause for its continued existence. Al-Ghazālī argues that on account of the same connection between the body and the soul, it is not unlikely (*lā yabʿudu*) that the body be a condition for the soul's continued existence (*baqāʾ*), such that if this relation is severed the soul would cease to exist (*Tahāfut*, 202–3 / 335–7). Even if, as Ibn Sīnā maintains, the connection between each pair of body and soul is due to an obscure mutual correspondence (*munāsaba majhūla*) between the two, which connects both entities without making the soul ontologically dependent on the body as an effect is to its cause, it may (*laʿalla*, *lā yabʿudu*) still be the case that this mutual correspondence be such in nature that its severance leads to the passing away of the soul (*Tahāfut*, 202–5 / 337–9). Ibn Sīnā writes that the mutual correspondence is obscure to us (*khafiya ʿalaynā*; Ibn Sīnā, *al-Shifāʾ*, *al-Ṭabīʿiyyāt*, *al-Nafs*, 225; *al-Najāt*, 378). If the soul passes away with the death of the body—al-Ghazālī then remarks without committing himself to this view—God may bring it back into existence when He resurrects the body. He concludes that Ibn Sīnā's foregoing proof for the soul's surviving the death of the body is unreliable (*lā thiqa bi-l-dalīl*) (*Tahāfut*, 204.18 / 339.1). There are important differences between this argument and the one described in *al-Iqtiṣād*: there is only partial overlap among the antecedents, and the consequent here

ment is based closely, often verbatim, on Avicenna's refutation of theological conceptions of bodily resurrection in his eschatological work, *The Epistle on "the Return" for the Feast of Sacrifice* (*al-Risāla al-Aḍḥawiyya fī l-maʿād*), a key source that hitherto has remained unidentified. To this, al-Ghazālī adds further sub-arguments compiled from other Avicennan works, especially *al-Shifāʾ*. The Avicennan argument, as set out by al-Ghazālī, is that all conceivable models of bodily resurrection, be they actually-held beliefs or purely hypothetical models, are impossible. The following three models are eliminated in turn.[23]

The first model is that a human consists of the body alone, animated by the accident of life, and that no soul exists; so resurrection only involves restoring the structure of the body and endowing it with life.[24] This view is rejected by Avicenna on the aforementioned grounds that since the individual human being ceases to exist after death the "restored" body would not in fact be the same as the original body, but only a replica thereof, which is created anew (*ustuʾnifa*).[25] Restoration, in the sense of re-existentiation, is inconceivable.

The second model is that a human consists of body and soul (*nafs*), that the soul survives the death of the body, and that God resurrects the individual by reconstituting his or her body out of its original particles and returning the soul to it.[26] There is no indication whether the soul hypothesised here is material or immaterial. This model is rejected on the grounds that the "original particles" of the body are either those that constituted it at the moment of death, or those that remained constant in the body throughout the individual's life. The former possibility cannot be the case, as it implies that some inhabitants of heaven would be emaciated or mutilated, a truly discommodious state of affairs. The latter too can be eliminated on the grounds that the particles of one human body can become constituents of another either directly through cannibalism or indirectly through the food chain, and that a particle constituting one bodily organ can be cycled within the body to become a constituent of

---

is that the soul's existence may be dependent on its connection to its original body, as opposed to any body whatsoever.

23 al-Ghazālī, *Tahāfut al-falāsifa*, ed. Marmura 215–17, ed. Bouyges 356–63; cf. Ibn Sīnā, *al-Risāla al-Aḍḥawiyya*, ed. Lucchetta 21–97, ed. ʿĀṣī 91–114.

24 This conception of man is found in earlier Ashʿarism, and is attributed to Abū l-Ḥasan al-Ashʿarī and al-Bāqillānī, see my "Classical Ashʿarī Anthropology," 466–70.

25 al-Ghazālī, *Tahāfut al-falāsifa*, ed. Marmura 215–17, ed. Bouyges 356–7; 358–60; cf. Ibn Sīnā, *al-Shifāʾ*, *al-Ilāhiyyāt*, 28–29; Ibn Sīnā, *al-Risāla al-Aḍḥawiyya*, ed. Lucchetta 63–69, ed. ʿĀṣī 103–4.

26 al-Ghazālī, *Tahāfut al-falāsifa*, ed. Marmura 215, ed. Bouyges 357.

multiple other organs in succession, and hence would need to be returned to all these organs at once.[27]

The third is that a human consists of body and soul, that the soul survives the death of the body, and that resurrection involves restoring the soul to a body, which need not consist of the matter of the original body.[28] Again, there is no clear indication whether the soul hypothesised here is material or immaterial.[29] The philosophers reject this model on two grounds. First, since human souls are infinite in number, they would need an infinite number of bodies; however, the world contains only a finite amount of matter.[30] Second, the notion that after a soul departs from a body it promptly becomes connected to a different body—otherwise known as metempsychosis (*tanāsukh*)—is disproved on the grounds that the soul can only become connected to specially-prepared matter, i.e. a newly-formed foetus. This, however, is impossible, for once a new foetus takes form, it will necessarily receive a newly-originated soul from the celestial principles, and no individual foetus can receive two souls at once.[31]

All three models are theological, in the sense that they assume that God acts directly and voluntarily on particular material objects. So from the point of view of dialectical tactics, the easiest and most efficient response would have been for al-Ghazālī to do exactly the same as he does in *al-Iqtiṣād*, that is, to defend the lowest common denominator among the three models, which is bodily resurrection as taught in revelation, and to avoid discussing the soul.[32]

Nonetheless, he chooses to base his response on the third model. He does this by proposing a hypothetical account of bodily resurrection on the basis of this model, and challenging the philosophers to refute it:

---

27 Ibid. ed. Marmura 217–18, ed. Bouyges 360–2; cf. Ibn Sīnā, *al-Risāla al-Aḍḥawiyya*, ed. Lucchetta 77–81, ed. ʿĀṣī 107–8.

28 al-Ghazālī, *Tahāfut al-falāsifa*, ed. Marmura 215, ed. Bouyges 357.

29 I take the expression "matter" (*mādda*) here (*Tahāfut*, 217.20 / 357.11) to be simply a reference to the matter of the body, rather than an intentional indication that the soul is immaterial.

30 al-Ghazālī, *Tahāfut al-falāsifa*, ed. Marmura 217, ed. Bouyges 362; cf. Ibn Sīnā, *al-Risāla al-Aḍḥawiyya*, ed. Lucchetta 69, ed. ʿĀṣī 104. On this problem, see Marmura, "Avicenna and the Problem of the Infinite Number of Souls."

31 al-Ghazālī, *Tahāfut al-falāsifa*, ed. Marmura 218, ed. Bouyges 362–3; cf. Ibn Sīnā, *al-Risāla al-Aḍḥawiyya*, ed. Lucchetta 83–85, 125–37, ed. ʿĀṣī 109; 122–5; *idem*, *al-Shifāʾ*, *al-Ṭabīʿiyyāt*, *al-Nafs*, 233–4.

32 This is the same as the first of the three models, without the denial of the existence of the soul.

> How would you disprove one who chooses the last alternative and holds that the soul continues to exist after death, that it is a self-subsisting substance, and that this view is not contrary to revelation, but indeed is evidenced in revelation?[33]

He goes on to cite a selection of relevant revealed evidence. To substantiate his challenge, the third model is then developed along philosophical lines: the soul hypothesised here is explicitly stated to be a separate, immaterial substance. So it survives the death of the body, which serves merely as its instrument. The identity of the individual is preserved in the continued existence of the soul, rather than in the body. So resurrection can occur by restoring the soul,

> to a body, whichever body this may be, whether it be [composed] of the matter of the original body, or a different matter (*raddu-hā ilā badan, ayy badan kāna, sawāʾ kāna min māddat al-badan al-awwal aw min ghayrihi*), or from matter created anew. For [the individual] is what he is by virtue of his soul, not his body (…).[34]

So, although the restored body—restored, that is, directly by God's power—would only be a replica of the original body, the individual would nonetheless be, properly-speaking, "restored" (*kāna dhālika ʿawdan muḥaqqaqan*). Al-Ghazālī claims that this philosophically-inspired hypothetical model can plausibly be argued to be in accordance with the teachings of religion, although it is not immediately clear in this passage whether or not this reflects his own conviction.

Al-Ghazālī then turns to the two philosophical counterarguments he mentioned earlier.[35] The first, which argues from the infinite number of souls, is confuted on the grounds that it assumes that the world is pre-eternal, a philosophical theory that had already been refuted in the first discussion of the *Tahāfut*. To the second counterargument, which proceeds by equating bodily resurrection to metempsychosis, he gives two responses. First, referring to bodily resurrection as "metempsychosis" is mere name-calling, and hence of no consequence. The philosophers may call it "metempsychosis" if they wished, as long as it is clear that the theological doctrine that al-Ghazālī defends involves the soul's return to a body in the hereafter, rather than in this

---

33 al-Ghazālī, *Tahāfut al-falāsifa*, ed. Marmura 217–18, ed. Bouyges 363.

34 Ibid., ed. Marmura 219, ed. Bouyges 364.

35 Ibid., ed. Marmura 219–20, ed. Bouyges 364–6.

world. Second, the claim that when a body becomes prepared to receive a soul one will be brought into being by the celestial principles hinges on the theory that the soul comes into being by natural causality, rather than by the activity of a voluntary agent; however the theory of natural causality has already been disproved earlier in the *Tahāfut*. Moreover, by the same natural theory of the soul's origination, it is conceivable (*lā yabʿudu*) that a new soul would only be brought into being in the absence of an already existing soul ready to become attached to the body. The obvious difficulty here is that the soul should become connected to another suitably-prepared body, not in the hereafter, but in this world, as soon as it departs from its original body. Al-Ghazālī resolves this problem by proposing that it is possible that the preparedness required for the "return" to matter of a soul that had already become perfected through managing a body be different from the preparedness required by a newly-generated soul to become connected to matter, and that it is hence possible that all the causes and conditions of preparedness—known only to God—for the former type of soul to return to a body can only come about in the hereafter, not in this world. He feels justified here to propose that aspects of the body-soul connection are known only to God, because in Discussion 19 he already cited Avicenna's own remark that the connection is in some respects "obscure."[36]

III Conviction *versus* Hypothesis

This response to Avicenna's refutation of the notion of bodily resurrection follows, in broad outline, the standard classical Ashʿarī pattern of dealing with "matters known through revelation" (*samʿiyyāt*), also encountered in *al-Iqtiṣād*: that is, to afford reason the role of establishing whether X is possible, and then to affirm X on the basis of revealed evidence. Al-Ghazālī's response consists of the above-described rational hypothesis concerning the nature of humans and the afterlife, combined with scriptural evidence affirming it as true (though with a qualification, as the present section will reveal): "This is taught in revelation, and is possible; therefore, it must be affirmed as true;" "What revelation teaches must be affirmed as true."[37]

---

36 See n. #22 above.

37 al-Ghazālī, *Tahāfut al-falāsifa*, ed. Marmura 220.14f. and 220.2, ed. Bouyges 365.8, 366.7f. Cf. ibid. 219.8 / 364.2f.: ".. and that is possible (*mumkin*) by ...," which follows a succinct interpretation of scriptural teachings on the afterlife, and introduces an explanation of their possibility.

How does this hypothetical model of the afterlife prove Avicenna wrong? Or, to throw the problem into sharper focus: How could an argument premised, at several points, on theistic doctrines that an Avicennist adversary would never concede prove *anything* against him? The doctrines in question are the creation of the world in time, the denial of the natural origination of the soul, the notion that God is a voluntary agent who acts directly on physical objects, and the view that revelation is a source of theological knowledge.

Yet I propose that although it is constructed on al-Ghazālī's own, rather than the philosophers', terms, the argument is, to a certain extent, legitimate. For it is set out defensively, as a response to Avicenna's refutation of the theological notion of bodily resurrection, rather than offensively, as a refutation of a positive Avicennan doctrine. It demonstrates that bodily resurrection is not impossible, but a logical possibility, though only if set against the framework of the arguer's own theistic system with which this view is shown to be coherent. This defensive objective justifies al-Ghazālī's resort in the model postulated to elements rooted in theistic doctrines that were already defended earlier in the book. Had his immediate purpose been to refute a positive Avicennan doctrine, he would not have been justified to premise his argument on any views that had not already been conceded by the philosophers.

The argument is particularly resonant with the description in the original reading of ¶ 2 in the above-quoted passage from *al-Iqtiṣād*: an immaterial soul is "affirmed" as a starting point, and the soul's return to a body, be it its original body or a different one, is then "postulated." By showing that no impossibility follows from this "postulation," al-Ghazālī proves that the soul's return to a body is possible. However, the argument does not match the description in ¶ 3, in which it is claimed that the philosophers are "forced to concede that they must affirm (*wujūb al-taṣdīq bi-*) the resurrection." Nor, for that matter, does it match the modified reading of ¶ 2. So the actual argument in the *Tahāfut* is by no means an *ad hominem* argument (*ilzām*), as claimed in both ¶ 2 and ¶ 3, but in fact a much weaker argument which shows that if certain non-philosophical, Ashʿarī doctrines are granted, one must then concede the possibility of bodily resurrection. The argument is portrayed in *al-Iqtiṣād* as much more potent than it really is.[38]

---

38 By contrast, the two *ad hominem* arguments described in the discussion of the pre-eternity of the world in *al-Iqtiṣād* (p. 104–5) are genuinely *ad hominem* (cf. *Tahāfut al-falāsifa*, ed. Marmura 25, 26–7, ed. Bouyges 42–3; 45–6). Both arguments, incidentally, are premised on the classical *kalām* all-or-none principle (on which see my "Argument from Ignorance," 194; 211–14).

The above reading raises the question whether the views that constitute the eschatological model that al-Ghazālī sets out are purely hypothetical and mooted for the sake of argument, or whether they reflect actual commitments of his. I propose that they are a mixture of conviction and hypothesis, as I explain in what follows. Al-Ghazālī's choice to develop an eschatological model on the basis of the third conception of the nature of humans and the afterlife, cumbersome and heavy on philosophical content as it is, rather than the minimal common denominator as he does in *al-Iqtiṣād*, must either serve a serious dialectical purpose, or attest a genuine preference for this model. The former possibility can be eliminated on the grounds that the argument in question is in fact not *ad hominem*, and hence does not include any Avicennan views conceded for the sake of argument. It follows that the eschatological model postulated consists of views that are either fully or partly representative of al-Ghazālī's own views. It cannot be fully representative of his views, since he tells us that one or more views "do not correspond to what we ourselves believe" (¶ 2). So it is only partly representative. And I propose that the views to which he is committed are the main central theses (roughly corresponding to the brief initial outline of the third conception of humans and the afterlife):[39] above all, the doctrines of the immaterial rational soul, the soul's surviving the death of the body, and its posthumous return to a body.[40]

As to the view or views that "do not correspond to what we ourselves believe," this, to my mind, is an element of the hypothetical process through which the soul returns to a body, which al-Ghazālī sets out in response to the Avicennan refutation of all three theological conceptions of human ontology and the afterlife. More specifically, it is the notion that the body to which the soul returns is not necessarily the body to which it was originally connected, but can possibly be an entirely other lump of matter. This notion is mentioned twice explicitly in the passage in question in *al-Iqtiṣād*: "… it [the soul] returns to the governance of a body, *whether it be the very same body of the individual or another*" (¶ 2); and "… the soul returns to the governance of *some body or other*

---

39 See p. 122 above.

40 That said, the philosophical doctrine of the absolute indestructibility, and hence eternity (*sarmadiyya*), of the soul is refuted (*ibṭāl*) in Discussion 19. Compare this to al-Ghazālī's opposition to the doctrine of the post-eternity of the world (*abadiyya*) in the second discussion of the *Tahāfut*. By contrast, the immateriality of the rational soul is not refuted, though the philosophers' proofs for it are challenged in the 18th discussion. Al-Ghazālī may have believed that the soul's continued existence following the death of the body is not necessary, but dependent on God's will, a question that falls outside the scope of our present study.

(*badan min al-abdān*)" (¶ 3).[41] In the broader context of the passage, this is the most relevant element of the supposed *ad hominem* argument (if, for a moment, we take this characterisation of the argument at face value). For, as we have seen in Part I above,[42] the preceding discussion in *al-Iqtiṣād* recognises as possible only two theories of restoration: according to one, accidents pass away but atoms do not, so the individual's body is reconstituted out of its original atoms; according to the other theory, God annihilates the whole world and then recreates it, including human bodies, *ex nihilo*, and the identity of the original matter of an individual's body is preserved in God's knowledge. By contrast, in the model hypothesised in the *Tahāfut*, atoms do not pass away, and the individual body may be reconstituted out of any atoms, be they its original atoms or altogether different ones. Moreover, the soul's return to a body seems to be a natural process, since it depends on the readiness of matter, albeit perhaps with an element of direct divine activity. This model, as al-Ghazālī himself admits, is precariously close to metempsychosis (*tanāsukh*), a heretical doctrine that he would never genuinely concede or wish to be associated with.

This reading is confirmed by the sense in which "*ilzām*" occurs in ¶ 2 (again, reading the text at face value). This term can refer either to an *ad hominem* argument as a whole (the process of forcing the opponent to concede such and such), or more narrowly to the view that the opponent is forced to concede (the consequent). In the clause, "an *ilzām* that does not correspond to what we ourselves believe," it most likely refers to the consequent, since belief normally consists of an assertion, rather than an argument. This is echoed in ¶ 3: "we forced [the philosophers] (*alzamnā-hum*) ... to concede that they must affirm the resurrection, which is for the soul to return to the governance of some body or other." It is, therefore, precisely the consequent that "does not correspond to what we ourselves believe."

So, the view that al-Ghazālī affirms in the *Tahāfut* for the sake of argument, without actually subscribing to it, is not the theory of the immaterial soul, but only the *process* through which the soul becomes reconnected to a body. This reading suggests that when he wrote the *Tahāfut* and the *Iqtiṣād*, the author had already adopted the theory of the immaterial soul, but had not fully worked out a solution to the knotty problem of the process of bodily resurrection and the soul's return to the body. He hazards a wild guess of such a process in order to complete his hypothetical eschatology, but leaves it as a speculative

---

41 These echo al-Ghazālī, *Tahāfut*, ed. Marmura 219, ed. Bouyges 364. See n. #*34* above.

42 See pp. 114–15 above.

and conjectural possibility unsupported by scriptural evidence.[43] Later, when he writes *al-Iqtiṣād* to a significantly different crowd of readers, he finds it necessary to spell out this non-commitment explicitly.

IV The Economy of Knowledge

Although, in *al-Iqtiṣād*, al-Ghazālī does not dissociate himself from the doctrine of the immaterial soul, he effectively distances himself from it by associating it with the philosophers, as he introduces it with, "according to them" (*ʿinda-hum*) (¶ 2). This, combined with the fact that in the same discussion he propounds a thoroughly materialist eschatology, has led recent commentators to conclude that in this work al-Ghazālī champions a classical-Ashʿarite anthropology, as opposed to the philosophically-influenced substance dualism he clearly espouses in other works.[44] This interpretation is seriously off the mark, albeit probably precisely the sort of reading that the author himself wanted most of his readers to arrive at.

The confusion is resolved once we consider the distinction that classical Ashʿarīs make between the human body and the spirit (*rūḥ*, *nafs*), which too is material, though whether it consists of atoms or accidents was a matter of disagreement. Some, including al-Juwaynī, considered the spirit to consist of atoms that are seeded in the body, but are not of the body. Life, knowledge, thinking and perception are explained as attributes of the body, rather than of the spirit, which has no activities of its own. Consequently, the punishment and inquisition of the tomb are experienced, not by the spirit, which departs from the body at death, but by the body—or only a part thereof, often said to be some atoms of the heart (literally)—in which God creates life and perception.[45] Now, what al-Ghazālī does in *al-Iqtiṣād* is to take advantage of the duality already present in earlier Ashʿarism (where, as mentioned, it is entirely materialist), and to concentrate exclusively on eschatological occurrences that take place in the body, including the restoration of the body, the punishment it

43 So, al-Ghazālī's statement that "this is taught in revelation (*al-sharʿ*)" (*Tahāfut*, 220 / 365, 366) refers to body-soul dualism and bodily resurrection, but not the process as such, on which there is nothing in revelation.

44 See, for instance, Marmura, "Bodily Resurrection," 282; 285, and Gianotti, *Unspeakable Doctrine of the Soul*, 68 ff.

45 On this subject, see my "Classical Ashʿarī Anthropology," 443–9; 465–74. On that a sound bodily structure is not a condition for life and other animate attributes, see also 451 ff.

experiences in the tomb and the inquisition by Munkar and Nakīr.[46] Whether he believes the soul to be material or immaterial, al-Ghazālī can still plausibly maintain that these occurrences all take place in the body. Yet the book says nothing on the nature of the soul. It is nowhere said to be material, nor in fact can its materiality be inferred simply from al-Ghazālī's views on posthumous occurrences in the body. For it is perfectly arguable that all his views on the occurrences involved in bodily eschatology can fit, like small pieces of a jigsaw puzzle, into a larger, dualist theory of the nature of humans and the afterlife, in which the soul is elevated to the status of an immaterial substance.

That al-Ghazālī refrains from expressing any views on the soul in this book is confirmed explicitly in the concluding part of the above-quoted passage from his discussion on resurrection. He writes (¶ 4):

> To discuss this subject further to get to the truth of the matter would lead us to investigate the spirit (*rūḥ*), the soul (*nafs*), life and the reality (*ḥaqīqa*) of each. However, creedal works (*muʿtaqadāt*) are not suited to delving to these great depths in rational subjects (*maʿqūlāt*). Accordingly, what we have said suffices for establishing the right balance of belief (*al-iqtiṣād fī l-iʿtiqād*) in order to confirm what is taught in revelation.

Al-Ghazālī clearly has more to say on the ontological and anthropological aspects of the afterlife, but chooses to include none of it in his *kalām* work, not even a statement on whether the soul is material or immaterial. He explains his evasiveness by pointing out that creedal compendia are not the appropriate framework to treat these subjects, which he characterises as (i) difficult and (ii) rational.[47] The echo of the book's title in the concluding sentence underscores the economy of theological truth that determines its intended scope, and consequently the exclusions. The expression "*iqtiṣād*" refers to striking the right balance—i.e. moderation—in the exposition of theology, which can be analysed in terms of the discipline's means and objectives.[48]

The balance in the epistemological "means" lies in the soundly-structured application of rational and revealed evidence, which steers clear of the two

46 The "part" (*juzʾ*) of the heart or the internal parts (*bāṭin*) mentioned in this context (*al-Iqtiṣād*, 216–18) is simply one or more atoms of the body. Al-Ghazālī's treatment of these subjects is consonant with earlier Ashʿarī views and language.

47 On rendering "*muʿtaqadāt*" as "creedal works," see n. 13 above.

48 For earlier discussions of the sense intended by "*iqtiṣād*" here, see Makdisi, "The Non-Ashʿarite Shāfiʿism of Abū Ḥāmid al-Ghazzālī," 249–50; Frank, *Al-Ghazālī and the Ashʿarite School*, 71 ff.

extremes of fideism and excessive rationalism which oversteps its bounds, represented respectively by traditionalist theology and philosophy. A case in point is that, in *al-Iqtiṣād*, the primary doctrines of theology (e.g. the existence of God, His attributes, and the possibility of prophecy) are established, in keeping with classical Ashʿarism, on strictly rational grounds, whereas in certain other topics the role of reason is reduced to the task of recognising the possible from the impossible while revelation is promoted to being the principal source of knowledge.

As to the "objective" of *kalām*, al-Ghazālī considers it to consist of the corroboration and defence of the core doctrines of orthodoxy against the specious doctrines and arguments of opposing schools of thought, for the benefit of educated, but non-specialist believers.[49] Assent is required to the bare minimum of doctrines, using the minimum amount of evidence, which spares such believers having to delve deeper (*taghalghul*) into, and to get to the truth of (*taḥqīq*) more advanced theological questions through critical enquiry (*baḥth*). Al-Ghazālī's theological "moderation" in this respect contrasts with the classical Ashʿarī position that *kalām* is the exclusive path to theological knowledge, and not merely a defensive shield for orthodoxy. To him, it is only an art (*ṣanʿa*) geared, first and foremost, to dialectic (*jadal*) and persuasion (*iqnāʿ*). Knowledge (*ʿilm*) is obtained, not by means of *kalām*, but through a higher theology reserved for the qualified few.

That said, the views that he supports in one genre should, *as much as possible*, dovetail with those advanced in a different genre; the two sets of views, albeit often disparate, should ideally fit into a structured, and more or less coherent larger system, although this coherence is often not so obvious when considered from the lower strata of the system. Al-Ghazālī, in my view, strives to maintain consistency among the views put forth in his different works. However, I say that he tries to do this "as much as possible," because he achieves this in varying degrees of success, as we shall see in the next section.[50]

Now, al-Ghazālī's claim to have struck the "right balance" in his treatment of resurrection refers to both the means and objectives of the book. First, following earlier Ashʿarīs, he bases eschatological doctrines primarily on the teachings of revelation, restricting the role of reason to ascertaining the possibility of the

49 Shihadeh, "From al-Ghazālī to al-Rāzī," 142–8.

50 I propose this reading as an alternative—one that is charitable but critical—to both the traditional (medieval and contemporary) view that al-Ghazālī's oeuvre is thoroughly self-contradictory and disingenuous, and the contrary view that everything in his system—novel, complex and ambitious as it is—fits neatly and readily into place. Much of his system was still work in progress.

occurrences and states of affairs in question, and to refuting unorthodox doctrines. Second, it contains the minimum amount of investigation needed to confirm the eschatological teachings of scripture (namely, proving the possibility of bodily resurrection), and refrains from more advanced, and in this context unnecessary, research aimed at discovering the realities of the soul, the spirit and life. So the picture painted in *al-Iqtiṣād* is partial and governed by the limitations of the book's scope and objectives. The eschatological views propounded, though remarkably consonant with classical Ashʿarī doctrines, are meant to represent, not al-Ghazālī's full doctrine of the afterlife, but only one part—the corporeal part—thereof; they are arguably not incompatible with the body-soul dualism advocated in other works, though it goes beyond the scope of our present study to argue this in detail.

It is little wonder, therefore, that al-Ghazālī classes psychology and anthropology among "rational subjects" (*maʿqūlāt*) (¶ 4), a label that comes into sharp contrast, first, with "matters known through revelation" (*samʿiyyāt*), the broad rubric under which the human spirit and eschatology are normally included in *kalām* works, and second, with "creedal works" (*muʿtaqadāt*) in general, which confirms that the subject belongs to higher theology, not to *kalām*. In other words, approaching psychology as a rational subject would be out of place in *al-Iqtiṣād* since it contrasts with the "means," namely the classical Ashʿarī view that the soul is knowable through revelation rather than reason, and the "objectives," namely establishing the core doctrines of orthodoxy and avoiding superfluous and complex investigation. So, unlike earlier Ashʿarīs, al-Ghazālī subscribes to a fundamentally rational theory of the soul, one, moreover, in which a distinction is made between the soul (*nafs*), i.e. the human soul, and the spirit (*rūḥ*), i.e. the pneuma.[51] What becomes evident in ¶ 4 is that, despite his evasiveness, al-Ghazālī offers a subtle, yet unambiguous, hint that he is committed to the theory of the rational soul and that he discusses it in other, more relevant and more advanced works.

V *Iqtiṣād*, General Ontology

Al-Ghazālī has a further, more pressing motive to omit any reference to immaterial souls in *al-Iqtiṣād*, which probably also partly explains the conspicuous

---

51 Earlier Ashʿarīs affirm the spirit primarily on the basis of scriptural evidence of its existence; they use "*nafs*" and "*rūḥ*" interchangeably (Shihadeh, "Classical Ashʿarī Anthropology," 465 ff.). On al-Ghazālī's distinction between the rational soul and the pneuma in the *Iḥyāʾ*, see Frank, *Al-Ghazālī and the Ashʿarite School*, 56.

absence of a direct discussion of the subject in a book such as the *Iḥyāʾ*, to whose objectives this subject seems highly germane. For this we need to turn to the first two theological doctrines treated in his *kalām* compendium, namely the creation of the world *ex nihilo* and the existence of God, the context in which atomism is normally introduced in classical *kalām* sources.[52]

Several points in the chapter on God's existence register quite explicitly al-Ghazālī's commitment to the atomism of earlier Ashʿarīs, most obviously his definition of "the world" (*al-ʿālam*) as everything (*kull mawjūd*) other than God, by which "we mean all bodies and their accidents."[53] Another case in point is his division of beings into space-occupying ones (*mutaḥayyiz*), which are either atoms (*jawhar*) or bodies agglomerated of atoms, and beings that are not space-occupying, which either subsist in atoms, or do not subsist in any substrate but are self-subsisting: the former are the accidents, the latter category includes only God.[54] This division of beings, of course, leaves no room for created immaterial beings, including immaterial human souls. Frank tries to resolve the contradiction between this general ontology and substance dualism by concentrating on al-Ghazālī's application of the expression "*jawhar*," which he attempts to interpret in a way that allows for the possibility of created immaterial entities.[55] He argues from details that al-Ghazālī leaves unsaid in *al-Iqtiṣād*, comparing the text both with some of his other works, including non-*kalām* texts, and with earlier Ashʿarī sources. For instance, he points out that "nowhere in the *Iqtiṣād* (...) does al-Ghazālī say of the *jawhar* that as such it has volume (*ḥajm*), as does al-Juwaynī (...),"[56] and that "al-Ghazālī conspicuously avoids asserting the traditional thesis that created beings must either occupy space or reside in subjects that occupy space (...), as does al-Juwaynī (...)."[57] As it happens, the latter point is factually incorrect; for, as I have just mentioned, al-Ghazālī does assert this traditional view.[58] Frank's reading, as has already been rightly remarked, "makes too much of too little,"[59] as none of the evidence he provides in this regard is of consequence. However, the more

52 As I intend to show in a forthcoming study, the philosophical theory of the rational soul had several problematic implications in the context of classical *kalām*. The implication discussed here is, in my assessment, the most pertinent in *al-Iqtiṣād*.

53 al-Ghazālī, *al-Iqtiṣād*, 24.

54 Ibid. 24.

55 Frank, *Al-Ghazālī and the Ashʿarite School*, 48–55.

56 Ibid., 53.

57 Ibid., 55.

58 See, for instance, the statement that every existent other than God is either a body or an accident, n. 53 above.

59 See Gianotti's criticism in *Unspeakable Doctrine of the Soul*, 80–3.

serious shortcoming of this reading is that it concentrates almost exclusively on the concept "*jawhar*" without paying due attention to the argument in which it appears.

Al-Ghazālī could not possibly have intended "*jawhar*" in this context to include both material and immaterial substances, as that would have nullified his proofs for both the creation of the world and consequently the existence of God. To prove the creation of the world *ex nihilo*, he uses the traditional four-step argument from accidents, derived in particular from the version propounded by al-Juwaynī, which in general outline goes as follows: (i) accidents exist; (ii) all accidents are temporally-originated; (iii) substances (*jawhar*), i.e. atoms, cannot be devoid of accidents; (iv) what cannot be devoid of, and hence cannot pre-exist, temporally-originated things must itself be temporally-originated, since an infinitely-regressive series of past temporally-originated events is impossible; therefore, the world, defined as the totality of atoms and accidents, is created *ex nihilo*.[60] Affirming the possibility of incorporeal beings other than God—that is, of a third class of primary created beings, comprising self-subsisting entities that, unlike atoms, are not space-occupying, and unlike accidents, do not inhere in a space-occupying substratum—will immediately undermine the third step in the argument. For, following the earlier *kalām* tradition, al-Ghazālī argues from a particular class of accidents to prove that no atom can be devoid of accidents belonging to that class, and hence the more general principle that no atom can be devoid of any accidents whatsoever. His accidents of choice, following al-Juwaynī, are the contraries of motion and rest, one of which must exist in every atom in the world.[61] However, if substances divide into atoms and immaterial entities, then the argument will fail to prove the temporal origination of the latter, since they cannot contain any accidents (strictly in the classical *kalām* sense of the term), certainly neither motion nor rest. It will follow that there may exist, in the world, substances that have not been proved to be created *ex nihilo*; so it will not follow that the world as a whole is created *ex nihilo*. If this argument proves unsound, then so too will the argument from creation *ex nihilo* for the existence of God, which goes as follows: All that is originated in time must be originated by a cause; the world is originated in time; therefore the world is originated by a cause.[62] Any half-decent theologian, not to mention al-Ghazālī, would have been aware of

60 Al-Ghazālī, *al-Iqtiṣād*, 26–34; cf. al-Juwaynī, *al-Shāmil*, 123–262; *al-Irshād*, 17–27. On the proof from creation *ex nihilo* for the existence of God, see Davidson, *Proofs for Eternity, Creation, and the Existence of God*, 134 ff.

61 al-Ghazālī, *al-Iqtiṣād*, 28; cf. al-Juwaynī, *al-Irshād*, 18.

62 al-Ghazālī, *al-Iqtiṣād*, 24.

the disastrous implications that follow out of suggesting the possibility of immaterial beings, let alone affirming their existence.

There is evidence in later *kalām* sources confirming the incompatibility argued here between the notion of immaterial beings and the classical *kalām* argument from accidents. This point is made in Sayf al-Dīn al-Āmidī's (d. 631/1233) philosophical work *al-Nūr al-bāhir fī l-ḥikam al-zawāhir* (*Splendid Light on Bright Wisdom*), where he criticises the argument on account of "a failure to prove that everything other than the Necessary Existent through Itself must contain accidents," since it neglects to consider separate entities, which are completely free from matter.[63] The same point is implied in the chapter on theological and philosophical proofs for the existence of God in Naṣīr al-Dīn al-Ṭūsī's (d. 672/1274) *Qawāʿid al-ʿaqāʾid* (*The Rules of What-To-Believe*), which opens as follows:

> *Chapter One, On Proving the Producer of the World.* "The world" refers to everything other than God, exalted. What is other than God, exalted, are either substances (*jawāhir*) or accidents. If substances are proven to require a Producer, then it will follow that accidents require Him, since they require what [substances] require.
>
> *Kalām* theologians *deny the existence of incorporeal substances* (*jawāhir ghayr jismāniyya*), as will be explained later. So they first prove that bodies and substances [i.e. atoms] are created in time, and then argue from this to prove that they have a pre-eternal creator. They use different ways to prove that bodies are created in time. One of them is that they say: Bodies cannot be devoid of created things [i.e. accidents]; and all that cannot be devoid of created things must [itself] be created; therefore, all bodies are created. This proof is based on the affirmation of four claims: first, the affirmation of the existence of [accidents[64]]; second, establishing that no body can be devoid of them; third, establishing that all [accidents] are created in time; fourth, establishing that all that cannot be devoid of created things is itself created.[65]

63 al-Āmidī, *al-Nūr al-bāhir*, 5:220. I am grateful to Laura Hassan (SOAS), who is currently preparing a study on aspects of al-Āmidī's philosophical and theological thought, for bringing this passage to my attention.

64 The text here and in the third claim reads 'created things' (*ḥawādith*), which in this case refers to accidents.

65 Naṣīr al-Dīn al-Ṭūsī, *Qawāʿid al-ʿaqāʾid*, in: al-Ḥillī, *Kashf al-fawāʾid*, 133; 135.

The two other proofs of creation *ex nihilo* are drawn from Fakhr al-Dīn al-Rāzī (d. 606/1210) and are of no relevance here. In his commentary on this passage, al-Ṭūsī's student Ibn Muṭahhar al-Ḥillī (d. 726/1325) distinguishes two definitions of "the world," namely (1) "everything other than God" and (2) "the heavens and the earth and what is in between," which in contrast to the former definition excludes immaterial substances, if their existence is affirmed.[66] In the former definition—the one used by classical *kalām* theologians and, as we have seen, by al-Ghazālī—no such exclusion is possible.

Al-Ghazālī would have classed the proposition that the world consists exclusively of atoms and accidents, which he deploys in the argument from accidents, as a "purely estimative proposition" (*wahmiyya ṣirfa*), understood as a proposition that may seem to be certain and primary (*awwaliyya*), but in fact is false (*kādhiba*) and stems from the estimative faculty's tendency to judge matters that lie beyond the senses no differently than it judges familiar sensory things.[67] Indeed, in his logical works, al-Ghazālī reproduces, with slight adjustments, two closely-related examples given by Avicenna for precisely this class of propositions: namely, that a being that has no definite location (*jiha*) is impossible, and that a self-subsistent being that is neither connected to the world nor disconnected from it, and neither inside the world nor outside it, is impossible. Both propositions amount to a rejection of the possibility of created immaterial beings.[68]

So, al-Ghazālī had a choice between (1) employing the conventional *kalām* argument from accidents and avoiding any discussion of immaterial souls anywhere in the book, and (2) undertaking an overhaul of the discussion of creation and God's existence. Although I suspect that he might have considered the latter option, he chose the former, despite the false reasoning it involved and its contradicting the substance dualism he championed elsewhere. To appreciate why he does so, we should first revisit his *low view* of the nature and objectives of *kalām*, not only that practised by earlier *mutakallimūn*, but also by implication his own *kalām* output.

As already mentioned, al-Ghazālī's top priority in *al-Iqtiṣād* and other *kalām* works was persuasion, rather than knowledge. He demotes *kalām* to a mere therapeutic dialectical art that is instrumental only in producing assent in the central doctrines of orthodoxy among a certain class of people, namely simple

66 al-Ḥillī, *Kashf al-fawāʾid*, 133–4.

67 On al-Ghazālī's notion of "estimative proposition" and its Avicennan background, see Griffel, "Al-Ghazālī's Use of 'Original Human Disposition' (*fiṭra*)," 16f., 22–24, 28.

68 al-Ghazālī, *Miḥakk al-naẓar*, 52–3; *idem*, *Miʿyār al-ʿilm*, 129–30; cf. Ibn Sīnā, *al-Shifāʾ*, *al-Manṭiq*, *al-Burhān*, 64–5; *idem*, *al-Najāt*, 115–18.

believers who adhere to the teachings of religion on the basis of uncritical imitation (*taqlīd*) but are intellectually a step above the illiterate believer, and have begun to question or doubt their inherited beliefs either by their own thinking or due to external influences. To remedy (*muʿālaja*) their doubts and restore their peace of mind (*ṭumaʾnīna*), al-Ghazālī prescribes that they be spoken to in ways that are persuasive and acceptable to them (*kalām muqniʿ maqbūl ʿinda-hum*). If at all possible, one should simply describe these doubts as evil or absurd, or cite a Qurʾānic verse, *ḥadīth* or statement of a respected person, and only resort to dispensing rational arguments should such basic means fail.[69] Yet, to be efficacious in producing assent, arguments used by the *kalām* theologian must be simple and start from premises that are readily acceptable to the target audience. They need not be demonstrative arguments, since their purpose is not to provide knowledge of reality (*ʿilm, taḥqīq*). For this reason, many of the arguments that al-Ghazālī himself advances in a *kalām* setting fall below the standards of apodicticity set out, following the Aristotelian tradition, in his logical works. He tells us that his main *kalām* work, *al-Iqtiṣād*, is superior to earlier *kalām* sources, since it goes further towards critical enquiry (*taḥqīq*) and knowledge (*maʿrifa*)—without fully providing either—than the conventional (*rasmī*) *kalām* of earlier theologians.[70] The difference is only one of degree; for the book is still, to a great extent, executed along the conventions (*rasm*) of classical *kalām*.

Al-Ghazālī's arguments for the existence of God and the creation of the world in time are a perfect case in point. Of his aforementioned two options—either (i) to follow, and to refine as much as possible, the traditional method, or (ii) to employ different proofs for these two doctrines—only the former option was feasible, and that is for at least three reasons. First, had he decided to dispense with the proof from accidents, he would have had to find alternative proofs for creation *ex nihilo* and the existence of God. For the latter doctrine, he could have adapted Avicenna's argument from contingency (*imkān*),[71] yet that was still closely associated with widely-condemned philosophical doctrines, particularly the conception of God as a necessitating cause.[72] In any case, al-Ghazālī would not have found an alternative proof for

---

69 al-Ghazālī, *al-Iqtiṣād*, 11; cf. Shihadeh, "From al-Ghazālī to al-Rāzī," 142–8.

70 al-Ghazālī, *al-Arbaʿīn*, 24; idem, *Jawāhir al-Qurʾān*, 81.

71 As he does in one of his *Maḍnūn* texts, see al-Ghazālī, *Kitāb al-Maḍnūn bihī ʿalā ghāyr ahlihī*, in: *Majmūʿah-yi falsafī-yi Marāgha*, 1–62, esp. 9–10. This work is of unquestionable authenticity, most evidently because it refers on p. 3 to the author's *Jawāhir al-Qurʾān*.

72 That said, this argument was later adapted to a theistic worldview, as can be observed in the works of Fakhr al-Dīn al-Rāzī and later Ashʿarīs.

creation *ex nihilo* that did not start from change undergone by material entities and as such applied to immaterial entities, which are neither observably subject to change nor always demonstrably so. Second, even if it was possible to devise or borrow an alternative argument that proved the createdness *ex nihilo* of both material and immaterial beings, excluding God, it would have appeared at the very least a proof so alien and potentially contentious that it would have sharply deviated from the author's declared objective of writing an accessible and rather conservative theological compendium that efficaciously produced assent in the central doctrines of orthodoxy and left its target readers with no nagging doubts. Introducing arguments associated with unorthodox schools of thought, not least the philosophers, in a subject as cardinal as the existence of God might have even appeared sacrilegious: a danger confirmed by al-Ghazālī's frequent arguments against the condemnation of views simply on account of their unorthodox provenance or associations.[73] Any major shift in the paradigm in a conservative book such as *al-Iqtiṣād*, by introducing unconventional doctrines, arguments or formats, would have been controversial and counterproductive. Third, the argument from accidents had itself acquired something of the status of an incontrovertible dogma in classical *kalām*.[74]

It is for these reasons that our theologian chooses to employ an unsound but conservative and persuasive argument to prove the creation of the world *ex nihilo*. But he leaves us clues as to his concessionary, probably reluctant, nod to convention: at one point in the argument from accidents, he tells us that the existence and temporality of accidents—respectively, the first and second principles of the argument—are self-evident and incontrovertible, but he nonetheless goes on to prove both premises "to uphold the conventional method" (*li-iqāmat al-rasm*).[75] And in *al-Risāla al-Qudsiyya*, another *kalām* text, he maintains that the existence of God can be recognised simply by the innate disposition (*fiṭra*) of humans or by contemplating signs of design in the world, but nonetheless goes on to set out the conventional Ashʿarite arguments for creation and the existence of God "in emulation of scholars who practised rational theology" (*al-iqtidāʾ bi-l-ʿulamāʾ al-nuẓẓār*).[76]

---

73 For instance, al-Ghazālī, *al-Munqidh*, 21ff.; *Tahāfut*, ed. Marmura 5–7, ed. Bouyges10–13; *Miʿyār al-ʿilm*, 131.

74 As pointed out, for instance, by Ibn Khaldūn (d. 808/1406), *al-Muqaddima*, 3:35, 95–96; Engl. transl. 3:52–53. 144. On the principle of "the conversion of evidence" (*inʿikās*), which led to this view, see my "Argument from Ignorance," 204–5 and 217–20.

75 al-Ghazālī, *al-Iqtiṣād*, 27.

76 al-Ghazālī, *al-Risāla al-Qudsiyya*, 80.26, 98. The text is also part of al-Ghazālī, *Iḥyāʾ*, 1:183.4. In this passage, *naẓar* refers to the practice of *kalām*.

Conclusion

Let us conclude by quickly summarising our main findings. First of all, I have shown that it would be wrong to read the discussion of eschatology in *al-Iqtiṣād* as advocating a standard materialist classical *kalām* anthropology straight and simple, one that rejects, and clashes with, the substance dualism that al-Ghazālī propounds in other works of his. The anti-philosophical argument he refers to is not at all an argument against the theory of the immaterial soul; moreover, the partial, selective eschatology he sets out provides fragmentary details of the afterlife of the body, but explicitly avoids spelling out any views on the nature or afterlife of the soul. Instead, he includes a subtle hint, to be decoded by the more discerning readers, at the substance dualism he subscribes to in other works written around the same period, shortly before or after *al-Iqtiṣād*.

I have also argued that the general ontology put forth in the beginning of *al-Iqtiṣād* is none other than classical Ashʿarī atomism, most importantly because atomism must be premised in the classical-*kalām* argument from accidents for the creation of the world *ex nihilo*, which in turn is premised in the cosmological proof from creation *ex nihilo* for the existence of God. Al-Ghazālī had little choice in this book but to commit this obvious contradiction of substance dualism, due, as we have just seen, to his conception of *kalām* as an inherently conservative art meant, first and foremost, to persuade average believers of orthodox tenets, as opposed to a genuine science.

This article has concentrated on *al-Iqtiṣād*, an undated book that was completed either in, or shortly after, 488/1095, following his completion of the *Tahāfut*.[77] It gives a snapshot of his thinking around the same period, during which he also published his most important book, the *Iḥyāʾ*. Whether in works written later on in his life he develops a different, possibly freer, more confident and more consistent approach to dealing with the conundrum of substance dualism in the context of Ashʿarī theology falls outside the purview of our study, and remains to be seen.[78] In any case, what we have here is an

---

77 The *Tahāfut* was completed on 11 Muḥarram 488/21 January 1095, as stated in one manuscript (see Bouyges's introduction to his edition of the *Tahāfut*, p. ix). For a brief chronology of al-Ghazālī's works, including *al-Iqtiṣād*, see Treiger, *Inspired Knowledge*, 11–14.

78 Al-Ghazālī tells us in *al-Munqidh*, 45, that between the years 490–500/1097–1107, he became certain on "countless grounds," including direct experience (*dhawq*), demonstrations and religious grounds, that man consists of body and soul. I read this as indicating that he became more profoundly committed to this doctrine, largely (as he would say) due to the direct experience offered by Sufi practice, rather than as evidence of a lack of commitment prior to this date. (See also Frank Griffel's reading of the passage in *Al-Ghazālī's Philosophical Theology*, 285.)

important early episode in the process through which the theory of the rational soul became accommodated in Ashʿarī thought.

Bibliography

Abū Saʿda, Muḥammad Ḥ. *al-Āthār al-sīnawiyya fī madhhab al-Ghazālī fī l-nafs al-insāniyya.* Cairo: Dār Abū Ḥarbiyya, 1991.

al-Āmidī, ʿAlī ibn Abī ʿAlī. *al-Nūr al-bāhir fī l-ḥikam al-zawāhir* [Facsimile of MSS Ankara, Dil ve Tarih-Coğrafya Fakültesi, Ismail Saib, 631, 2866, 4624 and 4830]. 4 vols. (vols. 1–3 and vol. 5; vol. 4 is missing). Frankfurt: Institut für Geschichte der Arabisch-Islamischen Wissenschaften, 2001.

Davidson, Herbert A. *Proofs for Eternity, Creation, and the Existence of God in Medieval Islamic and Jewish Philosophy.* New York: Oxford University Press, 1987.

Druart, Thérèse-Anne. "The Human Soul's Individuation and its Survival after the Body's Death: Avicenna on the Causal Relation between Body and Soul." *Arabic Sciences and Philosophy* 10 (2000): 259–73.

Frank, Richard M. *Al-Ghazālī and the Ashʿarite School.* Durham, NC: Duke University Press, 1994.

al-Ghazālī, Abū Ḥāmid. *al-Arbaʿīn fī uṣūl al-dīn.* Edited by M. Ṣ. al-Kurdī. Cairo: al-Maṭbaʿa al-ʿArabiyya, 1344 [1925].

———. *Iḥyāʾ ʿulūm al-dīn.* 16 vols. Cairo: Lajnat Nashr al-Thaqāfa al-Islāmiyya, 1356–1357 [1937–1938].

———. *al-Iqtiṣād fī l-iʿtiqād.* MS Dublin, Chester Beatty, Ar 3372.

———. *al-Iqtiṣād fī l-iʿtiqād.* Edited by I. A. Çubukçu and H. Atay. Ankara: Nur Matbaasi, 1962.

———. *al-Iqtiṣād fī l-iʿtiqād.* Edited by M. ʿImrān. Cairo: Dār al-Baṣāʾir, 2009.

———. *al-Iqtiṣād fī l-iʿtiqād.* Edited by A. M. al-Sharfāwī. Jeddah: Dār al-Minhāj, 2012.

———. *Jawāhir al-Qurʾān wa-duraruhu [wa-Kitāb al-Arbaʿīn fī uṣūl al-dīn].* Edited by Kh. M. Kāmil and ʿI. al-Sharqāwī. Cairo: Maṭbaʿat Dār al-Kutub wa-l-Wathāʾiq al-Qawmiyya, 1432/2011.

———. *Miḥakk al-naẓar fī l-manṭiq.* Edited by M. B. al-Naʿsānī al-Ḥalabī and M. al-Qabbānī al-Dimashqī. Cairo: al-Maṭbaʿa al-Adabiyya, w. d. [1925].

———. *Miʿyār al-ʿilm fī fann al-manṭiq.* Edited by M. Ṣ. al-Kurdī. Cairo: al-Maṭbaʿa al-ʿArabiyya, 1346/1927.

———. *al-Munqidh min al-ḍalāl / Erreur et délivrance.* Edition (following J. Ṣalībā and K. ʿAyyād) and French transl. by F. Jabre. Beirut: Commission libanaise pour la traduction des chefs-d'œuvre, 1969.

———. *al-Risāla al-Qudsiyya.* Arabic edition and English transl. in: Abdel Latif Tibawi. "Al-Ghazālī's Sojourn in Damascus and Jerusalem." *Islamic Quarterly* 9 (1965): 65–122.

———. *Tahāfut al-falāsifa.* = *The Incoherence of the Philosophers / Tahāfut al-falāsifa.* Edited and transl. by M. E. Marmura. 2nd ed. Provo: Brigham Young University Press, 2000.

———. *Tahāfut al-falāsifa.* = *Tahâfot al-Falâsifat ou «Incohérence des Philosophes.»* Edited by M. *Bouyges*. Beirut: Imprimerie Catholique, 1927.

Gianotti, Timothy J. *Al-Ghazālī's Unspeakable Doctrine of the Soul: Unveiling the Esoteric Psychology and Eschatology of the Iḥyāʾ.* Leiden: E. J. Brill, 2001.

Griffel, Frank. "Al-Ġazālī's Concept of Prophecy: The Introduction of Avicennan Psychology into Ašʿarite Theology." *Arabic Sciences and Philosophy* 14 (2004): 101–44.

———. *Al-Ghazālī's Philosophical Theology*. New York: Oxford University Press, 2009.

———. "Al-Ghazālī's Use of 'Original Human Disposition' (*fiṭra*) and Its Background in the Teachings of al-Fārābī and Avicenna." *The Muslim World* 102 (2012): 1–32.

———. "Review of Timothy J. Gianotti, Al-Ghazālī's Unspeakable Doctrine of the Soul: Unveiling the Esoteric Psychology and Eschatology of the Iḥyāʾ." *Journal of the American Oriental Society* 124 (2004): 108–11.

Hennig, Boris. "Ghazali on Immaterial Substances." In *Substance and Attribute in Islamic Philosophy: Western and Islamic Tradition in Dialogue*. Edited by C. Kanzian and M. Legenhausen. Heusenstamm: Ontos Verlag, 2007. 55–66.

al-Ḥillī, Ibn Muṭahhar al-Ḥasan ibn Yūsuf. *Kashf al-fawāʾid fī sharḥ Qawāʿid al-ʿaqāʾid.* Edited by Ḥ. M. al-ʿĀmilī. Beirut: Dār al-Ṣafwa, 1413/1993.

Ibn Sīnā, al-Ḥusayn ibn ʿAbdallāh. *al-Najāt min al-gharaq fī baḥr al-ḍalālāt*. Edited by M. T. Dānishpazhūh. Tehran: Intishārāt-i Dānishgāh-i Tihrān, 1364/1985.

———. *al-Risāla al-Aḍḥawiyya fī l-maʿād.* = *Epistola sulla vita futura.* Edition and Italian transl. by F. Lucchetta. Padua: Editrice Antenore, 1969.

———. *al-Risāla al-Aḍḥawiyya fī l-maʿād.* Edited by Ḥ. ʿĀṣī. Beirut: al-Muʾassasa al-Jāmiʿiyya li-l-Dirāsāt wa-l-Nashr wa-l-Tawzīʿ, 1404/1984.

———. *al-Shifāʾ, al-Manṭiq, al-Burhān.* Edited by A. al-ʿAfīfī and I. Madkūr. Cairo: al-Maṭbaʿa al-Amīriyya, 1375/1956.

———. *al-Shifāʾ, al-Ṭabīʿiyyāt, al-Nafs* = *Avicenna's De anima (Arabic text): Being the Psychological Part of Kitāb al-Shifāʾ*. Edited by F. Rahman. London: Oxford University Press, 1959.

———. *al-Shifāʾ, al-Ilāhiyyāt* = *The Metaphysics of The Healing / al-Shifāʾ: al-Ilāhiyyāt. A Parallel English-Arabic Text.* Edited and transl. by M. E. Marmura. Provo (Utah): Brigham Young University Press, 2005.

al-Juwaynī, ʿAbd al-Malik ibn ʿAbdallāh. *Kitāb al-Irshād.* Edited by M. Mūsā and ʿA. ʿAbd al-Ḥamīd. Cairo: Maktabat al-Khānjī, 1950.

———. *al-Shāmil fī uṣūl al-dīn*. Edited by ʿA. S. al-Nashshār, F. B. ʿAwn, and S. M. Mukhtār. Alexandria: Munshaʾat al-Maʿārif, 1969.

Ibn Khaldūn, ʿAbd al-Raḥmān ibn Muḥammad. *al-Muqaddima*. Edited by ʿA. al-Shaddādī. 3 vols. Casablanca: Bayt al-Funūn wa-l-ʿUlūm wa-l-Ādāb, 2005.

———. *The Muqaddimah. An Introduction to History*. English translation by F. Rosenthal. 2nd ed. 3 vols. Princeton: Princeton University Press, 1967.

Kukkonen, Taneli. "Receptive to Reality: Al-Ghazālī on the Structure of the Soul." *The Muslim World* 102 (2012): 541–61.

Majmūʿah-yi falsafī-yi Marāgha / A Philosophical Anthology from Maragha. Containing Works by Abū Ḥāmid Ghazzālī, ʿAyn al-Quḍāt al-Hamadānī, Ibn Sīnā, ʿUmar ibn Sahlān Sāvi, Majduddīn Jīlī and others. Facsimile edition with introductions in Persian and English by Nasrollah Pourjavady. Tehran: Markaz-i Nashr-i Dānishgāh, 1380/2002.

Makdisi, George. "The Non-Ashʿarite Shāfiʿism of Abū Ḥāmid al-Ghazzālī." *Revue des Etudes Islamiques* 54 (1986): 239–57.

Marmura, Michael E. "Avicenna and the Problem of the Infinite Number of Souls." *Mediaeval Studies* 22 (1960): 232–9.

———. "Al-Ghazālī on Bodily Resurrection and Causality in the *Tahāfut* and the *Iqtiṣād*." In *Probing in Islamic Philosophy: Studies In The Philosophies Of Ibn Sina*. Binghamton, NY: Global Academic Publishing, 2005.

Nakamura, Kojiro. "Was Ghazālī an Ashʿarite?" *Memoirs of the Research Department of the Toyo Bunko* 52 (1993): 1–24.

Shihadeh, Ayman. "The Argument from Ignorance and Its Critics in Medieval Arabic Thought," *Arabic Sciences and Philosophy* 23 (2013): 171–220.

———. "Classical Ashʿarī Anthropology: Body, Life and Spirit." *The Muslim World* 102 (2012): 433–77.

———. "From al-Ghazālī to al-Rāzī: 6th/12th Century Developments in Muslim Philosophical Theology," *Arabic Sciences and Philosophy* 15 (2005): 141–79.

Sīdbī, Jamāl R. *Naẓariyyat al-nafs bayna Ibn Sīnā wa-l-Ghazālī*. Cairo: al-Hay'a al-Miṣriyya al-ʿĀmma li-l-Kitāb, 2000.

Treiger, Alexander. *Inspired Knowledge in Islamic Thought: Al-Ghazālī's Theory of Mystical Cognition and Its Avicennian Foundation*. Abingdon and New York: Routledge, 2012.

Walton, Douglas N. *Ad Hominem Arguments*. Tuscaloosa (Ala.): The University of Alabama Press, 1998.

CHAPTER 6

Al-Ghazālī's Veil Section

Comparative Religion before Religionswissenschaft?

Anna Ayşe Akasoy

History of Religion in Political Controversies

On September 12, 2006, the then just recently elected Pope Benedict XVI delivered a lecture on "Faith, Reason and the University" at his former academic home in Regensburg.[1] In this lecture, he quoted what has become a notorious statement of the fourteenth-century Byzantine emperor Manuel II Palaiologos (reg. 1391–1425), according to whom Muhammad had brought nothing new and only evil to the world and Islam was merely spread by violent means. Christianity, in contrast, Benedict XVI argued, combined the best of two worlds: Greek rationalism and Biblical faith, and Christians should remain committed to the harmony between these.

Many Muslims rushed to defend their religion against this representation, and although the Pope was quick to point out that he did not share Manuel's view, the spirit in which he had quoted the emperor was probably well-captured. Unlike John Paul II, Benedict XVI was no great advocate of interfaith dialogue, and if he decided to touch the subject of Islam, which was bound to catch the attention of an audience beyond the small circle of Regensburg professors, why were his comments so limited, superficial and biased? Curiously, the Pope emphasized that a dialogue of religions and cultures was only possible if reason was liberated from its empirical shackles. He did not seem to envisage such dialogue with Islam though, since he took it for granted that Muslims do not try to achieve knowledge of God by rational means at all, neither in the fourteenth century nor today.

A lot of ink has been spilled over the Pope's address. Objections have been raised not only by Muslims, but also by Protestants and secularists. I would like to focus here on historical references as a rhetorical strategy and on the difficulties of quoting past views to support an argument directed at a contemporary audience. A historical example seems perfectly plausible in the context of a lecture about the university where, according to the Pope, theologians, historians, philosophers and philologists commonly serve a single rationality.

1 Benedict XVI, "Faith, Reason and the University: Memories and Reflections."

 | DOI 10.1163/9789004307490_007

In such an environment, it is not necessary to spell out in which ways a statement made in the fourteenth century has to be modified to fit a twenty-first-century purpose. While references to past views form part of a general habitus in the humanities, they are hardly gratuitous in philosophical and political arguments and their usage deserves closer scrutiny both for the sake of understanding the historical case and for the sake of our contemporary debate.

That people evoke past authorities is neither surprising nor should they be criticized for this. It seems an anthropological principle that we define ourselves as members of collectives that have been historically formed. History—whether "ordinary" human or salvation history—is crucial for the self-definition of religious communities. Their truth claims, especially regarding related communities, often rely on historical sequence. Preference given to the temporal priority of appearance establishes the superiority of the earlier movement based on principles such as intellectual property, that essence lies in origins, and that the rule of cultural developments is corruption, while emphasis on temporal posterity supports the superiority of the later movement based on the principles of supersession and evolution.

In debates concerning the oft-cited "clash of civilizations," historical encounters are frequently regarded as setting the framework for today. Historical references can be made in a critical or hostile spirit as well as with the opposite purpose. Violent conflicts are seen as a legacy to be overcome, peaceful collaborations a model to be emulated. If we have reached the famous end of history, then nothing can be that has not already been. That is why Islam needs a Martin Luther or an Enlightenment, and that is why without the historical utopia of Muslim Spain we are all doomed.

Those actively involved in these debates as religious authorities within their respective communities typically have an interest in the history of religious and philosophical doctrines, which, after all, is their profession. Medieval authors who wrote about religious diversity already tended to treat religions as sets of doctrines and thus equate religion with faith. In the confrontation between two proselytizing religions—Islam and Christianity—this may have made sense. Yet, there has always been more to being a follower of a certain religion. Islam, to mention but one example, started as a tribal religion. A lot of interfaith dialogue perpetuates these features of medieval discourse. Such conservative tendencies are hardly surprising given that they support the authorities and elites of the communities. Representatives of religious groups, including Benedict in the lecture mentioned above, show much less interest in socio-economic matters, such as inheritance laws in medieval France, which may have contributed to the Crusader movement. Such circumstances change, but the spirit of a religion, it is often assumed, remains the same.[2]

Medieval Models for Religious Thought in the Twenty-First Century

Who are the historical authors frequently cited in politicized Western European discussions about past religious encounters and why are they so popular? For Catholics, one may think of Thomas Aquinas (d. 1274) who was indebted to Arabic philosophy and who, I would like to add as an afterthought to an earlier point, should make us reconsider to what extent Benedict's "Greek" legacy is actually exclusively Greek. On the Muslim side, Averroes (Ibn Rushd, d. 595/1198) seems to show that rationalism and "Enlightenment" are part of the Islamic heritage and do not need to be imported from the West. More famous in the history of interfaith dialogue is the Catalan missionary Ramon Llull (d. 1315), himself no stranger to Arabic philosophy, who designed a quasi-mathematical system that was meant to demonstrate any truth and allow a comprehensive description of the world and God.[3] What makes Llull so appealing to us today is, among other things, that he presented his philosophy in form of charming tales in which representatives of different religions meet in a respectful way. Llull believed that by settling their doctrinal disagreements religious leaders could achieve world peace. Such hopes are still expressed today, although again often by those who have an interest in highlighting the importance of religious doctrine.

Llull's insight that dialogue is not possible if everyone simply points to the truth of their respective revelation resembles al-Ghazālī's doubt in his autobiography, a text which is quoted outside the narrow circle of Ghazalian experts. Other parallels too explain why these two medieval authors appear frequently in modern interfaith dialogue. In particular those who are spiritually committed will find kindred souls in the two men who have distinguished mystical sides. Both are also examples of "the best of both worlds," combining philosophical rigour and a piety that many believers can identify with today. Likewise, they do not offer as much room for doubt about the relationship between

2 For example, see Ramadan, *Western Muslims and the Future of Islam*, 9, on essential and changing aspects of religion. The focus on dogma in religious encounter extends to the study of these encounters. See Küng and van Ess, *Christentum und Weltreligionen*.

3 For a more detailed discussion of the following see Akasoy, "Al-Ghazālī, Ramon Llull and Religionswissenschaft," 33–59.

philosophy and religion as Averroes or Avicenna (Ibn Sīnā, d. 428/1037)—although, as is well known, these questions are the subject of controversy.

Like any form of name-dropping, references to these and other past writers may be a rhetorical device for demonstrating learnedness and create community. If we want to take them seriously as philosophers, however, the cumbersome task of translating medieval ethics into the contemporary world becomes unavoidable. What can we learn from al-Ghazālī? In order to deal with such questions we have to address the relevant debates and the concepts involved in them first. A fairly long preliminary discussion will be necessary before we return to al-Ghazālī.

Religion in the Public Debate

As the debates which followed Benedict's Regensburg address revealed, a *Kulturkampf* is taking place in Western Europe concerning religion and its role in public life. The Pope made reference to two of the most contested aspects: religious diversity and the relationship between religion and rationalism. What is at stake in the public debate, however, is not merely the extent to which religious communities should engage in interfaith dialogue or the acceptance of scientific theories which seem contrary to religious doctrines. Prominent intellectuals declare religion itself a phenomenon unsuitable for the enlightened human mind of the twenty-first century and significant parts of the general population too consider themselves non-confessional or even atheists.[4]

Just how contested the category of religion is became obvious during the United Kingdom census of 2011, which included the question "What is your religion?" Although answering the question was voluntary and one could tick a "no religion" box, some criticized the very presence of the category in the questionnaire. Religion, it was sometimes argued, was not unavoidable like ethnic identity or gender with all their different options, but rather like soccer or football. Thus, one should not assume, by default, that the category applies to everyone. Some people are passionate fans of Manchester United, some have a general interest in soccer, others support their national team every two years without knowing the offside rule, many have no interest at all in this sport. Likewise, if we use a definition of religion like that implied in the UK Census, i.e., belonging to a certain community defined by metaphysical beliefs in the supernatural, sacred rituals, authorities and a historically formed

---

4 A 2004 survey conducted by the BBC reveals different shapes and shades of being non-religious. See "UK among most secular nations," *BBC News*, February 26, 2004.

identity, many Britons may feel they have no such affiliation or only one of general cultural tradition.

The Academic Study of the History of Religion

Historians of religion in the Atlantic to Oxus region in the medieval period, at least in their professional capacity as critical students of human culture, can follow these political debates without any consequences for their work.[5] After all, most of the individuals we study would have been perfectly happy to tick one of the boxes in the United Kingdom's Census. (Although one might wonder which options would have been listed, which institution would have had an interest in organizing such a survey, and which box, for example, Central Asians in the period of the first Islamic incursions would have ticked.) However, some of the problems which are discussed in the public arena or become obvious in the analysis of these controversies have counterparts in the study of religion and its history. Here too, the category of religion is often contested and undertheorized.

Few historians of religion in the medieval world would probably create as seamless a connection between past and present believers as implied in Benedict's reference to Manuel II and his Persian interlocutor. Debates about expressions such as "Islamic history," "Islamic world" or "Islamic culture" testify to the sensibility of scholars regarding problems involved in the category of religion and the dangers of essentialising. And yet, no suitable alternative has been established—Hodgson's "Islamicate"[6] has been adopted only by a minority of scholars, others perhaps being circumspect of the underlying distinction between religion and civilization or culture. Thus, most scholars continue to use "Islamic" and "Muslim" as well as "religion" and related terms as part of their analytical vocabulary. The politicized standing of religion in the modern world may be an opportunity for historians to rethink these categories.

---

5 Like any discussion of whether concepts known in the present world may have existed in historical cultures and to what extent we can use such concepts if we write about these cultures, the present discussion faces the problem of a hermeneutic circle. See Krech, "Dynamics in the History of Religions: Preliminary Considerations on Aspects of a Research Programme," 20.

6 Hodgson, *The Venture of Islam*, 57–60.

Religion is Like Soccer and Islam is Like Spanish

While representatives of the religious communities often uphold the continuity of their traditions, social scientists present a very different picture. They employ various strategies in order to deconstruct the seemingly unchanging nature of religion. One tendency is to expand this category based on its social functions. Comparing religion and soccer is an argument along such lines. From an anthropological or phenomenological point of view, soccer has a lot in common with religion—there are rituals and priests, prophets and worship, ethics and rules, pilgrimages and sacred sites, orthodoxies, heterodoxies and unbelievers. It can be exhilarating and humbling, uniting and dividing. To others, this comparison may not seem entirely convincing. Most obviously, inflating the term religion bears the risk of rendering it meaningless.[7] In his *Introducing Anthropology of Religion*, Jack David Eller, for instance, explains in very broad terms that, "religion is the discourse, the language and practice, or the means by which human society and culture is extended to include the nonhuman."[8] While it certainly is plausible to consider a pet cemetery part of the sphere of religion, this does not apply to the numerous veterinarians, pet toy shops, dog walking grounds, and cat nail parlours, let alone the coexistence of human and nonhuman animals in rural areas.

Furthermore and more specifically, for most soccer fans, their "religion" concerns a fairly small area of their daily lives, their interactions with others and the world at large. Soccer fails to address some typical religious concerns. Thus, Volkhard Krech defines religion in the following way:

> "The legitimisation and reassurance method that I hypothetically identify as religion has to do with *reassurances by the ultimate authority; with an understanding on how to deal with what is considered unavailable and inescapable*. Religion establishes different ways of dealing with the unavoidable. (…) Religion has to do with the problem of how one can describe the transcendence *that cannot be represented in everyday experience* with immanent means, so how one can transform the unavailable into the available or the unsayable into the sayable."[9]

7 Similar problems have plagued historians of medieval Western Europe for a long time. See, among numerous publications on the difficulties involved in the concept of the state, Davies, "The Medieval State: The Tyranny of a Concept?"

8 Eller, *Introducing Anthropology of Religion*, 9.

9 Krech, "Dynamics in the History of Religions," 23 and 24.

Only a very small minority of soccer fans would probably recognize such an ultimate authority in the sphere of soccer. What the transcendent in this sphere might be I find difficult to imagine. The rituals, rules and authorities of soccer may simply be "nonreligious cognates."[10]

One could also think of religions as comprehensive doctrines in John Rawls's sense. Rather than like Manchester United, Islam would be like utilitarianism. The ambition of Rawls's political liberalism is to create a framework for fair interactions among people who subscribe to different and mutually exclusive comprehensive doctrines. (Political liberalism does not count as a comprehensive doctrine.) But religion is clearly more than, very broadly speaking, a set of doctrines and cultural values. In 1999, the social scientists Aristide Zolberg and Long Litt Woon explained "Why Islam is like Spanish."[11] They compared modes of exclusion in Western Europe against Muslims and in the United States against Hispanics. Both groups are ethnically defined and seen as culturally alien and threatening. Interestingly, the two authors emphasize the great insistence in Europe on the Christian legacy, which runs counter to the impression one gains in many writings about "Islam" and "the West," the former representing religiosity, the latter secularism.

Another tendency in the social sciences aims at a more fundamental deconstruction of religion, as frequently associated with the work of the anthropologist Talal Asad.[12] Among many historians of modern Western Europe who are inspired by his research, it counts as a truism that the category of religion, in particular insofar as it is opposed to the secular, is a product of the Enlightenment. Two historical developments may be adduced to support such a thesis. Firstly, the academic study of religion ("religious studies" as opposed to "theology") as it is practised at many Western universities is characterised by the fact that although students may have a stake in the truth claims of the religions they study, this is not supposed to inform their arguments. This principle requires a critical distance from religion which developed in larger circles only during the Enlightenment. Secondly, the idea of world religions emerged in the context of European colonialism and famously led to the creation of new religions such as Hinduism. Religious studies and classifications were an

10 Eller, *Introducing Anthropology of Religion*, xiv.

11 Zolberg and Woon, "Why Islam is like Spanish: Cultural Incorporation in Europe and the United States."

12 Asad, *Formations of the Secular*.

instrument of power. It was also in the course of these developments that the secular was equated with progress and modernity.[13]

As a result of this deconstruction of religion and the unearthing of the Orientalist mechanisms of religious studies, it seems doubtful that we can apply the category of religion to a period long before the Enlightenment and in an area outside of Western Europe and that we can find traditions of religious studies there. And yet, a lot can be said in favour of maintaining the category for medieval Islam. First of all, the Orientalizing nature of Western religious studies is much more obvious for encounters that first occurred only during the colonial period than for Islam. Eller shows how insufficient concepts primarily associated with Christianity are to describe, for instance, native religion in Australia. Eller cautions against imposing a "Western" concept of religion, but this "Western" concept is not quite as homogeneous and isolated as the criticism of such a mechanism suggests. Not only is Christianity diachronically and geographically diverse,[14] it is also deeply entangled with other religions, notably Judaism and Islam. Christianity and Islam emerged in "sectarian milieus" and the three religions developed in environments where the other religions played a crucial role. Although we have to be mindful of "Orientalizing" Islam and imposing concepts that, for one reason or another, are not suitable, the risk of completely distorting our object of study seems significantly lower.

To trace the development of a concept often means linguistic archaeology. The Arabic word "*dīn*" suggests that a category best translated as religion (as opposed to *īmān*, *umma*, *milla*, *sharīʿa* etc.) may have existed in medieval times in the Islamic world.[15] Modern authors sometimes use medieval Latin sources in order to explore the meaning of *dīn* and frequently discover discrepancies between Arabic and Latin antecedents of the concept of religion. In his interpretation of Petrus Alfonsi's "religious dialogue," Leor Halevi points out that *dīn* is rendered as *lex* where modern translators would deem "religion" more suitable.[16] Carl W. Ernst and Louis Gardet discuss differences between *dīn*

---

13 See Habermas, "Mission im 19. Jahrhundert. Globale Netze des Religiösen," and eadem, "Wissenstransfer und Mission. Sklavenhändler, Missionare und Religionswissenschaftler."

14 The ways confessional differences among German Christian scholars on Oriental Studies, have been analyzed by Marchand, *German Orientalism in the Age of Empire: Religion, Race, and Scholarship*.

15 Surveys of different meanings of *dīn* in the Qurʾān and early Islamic literature can be found in Louis Gardet's article "dīn," in *Encyclopaedia of Islam. New Edition*, 2:293–96; van Ess, *Theologie und* Gesellschaft, 4:565–67, and Ernst, *Following Muhammad: Rethinking Islam in the Contemporary World*, 65.

16 Halevi, "Lex Mahomethi: Carnal and Spiritual Representations of Islamic Law and Ritual in a Twelfth-Century Dialogue by a Jewish Convert to Christianity," 331–32.

and the Latin *religio*. Needless to say, the latter is not identical with the modern English "religion."

Despite long debates, "Islamic culture" and "Islamic world" are terms which have not been thrown overboard, not least because they appear to reflect the worldview of medieval people and the social and political significance of religious affiliations in the medieval period. With the Muslim conquests, Islamic legislation that is sensitive to confessional identity, and scholarly writing about different religious communities, we may have mechanisms that are not too dissimilar from Orientalism. An observation to this effect was made in 1988 by Steven Wasserstrom, but it seems that his recommendation went mostly unheeded in subsequent scholarship: "It may prove significant for future historians of the history of religions to study Islamicate history of religions as a function of the domination of Islamicate civilization over the 'others' within its cultural purview."[17] In addition to what has been mentioned above, further parallels can be identified between modern Western European religious studies and Islamic histories of religion. For the former, Jacques Waardenburg, for example, considered the encounters with new peoples crucial for an attitude to religion and religious diversity that aims at a more objective picture.[18] This observation can also be made for medieval authors such as al-Bīrūnī (d. ca. 442/1050) or Rashīd al-Dīn Fażlallāh (d. 718/1318). Waardenburg brings this new attitude in the West in connection with travel accounts—here too, one can draw a parallel to Muslim travelogues. The early tenth-century Arab traveller Ibn Faḍlān (fl. 309/922), for example, is with his travelogue of a trip to the Volga a valuable source for religious practices in Western Eurasia.[19] While Ibn Faḍlān as the caliph's envoy made a few disparaging comments, there is no reason to assume that his descriptions were distorted by polemical intentions.

Bringing together the discourse about religion as an analytical category in the study of Islamic history and culture on the one hand and among modernists and social scientists on the other hand potentially results in fundamental challenges of the parameters of one of the two fields: either the idea of a Western, (early) modern, Orientalist construction of "religion" is itself Orientalist since it does not consider the possibility that the category existed in other historical and cultural spheres, or the way we have used this category for the

---

17 Wasserstrom, "Islamicate History of Religions?", 411.

18 For this and the following see Waardenburg, *Classical Approaches to the Study of Religion: Aims, Methods and Theories of Research*, 7.

19 See now the new translation of Ibn Faḍlān's report in *Ibn Fadlan and the Land of Darkness: Arab Travellers In the Far North*, 1–58.

medieval Islamic world has been seriously misinformed and distorted by our own attitude to religion.

While the present article is not the place to conduct such an analysis in any serious manner, I would like to discuss what some of the problems outlined above imply for the study of a medieval thinker such as al-Ghazālī. Whether we would like to analyse his views for their own sake, trace his impact or argue for (or against) a greater influence, we should be mindful of the difficulties involved in some of our concepts. The social sciences in particular are Pandora's box to the historian.

Al-Ghazālī's Veil Section

In the famous veil section in his *Mishkāt al-anwār* (*Niche of Lights*), al-Ghazālī classifies the followers of different worldviews according to the veils of light and darkness which separate them from the Truth and which determine their beliefs and actions.[20] In this particular section of the treatise, al-Ghazālī comments on the *ḥadīth* according to which God has seventy veils of light and darkness and if He were to lift them, His sight would burn whoever sees Him. Humankind is divided into three groups depending on whether someone is veiled by darkness alone, by light alone or by a combination of both. In the main part of the veil section, al-Ghazālī discusses the three categories and who belongs to each of them.

Those veiled by darkness alone are *mulḥida* who do not believe in God or the Last Day and who are interested in this world only. Among them are materialists who only see the force of nature and those dominated by their animal souls. The latter are divided into four types. (1) The first type are hedonists. (2) The second type are those who enjoy using power, often in a sadistic way. Al-Ghazālī counts among them Bedouins (*al-aʿrāb*), Kurds and many stupid people (*ḥamqā*). (3) The third type are obsessed by property, (4) the fourth by fame and honour. This category also includes those who declare themselves Muslims without truly believing and for opportunistic reasons.

Although the groups discussed as part of the first category are marked by metaphysical premises (i.e., there is no divinity and life ends with death, there is no hereafter), their most important features are their motivations and desires. It is also important to underline that this represents the principal method of classifying people in the veil section. Frequently, the established religious communities constitute the structure of texts about other religions.

20 al-Ghazālī, *Mishkāt al-anwār*, 175–82; Griffel, *Al-Ghazālī's Philosophical Theology*, 245–60.

In the veil section, these labels are less significant and the boundaries between collectives fuzzy. Notably, the first category includes people who declare themselves Muslims.

The groups included in the second category, veiled by veils of light and darkness, are defined by epistemological features. The three sources of darkness are sense, imagination and corrupt rational comparisons. (I) The people of the first sub-category go beyond their own souls and desires and acknowledge a divinity, but they are limited by their senses. Among them are (1) idol worshippers who fabricate idols of precious materials since they are capable of worshipping might and beauty, but they cannot go beyond that; and (2) a "community of the furthest Turks" who have neither *milla* nor *sharīʿa* and who revere beautiful things in nature. What makes them superior to the idol worshippers is that they do not limit their worship to individual things (i.e., they are not bound to material objects, they transcend them) and they do not venerate man-made objects; (3) fire worshippers recognize the luminous of the divinity that goes beyond ordinary beauty and is dangerous; (4) star worshippers recognize that fire can be under human control and focus on the radiance and elevation of the heavenly bodies; (5) sun worshippers choose the supreme celestial being; (6) light worshippers have transcended such boundaries of the divine and attribute evil things to the divinity's antagonist. They are dualists.

(II) The second sub-category are superior to those limited by their sense perception, but they are limited by their imagination. They worship something existing that sits on the throne. Al-Ghazālī in this category mentions anthropomorphists (*al-mujassima*) and the Karramites, who are also known for their anthropomorphism, although he does not list any doctrinal details. The superior groups within this category deny that God has a body. That al-Ghazālī is particularly concerned with the issue of attributes here becomes obvious when he describes the (III) third subgroup of people limited by their imagination as those who worship a divinity that is hearing, seeing, speaking, knowing, powerful, desiring and living, but they fail to appreciate the transcendent nature of the deity. Rather, they understand the attributes along the lines of human perceptions.

Al-Ghazālī presents a few examples of those who are veiled by veils of light alone. (1) One of them realizes that these attributes apply in different ways to humans than to the deity. (2) The second group realize that they are angels who are the movers of the heavens and that the Lord moves the furthest celestial body. (3) Superior to them are those who understand that this relationship is not one of direct contact. Finally, the most elevated category are those who "have arrived" (*al-wāṣilūn*). They have realized that none of the above applies to the divinity, who is also the creator of what others consider the divinity.

Among this group are also the "elite of the elite" (*khawāṣṣ al-khawāṣṣ*) who perceive nothing but His face, i.e., have a superior mystical experience.

This classification of people according to their beliefs, motivations and actions has intrigued scholars for a long time.[21] They have been particularly interested in identifying those groups which al-Ghazālī merely alludes to, wondering why other groups are not included and aligning the hierarchy with statements al-Ghazālī made, for example about philosophers, in other texts. What interests us here is the understanding of religion in this passage, which seems to extend further than the two elements often cited as fundamental to a pre-modern concept of religion, namely community and religious law. Thus, the remotest Turks have neither of these, but can still be classified according to their objects of worship in the second category (and not even among the *mulḥida* who don't believe in God and the Day of Judgment).

In an article published in 1991, Hermann Landolt suggested that the concept of religion in the veil section resembled that of modern religious studies.[22] He cites a distinction discussed by Charles Adams according to which comparative views of religion are characterized by two elements: *epoché*, the irenic bracketing of one's own religious convictions, and the attempt to develop a taxonomy which reflects one's own background.[23] Both, Landolt suggests, are represented in the "veil section." In order to explore this association of the veil section, comparative religion, and Religionswissenschaft, and to return to the more general problems outlined at the beginning of this article, we will begin with a survey of different views regarding comparative religion in the medieval period, discuss briefly features of an Islamic attitude to religious diversity and the relationship between comparative religion and Religionswissenschaft and then draw a few conclusions regarding the veil section.

Comparative Religion in Medieval Islamic Literature

Among historians of religious studies, views differ as to when comparative religion emerged as an autonomous academic exercise that was not determined

21 For an overview of Western interpretations of the veil section in al-Ghazālī's *Mishkāt al-anwār* see Griffel, "Al-Ghazālī's Cosmology in the Veil Section of His *Mishkāt al-Anwār*," 27–31, and idem, "The Western Reception of al-Ghazālī's Cosmology from the Middle Ages to the 21st Century," 47–52.

22 Landolt, "al-Ghazālī and '*Religionswissenschaft*:' Some Notes on the *Mishkāt al-Anwār*."

23 Landolt, "al-Ghazālī and '*Religionswissenschaft*,'" 28; Adams, "Islamic Religious Tradition," esp. 38ff and 49–50, where Adams distinguishes different modern Western approaches to Islam.

by apologetic and polemical aims. In a frequently-cited study, Hans G. Kippenberg explored the rhetorical strategies used by historians of religion in the modern period against the backdrop of the rise of science.[24] Histories of religion were part of philosophies of religion which tried to preserve a part of human culture that did not succumb to the principles of modern rationalism. The bulk of Kippenberg's monograph is a historical survey which begins with Thomas Hobbes. The author does not discuss any earlier cases and why they may or may not fall into the same category. Kippenberg's study—like Talal Asad's work—is taken to exclude the possibility of comparative religion existing in the pre-modern period and outside of Western Europe or at least to declare such cases insignificant. Manuel Vásquez, for instance, summarized that Kippenberg "convincingly demonstrates that the comparative study of religion is a historical artefact, the rise of which is intimately bound up with the process of modernization in Europe."[25]

Eric J. Sharpe presented a slightly different picture in his earlier study on the history of comparative religion. While devoting the main part of his book to more or less the same protagonists as Kippenberg and seeing the beginning of the modern study of religion in the late nineteenth century, Sharpe also paid attention to the "antecedents" of comparative religion. These precursors of the academic discipline fulfilled fairly simple conditions and developed virtually simultaneously with religions. "Comparative religion (…) usually presupposes, if it does not absolutely require, a certain degree of detachment from a dominant religious tradition, and a degree of interest in the religious beliefs and practices of others."[26] It may thus not surprise that Sharpe identifies the first antecedents of comparative religion in classical antiquity. On the Muslim side, al-Ṭabarī, al-Masʿūdī and al-Bīrūnī are only mentioned in passing. "The honour of writing the first history of religion in world literature seems (…) to belong to the Muslim Shahrastānī. (…) This outstanding work far outstrips anything which Christian writers were capable of producing at the same period."[27] Although Wasserstrom had commented along similar lines in 1988 that, "there is general agreement among historians of the history of religions that Islamicate civilization produced the greatest premodern historical studies of world religions,"[28] medieval Islamic literature plays a fairly small role in modern accounts of the academic study of religion. Kippenberg and Sharpe reflect the

24 Kippenberg, *Discovering Religious History in the Modern Age.*

25 Vásquez, "Studying Religion in Motion: A Networks Approach," 154.

26 Sharpe, *Comparative Religion*, 2.

27 Ibid., 11.

28 Wasserstrom, "Islamicate History of Religions?" 408.

general state of the debate—if pre-modern religious studies are part of the picture, they are not discussed in much detail.

Jacques Waardenburg is a noteworthy exception in this regard. Rather than merely affirming the pioneering role of al-Shahrastānī (d. 548/1153) and his *Book of Religions and Sects* (*Kitāb al-Milal wa-l-niḥal*), he explored how medieval Muslim writers developed a distinctive history of religions. Like many others, Waardenburg sees the beginning of the study of religion as an autonomous discipline in the nineteenth century and identifies the scholar of Indian studies Max Müller (1823–1900) as an early protagonist. Sharpe calls Müller's *Introduction to the Science of Religion* (1873), "the foundation document of comparative religion in the English-speaking world."[29] At the same time, Waardenburg does not restrict his definition of comparative religion or even religious studies to this modern development. Instead of insisting that the study of religion has to follow the ideal of an objective description which requires a strictly secularized attitude to religion, Waardenburg also allows for a normative understanding of religion as part of religious studies.[30]

One may indeed wonder what the criteria for the critical distance to religion are that is often considered crucial for the academic study of religion in the modern period and whether such an attitude has to be present in a specific writer, or also among his contemporaries. Al-Shahrastānī famously declared: "I impose upon myself the obligation to present the view of each sect as I find them in their works without favour or prejudice, without declaring which are correct and which are incorrect, which are true and which are false."[31] While such words, if written by a scholar in nineteenth-century Western Europe, may have been taken as a typically modern academic attitude to religion, the period in which al-Shahrastānī lived seems to make the association with other attitudes more plausible to present-day scholars. Although he is not concerned with histories of religion, Adam Gaiser sees the *Kitāb al-Milal wa-l-nihal* in the context of heresiography, in particular of the Isma'ilite and Ash'arite traditions and points out parallels in Abū Tammām's (fl. *c.* 350/961) heresiographical *Book of the Tree* (*Kitāb al-Shajara*).[32] The line between the history of religion and

29 Waardenburg, *Classical Approaches to the Study of Religion*, 6–14; Sharpe, *Comparative Religion*, xi.

30 Waardenburg, *Perspektiven der Religionswissenschaft*, 20.

31 al-Shahrastānī, *Kitāb al-Milal wa-l-niḥal*, 5; French transl. 1:114. See Gaiser, "Satan's Seven Specious Arguments: al-Shahrastānī's Kitāb al-Milal wa-l-Nihal in an Ismaili Context," 179.

32 Ibid., 181–83. On Abū Tammām's heresiography see Madelung and Walker, *An Ismaili Heresiography*. It might be worth exploring parallels between al-Ghazālī's treatment of religious diversity in the veil section and the Isma'ilite heresiographies. They combine doctrinal commitment with discussions of religious diversity and were written in a

heresiography is difficult to draw and becomes even more difficult if one follows Waardenburg's suggestion to loosen the criterion of a non-normative attitude.

The different attitudes of Kippenberg and Sharpe on the one hand and Waardenburg on the other certainly owe a lot to their respective fields of expertise. They also reflect the two tendencies among social scientists outlined above. If we accept that our academic disciplines are the products of a culture set in history, we may either restrict our perspective to this environment alone (without making any claims as to whether, where and when a discipline existed outside of this area), or we may expand our perspective and define those criteria non-essential which we identify as culturally specific.

An Islamic "Theology of Religion"

As we have seen from Landolt's quotation of Adams, many historians of the study of religion approach the subject from the latter inclusive perspective and acknowledge or elaborate on the second point, the taxonomy which reflects their background. Thus, Wasserstrom remarked that, "[i]n all instances of Islamicate history of religions, its governing concern, in the final analysis, is the relation of the groups studied to Islam."[33] Likewise, according to Waardenburg, Islamic classifications of different religions reveal "typically Islamic criteria."[34] Muslim authors combined, "empirical research (...) that employs philological, literary, historical, and social scientific methods"[35] and the Qurʾānic taxonomy and assessment of other religions that reflected the late antique landscape.[36] Waardenburg saw an entire Islamic "theology of religions" at work which one might also recognize in the veil section: "There is one God, whom human beings have to become conscious of, to whom they should surrender, and whose will is that they obey the religious prescriptions."[37] Further elements that Waardenburg considers part of this "theology of religions" are not

similar historical milieu. Gaiser, "Satan's Seven Specious Arguments," 184, specifies Khorasan in the 4th/10th to 6th/12th centuries.

33 Wasserstrom, *Islamicate History of Religions?*, 410–11, states: "Whether this concern is predominantly determined by the abstract polarity of dispassionate scholarship/engaged polemic, or by the practical polarity of tolerance/coercion, or some combination of these, the ultimately determinative opposition was that of Islam/non-Islamic religions."

34 Waardenburg, *Muslims and Others: Relations in Context*, 24.

35 Ibid., 25.

36 Ibid., 25.

37 Ibid., 165.

mentioned explicitly in the veil section. Thus, while *The Niche of Light* is an esoteric interpretation of a passage in the Qurʾān and the veil section provides commentary of a *ḥadīth*, revelation and prophecy do not appear as topics in the classification of religious groups (unless one counts the absence of *sharīʿa* in the case of the remotest Turks).

Although the Qurʾānic taxonomy of religions does not provide the predominant framework in the veil section, there are elements of it in the passage. As Landolt had already pointed out, in verses 74–79 of *sura* 6, Abraham recognizes that the idol worshipping of his ancestors is a mistake. God shows him the realms of the heavens and the earth. Abraham contemplates ever higher heavenly bodies (a star, the moon, the sun). Every time he sees a body rising he thinks that it must be his Lord. Every time it sets, he realizes that this cannot be the case. Finally, he worships God as the creator.

Likewise, al-Ghazālī seems to make the last point in Waardenburg's Islamic "theology of religions" only implicitly: "There is one monotheistic Religion that is, beyond empirical Islam, the primordial and eternal Islam, radically opposed to all forms of idolatry or 'associationism' and to all forms of disobedience to the basic rules of religion."[38] In the veil section, there is no radical opposition between two sets of beliefs, but rather a very detailed hierarchy in which "Islam" is no homogeneous entity that automatically occupies the highest place in the taxonomy.

Scholars have indeed wondered about the selection of religious communities in the veil section and about the absence of Jews and Christians in particular.[39] These two groups are not only crucially important for the Qurʾānic taxonomy of religions, but also figure prominently in heresiographies. Al-Ghazālī does not seem to be basing himself on any prior list of communities, but selects them according to the needs of his spiritual and intellectual epistemology. He notes several times that more could be said about a sect and that there are further sects which fit into a given category.

The Islamic character of classifications of religions composed by medieval Muslims also becomes obvious when they reflect internal debates. As Waardenburg pointed out, they sometimes associated certain other religions with Muslim sects.[40] Both aspects are present in the veil section. The divine

38 Ibid., 165.

39 Gairdner, "Al-Ghazālī's Mishkāt al-Anwār and the Ghazālī-Problem," 129–30. Gairdner suggested that al-Ghazālī did not know where in the category of those veiled by light and darkness Jews and Christians were. Khalil, *Islam and the Fate of Others: The Salvation Question*, 29.

40 Waardenburg, *Muslims and Others*, 165.

attributes can be recognized behind the reasons why the idol worshippers and others in the same category worship objects. Later on in the classification, al-Ghazālī discusses the problem of the *ṣifāt* more explicitly. Muslim sects are placed in the same categories as non-Islamic religions. The judgmental or normative attitude which comes with a confessionally committed approach is reflected in the explicit hierarchy in which some forms of belief are superior to others. Al-Ghazālī, however, does not refute other doctrines in the way this is sometimes done in heresiographies.

While the veil section has thus several features which have been discussed for medieval Islamic comparative religion, the modern academic appreciation of religion Landolt invokes with the German term Religionswissenschaft typically also features an abstract notion of religion. As far as I can see, Waardenburg does not consider such a theorized understanding of religion necessary for comparative religion. Landolt's choice of terminology in his translations of passages from the veil section suggests that al-Ghazālī had such a more general sense. Arabic "*ta'alluh*," for instance, he renders as "religiosity."[41] Al-Ghazālī's main concern in the veil section seems to be with approaches to the divine and if there is a concept of religion, it is implicit and selective. While many elements commonly associated with (the Islamic) religion are not mentioned in the veil section, the elements which appear in categories two and three are more typically associated with religion. Metaphysical and cosmological beliefs determine what human beings can and should want to achieve. As the inclusion of the opportunistic Muslims in the first category shows, al-Ghazālī is interested in what people actually believe. Apart from the opportunistic Muslims, people's superficial and actual beliefs are identical. Nobody in this reckoning is an opportunistic idol worshipper. Human actions (for the second and third categories acts of worship) are an important expression of beliefs.

There are two further elements in Waardenburg's survey which can be used to analyse the way al-Ghazālī deals with religious diversity in the veil section and what understanding of religion he implied. Firstly, Waardenburg observes that the judgments of *mutakallimūn* and *fuqahā'* "concern the religious systems—doctrines, prescriptions, and rites—rather than the individual people adhering to them."[42] While it is indeed the case that al-Ghazālī classifies religious movements as collectives with collective beliefs and practices, his account also has a component that individuals can identify with. Not least, the question of actual belief has to be posed on an individual level. The veil section

41 This is bound to be a controversial translation. A translation as something to the effect of "coming closer to God" would probably provoke less criticism.

42 Waardenburg, *Muslims and Others*, 165.

contains elements of a *kalām* discourse, but does not concern itself with any legal problems. It resembles a religious anthropology insofar as it explores why humans venerate gods. Modern anthropology may help us to gain further insights into al-Ghazālī's approach.

If we compare al-Ghazālī's method to that of modern anthropologists, the difference could hardly be greater. Thus, Eller explains that, "[a]nthropology may attempt to explain *what* a society believes, but it is not ours to ask 'how they can believe it,' since such a prejudicial attitude presupposes that it is a thing that is hard—or bad—to believe."[43] In the anthropological study of religion, the focus lies on lived social practices rather than doctrines and what is "in people's heads."[44] These are precisely the questions al-Ghazālī is concerned with in the veil section: what is in people's heads and how can they believe it? If not by working with methods comparable to those of the medieval scholar, modern anthropology may provide us with insights to analyse his work. Talal Asad explains that, "[w]hat is distinctive about modern anthropology is the comparison of embedded concepts (representations) between societies differently located in time or space. The important thing in this comparative analysis is not their origin (Western or non-Western), but the forms of life that articulate them, the powers they release or disable."[45]

In order to explore the concept of religion which underlies the veil section along such lines we would have to ask a number of questions which might be too difficult to answer. While we may be fairly well informed about the author, we cannot be sufficiently certain about the readership or how al-Ghazālī's readers would have related his statements to actual non-Muslims. A question which might help to get further insights into such issues is genre and how the veil section relates to histories of religion that resemble heresiographies, as well as to legal assessments of non-Muslims. Both lend themselves more obviously to an analysis of power structures.

The Veil Section and Religionswissenschaft

Do the two features of a comparative view of religion that Landolt has pointed out then suffice to mark the veil section as an example of such an exercise? As we have seen from the above, key concepts in the study of the history of religion are contested, so much so that several answers to this question are

43 Eller, *Introducing Anthropology of Religion*, xiii.

44 Ibid., 3.

45 Asad, *Formations of the Secular*, 17.

possible. If we follow Sharpe and in particular Waardenburg and identify comparative religion in the medieval Islamic world, it might be possible to extend the list of usual suspects (notably al-Bīrūnī and al-Shahrastānī). Al-Maqdisī (or: al-Muqaddasī , fl. 355/966), whose *Book of Creation and of History* (*Kitāb al-Badʾ wa-l-taʾrīkh*) usually counts as historiography, also compares elements of different religions.[46] This author would be an interesting point for comparison with early modern Western authors. As Sharpe pointed out, "as the nineteenth century advanced, it became increasingly clear that the real focus of the study of religion was to be located, not in transcendental philosophy, but in the altogether this-worldly categories of history, progress development and evolution."[47] How much value did medieval Muslim authors such as al-Maqdisī find in the history of religion and did they see past religions as a proof for the existence of God?

As already stated, one of the main risks of extending analytical categories is that the defining criteria can be watered down. Both elements that Landolt mentioned can also be identified among pre-modern Western authors of inter-religious dialogues such as the above-mentioned Ramón Llull and may simply reflect a way of philosophically-informed medieval scholars to write about religious diversity. Furthermore, a "comparative view of religion" is not necessarily identical with "comparative religion," let alone with "Religionswissenschaft," and even a non-judgmental attitude may not make the crucial difference.

Then again, comparative religion may not be the only exercise known from religious studies which can be identified in the veil section. Sharpe, for example, distinguished different types of comparative religion: "the history of religion, the psychology of religion, the sociology of religion, the phenomenology of religion and the philosophy of religion."[48] While the veil section does not develop some of these aspects, it may count as a psychology or phenomenology of religion and should thus be assessed primarily as an exercise in that discipline rather than in comparative religion. Waardenburg distinguishes three basic patterns in the academic study of religion: (1) to study religions as part of a different academic discipline, (2) to examine more specific religious beliefs and practices (such as similarities or other classifications), and (3) to contextualize religious phenomena within their social and historical settings.[49] The fact that religions are not the primary topic in *Mishkāt al-anwār* connects it to the first pattern. One may recognize in the veil section an endeavour

46 Maqdisī, *Le Livre de la creation et de l'histoire*, 1:63 (Arabic text).

47 Sharpe, *Comparative Religion*, 24.

48 Ibid., xiii.

49 Waardenburg, *Perspektiven der Religionswissenschaft*, 18.

which Sharpe describes as an insight of the late nineteenth century: "to understand religion inevitably involves comparison."[50] One may add to this: to understand one's own religion inevitably involved comparison. The latter reflects the attitude to religious diversity in medieval inter-religious dialogues, while the former seems to require a more abstract notion of religion. The examination of different ways of *ta'alluh*, or striving for the divine, parallels the second pattern that Waardenburg described. Elaborating on this pattern, he explains that scholars can look for basic structures which appear in different ways in different religions, or they can establish typologies of certain religious phenomena. This description does not seem to be too different from al-Ghazālī's veil section. Curiously, Waardenburg points out that scholars who are more spiritually engaged tend to approach religion using the second pattern.[51]

In certain respects, the approach to religious diversity in the veil section mirrors that of the UK government. Religion (or, in terms of the veil section, approaching the divine) is a category that applies to everybody. Even those who do not have any positive religious beliefs can still be classified. Both Landolt and William H. T. Gairdner intimated that al-Ghazālī developed a philosophy of religion—rather than a religious philosophy—in his veil section, which seems to require a meta-perspective on religion. As the scholarship discussed above shows, it is not at all clear that the veil section fulfils the necessary conditions. Kippenberg, for example, entitled his first chapter "From the Philosophy of Religion to the History of Religions." Even the earliest authors discussed in this chapter such as Hobbes or Hume had a more elaborate concept of religion than what we can see in the veil section. For academics who study the history of religion it is important to know where al-Ghazālī's veil section stands in this respect—for reasons of intellectual rigour, if nothing else. But—to return to the point where this article has started—for those who refer to historical authorities in political debates too it is critical to know what understanding of religion transpired in a text such as the veil section.

Al-Ghazālī and Modern Religious Philosophy

Back thus from the historians of religion to those who express their own views on religion and faith. One can easily use al-Ghazālī to preach to the converted, but does he have anything to offer to those who believe that Islam is like

50 Sharpe, *Comparative Religion*, xii.

51 Waardenburg, *Perspektiven der Religionswissenschaft*, 18–19.

Manchester United? In other words, al-Ghazālī can be said to have presented a religious philosophy in his *Niche of Lights* (as well as in other works) and this philosophy probably appeals to those with similar inclinations. A philosophy of religion, however, does not require commitment of faith. What then could al-Ghazālī's message to the twenty-first-century unbeliever be? Atheists may very well stop reading after finding themselves insulted in the first few sentences. A sceptical reader might appreciate al-Ghazālī's radicalism in his autobiography,[52] but the solution is rather disappointing. A light in the heart turns on the presence or absence of faith and is thus not much better than a reference to the truth of one's scripture. The problems involved in the position of religion in the veil section reflect more general difficulties of translating medieval thought into the modern period.

Then again, al-Ghazālī's is hardly a uniquely medieval way of arguing. Since we have no empirical evidence for the existence of God, believers still struggle to demonstrate the truth of their faith and the solutions they find sometimes resemble that of al-Ghazālī. Tariq Ramadan, for instance, in his *Western Muslims and the Future of Islam*, presents an interpretation of Islam that reconciles faith and reason, although this interpretation promises success primarily among those who already share similar views.

Those who are not already sympathetic to Ramadan's views will probably find his arguments unpersuasive. The author, not unlike al-Ghazālī, describes faith as the most natural part of the human being, whereas many today believe that the most natural is what is most deeply rooted in our genetic makeup and what is visible in apes. They will neither see the spark in their hearts Ramadan evokes nor read the divine in the book of nature. For those whose views are rooted in post-metaphysical traditions, it is presumptuous to assume, as Ramadan does, that the primary responsibility of the human being lies in seeking the divine.

Among the numerous criticisms which have been directed against Tariq Ramadan is his account of Islamic intellectual history which, to put it in a nutshell, begins with al-Ghazālī and continues with Ibn Taymiyya (d. 728/1328). Critics such as the German-Lebanese Ralph Ghadban identify al-Ghazālī with the end of reason as an autonomous capacity.[53] This limitation of reason does not strike me as an exclusively Islamic affair. Even though Ramadan dismisses

52 See his chapter on the "inroads of skepticism" (*madākhil al-safsaṭa*) in al-Ghazālī, *al-Munqidh min al-ḍalāl*, 12–14.

53 See Ghadban, *Tariq Ramadan und die Islamisierung Europas*, 71 for Ramadan's account of Islamic intellectual history.

"the West" as decadent and secular, his interpretation of Islam is reminiscent of the Pope's agenda for the Christian faith.

In my opinion, interfaith dialogue never possessed the key to world peace, but I also sympathize with Jürgen Habermas' challenge that those who believe that religion is like soccer should try to understand the point of view of those who believe that religion is like gender. As we have seen from the Pope's address, the dividing line does not lie between "religious Islam" and "secular West," but rather runs through both spheres. When it comes to an agreement about the principles according to which we should interact, there is nothing wrong with paying respect to our pre-modern intellectual ancestors. Yet, as Habermas has pointed out in his debate with Benedict XVI, acknowledging the religious foundation of modern political philosophy as a historical development does not grant it a constitutive function for this philosophy, which is post-metaphysical. In view of the difficulties of aligning al-Ghazālī's taxonomy of religion and "Religionswissenschaft," one should wonder to what extent al-Ghazālī is rather too easily transposed into a modern setting not only in matters of religious diversity, but also regarding faith and reason.

Conclusions

As this article has shown, the gap between medieval and modern writing about religion is difficult to bridge, but the project of writing about the understanding of religion among medieval Muslims is not pointless. In his study of the formation of the secular, Talal Asad argued that, "[a]ny discipline that seeks to understand 'religion' must also try to understand its other."[54] While the secular might be the other of religion in the modern day, establishing the other for the medieval period is more difficult. According to the modern prejudice, the medieval world was so permeated by religion that it was impossible to transcend this category. The hierarchy in the veil section reflects the difficulties of this situation. While every human being can be subject to this classification, the other of religion is also the absence of transcendental doctrines and of belief in the divine. It is something that is as yet nameless.

Another question which would be important to explore is the extent to which the concept of religion in medieval Islamic societies was different from concepts of religion in the milieu in which Islam first emerged. It has often been said that Muhammad's movement reflected the late antique model in which empire was defined by an emperor, a religion, a language and a capital.

54 Asad, *Formation of the Secular*, 22.

Modern Western scholarship about the Muslim conquests is a picture book case for how much historians have been struggling with the category of religion. While there is a tendency to "reduce" religion, i.e., explain it only in terms of something else (e.g., Muslims conquered to achieve material gains), other accounts attribute agency to religion in ways that more anthropologically-informed historians consider critically ("Islam made Muslims conquer"). A different concept of religion may have developed by the time al-Ghazālī was writing.

The veil section is not the most obvious starting-point for an exploration of these questions. Al-Fārābī's (d. 339/950–51) works may lend themselves much more to such an analysis. For the field of Ghazali-studies, however, it is important to assess what kind of concept of religion he had. Furthermore, texts about religious diversity reveal significant insights into a more wide-spread understanding of religion that the works of the *falāsifa* may not capture.

Historical references come with considerable pitfalls, whether we are dealing with more normative views such as the Pope's address or more analytical approaches such as Landolt's study. Especially in philosophically engaged ways of dealing with the history of ideas, we cannot simply assume that rhetorical interpolations of past and present are understood in the way we mean them. Although tedious perhaps, we need to spell out why we refer to historical figures and what that implies for our own views.[55]

Bibliography

Adams, Charles J. "Islamic Religious Tradition." In *The Study of the Middle East: Research and Scholarship in the Humanities and Social Sciences*. Edited by L. Binder. New York: John Wiley & Sons, 1976. 29–95.

Akasoy, Anna. "Al-Ghazālī, Ramon Llull and Religionswissenschaft." *The Muslim World* 102 (2012): 33–59.

al-Akiti, M. Afifi and H. A. Hellyer. "The Negotiation of Modernity through Tradition in Contemporary Muslim Intellectual Discourse: The Neo-Ghazālian, Attasian Perspective." In *Knowledge, Language, Thought and the Civilization of Islam. Essays in Honor of Syed Muhammad Naquib al-Attas*. Edited by Wan Mohd *et al.* Skudai (Malaysia): UTM Press, 2010. .

55 A good example in that respect is al-Akiti and Hellyer, "The Negotiation of Modernity through Tradition in Contemporary Muslim Intellectual Discourse: The Neo-Ghazālian, Attasian Perspective," 119–34.

Asad, Talal. *Formations of the Secular: Christianity, Islam, Modernity.* Stanford: Stanford University Press, 2003.

Benedict XVI. "*Faith, Reason and the University: Memories and Reflections.*" Lecture given at the University of Regensburg on 12 September 2006. Transcript and translation from The Holy See: <http://www.vatican.va/holy_father/benedict_xvi/speeches/2006/september/documents/hf_ben-xvi_spe_20060912_university-regensburg_en.html> (last accessed Sept. 29, 2014).

Davies, Rees. "The Medieval State: The Tyranny of a Concept?" *Journal of Historical Sociology* 16 (2003): 280–300.

Eller, Jack David. *Introducing Anthropology of Religion: Culture to the Ultimate.* New York: Routledge, 2007.

Encyclopaedia of Islam. New Edition. Edited by an editorial committee consisting of H. A. R. Gibb *et al.* 13 vols. Leiden and London: Luzac and Brill, 1954–2009.

Ernst, Carl W. *Following Muhammad: Rethinking Islam in the Contemporary World.* Chapel Hill: The University of North Carolina Press, 2003.

Gairdner, William H. T. "Al-Ghazālī's *Mishkāt al-Anwār* and the Ghazālī-Problem." *Der Islam* 5 (1914): 121–53.

Gaiser, Adam R. "Satan's Seven Specious Arguments: al-Shahrastānī's Kitāb al-Milal wa-l-Nihal in an Ismaili Context." *Journal of Islamic Studies* 19 (2008): 178–95.

Ghadban, Ralph. *Tariq Ramadan und die Islamisierung Europas.* Berlin: Hans Schiler, 2006.

al-Ghazālī, Muḥammad ibn Muḥammad. *Mishkāt al-anwār wa-miṣfāt al-asrār.* Edited by ʿAbd al-ʿAzīz ʿIzz al-Dīn al-Sayrawān. Beirut: ʿĀlam al-Kutub, 1407/1986.

———. *al-Munqidh min al-ḍalāl / Erreur et délivrance.* Edition and French transl. by F. Jabre. Beirut: Commission libanaise pour la traduction des chefs-d'œuvre, 1969

Griffel, Frank. *Al-Ghazālī's Philosophical Theology.* Oxford: Oxford University Press, 2009.

———. "Al-Ghazālī's Cosmology in the Veil Section of His *Mishkāt al-Anwār.*" In *Avicenna and his Legacy: A Golden Age of Science and Philosophy.* Edited by Tzvi Langermann. Turnhout (Belgium): Brepols. 2009. 27–49.

———. "The Western Reception of al-Ghazālī's Cosmology from the Middle Ages to the 21st Century." *Dîvân: Disiplinlerarası Çalışmalar Dergisi / Dîvân: Journal of Interdisciplinary Studies* 16 (2011): 33–62. <http://www.divandergisi.com/>

Habermas, Rebekka. "Mission im 19. Jahrhundert. Globale Netze des Religiösen." *Historische Zeitschrift* 287 (2008): 629–79.

———. "Wissenstransfer und Mission. Sklavenhändler, Missionare und Religionswissenschaftler." *Geschichte und Gesellschaft* 36 (2010): 257–84.

Halevi, Leor. "Lex Mahomethi: Carnal and Spiritual Representations of Islamic Law and Ritual in a Twelfth-Century Dialogue by a Jewish Convert to Christianity." In *The Islamic Scholarly Tradition: Studies in History, Law, and Thought in Honor of Professor Michael Allan Cook.* Edited by A. Q. Ahmed *et al.* Leiden: Brill, 2011. 315–42.

Hodgson, Marshall G. S. *The Venture of Islam. Conscience and History in a World Civilization*. Vol. 1. *The Classical Age of Islam*. Chicago: University of Chicago Press, 1974.

Ibn Faḍlān, Aḥmad. *Ibn Fadlan and the Land of Darkness: Arab Travellers In the Far North*. Translated by P. Lunde and C. Stone. London: Penguin, 2012.

Khalil, Mohammad Hassan. *Islam and the Fate of Others: The Salvation Question*. Oxford: Oxford University Press, 2012.

Kippenberg, Hans G. *Discovering Religious History in the Modern Age*. Princeton: Princeton University Press, 2002.

Krech, Volkhard. "Dynamics in the History of Religions: Preliminary Considerations on Aspects of a Research Programme." In *Dynamics in the History of Religions between Asia and Europe: Encounters, Notions, and Comparative Perspectives*. Edited by Volkard Krech and Marion Steinicke. Leiden: Brill, 2011. 15–70.

Küng ,Hans and Josef van Ess. *Christentum und Weltreligionen. Islam*. Munich: Piper, 1994.

Landolt, Hermann. "Ghazālī and '*Religionswissenschaft*.' Some Notes on the *Mishkāt al-Anwār*." *Asiatische Studien* (Zurich) 45 (1991): 19–72.

Madelung, Wilferd and Paul E. Walker. *An Ismaili Heresiography: The "Bāb al-shayṭān" From Abū Tammām's Kitāb al-Shajara*. Leiden: Brill, 1998.

al-Maqdisī, al-Muṭahhar ibn Ṭāhir. *Kitāb al-Badʾ wa-l-taʾrīkh / Livre de la création et de l'histoire*. Edition and French transl. by Clément Huart. 6 vols. Paris : Leroux, 1899–1919.

Marchand, Suzanne L. *German Orientalism in the Age of Empire: Religion, Race, and Scholarship*. Cambridge: Cambridge University Press, 2009.

Ramadan, Tariq. *Western Muslims and the Future of Islam*. Oxford: Oxford University Press, 2005.

al-Shahrastānī, Muḥammad ibn ʿAbd al-Karīm. *al-Milal wa-l-niḥal = Book of Religious and Philosophical Sects*. Edited by William Cureton. 2 vols. London: Printed for the Society for the Publication of Oriental Texts, 1842–46.

——— *Livre des religions et des sects*. French translation by Daniel Gimaret, Jean Jolivet, and Guy Monnot. 2 vols. Louvain/Paris: Peeters/UNESCO, 1986–93.

Sharpe, Eric J. *Comparative Religion*: A History. La Salle (Il.): Open Court, 1986.

"UK among most secular nations," *BBC News*. Last updated: February 26, 2004. <http://news.bbc.co.uk/2/hi/programmes/wtwtgod/3518375.stm> (last accessed Sept. 29, 2014).

van Ess, Josef. *Theologie und Gesellschaft im 2. und 3. Jahrhundert Hidschra: Eine Geschichte des religiösen Denkens im frühen Islam*. Berlin and New York: Walter de Gruyter, 1997.

Vásquez, Manuel A. "Studying Religion in Motion: A Networks Approach." *Method and Theory in the Study of Religion* 20 (2008): 151–84.

Waardenburg, Jacques. *Classical Approaches to the Study of Religion: Aims, Methods and Theories of Research.* Berlin: Walter de Gruyter, 1999.

———. *Muslims and Others: Relations in Context.* Berlin: Walter de Gruyter, 2003.

———. *Perspektiven der Religionswissenschaft.* Würzburg: Echter, 1993.

Wasserstrom, Steven M. "Islamicate History of Religions?" *History of Religions* 27 (1988): 405–11.

Zolberg, Aristide R. and Long Litt Woon, "Why Islam is like Spanish: Cultural Incorporation in Europe and the United States." *Politics & Society* 27 (1999): 5–38.

CHAPTER 7

Is There an Autograph of al-Ghazālī in MS Yale, Landberg 318?

Frank Griffel

The 900th anniversary of al-Ghazālī's death in 2011 was an event not only celebrated at conferences and academic meetings but also on the book-market. 2010 and 2011 saw the publication of two new editions of al-Ghazālī's most influential work *The Revival of the Religious Sciences* (*Iḥyāʾ ʿulūm al-dīn*) that are both based on an original study of manuscripts. This is very welcome, after for more than 150 years every new edition of this work simply copied its text from a previous print. The more impressive of these two new books is the ten-volume edition published by Dār al-Minhāj in Jeddah, Saudi Arabia. Its editors are identified as a "Scholarly Commission at the Dār al-Minhāj Center for Scholarly Editions."[1] If the editors indeed used all 17 manuscripts—among them are the oldest known textual witnesses of *Iḥyāʾ ʿulūm al-dīn* from the 6th/12th century—and the one earlier print listed and described in the introduction they have truly done an impressive feat.[2] Seven years, they say, they labored on this edition. Unfortunately, however, the editors do not establish a stemma of manuscripts nor do they inform us whether they prioritized some over others. In their explanation of the editorial process they remain silent about their decision making in case of conflicting variants.[3] In fact, the edition rarely ever mentions variant readings among the textual sources that are used. Its footnotes are limited to the verification of *ḥadīth* and of passages that al-Ghazālī quotes from earlier books. This omission significantly limits the

---

1 *al-Lajna al-ʿIlmiyya bi-Markaz Dār al-Minhāj li-l-Dirāsāt wa-l-Taḥqīq al-ʿIlmī.* Muḥammad Ghassān Nuṣūḥ ʿAzqūl al-Ḥusaynī signs as "supervisor over the editorial work and the publication" (*al-mushrif ʿalā aʿmāl al-buḥūth wa-l-nashr*) at the Dār al-Minhāj Center for Study and Scholarly Editions (1:111). Muḥammad ʿAbd al-Raḥmān Shumayla al-Ahdal signs the preface of the book (1:33) and ʿUmar Sālim S. Bājkhīf, the owner of Dār al-Minhāj, the *silsila* of the book's transmission from al-Ghazālī to the scholars who worked on this edition.

2 al-Ghazālī, *Iḥyāʾ ʿulūm al-dīn* (ed. Dār al-Minhāj), 1:51–81. These manuscripts come from seven different libraries. The great majority of them are from three libraries, the Gazi Husrev Bey Library in Sarajevo, the Chester Beatty Library in Dublin, and the Staatsbibliothek Preussischer Kulturbesitz in Berlin.

3 al-Ghazālī, *Iḥyāʾ ʿulūm al-dīn* (ed. Dār al-Minhāj), 1:100–107.

 | DOI 10.1163/9789004307490_008

editorial value of the print. Only future studies will be able to determine whether the text established in this edition truly is an improvement over the modern *textus receptus* of the *Iḥyāʾ*. Right now one can only say that this new 10-volume edition is a significant publishing event.[4]

The second new edition in 6 volumes comes out of Damascus and uses far fewer manuscripts. Its editors clarify that they compared the *textus receptus* with seven manuscript copies from the Chester Beatty Library in Dublin and the Ẓāhiriyya collection in Damascus, some of them going back to the mid-6th/12th century. Unlike the first mentioned edition, however, this one is heavily footnoted. In addition to *ḥadīth*-verifications, it lists variant readings from the manuscripts and reproduces relevant passages from al-Murtaḍā al-Zabīdī's (d. 1205/1791) voluminous commentary on the *Iḥyāʾ*. Whereas the benefit of the first mentioned edition is pending on the quality of the text it produced, the usefulness of this one is immediately apparent: It provides variants where before there were none and by printing the corresponding page reference of the Būlāq-print of al-Murtaḍā al-Zabīdī's commentary, it offers easy access to the commentary, which is now available on the Internet as PDFs. In its 6th volume, the new edition also features an alphabetical index of *aḥādīth* quoted in the *Iḥyāʾ*, something no other edition ever did.[5]

4 The new Dār al-Minhāj edition of *Iḥyāʾ ʿulūm al-dīn* notes that its publication coincided with the 900th anniversary of al-Ghazālī's death according to the Common Era (cf. ibid., 1:50). Thus, it came too late to be included in the research of this volume yet its pagination is included in the index of passages from the *Ihyāʾ*.

5 This edition was established by ʿAlī Muḥammad Muṣṭafā and Saʿīd al-Maḥāsinī and published 1431/2010 by Dār al-Fayḥāʾ and Dār al-Manhal in the Ḥalbūnī district of Damascus. It is, however, poorly distributed outside of Syria and hardly available at Western libraries. This might be an effect of the civil war that broke out in Syria in the Spring of 2011. The editors of this edition state (1:15) that they used the *textus receptus* from the margins of al-Zābīdī's commentary as the base text (*aṣl*) and compared it with three manuscript copies. The details the editors provide on the manuscripts (1:105–7) reveal that they used four different volumes from the Chester Beatty Library in Dublin (nos. 3353, 3429, 4051, and 5124) and three volumes from the Ẓāhiriyya collection at al-Asad National Library in Damascus (film nos. 1629, 2988, 9738). The editors present the latter three volumes as parts of a single set, referring to them with a single manuscript signum. They do the same with MSS Chester Beatty 3353, 5134 and 3429 and thus believed that they dealt with three different sets of manuscripts of the *Iḥyāʾ*. The description of these volumes, however, reveals that all seven copies were copied by different copyists at different times and have different numbers of lines on one pages, suggesting that not any of them were part of a common set of volumes. I am grateful to Ayman Shihadeh who alerted me to the existence of this new edition.

This is only the third time in the history of Arabic printing that a text of the *Iḥyāʾ ʿulūm al-dīn* was transferred from manuscript to the printed press.[6] The first was the *editio princeps* published in 1269/1853 at the Būlāq Press near Cairo under the supervision of Muḥammad ibn ʿAbd al-Raḥmān Quṭṭa al-ʿAdawī (d. 1281/1864) who used, "the best testimonies at the Khedival library."[7] The text of this edition has been copied from one reprint to the next and is still the basis of the modern *textus receptus* that can be found in almost all editions that are currently on the Arabic book-market. Forty years after this *editio princeps*, in 1311/1894, the Maymaniyya Press in Cairo published a 10-volume edition of al-Murtaḍā al-Zabīdī's monumental commentary to the *Revival*, *Itḥāf al-sāda al-mutaqqīn* (*The Gift of the God-Fearing Sayyids*). Like the *editio princeps* it was established on the basis of unidentified manuscript(s). When al-Murtaḍā al-Zabīdī wrote his commentary in the years before 1201/1787,[8] he collated several manuscripts of the *Iḥyāʾ* that were available to him in Cairo and he notes variants among them in his commentary. This means the text of the *Iḥyāʾ* included within al-Zabīdī's commentary is a textual witness independent of that printed in 1269/1853. When al-Zabīdī's commentary was put to print, it was the second time that a text of the *Iḥyāʾ* was transferred from manuscript(s) to printed book.[9] After almost one-hundred and sixty years of being in print, the two editions of Jeddah and Damascus mark only the third time that happened. They are the first "modern" editions of the *Iḥyāʾ* that at least identify its textual sources.

The new edition out of Jeddah is particularly relevant for a smaller text of al-Ghazālī that is often printed together with his *Revival*. *The Dictation on Difficult Passages in the Revival* (*al-Imlāʾ fī mushkil al-Iḥyāʾ*)[10] is a text written in response to readers's complaints about certain teachings in *Iḥyāʾ ʿulūm al-dīn*. We assume that this happened as part of the controversy al-Ghazālī was involved in after he began teaching at the Niẓāmiyya *madrasa* in Nishapur in 499/1105.[11] The only printed version that was available before this new edition

---

6 I mean by "printed press" the one with moveable types. Not counted here are lithograph editions of the text established in Tehran and in India, mostly Lucknow, during the second half of the 19th century.

7 See the colophon in the 4-volume *Iḥyāʾ*-print of Būlāq: Dār al-Ṭibāʿa wa-l-Waqāʾiʿ al-Miṣriyya, 1269 [1853], 4:341. For more details see my *Al-Ghazālī's Philosophical Theology*, 15.

8 Reichmuth, *The World of Murtaḍā al-Zabīdī*, 110.

9 This edition also includes the *textus receptus* in its margins.

10 The text is also known under other but at the end quite similar titles, such as *al-Imlāʾ fī ishkālāt al-Iḥyāʾ*. Badawī, *Muʾallafāt al-Ghazālī*, 323, documents the different titles and their usage.

11 Garden, *The First Islamic Reviver*, xii, 13–14.

goes back to the *editio princeps* in the margins of the Maymaniyya Press edition of al-Murtaḍā al-Zabīdī's commentary on the *Revival*.[12] That edition, however, is based on a manuscript which represents not the original recension of the text. It seem that the pages of this manuscript, or an earlier one that this one depends on, got mixed up. The divisions in this printed text, for instance, do not match the description al-Ghazālī gives of his agenda in the book.[13] The disarray of text is arbitrary and it is so severe, for instance, that the important chapter on al-Ghazālī's famous dictum that there is, "in possibility nothing more wondrous than the form of this world" (*laysa fī l-imkān abdaʿ min ṣūrat hādhā l-ʿālam*) is only in its first half original while the second half comes from an earlier chapter that comments on the Sufi saying: "Divulging the secret of Lordship is unbelief" (*ifshāʾ sirr al-rubūbiyya kufr*). This led to serious misunderstandings even in my own work.[14] Scholars have noted the discrepancies in the printed versions and have bemoaned the poor quality of all printed texts of *al-Imlāʾ*.[15] This new edition of the *Iḥyāʾ* includes in its first volume a new edition of *al-Imlāʾ ʿalā mushkil al-Iḥyāʾ* based on seven manuscripts[16] providing finally—after more than 120 years—a printed version of the original recension of the work.[17]

---

12 al-Zabīdī, *Itḥāf al-sāda*, 1:41–252 (margins). The new 6-volume edition out of Damascus reproduces this defective *textus receptus* (6:539–95).

13 al-Zabīdī, *Itḥāf al-sāda*, 1:44–47 (margins).

14 See, e.g. my *Al-Ghazālī's Philosophical Theology*, 231. The paragraph in the middle of that page is based on a passage that does not belong to this chapter. The wrong text is e. g. printed in al-Ghazālī, *al-Imlāʾ fī ishkālāt al-Iḥyāʾ* (ed. Cairo 1937–38), 3084.14–3085.5, the correct one is printed in idem, *Iḥyāʾ ʿulūm al-dīn.* (ed. Dār al-Minhāj), 1:344.11–345.*ult.*

15 See al-Akiti, *The Maḍnūn of al-Ghazālī: A Critical Edition of the Unpublished Major Maḍnūn with Discussion of His Restricted, Philosophical Corpus*, 2:293 and my *Al-Ghazālī's Philosophical Theology*, 347, n. 64. In *The Maḍnūn of al-Ghazālī*, 2:293 and in "Index to Divisions of al-Ghazālī's Often Cited Public Works," 149–50, al-Akiti establishes a "correction of the pagination of the *Imlā*" that allows the reader of the most widespread printed recension to convert it to a more original one.

16 These manuscripts are from Dār al-Kutub al-Miṣriyya in Cairo, the King ʿAbd al-ʿAzīz Library in Riyadh, Chester Beatty Library in Dublin, and Millet Yazma Eser Kütüphanesi in Istanbul. The oldest one is MS Feyzullah Efendi 2123 from Millet Kütüphanesi, which, according to the editors (1:91) was copied in 656/1258 or (1:353) in 646/1248. According to Şeşen, *Mukhtārāt min al-makhṭūṭāt al-ʿarabiyya al-nādira fī maktabāt Turkiyā*, 636, however, that volume was copied in 696/1296–97. In my own study of the manuscript I cannot decide either and must admit that the number of the year in the collophon on fol. 77b is very hard to read.

17 al-Ghazālī, *Iḥyāʾ ʿulūm al-dīn* (ed. Dār al-Minhāj), 1:213–353.

A Handwritten *ijāza* by al-Ghazālī?

In the first volume of the new edition, its editors also include a reproduction of a page from MS Yale University, Beinecke Rare Book and Manuscript Library, Landberg 318 together with the claim that the page contains an autograph by al-Ghazālī. The assumed autograph is an *ijāza* on fol. 230a that al-Ghazālī seems to have written with his own hand. The editors transcribe the text of the *ijāza* into plain Arabic yet offer little additional information other than writing that this is "an example of al-Ghazālī's handwriting" and "a picture of al-Ghazālī's handwriting."[18] If that were the case, the manuscript at Yale University would be—as far as I know—our only material connection with the life of the great scholar.

Despite his prominence among Muslim scholars, there are no surviving artifacts from al-Ghazālī's life. We know of no manuscript written or copied by him and no autograph note. The same seems to be true for manuscripts of his works copied during his lifetime.[19] Even manuscripts that were copied soon after his death are extremely rare and valuable.[20] Ṭabarān-Ṭūs, the place where al-Ghazālī was born, no longer exists. Nishapur is today only a faint shadow of what the city was when al-Ghazālī studied and taught there. In Baghdad, we know where the Niẓāmiyya *madrasa* once was but no significant remains are left of that building nor of others where he stayed. We are told that once there was in Damascus a small Sufi-*madrasa* named after al-Ghazālī, but that building is gone just like his chamber in one of the minarets of the Umayyad mosques.[21] In Mamluk times, a new minaret replaced the old, taking with it

---

18 "*ṣūra ʿan khaṭṭ al-Imām al-Ghazālī,*" "*anamūdhaj li-khaṭṭ al-Imām al-Ghazālī;*" ibid. 1:209–211.

19 In my "Ms. London, British Library Or. 3126: An Unknown Work by al-Ghazālī on Metaphysics and Philosophical Theology," I try to show that the London manuscript described therein is very old and may date to al-Ghazālī's lifetime. The general conclusions are confirmed by Afifi al-Akiti in his analysis of the codex (*The Maḍnūn of al-Ghazālī: A Critical Edition of the Unpublished Major Maḍnūn with Discussion of His Restricted, Philosophical Corpus*, 2:294–336). He suggests that a marginal note on fol. 14b of this manuscript may be by al-Ghazālī's hand (2:330–36).

20 One example is MS Istanbul, Şehit Ali Paşa 1712, containing three works of al-Ghazālī (*Iljām al-ʿawāmm*, *al-Munqidh min al-ḍalāl*, and *Fayṣal al-tafriqa*) that were—according to the three colophons—copied between Dhū l-Qaʿda 508 and Shawwāl 509 (April 1115–February 1116). I am, however, not entirely convinced that the material evidence of the manuscript supports those dates. These colophones may have been copied from an earlier mansucript.

21 Cf. my *Al-Ghazālī's Philosophical Theology*, 44.

any recollection of al-Ghazālī's cell. In Jerusalem, a small *madrasa* (a *zāwiya*) above the Gate of Mercy to the Ḥaram al-Sharīf was known as the place where al-Ghazālī had stayed and taught. This information comes to us from the 10th/16th century but turned out to be wrong. The *madrasa* in question was built in the Ayyubid period almost a century after al-Ghazālī's death.[22]

The destruction of everything connected with al-Ghazālī's life goes so far that even his grave can hardly be identified. It is most likely in or near the so-called Hārūniyya, a mausoleum that stands alone within the field of ruins that was once Ṭabarān-Ṭūs. The current building, however, has been dated to the early 8th/14th century and thus may not be al-Ghazālī's original mausoleum.[23] Following Ernst Diez, who was the first to describe and analyze the building, Iranian scholars still see in it a monument that was built to the memory of al-Ghazālī[24] and it is indeed possible that the unknown patron who commissioned the building choose the place known as al-Ghazālī's grave for it to be built on. The mausoleum, however, bears no inscription and there is no marked grave anywhere within it or closeby. A British traveler who visited the place in 1880—and took it to be the mausoleum of the poet Firdawsī (d. 411/1020)—reports of fragments of a stone coffin at the center of the building and of inscriptions that other travelers had stolen only a few years before his visit.[25] If ever there was a connection between the so-called Hārūniyya and al-Ghazālī, it too is lost in history.

A hand-written note of the great Imām would, therefore, be a sensation and it would significantly enhance the value of the manuscript that bears it. Such increase in value is true today just as it was nine centuries ago and this alone

22 Ibid., 45–47.

23 Wiber, *The Architecture of Islamic Iran: The Ilkhānid Period*, 145–46 (#50). Wiber follows Pope, *A Survey of Persian Art*, 2:1072–76, in his dating of the building to the early 8th/14th century. I am grateful to Sheila Blair of Boston College for pointing me to literature on the dating of the Hārūniyya.

24 *Dayirat al-maʿārif-i bināhā-yi tārīkhī-yi Īrān dar dawrat-i Islāmī*, 10–12. See the extensive description of the building (here: *Der Kuppelbau in Ṭūs*) in Ernst Diez, *Churasanische Baudenkmäler*, 55–62. Diez points out (pp. 59–60) that both Yāqūt (d. 626/1229), *Muʿjam al-buldān*, 3:361, and Ibn Baṭṭūṭa (d. 770/1368–9), *Riḥla*, 3:77, report the existence of a prominent grave (*qabr*) for al-Ghazālī in Ṭabarān-Ṭūs. Diez concedes that the stucco-ornaments of the building speak for a date of construction later than the 6th/12th century, "but this should not lead to conclusions given the widespread habit of renewing these decorations." A waterpainting of the Hārūniyya in the ruins of Ṭābarān-Ṭūs is on the front binding of this book. It was published by Diez in his *Die Kunst der islamischen Völker*, table 3.

25 O'Donovan, *The Merv Oasis*, 2:15–16.

must prompt us to take a close and skeptical look at the evidence. The increase in value might attract forgeries. In the following I will briefly explain the evidence and decide whether al-Ghazālī really left an autograph in that manuscript.

Three Notes at the End of a Manuscript of al-Ghazālī's *al-Wajīz*

The note in question is written at the end of a complete manuscript of al-Ghazālī's book *al-Wajīz fī fiqh madhhab al-Imām al-Shāfiʿī* (*The Succinct Book on Shafiʿite Substantial Law*). This manuscript is the oldest known copy of the work and in itself an important witness. It was copied in the month of Shawwāl 507/March-April 1114, less than three years after al-Ghazālī's death in Jumāda II 505/December 1111. This dating of the manuscript goes back to Leon Nemoy's catalogue of the Arabic manuscripts at Yale from 1956 and is based on his reading of the colophon at the end of the text of *al-Wajīz* as well as other criteria.[26] The paper of the book is old oriental paper and the style of the handwriting is Seljuq, putting the production of this book at any time before the 8th/14th century. The year in that colophon, however, is not entirely unambigious (see the reproduction of fol. 230a at the end of this chapter). Nemoy must have read the brief colophon as follows:

فوافق الفراغ صبح يوم الأحد خامس وعشرين شوال سنة سبعة خمسماية.

> "[Copying this manuscript] was completed on the morning of Sunday, 25 Shawwāl 507."

A look at the conversion tables for the Muslim calendar reveals that 25 Shawwāl 507 is equivalent to 4 April 1114 but fell on a Saturday and not a Sunday.[27] This difference of one weekday, however, is not unusual. Pre-modern date keeping was not always precise and may also have differed temporarily from region to region due to the uncertainty of the beginning and the end of Ramaḍān, where the calenderial day may be overruled by the sighting of the crescent moon.

26 Nemoy, *Arabic Manuscripts in the Yale University Library*, 109 (#999). Cf. also Nemoy's record card on this manuscript within the card catalogue of Arabic manuscripts that he prepared and that is available on request at the Beinecke Rare Book and Manuscript Library, Yale University.

27 Wüstenfeld, *Wüstenfeld-Mahler'sche Vergleichungs-Tabellen zur muslimischen und iranischen Zeitrechnung*, 12.

Shawwāl is the month after Ramaḍān, and discrepancies of this kind are most likely at this time of the Muslim year.

There is a second very strong argument for the fact that this manuscript was copied *after* al-Ghazālī's lifetime and that is the eulogy used in the book's title. The current title page bears numerous remarks, among them owner-notes and notices about its date and content. The original title of the book, written by the hand of its copyist, is in the first three lines on the title page and reads:

كتاب الوجيز في الفقه
من تحارير الشيخ الإمام حجة الإسلام ابي حامد محمد بن محمد بن محمد الغزالي الطوسي
رحمة الله عليه و رضوانه

> "*The Succinct Book on Jurisprudence* from among the compositions of the master, the Imām, Proof of Islam, Muḥammad ibn Muḥammad ibn Muḥammad al-Ghazālī al-Ṭūsī, may God have mercy on him and be pleased with him."

The formula "may God have mercy on him" (*raḥmatu Llāh ʿalayhī*) is only used if the person after whose name it follows is already dead. Given that this note is written by the hand of the original copyist—which we will call Hand 1—when he made the copy, it confirms that al-Ghazālī had already passed away when this manuscript was produced.

After the end of the text of *al-Wajīz* follow three different notes by apparently three different readers. All three call into question whether this copy was completed in Ramāḍān 507, two years and three months after al-Ghazālī's death. While this first prompted me to doubt Nemoy's reading of the year 507 AH, I have eventually concluded that this reading is indeed correct. This manuscript has the consistent appearance of a book that was copied over two years after al-Ghazālī's death. If this manuscript was indeed copied in 507, there must be something wrong with the three notes at its end.

The first of the three notes is an *ijāza*, i. e. a license or confirmation of graduation for studying the book with a teacher. This first *ijāza* on fol. 230a is written in Hand 2 and reads:[28]

28 The text of *al-Wajīz* is, in fact, followed be a brief note in red ink saying: "We seek help from Him and there is no power and no strength other than with God, the All-knower, the All-magnificent." It is difficult to determine whether this note is in the handwriting of the original scribe (Hand 1)—to me it appears to be so. That, however, has no effect on my argument and I neglect this note here.

الحمد لله رب العالمين نحمده ونستعينه ونستغفره ونعوذ بالله
من شرور أنفسنا و من سيئات أعمالنا وصلى ألله
على سيدنا محمد وآله وصحبه وسلم. وبعد فقد قرأ
عليّ العبد الصالح الموفق الفالح تاج الدين بن أحمد الطوسي
الشافعي جميع كتابنا الموسوم بالوجيز قراءةَ تحقيقٍ و عرفانٍ
وتدقيقٍ وإتقانٍ وشرحتُ له في ذلك ما يسره ألله عليّ
وقد استخرتُ ألله تعالى وأجزتُ له بلّغه ألله في
الدارين أمله ان يَقرَأه ويُقرِأه بما قرأه عليّ وألله أعلم
قال ذلك وكتبه محمد بن محمد بن محمد الغزالي الطوسي
الشافعي حامداً مصلياً مسلماً والحمد لله وحده[29]

"Praise to God, Lord of the Worlds. We praise Him and we ask Him for help and for forgiveness and we seek refuge with Him from the bad impulses in our souls and the bad effects of our actions. May God bless our master Muḥammad and his family and companions and grant [them] salvation. Now then: The pious, prosperous, and successful servant Tāj al-Dīn ibn Aḥmad al-Ṭūsī al-Shāfiʿī studied with me the whole of our book that is named *The Succinct One*. The study was analytic, inspired [by Sufi knowledge], detailed, and complete. In it I explained to him what God made easy for me [to understand]. I ask God, exalted, for guidance and I license [Tāj al-Dīn]—may God make him achieve what he hopes for in this world and the next—to read and to teach what he studied with me; and God knows best. The one who says this and who writes this down is Muḥammad ibn Muḥammad ibn Muḥammad al-Ghazālī al-Ṭūsī al-Shāfiʿī, [and he does so] thankfully, asking for blessing and for salvation and praise be to God alone."

This is a license of teaching (*ijāzat al-tadrīs*) issued by al-Ghazālī himself. It is signed by his name and confirms that the student named therein studied "the whole of our book (...) *al-Wajīz*" with Muḥammad ibn Muḥammad ibn Muḥammad al-Ghazālī. But how is this to square with the fact that the manuscript was almost certainly copied after al-Ghazālī had passed away? Leon Nemoy thought he could solve this problem by assuming the *ijāza* was issued by one of al-Ghazālī's sons by the name of Muḥammad. In his catalogue of

---

29 See the transcription of the handwritten texts on this page in al-Ghazālī, *Iḥyāʾ ʿulūm al-dīn* (ed. Dār al-Minhāj),1:210 .

Arabic manuscripts at Yale he notes that this book bears an "autograph ijāza by Muḥammad ibn Muḥammad ibn Muḥammad al-Ghazzālī, presumably the author's son."[30] Nemoy obviously overlooked the personal pronoun in *jamīʿ kitābinā* ("the whole of *our* book")—a not unlikely oversight given the careless way this *ijāza* is written.

Before we rush to judgment over this *ijāza* let us first take a look at the other two notes at the end of this book. Next follows a remark at the bottom of fol. 230a. It is signed by some unknown Taqī al-Ḥiṣnī and written in Hand 3:

الحمد لله
تشرّفتُ من فضل ألله تعالى وإحسانه عليَّ بتبرّكي بخطّ
شيخ الشريعة والحقيقة وأسها سيدي الشيخ محمد بن محمد بن محمد
الإمام الغزالي رضي ألله تعالى عنه صاحب الوجيز بواسطة
مولانا مالكه السيد الشريف السيد حسن العجلاني الحسيني أعاد ألله تعالى
علينا وعليه مع فروعنا من نفحات الإمام الغزالي آمين التقي الحصني كاتبه

> God be praised! Through God's, the exalted's favor and his beneficence to me, I am honored with being blessed by the handwriting of the master of *sharīʿa* and [the master] of truth and its foundation, my lord, the master Muḥammad ibn Muḥammad ibn Muḥammad al-Imām al-Ghazālī, may God the exalted be pleased with him, the author of *al-Wajīz*. [That I am blessed comes] through the mediation of our patron and the owner [of the hand-writing] the noble master of *sharīʿa*, the *sayyid* Ḥasan al-ʿAjlānī al-Ḥusaynī, may God continue [to provide] for us together with [these] branches of ours from the breaths of Imām al-Ghazālī. Amen! Al-Taqī al-Ḥiṣnī wrote this.

Here, the unknown reader al-Taqī (or: Taqī al-Dīn) al-Ḥiṣnī (or: al-Ḥuṣnī) expresses in rather baroque Arabic his gratitude to God and to the owner of the book, Ḥasan al-ʿAjlānī al-Ḥusaynī for reading al-Ghazālī's handwriting. This note can be dated to some time in or after 1096/1685. On the title page of the book there is an owner note of someone signing as Ḥasan ibn ʿAjlān al-Ḥusaynī—dated 1096 AH—and right next to it in a different hand the owner note of Muḥammad ibn ʿAjlān al-Ḥusaynī, who may have been the brother of Ḥasan, dated 1094 AH. It seems quite possible that the note on the last page was

30 Nemoy, *Arabic Manuscripts in the Yale University Library*, 109 (#999). In *Al-Ghazālī's Philosophical Theology*, 305, n. 263, I accepted that judgment.

written a long time—probably more then five centuries—after the first.The last sentence can also be read as an allusion to the title of a famous book on Andalusi poetry and prose by al-Maqqarī (d. 1041/1632)—*The Breath of Perfume from the Branch of Lush Andalus* (*Nafḥ al-ṭīb min ghuṣn al-Andalus al-raṭīb*), which would equally date the note after the early 11th/17th century.

Nemoy, who had concluded that the *ijāza* right above this text was by al-Ghazālī's son, understood the meaning of this note but assumed its author had misunderstood the earlier note. In his card catalogue of the Arabic manuscripts at Yale he writes: "the owners note under it, implying that the ijazah is by the author himself, is patently mistaken."

Finally, there is on the very last page of the book, on fol. 230b, a second *ijāza* that stretches over almost the whole page. Both the handwriting as well as the ink used in this *ijāza* seems to be the same as in the *ijāza* a page before that is signed by al-Ghazālī. In fact, the appearance of this *ijāza*—with its frame and the space between the lines—is very similar to the one on fol. 230a. The same applies to parts of its text:[31]

الحمد لله ربّ العالمين
المحمود على كل حال وصلى ألله على سيدنا محمد وعلى آله وصحبه
خير صحبٍ وآلٍ وبعد فإن الأخ في ألله والرفيق الى الله حضر لديّ
و قرأ عليَّ هو الشيخ الإمام والحِبر الهمام الزاهد العابد سيدنا (؟) الشيح
شهاب الدين أحمد بن قطب الوقت والأوان في العالم وإنسان عين
أعيان أهل النُصرة والتمكين محي الدين محمد بن المرزبان الشافعي
جميع كتّاب الوجيز لحجّة الإسلام أبي حامد الغزالي رضي الله عنه قراءةَ
إتقانٍ وتحقيقٍ وعرفانٍ وتدقيقٍ أحسن فيها وأجاد و أفاد حفظه
الله تعالى واستعاد وقد استخرتُ الله تعالى وأجزتُ له بلّغَه الله
في الدارين أملَه ان يروي من جميع ما تُحّدث لي وعنى روايةً وبأصحّه
الى سند وإضافته شرطَ المعتبَر عند أهل الأثر وكان ذلك في
أواخر شهر رمضان المعظّم سنة سبعة وخمسمايه والحمد لله تع
قال ذلك وكتبه الفقير الى ألله في قصبة (؟) الغربية أحمد بن أحمد
ابن عبد الرحمان الجيلي الشافعي الأشعري عُفي عنهم

31 I am grateful to Adel Allouche of Yale and Yasin Apaydin of Istanbul University for their paleographic assistance.

> Praise to God, Lord of the Worlds. [He is] thanked for all circumstances! May God bless our master Muḥammad and his family and companions—the best companions and the best family. Now then: The brother in God and the companion [on the way] to God stayed with me and studied with me. He is the master, the Imām, the ink [of good writing], the eager, the ascetic, the servant, our lord (?), the master Shihāb al-Dīn Aḥmad, the pole of times in this world, the pupil of the eyes of the people[32] who provide support (*nuṣra*) and strengthening, Muḥyī l-Dīn Muḥammad ibn al-Marzubān al-Shāfiʿī. [He studied with me] the whole of the book *The Succinct One* by the Proof of Islam Abū Ḥāmid al-Ghazālī, may God be pleased with him. The study was thorough, analytic, inspired [by Sufi knowledge], and detailed in the best way. He is [now] proficient and accomplished. May God preserve him and may He continued to do so.
>
> I ask God, exalted, for guidance and I license [Muḥyī l-Dīn]—may God make him achieve what he hopes for in this world and the next—to transmit all *ḥadīth* material [that has come] to me and [that has been narrated] on my authority according to what is most correct in [being traced] to a transmitter (*sanad*) and adding to it in accordance with the considerations that the *hadīth*-scholars have.[33]
>
> This is done at the end of the glorified months of Ramaḍān 507, thanks to God the exalted. The one who says this and who writes it down is the one who is in need of God at the western fortress (?), Aḥmad ibn Aḥmad ibn ʿAbd al-Rahmān al-Jīlī al-Shāfiʿī al-Ashʿarī. May they (*scil.* all those mentioned in this *ijāza*) be excused.

A number of phrases in the *ijāza* are difficult to read and even more difficult to translate so that there remains quite a degree of ambiguity over the detailed phrasing of it. There is an evident overlap between the text of this *ijāza* and the one a page before. The central sentence, "I ask God, exalted, for guidance and I license [NN]—may God make him achieve what he hopes for in this world and the next—to teach…," appears in both documents. The same applies to the description of the kind of study the student had undertaken, characterizing it as being inspired by analytic inquiry (*taḥqīq*), Sufi inspiration (*ʿirfān*), completeness (*itqān*), and detail (*tadqīq*). Such similar or even identical wording may be due to a shared standard within the genre of *ijāza* at this time or because the second *ijāza* drew inspiration from the first—the one signed by the great scholar al-Ghazālī.

---

32 A wordplay on two of the many meanings of the Arabic word "*ʿayn*."

33 The English is deliberately unclear to reflect the original where it is equally clear what is to be added here.

Despite ambiguity in the details of the text of the second *ijāza*, the main points are clear. The Shāfiʿite jurist and Ashʿarite theologian Aḥmad ibn Aḥmad ibn ʿAbd al-Rahmān al-Jīlī grants a license of transmission (*ijāzat al-riwāya*) to Shihāb al-Dīn Muḥammad ibn al-Marzubān, a man who receives lofty praise in this document, maybe because of his distinguished position as the member of a family of landed proprietors (Pers. *marzbān*). This license is dated to the last days of the month of Ramaḍān 507 which fell into early March 1114. It is thus dated almost exactly one month before the copying of the book on whose last page we find it was completed. Something else is curious: The last phrase in the *ijāza* ("May they be excused.") seems to suggest that all three people mentioned therein, Aḥmad al-Jīlī the teacher, Muḥammad ibn al-Marzubān the student, and al-Ghazālī as the author of the book, have already passed away.

If we look at this manuscript we see that there is a consistency in the information about its main text being copied in 507/1114 and being completed on Saturday, 25 of Shawwāl of that year. The main text of *al-Wajīz* is followed by two *ijāza*s in what I would say is one identical handwriting (Hand 2). That both *ijāza*s are written in the same hand shows, for instance, in the way words like *al-shāfiʿī* or *ballaghahū* are written. They are thus in the same handwriting while signed by two different scholars. These two *ijāza*s are also chronologically inconsistent with the manuscript we find them in. The first pretends to be signed by al-Ghazālī himself, despite the fact that the title page of the book that it is written in confirms that he was already dead. The second *ijāza* pretends to be issued one month before the text of the last page in this book was put to paper. These two *ijāzas* are written on the very same leaf on which the text of *al-Wajīz* ends, the first on its front and the second on its back page. Even if we assume this *ijāza* was issued while this book was being copied, how could its author know on which leaf to put it?

One explanation is that both *ijāza*s are crude forgeries, put into this book to enhance its market value and/or to establish the scholarly credentials of their two recipients. But that would not explain why no attempts were made to better cover-up the forgery, by, for instance, simply changing the date of the latter of two *ijāza*s by just one or two months. If this *ijāza* is a forgery and the study described therein never took place, then it would have mattered little whether it was issued in Ramaḍān 507 or two months later in Dhū l-Qaʿda. Yet the earlier date leads even a cursory reader of the *ijāza* into suspicion.

The most likely explanation is that the two *ijāza*s are neither forgeries nor are they fully authentic. They are both copies of authentic *ijāza*s. They appear at the end of this particular manuscript of *al-Wajīz* because they have been copied from another manuscript—one that was older and indeed available during al-Ghazālī's lifetime. The frames around the two *ijāza*s are there to indicate that they are not an original part of the book. Maybe the earlier manuscript they were in sustained significant damage and could no longer be used for study. Maybe the recipients of these two *ijāza*s were eager to preserve these records of their academic accomplishments. The best way to do that was, of course, to copy the two *ijāza*s into another manuscript of *al-Wajīz*. This explains why both *ijāza*s appear to be in the same handwriting, why their dating conflicts with the dating of the manuscript, and why al-Ghazālī appears to have signed a text that was evidently written after his death. He never truly signed the text. The phrase, "the one who says this and who writes this down is (…) al-Ghazālī," was, like the rest of the *ijāza* not written by al-Ghazālī's hand. It was written by someone who copied these words from a different book or a piece of paper.

What we have here then is—in all likelihood—not the handwriting of al-Ghazālī but a copy of an *ijāza* that the great master issued himself.

Bibliography

al-Akiti, Muhammad Afifi. *The Maḍnūn of al-Ghazālī: A Critical Edition of the Unpublished Major Maḍnūn with Discussion of His Restricted, Philosophical Corpus*. 3 vols. PhD dissertation, Worcester College, Oxford University, 2007.

———. "Index to Divisions of al-Ghazālī's Often Cited Public Works." *Muslim World* 102 (2012): 70–200.

Badawī, ʿAbd al-Raḥmān. *Muʾallafāt al-Ghazālī*. 2nd ed. Kuweit: Wikālāt al-Maṭbūʿāt, 1977.

Dayirat al-maʿārif-i bināhā-yi tārīkhī-yi Īrān dar dawrat-i Islāmī / Encyclopedia of the Iranian Historical Movements in the Islamic Era. Tehran: Ḥawzah-yi Hunārī, 1376 [1997].

Diez, Ernst. *Churasanische Baudenkmäler*. Band 1. (Berlin: Dietrich Reimer, 1918).

———. *Die Kunst der islamischen Völker* (Berlin: Akademische Verlagsgesellschaft Athenaion, 1915),

Garden, Kenneth. *The First Islamic Reviver. Abū Ḥāmid al-Ghazālī and His Revival of the Religious Sciences*. New York: Oxford University Press, 2014.

al-Ghazālī, Muḥammad ibn Muḥammad. *Iḥyāʾ ʿulūm al-dīn*. 16 parts. Cairo: Lajnat Nashr al-Thaqāfa al-Islāmiyya, 1356–1357 [1937–1938].

———. *Ihyaʾ ʿulūm al-dīn*, 10 vols. (introductory volume + 9 numbered vols.) Jeddah: Dār al-Minhāj: 1432/2011.

———. *Ihyaʾ ʿulūm al-dīn*. Edited by ʿA. M. Muṣṭafā and S. al-Maḥāsinī. 6 vols. Damascus: Dār al-Fayḥāʾ and Dār al-Manhal, 1431/2010.

———. *al-Imlāʾ fī ishkālāt al-Iḥyāʾ*. In: *Iḥyāʾ ʿulūm al-dīn*. 16 parts. Cairo: Lajnat Nashr al-Thaqāfa al-Islāmiyya, 1356–1357 [1937–1938]. 6:3035–3095.

———. *al-Wajīz fī fiqh madhhab al-Imām al-Shāfiʿī.* Edited by ʿA. Muʿawwaḍ and ʿĀ. ʿAbd al-Mawjūd. 2 vols. Beirut: Dār al-Arqam ibn Abī l-Arqam: 1418/1997.

Griffel, Frank. *Al-Ghazālī's Philosophical Theology.* New York: Oxford University Press, 2009.

———. "Ms. London, British Library Or. 3126: An Unknown Work by al-Ghazālī on Metaphysics and Philosophical Theology." *Journal of Islamic Studies* 17 (2006): 1–42.

Ibn Baṭṭūṭa, Muḥammad ibn ʿAbdallāh. *Riḥla = Voyages d'Ibn Batoutah.* Texte arabe accompagné d'une traduction par C. Defrémery et B. R. Sanguinetti. 4 vols. Paris : Imprimerie impériale, 1853–1858.

Nemoy, Leon. *Arabic Manuscripts in the Yale University Library* (New Haven: Connecticut Academy of Arts and Sciences, 1956).

O'Donovan, Edmond. *The Merv Oasis. Travels and Adventures East of the Caspian During the Years 1879–80–81, Including Five Months' Residence Among the Tekkés of Merv.* 2 vols. New York: G. P. Putnam's Sons, 1883.

Pope, Arthur Upham (ed.) *A Survey of Persian Art, From Prehistoric Times to the Present.* 18 vols. London, New York : Oxford University Press, 1938–2005.

Reichmuth, Stefan. *The World of Murtaḍa al-Zabīdī (1732–91). Life, Networks and Writings.* Cambridge: Gibb Memorial Trust, 2009.

Şeşen, Ramazan (also: Ramaḍān Shishin). *Mukhtārāt min al-makhṭūṭāt al-ʿarabiyya al-nādira fī maktabāt Turkiyā.* Edited by Ekmeleddin Ihsanoğlu. Istanbul: İSAR, 1997.

Wilber, Donald. *The Architecture of Islamic Iran: The Ilkhānid Period.* Princeton: Princeton University Press, 1955.

Wüstenfeld, Ferdinand. *Wüstenfeld-Mahler'sche Vergleichungs-Tabellen zur muslimischen und iranischen Zeitrechnung mit Tafeln zur Umrechnung orient-christlicher Ären.* Edited and improved by J. Mayr and B. Spuler. Wiesbaden: F. Steiner 1961.

Yāqūt al-Ḥamawī al-Rūmī: *Muʿjam al-buldān = Jacut's Geographisches Wörterbuch.* Edited by Ferdinand Wüstenfeld. 6 vols. Leipzig: F.A. Brockhaus, 1866–73.

al-Zabīdī, al-Murtaḍā Muḥammad ibn Muḥammad. *Itḥāf al-sāda al-muttaqīn bi-sharḥ Iḥyāʾ ʿulūm al-dīn.* 10 vols. Cairo: al-Maṭbaʿa al-Maymaniyya, 1311 [1894].

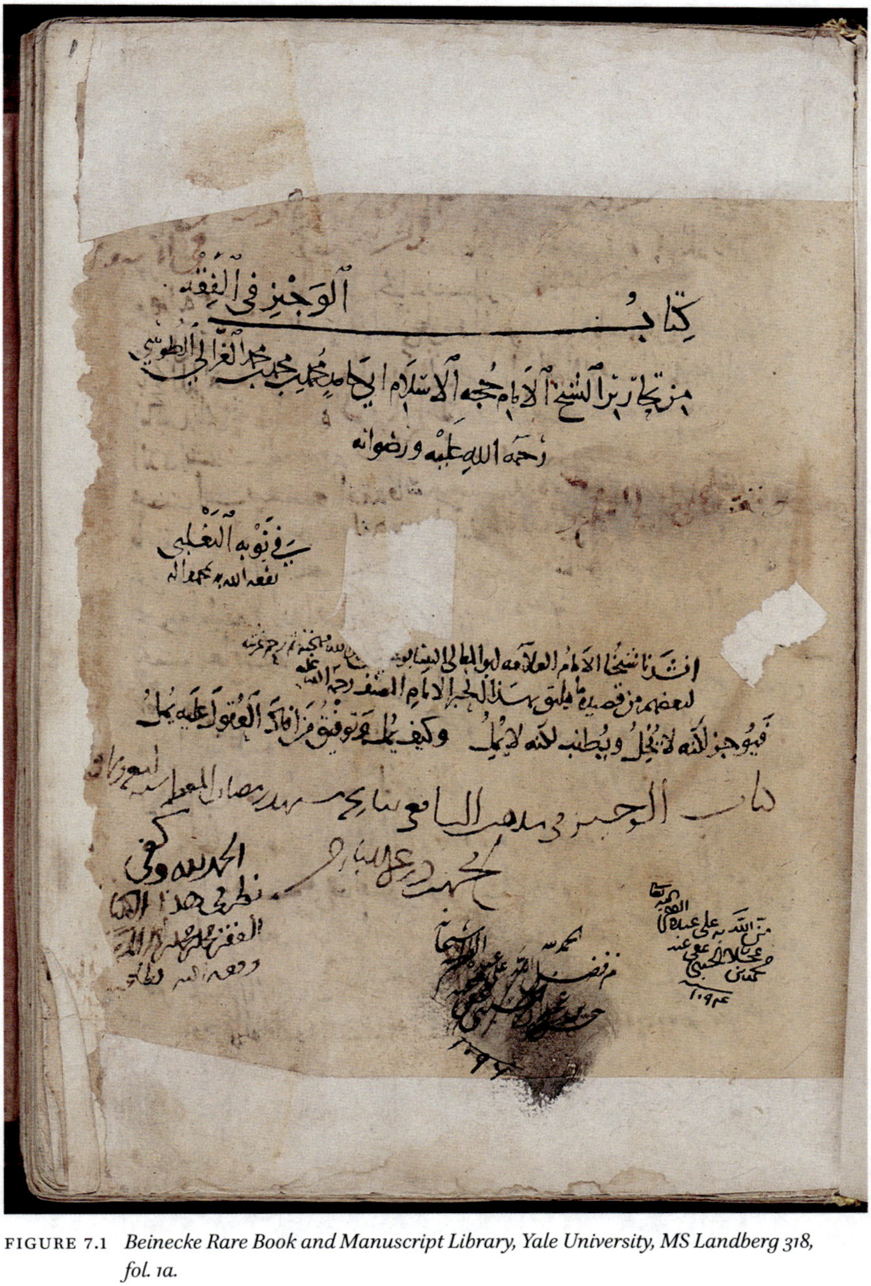

FIGURE 7.1 *Beinecke Rare Book and Manuscript Library, Yale University, MS Landberg 318, fol. 1a.*

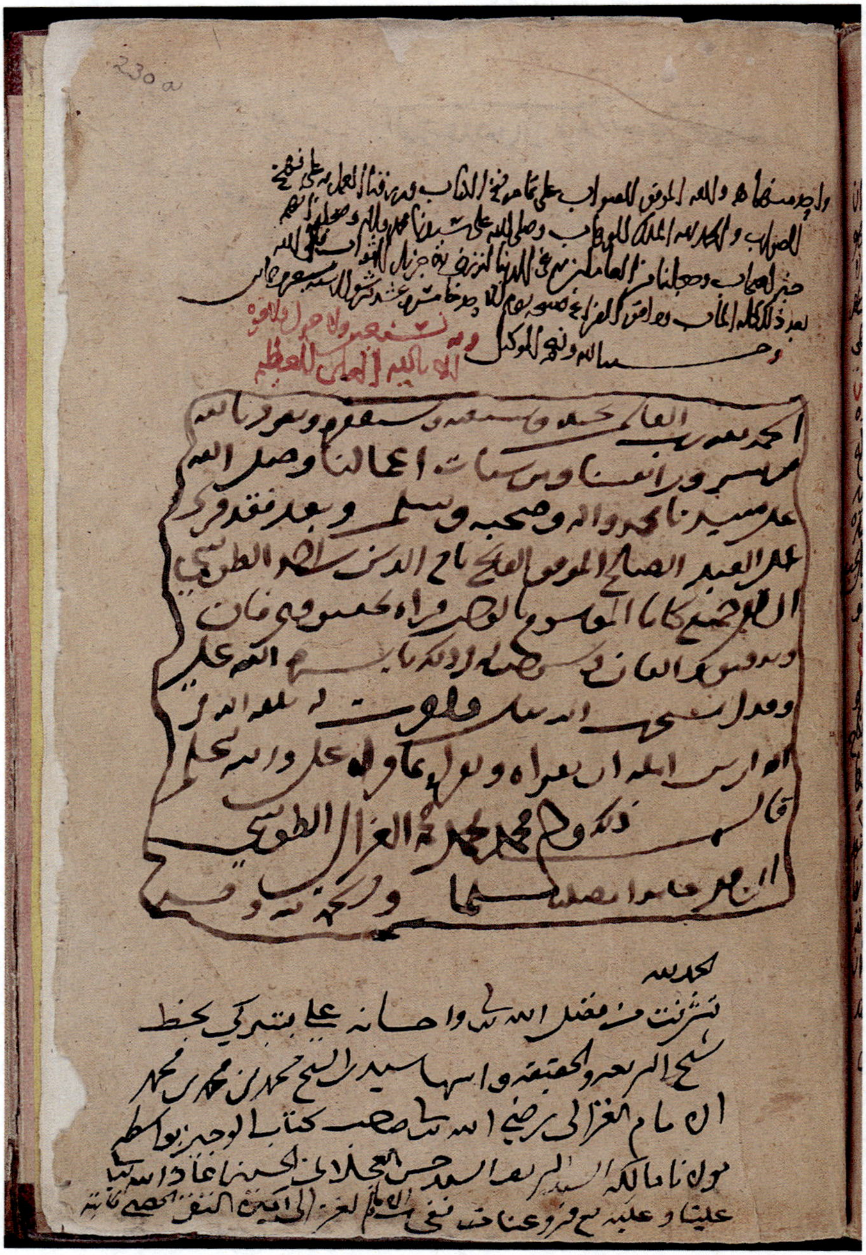

FIGURE 7.2 *Beinecke Rare Book and Manuscript Library, Yale University,* MS *Landberg 318, fol. 230a.*

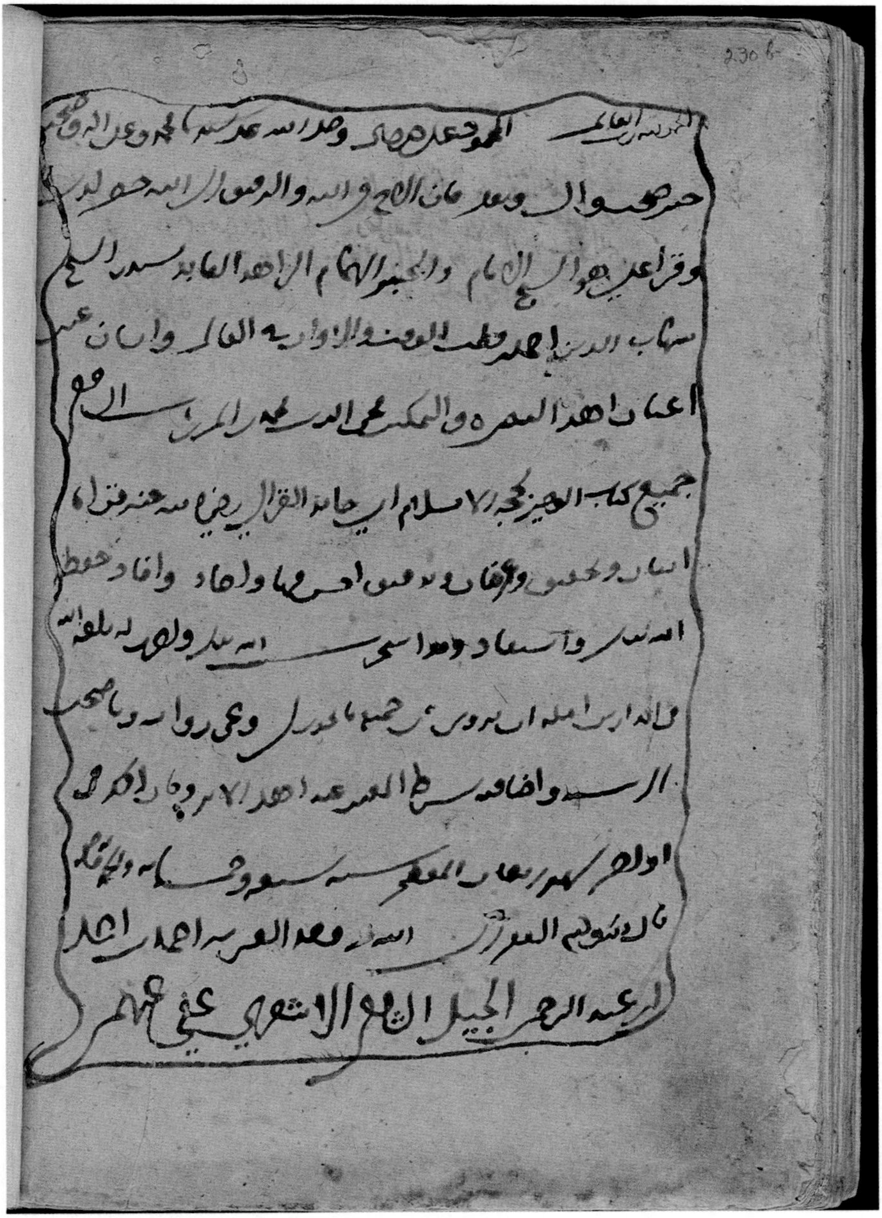

FIGURE 7.3 *Beinecke Rare Book and Manuscript Library, Yale University, MS Landberg 318, fol. 230b*

PART 2

Al-Ghazālī's Influence

CHAPTER 8

Intuition, Intellection, and Mystical Knowledge

Delineating Fakhr al-Dīn al-Rāzī's Cognitive Theories

Damien Janos

Introduction

In the twenty-first book of his *Revival of the Religious Sciences* (*Iḥyāʾ ʿulūm al-dīn*), al-Ghazālī reports a parable (*mithāl*) that has since become famous and legendary: A group of Byzantine painters—symbolizing philosophers and theoretical scholars—are pitted in a contest against a group of Chinese artists—symbolizing the Sufi masters. Each group was asked to paint an image on opposite walls of a room divided by a curtain. Whereas the Byzantines created a magnificent drawing rich in color and precious materials, the Chinese artists polished the walls of the room to the extent that it could purely and faithfully reflect the image on the opposite side. When the curtain was withdrawn the room had two magnificent and very similar paintings, produced, however, by very different methods. In this highly allegorical story on the merits of discursive philosophical knowledge and Sufi self-cultivation, al-Ghazālī does not betray any preference for either side but seems to recognize these two methods as valid approaches to cultivating one's intellectual and spiritual abilities.[1]

Although al-Ghazālī's treatment of this issue is striking, discussions about the relation of mystical and philosophical knowledge reappear in various forms throughout Arabic intellectual history and received divergent formulations in the works of different authors. The aim of the present contribution is to address the way in which this problem crystallized in the works of the famous philosopher and theologian Fakhr al-Dīn al-Rāzī (d. 606/1210). More specifically, this study will discuss Fakhr al-Dīn's views on cogitative and intuitive knowledge, and how the latter in particular relates to mystical

* This article has greatly benefited from the constructive comments of various colleagues. I am grateful notably to Sophia Vasalou and Alexander Treiger for their insight. However, I am most indebted to Frank Griffel for his invaluable and incisive feedback on previous drafts of this article.

1 al-Ghazālī, *Iḥyāʾ ʿulūm al-dīn*, 8:1382; see also Griffel, *Al-Ghazālī's Philosophical Theology*, 263–65.

 | DOI 10.1163/9789004307490_009

knowledge. Two pressing questions in this regard concern, first, the extent to which al-Rāzī's theory of human cognition relies on Avicenna's (Ibn Sīnā, d. 428/1037) psychology and theory of intuition, as well as on the tradition that developed after Avicenna, notably in the works of al-Ghazālī, and second, how al-Rāzī assessed the other approaches to knowledge practiced during his day, notably the approach of the Sufis. It is by now acknowledged that al-Rāzī entertained some interest in the Sufi tradition, while continuing to be an Avicennian thinker in many fundamental ways until the very end of his life. This duality can be explained by the sustained process of assimilation and transformation of Avicennian philosophical concepts within *kalām* after the death of *al-shaykh al-ra'īs* and by the wide influence of the Sufis in the society of al-Rāzī's time. Yet the co-existence of these ideas and their function in al-Rāzī's thought remain to be examined in detail.[2]

The present article proposes to tackle these issues in light of key passages drawn from al-Rāzī's corpus, many of which are here translated into English and analyzed for the first time. I begin with an examination of how Fakhr al-Dīn conceived of the nature of mystical knowledge and of its relation to the various faculties of the human intellect. I then proceed to elucidate its connection with philosophical knowledge and address the issue of their potential compatibility, exploring in the process the more general question of how al-Rāzī regarded the relation between Avicennian philosophy and Sufism. In the last section of the article, I examine the repercussions that al-Rāzī's cognitive theories have on the issue of the knowability of God.

1 Intuition and Mystical Knowledge

In a recent article, Ayman Shihadeh has shed some valuable light on al-Rāzī's relation to Sufism and the impact that mystical cognitive ideas had on the great Ash'arite thinker. In this study, Shihadeh argues that toward the end of his life, and as a result of his increasing skeptical outlook, al-Rāzī turned to Sufism and embraced a new cognitive theory based on mystical concepts and practices. Accordingly, two distinct cognitive theories can be found in Fakhr al-Dīn's works: the first consists in syllogistic, discursive knowledge and the other in what—for want of a better word—may be called mystical or esoteric knowledge. The latter kind of knowledge amounts to non-discursive and non-syllogistic knowledge that is conveyed in the form of divine disclosures, which

2 For a recent study on another aspect of al-Rāzī's epistemology and its relation to Ibn Sīnā, see Eichner, "'Knowledge by Presence.'"

are granted by God directly to some of his creatures. According to Shihadeh, these two kinds of knowledge are unrelated and autonomous, as well as incompatible insofar as the mystical knowledge received through divine illuminations does not rest on the discursive and reflective operations of the intellect.[3]

Shihadeh's article is meritorious in that it is the first study entirely dedicated to the issue of al-Rāzī's relation to Sufism, with regard to which it contributes valuable historical and biographical insight. As Shihadeh argues, there can be little doubt that al-Rāzī in his late works, and notably in his *Long Commentary on the Qur'an* (*al-Tafsīr al-kabīr aw Mafātīḥ al-ghayb*), *The Elevated Subjects* (*al-Maṭālib al-ʿāliya*), and *Flashlights of Proofs* (*Lawāmiʿ al-bayyināt*), shows a marked interest in Sufi ideas and terminology, which he borrows liberally to enrich his own doctrinal expositions.[4] More specifically, as Shihadeh noticed, al-Rāzī appears to be elaborating on a particular brand of philosophical Sufism he inherited from al-Ghazālī, a topic which I discuss briefly at the end of the article. Finally, Shihadeh's argument that Fakhr al-Dīn grew progressively weary of the traditional syllogistic method embraced by the philosophers is thought-provoking. All in all, then, it seems undeniable that the late al-Rāzī shows a pronounced interest in Sufism.[5]

---

3 Shihadeh, "The Mystic and the Sceptic in Fakhr al-Dīn al-Rāzī." For our purposes, Shihadeh's main arguments can be summarized as follows: (1) al-Rāzī converted to Sufism (103, 117); (2) mystical knowledge is unrelated and antithetical to philosophical knowledge insofar as it is non-syllogistic and not properly conceivable by the intellect (113, 115); these two kinds of knowledge are in fact dichotomic (114); and (3) Sufi knowledge is also unrelated to intuition (*ḥads*) (115–16).

4 al-Rāzī, *al-Maṭālib al-ʿāliya min al-ʿilm al-ilāhī*; idem, *al-Tafṣīr al-kabīr*, and idem, *Lawāmiʿ al-bayyināt fī l-asmāʾ wa-l-ṣifāt*. The first two works will form the backbone of the following analysis. For the chronology of al-Rāzī's oeuvre and the dating of these works, see Griffel, "On Fakhr al-Dīn al-Rāzī's Life and the Patronage He Received." That *al-Tafsīr al-kabīr* and *al-Maṭālib al-ʿāliya* are Fakhr al-Dīn's two last major works is well known. *Lawāmiʿ al-bayyināt* is not included in Griffel's list, but according to Gloton in the introduction to his French translation, *Traité sur les noms divins*, 27, it can be dated to 595/1198–99 on the basis of a statement appearing at the end of the treatise. However, no concrete indication of the treatise's date of composition can be found there, and it is unclear on what grounds Gloton reached this conclusion.

5 Shihadeh's article is the first to focus entirely on al-Rāzī's relation to Sufism, but for the bibliographic record, one should cite the following studies, which have touched on the subject: Gramlich, "Fakhr ad-Din ar-Razis Kommentar zu Sure 18, 9–12," Haywood, "Fak͟hr al-Dīn al-Rāzī's Contribution to Ideas of Ultimate Reality and Meaning," Nasr, "Fak͟hr al-Dīn al-Rāzī," and more recently Lewis, *Rumi: Past and Present, East and West*, and Lagarde, *Les secrets de l'invisible: essai sur le Grand commentaire de Faḫr al-Dîn al-Râzî*, especially 35 and 108. Although

In what follows, I intend to build on the insight provided by Shihadeh by focusing closely on the relation between philosophical and mystical cognition in al-Rāzī's works. In this connection, Shihadeh's interpretation strikes me as problematic with regard to two specific points: First, it claims that al-Rāzī considered mystical knowledge to be distinct from, and unrelated to, philosophical knowledge in general and intuitive knowledge in particular. In other words, mystical knowledge, as opposed to the knowledge acquired by intuition and cogitation, is non-syllogistic in form and not grounded in logic, and transcends the normal operations of the human intellect. Second, and as a corollary, it presents Sufism and philosophy as two irreducible cognitive alternatives, which are fundamentally incompatible with one another. Shihadeh argues that since al-Rāzī regards Sufi knowledge as being superior and unrelated to philosophical knowledge, the latter consequently becomes superfluous and ineffectual. In Shihadeh's eyes, this explains why al-Rāzī allegedly abandoned the philosophical approach and turned to the transcendent and immediate cognitive approach of the Sufis.

In view of the fact that al-Rāzī sometimes describes one mode of cognition as being cogitative and syllogistic, the other as being immediate and conveyed in the form of divine disclosures, the inclination to conclude that he upheld two distinct and irreconcilable theories of how human beings acquire knowledge is understandable. But as I shall argue below, I believe that al-Rāzī conceives of both methods as being not only compatible, but as forming the two branches of a single cognitive tree. Moreover, both theories are integrated in a psychological framework that Fakhr al-Dīn borrows from Avicenna and which makes the concept of intuition the cornerstone of all superior forms of human cognition. Since Shihadeh does not provide the broader psychological background of al-Rāzī's alleged mystical theories, it seems necessary to begin the following analysis with a short account of the structure of al-Rāzī's noetics. Accordingly, I devote some paragraphs to discussing Fakhr al-Dīn's views on the faculties of the human intellect, as well as on intuition and cogitation, subsequently addressing the question of how al-Rāzī defined mystical knowledge. The starting point of my analysis is al-Rāzī's *Commentary* on Avicenna's *Pointers and Reminders* (*Sharḥ al-Ishārāt wa-l-tanbīhāt*). Although this work provides valuable insight into al-Rāzī's interpretation of Avicenna's doctrines

---

Lagarde's work devotes considerable space to discussing the place of mysticism in al-Rāzī's thought in *al-Tafsīr al-kabīr*, it does not provide an analytical treatment of the subject. More relevant to the topic at hand are the comments by Abrahamov, "Faḫr al-Dīn al-Rāzī on the Knowability of God's Essence and Attributes," 221 ff. on the mystical material in *al-Maṭālib al-ʿāliya*.

and may reflect his own beliefs, it remains a commentary and as such its contents can only be cautiously attributed to al-Rāzī himself. However, as I will show subsequently, the ideas Fakhr al-Dīn develops in this work are fully compatible with those he articulates in his other, more personal, works, such as *The Eastern Investigations*, *The Elevated Subjects*, and the *Long Commentary*.

Following Avicenna and other Avicennian philosophers, al-Rāzī divides the human intellect into four main stages or faculties: (1) the material intellect (*al-ʿaql al-hayūlānī*); (2) the dispositional intellect (*al-ʿaql bi-l-malaka*); (3) the actual intellect (*al-ʿaql bi-l-fiʿl*); (4) and the acquired intellect (*al-ʿaql al-mustafād*). For our present purposes, I will focus only on the second and third stages, that is, the stages of the dispositional and actual intellect. The second stage, al-Rāzī informs us, develops when the primary or axiomatic sciences (*al-ʿulūm bi-l-awwaliyyāt* or *al-ʿulūm al-awwaliyya*) have been fully assimilated. These primary sciences consist of the primary intelligibles (*maʿqūlāt uwwal*) and axioms without which further knowledge would not be possible, such as the law of non-contradiction or the knowledge that the whole is greater than the part. These intelligibles are quickly or even spontaneously grasped by the intellect during its early formation, albeit possibly through the intermediary of experience and sense perception, and they represent the cognitive foundation on which further knowledge, that is, the secondary theoretical sciences (*al-ʿulūm al-naẓariyya*), can be acquired by the actual intellect. In other words, the dispositional intellect may be predicated of the human rational soul when the latter possesses the intelligibles that are both primary and universal and is potentially capable of elaborating synthetic and syllogistic knowledge.[6]

Al-Rāzī then proceeds to explain that the acquisition of knowledge in the dispositional intellect, or more precisely at this point in the actual intellect, can occur in two basic ways: either through study and cogitation (*ṭalab* and *fikr* respectively) or through intuition (*ḥads*). The latter is essentially, according to the Avicennian tradition, the ability of the intellect to intuit the middle term of a syllogism and therefore to obtain syllogistic knowledge without having to undergo the habitual sequential procedures required by logical cogitation. Al-Rāzī's *Commentary* on Avicenna's *Pointers and Reminders* provides a clear statement to this effect:

> **Text 1:** The disposition (*istiʿdād*) for the conversion of these primary sciences (*al-ʿulūm al-awwaliyya*) into the theoretical sciences (*al-ʿulūm*

6 For this breakdown of the different kinds of intellectual faculties and for a description of the dispositional intellect (*al-ʿaql bi-l-malaka*) in particular see: al-Rāzī, *Sharḥ al-Ishārāt*, ed. Tehran 2:269:1ff.; ed. Cairo 1:154.10ff.; idem, *al-Maṭālib*, 7:279–280 and 2:417–418.

al-naẓariyya) occurs either by means of assiduous [effort] and study (*al-jidd wa-l-ṭalab*), and this is reflection (*al-fikr*), or (...) without yearning (*shawq*) and study, and this is intuition (*al-ḥads*).[7]

Al-Rāzī elaborates on this distinction a few pages later, providing valuable information on the nature of intuition:

> **Text 2:** Know that intuition (*ḥads*) and reflection (*fikr*) are similar in one aspect and differ in another. What they have in common is that each one of them is a motion that occurs in the mind (*ḥaraka taʿriḍu li-l-dhihn*) from the middle term [of a syllogism, *al-ḥadd al-awsaṭ*] to the thing sought (*al-maṭlūb*). As for their difference, it lies in the fact that in reflection, the thing sought is first posited, and the middle term leading to it is then investigated. And it may happen that the investigator finds it (*scil.* the middle term), in which case he is led to the thing sought, or it may happen that he (*scil.* the investigator) does not find it, in which case his reflection stagnates. But in the case of intuition, the middle term is first present in the mind, then the mind is led by it to the thing sought. This may happen without yearning to obtain the middle term. In this case, the cognizance (or awareness, *al-shuʿūr*) of the middle [term] precedes that of the thing sought. But there may be a yearning to reach it [the middle term], in which case the cognizance of the middle [term] is posterior to the cognizance that something is sought, although the acquisition of the middle [term] by the mind barely follows the appearance of this yearning. But in the case of reflection, the delay [between the yearning and the acquisition of the middle term] may be great.[8]

---

7 al-Rāzī, *Sharḥ al-Ishārāt wa-l-tanbīhāt*, ed. Tehran 2:269:6–10; ed. Cairo 1:154.13–15. All English translations cited in this article are my own.

8 al-Rāzī, *Sharḥ al-Ishārāt*, ed. Tehran 2:271:15–272.6; ed. Cairo 1:156.4–20. The subtle distinction al-Rāzī makes between various kinds of logical awareness or cognizance (*shuʿūr*) would deserve further investigation, which cannot be conducted here. More generally, this passage suggests that al-Rāzī did not regard the distinction between cogitation (*fikr*) and intuition (*ḥads*) as a hard or absolute one, since they essentially lead to the same kind of knowledge. His main point seems to focus on the different speed with which both processes unfold. That we are dealing with a soft distinction seems supported by the fact that (a) the philosopher may override this distinction and possess both skill in syllogistic cogitation and a very developed intuition; and (b) it seems necessary to always assume some degree of intuitive competence in syllogistic reasoning, as the person utterly devoid of intuition is considered a fool by al-Rāzī and could not be able to engage in any kind of learning process (see Text 6 below). In

This highly informative passage broadly contrasts cogitation to intuition, as the previous one had, but in addition it provides more specific insight into the different kinds of relations between intuition and the awareness and intention of solving a particular logical problem. Of particular interest is al-Rāzī's view that the act of intuition can be either prior or posterior to the yearning or desire (*shawq*) for a specific solution, which alters the sequential relation between intuition and the awareness of this goal. Hence, intuition can be either immediate or quasi-immediate and precede the thing sought, or a short amount of time may elapse between the awareness of the thing sought and the act of intuition itself.[9]

Furthermore, it is important to stress that although al-Rāzī, following Avicenna himself, is keen on stressing the difference between these two cognitive modes he believes that they ultimately lead to the acquisition of the same kind of knowledge. For intuitive knowledge is intellectual (in the sense that it is acquired by the dispositional or actual intellect, themselves stages of the rational part of the human soul) and it is also syllogistic in nature (in the sense that it is organized into sciences and that it is built on the foundation of even more fundamental epistemological principles, i.e., the primary intelligibles). In other words, cogitation and intuition produce identical knowledge, although they differ with regard to the speed and manner in which this knowledge is

---

any case, it will be shown below that the ideal knowers are for al-Rāzī those who combine the cognitive and intuitive approaches to maximize their acquisition of knowledge.

9 The definition of both cogitation and intuition as a motion (*ḥaraka*) of the mind seems a crucial point, since it implies that even though intuition may be described loosely as being immediate and non-discursive (at least when compared with cogitation), it is not absolutely so, since a motion necessarily involves development in time. This explains why I am using the slightly contrived expression "quasi-immediate" to describe the act of intuition. However, when compared with cogitation, intuition would indeed appear to be immediate. This in my view is what justifies al-Rāzī's use of a metaphorical language of illumination and disclosure to describe intuitive knowledge; see the discussion below in Section III. The temporal aspect of intuition as a cognitive phenomenon that can elapse over a shorter or longer period of time is addressed by Ibn Sīnā in some of his works; see for instance Ibn Sīnā, *al-Mabdaʾ wa-l-maʿād*, 115–117. Ibn Sīnā also seems to have been aware of the difficulty as to whether intuitive knowledge is completely immediate and non-discursive. In *al-Shifāʾ*, *al-Ṭabīʿiyyāt*, *al-Nafs*, 249.20–21, he is uncertain whether people endowed with the highest intuition and the saintly faculty access the middle terms "all at once or *almost* all at once" (*immā dufʿatan wa-immā qarīban min dufʿatan*). On intuition in general in Ibn Sīnā's philosophy and on the issue of intuition as a movement of the soul, see Gutas, "Intuition and Thinking: The Evolving Structure of Avicenna's Epistemology," and idem, *Avicenna and the Aristotelian Tradition*, 179–201.

acquired. While cogitation is slow, arduous, and fully discursive, the intuitive act is quasi-immediate.[10]

Finally, as al-Rāzī explains in other passages of his works, intuition exists in various degrees in different individuals, and it is therefore infinitely malleable and perfectible. Some people are almost entirely devoid of it, others possess it to some moderate extent, while still others have an intuition that is so powerful that it endows them with the quasi-immediate knowledge of a vast number of middle terms and even of entire sciences without exertion or study. Both with regard to cogitation and intuition, then, the human aptitude for learning is characterized by drastic variations with regard to the difficulty or ease with which these processes operate.[11] It should be noted that the basic distinction between intuition and cogitation, as well as the various features of intuition discussed above, can be found in an almost similar form not only in *Pointers*, on which al-Rāzī was here commenting, but also in many other writings by Avicenna.[12]

Now, according to al-Rāzī, the highest part of this intuitive faculty is called "the saintly faculty" or "the saintly soul" (*al-quwwa al-qudsiyya* or *al-nafs al-qudsiyya*). As al-Rāzī explains in his *Commentary on Pointers and Reminders*:

---

10 Al-Rāzī seems to be in agreement with Ibn Sīnā in defining intuitive intellectual knowledge as being syllogistic in nature; see Adamson, "Non-Discursive Thought," 92–94, 98, 104, who concludes that all intellectual knowledge for Ibn Sīnā, including non-discursive knowledge, is structured syllogistically.

11 See especially al-Rāzī, *Sharḥ al-Ishārāt*, ed. Tehran 2:268.14ff.; ed. Cairo 1:153.34 ff.; and idem, *al-Maṭālib*, 7:280.3–9. See also Texts 4 and 6 discussed below.

12 See notably Ibn Sīnā, *al-Mabdaʾ wa-l-maʿād*, 115–117; idem, *al-Shifāʾ*, *al-Ṭabīʿiyyāt*, *al-Nafs*, 248–250; idem, *al-Ishārāt wa-l-tanbīhāt*, 2:392–395; and idem, *al-Mubāḥathāt*, ed. Bīdārfar 106–7, ed. Badawī 231. In his seminal article, "Intuition and Thinking," Gutas broadly distinguishes two main stages in Ibn Sīnā's theory of intuition, the "standard version" typical of the early and middle phases of Ibn Sīnā's life and the "revised version" elaborated in Ibn Sīnā's late works. It is highly improbable in my view that al-Rāzī would have distinguished between these two versions, as his own theory of intuition incorporates doctrinal features that according to Gutas are incompatible and belong to one version or the other. For instance, al-Rāzī sharply distinguishes intuition from cogitation, which is a feature of the "revised version," but he also defines both as a movement of the mind, a claim more characteristic of the "standard version." The main point here is that al-Rāzī relies directly on Ibn Sīnā's theory of intuition, especially in the form in which this doctrine would have been accessible to him in *al-Shifāʾ* and *al-Ishārāt*, and that he uses it as the cornerstone for his interpretation of both philosophical and mystical knowledge, as we shall see shortly.

> **Text 3:** As for the upper limit [of intuition], it is the noble and exalted intuitive faculty, and this is [the faculty] whose oil can almost radiate with light.[13]

Shortly after, he adds: "And he (*scil.* Avicenna) said that the saintly faculty is one of the different kinds of intuition (*nawʿ min anwāʿ al-ḥads*)."[14] According to al-Rāzī, then, this faculty is firmly inscribed in an Avicennian noetical framework. It is an exalted and pure form of intuition, which is associated with the dispositional and actual intellects. These stages of the intellect are the locus for the transition from primary, spontaneous knowledge to theoretical, syllogistic knowledge, and it is at this level that both cogitation and intuition are embedded.[15]

A longer description of the saintly faculty and of its characteristics appears in *The Eastern Investigations*, which is fully in harmony with the evidence from al-Rāzī's commentary on *Pointers* that has been discussed thus far:

> **Text 4:** This human being [who possesses a superior intuition] becomes cognizant of the true existence of things without study and yearning (*min ghayr ṭalab minhu wa-shawq*). His mind (*dhihnuhū*) is led to the conclusions [of syllogisms, *al-natāʾij*] without assiduous effort in this matter, then from these conclusions to others, until he encompasses the ends of these human pursuits and the exalted degrees [of knowledge]. This faculty is called the saintly (*al-qudsiyya*) [faculty], and it is distinguished from the rest of souls both quantitatively (*bi-l-kam*), because it has a greater access to the middle terms, and qualitatively (*bi-l-kayf*), because it is faster in moving (*asraʿ intiqālan*) from the [first] principles to the secondary [principles] and from the premises to the conclusions (*min al-mabādiʾ ilā l-thawānī wa min al-muqaddimāt ilā l-natāʾij*). It also

---

13 al-Rāzī, *Sharḥ al-Ishārāt*, ed. Tehran 2:269.12–13; ed. Cairo 1:154.21–23: *wa-ammā al-ṭaraf al-aʿlā wa huwa al-quwwa al-ḥadsiyya al-sharīfa al-bāligha wa hiya allatī yakādu zaytuha yuḍīʾu.* The expression *al-quwwa al-ḥadsiyya al-sharīfa al-bāligha* refers to the saintly faculty and is sometimes used by al-Rāzī interchangeably with the terms *al-quwwa al-qudsiyya*. Al-Rāzī's discussion of the various degrees of intuition in this passage is enriched with references to light symbolism and particularly to the Light Verse in *Sūrat al-nūr* (Q 24:35).

14 al-Rāzī, *Sharḥ al-Ishārāt*, ed. Tehran 2:273.5–6; ed. Cairo 1:156.39.

15 al-Rāzī, *Sharḥ al-Ishārāt*, ed. Tehran 2:267–74; ed. Cairo 1:153–156. The localization of the saintly faculty (*al-quwwa al-qudsiyya*) at the level of the dispositional intellect is clear in this passage of *Sharḥ al-Ishārāt* as well as in the following passage: al-Rāzī, *al-Mabāḥith al-mashriqiyya*, 2:417–418.

> differs from the other souls in another way, namely, that the other souls determine the goals and then search for the middle terms leading to them, whereas in the case of the saintly souls, the middle term occurs in the mind and leads it to the sought conclusion, with the awareness (*al-shuʿūr*) of the middle term preceding the awareness of the thing sought.[16]

Apart from explicitly identifying the saintly faculty as a kind of superior intuition, as Text 3 already implicitly had, this passage provides valuable insight into the kind of knowledge produced by the saintly faculty. According to al-Rāzī, the saintly faculty is comparable to both cogitation and lower forms of intuition in that it produces syllogistic knowledge, that is, knowledge that is organized logically and consists of primary and secondary principles and premises and conclusions. The main differences are, first, the speed and ease with which those blessed with the saintly faculty can access these principles and conclusions when compared to those limited to syllogistic reasoning or lower forms of intuition; and, second, the fact that in those blessed with the saintly faculty, awareness of the middle term precedes awareness of the thing sought. In light of this evidence, it is clear that the kind of knowledge derived from the saintly faculty is essentially the same as that reached through syllogistic reasoning. But whereas ratiocination is slow and discursive, intuition, and especially the saintly faculty, enable one to acquire this knowledge immediately or quasi-immediately and without effort. In fact, as is implied in Texts 4 and 6, this faculty makes it possible—at least in principle—for the entirety of the theoretical sciences (*al-ʿulūm al-naẓariyya*) to be acquired without reflection or study. Hence, what differs is the mode of reaching this knowledge, not the nature of the knowledge itself. This point will be crucial for the following discussion of al-Rāzī's views on mystical knowledge.

As mentioned above, al-Rāzī's exposition of intuition—including the definition of the saintly faculty as the highest kind of intuition—is directly indebted to Avicenna, even though it consists of features that are not always juxtaposed in the same account by Avicenna himself. For our present purposes, however, an important question arises: What kinds of individuals are liable to develop the saintly faculty? Al-Rāzī generally attributes the saintly faculty to prophets and relies on it to explain the phenomena of revelation and prophecy. In this context, it is generally called the "prophetic saintly faculty or soul" (*al-quwwa al-qudsiyya al-nabawiyya*). It enables prophets to access the knowl-

16 al-Rāzī, *al-Mabāḥith al-mashriqiyya*, 1:353.21–354.9.

edge and obtain the instructions they need to carry out their spiritual mission.[17] In attributing an exalted form of intuition to the prophets, namely the saintly faculty, al-Rāzī is merely following Avicenna, and later al-Ghazālī, and adapting Avicennian psychological notions to explain this dogma.[18]

Yet al-Rāzī in various other passages intimates that the saintly faculty also characterizes other groups, namely, the Sufi masters (*al-awliyāʾ*) and philosophers (*al-ḥukamāʾ*). With regard to the Sufi masters, Fakhr al-Dīn in his commentary on *Sūrat al-nūr* writes (citing al-Ghazālī):

> **Text 5:** The fifth: the saintly faculty by which prophets and some friends [of God] are characterized, and through which the hidden decrees and lordly secrets are manifested.[19]

As for the fundamental similarity in the way knowledge is acquired by the intellect of prophets and philosophers, it is stressed in the following passage of *The Elevated Subjects*:

> **Text 6:** Know that the degrees of facility and difficulty (related to the acquisition of knowledge by the dispositional and actual intellects) are not fixed, but it is as if they were infinite (*ghayr mutanāhiya*). Just as (this disposition) may be entirely lacking, as is the case of the fool who possesses no inclination whatsoever toward acquisition and study, likewise, it may by way of increase result in someone who is perfect (*al-kāmil*) and who acquires the syllogistic combinations (*al-tarkībāt*) to their utmost

---

17 See for instance, al-Rāzī, *al-Tafsīr al-kabīr*, 23:234.11–12 (*ad* Q 24:35); and idem, *al-Mabāḥith al-mashriqiyya*, 2:418.1–2.

18 See Marmura, "Avicenna's Psychological Proof of Prophecy," and Griffel, "Al-Ġazālī's Concept of Prophecy: The Introduction of Avicennan Psychology into Ašʿarite Theology," 111–112, who briefly discusses the saintly faculty in Ibn Sīnā and al-Rāzī in the context of his discussion of al-Ghazālī's proofs for prophecy. See also the illuminating discussion in Treiger, *Inspired Knowledge*, 74–79. Ibn Sīnā, al-Ghazālī, and al-Rāzī all seem therefore to agree that the saintly faculty represents the purest and highest part of the intuitive faculty and is the privilege of prophets. In spite of the fact that the terminology between the two later thinkers differs slightly (al-Ghazālī's *al-rūḥ al-qudsī* is not found in al-Rāzī, who refers instead to *al-quwwa al-qudsiyya* or *al-nafs al-qudsiyya*), their theory is similar and grounded in Avicennian psychology. However, al-Rāzī, more than al-Ghazālī and even Ibn Sīnā, is explicit in situating this faculty at the level of the dispositional intellect.

19 al-Rāzī, *al-Tafsīr al-kabīr*, 23:233.12–14 (*ad* Q 24:35): *wa khāmisuhā al-quwwa al-qudsiyya allatī takhtaṣṣu bihā l-anbiyāʾ* (…) *wa-baʿḍ al-awliyāʾ wa tatajallā fīhā lawāʾiḥ al-ghayb wa-asrār al-malakūt.*

> degree and in a perfect order, without striving toward study (*min ghayr saʿy fī l-ṭalab*). The possessors of this perfection (*al-kamāl*) are the greatest prophets and the perfect philosophers (*al-anbiyāʾ l-muʿaẓẓamūna wa-l-ḥukamāʾ l-kāmilūna*). And some among the Sufis call this kind of knowledge the mystical knowledge (*al-ʿilm al-ladunī*), a [phrase] taken from [the Qurʾanic passage]: "and we had taught him knowledge that comes from Us" (*wa-ʿallamnāhū min ladunnā ʿilm*^{an}, Q 18:65).[20]

This passage puts forth the striking claim that some philosophers (*al-ḥukamāʾ*) can acquire the uppermost kind of intuition, and presumably the saintly faculty itself. These philosophers' knowledge, the intuitive way through which they obtain it, and the perfection they derive from it, are compared to those of the prophets. Although Text 6 does not mention the saintly faculty literally, it is implicit in al-Rāzī's reference to the cognitive perfection (*kamāl*) these individuals attain and in the fact that they acquire these syllogistic sciences or combinations (*al-tarkībāt*) without "striving toward study." It is also worthwhile noticing that al-Rāzī establishes a deliberate and strategic link with the Sufis, who, according to him, apply their own terminology to describe a similar kind of cognitive phenomenon. The main implications are, first, that the Sufis also should be included among those who have reached the highest peaks of the intuitive faculty (as Text 5 had already indicated), and, second, that the intuitive knowledge acquired by the prophets, mystics, and philosophers is essentially the same and varies only in degree. According to al-Rāzī, then, the prophets, saints, and philosophers are the three groups who have access to the highest reaches of intuition and may acquire the saintly faculty.

Fakhr al-Dīn's view that Sufi masters and philosophers also have access to the saintly faculty may appear surprising at first sight. Prophets are as a rule set apart from the rest of humanity in the Islamic tradition as a result of their special religious mission and the divine knowledge of which they are the exclusive recipients. But al-Rāzī's move is in fact justified by the very structure of his noetics and his theory of intuition and the saintly faculty. Recall that intuition is, on al-Rāzī's psychological account, infinitely perfectible, so that it

---

20 al-Rāzī, *al-Maṭālib al-ʿāliya*, 7:280.3–9. The text of al-Saqqā's edition of *al-Maṭālib al-ʿāliya* has been checked with that of MS Kayseri, Reşit Efendi 503, fol. 329b, a copy not used by al-Saqqā. Although its relationship to the autograph is not as close as Ramazan Şeşen claims in his description of it (in *Mukhtārāt min al-makhṭūṭāt al-ʿarabiyya al-nādira fī maktabāt Turkiyā*, 658), the manuscript is of high value due to its comparison with others noted in its margins. It was copied shortly after 1165/1752. The variant readings of the manuscript in this passage are minor and hardly affect the translation.

is *theoretically* possible for most or many individuals to reach the level of the saintly faculty. Being merely a rarefied and pure form of intuition, the saintly faculty is potentially accessible to human beings who tread the path of knowledge and self-purification and increase their intuitive faculty sufficiently to reach this exalted state. Granted the existence of a natural inclination or talent (*fiṭra*) that allows it, each person can infinitely perfect his or her intuition and strive to attain this state. This explains why, according to al-Rāzī, certain philosophers can acquire a very high form of intuition and even in theory the saintly faculty. Moreover, it is important to stress that prophets, Sufi masters, and philosophers who possess this exalted intuitive faculty acquire what is in essence intellectual, syllogistic knowledge, and even entire sciences, albeit without effort and striving.

That al-Rāzī attributed the saintly faculty or a superior form of intuition (at least potentially) to other individuals apart from prophets is clear enough from the previous passages, but it is also supported by evidence gleaned from his *Commentary on Pointers and Reminders*. After surveying the various grades of knowers (*al-ʿārifūn*), al-Rāzī concludes that the most advanced among them possess "the noble and perfect saintly soul" (*al-nafs al-sharīfa al-kāmila al-qudsiyya*).[21] Hence, there can be little doubt that al-Rāzī extended this concept to include not only prophets, but also other individuals not blessed specifically with the prophetic vocation. This does not mean, however, that prophets, Sufi masters, and philosophers possess exactly the same knowledge or with equal clarity. The degrees of intuition, even at this superior level, are virtually infinite and vary from one individual to the other, so that there are presumably gradations distinguishing those who have reached this exalted state as well.[22]

In light of the foregoing, it becomes easier to understand why al-Rāzī often describes the possessors of the saintly faculty as being the recipients of "divine illuminations" and "disclosures" (*ishrāq*, *tajallā*, *kashf*, and *mukāshafāt* are the terms most commonly used by al-Rāzī for this purpose; see for instance Text 5 above and Texts 9 and 10 below). In al-Rāzī's eyes, intuition and the saintly faculty are the medium through which insights from the divine world are communicated to humans. However, these do not constitute a special, non-logical

21 al-Rāzī, *Sharḥ al-ishārāt*, ed. Tehran 2:604.15–19; ed. Cairo 1: 2:111.35–37. I shall return to these *ʿārifūn* at the end of my paper.

22 Although al-Rāzī does not explain what factors differentiate the various saintly souls, one may surmise that variations in both nature (*fiṭra*) and the degrees of spiritual purification attained are the two main criteria. At any rate, we may conclude that al-Rāzī's psychology is structured according to highly nuanced classifications, with distinctions pertaining not only to different intellectual faculties, but to different degrees and levels within a single faculty.

or supra-intellectual kind of knowledge, but rather a kind of intellectual and syllogistic knowledge that is grasped quasi-immediately and without effort. It is therefore—at least metaphorically—comparable to a kind of disclosure or illumination of the mind or heart. In other words, it seems that al-Rāzī deploys mystical terminology to describe a cognitive phenomenon that is perfectly accountable on Avicennian psychological grounds.[23]

To sum up, several important points have been established. Mystical knowledge, according to al-Rāzī, is essentially quasi-immediate, intuitive, intellectual knowledge acquired by the dispositional and actual faculties. These are among the four stages of the human intellect in the tradition of Avicennian noetics to which Fakhr al-Dīn subscribed. By implication, this means that mystical cognition is not antithetical to the operations of the intellect. Rather, it is grounded in the faculties of the rational soul (*al-nafs al-nāṭiqa*), where intuition and its most refined and exalted part, the saintly faculty, are located. In other words, mystical knowledge for al-Rāzī is not an irrational or supra-rational form of knowledge that would stand in stark contrast to reflection and syllogistic reasoning, but is essentially and qualitatively the same kind of knowledge as reflective knowledge, albeit one which has been acquired without effort or study. Unlike cogitation, it does not follow the temporal sequences of a syllogism, but ultimately it results in the same kind of syllogistic knowledge that reasoning (*fikr*) otherwise leads to. It is also intellectual in the sense that it presupposes the healthy activity of the dispositional and actual intellects and the thorough internalization of the primary sciences or intelligibles, a necessary step for all further theoretical and metaphysical knowledge to develop. Finally, this highly developed intuitive ability characterizes not only prophets, but also Sufis and philosophers, who in al-Rāzī's view can be blessed with this special cognitive state.

Just as al-Rāzī—following Avicenna—had proffered a psychological explanation to account for prophetic knowledge, he similarly articulated a psychological explanation of mystical knowledge, essentially identifying it with the intellectual intuition of the prophets and philosophers. In both cases, the crux of his argumentation relies on the key notions of intuition and the saintly faculty, which he borrowed directly from Avicenna, but which, as we shall see

23 Ibn Sīnā himself used some of these terms with a similar purpose in mind; see Gutas, *Avicenna and the Aristotelian Tradition*, 343–346. The connection al-Rāzī establishes between the saintly faculty and these divine illuminations is also apparent in various passages of *al-Tafsīr al-kabīr*, among which see, for instance, 23:233–234 (*ad* Q 24:35), where al-Rāzī resorts to a rich vocabulary of light to describe noetical categories. I will return to this point later on in connection with Ibn Sīnā's *al-Ishārāt*.

in the next section of this article, he creatively adapted to suit his own needs. Further extending this line of argumentation, it should be noted that all knowledge for al-Rāzī is intellectual (*ʿaqlī*), since he defines the angels either as pure intellects or noble rational souls, and since he regards God Himself as the possessor of intellectual knowledge.[24]

II The Cogitative Method and the Path of Spiritual Purification

We saw in the previous section that Fakhr al-Dīn establishes an important distinction between intuition and cogitation qua cognitive modes. There is another central distinction that one finds in the Razian texts, this time between cogitation and syllogistic study (*fikr* and *ṭalab*) on the one hand and exercises of spiritual purification (*riyāḍāt*) on the other. The task of this section is to shed light on how these two sets of distinctions correlate, and to settle the issue of whether al-Rāzī conceived the latter distinction as being antithetical or complementary. As we shall see, this issue of compatibility has a direct bearing on al-Rāzī's conception of the relation between mysticism and philosophy and on the nature and goal of philosophy.

Fakhr al-Dīn sometimes contrasts what may be called a theoretical and cogitative approach and a practical approach consisting of exercises of mental purification. Two clear accounts embodying this distinction appear in *The Elevated Subjects* and in the *Long Commentary*:

> **Text 7**: Human souls (or spirits, *al-arwāḥ al-bashariyya*) may be classified in two kinds [or species, *nawʿayn*]: there are those whose illumination and power (*ishrāquhā wa-quwwatuhā*) are brought about by the purification and the cleansing of the soul (*al-taṣfiya wa taṭhīr al-nafs*) from everything that is not God, and others [whose illumination and power] are brought about by forming demonstrative proofs that are certain (*tarkīb al-barāhīn al-yaqīniyya*). The first are the prophets and friends [of God, *al-anbiyāʾ wa-l-awliyāʾ*], the second the philosophers (*al-ḥukamāʾ*).[25]

This passage explains that the illumination and empowerment of the human soul can be brought about in two ways: either through kathartic exercises aimed at increasing the mind's focus on God, or through a rigorous training in the philosophical syllogistic arts. As the two methods are ascribed to the

24 al-Rāzī, *al-Maṭālib al-ʿāliya*, 7:17–19.

25 al-Rāzī, *al-Maṭālib al-ʿāliya*, 7:283.9–11. MS Kayseri, Reşit Efendi 503, foll. 330a–330b.

prophets and Sufi masters and philosophers respectively, the excerpt indicates that al-Rāzī did perceive a distinction between philosophy and mysticism, not, however, with regard to the kind of knowledge that characterizes these disciplines, but to the different approaches accessible to human beings for attaining what is fundamentally the same kind of knowledge.

In another passage written in the same vein, which belongs to al-Rāzī's commentary on Sura 12 (*Sūrat Yūsuf*), *he* contrasts the approaches of the mystics and philosophers, this time with regard to the order of study and to how these groups implement the various learned disciplines:

> **Text 8:** What is meant by judgment (*al-ḥukm*) is practical philosophy (*al-ḥikma al-ʿamaliyya*), and what is meant by science (*al-ʿilm*) is theoretical philosophy (*al-ḥikma al-naẓariyya*). Here (*scil.* in the case of the mystics) practical philosophy precedes theoretical philosophy, because the practitioners of spiritual exercises (*aṣḥāb al-riyāḍāt*) [first] occupy themselves with practical philosophy and then ascend from there to theoretical philosophy. As for the people of intellectual concepts and spiritual theories (*aṣḥāb al-afkār al-ʿaqliyya wa-l-anẓār al-rūḥāniyya*), they first attain theoretical philosophy and then descend from there to practical philosophy.[26]

The "people of intellectual concepts and spiritual theories" are in the context of these different branches of *ḥikma* none other than the philosophers. The emphasis here is on the order in which the sciences are implemented. The philosophers begin with theory and end with practical philosophy, whereas the mystics begin with this science and only subsequently proceed to theoretical philosophy. Practical philosophy here is to be construed not only in terms of ethics, but also as including exercises of spiritual purification. Al-Rāzī's ascription of both practical and theoretical philosophy to the mystics is in itself noteworthy and reflects his highly idiosyncratic view of the relation between philosophy and mysticism, which will be further explored below. The Sufis themselves would surely not have referred to their sciences using this kind of terminology. At any rate, from this passage we may infer yet again that for al-Rāzī the main distinction lies not in the kind of knowledge that is sought by these various groups, but rather in their approach to knowledge and the means of cultivating it.

That Fakhr al-Dīn in fact did not perceive the philosophical and mystical approaches as being antithetical or incompatible, but as forming a single

26 al-Rāzī, *al-Tafsīr al-kabīr*, 18:111.19–21 (*ad* Q 12:22).

integrated discipline, is ascertained in the following quote from the *Long Commentary*. Here, al-Rāzī expounds on the passage in Sura 18 where the Qur'an clarifies how the enigmatic master of Moses, a figure who in the Qur'an is only referred to as "one of Our servants" and who is usually identified with the prophet Khiḍr, acquires his superior knowledge:

> **Text 9:** His (*scil.* God's) saying: "We had taught him knowledge that comes from Us,"[27] explains that he (*scil.* the prophet Khiḍr) acquired these sciences from God without an intermediary. The Sufis call the sciences acquired by means of disclosures (*bi-ṭarīq al-mukāshafāt*) the mystical sciences (*al-ʿulūm al-laduniyya*), and the master Abū Ḥāmid al-Ghazālī composed a treatise entitled *Risāla fī ithbāt al-ʿulūm al-laduniyya*.[28] The truth of the matter with regard to this topic is as follows: When we perceive something and conceive it as being existent, either by passing judgment over it, and this is *taṣdīq*, or without judgment, and this is *taṣawwur*, both of these parts (*qismayn*) are either theoretical (*naẓariyy^an^*) and reached without acquisition and study (*kasb wa-ṭalab*), or they are acquired (*kasbiyy^an^*). The acquired sciences (*al-ʿulūm al-kasbiyya*) are not present in the soul's substance (*fī jawhar al-nafs*) from the outset, but they can certainly be obtained by following a method (or way, *ṭarīq*) that consists of two parts (*qismayn*): One part requires that man synthesize these innate and theoretical sciences until he reaches through [the act of] synthesis the information about what he did not know. This is the method called reflection (*al-naẓar*), ratiocination (*al-tafakkur*), methodical investigation (*al-tadabbur*), close examination (*al-taʾammul*), deliberation (*al-tarawwī*), and inference (*al-istidlāl*). This kind of learned acquisition is the method that is performed only through effort and investigation (*bi-l-jahd wa-l-ṭalab*). The second way is for man to endeavor by means of ascetic exercises and spiritual striving (*al-riyāḍāt wa-l-mujāhadāt*) to lessen his sensual and imaginative faculties. When these are weakened, the rational faculty (*al-quwwa al-ʿaqliyya*) is strengthened and the divine lights illuminate the substance of the intellect (*jawhar*

27 Q 18:65: *wa-ʿallamnāhū min ladunnā ʿilm^an^*.

28 The *Risāla fī ithbāt al-ʿulūm al-laduniyya* that al-Rāzī ascribes to al-Ghazālī is most probably *al-Risāla al-Laduniyya*, attributed to al-Ghazālī and available in prints since the early 20th century. Recently, a manuscript version of the text (titled *Risāla fī al-ʿilm al-ladunī*) was published in facsimile in *Majmūʿah-yi falsafī-yi Marāgha / A Philosophical Anthology from Maragha*, 100–20 and has revived the debate on the text's attribution to al-Ghazālī. The tendency presently is to regard it as an authentic treatise of al-Ghazālī.

> *al-ʿaql*), profound insights are acquired, and the sciences (*al-ʿulūm*) are perfected without the intermediary of striving and aiming for ratiocination and close examination. This [approach] is called the mystical sciences (*al-ʿulūm al-laduniyya*).[29]

This excerpt is drawn from a longer passage in which al-Rāzī intends to distinguish the theoretical sciences (*al-ʿulūm al-naẓariyya*), which are present in the human soul from the outset, from the acquired sciences (*al-ʿulūm al-kasbiyya*), which are acquired either gradually over a period of time (through cogitation) or instantaneously (through intuition).[30] Although al-Rāzī does not mention intuition by name in this excerpt, it is clear that the second way or part of the method (*ṭarīq*) he describes, where knowledge and the sciences are acquired "without the intermediary of striving and aiming for ratiocination and close examination," is nothing other than intuitive knowledge. This passage therefore displays the customary Razian distinction between intuitive

29 al-Rāzī, *al-Tafsīr al-kabīr*, 21:149.27–150.13 (*ad* Q 18:65). It is possible that in this passage and the one following it al-Rāzī intends primarily to discuss prophetic knowledge, as the Qurʾanic verse alluding to Khiḍr provides the starting point of the discussion. However, the tenor of the passage is close to some of the other excerpts discussed previously that do not limit this kind of cognition to prophets alone. Moreover, the fact that the second approach consisting of spiritual exercises is thoroughly integrated in what (I will argue below) is an overarching philosophical method suggests otherwise.

30 The distinction al-Rāzī makes here between the acquired and theoretical sciences is unusual, since he habitually regards the theoretical sciences as being acquired. In fact, al-Rāzī much more frequently contrasts the innate or spontaneous sciences (*al-ʿulūm al-badīhiyya*), consisting of the primary intelligibles, to the theoretical sciences (*al-ʿulūm al-naẓariyya*), which are acquired and elaborated on the basis of the spontaneous sciences. Here the theoretical sciences seem to have taken the place of the spontaneous sciences. This can perhaps be explained by al-Rāzī's intention: his aim here is to emphasize that both syllogistic reasoning *and* the exercises of purification are processes and practices that unfold in time and that lead to a knowledge that is therefore acquired. Even though the intuitive cognition to which the second way leads is itself immediate, the path to perfecting the intuitive faculty is on the other hand long and arduous. Al-Rāzī's classification of the sciences should also be contrasted to the common Sufi distinction between the acquired sciences (*al-ʿulūm al-kasbiyya*) and the bestowed sciences (*al-ʿulūm al-wahbiyya*), expressions which al-Rāzī does not use, and which constitute yet another indication that he did not embrace the Sufi cognitive model. Unlike the Sufis, who believe that divine illuminations bear no connection with syllogistic knowledge and who thus regard the acquired and bestowed sciences as independent from one another, al-Rāzī believes that what the Sufis call mystical knowledge is in fact intuitive knowledge consisting of immediately acquired syllogistic knowledge. I am grateful to Eliza Tasbihi for sharing her insight into the Sufi tradition on this subject.

and reflective knowledge with which we are well acquainted by now. But several points should be stressed at the present juncture. First, it should be noted that al-Rāzī presents these approaches to knowledge as two parts (*qismayn*) of a single method or way (*ṭarīq*). Not only are they not antithetical or contradictory, but they are described by al-Rāzī himself as being compatible and complementary and as forming the two branches of a single cognitive tree. Moreover, it is clear that the second part is itself to be understood as leading to a kind of knowledge that, while intuitive, remains intrinsically intellectual and syllogistic in nature. This hypothesis is borne out by the terminology used to describe the second part: "the rational faculty" and "the substance of the intellect" are designated as the locus of reception of this knowledge, which consists of "sciences." Although al-Rāzī does not mention intuition or the saintly faculty by name in this passage, their role is implied, since we saw that intuition is the faculty that allows humans to acquire scientific knowledge quasi-immediately and without effort. Finally—and this is crucial—al-Rāzī explains that acquisition of this intuitive and immediate knowledge occurs thanks to the practice of ascetic and spiritual exercises.

In light of the evidence adduced above, it appears that the distinction Fakhr al-Dīn draws between cogitation and study on the one hand and exercises of spiritual purification on the other overlaps significantly with the other distinction he establishes between cogitation and intuition, which I discussed in the first section of this study. In many of the excerpts discussed above, and especially in Text 9, intuitive knowledge acquired without effort is associated with the practice of mind purification and spiritual introspection, the implication being that such ascetic practices predispose the intellect for the acquisition of intuitive knowledge. Moreover, the combination *ḥads/riyāḍāt* is also identified by al-Rāzī with the esoteric knowledge of the Sufis, thus furnishing additional evidence that he was intent on connecting the philosophical approach with the mystical one in a fundamental way. As in Text 6, al-Rāzī explicitly refers to the Sufi position in an attempt to emphasize the intrinsic compatibility and harmony of these various cognitive approaches. But Text 9 goes even further in this direction, for it claims that what the Sufis call mystical knowledge is in fact a part of Fakhr al-Dīn's overarching philosophical method.

Another explicit statement concerning the interrelatedness of these various disciplines can be found in a passage of *The Elevated Subjects*, when al-Rāzī writes:

> **Text 10**: If it happens that this person has become perfect in the method of reflective proof (*al-istidlāl al-fikrī*) and is also granted perfection in the path of purification and spiritual exercises (*ṭarīqat al-taṣfiya wa l-riyāḍa*), and if his soul is originally disposed to experiencing these states (*wa kānat nafsuhū fī mabdaʾ l-fiṭra ʿaẓīmat al-munāsaba li-hādhihi l-aḥwāl*),

> then this person reaches the furthest limits of these exalted stages and stations (*kāna dhālika l-insān wāṣilan fī hādhihi l-madārij wa l-maʿārij ilā aqṣā l-ghāyāt*).[31]

In this excerpt, al-Rāzī outlines three criteria or conditions that must be fulfilled for one's mind to be receptive to the divine disclosures and to reach the highest level of (intuitive) knowledge. The first is reflective reasoning (*al-istidlāl al-fikrī*) in the form of study and ratiocination, under which categories al-Rāzī includes all forms of syllogistic reasoning. The second consists of exercises of spiritual purification (*ṭarīqat al-taṣfiya wa-l-riyāḍa*), which are destined to clear the heart from any superfluous thought and to direct one's mind toward the divine world exclusively. Finally, the third is the possession of a talent or innate nature (*fiṭra*) inclined to such pursuits. Like Text 9, then, Text 10 indicates that reflective training and exercises of spiritual purification are complementary and necessary if one is to reach the highest stage of intuition. The notion of a natural inclination is important, as it suggests that some people may never obtain these cognitive illuminations, even though they may engage in intellectual striving and spiritual exercises during much of their life. Yet at the same time it implies that, given a nature inclined to knowledge, the acquisition of a fully developed saintly faculty and of the highest kind of knowledge that accompanies it is at least theoretically possible for several people. These achievements result from natural and psychological dispositions that are potentially common to most, if not all, human beings. In this regard, we notice that al-Rāzī adopts a very pragmatic and naturalistic approach to his account of human cognition.[32]

Fakhr al-Dīn unfortunately does not specify which ascetic or devotional exercises he has in mind, and whether these exercises correspond to some of the standard Sufi practices, such as fasting, *dhikr*, etc. But it is clear that they are in his view an efficient means of self-purification and of preparing the intellect for accessing the highest sphere of knowledge.[33] At any rate, we may conclude from the previous excerpts that, although al-Rāzī is broadly relying on Sufi terminology and ideas of spiritual purification, and although he also mentions the stages and stations usually associated with Sufi spirituality, he

---

31 al-Rāzī, *al-Maṭālib*, 1:58.18–59.2. MS Kayseri, Reşit Efendi 503, fol. 6a.

32 The same may be said of Ibn Sīnā's conception of intuition as well. According to Hasse, *Avicenna's De anima*, 164, intuition is an "inborn intellectual power" that can nonetheless be trained and perfected through practice.

33 Treiger, *Inspired Knowledge*, 37–38, discusses what appear to be similar spiritual exercises in connection with al-Ghazālī.

does not relinquish the importance of reflective reasoning for accessing such exalted states. In fact, in this passage, he considers intellectual study a requisite for such pursuits. In brief, Text 10 agrees with Texts 8 and 9 in describing logical cogitation and ascetic exercises as the two aspects or branches of a single cognitive program, although it adds the important notion of innate nature or talent. Hence, according to al-Rāzī, it is philosophically advisable to tread the path of self-purification and the path of syllogistic training side by side.

One point requires additional clarification. Although Text 10 claims that all of these conditions must be fulfilled before one can be receptive to the divine illuminations, it is possible, and in fact likely, that in the case of those who have already attained the saintly faculty, logical cogitation becomes superfluous and even pointless. This seems substantiated by Text 7, which is less harmonizing in tone, and which also intimates that some individuals may reach the highest peaks of knowledge without engaging in cogitation and syllogistic reasoning. This is also independently confirmed by the three qualities that in al-Rāzī's view characterize the prophet: a strong intuitive faculty (i.e., the saintly faculty), a strong imaginative faculty, and a strong practical faculty.[34] None of these calls for or implies philosophical reflection. Hence, it may be possible for some rare individuals to reach the saintly faculty without engaging in syllogistic training and simply by performing spiritual exercises and/or by being endowed with a special nature. However, and while this might be true, it is worth stressing once more that the kind of knowledge they reach is essentially syllogistic in nature and the same as that attained through cogitation and the syllogistic sciences.

In view of these remarks, it would seem that the program al-Rāzī outlines in Texts 9 and 10 is aimed at individuals standing outside the sphere of prophecy. It appears that for the majority of people, al-Rāzī considers both striving in the way of syllogistic reasoning and exercises of purification as contributing to perfecting one's intellectual nature. By implication, this would mean that this passage is addressed primarily to those still ascending the path of intuitive knowledge and who may still benefit from ratiocination and syllogistic training. It is presumably the program Fakhr al-Dīn had in mind for most aspiring *ʿārifūn*, including possibly himself. And this is presumably the main difference between the prophets and the philosophers in al-Rāzī's mind. While individuals from both groups may obtain the saintly faculty and the highest knowledge

34 Al-Rāzī is relying directly on Ibn Sīnā: see for instance, *al-Mabdaʾ wa-l-maʿād*, 115 ff., as well as Griffel, "Al-Ġazālī's Concept of Prophecy," 114 ff. In Ibn Sīnā, however, there is the question of whether these three qualities refer to different kinds of prophecy; see Hasse, *Avicenna's De anima*, 155 ff. and al-Akiti, "The Three Properties."

accessible to human beings, the philosophers must as a rule go through this two-branched program, while the prophets may dispense with this approach.[35]

In sum, al-Rāzī in these passages upholds the intrinsic compatibility and harmony of the philosophical, theoretical method of cogitative reasoning and of the practical method of spiritual exercises lying at the core of the mystical way. The principal aim of these exercises is to hone one's intuitive faculty by purifying the mind and making it more receptive to the divine disclosures. Fakhr al-Dīn's main contribution in this regard was to provide a clear, integrated, and overarching method (*ṭarīq*) consisting of these two activities. Al-Rāzī's harmonization of what has traditionally been perceived as elements belonging to different disciplines amounts to a creative synthesis of the various trends existing during his time, chiefly the Avicennian and mystical traditions. Moreover, the evidence gathered thus far indicates that Fakhr al-Dīn himself perceived this system as being primarily philosophical in nature, since he is effectively bringing Sufi terms and concepts within the fold of Avicenna's psychology and construing them in light of his theory of intuitive knowledge. In spite of this, the extent to which he relied on an Avicennian precedent to achieve this project remains to be carefully investigated. Below I examine some antecedents that can explain al-Rāzī's accomplishment and analyze in more detail al-Rāzī's perception of the relation between Sufism and philosophy in the trail of Avicenna's *Pointers*.

III Al-Rāzī's Interpretation of Avicenna's *Pointers* and Its Relation to al-Ghazālī's Works

The previous analysis showed that al-Rāzī considered mystical knowledge to be essentially similar to the intuitive knowledge described in the works of the philosophers. Yet the relation between Sufism and Avicennian philosophy as

35 Nevertheless, some ambiguity subsists as to how the prophets reach the saintly faculty, a point left hanging by al-Rāzī. Two explanations in my view are possible: either they are born with a special nature or talent (*fiṭra*) that spontaneously endows them with such a special ability (the naturalistic explanation), or they reach it as a result of both having a natural inclination to spiritual knowledge and assiduously cultivating this nature through spiritual exercises (the developmental explanation). In this connection, it should be said that the Achilles' heel of al-Rāzī's cognitive theory is the very concept of the saintly faculty, which called for additional distinctions and qualifications on his part. Although it plays a crucial role in his explanation of the superior cognition of prophets, Sufi masters, and philosophers, al-Rāzī is laconic as to how it functions in its details and what the differences between these various cases are.

Fakhr al-Dīn conceived it and the issue of where he situated himself along this decidedly fluctuating line require a closer investigation. In this connection, two main questions emerge: First, did al-Rāzī regard his intellectual method (*ṭarīq*) as lying closer to Sufism or to Avicennian philosophy, assuming that this distinction even applied in his mind? And second, did Fakhr al-Dīn believe Avicenna himself to have been engaged in such a harmonizing endeavor?

These are thorny problems whose resolution would require a deeper analysis of al-Rāzī's oeuvre and of his thought as a whole. However, some tentative conclusions founded on several critical points may nevertheless be sketched. The first point is that al-Rāzī is consistent in referring to the Sufis as a separate and distinct group. He usually speaks about them in the third person, using standard formulas such as: "the Sufis say (*qāla l-ṣūfiyya*) ..." or "some among the Sufis say (*qāla baʿḍ min al-ṣūfiyya*) ..." to refer to their views (this is the case of Texts 6 and 9 above). These rather aloof references suggest that al-Rāzī did not identify directly with the Sufi camp. This is especially true of Text 9, where he exposes his view of the ideal philosophical method and notes almost incidentally at the very end of the passage that the Sufis employ their own terms to describe the second part of this method.

Corroborating this point is the fact that the Sufi reports on al-Rāzī that have been preserved usually depict him in an unfavorable light, if not in a directly polemical manner.[36] A crucial document often referred to in this connection, namely, Muhyī l-Dīn Ibn ʿArabī's (d. 638/1240) letter to al-Rāzī, would seem to support the view that Fakhr al-Dīn was not regarded as a mystic by the Sufis themselves. This letter, whose date remains somewhat uncertain, is hortatory and rather encouraging in tone, but its tenor and contents imply that al-Rāzī was not a member of the mystical path, since it was precisely Ibn ʿArabī's aim to attempt to convert the Persian thinker, whose philosophical or theological works he had come across, to the Sufi cause.[37]

Furthermore, judging from the evidence discussed in this article, it seems that al-Rāzī's debt to Sufism can be limited to two specific aspects, which, in the final analysis, indicate Fakhr al-Dīn's creative assimilation of mystical notions for his own philosophical purposes, rather than a straightforward embrace of *taṣawwuf*. First, he borrows from Sufism a distinct set of terms to describe the knowledge acquired through intuition, or rather the intuitive act

36 Shihadeh, "The Mystic," 103; Lewis, *Rumi: Past and Present*, 57–60.

37 Ibn ʿArabī, *Risālat al-shaykh ilā l-imām al-Rāzī*. See also Gloton's remarks in his introduction to Fakhr al-Dīn al-Rāzī, *Traité sur les noms divins*, 27–28; and Vâlsan, "Épître adressée à l'Imâm Fakhru ad-Dîn al-Râzî par le cheick al-Akbar Muḥyî ad-Dîn Ibn ʿArabî," who provides a French translation of the letter with notes.

and experience of acquiring this superior knowledge. Accordingly, al-Rāzī mentions the spiritual tasting (*dhawq*) and the disclosures (*mukāshafāt*) associated with the true seeker. Al-Rāzī also mentions the "states" (*aḥwāl*), "stations" (*maqāmāt*), "degrees" (*darajāt*), and "ascending points" (*maʿārij*) associated with this kind of knowledge. However, it is clear that he is adapting this terminology to his own needs and that, unlike the Sufis, he is using it symbolically or metaphorically to describe what is in essence the acquisition of syllogistic knowledge by the intellect through intuition (Texts 5, 6, 7, and 9). Al-Rāzī's departure from the Sufis is also explicit in the way he consistently refers to the various sciences as either spontaneous (*badīhiyya*) or acquired (*kasbiyya*), practical (*ʿamaliyya*) or theoretical (*naẓariyya*), which is in line with the Avicennian tradition, but which on the other hand departs from the Sufis' distinction between the acquired sciences (*al-ʿulūm al-kasbiyya*) and those that are "given" (*al-wahbiyya*).[38]

The second aspect of al-Rāzī's putative debt to Sufism is the frequent reference to ascetic exercises or exercises of spiritual purification (*al-riyāḍāt*). But in this case as well, and as we saw above, al-Rāzī is not simply borrowing this idea from the Sufis, but adapting it for his own purposes and integrating it in his philosophical program as one of its two main parts (*qismayn*). These exercises are directly connected with his theory of intuitive knowledge, since they constitute an efficient way of perfecting one's rational faculty and especially one's intuitive faculty (Texts 7, 9, and 10). The fundamental connection between these ascetic exercises and the betterment of the rational soul is vindicated by the intellectualist framework in which these practices are discussed: their primary aim is to prepare the intellect (*al-ʿaql*) for the intuitive acquisition of the intelligibles and sciences by mitigating or even obliterating the lower aspirations of the soul and its attachment to the corporeal world. The elements in al-Rāzī's works that can putatively be traced to Sufism therefore seem to have assumed a particular form and function in his philosophical system.

Even then, one may wonder to what extent these two aspects really derive from Sufi sources, as opposed to, say, Avicenna's works, which already show an awareness of the relation between philosophy and mysticism. It is significant that the points discussed above apparently had, in al-Rāzī's eyes, an Avicennian precedent, especially as they were expounded in the last section of Avicenna's *Pointers*. Al-Rāzī was well acquainted with this text, which he commented

---

38 We saw above that the intuitive knowledge that characterizes the higher cognition of the Sufi masters and some philosophers is for al-Rāzī acquired, and hence contrasts sharply with the 'given' or 'granted knowledge' of the Sufi tradition.

upon during the 1180s or early 1190s. This affiliation with the Avicennian corpus is important insofar as it suggests that al-Rāzī's main incentive for the conceptualization of Sufism and its relation to philosophy likely resulted from a process of exegesis of this seminal Avicennian text and a consideration of the interest it generated—and this regardless of Avicenna's ideological position regarding mysticism.[39] In *Pointers*, Avicenna had articulated a theory of the ideal knower (*ʿārif*) who has acquired a philosophical education and who in addition performs exercises of spiritual purification. One specific point that could have inspired al-Rāzī is that in Avicenna's classification, the qualities of the ascetic, the worshipper, and the knower can overlap.[40] More specifically, the idea that ascetic exercises, when practiced by the knowers, can increase their intellectual receptivity to the truth seems to have had an impact on Fakhr al-Dīn.[41] In that sense, al-Rāzī's description of the perfect philosopher who combines practice and theory, asceticism and reflection, in the *Long Commentary* and *The Elevated Subjects* is likely to have been partially modeled on the Avicennian *ʿārif*.

Moreover, many of the more evocative terms used by al-Rāzī to describe the highest intuitive knowledge of the philosophers and Sufi masters could have been gleaned from this Avicennian source, as well as from Avicenna's commentary on *Theology of Aristotle*.[42] Even Avicenna's *On the Provenance and*

---

39 For a study of al-Rāzī's exegetical approach to the *Ishārāt* and his place in the commentary tradition on this work, see Wisnovsky, "Avicennism and Exegetical Practice," and idem, "Towards a Genealogy of Avicennism," esp. 323–338. Modern accounts about the nature and underlying motives of Ibn Sīnā's discussion in the last two *namaṭ* of *al-Ishārāt* have varied widely; while some scholars have interpreted it as a Sufi work, others prefer to stress its philosophical dimension. I will not engage here with this controversy, nor refer to the large literature on this topic, as my focus in this present article is on al-Rāzī's interpretation of *al-Ishārāt*. With regard to Ibn Sīnā himself, I will limit myself to making a suggestion below as to how he may have interpreted mystical knowledge in light of his epistemology.

40 Ibn Sīnā, *al-Ishārāt*, 199.7–8: "and these [definitions] may overlap with one another."

41 Ibn Sīnā, *al-Ishārāt*, 199.9ff. This passage, which calls for the lower faculties of the mind to be tamed through exercises for the sake of an easier access to the truth, bears striking similarities with Text 9 above.

42 The terminology that al-Rāzī deploys not only in *Sharḥ al-Ishārāt*, but also in *al-Tafsīr al-kabīr* and *al-Mabāḥith al-ʿāliya*, appears partly in Ibn Sīnā's *al-Ishārāt wa-l-tanbīhāt* (*darajāt, maqāmāt, shurūq, nūr, riyāḍāt*, etc.; see Ibn Sīnā, *al-Ishārāt*, 198–99, 202.18ff.). In his commentary on *The Theology of Aristotle*, Ibn Sīnā also resorts to some terms (*tajliya, mushāhada, ṭaʿm*) that could be thought at first glance to express Sufi ideas, but which according to Adamson are unrelated to Sufism. In fact, these terms are consistent with Ibn Sīnā's epistemology and are used merely to describe the experience of acquiring the

Destination, an early and formative work chronologically separated from *Pointers* by some two decades, associates a symbolic terminology of light and illumination with the higher intuitive knowledge of the prophets.[43] This practice is reiterated much later in Avicenna's *The Discussions* (*al-Mubāḥathāt*), which describe the acquisition of knowledge through intuition as a kind of "divine effluence" (*fayḍ ilāhī*).[44] Hence, it would seem that both Avicenna and al-Rāzī conceived of the highest form of intellection and intuition as a quasi-immediate cognitive phenomenon, which, as such, could be adequately described by means of a language of emanation and illumination. This practice should be seen chiefly as a development internal to Avicenna's philosophy and one not directly related to Sufism, even though some of the terms themselves may have been borrowed from this discipline. Nevertheless al-Rāzī's use of this terminology and the emphasis he places on ascetic exercises, even if likely inspired by specific elements he found in Avicenna's philosophy, should be regarded as an original elaboration on these Avicennian works.

In light of the foregoing, al-Rāzī's commitment to a harmonizing project that seeks to construe prophetic, mystical, and philosophical knowledge by means of the concept of intuition and more generally within an Avicennian epistemological framework was rendered feasible by his ingenious exegesis of the Avicennian texts. This in turn suggests that al-Rāzī regarded his method and project as being chiefly inscribed in the Avicennian philosophical tradition. It may even be that he considered Avicenna himself to have embarked on this project and to have gestured toward the solution he formulated in his works. In spite of this, the extent to which Fakhr al-Dīn regarded himself merely as reiterating an already formulated Avicennian position or as completing a project that the *al-shaykh al-raʾīs* did not have the time to bring to fruition should remain an open question. Moreover, Fakhr al-Dīn's attitude ultimately says less about Avicenna than it does about his interpretation of Avicenna,

---

highest kind of intellectual, syllogistic knowledge; Adamson, "Non-Discursive Thought," 108–111; see also Gutas, *Avicenna and the Aristotelian Tradition*, 343–346. This study reaches a similar conclusion with regard to Fakhr al-Dīn's works. Naturally, this does not mean that Ibn Sīnā and Fakhr al-Dīn used these terms with the same purpose in mind, but the fact remains that many of them are already found in the Avicennian texts, where they are employed to describe the highest intellectual knowledge attained by the rational soul.

43 Ibn Sīnā, *al-Mabdaʾ wa-l-maʿād*, 116–17. In this connection, see also the preserved fragment of Ibn Sīnā's commentary in Sebti and De Smet, "Avicenna's Philosophical Approach to the Qur'an in the Light of his *Tafsīr sūrat al-Iḫlāṣ*."

44 Ibn Sīnā, *al-Mubāḥathāt*, ed. Bīdārfar 107.7; ed. Badawī 231.7. For an English translation of this passage and a discussion of the text, see Gutas, "Intuition and Thinking," 15.

which should be regarded as yet another intriguing development of the post-Avicennian philosophical tradition.

In addition to this obvious Avicennian connection, Fakhr al-Dīn's interpretation was also likely shaped by al-Ghazālī's own attempt to reconcile the Avicennian legacy with the theological and mystical theories of his time.[45] As Alexander Treiger has convincingly shown, al-Ghazālī developed his own brand of Avicennizing Sufism, interpreting mystical theories "on the basis of Avicenna's noetics and theory of prophecy."[46] More specifically, there are numerous parallels between al-Ghazālī and al-Rāzī with respect to their handling of specific cognitive ideas. For instance, they both share a common set of terms to express the higher cognitive mode of the Sufi masters and *ʿārifūn*, which they nonetheless construe in light of Avicennian psychology and especially in connection with intuition.[47] In addition to this terminological and conceptual parallel, one finds a similar tendency in their works to erect hierarchies of seekers on the basis of their understanding of divine oneness (*tawḥīd*). They also place a particular emphasis on the pronoun *huwa* ("he"), which in their eyes encapsulates the core of spiritual knowledge. Like al-Ghazālī, al-Rāzī believed that protracted meditation on this word is conducive to a special cognitive disclosure of the divine oneness, which he nonetheless describes in Avicennian metaphysical terms.[48]

---

45 This hypothesis was raised, but not explored, by Shihadeh, "The Mystic," 118. For insight into the period between al-Ghazālī and al-Rāzī, see Shihadeh, "From al-Ghazālī to al-Rāzī."

46 Treiger, *Inspired Knowledge*, 103, but see also 42 ff.; idem, "Monism and Monotheism in al-Ghazālī's *Mishkāt al-anwār*," 16–17. Although he recognizes the Sufi provenance of many of the technical terms employed by al-Ghazālī, Treiger is nevertheless intent on connecting al-Ghazālī chiefly with the Avicennian tradition. His main thesis is that al-Ghazālī's cognitive theories and his interpretation of such technical terms is chiefly indebted to Ibn Sīnā. Treiger's conclusions are thus in harmony with the results of the present study. For a different interpretation of al-Ghazālī's cognitive theories and position with regard to the knowability of God, see Abrahamov, "Al-Ghazālī's Supreme Way to Know God."

47 For insight into al-Ghazālī's conception of the "mystical sciences," see Treiger, *Inspired Knowledge*, 66, 71–72, 74, 146–147 n. 47. Pages 74–79 discuss specifically the relation between intuition and the "saintly spirit" (*al-rūḥ al-qudsī*), which is clearly equivalent to al-Rāzī's *al-quwwa al-qudsiyya*. Both authors also describe the higher cognitive state this faculty or spirit leads to in terms of a spiritual tasting (*dhawq*), divine disclosures (*mukāshafāt*), etc. Moreover, they both attribute the saintly faculty to prophets and Sufi masters. There are therefore numerous parallels between the two thinkers. But al-Rāzī, in contrast to al-Ghazālī, explicitly attributes the highest intuition to philosophers as well, as we saw in connection with Text 6.

48 al-Rāzī, *al-Tafsīr al-kabīr*, 1:149.25–26; 32:179.18–20 (*ad* Q 112). Interestingly, the latter passage can also be found in two other works by al-Rāzī, *al-Maṭālib al-ʿāliya*, 3:259 and

Yet there are also important differences between these three thinkers. Avicenna establishes the supremacy of philosophical learning and the demonstrative method, and he defines the prophet as a full-fledged philosopher who possesses syllogistic knowledge in its entirety through his ability to connect with the Agent Intellect. Avicenna thereby rejects the claim made by the theologians concerning the special and superior status of knowledge through inspiration (*ilhām*). Al-Ghazālī, in contrast, defends the superior cognition attained by prophets and Sufi masters through inspiration over the philosophical method, although he incorporates some philosophical ideas in his own works.[49] Indeed, al-Ghazālī seems to have maintained a sharp distinction between the prophets and Sufi masters on the one hand and the philosophers on the other, curtailing, especially in his work *The Deliverer from Error* (*al-Munqidh min al-ḍalāl*), the scope of the philosophers' knowledge. Al-Rāzī is considerably closer to Avicenna than al-Ghazālī on this specific point, since he considers the best philosophers to be (at least potentially) able to attain the cognitive level of prophets and Sufi masters and to reach the highest intuitive cognition and even the stage of the saintly faculty (as Text 6 explicitly states, and as Texts 9 and 10 imply). This point, which builds on al-Fārābī's and Avicenna's theories of the philosopher-prophet, endows the philosophers with a higher status than that which can be found in al-Ghazālī's works. What is more, it is possible that al-Rāzī goes beyond Avicenna himself, since the latter recognizes the superior cognition of the prophet-philosopher over that of other philosophers, and he at any rate does not explicitly ascribe the saintly faculty to individuals other than the prophets in his main works, even though the structure and nature of his psychological doctrines would allow such an idea.[50]

Lawāmiʿ al-bayyināt, 299–300. The present author is preparing an English translation of this passage in the context of a study of al-Rāzī's views on divine unity. On al-Ghazālī's spiritual digressions on the term *huwa* and on his esoteric declaration of faith *lā huwa illā huwa*, see Treiger, "Monism," 2, 5, 14–15.

49 For a brief but insightful discussion of this point in al-Ghazālī, see Griffel, *Al-Ghazālī's Philosophical Theology*, 99–101 and Treiger, *Inspired Knowledge*, 156, note 2.

50 That other individuals apart from prophets, especially some philosophers, may reach the highest degrees of the intuitive faculty and even the saintly faculty is nonetheless implied in Ibn Sīnā's writings and in his general treatment of intuition; see notably the passage of *The Discussions* mentioned below. Not only does he regard intuition as being infinitely perfectible, like al-Rāzī, but Ibn Sīnā is also known to have made rather bold claims concerning his own intuitive ability as a philosopher. But the formulation of this issue seems skewed by the fact that for Ibn Sīnā, the prophet is also a philosopher, so the more pressing and precise question is whether a philosopher who is not at the same time a prophet can access this faculty. In other words, does the philosopher who reaches the saintly

When compared to al-Ghazālī, then, al-Rāzī's position essentially amounts to a vindication of the philosophical tradition and of Avicennian epistemology in particular.

Furthermore, al-Rāzī develops a synthetic method that reconciles both syllogistic reasoning and exercises of spiritual purification in a manner and form that cannot be found as such in the Avicennian and Ghazalian works. In aiming for this new and integrated philosophical model, and in defining the curriculum of the ideal *ʿārif* in this light, al-Rāzī significantly elaborated on these two thinkers. His account is more explicit than the information that can be found in Avicenna's *Pointers* and al-Ghazālī's works. When compared to al-Ghazālī's views in particular, Fakhr al-Dīn attributes a more central and important role to philosophical thinking in the education of the aspiring *ʿārif*.

Finally, one of the most striking features of al-Rāzī's treatment of this issue—and one which does not appear as such in *Pointers* and in al-Ghazālī's works—is his repeated and explicit claim that what the Sufis call mystical knowledge (*al-ʿilm al-ladunī*) is in fact a kind of intellectual, intuitive knowledge, which is comparable and even similar to the knowledge that the philosophers acquire through intuition. In Fakhr al-Dīn's cognitive template, this intuitive knowledge can be attained by Sufi masters, prophets, and philosophers alike. What is particularly noteworthy is that al-Rāzī attributes this intellectualist theory to the Sufis themselves, thereby collapsing the "mystical sciences" (*al-ʿulūm al-laduniyya*) and the structured, essentially syllogistic sciences acquired through intuition into a single, overarching theory. Apart from his aim of developing or refining the philosophical model he inherited from Avicenna, al-Rāzī's intention in doing so might have been to appeal to the Sufis by underlining the essential congruity and compatibility of their approaches and spiritual goals.

In brief, then, al-Rāzī's interpretation of Sufism was likely inspired by the Avicennian *Pointers* tradition and other Avicennian texts, mediated through al-Ghazālī's works. However, al-Rāzī tapped into these precedents creatively, elaborating in the process his own ideal of the philosopher or knower and a quite distinct and (as far as I can see) innovative interpretation of how mystical knowledge relates to philosophical knowledge. The result was the creation of a philosophical method (*ṭarīq*), which from our perspective combines mystical and philosophical aspects, but which from al-Rāzī's standpoint was almost

faculty automatically become a kind of prophet? Regardless of this question, the fact remains that the Avicennian texts are not as explicit on this matter, especially when compared with Text 6 above, which distinguishes the prophets from the philosophers but ascribes the highest intuitive knowledge to both.

certainly regarded as an integrated and holistic philosophical approach to knowledge, which he consistently calls *al-ḥikma* or *al-maʿrifa*, or even *al-ʿilm*, and its practitioners, *ḥukamāʾ* and *ʿārifūn*. Fakhr al-Dīn's primary aim was not to demonstrate the superiority of mysticism over philosophy, as Shihadeh claimed in his article. Rather, it was an attempt to merge the philosophical and mystical currents into one stream and show the essential agreement of their cognitive contents and the intrinsic compatibility of their method and practice.[51] Yet, there can be little doubt that al-Rāzī regarded this project chiefly as a philosophical venture that he inherited from Avicenna. Moreover, it appears that neither he nor the Sufis considered that he truly belonged to the Sufi camp.

In view of the foregoing, the existing evidence does not justify the notion of a "conversion" to mysticism on the part of al-Rāzī, if mysticism is construed as an antithesis, or even an alternative, to philosophy. The situation appears to be quite different and more nuanced. Fakhr al-Dīn perceived himself as a *ḥakīm*, a philosopher, until the very end of his life, engaging in philosophical disputes well into his late years and in his two major last works, *The Elevated Subjects* and the *Long Commentary*.[52] More to the point, al-Rāzī seems intent on showing that there is no real qualitative difference between the knowledge sought by philosophy and that sought by mysticism. In this respect, it is true that he, like al-Ghazālī, fully condones the ascetic exercises of self-purification characteristic of the Sufi path. But again, these practices are deliberately integrated within an Avicennian epistemological framework, since their aim is to strengthen the intuitive faculty, which for al-Rāzī is the chief and only means, together with cogitation, of acquiring superior metaphysical knowledge. Hence, to describe Fakhr al-Dīn's ideal *ʿārif*, and by implication,

---

51 A word with regard to chronology is in order. If Ibn Sīnā's *al-Ishārāt* did play such a seminal role in shaping al-Rāzī's approach to Islamic mysticism, then al-Rāzī may have begun elaborating his new intellectual system possibly as early as 1184, when he started work on his *Sharḥ al-Ishārāt*. At any rate, he is aware of the doctrines of the Sufis in this commentary and refers to them on various occasions in a way that prefigures his treatment of human knowledge in his very last works, *al-Tafsīr al-kabīr* and *al-Maṭālib al-ʿāliya*. We also find in *Sharḥ al-Ishārāt* the same effort toward a harmonization of *falsafa* and *taṣawwuf* that we find in al-Rāzī's late works, and the concepts of intuition (*ḥads*) and the saintly faculty (*al-quwwa al-qudsiyya*) as a locus for divine illuminations are already articulated in this work. There can be little doubt that *Sharḥ al-Ishārāt* is connected with al-Rāzī's *al-Tafsīr al-kabīr* and *al-Maṭālib al-ʿāliya* and that his interest in reconciling mysticism with Avicennian philosophy was already apparent during this earlier period.

52 Street, "Concerning the Life and Works of Fakhr al-Dīn al-Rāzī," 140, 145–6, makes a similar point with regard to al-Rāzī's late interest in theology.

al-Rāzī himself, as a Sufi, seems more misleading than illuminating and obscures his intricate and sophisticated views on the relation between philosophy and mysticism.

The foregoing conclusions could have serious implications for our understanding of the pre- and post-Razian philosophical traditions. The first implication is that al-Rāzī's exegesis of the Avicennian texts may help us to better understand retrospectively how Avicenna himself *may* have envisaged the relation between Sufism and philosophy. Naturally, al-Rāzī's interpretation of Avicenna's *Pointers* is not to be conflated with Avicenna's views, which should be kept distinct and the correct interpretation of which remains moot. Yet, and this is a fact, the Avicennian works contain some of the core features of Fakhr al-Dīn's later philosophical synthesis: they deploy a specific vocabulary of illumination to describe the acquisition of the highest intellectual knowledge, and they also place an emphasis on practical exercises of spiritual purification. Moreover, although decisive evidence is lacking in this regard, Avicenna, like al-Rāzī, probably regarded mystical knowledge as an exalted form of intuition—as he had already done with regard to prophecy—with the implication that he would have explained mystical knowledge in light of a central concept of his psychology and hence brought it within the fold of philosophy. It should be noted that in *The Discussions*, Avicenna (or one of Avicenna's disciples on behalf of the master) attributes the saintly faculty to "some people" (*min al-nās baʿḍuhum*), as opposed to the prophets specifically.[53] As this work puts forth what Gutas called Avicenna's "revised version" of the theory of intuition, it is possible that by this late stage Avicenna had extended the saintly faculty to other individuals apart from prophets, and possibly to some Sufi masters and philosophers, or to some of the "knowers" (*ʿārifūn*) mentioned in his *Pointers*.

Hence, bearing in mind the pitfalls of extrapolation and retrospective interpretation, the evidence found in al-Rāzī suggests that Avicenna was not a Sufi in the traditional sense, as has been claimed by some scholars.[54] Rather, Avicenna possibly set a precedent for al-Rāzī's more consummate project of defining mystical knowledge in light of philosophical categories and of creating an overarching philosophical system containing both theoretical and practical or applied aspects. Even though decisive evidence is missing at this point in time, I suspect that this project would have been facilitated by Avicenna's interpretation of mystical knowledge as a kind of intuitive knowledge that is essentially intellectual and organized syllogistically. As in the case of al-Rāzī,

53 Ibn Sīnā, *al-Mubāḥathāt*, ed. Bīdārfar 107.7–9; ed. Badawī 231.7–8.

54 See for instance Shams Inati's introduction in *Ibn Sīnā and Mysticism*, especially 62–64.

such an attempt at co-opting Sufism would not have affected the core of Avicenna's metaphysics or physics (including his psychology), but would have contributed mainly to a redefinition of philosophy as a kind of holistic system and praxis.

The second implication pertains precisely to the latter point and to the way philosophy was practiced as a discipline and way of life during the classical and post-classical periods. Much valuable insight has been generated on this topic with regard to the late-antique tradition by Pierre Hadot and others, and this issue continues to be hotly discussed and debated among classicists. Yet it has barely been broached with regard to the Arabic philosophical tradition.[55] If my interpretation of al-Rāzī's overarching intellectual project as exposed above is correct, then it would represent a first step toward a better understanding of the "praxis" of philosophy in the post-classical Islamic context. Indeed, the Sufi or ascetic dimension that Fakhr al-Dīn incorporates in his own brand of philosophy constitutes the latter's practical, performative, and devotional aspects. Its chief aim was nonetheless theoretical in that it was designed to prepare the rational soul of the knower for the reception of higher intellectual cognition and metaphysical knowledge. While this praxis consisted presumably of very concrete exercises or activities, such as fasting, meditation, praying, and in general the conscious shunning of all corporeal attractions, its sole or main purpose was the purification and betterment of the rational soul in general and of the intuitive faculty in particular. In outlining this dual practical and theoretical program for the aspiring knowers (*ʿārifūn*) and philosophers (*ḥukamāʾ*), al-Rāzī effectively created an integrated system that probably had a lasting and profound influence on subsequent Islamic intellectual history, but whose ramifications remain to be precisely mapped out.

There is, finally, a third repercussion, whose theological and epistemological importance deserves a detailed treatment of its own.

IV One Crucial Theological and Epistemological Implication: The Question of the Knowability of the Divine Essence

In the last part of this article, I wish to explore briefly one important repercussion that al-Rāzī's cognitive theories have on his theology, namely, his views regarding the human knowability of God. The question of whether humans can know God's essence is addressed by Fakhr al-Dīn in various sections of his works, and it undoubtedly puzzled him throughout his life, as he returned to

55 For a recent attempt, see Azadpur, *Reason Unbound*.

this topic over and over again. It was also a question addressed by the Ashʿarites—the theological school Fakhr al-Dīn nominally adhered to—who put forth their famous theory of the *bi-lā kayf*, as well as by al-Ghazālī and the *falāsifa*, with whose views on the matter al-Rāzī was acquainted.[56] With regard to al-Ghazālī and al-Rāzī, this theological issue was the object of a detailed article by Binyamin Abrahamov published some years ago. Abrahamov argues that al-Rāzī sometimes follows al-Ghazālī in claiming that the divine essence is knowable to some extent, but that in his late works Fakhr al-Dīn became increasingly skeptical about the possibility of knowing God and ultimately deemed it impossible.[57] Abrahamov's article aptly exposes and contextualizes some of the main arguments al-Rāzī seemingly mustered in defence of the thesis of the unknowability of the divine essence and discusses many key passages dealing with this issue. In spite of this, Abrahamov's conclusions do not take into account the complexity of al-Rāzī's cognitive theories as detailed above and should therefore be complemented by a short note on how intuitive cognition fits in this picture.

It should be underlined in the first place that al-Rāzī in many instances seems to have considered it possible for humans to acquire insight or illuminations into this utmost object of cognition that is the divine essence. In fact, Fakhr al-Dīn asserts repeatedly and quite routinely in the *Long Commentary* that knowledge of God's essence (*dhāt Allāh*) represents the highest object of knowledge (*ashraf al-maʿlūmāt*). Since al-Rāzī does not mention any caveat (such as that this object is conceivable "only as far as is possible for humans"), the implication seems to be that it is an object of knowledge (*maʿlūm*) and part of a science (*ʿilm*) that can be known for certain.[58] In his commentary on Sura 112 (*Sūrat al-ikhlāṣ*), he goes so far as to state that this *sūra* is worth one third of the Qur'an, precisely because "this *sūra* comprises the knowledge of the divine essence" (*wa hādhihī l-sūra mushtamila ʿalā maʿrifat al-dhāt*).[59] In *The Elevated Subjects* al-Rāzī also describes the knowledge of the divine essence as the highest theological goal and the noblest theological inquiry.[60]

---

56 For a brief treatment of this issue in the theological tradition, see Abrahamov, "Faḫr al-Dīn al-Rāzī," 204–7; for al-Ghazālī, see Shehadi, *Ghazali's Unique Unknowable God*, and Abrahamov, "Al-Ghazālī's Supreme Way to Know God"; and for Ibn Sīnā, Adamson, "Non-Discursive Thought," 105–11.

57 See Abrahamov, "Faḫr al-Dīn al-Rāzī," especially 207–211 for the relation between al-Ghazālī and al-Rāzī.

58 al-Rāzī, *al-Tafsīr al-kabīr*, 2:87.12–14, 87.26–27 (*ad* Q 2:21–22); 32:176.28–29 (*ad* Q 112).

59 Ibid., 32:176.29–177.1 (*ad* Q 112).

60 al-Rāzī, *al-Maṭālib al-ʿāliya*, 1:367.6–7; cf. *al-Tafsīr al-kabīr*, 2:87.26–28 (*ad* Q 2:21–22).

A similar view is put forth in the *Commentary on Pointers and Reminders*, dated considerably earlier. Toward the end of the treatise, al-Rāzī elaborates a three-fold hierarchy of seekers, which seems directly inspired by the Avicennian text, and which classifies these various groups depending on their spiritual proximity to God. The first and highest group venerates God in Himself, whereas the second group includes the divine attributes in its conception of the divine being. Finally, the seekers of the third group worship God chiefly for the perfection of their own soul. What is significant is that al-Rāzī explicitly states that the object of knowledge and worship of the first group is nothing other than God's essence (*dhātuhu taʿālā*).[61] And in another passage of the same work, he explains that the main preoccupation of the highest kind of seeker "is to be immersed in God's essence" (*al-istighrāq fī dhāt Allāh*).[62]

But even in *The Elevated Subjects*, the work which represents the main focus of Abrahamov's article, al-Rāzī deliberately leaves open the issue of whether it is possible for human beings to attain a special cognition of the divine essence. He writes:

> **Text 11:** We then say: This is the sum of the discussion concerning the fact that this knowledge (*ʿilm*) (*scil.* of God's essence) has not been attained by human beings (*gayr ḥāṣil li-l-bashar*). As for the question of whether it has been attained by angels, the assumption is that it has not. But is this cognition [at all] possible for angels and for humans (*fa-hal yumkinu ḥuṣūl hādhihī l-maʿrifa li-l-malāʾika aw li-l-khalq*)? There is uncertainty concerning this point.[63]

This passage, which appears at the very end of a section devoted to the issue of the knowability of God, suggests that the aging al-Rāzī had not definitively made up his mind concerning the human capacity of knowing the divine essence. At first sight, the statement could be read as contrasting a kind of knowledge (*ʿilm*) with a kind of cognition (*maʿrifa*), the two being qualitatively different. But al-Rāzī seems to use these two terms interchangeably in his works. Hence, his main point here is probably not between two contrasting

61 al-Rāzī, *Sharḥ al-Ishārāt*, ed. Tehran 2:600.18–19; ed. Cairo 2:109.33.

62 al-Rāzī, *Sharḥ al-Ishārāt*, ed. Tehran 2:593.12–13; ed. Cairo 2:105.13–15; "*al-istighrāq*" may also be translated as "to be fully preoccupied by."

63 al-Rāzī, *al-Maṭālib al-ʿāliya*, 2:98.7–10; MS Kayseri, Reşit Efendi 503, fol. 71a. To preserve the intended meaning of the passage, I translated *gayr ḥāṣil li-l-bashar* as "has not been attained by human beings," rather than "is not attainable by human beings," since al-Rāzī raises the question immediately after as to whether this knowledge is at all possible theoretically, a question which would be meaningless if the first sentence was construed as an absolute negation.

kinds of knowledge, but between two considerations: on the one hand, that in general this knowledge has not been attained by humans and angels, and on the other hand, that it is perhaps possible for some individuals to attain it under special circumstances.[64]

It is at this juncture that al-Rāzī's uncertainty concerning this point should be connected with his theory of intellectual intuition and especially the saintly faculty. Indeed, the latter concept may constitute the key to the problem. As we saw in the previous sections of this article, Fakhr al-Dīn believes that the scope and power of intuition are theoretically unlimited. Intuition, and the saintly faculty itself, may exist at various degrees in different individuals, depending on such factors as their personal talent or innate nature and the assiduity with which they perform intellectual and spiritual exercises. A corollary of this is clearly that the objects to which intuition applies are also virtually unlimited or at least vary greatly in both depth and nature: those people utterly devoid of intuition will learn very little, while those endowed with the saintly faculty will have access to metaphysical knowledge that will remain forever hidden to others. This would apply particularly to certain immaterial beings removed from the realm of human sense perception, and whose intellectual apprehension would be impossible for people unendowed with a strong intuitive faculty.

In view of this, it cannot be completely excluded that al-Rāzī believed some individuals advanced enough on the cognitive path and the possessors of an intuitive faculty such that their knowledge would extend to the divine essence itself. Returning for a moment to the discussion in the first part of this paper, Fakhr al-Dīn's adherence to a higher form of intuitive knowledge that bypasses the normal operations of discursive thinking (*fikr*) probably explains why he occasionally intimated that this knowledge is after all possible. As a corollary, this would mean that al-Rāzī's elaborate arguments seemingly against the knowability of God's essence and reality, as articulated for instance in *The Elevated Subjects*, were probably not meant to negate the possibility of this kind of knowledge *per se*, but merely the capacity of the intellect to reach it

64 If the semantic distinction between *ʿilm* and *maʿrifa* is maintained, then there is another way of reading the passage: on the one hand, humans and angels cannot know God through reflective knowledge (*ʿilm*); on the other hand, it is possible that a select few from among them may know God through a superior kind of intuitive knowledge (*maʿrifa*), probably those blessed with the saintly faculty. But in either case, and assuming that he did believe such knowledge to be possible, al-Rāzī's point would be identical in one major respect: only very few from among God's creatures would be able to reach cognition of the divine essence, which would occur through their perfected saintly faculty. These special circumstances explain al-Rāzī's cautious tone when dealing with the issue of the human knowability of God.

solely through discursive thought and by means of argumentative tools. In the interpretation I am suggesting here, knowledge of God's essence would be both intellectual and syllogistic in nature (since all knowledge for Fakhr al-Dīn is structured syllogistically), but reserved to those who have accessed the peaks of intuition (as opposed to those who engage mostly in cogitation and/or possess a weak intuitive faculty).[65] At any rate, given al-Rāzī's increasingly complex views on human cognition and the role of intuition, we can better understand the underlying ambiguity and uncertainty that can be detected in his works concerning the issue of the knowability of God.

Conclusion

In the course of this study, I adduced and analyzed various passages taken from Fakhr al-Dīn al-Rāzī's corpus with the aim of establishing a series of points. First, I showed that al-Rāzī defines mystical knowledge as a kind of intuitive intellectual knowledge acquired quasi-immediately or immediately. He does not oppose a "philosophical" cognitive theory to a "mystical" one. Rather, intuitive cognition, which is shared by both mystics and philosophers, is a general, if variable, feature of the human intellect and leads to the acquisition of knowledge that is accountable to the laws of logic and organized syllogistically. Fakhr al-Dīn's entire argumentation in support of this claim revolves around the concepts of intuition and especially the saintly faculty, the highest form of intuition obtainable by human beings. I argued that al-Rāzī developed a complex cognitive theory whose main building blocks are Avicennian, although he also draws generously on Sufi terms and notions, which he deliberately integrates within this Avicennian epistemological paradigm.

Second, I showed that al-Rāzī does distinguish between different *approaches* or *methods* of acquiring knowledge, one based on reflection, the other on intuition, a distinction which partly overlaps with another distinction he draws

65 It is worthwhile comparing Fakhr al-Dīn's view on this issue to that of Ibn Sīnā. According to the latter in his commentary on *The Theology of Aristotle*, the intellect can know only God's effects and "traces" in the world through its normal cogitative processes, but it can obtain insight into the divine essence through a divine disclosure from God, which is grasped by the intellect "insofar as is possible." Although Ibn Sīnā does not explicitly connect this revealed knowledge with intuition in this specific passage, this knowledge is intellectual and syllogistic in nature; see Adamson, "Non-Discursive Thought," 106–10, especially 110. Given that the saintly faculty represents the most exalted cognitive stage according to Ibn Sīnā, as it does for al-Rāzī, it is clear that the highest knowledge of God that human beings can achieve would have to rely on this faculty.

between the way of reflection and the way of spiritual discipline. The main difference for al-Rāzī lies not in the nature of the knowledge produced by these approaches, but in the methods employed for training and preparing the intellect for the acquisition of theoretical knowledge. Fakhr al-Dīn regarded these various approaches as being not only compatible, but as forming the two branches of a single, integrated philosophical system, which included both theory and practice. Al-Rāzī devised this synthetic system by elaborating on the Avicennian *Pointers* tradition and on al-Ghazālī's works, but when compared to his predecessors he provides a more systematic and seamless interpretation of how mystical exercises can be reconciled with and benefit theoretical knowledge. Ultimately, al-Rāzī provides a compelling formulation of a holistic philosophical praxis. A crucial implication of this achievement is that al-Rāzī did not "convert" to Sufism; rather, he integrated specific ascetic practices within an Avicennian philosophical paradigm, which he also transformed considerably in the process. Fakhr al-Dīn's mature and fully worked out cognitive theories are indeed complex and subtle and may very well be the "keys" (*mafātīḥ*) that became associated with his *Long Commentary*, alternatively known as *The Keys to the Unseen* (*Mafātīḥ al-ghayb*).

Bibliography

Abrahamov, Binyamin. "Faḫr al-Dīn al-Rāzī on the Knowability God's Essence and Attributes." *Arabica* 49 (2002): 204–30.

———. "Al-Ghazālī's Supreme Way to Know God." *Studia Islamica* 77 (1993): 141–68.

Adamson, Peter. "Non-Discursive Thought in Avicenna's Commentary on the *Theology of Aristotle*." In *Interpreting Avicenna: Science and Philosophy in Medieval Islam*. Edited by J. McGinnis. Leiden Brill, 2004. 87–111.

Al-Akiti, M. Afifi. "The Three Properties of Prophethood in Certain Works of Avicenna and al-Ġazālī." In *Interpreting Avicenna: Science and Philosophy in Medieval Islam*. Edited by J. McGinnis. Leiden Brill, 2004. 189–212.

Azadpur, Mohammad. *Reason Unbound: On Spiritual Practice in Islamic Peripatetic Philosophy*. Albany: State University of New York Press, 2011.

Eichner, Heidrun. "'Knowledge by Presence,' Apperception and the Mind-Body Relationship. Fakhr al-Dīn al-Rāzī and al-Suhrawardī as Representatives of a Thirteenth Century Discussion." In *In the Age of Averroes. Arabic Philosophy in the Sixth/Twelfth Century*. Edited by P. Adamson. London: Warburg Institute, 2011. 117–40.

al-Ghazālī, Muḥammad ibn Muḥammad. *al-Risāla al-Laduniyya*. Edited by Muḥyī al-Dīn Ṣabrī al-Kurdī. Cairo: Maktabat Kurdistān al-ʿIlmiyya, 1327 [1909].

———. *Iḥyāʾ ʿulūm al-dīn*. 16 vols. Cairo: Lajnat Nashr al-Thaqāfa al-Islāmiyya, 1356–1357 [1937–1938].

Gramlich, Richard. "Fakhr ad-Din ar-Razis Kommentar zu Sure 18, 9–12." *Asiatische Studien* (Zürich) 33 (1979): 99–152.

Griffel, Frank. "Al-Ġazālī's Concept of Prophecy: The Introduction of Avicennan Psychology into Ašʿarite Theology." *Arabic Sciences and Philosophy*, 14 (2004): 101–44.

———. "On Fakhr al-Dīn al-Rāzī's Life and the Patronage He Received." *Journal of Islamic Studies* 18 (2007): 313–44.

———. *Al-Ghazālī's Philosophical Theology*. New York: Oxford University Press, 2009.

———. "Fakhr al-Dīn al-Rāzī." In *Encyclopedia of Medieval Philosophy: Philosophy between 500 and 1500*. Edited by H. Lagerlund. 2 vols. Dordrecht: Spinger, 2011. Vol. 1. 341–45.

———. "Between al-Ghazālī and Abū l-Barakāt al-Baghdādī: The Dialectical Turn in the Philosophy of Iraq and Iran during the Sixth/Twelfth Century." In *In the Age of Averroes*, ed. P. Adamson. London: Warburg Institute, 2011. 45–75.

Gutas, Dimitri. *Avicenna and the Aristotelian Tradition: Introduction to Reading Avicenna's Philosophical Works*. Second, Revised and Enlarged Edition, Including an Inventory of Avicenna's Authentic Works. Leiden; Boston: Brill, 2014 [1988].

———. "Intuition and Thinking: The Evolving Structure of Avicenna's Epistemology." In *Aspects of Avicenna*. Edited by R. Wisnovsky, Princeton: Markus Wiener, 2001. 1–38.

Hasse, Dag N. *Avicenna's De anima in the West. The Formation of a Peripatetic Philosophy of the Soul 1160–1300*. London / Turin: The Warburg Institute / Nino Aragno Editore, 2000.

Haywood, John A. "Fakhr al-Dīn al-Rāzī's Contribution to Ideas of Ultimate Reality and Meaning." *Ultimate Reality and Meaning* 2 (1979): 264–91.

Ibn ʿArabī, Muḥyī al-Dīn Muḥammad ibn ʿAlī. *Risālat al-shaykh ilā l-imām al-Rāzī*. In *Rasāʾil Ibn al-ʿArabī*. 2 Parts. Hyderabad: Dāʾirat al-Maʿārif al-ʿUthmāniyya, 1948. Part 1. 2–14.

Ibn Sīnā, al-Ḥusayn ibn ʿAbdallāh. *Ibn Sīnā and Mysticism, Remarks and Admonitions: Part Four. An English Translation of the Fourth Part (Sufism) of Avicenna's al-Ishārāt wa-al-tanbīhāt*. Translated by Sh. C. Inati. London; New York: Kegan Paul International, 1996.

———. *al-Ishārāt wa-l-tanbīhāt*. Edited by J. Forget. Leiden: E. J. Brill, 1892.

———. *al-Mabdaʾ wa-l-maʿād*. Edited by ed. ʿAbd Allāh Nūrānī. Tehran: Mu'assasah-i Muṭālaʿāt-i Islāmī, Dānishgāh-i MacGill, bā hamkārī-i Dānishgāh-i Tihrān, 1984.

———. *al-Mubāḥathāt*. Edited by M. Bīdārfar. Qom (Iran): Intishārat-i Bīdārfar, 1371/1413 [1992].

———. *al-Mubāḥathāt*. In *ʿAristū ʿinda l-ʿarab*. Edited by ʿA. Badawī. 2nd edition. Kuwait: Wikālat al-Maṭbūʿāt, 1978.

———. *al-Shifāʾ, al-Ṭabīʿiyyāt, al-Nafs = Avicenna's De anima (Arabic text): Being the Psychological Part of Kitāb al-Shifāʾ*. Edited by Fazlur Rahman. London: Oxford University Press, 1959.

Jomier, Jacques. "Qui a commenté l'ensemble des sourates al-ʿAnkabūt à Yāsīn (29–36) dans 'le tafsīr al-kabīr' de l'imām Fakhr al-Dīn al-Rāzī?" *IJMES* 11 (1980): 467–85.

———. "Les *Mafātīḥ al-ghayb* de l'imām Fakhr al-Dīn al-Rāzī. Quelques dates, lieux, manuscrits." *MIDEO* 13 (1977): 253–90.

Lagarde, Michel. *Les secrets de l'invisible: essai sur le Grand commentaire de Faḫr al-Dîn al-Râzî*. Beirut: Albouraq, 2009.

Lewis, Franklin D. *Rumi: Past and Present, East and West*. Oxford: Oneworld, 2000.

Majmūʿah-yi falsafī-yi Marāgha / A Philosophical Anthology from Maragha. Containing Works by Abū Ḥāmid Ghazzālī, ʿAyn al-Quḍāt al-Ḥamadānī, Ibn Sīnā, ʿUmar ibn Sahlān Sāvi, Majduddīn Jīlī and others. Facsimile edition with introductions in Persian and English by Nasollah Pourjavadi. Tehran: Markaz-i Nashr-i Dānishgāh, 1380/2002.

Marmura, Michael E. "Avicenna's Psychological Proof of Prophecy." In *Journal of Near Eastern Studies*. 22 (1963): 46–56.

Nasr, Seyyid Hossein. "Fakhr al-Dīn Rāzī." In *A History of Muslim Philosophy*. Edited by M. M. Sharif. 2 vols. Wiesbaden: Harrassowitz, 1963–66. Vol. 1, 642–55.

al-Rāzī, Fakhr al-Dīn Muḥammad ibn ʿUmar. *al-Arbaʿīn fī uṣūl al-dīn*. Ḥydarabad: Maṭbaʿat Majlis Dāʾirat al-Maʿārif al-ʿUthmāniyya, 1934.

———. *Lawāmiʿ al-bayyināt fī l-asmāʾ wa-l-ṣifāt*. Edited under the title *Sharḥ asmāʾ Allāh al-ḥusnā* by Ṭāhā ʿAbd al-Raʾūf Saʿd. Cairo: Maktabat al-Azhariyya li-l-Turāth, 1420/2000.

———. *Traité sur les noms divins: Lawâmiʿ al-bayyinât fī al-asmâʾ wa al-çifât* (*Le Livre des Preuves Éclatantes sur les Noms et les Qualités*. Translated into French by M. Gloton. Beirut: Les Éditions Al-Bouraq, 1421/2000.

———. *al-Mabāḥith al-mashriqiyya fī ʿilm al-ilāhiyyāt wa-l-ṭabīʿiyyāt*. 2 vols. Tehran: Maktabat al-Asad, 1966 [photostatic reproduction of the Hyderabad 1923–24 edition].

———. *al-Maṭālib al-ʿāliya min al-ʿilm al-ilāhī*. Ed. Aḥmad Ḥijāzī al-Saqqā. 9 parts in 5 vols. Beirut: Dār al-Kitāb al-ʿArabī, 1987.

———. *Sharḥ al-Ishārāt wa-l-tanbīhāt*. Edited by ʿAlī Reża Najafzādah. 2 vols. Tehran: Anjuman-i Āsār va-Mafākhir-i Farhangī, 1383–84 [2004–06].

———. *Sharḥ al-Ishārāt wa-l-tanbīhāt*. In the margins of *al-Kitāb al-mawsūm bi-sharḥay al-Ishārāt li-l-khwājah Naṣīr al-Dīn al-Ṭūsī wa li-l-imām Fakhr al-Dīn al-Rāzī*. 2 vols. in 1. Cairo: al-Maṭbaʿa al-Khayriyya, 1325 [1907].

———. *al-Tafsīr al-kabīr* [*aw Mafātīḥ al-ghayb*]. 32 vols. Cairo: al-Maṭbaʿa al-Bahiyya al-Miṣriyya, n. d. [*c*. 1933].

Sebti, Meryem and Daniel de Smet. "Avicenna's Philosophical Approach to the Qurʾan in the Light of his *Tafsīr sūrat al-Iḫlāṣ*." *Journal of Qurʾanic Studies* 11 (2009): 134–48.

Şeşen, Ramazan (also: Ramaḍān Shishin). *Mukhtārāt min al-makhṭūṭāt al-ʿarabiyya al-nādira fī maktabāt Turkiyā*. Edited by Ekmeleddin Ihsanoğlu. Istanbul: ISAR, 1997.

Shehadi, Fadlou. *Ghazali's Unique Unknowable God: A Philosophical Critical Analysis of Some of the Problems Raised by Ghazali's View of God as Utterly Unique and Unknowable*. Leiden: Brill, 1964.

Shihadeh, Ayman. "The Mystic and the Sceptic in Fakhr al-Dīn al-Rāzī." In *Sufism and Theology*. Edited by A. Shihadeh. Edinburgh: Edinburgh University Press, 2007. 101–22.

———. "From al-Ghazālī to al-Rāzī: 6th/12th Century Developments in Muslim Philosophical Theology." *Arabic Sciences and Philosophy* 15 (2005): 141–79.

Street, Tony. "Concerning the Life and Works of Fakhr al-Dīn al-Rāzī." In *Islam: Essays on Scripture, Thought and Society: A Festchrift in Honour of Anthony H. Johns*. Edited by P. G. Riddell and T. Street. Leiden: Brill, 1997. 135–46.

Treiger, Alexander. *Inspired Knowledge in Islamic Thought: Al-Ghazālī's Theory of Mystical Cognition and its Avicennian Foundation*. London: Routledge, 2012.

———. "Monism and Monotheism in al-Ghazālī's *Mishkāt al-anwār*." *Journal of Qur'anic Studies* 9 (2007): 1–27.

Vâlsan, Michel. "Épître adressée à l'Imâm Fakhru ad-Dîn al-Râzî par le cheick al-Akbar Muḥyî ad-Dîn Ibn ʿArabî." *Etudes traditionnelles* 366–367 (1961): 242.

Wisnovsky, Robert. "Avicennism and Exegetical Practice in the Early Commentaries on the *Ishārāt*." *Oriens* 41 (2013): 349–378.

———. "Towards a Genealogy of Avicennism." *Oriens* 42 (2014): 323–363.

CHAPTER 9

Fakhr al-Dīn al-Rāzī's Use of al-Ghazālī's *Mishkāt* in His Commentary on the Light Verse (Q 24:35)

Jules Janssens

As early as 1975, Hava Lazarus-Yafeh pointed out that Fakhr al-Dīn al-Razī (d. 606/1210) in his commentary on the Light Verse (Q 24:35) in his *al-Tafsīr al-kabīr* (*The Long Qur'an-Commentary*) relied heavily on al-Ghazālī's *Mishkāt al-anwār* (*Niche of Lights*).[1] But it was not until 1991 that a scholar, namely Hermann Landolt in his seminal study "Al-Ghazālī and 'Religionswissenschaft,'" paid explicit attention to the nature of this usage.[2] Among other aspects, Landolt emphasizes that Fakhr al-Dīn does not follow the order of the discussion in al-Ghazālī's *Mishkāt*. Al-Rāzī, though, largely supports al-Ghazālī's opinion that God is the only light, yet says nothing of the latter's controversial interpretation of the divine face (*wajh Allāh*) as the source from which all being emanates.[3] In the section of the *Tafsīr* dealing with the so-called "veils-tradition," in which different groups of worshippers are classified according to how much they are veiled by light and/or darkness, al-Rāzī places, if we follow Landolt, all *falāsifa*—the "naturalists" as well as those who look to the movers of the spheres—in the second highest class of those veiled by light and darkness. Despite the use of a philosophical language, al-Rāzī reserves the highest class of those veiled by pure light, Landolt argues, for the defenders of a classical (Ashʿarite) attributism.[4] He stresses that even if in this last case al-Rāzī offers an interpretation that critically deviates from al-Ghazālī's *Mishkāt*, this would not prove that the actual third section of the *Mishkāt* is a forgery, as William M.

1 Lazarus-Yafeh, *Studies in al-Ghazālī*, 45, n. 32.

2 Landolt, "al-Ghazālī and 'Religionswissenschaft,'" 64–72. Landolt also discusses the *Risālah-yi taʾwīlāt-i mushkilāt al-aḥādith al-mushkila*, where one finds many similarities with the first two parts of Fakhr al-Dīn al-Rāzī's commentary on the light verse. Nasrollah Pourjavady, who first edited and later translated the text (Pourjavady, "Fakhr-i Rāzī va-Mishkāt al-anvār-i Ghazzālī," 226–29, and idem, "Fakhr-e Râzî und Ghazzâlîs *Mishkât al-anwâr* (Lichternische)," 63–66) inclines toward ascribing it to al-Rāzī, but this needs further examination.

3 al-Ghazālī, *Mishkāt al-anwār*, 137–38.

4 Landolt, "al-Ghazālī and 'Religionswissenschaft,'" 67; al-Rāzī, *al-Tafsīr al-kabīr*, 23:231.11–26.

 | DOI 10.1163/9789004307490_010

Watt had claimed,[5] but is more likely the expression of the desire of Fakhr al-Dīn to maintain the image of al-Ghazālī as an "orthodox theologian."

More recently, Soraya M. Hajjaji-Jarrah dealt anew with the first two sections of al-Rāzī's commentary on the Light Verse.[6] She mainly agrees with Landolt's views, but particularly stresses the presence of monism or of what resembles the idea of "unity of being" in al-Rāzī's commentary. Unfortunately, none of these publications offers a detailed survey of the passages in Fakhr al-Dīn's *Tafsīr* that are derived from, or at least clearly inspired by the *Mishkāt*. In order to fully and correctly grasp al-Rāzī's debt to the latter, it is important to know precisely what he literally reproduces, as well as the exact degree and nature of his rewordings when present. Undoubtedly important to note also is the presence of any additions or omissions. Even if Landolt's interpretation is generally thought to be the most valuable, it is hoped that this more detailed analysis will offer further substantial evidence for his view, while adding (minor) nuances. Let me add that the analysis , which follows, will not deal with minor differences. These probably result from editorial mistakes, especially in the case of al-Rāzī's *Tafsīr* of which no critical edition is available.[7]

Fakhr al-Dīn al-Rāzī starts his commentary on the Light Verse with the rejection of those who interpret, as he claims the Manicheans did, God's being as "light" in terms of body or bodily form. But if it is neither body nor bodily form, what is it? Al-Rāzī gives four possible interpretations, but only after noting that the argument that God is light is in need of further explanation. This means that it cannot be taken literally and has to be subject of *taʾwīl* ("allegorical interpretation"). The four retained alternatives are: (1) God's light is His guidance; (2) God's light is His ruling over heavens and earth; (3) God's light is His organization of heavens and earth; and (4) God's light is His figurative "enlightening" of heavens and earth. Using the language at the end of

5 Watt, "A Forgery in al-Ghazālī's *Mishkāt?*"

6 Hajjaji-Jarrah, "'*Ayāt al-nūr*:' A Metaphor for Where We Come From, What we Are, and Where We Are Going," 170–74.

7 al-Rāzī, *al-Tafsīr al-kabīr*, 23:222–38. The edition I use is one of the standard ones, included by Michel Lagarde in his *Index du Grande Commentaire de Faḫr al-Dīn al-Rāzī*, 60–80. It was prepared by a "committee of editors" (*hayʾat al-taṣḥīḥ*, p. *ghayn* in vol. 1) that was, according to G. C. Anawati in *EI²*, 3:754, headed by Muḥammad Muḥyī l-Dīn ʿAbd al-Ḥamīd (1900–72). The edition provides no information on its textual bases. The text of al-Rāzī's commentary on Q 24:35 has also been reproduced in Sayrawān's edition of al-Ghazālī, *Mishkāt al-anwār*, 79–109. Recently it has been translated into English in Hamza and Rizvi (eds.), *An Anthology of Qur'anic Commentaries*, 1:384–408, though that translation should be used with much caution.

the Qur'anic verse ("Allah guideth unto His light whom He will") as justification,[8] al-Rāzī expresses his preference for the first interpretation, but without outright rejecting them. It is only after laying this basic framework that he for the first time mentions al-Ghazālī by name. Al-Rāzī stresses that the latter had devoted a complete book to the explanation of the Light Verse, namely, as explicitly mentioned, *Mishkāt al-anwār*.[9] He declares that he will relate the upshot of that work, as well as adding some new elements. More importantly, he insists that he will offer what he calls an impartial judgment (*inṣāf*). Thus, he makes it clear that he will not simply copy his predecessor's view, but that he will expand on it and add critical commentary. What follows will explore how he achieves this well-defined goal.

Al-Rāzī begins his report of al-Ghazālī's *Mishkāt al-anwār* with a summary of its introduction and the beginning of the first part (*faṣl*) including its first "fine point" (*daqīqa*). In conformity with his source, despite occasional differences in the wording, al-Rāzī argues two main points, first, that "light" refers to what illuminates other entities, e.g. the sun, the moon, and fire, but that in order for light to fulfil its purpose, i.e. to be visible and make things visible, there has to be a seeing soul (*al-rūh al-bāṣira*). Second, al-Rāzī stresses al-Ghazālī's notion that the human intellectual power (*al-quwwa al-ʿāqila*), is more properly called light than the seeing soul.[10]

Then he concentrates on the difference between outer and inner sight in humans, stressing the absolute superiority of the latter over the former. Indeed, the inner sight is free of all the deficiencies that qualify the outer. Although the wording is more concise, and thus far from identical, it is clear that the beginning of the second section of *Mishkāt*'s first part directly inspired Fakhr al-Dīn.[11] However, there is one detail that deserves special attention. In line with al-Ghazālī, al-Rāzī identifies the inner eye with the intellecting power (*al-quwwa al-ʿāqila*). However, in sharp contrast with his predecessor, he makes no reservation whatsoever. He omits the former's affirmation in *Mishkāt* that the same power can also be designated by other terms, such as "spirit" (*rūḥ*) or "human soul" (*al-nafs al-insānī*). Certainly, al-Ghazālī does not further develop the implications of these possible alternatives, because such examination could in his view confuse the less gifted reader. In this sense, al-Rāzī may have judged it better to not mention them at all. Perhaps of greater significance is the fact that he, in the present context, never uses the word "heart" (*qalb*),

8 Translation by Pickthall, *The Meaning of the Glorious Koran*, 256.

9 See al-Rāzī, *al-Tafsīr al-kabīr*, 23:224.19–20.

10 Ibid., 23:224.22–225.2; al-Ghazālī, *Mishkāt al-anwār*, 119.1–121.14.

11 al-Rāzī, *al-Tafsīr al-kabīr*, 23:225.2–5; al-Ghazālī, *Mishkāt al-anwār*, 121.16–122.14.

although al-Ghazālī in his *Mishkāt* explicitly situates the inner eye in the heart. The word "heart" is rich in meaning in al-Ghazālī, but here it clearly expresses a human's ideal reality, i.e. a principle of both practical and theoretical knowledge that includes knowledge of God inside the framework of the religious law.[12] As such, the term belongs to the domain of Sufism, as does the term "spirit." In avoiding this terminology, Fakhr al-Dīn seems to distance himself from any kind of Sufism, or even from a Sufi-oriented perspective. He clearly wants to avoid any ambiguity in this respect, and therefore is satisfied in using the usual philosophical-theological term "intellect." This attitude sharply contrasts with that of his predecessor, in whose works one often finds combinations of terms derived from different intellectual traditions while it is not always clear which is the prevalent perspective.[13]

In the next section of both commentaries, the discussion of the superiority of the "light of reason" over the "light of the physical eye" and the shortcomings (singl. *naqīṣa*) of sensible perception, al-Rāzī shows an even stronger tendency to prefer philosophical terminology over Sufi terminology, and perhaps of philosophy, or more precisely, philosophical theology, over Sufism. Again, al-Rāzī's analytical ordering of his own *Tafsīr* has a solid base in the *Mishkāt*, although it is much ampler and contains significant rewording as far as the seven shortcomings are concerned.[14]

Both work have seven shortcomings of the physical eye in common. Their list can be established as follows ("T" refers to al-Rāzī's *Tafsīr*, "M" to al-Ghazālī's *Mishkāt*):[15]

T1=M1: sensation possesses no self-awareness;
T7=M2: vision is dependent on the being near to or far away from its object;
T8=M4: sensation can only deal with the outward aspects of things, not with the inward;
T10=M5: sensation is always limited in its scope;
T12=M6: sensation cannot grasp what is infinite;
T18=M3: sensation cannot grasp what is veiled;
T20=M7: sensation is open to errors.

---

12 See Jabre, *Essai sur le lexique de Ghazali*, 236.

13 Regarding a case of al-Ghazālī's wavering between philosophy and Sufism, see my "Al-Ghazālī between Philosophy (*Falsafa*) and Sufism (*Taṣawwuf*): His Complex Attitude in the Marvels of the Heart (*'Ajā'ib al-Qalb*) of the *Iḥyā' 'Ulūm al-Dīn*."

14 al-Rāzī, *al-Tafsīr al-kabīr*, 23:225.5–228.10; al-Ghazālī, *Mishkāt al-anwār*, 123.1–127.9.

15 A similar list (although with one modification - see infra, n. 18) has been given by Landolt, "Al-Ghazālī and 'Religionswissenschaft,'" 68, n. 202.

Both works explicitly deny that any of these limitations also apply to reason. Notwithstanding this basic content agreement, there are important variations in the very wording. This can be illustrated this by way of two examples:

(1) In T1, al-Rāzī affirms that the visual power does not perceive itself (*al-quwwa al-bāṣira lā tudriku nafsahā*), while al-Ghazālī simply states: "the eye does not perceive itself (*al-ʿayn lā tabṣuru nafsahā*)". It is obvious from a philosophical point of view that Fakhr al-Dīn's formulation is technically superior. His deeper involvement with philosophy shows also when al-Rāzī stresses that we cannot perceive our own act of perception nor its instrument. This mirrors Avicenna (Ibn Sīnā, d. 428/1037), when he states: "Each faculty, which perceives through an instrument, does not perceive itself, nor its instrument, nor its act of perception."[16] Without discussing the complex issue of the inner senses in Avicenna's thought, it is clear that by this instrumentally mediated perception he means visual sensation, not reason.

(2) In T20 al-Rāzī remains sober in presenting the failure of visual perception. Contrary to al-Ghazālī, who offers several examples, al-Rāzī is satisfied with giving only one, i.e. the perception of something that is in motion as being at rest, or vice versa (alluded to by al-Ghazālī, when he mentions that the eye perceives the stars as being at rest). More strikingly, however is Fakhr al-Dīn's replacement of what is considered a weak *ḥadīth* (relating a question of the Prophet to the archangel Gabriel about the motion of the sun), which constitutes the ultimate example of vision's weakness in *Mishkāt*, by the sober affirmation that "reason is the judge and sensation is what is judged upon." This statement reflects a philosophically-inspired idea. Again, although not acknowledged, the ultimate inspiration may stem from Avicenna, specifically when he declares that only the judgment of reason is decisive.[17]

In addition to the seven shortcomings already mentioned, Fakhr al-Dīn develops thirteen others. In other words, he substantially expands upon the list in the *Mishkāt* at least at first glance. Three of these additional imperfections, can be directly connected to elements present in al-Ghazālī's elaboration of the seven shortcomings:

16 Ibn Sīnā, *al-Shifāʾ*, *Kitāb al-Nafs*, 219.16–17.

17 Ibid., 167.1–2.

- T4, in which al-Rāzī stresses that sensation, contrary to reason, cannot grasp a multitude of sensations at any given time. This is a slightly modified version of M5, where al-Ghazālī insists that the eye sees only a fraction of what exists and hence is limited in its scope, in sharp contrast with intelligence, which encompasses the entirety of being;[18]
- T9 states that reason is able to perceive God, unlike sensation, which perceives only forms and colors. This can be considered the logical conclusion of M4, according to which the exterior eye perceives the exterior things only in their exteriority, not the reality of things which is only accessible to reason;
- T17 strongly emphasizes that sensation, contrary to reason, is restricted by the physical dimensions of things. This relates to al-Ghazālī's M7 and his discussion of the dependence of vision on the distance between the eye and the seen object.

The formulation of the other ten shortcomings seems to be original to al-Rāzī. However, some of them can easily be linked to al-Ghazālī:

- T13, in which Fakhr al-Dīn says that through their faculty of reason humans share with God the perception of the realities of things, while through their sensitive powers they resembles beasts, reminds one clearly of the well-attested Ghazalian idea that humans stand midway between angels and beasts, as expressed, for example, in the beginning of the fifth chapter of *Mīzān al-ʿamal* (*Scale of Action*): "Man has been created according to a rank that is between that of the beast and that of the angel."[19]
- T19, in which the intellect is compared to a ruler and sensation to a servant. This can also be linked to *Mīzān al-ʿamal*, in this case to its 10th chapter, in which reason is presented as a good counselor and the faculties of envy and anger as its servants.[20]

The eight other shortcomings, which al-Rāzī adds, do not show such close links to al-Ghazālī's writings. Rather they reveal philosophical, particularly Avicennian influences. A direct correspondence with, or at least inspiration from, Avicenna's *Kitāb al-Nafs* (*De anima*), of *al-Shifāʾ*, is always detectable:

---

18 According to Landolt, "Al-Ghazālī and 'Religionswissenschaft,'" 68, n. 202, T4, not T10, corresponds to M5. Certainly, there exist similarities between them, but T10 underlines with M5 the limitation in scope of sensation and the being all-encompassing of reason. In this sense, the direct correspondence between T10 and M5 looks more probable.

19 al-Ghazālī, *Mīzān al-ʿamal*, 25.7–8, which is itself influenced by al-Rāghib al-Iṣfahānī's *Kitāb al-Dharīʿa*; see my "Al-Ghazālī's *Mīzān al-ʿamal*," 125.

20 al-Ghazālī, *Mīzān al-ʿamal*, 45–47 (itself also influenced by al-Rāghib al-Iṣfahānī, *Kitāb al-Dharīʿa*, 126–27).

- T2: only reason is able to grasp universals (*kulliyyāt*);[21]
- T3: sensitive perception, contrary to reason, is not conclusive (*muntij*);[22]
- T5: sensation cannot perceive at once something strong and something weak;[23]
- T6: the faculties of perception, contrary to those of reason, weaken after the age of forty;[24]
- T11: reason, contrary to sensation, can unify the multiple and multiply what is one;[25]
- T14: there is a need for the presence of an external object in sensation, not in intellection;[26]
- T15: the existence of external things, which al-Rāzī in genuinely Avicennian terms qualifies as possible in their essence, always follows an act of knowledge, while sensation always follows the existence of things outside;[27]
- T16: reason, contrary to sensation, requires no instruments.[28]

Hence, the presence of a strong Avicennian influence cannot be denied. This in no way implies a radical rupture with al-Ghazālī's exegesis, or with his basic thought. In fact, al-Ghazālī adhered to an Avicennian-inspired philosophical theology that developed a complex attitude toward philosophy.[29] Moreover, al-Ghazālī himself stresses in the second introduction to the *Tahāfut al-falāsifa* (*The Incoherence of the Philosophers*) that one must not refute philosophical doctrines that do not clash with any religious principle.[30] In this sense, the

21 Ibn Sīnā, *al-Shifāʾ*, *Kitāb al-Nafs*, 40.4. Let me stress that in the present context there is no doubt that the term *kulliyyāt* means "universals," not "complex issues" as rendered in the English translation of al-Rāzī's commentary on the Light Verse in Hamza and Rizvi, *An Anthology of Qur'anic Commentaries*, 389.

22 Ibn Sīnā, *al-Shifāʾ*, *Kitāb al-Nafs*, 207.12–3.

23 Ibid., 219.1–3.

24 Ibid., 219.10–5.

25 Ibid., 239.3–12.

26 Ibid., 218.1–9.

27 Ibid., 58.3–6. I have not found, however, a direct source for the idea that the existence of the possible beings is always preceded by an act of intellection, but al-Rāzī's affirmation reminds of Ibn Sīnā's idea of God's creative knowledge. See for example Ibn Sīnā, *The Metaphysics of The Healing / al-Shifāʾ: al-Ilāhiyyāt*, 294.14–295.6. The act of knowledge that precedes the existence of the external things is undoubtedly on the part of God or a celestial intellect, even if al-Rāzī does not explicitly mentions this.

28 Ibn Sīnā, *al-Shifāʾ*, *Kitāb al-Nafs*, 216.18–217.4.

29 See e.g., Griffel, *Al-Ghazālī's Philosophical Theology*, 97–109; see also my "Al-Ghazālī's *Tahāfut*: is it really a rejection of Ibn Sīnā's philosophy?" 15–17.

30 al-Ghazālī, *The Incoherence of the Philosophers / Tahāfut al-falāsifa*, 5.18–19.

dominance of reason over sensation undoubtedly is, in al-Rāzī's view, a doctrine of natural philosophy that is religiously neutral.

Despite his substantial additions to the number of sensation's shortcomings, Fakhr al-Dīn's treatise remains largely faithful to its Ghazalian source. The only striking divergence from al-Ghazālī is an omission, namely the absence of any mention of the inner senses of imagination and estimation, which occupy an important place as possible sources of error in *Mishkāt*.

The next point raised by Fakhr al-Dīn discusses the distinction between "given" knowledge and acquired knowledge and closely follows al-Ghazālī.[31] But he articulates the former of the two in a slightly modified way: not just as (immediately) present, but as, although innate, not belonging to the concomitants of the human substance, and hence needing a cause to become actively illuminating. Perhaps he wants to stress also that in this case (having to do with "necessary," i.e. axiomatic truths, reformulated by al-Rāzī in *kalamic* terms of "soundness of states") there is a need for an "instructor-guide" (*murshid*), as is the case in speculative matters—the latter clearly recognized by al-Ghazālī. In almost identical terms, al-Rāzī presents the Qur'ān as this "instructor-guide:" its light may be compared with the light of the sun, while the light of the intellect resembles that of the eye in vision. To substantiate this view, he follows his predecessor and quotes Q 64:8 and 4:174.

Hereafter, Fakhr al-Dīn omits a complete section of the *Mishkāt*. In this section, special attention is paid to the difference between the inner and the outer eye, the former belonging to the celestial and the latter the terrestrial world.[32] The celestial world (*al-malakūt*) is described as exceeding normal perception. Nevertheless, humans, provided they are correctly disposed, are able to travel to that world. The details of this "ascension" constitute the majority of the section and are highly mystical in tone. Given that the section is presented as a "complement" (*takmila*), one cannot ignore the possibility that it was not present in the copy al-Rāzī had at his disposal. But this is at best a hypothesis, and not necessarily the best one. In what precedes, we already discovered a tendency in al-Rāzī to offer a *kalamic*-philosophical rewording of al-Ghazālī's work and to avoid outspoken mystical ideas. In what follows, the same tendency will also come to the fore. Thus, al-Rāzī's omission most likely results from a conscious choice.

Having omitted this "mystical" part, Fakhr al-Dīn resumes with *Mishkāt*. Agreeing with al-Ghazālī, he insists that it is Muḥammad who is referred to in the Qur'ānic saying, "a lamp that giveth light" (Q 33:46), and that which

---

31 al-Rāzī, *al-Tafsīr al-kabīr*, 23:228.10–18; al-Ghazālī, *Mishkāt al-anwār*, 128.13–130.6.

32 al-Ghazālī, *Mishkāt al-anwār*, 130.7–133.5.

enlightens other things so that they become visible is properly called a "lamp."[33] Compared to his source, he seems to stress particularly the superiority of the Prophet's (intellectual) light over the (physical) light of the sun. However, this is still in line with the *Mishkāt*'s general perspective. Again in full accordance with al-Ghazālī, al-Rāzī points out that the Prophet's light has its source in a still higher light, although he identifies that light with the light coming from the angelic spirits (*al-arwāḥ al-malāʾika*), while al-Ghazālī had expressed it symbolically in terms of a "fire", the origin of which is "the eminent divine spirit" (*al-rūḥ al-ilāhiyya al-ʿulwiyya*).[34] It is striking that to demonstrate this idea al-Rāzī quotes only Qur'anic verses, while al-Ghazālī mainly evokes a very weak tradition.[35] Another point that deserves particular attention is al-Rāzī's addition of a philosophically inspired justification of the eminence of the angels over the prophets: the cause has to be more powerful than the effect.

Fakhr al-Dīn, again in line with *Mishkāt*, underlines the existence of a hierarchy in the celestial spirits, related to whether they are giver or receiver.[36] However, he inverses the order of al-Ghazālī's explanation. He begins by emphasizing, based on Q 81:21, that the archangel Gabriel occupies the highest rank among the angels. This sharply contrasts with al-Ghazālī's suggestion that the archangel Isrāfīl may be superior to Gabriel. Given that there is no mention of Isrāfīl in the Qur'ān, where it is clear that Gabriel occupies the highest rank among the angels, al-Rāzī's rewording makes much sense. As for al-Ghazālī, he likely based his suggestion not on the well-known traditional view of Isrāfīl as the angel of resurrection, but rather on him being the angel of the Throne (*al-ʿarsh*) who veils God from the sight of the angels. This idea is, for example, present in the mystical Qur'anic Commentary, ascribed to al-Tustarī.[37] Hence the rejection of a mystical approach may have also played a role in al-Rāzī's replacing Isrāfīl with Gabriel. Al-Rāzī then repeats, not without amplification, al-Ghazālī's example of the reflection of moonlight on a mirror fixed upon a wall, stressing that what is the closest to the source is also the most powerful. Worthy of attention is al-Rāzī's acceptance of a similarity between the celestial and the terrestrial realms as far as a distinction between higher and lower lights is concerned. Hence, he does not exclude the existence of a certain

33 al-Rāzī, *al-Tafsīr al-kabīr*, 23:228.18–23; al-Ghazālī, *Mishkāt al-anwār*, 133.7–13.

34 al-Rāzī, *al-Tafsīr al-kabīr*, 23:228.23–29; al-Ghazālī, *Mishkāt al-anwār*, 133.15–134.11.

35 On that tradition see Elschazlīs comment in his German translation al-Ghazālī, *Die Nische der Lichter*, 70, note 46.

36 al-Rāzī, *al-Tafsīr al-kabīr*, 23:228.29–229.9; al-Ghazālī, *Mishkāt al-anwār*, 135.2–18.

37 See Böwering, *The Mystical Vision of Existence in Classical Islam*, 138.

parallelism between these two worlds. Nevertheless, this idea never occupies the same central place it does in *Mishkāt*.

Fakhr al-Dīn affirms together with al-Ghazālī that God is the greatest light.[38] But whereas al-Ghazālī offers a purely rational justification, namely that there has to be an ultimate source of light that is purely illuminating while not being illuminated itself—a notion that may have been inspired by the Aristotelian argument for the unmoved mover—al-Rāzī opts for a Qur'anic foundation, quoting Q 38:78. Hereafter, he omits as section of *Mishkāt*, entitled *ḥaqīqa*, in which al-Ghazālī underlines that with the exception of God, nothing can be referred to appropriately "light."[39] Since all lights other than God borrow their light from an external source, they can at best be qualified as a "light" only in a metaphorical sense. Al-Rāzī does not reject this idea but integrates it in his somewhat amplified version of the *ḥaqīqa* that follows next in *Mishkāt*.[40] Having once again stressed a parallel between the lights in the lower world and those in the upper world, he points out—as does al-Ghazālī in *Mishkāt*—that they all are possible in themselves, and therefore are pure darkness when considered by themselves. In genuine Avicennian terms, he says that possible in itself is pure non-being, while requiring something external for its being.[41] The formulation in the *Mishkāt* is less precise, at least from an Avicennian point of view, since it simply distinguishes between what has being in itself and what has being through another. Elsewhere al-Ghazālī adopts the Avicennian distinction in its original sense, such as in *al-Maqṣad al-asnā fi sharḥ maʿānī asmāʾ Allāh al-ḥusnā* (*The Highest Goal in Explaining the Beautiful Names of God*), wherein the discussion of the name *al-ḥaqq*, he states:

> The possible in itself, necessary through another is true in one respect, nugatory in another. Hence, considered in itself it has no existence, and so is nugatory. Considered from something else it acquires existence, and so, from this facet that follows (Him who) bestows existence, it is existent. From this latter point of view it is true, and from the point of view of itself it is nugatory. Therefore the Most High said: "Everything is perishing save His Face" (Q 28:88).[42]

38 al-Rāzī, *al-Tafsīr al-kabīr*, 23:229.9–11; al-Ghazālī, *Mishkāt al-anwār*, 136.2–7.

39 al-Ghazālī, *Mishkāt al-anwār*, 136.9–137.2.

40 al-Rāzī, *al-Tafsīr al-kabīr*, 23:229.11–24; al-Ghazālī, *Mishkāt al-anwār*, 137.4–15.

41 This reminds one, of course, of Ibn Sīnā's well-known distinction between the "necessary in itself" and the "possible in itself, necessary through another.' For the idea that the possible in itself deserves non-being, see, e.g., Ibn Sīnā, *The Metaphysics of The Healing / al-Shifāʾ: al-Ilāhiyyāt*, 284.4–5.

42 al-Ghazālī, *al-Maqṣad*, 137.9–13. Treiger, "Monism and Monotheism in al-Ghazālī's *Mishkāt al-anwār*," 9, already acknowledged al-Ghazālī's debt to Ibn Sīnā in this passage.

This wording is very close to Avicenna in *al-Ilāhiyyāt*, (*Metaphysics*) of *al-Shifāʾ* (*The Healing*):

> [As for] the rest of things [i.e. other than the Being Necessary By Virtue of Itself], their quiddities, as you have known, do not deserve existence; rather, in themselves and with the severing of their relation to the Necessary Being, they—deserve non-existence. For this reason, they are all in themselves nugatory, true [only] through Him and, with respect to the facet [of existence] that follows Him, realized. For this reason, "everything perishes save His face" (Q 28:88).[43]

In light of this, the wording of the *Mishkāt* appears as merely non-technical rather than expressing a true divergence from Avicenna's view. If this is correct, al-Rāzī specifies more accurately what al-Ghazālī had in mind. Perhaps of greater significance is Fakhr al-Dīn's proper use of the expression, "[God] overflows the light of being (or: existence) over them [*scil.*, the beings possible in themselves]" (*afāḍa ʿalayhā nūr al-wujūd*). Strikingly, this expression is also present in Avicenna's commentary on Sura 113 (*al-Falaq*). Since in that commentary Avicenna mainly deals with the problem of evil, the statement can be understood as expressing the idea that the existence of the good—or should one say: the good of existence?—is only possible in the metaphorical light of God.[44] Therefore, the expression "overflow the light of being" may constitute a tentative attempt to avoid pure monism, similar to the idea of "gradation of existence" (*tashkīk al-wujūd*).[45] It looks as if, at least in the present context, al-Rāzī has been more attentive to this Avicennian correction than al-Ghazālī. Moreover, al-Rāzī not only mentions God's "overflowing the light of being," but also his "overflowing the lights of knowledge" (*afāḍa ʿalayhā anwār al-maʿārif*) upon beings possible by themselves. Note that he, contrary to al-Ghazālī, does not speak of a single light. If on the ontological level nothing can be without having been directly granted the gift of existence by God, on the level of epistemology God still remains the ultimate source of illumination, whereas existence may be mediated by other instances. This reflects a genuinely *kalamic*

43 Ibn Sīnā, *The Metaphysics of The Healing / al-Shifāʾ: al-Ilāhiyyāt*, 284.14–16.

44 See my "Creation and Emanation in Ibn Sīnā," 461.

45 Treiger, "Monism and Monotheism in al-Ghazālī's *Mishkāt al-anwār*," 9 and 23, note 48, indicates that the notion of "gradation of existence" does not permit one to interpret Ibn Sīnā's system as a whole in a monistic sense. However, as he notes, one finds in his writings passages that are highly monistic in tonality. In other words, the tension between monism and monotheism, which Treiger reveals to be present in the *Mishkāt*, is already present in al-Ghazālī's Avicennian source. The whole issue merits a more detailed analysis, as already noted by Treiger.

position. Even if it is not as such present in *Mishkāt*, it certainly is not in contradiction with al-Ghazālī's overall view on creation and *divine* knowledge. However, compared to Avicenna, who defends the model of a creation that is "mediated" by the process of emanation, this constitutes an important rectification. In this sense it is certainly not amalgamated at random with al-Ghazālī's statements, as Hajjaji-Jarrah indeed suggests.[46]

After identifying God as the only true light, al-Rāzī omits two sections of the *Mishkāt*. The first is titled *ḥaqīqat al-ḥaqāʾiq*, "truth of the truths."[47] In it, al-Ghazālī deals with the *ʿārifūn*, "those who know," who realize the absolute uniqueness of God's existence and greatness and, at once, the existence of two faces in all that is not God, i.e. one directed toward themselves and another directed toward God. Al-Ghazālī concludes with the affirmation of an extremely negative theology, namely that only God knows Himself, while referring for further explanation to his *Maqṣad*. As to the second section, which is referred to as an *ishāra*, "pointer," in it al-Ghazālī clarifies in which ways—either by (acquired) scientific knowledge (*ʿirfān*^an^ *ʿilmiyy*^an^) or by (spontaneous) taste (*dhawq*^an^)—the *ʿārifūn* attain the ultimate reality of the truth, or better: Truth. In this context, al-Ghazālī also explains some of the most provocative Sufi sayings as related to a state of "drunkenness," expressing not a real unification with the Divine, but a resemblance of unification.[48] At the end al-Ghazālī notes that mysteries are hidden in all this that he is not at liberty to discuss. The apparent mystical elements in this section, even though they are expressed with critical caution, are in all likelihood the reason why Fakhr al-Dīn did not take these sections into account in his commentary.

Al-Rāzī uses elements of the conclusion of the first part of *Mishkāt*,for the formulation of two questions. The first asks to what degree the light of God is related to the heavens and the earth.[49] In his answer al-Rāzī follows closely al-Ghazālī, omitting only a few lines.[50] He stresses that both the higher and the lower world are filled with externally visible lights (perceived by visual perception) and internally visible lights (perceived though rational perception), all of them having their ultimate source in the light of lights. Hereafter follows in the *Mishkāt* one of al-Ghazālī's most monistic texts, in which he states that "There is no God but God" is the confession of divine unity (*tawḥīd*) of the

46 Hajjaji-Jarrah, "'*Ayāt al-nūr*:' A Metaphor for Where We Come From, What we Are, and Where We Are Going," 178–79, note 10.

47 al-Ghazālī, *Mishkāt al-anwār*, 137.16–139.2.

48 Ibid., 139.3–141.9.

49 al-Rāzī, *al-Tafsīr al-kabīr*, 23:229.24–230.9, reading *kam* instead of *lima* in 23:229.25.

50 al-Ghazālī, *Mishkāt al-anwār*, 142.8–144.1.

commoners, whereas "There is nothing but He" (*lā huwa illā huwa*) is the confession of unity of the elect.[51] In it, al-Ghazālī evokes the ascending phase of the spiritual realization of the *ʿārifūn* in which all multiplicity disappears in absolute singularity (*al-fardāniyya al-maḥḍa*) and pure unity (*al-waḥdāniyya al-ṣarfa*). Following this ascending phase there is a reverse descending phase where the multiplicity of this world is again accounted for, but now looked at from the perspective of the highest unity and singularity.[52] According to al-Ghazālī this is the last object of spiritual search, whereby he notes that the descent into the lowest heaven can be that of an angel, but not that of God as claimed by one of the Sufis, unless interpreted in a particular way. This double motion of spiritual realization, as well as the expression of monism, will become very central in the thought of one of the greatest Islamic mystic thinkers, Muhyī l-Dīn Ibn ʿArabī (d. 638/1240).[53] Hence, when exposing these ideas al-Ghazālī enters a profoundly mystical context. That al-Rāzī has not integrated them into his own commentary shows again his reluctance, or, at least, reticence to accept these kind of ideas. Moreover, it must be noted that al-Ghazālī explicitly states that he has not expressed the full truth of these matters clearly and completely because they probably will exceed the limits of understanding of his addressee. When he turns back to earth, Fakhr al-Dīn again closely mirrors him in the answer to the question: "If God is light, why is there need for a demonstration to establish it?" With al-Ghazālī he insists that the existence of God's light (in view of a human's interior insights) can be clarified by the existence of visible light (in order to see colors), but that there exists an important difference between them, namely that divine light, contrary to

51 Ibid., 144.1–145.1. This passage would need to be amended in Sayrawān's edition according to the evidence in the collection of al-Ghazālī's Persian letters (*Makātīb-yi fārisī-yi Ghazzālī*, 12) where he responds to the following question: "What does the *Imām al-Aʾimma* and *Ḥujjat al-Islām* [al-Ghazālī] answer to those who object to some of his sayings in *Mishkāt* and *Kīmiyāʾ*, such as that "There is no god but God" (*lā ilāha illā Allāh*) is the *tawḥīd* of the ordinary people and that "There is no one but He" (*lā huwa illā huwa*) is the *tawḥīd* of the elite?" (See the correction of the text of this edition by Krawulsky, *Briefe und Reden des Abū Hāmid Muhammad al-Gazzālī*, 79, 222.) The reading that *lā huwa illā huwa* is, according to al-Ghazālī, the *tawḥīd* of the elite is part of the manuscript tradition of *Mishkāt* and can, for instance, be found in A. ʿIzzat and F. Zakī al-Kurdī's *edition princeps* of *Mishkāt al-anwār* (Cairo: Maṭbaʿat al-Ṣidq, 1322 [1904–05]), 23.5. The passage has also been extensively analyzed by Treiger, "Monism and Monotheism in al-Ghazālī's *Mishkāt al-anwār*," 4–10 although he is unaware of the emendation suggested in al-Ghazālī's collection of letters.

52 al-Ghazālī, *Mishkāt al-anwār*, 145.1–146.5.

53 See e.g., Roger Deladrière in the introduction to Ibn ʿArabī, *La profession de foi*, 32–78.

visible light, cannot disappear.[54] In this latter respect, he does not hesitate to use al-Ghazālī's particular emphasis on the fact that the divine light, by the very force of its evidence, becomes invisible, or, in other words, due the violence of its manifestation, is hidden to the creatures. This time, again, al-Rāzī omits a paragraph that is mystical in tone. It distinguishes three categories of people, the highest of which consists of those who see all things through God.[55] Moreover, he omits the final paragraph, where al-Ghazālī clarifies that his affirmation that God is "with (*maʿa*) the things" has no local signification, but means that insofar as He reveals all things He is in one respect with them, while He is in another respect before and above them. This last omission undoubtedly results from a conscious decision by al-Rāzī, who already in describing the parallelism between visible and divine lights to avoid speaking of "God's being with all things." In fact, he only mentions God's "light" as being with "all things." I see in this a decision to avoid an outspoken monism. Al-Rāzī does not accuse al-Ghazālī of having defended monism, but he probably realized that even if his predecessor tried to qualify his monism, he nevertheless touched delicate issues, some of which—like the presence of God's "being with"—he was not able to settle in a coherent and comprehensive way. Hence, despite the kind of "abrogation" al-Ghazālī offered in the last paragraph of the *Mishkāt*, as Hajjaji-Jarrah has rightly observed, it is not so puzzling, as she believes, that al-Rāzī ceased to cite it.[56] Given that he had the "with" related to light and not to being, he may have judged that he had already qualified the involved monism in a substantial way. So, one can easily understand that Fakhr al-Dīn considers al-Ghazālī's explanation to be pleasant, but, above all, not in contradiction with his view that God's light primarily means His guidance.[57]

In the second part of his commentary, al-Rāzī no longer concentrates on the Light Verse itself, but on the famous, although non-canonical, *ḥadīth* of the seventy veils. He quotes it with the variants seven hundred and seven thousand in the same way as al-Ghazālī does in the heading of the third part of the *Mishkāt*.[58] Moreover, exactly as al-Ghazālī does, he starts his explanation by

54 al-Rāzī, *al-Tafsīr al-kabīr*, 23:230.10–25; al-Ghazālī, *Mishkāt al-anwār*, 146.9–147.1 and 148.1–15.

55 al-Ghazālī, *Mishkāt al-anwār*, 147.2–9. However, I must admit that due to homoioteleuton the paragraph may have been absent in the manuscript(s) of the *Mishkāt* that al-Rāzī had at his disposal.

56 Mahdi Hajjaji-Jarrah, "'*Ayāt al-nūr*:' A Metaphor for Where We Come From, What we Are, and Where We Are Going," 173.

57 al-Rāzī, *al-Tafsīr al-kabīr*, 23:230.25–29.

58 al-Rāzī, *al-Tafsīr al-kabīr*, 23:230.26–231.2; al-Ghazālī, *Mishkāt al-anwār*, 175.2–4. Al-Rāzī's debt to al-Ghazālī is hardly open to doubt since only the variant seven thousand seems

distinguishing between three major ways people may be veiled: by a mixture of light and darkness, by pure light, or by pure darkness.[59] Note that compared to the *Mishkāt*, here at the beginning of al-Rāzī's discussion the order has been inversed. Yet, when we look at the detailed discussion that follows this is no longer the case.

Al-Rāzī presents those who are veiled by pure darkness as people who are only preoccupied with bodily concerns: they do not wonder about the possibility of deducing from the sense-based reality the existence of a Necessary Being and, since all that is outside God is in itself pure darkness, these people do not realize either that their visibility is due to the latter's light.[60] At first, this formulation does not have much in common with al-Ghazālī's, which presents the first group veiled by darkness as "heretics" (*mulḥida*).[61] He, moreover, divides this group into two major categories: those who have searched a cause for this world and have assigned it to "natural disposition" (*ṭabʿ*), and those who are dominated by their own passions, specified according to four further subcategories.[62] As already observed by Landoldt, one can easily identify al-Rāzī's view with this second group of those who are veiled by pure darkness according to the *Mishkāt*.[63] Major common elements exist between the descriptions by al-Ghazālī and al-Rāzī of this second class. Even if al-Rāzī does not mention the four subcategories that al-Ghazālī distinguishes between, he admits the possibility of a further distinction, but stresses that it is unlimited because of the uncountable ways of being related to the body. Furthermore, he agrees with al-Ghazālī and presents those veiled in darkness as "atheists", insofar as they do not ask in any way whatsoever whether there is an ultimate cause for the existence of all things.

Landolt did not overlook that the first group in al-Ghazālī's classification of those who are veiled in pure darkness, is, in Fakhr al-Dīn's grouping, integrated into the second one, those veiled by a mixture of light and darkness. But does this description refer to the "naturalist philosophers," as Landolt claims?[64] If

---

well attested in the tradition collections, see the commentary of Elschazlī in al-Ghazālī, *Die Nische der Lichter*, 85, note 176 and of Deladrière in al-Ghazālī, *Le Tabernacle des Lumières*, 99, note 3.

59 al-Rāzī, *al-Tafsīr al-kabīr*, 23:231.2–4; al-Ghazālī, *Mishkāt al-anwār*, 175.5–9.

60 al-Rāzī, *al-Tafsīr al-kabīr*, 23:231.4–10.

61 In the Ashʿarite circles of al-Ghazālī's time the term *mulḥidūn* is more or less synonymous with that of *dahriyyūn*, who can be labeled "heretics" or almost "atheists" in the sense that, given their proclaiming the eternity of the world, they *de facto* deny the necessity of a God-Creator.

62 al-Ghazālī, *Mishkāt al-anwār*, 177.1–179.18.

63 Landolt, "Al-Ghazālī and 'Religionswissenschaft,'" 67.

64 Ibid.

I am hesitant to accept his interpretation, it is mainly because the connection between these people, who according to al-Ghazālī have made "nature" a cause for this world, and the naturalist philosophers is far from evident. Indeed, when one looks at *al-Munqidh min al-ḍalāl*, (*The Deliverer from Error*), one sees that the naturalist philosophers, although denying resurrection, do not deny the existence of a God-Creator.[65] With reference to Q 4:37 or Q 9:45, al-Ghazālī makes clear that the adherents of this group are characterized by both the denial of the existence of a God-Creator and of resurrection. In the view of *al-Munqidh*, the only philosophers who would fulfil this description are the so-called "materialists" (*dahriyyūn*). Landolt was maybe aware of this since he placed naturalist between quotation marks, but he does not say so explicitly.

Whatever the case may be, in Fakhr al-Dīn al-Rāzī these materialists appear in the second class, those veiled by a mixture of light and darkness.[66] They are presented as believing that contingent beings have no need for an external determining agent (*mu'aththir*)—and this is an aspect of darkness, but they have also a notion of self-sufficiency (*ghaniyya*), which is a divine characteristic of excellence—and this is an aspect of light. Besides those who make the "natural disposition" (*ṭabʿ*) the determining agent of the existing things, al-Rāzī mentions others who identify this agent either with movements (*ḥarakāt*) or the conjunction (*ijtimāʿ*) and separation (*iftirāq*) of the contingent things, or with their relation to the movements or movers of the spheres.[67] In other words, all those in the second group look for a cause to explain the existence of this world, but, at the same time, they make this cause part of the universe, which therefore they consider to be self-sufficient. Thus, there is in their view no need for the acceptance of the existence of a (transcendent) God. In this sense they can be qualified as "natural" philosophers in a broad sense, i.e. including the "materialists". This group is not present as such in al-Ghazālī. In fact, in his second class, he deals with different imperfect understandings of the godhead, which have their origin in the senses, imagination, or mis- taken intellectual analogies.[68] This distinction is completely absent in al-Rāzī's

65 al-Ghazālī, *al-Munqidh min al-ḍalāl*, 19.22.

66 al-Rāzī, *al-Tafsīr al-kabīr*, 23:231.11–19.

67 The reference is almost certainly to different schools of astronomy that held the position that the stars act autonomously without being put in place by God, a classical position associates with the *dahriyya* (I thank Frank Griffel for having drawn my attention to this), and offers as such a strong indication that al-Rāzī has first and foremost the "materialists" in mind.

68 al-Ghazālī, *Mishkāt al-anwār*, 180.1–183.7. A brief, but significant summary of this section is offered by Griffel, "Al-Ghazālī's Cosmology in the Veil Section of the *Mishkāt al-anwār*," 32–3.

depiction of the three veiled groups. Still, it seems that he has been influenced by the idea—well-expressed in *Mishkāt*—that the very acceptance of (one of) the divine characteristics is the expression of the being veiled by light: glory and beauty,[69] dominion and splendor[70] (181,6–7), etc. It is striking that al-Rāzī does not use any of these characteristics mentioned in *Mishkāt*; instead, he evokes the single, but highly relevant qualification of self-sufficiency, which as its active participle "self-sufficient" (*ghaniyy*) is one of God's ninety-nine beautiful names. In the work, which he devotes to the divine names, al-Rāzī, in Avicennian terms, emphasizes that God is the only truly self-sufficient, namely that He is the being necessary by virtue of itself, and that everything outside Him is in need of His giving it being.[71]

Contrary to al-Ghazālī, Fakhr al-Dīn does not point to a false comparison between creational (human) and divine qualities, but to the ascription of a typically divine characteristic to humans. In this sense he can include in this second class both the materialists, who do limit their causal research to the lower world, as well as those who look for a causal explanation in the higher world of the spheres and their motions, and even to the causes of these motions. The latter is reminiscent of al-Ghazālī's second group among the class of those who are veiled by pure light, as they are said to recognize a plurality of heavens and the existence of a mover for each of them.[72] However, al-Ghazālī adds that all these motions are regulated by the ultimate sphere, of which the Lord is the mover—in all likelihood meaning here the Aristotelian idea of the Unmoved Mover.[73] From al-Ghazālī's perspective, the positing of a unique principle seems to be part of coming to a genuine understanding of the divine. As for al-Rāzī, he seems unconvinced. Rather, he emphasizes that the positing of the cause of this world inside the universe demonstrates a very primitive understanding of god, not of a true understanding of God.

An even more profound change in perspective seems to come to the fore in al-Rāzī's description of the third class, those who are veiled by pure light. Al-Rāzī states that the way to full knowledge of God passes through the recognition of the negative and the relational attributes of God, which are infinite in number. Whenever humans arrive at (*waṣala*) one of its different degrees the ones higher than this are always being veiled from them.[74] Despite the use of a

69 al-Ghazālī, *Mishkāt al-anwār*, 180,13.

70 Ibid., 181,6–7.

71 al-Rāzī, *Lawāmiʿ al-bayyināt*, 330.

72 al-Ghazālī, *Mishkāt al-anwār*, 184.1–6.

73 Griffel, "Al-Ghazālī's Cosmology," 40–43.

74 al-Rāzī, *al-Tafsīr al-kabīr*, 23:231.20–24.

philosophical language, one cannot but detect here the expression of what Landolt has labelled a "theological attributism."[75] This has, at least at first sight, nothing in common with the cosmological approach that prevails in *Mishkāt*.[76] Hence, did al-Rāzī cheat in order to save the image of al-Ghazālī as "orthodox" theologian, as Landolt suggests?[77] Even if this looks likely, it must be noted that Fakhr al-Dīn clearly uses some expressions derived from *Mishkāt*. First of all, discussing negative (and relative) attributes is reminiscent of al-Ghazālī's expression that the true God is something holy, free of everything that we have attributed to Him.[78] Hence, both Fakhr al-Dīn and al-Ghazālī favour here a (kind of) negative theology. Furthermore, the idea of "arrival" is also present in the *Mishkāt*, since it introduces the fourth and highest category as "those who have arrived" (*al-wāṣilūn*). Certainly, al-Rāzī emphasizes that such "arrival" never concerns the very reality of God, whereas al-Ghazālī ultimately describes it in terms of "annihilation" (*fanā'*). However, earlier in the *Mishkāt*, al-Ghazālī pointed out that "annihilation" is not the "becoming one (*ittiḥād*) with God."[79] Finally, the idea of the existence of different degrees in the attainment of knowledge of God underlies both al-Rāzī's' *Tafsīr* as well as *Mishkāt*. Only al-Ghazālī adds that some of those who arrive have not climbed step by step all the stages that have been mentioned.[80] These similarities show that al-Rāzī indeed had at his disposal this actual section of the *Mishkāt*.[81]

---

75 Landolt, "Al-Ghazālī and 'Religionswissenschaft,'" 67.

76 al-Ghazālī, *Mishkāt al-anwār*, 183.8–185.15. Regarding the presence of a basically cosmological approach in this section, see Griffel, "Al-Ghazālī's Cosmology," 43–45.

77 Landolt, "Al-Ghazālī and 'Religionswissenschaft,'" 68.

78 al-Ghazālī, *Mishkāt al-anwār*, 184.20–21.

79 Ibid., 141.3–9. This fact is referred to in Griffel, "Al-Ghazālī's Cosmology," 46, note 52.

80 In this later case, al-Ghazālī perhaps offers a Sufi reformulation of Ibn Sīnā's concept of intuition (*ḥads*). Although this mode of knowledge is in the first place typical of the prophet (see Afifi al-Akiti, "The Three Properties of Prophethood in Certain Works of Avicenna and al-Ghazālī," 198, note 27; Treiger, *Inspired Knowledge in Islamic Thought*, 77–78), it can also be applied to some well gifted men (Sufis for al-Ghazālī, philosophers for Ibn Sīnā). Hence, these latter have quasi-prophetic powers; see Treiger, *Inspired Knowledge in Islamic Thought*, 65; and Janssens, "Al-Ghazālī between Philosophy (*Falsafa*) and Sufism (*Taṣawwuf*): His Complex Attitude in the *Marvels of the Heart* (*Ajā'ib al-Qalb*) of the *Iḥyā' 'Ulūm al-Dīn*," 628.

81 An additional element of evidence has been offered by Landolt, "Al-Ghazālī and 'Religionswissenschaft,'" 68–72, based on the small Persian treatise *Risālah-yi ta'wīlāt-i mushkilāt al-aḥādith al-mushkila* (see above n. 2), which, if not written by al-Rāzī himself, is highly Razian in nature.

The explanation of the symbolism of the Light Verse is the object of the third part of al-Rāzī's commentary.[82] He offers no less than ten interpretations, which were available at his time and which he considered worthy of attention. Everything indicates that he offers them according to the order of his preference, since he starts with the interpretation that he clearly states he prefers, namely that the light symbolizes divine guidance. This, he says, is also the view of the majority of the *mutakkallimūn*. Then al-Rāzī evokes the identification of the light with the Qur'an, followed by the Prophet, and by the knowledge of God as well as the legal prescriptions in the heart of the believers. Hereafter, he evokes al-Ghazālī's and Avicenna's explanations, after which he still mentions four other interpretations of the Light Verse. Apart from the first, most of these views are presented in very brief terms. However, when Fakhr al-Dīn comes to al-Ghazālī's view, and to a lesser degree to Avicenna's (nos. 5 and 6), he gives a rather detailed explanation.[83] Both stress the role of the human faculties of perception, but according to al-Rāzī's understanding only al-Ghazālī presents them explicitly as lights, whereas Avicenna just describes the way in which the human soul perceives. It is obvious that al-Rāzī is aware that the former was indebted to the latter, a fact that currently is generally acknowledged.[84] Nevertheless, al-Rāzī seems to detect in al-Ghazālī's explanation an implicit reference to the idea of guidance, namely in the explicit qualification of the human "perceptive" powers as "luminous" in the heading of the second pole (*quṭb*) of the second part of the *Mishkāt*.[85] However, this may simply be the result of al-Rāzī's desire to save the image of al-Ghazālī as "orthodox" theologian. I should stress that al-Rāzī's presentation of al-Ghazālī's view shows many literal correspondences with *Mishkāt*. Certainly, his presentation of the five human powers that lead to knowledge is less extensive than al-Ghazālī's and, as well, a few minor omissions and modifications come to the fore in the way he presents the latter's proper explanation of the Light Verse. But all in all he is respectful of al-Ghazālī's wording. I did not find anything fundamentally new in al-Rāzī's approach compared to what I have already mentioned and therefore omit any detailed discussion.

82 al-Rāzī, *al-Tafsīr al-kabīr*, 23:231.25–235.14.

83 Ibid., 23:233.6–234.16; 234.16–29 respectively.

84 See, e.g., Treiger, *Inspired Knowledge in Islamic Thought*, 75–77; Okumuş, "The Influence of Ibn Sīnā on al-Ghazālī in Qur'anic hermeneutics," 405–8.

85 al-Ghazālī, *Mishkāt al-anwār*, 165.1.

Conclusions

Having surveyed the differences between al-Ghazālī's *Mishkāt al-anwār* and Fakhr al-Dīn's commentary on the Light Verse in his *Tafsīr al-kabīr*, some conclusions are clear. We saw at the beginning that al-Rāzī declared that he would present to his readers what al-Ghazālī had achieved in his book.[86] When one specifically concentrates on the symbolism of the Qur'anic Light Verse, it is obvious that he succeeded in his task. All major passages that deal with the divine light have been incorporated in al-Rāzī's own commentary. Yet al-Rāzī does so not by blind imitation (*taqlīd*)—an attitude that his great predecessor had vehemently condemned (with the exception of the imitation of the Prophet).[87] Following his early announcement, he also critically approaches al-Ghazālī's text. He clearly values one of its most important ideas, i.e. God is light, even the only real light, so that outside of Him everything is darkness. One easily detects the presence of the Avicennian distinction between the unique Necessary Being By Virtues Of Itself and all other beings that are merely possible by themselves, necessary through another as the background for this. This Avicennian background has not detracted Fakhr al-Dīn. He is ready to accept some of the former's philosophical ideas, as al-Ghazālī had undoubtedly already done before him.[88] This becomes especially clear in his inclusion of Avicenna's commentary on the Light Verse among his list of those that offer possible, if not the best, still acceptable interpretation. I think two remarks are in place here:

1. Al-Ghazālī has never refuted philosophy as a discipline, he rather disagreed with some of its aspects—indicating that on some issues, namely those where the philosophers dispose of really demonstrative knowledge, they are to be followed;[89]
2. Avicenna has used some terminology, as well as some questions, from both *kalām* and the mysticism of his time—a fact that clearly facilitated the integration of his philosophy in the later developments of both disciplines, even if his own articulation was outspokenly philosophical in nature.[90]

---

86 *Anā anqulu muḥaṣṣil mā dhakarahū maʿa zawāʾid kathīra*; al-Rāzī, *al-Tafsīr al-kabīr*, 23:224.21.

87 Frank, "Al-Ghazālī on *taqlīd*. Scholars, Theologians, and Philosophers."

88 Among recent publications in this sense, see Griffel, *Al-Ghazālī's Philosophical Theology*, and Treiger, *Inspired Knowledge in Islamic Thought*.

89 See in this respect the second introduction to al-Ghazālī *The Incoherence of the Philosophers / Tahāfut al-falāsifa*, 5–7.

90 See Wisnovsky, *Avicenna's Metaphysics in Context*, 145–60 and 227–43 (regarding *kalam*)

So, both al-Rāzī and al-Ghazālī are in favor of what Shihadeh and Griffel have called a "philosophical theology."[91] More distressing for al-Rāzī seems to have been the presence of outspoken mystical passages in the text. Presumably, he was puzzled by them and saw no possibility for integrating them in his philosophical-theological approach. Rather than offering an arbitrary explanation, he has opted to omit them. In doing so, he does more than just give an impartial judgment, as he claimed at the outset of his work. Indeed, one has the strong impression that he attempted to qualify al-Ghazālī as an authentic *mutakallim*. This may at first sight look a somewhat unnatural move, but at closer inspection it may have a basis in *Mishkāt*. There, in the "conclusion" (*khātima*) of its second part, al-Ghazālī insists that light means guidance.[92] This is, in al-Rāzī's view, the prevailing opinion in *kalām*, and, moreover, his preferred one. Given that it is affirmed in a "conclusion"—even if it is not of the *Mishkāt* as a whole work, but only of one of its parts—Fakhr al-Dīn can have imagined that al-Ghazālī, after all, remained a good "theologian."[93] In the final analysis, al-Rāzī appears as a critical, but careful reader of the *Mishkāt*, a text that he highly esteems by giving it such a prominent place in his own commentary on the Light Verse. It is beyond doubt that he also held in high esteem its author, al-Ghazālī, who even nowadays continues to fascinate (and puzzle) many scholars' minds.

Bibliography

al-Akiti, M. Afifi. "The Three Properties of Prophethood in Certain Works of Avicenna and al-Ghazālī." In *Interpreting Avicenna: Science and Philosophy in Medieval Islam*. Edited by J. McGinnis. Leiden: Brill, 2004. 189–212.

Bowering, Gerhard. *The Mystical Vision of Existence in Classical Islam: The Qur'anic Hermeneutics of the Sufi Sahl at-Tustari*. Berlin: Walter de Gruyter, 1979.

and my "Ibn Sīnā: A Philosophical Mysticism or a Philosophy of Mysticism" (regarding mysticism).

91 Shihadeh, "From al-Ghazālī to al-Rāzī: 6th/12th Century Developments in Muslim Philosophical Theology," and Griffel, *Al-Ghazālī's Philosophical Theology*.

92 al-Ghazālī, *Mishkāt al-anwār*, 172.3.

93 It could be that the concerned conclusion was in al-Rāzī's copy of the *Mishkāt* not just the conclusion of the second section, but the conclusion of the whole work, given that he discusses the tradition on the "Veils" before exposing the proper exegesis of the Light Verse. However, in view of other modifications that one finds in al-Rāzī's dealing with the *Mishkāt*, this is far from being sure.

EI^2 = *Encyclopaedia of Islam. New Edition.* Edited by an editorial committee consisting of H. A. R. Gibb et al. 13 vols. Leiden and London: Luzac and Brill, 1954–2009.

Frank, Richard M. "Al-Ghazālī on *Taqlīd*. Scholars, Theologians, and Philosophers." *Zeitschrift für die Geschichte der arabisch-islamischen Wissenschaften* 7 (1991/92): 207–52.

al-Ghazālī, Muḥammad ibn Muḥammad. *The Incoherence of the Philosophers / Tahāfut al-falāsifa*. Edited and transl. by M. E. Marmura. 2nd ed. Provo: Brigham Young University Press, 2000.

———. *Mīzān al-ʿamal*. Edited by M. Ṣ. al-Kurdī. Cairo: al-Maṭbaʿa al-ʿArabiyya, 1342 [1923].

———. *Makātīb-yi fārisī-yi Ghazzālī be-nām-i Fażāʾil al-anām min rasāʾil Ḥujjat al-Islām*. Edited by ʿA. Iqbāl. Tehran: Kitābfurūsh-i Ibn Sīnā, 1333 [1954].

———. *al-Maqṣad al-asnā fī sharḥ maʿānī asmāʾ Allāh al-ḥusnā*. Edited by F. A. Shehadi. Beirut: Dār al-Mashriq, 1986.

———. *Mishkāt al-anwār wa-miṣfāt al-asrār*. Edited by ʿA. ʿI. al-Sayrawān. Beirut: ʿĀlam al-Kutub, 1407/1986.

———. *al-Munqidh min al-ḍalāl / Erreur et deliverance*. Edition and French transl. by F. Jabre. 2nd edition. Beirut: Commission libanaise pour la traduction des chefs-d'œuvre, 1969.

———. *Die Nische der Lichter.* German transl. by ʿA. ʿA. Elschazlī. Hamburg: Meiner, 2002.

———. *Le Tabernacle des Lumières.* French transl. by R. Deladrière. Paris: Editions du Seuil, 1999.

Griffel, Frank. *Al-Ghazālī's Philosophical Theology*. New York: Oxford University Press, 2009.

———. "Al-Ghazali's Cosmology in the Veil Section of His *Mishkāt al-anwār*." In *Avicenna and his Heritage: A Golden Age of Science and Philosophy*. Edited by Y. T. Langermann. Turnhout (Belgium): Brepols, 2009. 27–49.

Hamza, Feras, and Sajjad Sajjad (eds.) *An Anthology of Qur'anic Commentaries. Volume 1. On the Nature of the Divine.* Oxford: Oxford University Press in Association with the Institute of Ismaili Sudies, 2008.

Ibn ʿArabī, Muḥammad ibn ʿAlī. *La profession de foi.* French transl. by R. Deladrière. Paris: Editeur Actes Sud. 2010.

Ibn Sīnā. al-Ḥusayn ibn ʿAbdallāh. *al-Ishārāt wa-l-tanbīhāt*. Edited by J. Forget. Leiden: E. J. Brill, 1892.

———. *The Metaphysics of The Healing / al-Shifāʾ: al-Ilāhiyyāt. A Parallel English-Arabic Text.* Edited and transl. by M. E. Marmura. Provo (Utah): Brigham Young University Press, 2005.

———. *al-Shifāʾ. Kitāb al-Nafs.* Edited by Fazlur Rahman. London: Oxford University Press, 1959.

Jabre, Farid. *Essai sur le lexique de Ghazali; contribution à l'étude de la terminologie de Ghazali dans ses principaux ouvrages à l'exception du Tahāfut.* Beirut: Librairie Orientale, 1970.

Janssens, Jules. "Creation and Emanation in Ibn Sīnā." *Documenti e Studi sulla Tradizione Filosofica Medivale* 8 (1997): 455–477.

———. "Al-Ghazālī between Philosophy (*Falsafa*) and Sufism (*Taṣawwuf*): His Complex Attitude in the Marvels of the Heart (*'Ajā'ib al-Qalb*) of the *Iḥyā' 'Ulūm al-Dīn*." *The Muslim World* 101 (2011): 614–32.

———. "Al-Ghazālī's *Mīzān al-'amal*: An Ethical Summa Based on Ibn Sīnā and al-Rāghib al-Iṣfahānī." In *Islamic Thought in the Middle Ages: Studies in Text, Transmission and Translation, in Honour of Hans Daiber*. Edited by A. A. Akasoy and W. Raven. Leiden: Brill. 2008. 123–38.

———. "Al-Ghazālī's *Tahāfut*: Is It Really a Rejection of Ibn Sīnā's Philosophy?" *Journal of Islamic Studies* 12 (2001): 1–17.

———. "Ibn Sīnā: A Philosophical Mysticism or a Philosophy of Mysticism?" Paper presented at the International Colloquium "Mysticism without Bounds." Bangalore (India), January 2011.

Krawulsky, Dorothea. *Briefe und Reden des Abū Hāmid Muhammad al-Gazzālī.* Freiburg: Klaus Schwartz, 1971.

Lagarde, Michel. *Index de Grand Commentaire de Faḫr al-Dīn al-Rāzī.* Leiden: E. J. Brill, 1996.

Landolt, Hermann A. "Al-Ghazālī and 'Religionswissenschaft': Some Notes on the Mishkāt al-anwār for Professor Charles J. Adams" *Asiatische Studien* (Zurich) 45 (1991): 19–72.

Lazarus-Yafeh, Hava. *Studies in al-Ghazālī.* Jerusalem: Magnes Press, 1975.

Hajjaji-Jarrah, Soraya M. "'*Ayāt al-nūr*:' A Metaphor for Where We Come From, What we Are, and Where We Are Going." In *Reason and Inspiration in Islam: Theology, Philosophy and Mysticism in Muslim Thought: Essays in Honor of Hermann Landolt.* Edited by T. Lawson. London: I. B. Tauris, 2005. 169–181.

Okumuş, Mesut. "The Influence of Ibn Sīnā on al-Ghazālī in Qur'anic hermeneutics." *The Muslim World* 102 (2012): 390–411.

Pickthall, Mohammed Marmaduke. *The Meaning of the Glorious Koran.* Hyderabad: Government Central Press. 1938.

Pourjavady, Nasrollah. "Fakhr-i Rāzī va-Mishkāt al-anvār-i Ghazzālī." *Ma'ārif*, vol. 2 (1364 [1985]): 213–29.

———. "Fakhr-e Râzî und Ghazzâlîs Mishkât al-anwâr (Lichternische)," *Spektrum Iran* (Bonn), 2 (1989): 49–70.

al-Rāghib al-Iṣfahānī, Ḥusayn ibn Muḥammad. *Kitāb al-Dharī'a*. Edited by Ṭ. 'A. Sa'd. Cairo: Maṭba'at Ḥasān, 1973.

al-Rāzī, Fakhr al-Dīn Muḥammad ibn ʿUmar. *Lawāmiʿ al-bayyināt fī l-asmāʾ wa-l-ṣifāt*. Edited under the title *Sharḥ asmāʾ Allāh al-ḥusnā* by Ṭ. ʿA. Saʿd. 2nd ed. Cairo: Maktabat al-Azhariyya li-l-Turāth, 1420/2000.

———. *al-Tafsīr al-kabīr aw-Mafātīḥ al-ghayb*. 32 vols. Cairo: al-Maṭbaʿa al-Bahiyyah al-Miṣriyya, n. d. [*c.* 1933].

Shihadeh, Ayman. "From al-Ghazali to al-Razi: 6th/12th Century Developments in Muslim Philosophical Theology." *Arabic Sciences and Philosophy*, 15 (2005): 141–79.

Treiger, Alexander. *Inspired Knowledge in Islamic Thought: Al-Ghazali's Theory of Mystical Cognition and Its Avicennian Foundation*. London: Routledge, 2011.

———. "Monism and Monotheism in al-Ghazālī's *Mishkāt al-anwār*." *Journal of Qur'anic Studies* 9 (2007): 1–27.

Watt, William Montgomery. "A Forgery in al-Ghazālī's *Mishkāt*?" *Journal of the Royal Asiatic Society* (1949): 5–22.

Wisnovsky, Robert. *Avicenna's Metaphysics in Context*. Cornell: Cornell University Press, 2003.

CHAPTER 10

Ottoman Perceptions of al-Ghazālī's Works and Discussions on His Historical Role in Its Late Period

M. Sait Özervarlı

Historians commonly acknowledge al-Ghazālī's importance in the transformation of post-classical Islamic thought. In this chapter I shall discuss examples of commentated and abridged translations of his works from the Ottoman period and the impact these works had on Ottoman scholars. These provide insight into the different perceptions of his legacy in the early modern period and call attention to the various ways that al-Ghazālī was represented by prominent figures of the late Ottoman period. The number of al-Ghazālī's manuscripts collected and preserved in the libraries of Istanbul and Anatolia, including some copied in the modern era, show the level of attention and respect that the Ottomans had for his works. In pre-modern times al-Ghazālī was influential through several channels, mainly though his own works but also through commentaries on them, translations into Ottoman Turkish, and finally through criticisms of his positions. In the 19th and early 20th centuries, he was rediscovered and used as one of the sources of renewal of Islamic and rational disciplines. Modern Ottoman thinkers of Istanbul, such as İzmirli İsmail Ḥakkı (1869–1946), Mehmed Ali Ayni (1865–1945), and Elmalılı Ḥamdi [Yazır] (1878–1942) referred to al-Ghazālī and his concept of *iḥyāʾ* ("revival") extensively in their own efforts to renew Islamic theology and philosophy. Ottoman thinkers were mostly attracted to the eclecticism and mysticism of his thought, as well as to his promotion of logic in religious thought. However, more radical Ottoman modernists blamed al-Ghazālī for the decline of rationalism and philosophy. Modern authors of the late Ottoman and early republican period, such as Mehmed Şemseddin [Günaltay] (1883–1961) and Celal Nuri [İleri] (1882–1938), who will be discussed below, accused him of closing doors to philosophical thinking and having a negative impact on later generation of scholars. In this chapter, I shall first give an overview on the reception of al-Ghazālī in Ottoman Turkey—presented mostly through the adaptations and the translations of his work. In the second part of the chapter I shall take a closer look at the late Ottoman controversy on al-Ghazālī's role in the intellectual history of Islam.

 | DOI 10.1163/9789004307490_011

1 Major Ottoman Translations of and Commentaries on al-Ghazālī's Works

In this section, I will briefly describe some Ottoman translations and commentaries on al-Ghazālī's books from the classical to the modern period.[1] Early Ottomans were quite impressed by al-Ghazālī's interdisciplinary, multi-layered scholarship and regarded him as a religious authority, especially through his *Iḥyāʾ ʿulūm al-dīn* (*The Revival of the Religious Sciences*). Its rich theological, mystical, philosophical, and ethical content made the book an especially suitable means of reviving early Islamic scholarly thought and methodology. It was particularly interesting for scholars who pursued the task of revitalizing disciplines of Islamic thought and its methodology. The 17th century-bibliographer Katib Çelebi (d. 1067/1657) cites a common saying among scholars that if all other Islamic books disappeared, leaving only the *Iḥyāʾ*, it would be sufficient.[2] The earliest partial translation of the *Iḥyāʾ* into Ottoman Turkish covered only its first quarter on the norms of daily life (*rubʿ al-ʿādāt*) and was done by Bilalzade Meḥmed al-Ḥanafī (d.after 967/1560) in 1560. The autograph copy of the translator is held in an Istanbul manuscript library.[3] The translation leaves out the introduction and the first book with its harsh criticism of more traditional Islamic scholarship and starts only from the second book which discusses the creed of Islam. The Turkish text is written in an easy, clear style, but includes some structural difficulties that interrupt its fluency as the translator tried to be as literal as possible.

Another partial translation of the *Iḥyāʾ* into Turkish was done by Sheyhülislam Bostanzade Meḥmed Efendi (d. 1006/1598) in the 16th century, titled *Yanābiʿ al-yaqīn fī Iḥyāʾʿulūm al-dīn* (*The Sources of Certitude on The Revival of the Religious Sciences*) and is dedicated to Sultan Aḥmed I (reg. 1590–1617). From the introduction and table of contents it appears that the author intended to translate the full text, but he stopped in the middle of the second volume of the *Iḥyāʾ*. The translation may have some additional lost parts, or the author may have left it incomplete. In his highly eloquent introduction, the translator emphasizes his reasons for translating *Iḥyāʾ* for Ottoman readers: namely its comprehensiveness, that it collects together a large amount of

1 Two recent articles list and portray the translations of al-Ghazālī's works into Ottoman and modern Turkish. See Günaydın, "Gazâlî Tercümeleri," 63–90 and Yazar, "Gazzâlî'nin XIII–XIX. Yüzyıllar Arasında Batı Türkçesinde Tercüme Edilen Eserleri," 67–156. The latter is more detailed in its scope, descriptions and focus on manuscripts.

2 Katib Çelebi, *Kashf al-ẓunūn*, 1:23.

3 MS Istanbul, Süleymaniye Yazma Eser Kütüphanesi, Ayasofya 1720, foll. 1–164.

useful knowledge from different sources, and the lack of a similar work in Turkish.[4] In addition to these translations, the second chapter of the first book of *Iḥyāʾ* was also subject of a commentary by Ṣadreddinzade Meḥmed Emin Şirvani (d. 1036/1627) in the 11th/17th century. He touches upon some scholarly problems of his time, such as the excessive emulation of authorities (*taqlīd*), a subject on which al-Ghazālī has interesting things to say.[5]

The Ottoman encyclopaedic scholar and biographer Ṭaşköprüzade ʿIṣamaddin Aḥmed (d. 968/1561) added a long section on morality in the second part of his voluminous Arabic-language encyclopaedia *Miftāḥ al-saʿāda wa-miṣbāḥ al-siyāda* (*The Key of Happiness and the Light of Nobility*) on the classification of knowledge.[6] While the first three volumes have next to nothing to do with the subject matter of the *Iḥyāʾ*, and are instead about scholarly disciplines, from their definitions, subjects, and aims, the last two volumes of the book appear to be a shortened version of the *Iḥyāʾ*, even though the author nowhere acknowledges this. A close examination of the table of contents shows that Ṭaşköprüzade follows the structure in the *Iḥyāʾ* quite closely. In the introduction to the two last volumes, Ṭaşköprüzade says that he has divided it into four sections (singl. *shuʿba*): namely rituals (*ʿibādāt*), customs (*ʿādāt*), destructive actions (*muḥlikāt*), and saving actions (*munjiyyāt*).[7] These divisions are identical to al-Ghazālī's, with the minor difference that any main parts is named a *shuʿba* instead of a *rukn*. Similarly, sections are named *aṣl* ("root") in *Miftāḥ al-saʿāda* instead of *kitāb* ("book") in al-Ghazālī's *Iḥyāʾ*. Further subsections are called *maṭlab* ("question") instead of *bāb* ("chapter") though even these have the same content titles.[8] Ṭaşköprüzade sometimes merges a number of subsections into one, and in some cases he includes only the title of a section without its full text, probably to show that he aims at reproducing the order of al-Ghazālī's book. He follows the *Iḥyāʾ* not only in its structure but also in its content, in some cases using al-Ghazālī's sentences with only minor changes. He does differ, however, in his recommendations of further readings concerning jurisprudence. While al-Ghazālī recommends that readers see his *Khulāṣat al-mukhtaṣar* (*The Summary of the Abridged*), *al-Wasīṭ fī l-madhhab* (*The Middle Book on Substantial Law*), or *al-Basīṭ fī l-furūʿ al-madhhab al-Shāfiʿī* (*The*

---

4 See MS Istanbul, Süleymaniye Yazma Eser Kütüphanesi, Fatih 2574. The MS has 423 foll.

5 Şirvani, *Sharḥ Qawāʿid al-ʿaqāʾid li-l-Ghazālī*. For an analysis of al-Ghazālī's position on *taqlīd* see Frank, "Al-Ghazālī on *taqlīd*."

6 Kemaleddin Meḥmed Ṭaşköprüzade (d. 1030/1621), the son of the author later translated the book into Ottoman Turkish where it was known under the title *Mawżuʿat al-ʿulum*.

7 Ṭaşköprüzade, *Miftāḥ al-saʿāda*, 3:6–7.

8 A table of comparisons between the table of contents of both books is given by Sakallı, "Miftahu's-saâde—Ihyau ulumi'd-din Münasebeti," 71–78.

Extended Book on Shafi'ite Substantial Law) depending on the amount of detail they need, Ṭaşköprüzade suggests books from the Hanafite school, such as Burhān al-Dīn al-Marghīnānī's (d. 593/1197) *Bidāyat al-mubtadi'* (*The Commencement for the Beginner*), Ṣadr al-Sharīʿa al-Maḥbūbī's (d. 747/1346–47) *Wiqāyat al-riwāya fī masāʾil al-Hidāya* (*Protecting the Content of the Discussions in the Hidāya*), or Najm al-Dīn al-Nasafī's (d. 537/1142–43) *al-Manẓūma fī l-khilāfiyyāt* (*The Poetic Treatise on Controversial Subjects*).[9]

Birgivi Meḥmed Efendi's (d. 981/1573) *al-Ṭarīqa al-muḥammadiyya wa-l-sirāṭ al-Aḥmadiyya* (*The Path of Muhammad and Biography of Ahmad*) in Arabic is indeed a similar case. One of the most respected books in Ottoman society, Birgivi's text—although it underlines Sunni positions more emphatically than the original—looks like a summary of the *Iḥyā'*, especially regarding ethical issues. Many of its terms and divisions are derived from the *Iḥyā'*. Despite having been written by a Hanafite author, *al-Ṭarīqa al-muḥammadiyya* is often considered an inspiration for the 11th/17th century Kadızadeli movement and similar radical, proto-salafi groups. It emphases traditions (*ḥadīth*) and takes firm position against innovations. Birgivi's book, however which contains basic creeds, ethical conducts and spiritual practices, does not include extreme views. Rather, it resembles *Iḥyā'* in many ways, with quotes from al-Ghazālī cited by name.[10] The last part of its second chapter (*al-faṣl al-thālith* in *al-bāb al-thānī*) on piety (*taqwa*) closely follows al-Ghazālī's *Iḥyā'*, especially regarding destructive actions performed by the tongue, eyes, and other human organs, with the opposite actions that remedy their harms.[11] There are also passages that repeat the *Iḥyā's* wordings without a reference to al-Ghazālī.[12] Birgivi's popular appellation *muhyiddīn* ("Reviver of Religion") is another sign of his connection with the *Iḥyā'*. The main difference between Birgivi and al-Ghazālī is the latter's strict opposition to innovations and his harsh language towards contemporary Sufi groups—especially in the very last chapter of his book, which reminds of Ibn Taymiyya's position.

In the modern period, Yūsuf Aḥmed Sıdkı (1816–1903)—the father of the early republican statesman Ebül'ula Mardin (1881–1957) and the great grandfather of the well-known sociologist Şerif Mardin (b. 1927)—wrote a complete Turkish translation and commentary on the *Iḥyā'* titled *Masīr ʿumūm al-muwaḥḥidīn* (*The Journey of All Monotheists*) in nine volumes, which he presented to Sultan Abdülhamid II for publication in 1879. Due to political turbulence and

9 Ṭaşköprüzade, *Miftāḥ al-saʿāda*, 3:15.

10 Birgivi, *Sīrat al-rasūl aw al-ṭarīqa al-muḥammadiyya*, 56, 60, 129–30, 204, 304.

11 Ibid., 69–297.

12 Çağrıcı, "Gazzâlî'nin İhyâ'sı ile Birgivî'nin Tarîkat-i Muhammediyesi'nin Mukayesesi," 478.

its lengthy scope, it remained in manuscript and was never printed.[13] In the introduction, the translator presents his work as a service to Turkish speaking people of Anatolia (*diyar-i Rūm*), where he spent years as a visitor from Mardin, and highlights his preference for a clear and common language, instead of the stylistic literary method used in previous attempts, as his main motivation for creating a new translation. He also stresses his own original contributions to the translation: since al-Ghazālī was a Shafiʿite, and the majority of the audience of the translated text would be Hanafite, Sıdkı added changes especially where al-Ghazālī discussed religious obligations.[14] Throughout the book, the original Arabic text from the *Iḥyāʾ* are written in red ink with their Turkish translations underneath in black, allowing readers to compare both texts and see the additional notes.

Written originally in Persian, as a text directed to state officials and civil servants in the high administration, and a kind of short version of the *Iḥyāʾ*, al-Ghazālī's *Kīmyā-yi saʿādat* (*Alchemy of Happiness*) was another work that the Ottomans consistently translated and commentated upon. Its translators include Sehabi Husameddin bin Ḥüseyin (d. 971/1564), who produced *Tedbīr-i iksīr* (*The Management of Elixir*), a book commissioned by Sultan Süleyman I "the Magnificent" (reg. 1520–66) and highly rewarded after its completion; Vankulu Mehmed bin Mustafa's (d. 1000/1592) *Tercüme-i Kīmyā* (*The Translation of Alchemy*), which recommends its readers to refer to *Iḥyāʾ ʿulūm al-dīn* and also *Jawāhir al-Qurʾān* (*The Jewels of the Qurʾan*) as more sophisticated texts; and finally Nergisizade Meḥmed Bosnevi's (d. 1044/1635) *Iksīr-i devlet* (*The Elixir of the State*), a partial translation written during the reign of Sultan Murad IV (reg. 1623–40).[15]

The earliest Ottoman discussions, however, were on al-Ghazālī's polemics with philosophers. Scholars in the 15th and 16th centuries such as Hocazade (d. 893/1488), ʿAlāʾal-Dīn al-Ṭūsī (d. 887/1482), Kemalpaşazadeh (d. 940/1534), and Karabaghi (d. 942/1535), wrote commentaries and annotations to al-Ghazālī's *Tahāfut al-falāsifa* (*The Incoherence of the Philosophers*). I published a detailed

---

13 MS Istanbul, University Central Library, Turkish Manuscripts, nos. 5851 to 5859. Recently, the first of the nine volumes was published in a facsimile print of MS Istanbul, University Central Library, Turkish Manuscripts, no. 5851, and a parallel edition of the Ottoman Turkish text in Latin characters: Yūsuf Aḥmed Sıdkı, *Mesîru umûmi l-muvahhidîn şerh u terceme-i Kitâb-i Ihyâu ulûmi d-dîn.*

14 Sıdkı, *Masīr ʿumūm al-muwaḥḥidīn*; Sadık Yazar, "Gazzâlî'nin XIII–XIX. Yüzyıllar Arasında," 78–79.

15 For the descriptions and copies of these and other translations of *Kīmyā* see Yazar, "Gazzâlî'nin XIII–XIX. Yüzyıllar Arasında," 83–102.

analysis on the Ottoman *Tahāfut* literature in the first volume of this collection.[16] The Ottomans also translated and commented *Ayyūhā l-walad* (*Dear Child!*). The most widely circulating translation of this treatise was produced by the well-known author Gelibolulu Muṣṭafa ʿAli (d. 1008/1600). It bears the title *Tuḥfat al-ṣulāḥa* (*The Gift of Righteous People*) and is presented as a useful source for pious people and committed students. Katib Çelebi and Meḥmed Ṭahir both mention the book as one that offers detailed commentary with explanations on the text and on each topic. In 1655, ʿAli Halifa Antalyavi (d. after 1065/1655) produced a second, very literal translation during the reign of Sultan Meḥmed IV, while a more recent work written in 1887 by Meḥmed Reshid (d. 1358/1939), and dedicated to Abdülḥamid II, although titled as translation, is much more extensive than the original.[17]

The Persian treatise *Naṣīḥat al-mulūk* (*Councel for Kings*), though its attribution to al-Ghazālī is disputed, was also very popular, mostly through the Arabic version *al-Tibr al-masbūk fī Naṣīḥat al-mulūk* (*The Forged Sword in Counsel for Kings*). This Arabic translation was produced by Ṣafī l-Dīn Abū l-Ḥasan ʿAlī ibn al-Mubārak (fl. 571/1175). His Arabic version was translated into Ottoman Turkish—often with additions—by several authors, such as the historian and poet Ashıq Çelebi (d. 979/1572), the literary man ʿAlāʾī ibn Muḥibbī al-Shīrāzī (fl. 10th/16th century), and the poet Vücudi Meḥmed Efendi (d. 1021/1612).[18] In their introductions, they each emphasize the need of sultans and governors for scholarly advice on moral perfection and governing improvements. Since most rulers at the time spoke Turkish, it was wise to provide them with a book in this language.[19] These translations mostly include commentaries and are important because they were sources of Ottoman *naṣīḥatname*s (advice letters). It should be stressed that through these translations al-Ghazālī became a dominant influence on these *naṣīḥatname*s. Beginning in the 10th/15th and 11th/16th centuries, subject matters such as moral principles, politics, and administration for sultans were revived in Ottoman intellectual

16 Özervarlı, "Arbitrating between al-Ghazālī and the Philosophers."

17 For other Turkish translations of *Ayyūhā l-walad* and mistaken attributions see Yazar, "Gazzâlî'nin XIII–XIX. Yüzyıllar Arasında," 103–15.

18 *Tercüme-i Tibr al-mesbūk*, MS Topkapı Sarayı Müzesi Kütüphanesi, Bağdad Köşkü 351 and MS Nuruosmaniye 3741; *Natīcat al-sulūk*, Istanbul University Library, Turkish Manuscripts 6943, 6949 and MS Süleymaniye Yasma Eser Kütüphanesi, Hüsrev Paşa 313; *Rawayiḥ al-sulūk*, Istanbul University Library, Turkish Manuscripts 3235.

19 For more translations of *Naṣīḥat al-mulūk* into Turkish and their copies see Yazar, "Gazzâlî'nin XIII–XIX. Yüzyıllar Arasında," 115–33.

circles. This happened within the frame of discussions on the compatibility of religion and philosophy. Here, Ghazalian views were widely referred to and considered a source of authority. In his annotated Turkish translation of *Naṣīḥat al-mulūk*, which was double the size of the original work, ʿAla'i updated earlier controversies and addressed the current situation of Ottoman society.[20] The rise of a distinctively Ottoman genre of *naṣīḥatnāme* under Ghazalian influence coincided with the development of universal sovereignty. By applying this literature of advice to the Ottoman context of governance, and focusing on improvement of reality rather than admiration of ideals, the authors tried to add to the legitimacy of the Ottoman power against the Safavid and Mamluk dynasties.[21] Their work can be compared with al-Ghazālī's role in legitimizing and supporting the Seljuq dynasty under the Abbasid caliphate. Similar influences of al-Ghazālī can be seen on other genres, such as the *Siyāsetname*, which addresses signs of decline within the state, and *Layiha*, a memorandum which articulated viewpoints regarding possible dangers to society. *Akhlāq* literature, however, represented a more theoretical base for this kind of counsel or advice in moral and social philosophy. *Akhlāq-i ʿAlāʾī* by Kınalızade Ali (d. 979/1572), for instance, though supposed to be a Turkish version of the genre in line with Persian works like *Akhlāq-i Nāṣiri* by Naṣīr al-Dīn Ṭūsī (d. 672/1274) and *Akhlāq-i Jalālī* by Jalāl al-Dīn Davānī (d. 908/1502), is influenced by *Iḥyāʾ* throughout its text, particularly in the long section on spiritual illnesses, which are not included in Ṭūsī's and Davānī's books.[22]

Al-Ghazālī's purely theological works, such as *al-Iqtiṣād fī l-iʿtiqād* (*The Balanced Book on What-To-Believe*), did not receive the same attention among Ottoman scholars. Authors of philosophical theology in the classical Ottoman period were more interested in the books of Aḍud al-Dīn al-Ījī (d. 746/1345), Saʿd al-Dīn al-Taftāzānī (d. 792/1390), and al-Sharīf al-Jurjānī (d. 816/1413), rather than al-Ghazālī. The former authors were more sophisticated and simply superseded al-Ghazālī's work. They included and combined later discussions and thus captured the Ottoman scholarly environment better than al-Ghazālī. Al-Ghazālī's short intellectual autobiography, however, *al-Munqidh min al-ḍalāl* (*The Deliverer from Error*) enjoyed some popularity, and was translated by Meḥmed Veliyuddin, Zeyrekzade Meḥmed Efendi, and İbrahim

20 See Yılmaz, *The Sultan and the Sultanate: Envisioning Rulership in the Age of Süleyman the Lawgiver, 1520–1566*, 100–101.

21 Howard, "Genre and Myth in the Ottoman Advice for Kings Literature," 139.

22 Kınalızade, *Akhlaḳ-i ʿAlaʾi*, 169–321.

Giridi (d. after 1185/1771).[23] Commentary translations of theological treatises such as *Iljām al-ʿawāmm min al-kalām* (*Restraining the Ordinary People from the Science of Kalam*) by Aḥmed Rushdi (d. after 1302/1885)[24] and *al-Durra al-fākhira fi kashf ʿulūm al-ākhira* (*The Precious Pearl Revealing Knowledge about the Afterlife*) by Muallim Ömer Ḳastamoni were also published.[25]

These examples of translations, commentaries and influences show that al-Ghazālī was an important influence on Ottoman scholars and that they were interested in the variety of his oeuvre. His books and treatises had rich materials for them to explore and discuss. For the Ottomans, beginning in the 15th century, from the time of Meḥmed II (reg. 1444–81), al-Ghazālī was not just an author of Islamic texts, but also a model for combining and synthesizing various kinds of Islamic knowledge. For this reason *Iḥyāʾ ʿulūm al-dīn* received a great deal of attention among Ottomans, and in addition to its translation and commentaries, was widely emulated. The Ottoman Empire aimed at building a social order from among multi-ethnic and multi-religious communities, and therefore Ottoman thinkers were more interested in moral values that could help integrate different groups and in practical solutions to resolve the problems of their society rather than theory. It is not surprising that *Naṣīḥat al-mulūk* was one of the most translated and most widely read books, not only among the *ʿulamāʾ*, but also by literary men and administrators.

II Conflicting Images of al-Ghazālī in the Modern Period

Following this general background about the place and authority of al-Ghazālī's works in Ottoman intellectual history, I will now discuss how he and his works became a focus, both detested and adored, of modern debates. An examination of widely-read journals and books in the late 19th and early 20th centuries will show that al-Ghazālī was indeed a focus-point of controversies among rival circles in the modern Ottoman period. For Mehmed Şemseddin [Günaltay] (1883–1961), a professor of history and Islamic studies at the Ottoman

23 *Terjüme-i munqiẕ*, dated 1136/1724, Köprülü Kütüphanesi, Mehmed Asım Bey, no. 143; *Tercüme al-Munqıẕ min al-żalāl*, dated 1167/1754, Emel Esin Library, no. 233; *Munqıẕu min al-żalāl tercümesi*, dated 1185/1771, Istanbul University Library, Turkish Manuscripts 2229. Another translation in the late period by Zihni and Meḥmed Efendi was printed in Istanbul (Maṭbaʿa-i Amire) in 1870 and 1872.

24 See Ömer, *Taʿyīn al-waẓāʾif fi ḥaqq al-mutashābihāt.*

25 Ömer, *Ahiret ḥalleri.* For a short list of some printed translations of al-Ghazālī's works mostly from the last three decades of the 19th century, see Günaydın, "Gazâlî Tercümeleri," 68–70.

Darülfünün , a modern higher educational institution, and later a politician in the republican period, al-Ghazālī was as destructive to Islamic culture as the Crusaders. In his major work on philosophical theology, *Felsefe-yi Ula* (*First Philosophy*), published in 1920, he claims that the Muslim philosophical movement that began with the efforts of al-Kindī (d. *c.* 250/865) and reached its peak through genius abilities of Avicenna (Ibn Sīnā, d. 428/1037), was "gravely punched by merciless and effective strokes of al-Ghazālī." As a consequence, Muʿtazilite theories that, according to Şemseddin relied on ancient philosophy, lost their value. After al-Ghazālī more traditional and mystical theories replaced them.[26]

In another work written during the early republican period, Şemseddin emphasizes the negative impact of Ghazalian thought on Islamic intellectual history even more forcefully. To him "it was highly indicative that just months before the meeting of the Council of Claremont in 1095, al-Ghazālī wrote a book against al-Fārābī and Avicenna that would turn off the light of philosophy and secular sciences in the Muslim world."[27] Moreover, al-Ghazālī opposed sciences in favor of religion, and following his ten years of intellectual crisis, he started to act like the head of an inquisition committee. In Şemseddin's opinion, at his death al-Ghazālī had indeed achieved his goal of expelling and banishing philosophy. He was so influential among the Ottomans that although they were officially Maturidite, the *madrasa* system in Istanbul and other cities surrendered to the Ashʿarite school up until the Ottoman Empire's last days. In his interpretation of al-Ghazālī, Şemseddin underlines two aspects of his thought: anti-rationalism and mysticism. It is no coincidence that these were the two main targets of the modernist Ottomans in his time. In Şemseddin's view, al-Ghazālī gained such a high stature among his successors that they were obliged to exhaust themselves in the labyrinths of Ashʿarite interpretations, or to be buried by subjective methods of Sufism. He laments that bright intellects such as Fakhr al-Dīn al-Rāzī (d. 606/1210), Sayf al-Dīn al-Āmidī (d. 631/1233), Saʿd al-Dīn al-Taftāzānī, and al-Sharīf al-Jurjānī could not extract themselves from the ruling anti-rationalist and mystifying establishment that was created by al-Ghazālī. Similarly, scholars such as Jalāl al-Dīn Rūmī (d. 672/1273), Ṣadr al-Dīn Qūnawī (d. 673/1274), Yahya al-Suhrawardī (d. 587/1191), and Badr al-Dīn al-Simāwī (d. 823/1420) could not escape the atmosphere of negative mystical thinking.[28] Therefore, for Şemseddin Günaltay, al-Ghazālī was to blame for numerous undesired directions that the Islamic intellectual

26 Şemseddin, *Felsefe-yi Ula*, 357.

27 Şemseddin, "İslam Dünyasının İnhitatı Sebebi Selçuk İstilası Mıdır?", 10.

28 Ibid., 10–12.

history took and the problems this caused. He, however, judges the post-classical period in Islamic intellectual history according to the conditions of his own age with modern expectations in his mind.[29]

Celal Nuri [İleri] (1882–1938), a modernist thinker, journalist, and politician in the late Ottoman and early republican periods, for his part admired Ibn Rushd (d. 595/1198) and emphasizes his great impact on some enlightened Western philosophers. He also blamed Ottoman scholars for achieving much less than their potential by following al-Ghazālī instead of Ibn Rushd.[30] His interpretation of Islamic intellectual history—an interpretation that we today would call incorrect—seems, like that of Şemseddin, influenced by the French scholar Ernest Renan (1823–92) and other Western orientalists.[31] Renan was best known for his *Averroes et l'averroisme* of 1852. The two modern Ottoman intellectuals Namık Kemal (1840–88) and Ali Ferruh (1865–1907) criticised Renan.[32] A third refutation of Renan's views by the Russian Tatar Muslim ʿAtaullah Bayezidov (1846–1911?) was also translated into Turkish.[33] However, not only modernists disapproved al-Ghazālī's views. For instance, Şeyhülislam Muṣṭafa Ṣabri (1869–1954), one of the late Grand Muftis and a traditionalist scholar who spent his life in exile in Egypt during the republican period, criticized al-Ghazālī for his non-Ashʿarite views, such as doubting knowledge through senses and relying too much on intuition.[34]

In contrast to these interpretations, there were also very positive remarks about al-Ghazālī's place in Islamic intellectual history, mostly from reformist Ottomans: Ali Suavi (1839–1878), an activist intellectual and member of the Young Ottomans, wrote a series of articles in *Ulum Gazetesi* (Journal of Sciences, 1869–70), defending al-Ghazālī against critics. Suavi published the journal during his Paris exile in a lithograph print of his handwriting. In the first part of a set of Ottoman Turkish articles titled *al-Radd ʿalā man radda ʿalā l-Ghazālī* (*Refutation of Those who Refuted al-Ghazālī*), Suavi gives a short biography of al-Ghazālī, drawing attention to Latin and other Western translations of his works, as well as a recent call by the French Association of Sciences to translate his theological books for a stipend of 5,000 Francs. Suavi argued that

29 On Şemseddin see Çetinkaya, *Türkiye'nin Modernleşmesi Sürecinde Şemseddin Günaltay*, 39ff.

30 See Nuri İleri, *Tarikh-i İstiḳbal*, 73–105.

31 On Celal Nuri İleri see Herzog, *Geschichte und Ideologie: Mehmed Murad und Celal Nuri*, 88ff.

32 See Kemal, *Renan Müdafaʿanamesi*, 2 ff.; İbnürreşad, *Teshhir-i ebaṭil*, 1ff.

33 Bayezidov, *Redd-i Renan*, 6 ff.

34 Ṣabri, *Mawqif al-ʿaql wa-l-ʿilm wa-l-ʿālam*, 1: 266–70. On Mustafa Sabri see Bein, "Ulema and Activism in the Late Ottoman Empire," 67–90.

critics of al-Ghazālī highlighted his so-called "destruction" of philosophy, but they did not comprehend the ways and aims of his effort. Suavi considered a link between these criticisms and Orientalist writings, and refers to recent efforts by European scholars who criticized al-Ghazālī of imitating earlier scholars, and presenting his work as an obstacle to philosophical activity and rational approaches in religious thought. Suavi accused Western Orientalists—without naming names—of misunderstanding the *Tahāfut*-debate and wrongly siding with Ibn Rushd.[35] Referring to the *Tahāfut* commentaries written by Hocazade and ʿAlā al-Dīn al-Ṭūsī during the reign of Meḥmed II, Suavi suggested that a synthesis of the approaches of al-Ghazālī and Ibn Rushd had already been achieved by early Ottoman scholars, and that therefore the dispute was resolved. He recommended that European scholars study al-Ghazālī's philosophical theology by examining five works of the *Tahāfut*-tradition: al-Ghazālī's, Ibn Rushd's response, as well as Hocazade's and al-Ṭūsī's works alongside Kemalpaşazade's commentary on Hocazade's work. However, it seems that Suavi made this statement without himself examining the content of the Ottoman *Tahāfut* commentaries, since they were written without knowledge of Ibn Rushd's refutation. As I demonstrated in my article in the first volume of this work, the Ottoman scholars engaged in "judging" al-Ghazālī's *Tahāfut* compared his views only with the previous Muslim philosophers and softened his language in the three main accusations of disbelief.[36]

Suavi himself refers to Ibn Rushd's *Tahāfut al-tahāfut*, and quotes a couple of short lines from the book, yet he does not question that the Ottoman scholars knew this work. Although there were indeed some Ottoman thinkers before him who examined and referred to the philosophical works of Ibn Rushd, they lived in the 11th/17th century, more than a century after Hocazade's and al-Ṭūsī's works alongside Kemalpaşazade. The famous bibliographer Katib Çelebi, for instance, seems to have seen Ibn Rushd's book and refers to it in his *Kashf al-ẓunūn*. He describes al-Ghazālī's *Tahāfut al-falāsifa* in detail and mentions at the end of his short entry on that work the refutation of Ibn Rushd, quoting the beginning and the end.[37] The Ottoman philosopher and translator Yanyavi Esad Efendi (d. 1143/1730), who was known as "the Third Teacher" (*al-muʿallim al-thālith*) among the Ottomans, also referred to Ibn Rushd.[38]

35 Suavi, "al-Radd ʿalā man radda ʿalā l-Ghazālī," 346–47.

36 Cf. Özervarlı, "Arbitrating between al-Ghazālī and the Philosophers."

37 Çelebi, *Kashf al-ẓunūn*, 1:512–13.

38 Yanyavi, *al-Taʿlīm al-thālith*, MS Istanbul, Rağıb Paşa Kütüphanesi 824, fol. 2a. For Yanyavi's references to Ibn Rushd also see Özervarlı, "Yanyalı Esad Efendi's Works on Philosophical Texts as Part of the Ottoman Translation Movement in the Early Eighteenth Century."

However, references to Ibn Rushd and acknowledgments of him were not at all frequent among the Ottomans.[39] Therefore, it is not surprising to see Suavi's note about the existence of so many copies of al-Ghazālī's *Tahāfut al-falāsifa*, and Ottoman commentaries on his text, while being not able to find more than one copy of Ibn Rushd's *Tahāfut al-tahāfut* at the Şehid Ali Paşa Library in the Şehzadebaşı neighbourhood of Istanbul, a manuscript that is now at the library of the Süleymaniye *külliye*.[40]

After introducing Ibn Rushd and al-Ghazālī, Suavi explains the reasons why he supported the latter and why he rejected the arguments of Muslim philosophers in metaphysics. He compares the Muslim *falāsifa*'s claim of epistemological certainty in metaphysics to that of his contemporary, the German scientist Ludwig Büchner (1824–1899) about the eternality of matter. According to Suavi, al-Ghazālī accepted that demonstrative certainty exists in mathematical as well as the natural sciences and logic yet he rejected such certainty in the field of metaphysics, which to him is based on mere hypotheses and assumptions. Therefore, he argues, since al-Ghazālī did not object to philosophy in general and only criticized its hypothetical parts, he cannot be blamed for the decline of philosophical reasoning in Islam and for the spread of blind imitation (*taqlīd*). Suavi refers to al-Ghazālī's skeptical rationalism by quoting from the end of *Mīzān al-ʿamal* (*The Scales of* Action) on the value of doubt and the use of reason to save oneself from confusion.[41] Moreover, Suavi gives a short summary of al-Ghazālī's *Tahāfut* at the end of his article and points out that despite his claim that the *falāsifa* had fallen into apostasy on three questions, this accusation was softened by later commentators. The Ottoman scholar ʿAlāʾ al-Dīn Ṭūsī, for instance, in his re-working of the *Tahāfut* explained al-Ghazālī's first claim of apostasy due to the *falāsifa's* positions of the world's pre-eternality of the world with important references to other previous scholars, such as Fakhr al-Dīn al-Rāzī. The second issue regarding the position of God's knowledge of particulars was, according to Suavi, solved by Jalāl al-Dīn Davānī in his *Sharḥ al-ʿaqāʾid al-ʿAḍudiyya* (*Commentary on the Creed of ʿAḍud al-Dīn al-Ījī*). Finally, the third view about the spiritual resurrection and the denial of bodily pleasures, al-Ghazālī attributed in his book *Mīzān al-ʿamal* to both the Sufis and the *falāsifa*. Since Sufi opinions, Suavi argues, were generally approved by al-Ghazālī especially in *al-Munqidh*, a partial autobiography and one of his latest books, this remark should be regarded as a sign of later

39 Özervarlı, "Arbitrating between al-Ghazālī and the Philosophers."

40 Suavi, "al-Radd ʿalā man radda ʿalā l-Ghazālī," 350.

41 Ibid., 353–55.

flexibility by him on the issue of bodily resurrection.[42] As a member of the Young Ottoman movement of intellectuals, Ali Suavi was both interested in Western ideas as well as critical of them.[43] With others from this group, he wanted to reform Islamic thought, enable it to withstand modern challenges, and crate a harmonic synthesis between the new and the old. This is why he greatly esteemed and valued al-Ghazālī's revitalization efforts of Muslim scholarly disciplines. Still, he considered Ibn Rushd more a Western-type philosopher with no decisive connection to the Islamic world. By defending the Ghazalian approach, Suavi aimed at rejecting more critical comments on him by both Orientalist authors and their Ottoman followers.

Another late Ottoman and early Republican scholar, Aksekili Aḥmed Ḥamdi (also: Aḥmed Ḥamdi Akseki, 1887–1951)[44] defended al-Ghazālī's Sufi approach in particular against formal theological positions. In a series of articles in the journal *Maḥfil* where he presented the position of Sufis'—and more specifically that of al-Ghazālī's—on the soul (*rūḥ*), Ḥamdi emphasized the differences between Sufi interpretations and positions of the theologians and philosophers. He presents the definition of soul according to Sufis as an invisible intellect of divine grace (*latife-i mudrike-i rabbāniyye*), manifested in the body. Ḥamdi argued that al-Ghazālī had explained his ideas on the soul—to those who have deep knowledge and the capacity to understand—in most of his works, and especially in *al-Maḍnūn bihī ʿalā ghayri ahlihī* (*The Book to Be Withheld from Those For Whom it is Not Written*) and *al-Maḍnūn al-saghir* (*The Shorter Book to Be Withheld*). These two short texts became available in print in a collection of works by al-Ghazālī edited by Muṣṭafā Muḥammad al-Qashīshah and published in Cairo in 1303/1886 and. The collection was reprinted 1309/1891 by Aḥmad al-Bābī al-Ḥalabī.

Following a general introduction, Ḥamdi presents al-Ghazālī's main points on the soul, starting with his interpretations of Qur'anic verses 32:9 and 17:85, his metaphoric explanations of the soul as a mirror reflecting sunlight on an object, and his rejection of the soul as a part of the divine existence. In addition, Ḥamdi finds al-Ghazālī's opinion about the temporal origination (*ḥudūth*) of the soul within the early stage of the human embryo interesting and relevant to current biological theories. He regards this opinion as an example and

---

42 Ibid., 366–67.

43 On the members and views of the Young Ottomans and Ali Suavi, see Mardin, *The Genesis of Young Ottoman Thought*, 10–80 and 360–84.

44 On the life and works of Ḥamdi see Ertan, *Ahmet Hamdi Akseki*.

evidence of the harmony between Islamic philosophical thought and modern science.[45]

In the articles that followed, Ḥamdi focused on al-Ghazālī's concept of substance, describing the soul as a substance rather than an accident due to its independence and being beyond time and space. He points out that, according to al-Ghazālī, the high qualities of the soul do not make it identical to a divine reality. Its existence is dependent on God, whereas God exists with no dependency on anything external to Him. According to Ḥamdi, al-Ghazālī's emphasis on the difference between the two existences is related to avoiding any possible connection with incarnation and unification (*ḥulūl* and *ittiḥād*) of humans with God. However, Ḥamdi acknowledges that al-Ghazālī's clarifications only helps to understand the reflected part of the soul and not its reality. The soul's true reality (*ṣūret-i ḥaḳiḳiyye*) is beyond human rational capacity and can only be comprehended by intuition. Al-Ghazālī probably reached this understanding through his intuitional experiences, Ḥamdi suggests, but it is hard for anyone to explain that kind of knowledge through a terminology reflecting the physical senses.[46]

In another comparison, Ḥamdi suggested a similarity between al-Ghazālī's and Ibn 'Arabī's views on the determination and limitation of soul and body, and discussed other questions regarding the soul, such as its continuity and eternality, changeability and variability, and divisibility and multiplicity. Despite his admiration for al-Ghazālī's approach, Ḥamdi at the end admits that Ghazalian explanations do not solve all the existing problems regarding this issue. For instance, they do not provide certainty about the true nature and the essence of the soul and they do not fully explain the relation between soul and body. The lack of full clarification about these questions, however, is not due to the impossibility of perception but comes mainly from the human tendency to expect to understand in logical and rational ways.[47]

During the time that Ḥamdi published his articles on al-Ghazālī's theory of soul in the journal *Maḥfil*, a debate erupted between him and the editorial board of the journal. The editors added a short note at the beginning of the fourth part of his series of articles saying that the text *al-Maḍnūn bihī 'alā ghayri ahlihī*, which is referenced by Ḥamdi and which he attributed to al-Ghazālī, was actually not by him. The editors refer in their notes to well-known scholars such as Ibn al-Ṣalāḥ al-Shahrazūrī (d. 643/1245) and Tāj al-Dīn

45 Ḥamdi, "Ṣufiye-i Kiram Hażaratının Ruh Ḥakkındaki Tarz-ı Telakkileri," 44–45; Ḥamdi, "Ṣufiye-i Kiram Hażaratının Ruh Ḥakkındaki Tarz-ı Telakkileri," 60–62.

46 Ḥamdi, "Gazzali'nin Ruḥ Ḥakkındaki Telakkiyatı," 96–99.

47 Ibid., 99; Ḥamdi, "Gazzali'nin Ruḥ Ḥakkındaki Telakkiyatı," 133–34.

al-Subkī's (d. 771/1370) and their judgment of its lack of authenticity.[48] Most probably they relied on al-Subkī's entry of al-Ghazali in his al-*Tabaqāt al-Shafiʿiyya*, where he quotes Ibn al-Ṣalāḥ about the impossibility of the attribution of the book to al-Ghazālī. Al-Subkī agrees with Ibn al-Ṣalāḥ that the text of *al-Maḍnūn* teaches the eternality of the world, denies divine knowledge of the particulars, and excludes attributes of God, and that it therefore cannot be a work of al-Ghazali given that he himself accused others of apostasy because of such views.[49] However from this content description of al-Subkī, it seems clear that the text Ibn al-Ṣalāḥ and he saw was different from the two common versions of the *Maḍnūn*, which were read and discussed by the Ottomans. The existing manuscripts of the *Maḍnūns* in Ottoman Turkish libraries i.e. *al-Maḍnūn bihī ʿalā ghayri ahlihī* and *al-Maḍnūn al-saghīr*,[50] match the earliest Cairo editions. Until 2004, these were the only known texts of Ghazalian works bearing the title "*al-Maḍnūn*."[51] Another piece of evidence is Katib Çelebi's entry on *al-Maḍnūn bihī ʿalā ghayri ahlihī* in his *Kashf al-ẓunūn*, where he first cites the views of Ibn al-Ṣalāḥ and al-Subkī about the book, and then quotes the beginning and a brief description of the book. The text here also corresponds with the printed text of the Cairo editions.[52]

The recent discovery of another text titled "*al-Maḍnūn bihī ʿalā ghayri ahlihī*" by Nasrollah Pourjavady,[53] and its critical edition by Afifi al-Akiti as a part of his doctoral dissertation[54] strengthens the existence of different texts attributed to al-Ghazālī under the same title and the possibility that Ibn al-Ṣalāḥ and al-Subkī saw a version, that scholars of later centuries had no access to. The fact that Ibn Rushd refers to *al-Maḍnūn bihī ʿalā ghayri ahlihī* as one of al-Ghazali's books suggests the existence of authentic versions of texts bearing this title.[55] However, whether the text that Ibn al-Ṣalāḥ and al-Subkī saw was the same that Pourjavady printed and al-Akiti called "Major *Maḍnūn*" requires

48 Ḥamdi, "Gazzali'nin Ruḥ Ḥakkındaki Telakkiyatı," 118, fn. 1.

49 al-Subkī, *Ṭabaqāt al-shāfiʿiyya al-kubrā*, 6:257.

50 For some copies of the two more known versions of the *Maḍnūns* see MS Istanbul, Süleymaniye Yazma Eser Kütüphanesi, Ayasofya, 2075, 4810; Reisülküttab, 1198; Şehid Ali Paşa, 1190, 2825.

51 For the bibliographic details of the *Maḍnūns* published in Cairo see bibliography. These two texts are also translated into Turkish by Dursun Sabit Ünal and published in the volume *İki Madnun*.

52 See Katib Çelebi, *Kashf al-ẓunūn*, 2:1713.

53 See Pourjavady (ed.), *Majmūʿah-yi falsafī-yi Marāgha / A Philosophical Anthology from Maragha*, 1–62.

54 See the second volume of al-Akiti, "The *Maḍnūn* of al-Ghazalī."

55 Ibn Rushd, *al-Kashf ʿan manāhij al-adilla fī ʿaqāʾid al-milla*, 151.

further materials and comparisons. Late Ottomans discussed the authenticity of the book without having access to the version published in 2004. Yet this might have been the source of Ibn al-Ṣalāḥ and al-Subkī in their denial of its authenticity.

In the next article of the series, Ḥamdi responded to the editors with a long footnote, where he expressed his confusion about the editorial statement on the lack of authenticity of the source. He argues that the source of his articles was not *al-Maḍnūn* alone, but several works of al-Ghazālī of which *al-Maḍnūn* was just one. In the first part of the article, for instance, Ḥamdi claimed, he had pointed out that al-Ghazālī dealt with the issue of the soul in a number of books, yet his most detailed treatment was in *al-Maḍnūn* and *al-Maḍnūn al-ṣaghīr*. He invited the editors to reread the first part of his series of articles and pointed out that the editorial board was wrong to think that there was only one text called *al-Maḍnūn*. He lists three titles for the *Maḍnūn* corpus: (1) *al-Maḍnūn bihī ʿalā ghayri ahlihī* or *al-Maḍnūn al-kabīr*, (2) *al-Maḍnūn al-ṣaghīr* or *al-Ajwiba al-Ghazāliyya fī l-masāʾil al-ukhrawiyya* (*Ghazalian Answers to Questions on the Hereafter*), and (3) *al-Maḍnūn bihī ʿalā ahlihī*. He asks which *al-Maḍnūn* do Ibn al-Ṣalāḥ al-Shahrazūrī and al-Subki rejected to be al-Ghazālī's? Ḥamdi expects that the editors had to have a reason for accepting the views of the cited authorities on *al-Maḍnūn*. Relying on mere statements of others to reject the authenticity of a work, he suggests, was not worthy of scholarly attention.[56]

On behalf of the editorial board, a certain Hafız İbrahim carried on the debate by writing a separate article on the question of the authenticity of the several *Maḍnūns*.[57] In the introduction, he emphasizes that evaluations of al-Ghazālī's works had a practical importance because of his remarkable influence, and that this was the reason why the editorial board called attention to the passages by Ibn al-Ṣalāḥ and al-Subkī. İbrahim however, relying mainly on Katib Çelebi's quotes from the book, thought that the text of Ibn al-Ṣalāḥ and al-Subkī was the same text of *al-Maḍnūn bihī ʿalā ghayri ahlihī* that became available through the Cairo prints. As a result, he finds it difficult to validate Subki's claim that, "it clearly includes the pre-eternality of the world (*wa qad ishtamala ʿalā l-taṣrīḥ bi-qidam al-ʿālam*) in *al-Maḍnūn bihī ʿalā ghayri ahlihī*. He rather suggests that Ibn al-Ṣalāḥ and al-Subkī's understanding might be related to al-Ghazālī's diplomatic language (*idare-i kelam*) in reporting the teachings of the *falāsifa*.[58] İbrahim was, of course, not aware of another

56 Ḥamdi, "Gazzali'nin Ruḥ Ḥakkındaki Telakkiyatı,", 134–35.

57 İbrahim, "İmam Gazzali ve el-Mażnun Kitapları," 10:164–65.

58 Ibid. 165.

Maḍnūn-text and tried hard to reconcile al-Subki's words with the existing printed version of *al-Maḍnūn bihī ʿalā ghayri ahlihī*. In those, one does not find clear expressions of the pre-eternality of the world. By way of additional evidence, İbrahim argues that the text printed right after *al-Maḍnūn bihī ʿalā ghayri ahlihī*, namely *al-Maḍnūn al-ṣaghīr*, is equally unauthentic. İbrahim understands that this work is also known as *al-Nafkh al-rūh wa-l-taswiya* (*Breathing of the Spirit and the Shaping*) and he points to the fact that the *Iḥyāʾ*-commentator al-Murtaḍa al-Zabīdī (d. 1205/1791) listed it among the books that were not authored by al-Ghazālī,[59] and therefore should be considered unauthentic. İbrahim also argues that the question-and-answer-format of the *al-Maḍnūn al-ṣaghīr* provides yet another reason to doubt its attribution to al-Ghazālī.[60]

Hafız İbrahim then focuses on the teaching of the soul in *al-Maḍnūn al-ṣaghīr* and argues that the discussion there does not correspond with other works of al-Ghazālī. In the related section of the *Iḥyāʾ*, he points out that the nature of soul is not discussed. Instead, the book only discusses the soul's attributes and states. Finally, İbrahim quotes the two following passages—the first from the *Iḥyāʾ* and the second from *al-Maḍnūn al-ṣaghīr*—suggesting that both cannot come from one and the same author:

> The essence [of the soul] (…) is something that the Prophet, peace be upon him, did not talk about, and therefore no one else should talk about it.[61]
>
> This is the question on the mystery of the soul (*sirr al-rūḥ*) and the Prophet, peace be upon him, was not permitted to divulge it to those who are not eligible. If you are, however, eligible of it, listen and know that the soul is not a body and that….[62]

But the exchange does not end here. Ahmed Ḥamdi again responded to the points made by Hafız İbrahim on behalf of the editorial board in the form of a longer and highly polemical article in the twelfth issue of *Maḥfil*.[63] At the beginning he stresses that the real intention of İbrahim and the editors was not to question the authenticity of *al-Maḍnūn*, but rather to oppose the content of

59 al-Zabīdī, *Itḥāf al-sāda*, 1:44.
60 İbrahim, "İmam Gazzali ve el-Mażnun Kitapları," 165.
61 al-Ghazālī, *Iḥyāʾ ʿulūm al-dīn*, 8:1350.
62 al-Ghazālī, *al-Maḍnūn al-ṣaghīr*, 4. Cf. İbrahim, "İmam Gazzali ve el-Mażnun Kitabları," 165.
63 Ḥamdi, "İmam Gazzali ve el-Mażnun Kitabları," 12: 204–10.

the book and especially the theory of the unity of existence (*vaḥdet-i vücud*). The editors, he argues, thought that the simple rejections of *al-Maḍnūn* would be enough to disassociate al-Ghazālī with the idea of the unity of existence. Therefore their main objective was not the clarification of whether they were his books or not, but sidelining or rejecting them.

Following this brief introduction, Ḥamdi lists arguments presented by the editors and discusses their validity. He emphasizes that his main source in the articles on al-Ghazālī's views on the soul was *al-Maḍnūn al-saghīr*. Therefore, the editors should have demonstrated that the content of the text regarding the soul was in contradiction with al-Ghazālī's views in his other works. However, they instead underlined remarks of some earlier scholars about *al-Maḍnūn bihī ʿalā ghayri ahlihī*, which, in fact, take only a minor place in Ḥamdi's previous articles. Ḥamdi argues that the editors' main evidence regarding the forgery of the texts is the passage from al-Subkī about the existence of heretic views in *al-Maḍnūn*. However they do not verify the claim with their own inquiries into the textual evidence from al-Ghazālī's works. A fair examination of the longer *al-Maḍnūn* without an ardent theological approach, Ḥamdi goes on, would show that there al-Ghazālī does not express the pre-eternality of the world. In fact, al-Ghazālī did not intend to write *al-Maḍnūn* for general readers, but rather attempted to demonstrate certain truths to highly educated people of interest, and keep those who are not qualified away from such ideas. This is quite clear even from its title. In Ḥamdi's view, al-Ghazālī accepted that truths were multi-levelled and people should have access to knowledge according o their level.

Responding to the editor's reference to al-Subkī, Ḥamdi quotes other scholars, such as Ibn Khallikān (d. 681/1282) and ʿAbd al-Qādir al-ʿAydarūs (d. 1038/1628), who accepted the book as being among the authentic works of al-Ghazālī.[64] It is obvious, he affirms, that when al-Ghazālī's authorship of many of his books of similar contents, like *Mishkāt al-anwār* (*The Niche of Lights*), *Kitāb al-Arbaʿīn* (*The Book of Forty*), *Jawāhir al-Qurʾān* (*Jewels of the Qurʾān*) is certain, it would be illogical to express doubts about the *Maḍnūns*. Besides, Ḥamdi also discusses the term "*madsūs*" ("deceit" or "interpolated") used by al-Zabīdī, the commentator of *Iḥyāʾ* for *al-Maḍnūn al-ṣaghīr*, and argues that the term was usually employed by commentators to avoid criticism and gossip from common people toward scholars. He gives the example of ʿAbd al-Wahhāb al-Shaʿrānī (d. 973/1565), one of the commentators on Ibn al-ʿArabī, who used the same term for some of the latter's authentic works when it was impossible to defend their literal wording. In circumstances when

---

64 Cf. Ibn Khallikān, *Wafayāt al-aʿyān*, 4:218; al-ʿAydarūs, *Taʿrīf al-aḥyāʾ bi faḍāʾil al-Iḥyāʾ*, 9.

even the *Iḥyāʾ* was decreed to be burnt and was nicknamed *iḥyāʾ insilākh ʿan al-dīn*, "the revival of abandoning religion" and when al-Ghazālī had to defend himself against accusations of apostasy by writing his *Faysal al-tafriqa bayna al-Islām wa al-zandaqa* (*The Decisive Criterion for Distinguishing Islam from Clandestine Unbelief*), it was hard to fully defend al-Ghazālī's teachings publicly. Thus, it became necessary for the *Iḥyāʾ* commentator al-Zabīdī to deny the authenticity of *al-Maḍnūn al-ṣaghīr* (i.e. *Kitāb al-nafkh wa-l-rūḥ wa-l-taswiya*) which was directed against the common approach of the theologians, and to label it problematic. Ḥamdi reminds his readers that even *al-Mankhūl min ta'liqāt al-usūl* (*The Sifted among the Notes on the Methods of Jurisprudence*) was likewise denied as al-Ghazālī's work by other authorities; meaning that these kinds of statements from scholars regarding the authenticity of works cannot be relied upon.

Al-Ghazālī cannot be put under one label of scholarship, Ḥamdi argues, since there were multi-dimensional aspects of him: a theologian al-Ghazālī, a philosopher al-Ghazālī, a mystic al-Ghazālī, a jurist al-Ghazālī etc. His writings differ according to his various roles. It would be impossible, for instance, to have no difference between the writings of the philosopher al-Ghazālī and the jurist or even the theologian. The aim of theology was to protect the faith of common people from confusion that was caused by innovators, however al-Ghazālī aimed to go beyond the discourse of theologians and dealt with ontological questions. Therefore, it is only natural to see a difference between al-Ghazālī's words in the *Iḥyāʾ*, and his approach in the *Mishkāt*, *Jawāhir* or the *Maḍnūn*. The apparent contradiction, Ḥamdi points out, comes from addressing different people in accordance with their intellectual level. In *Iḥyāʾ* al-Ghazālī addressed more common people and did not touch on the essence of soul, which is a part of deeper spiritual knowledge. Here, he rather focused on moral purification and perfection of heart. However, in *al-Maḍnūn*, *Mishkāt*, *Jawāhir*, and *al-Arbaʿīn* he addressed only to those who have capacity to perceive hidden knowledge and truths, and therefore al-Ghazālī did not hesitate to use a mystical or philosophical terminology.

In a last step, Ḥamdi points out how the editors left the quotation from *Iḥyāʾ* incomplete. He argues that al-Ghazālī in fact explained the reason why he wouldn't discuss the essence of soul in the *Iḥyāʾ* in the previous and subsequent sentences of the passage, which the editors did not mention. The whole quoted passage is written to highlight the purpose of omitting elaborations on the essence of soul, expressing that the *Iḥyāʾ* was not the appropriate place to delve into the secrets of the issue.[65] By failing to reproduce the middle and last

65 Cf. al-Ghazālī, *Iḥyāʾ ʿulūm al-dīn*, 8:1350.

sentences of the passage, the editors seemed to conceal the perspective of al-Ghazālī from the readers. This way of informing, Ḥamdi suggests, can only be regarded as sophistry (*mughālaṭā*) by the experts of argumentation. In short, he concludes, there is no difference between al-Ghazālī's text in the *Iḥyā*ʾ, and his approach in the smaller *Maḍnūn*. The difference is in the distinction and particularity of the content of the two books. In support of this argument, he recalls another passage from the *Mishkāt*:

> Moreover, not every mystery is to be revealed or divulged; not every truth is to be laid bare or made plain, but "Noble hearts seal mysteries like the tomb." Or, as one of those who know has said: "To divulge the secret of the Godhead is to deny God." Or, as the Prophet has said: "There is a knowledge like the form of a hidden thing, known to none save those who know God." If then these speak of that secret, only the children of ignorance will contradict them. And howsoever many these ignorants be, the mysteries must from the gaze of sinners be kept inviolate. But I believe that your heart has been opened by the light and your consciousness purged of the darkness of ignorance. I will, therefore, not be so niggardly as to deny your direction to these glorious truths in all their fineness and all their divineness; for the wrong done in keeping wisdom from her children is not less than that of yielding her to those who are strangers to her.[66]

In this passage, Ḥamdi points out, al-Ghazālī clearly admits the need to hide some truths from certain unqualified readers and not show his higher books to them. Ḥamdi also refers to *Jawāhir al-Qur'ān* for a similar account.[67] Underlining these passages Ḥamdi tries to demonstrate the harmony between various texts of al-Ghazālī, and their correspondence to the *Maḍnūn* in order to show their authenticity. In his view, there is no strong evidence to refute or weaken the attribution of the two *Maḍnūn* texts to al-Ghazālī. The author, who wrote the *Mishkāt* and *Jawāhir*, would also write the smaller *Maḍnūn*, as a part of his upper level texts that shouldn't be presented to unqualified readers.[68] As for the number of the *Maḍnūn texts* attributed to al-Ghazālī, Ḥamdi explains that he used to think that there were three *Maḍnūns*, because earlier he had seen a text claimed to be a different *Maḍnūn*, but after his examination and

66 al-Ghazālī, *Mishkāt al-anwār*, 116–18. The English translation is from Gairdner, *Al-Ghazzālī's Mishkāt al-anwār*, 44.

67 Cf. al-Ghazālī, *Jawāhir al-Qur'ān*, 84–85.

68 Ḥamdi, "İmam Ghazzali ve el-Mażnun Kitabları," 12:208.

comparison, he now realized that it was almost the same text as the *al-Maḍnūn al-ṣaghīr*. Moreover, although it is written in the form of questions and answers, each passage starts with personal pronouns of the first and second persons instead of any use of the third person. Therefore, he assures that the text itself does not imply that it was written by a third person, as the editors argued in their comment.[69]

The debate shows that quite detailed and sophisticated discussions about the authenticity of al-Ghazālī's books and in particular of *al-Maḍnūn* continued into the late Ottoman period. In the earlier Ottoman period, those discussions usually happened in commentaries on or in translations of al-Ghazālī's works, many of which have not yet been studied. Now, in the modern period it happened in periodicals and journals. As an admirer of al-Ghazālī's mystical thought and an expert of his views on soul, Aḥmed Ḥamdi seems to be convinced by strong textual arguments about the authenticity of both the larger and smaller *Maḍnūn* treatises known to the public. On the other hand, Hafiz İbrahim, on behalf of the editorial of the journal *Maḥfil*, relied on historical criticism of the treatises and did not dare to trust in an already obscured text. The comment of Ibn al-Ṣalāḥ and al-Subkī were thus at the center of the debate. Both scholars based their arguments on the only available *Maḍnūn* texts and none of them was discussing the possible disappearance of other versions of the *Maḍnūns* in their time, and the probable availability of different copies to Ibn al-Ṣalāḥ and al-Subkī. Ahmed Ḥamdi was sure about the authenticity of the existent two versions of the *Maḍnūns* and therefore suggested not taking al-Subkī's criticism seriously. To him the content of the texts was in harmony with al-Ghazālī's other writings. Ḥamdi could not conceptualize that al-Subkī was talking about another version of *al-Maḍnūn*. Hafiz Ibrahim, however, paid great attention to al-Subkī's comment and preferred to follow his opinion as an earlier authority in Islamic intellectual history. He, too, could not imagine Subkī's possible reference to another different text. The existence of so many copies of *al-Maḍnūn bihī ʿala ghayr ahlihī* as well as *al-Maḍnūn al-saghīr* (also known as *Kitab al-Nafkh wa-l-rūḥ wall-taswiya* and *al-As'ila wa-l-ajwiba*) in Ottoman libraries under the name of al-Ghazālī directed them to focus only on those two texts. Although modern studies on Ghazalian texts by W. Montgomery Watt, Maurice Bouyges, Abd al-Rahman Badawī, H. Lazarus Yafeh, and George F. Hourani provided different answers about the *Maḍnūn's* attribution to al-Ghazālī, the above two texts have a certain reception in Muslim scholarship. In addition, Nasrollah Pourjavady's discovery of another text, which Afifi al-Akiti refers to as the "Major *Maḍnūn*" in his recent doctoral

69 Ibid., 12:209.

dissertation, brings new dimensions to the obviously vexed question of the *Maḍnūn*'s authenticity.[70]

To return to Ottoman scholars and their perspectives on al-Ghazālī, Mehmed Ali Ayni (1869–1945), a professor at Darülfünun and a devotee of mystical philosophy in the late Ottoman Empire, was another scholar interested in him. He translated Carra de Vaux's monograph on al-Ghazālī, published in Paris in 1902, with some changes and additions, into Ottoman Turkish. In this book Ayni mainly praises al-Ghazālī's critical approach and polemical proficiency. He underlines al-Ghazālī's efforts to examine philosophical views and texts, and emphasizes that he did not reject philosophical systems in totality, but attempted to question certain specific views. He assures that, if read carefully, it would be possible to realize that al-Ghazālī understood Avicenna's philosophy quite well. Praising his philosophical knowledge and thinking, Ayni stresses that al-Ghazālī's most interesting texts, like the *Tahāfut*, are not commonly found among the writings of Muslim philosophers and theologians.[71]

The two conflicting images of al-Ghazālī discussed so far amount to an almost complete opposition to or an equally complete appreciation for him. There are, however, cases where al-Ghazālī was evaluated in comparison with Muslim philosophers and Ibn Rushd. Şeyhülislam Musa Kazım (1858–1920), a Grand Mufti with a reformist approach—interestingly named after a Shiite imam—reviewed some questions raised in *Tahāfut* in a series of articles and later published his review as a treatise in his *Kulliyāt*.[72] In his discussion on the pre-eternity of the world, Musa Kazım highlights the similarities of argumentation between al-Ghazālī and Ibn Rushd and suggests that if both texts were examined carefully, especially on the precedence of divine existence, one would realize the lack of a large gap between the two in their ontology.[73] In Kazim's opinion, Ibn Rushd's accusation that al-Ghazālī misunderstands the views and the opinions of the *falāsifa* is not acceptable. Rather al-Ghazālī commanded a good knowledge of philosophical details on the topics. He tried to rewrite the views of the philosophers for polemical and dialectical reasons in religious and metaphysical matters without any alteration of ideas. In fact, al-Ghazālī's efforts helped Ibn Rushd to clarify some details of the arguments of the philosophers. On the other hand, Kazım points out that al-Ghazālī identified some of the views of the peripatetic philosophers with those of the "materialists" (*dahriyyūn*). For instance, despite his clarification at the

---

70 al-Akiti, "*The Maḍnūn of al-Ghazālī*," idem, "The Good, the Bad, and the Ugly of Falsafa."

71 Ayni, *Huccetülislam İmam Gazzali*, 3 ff. For further details on Ayni's thought see Akdemir, *Mehmed Ali Ayni'nin Düşünce Dünyası*, 31ff.

72 See Kazım, "İbn Rüshd'ün Meslek-i Felsefisi ve İmam Gazzali," 139–96.

73 Ibid., 150.

beginning of the third chapter of the *Tahāfut* that only materialists opposed God's being the originator (*sāniʿ*) of the world, throughout the chapter he criticizes the Muslim philosophers for playing some linguistic games about divine actions, and thus creating problems in relation to God's act of generating the universe. This, Kazım proposes, is like blaming people for a crime they have not committed. The peripatetic philosophers do not deny God's actions as generator. They see God as the primary and willing actor and they prove it through rational methods.[74]

Nevertheless, in the issue of resurrection al-Ghazālī did not mix the views of the Muslim philosophers with those of the *dahrīs*, Kazım verifies, and honestly acknowledges the *falāsifa*'s acceptance of the Hereafter. The only dispute that took place was on the form of resurrection. In Kazım's view, al-Ghazālī's arguments concerning the resurrection of body, especially his connecting it to divine power, is not strong. Many Muslim thinkers tried to balance or combine God's power with divine wisdom. In fact, the philosophers' reservations about bodily resurrection are related to beliefs in some religions that demand a resurrection of the exact same form of the buried body. However, human bodies have their physical conditions designed for this world and if they remained in the same form they would not be able to resist an eternal fire or absorb extraordinary rewards of paradise. Thus, in Islamic belief, bodies will have different structures and conditions in the Hereafter. As a result, Kazım maintains, al-Ghazālī's satisfaction of any kind of "body" in resurrection, different from the this-worldly one, is in fact sufficient for the philosophers to compromise with him, since their concern was having the same body in the two worlds[75]

Kazım, in conclusion, argues that Ibn Rushd, by living in Spain and having access to some Jewish, Christian, Ancient Greek, and Latin sources, had some advantage compared to other thinkers. But despite some of his exaggerations and mistranslations of some sources in the East, al-Ghazālī, too, was quite adequate in philosophical discussions—contrary to Ibn Rushd's criticism of him. However, there are always disputes among thinkers, and disagreements within philosophical schools. The disputes between individual philosophers of each school may be more significant than those between al-Ghazālī and some of these schools. Therefore, al-Ghazālī's criticisms of Muslim or other philosophers, in Kazım's opinion, should not be regarded as a move for destruction of philosophy.[76]

---

74 Ibid., 161–63.

75 Ibid., 175, 190–91.

76 Ibid., 195–96. On other aspects of Kazım see Reinhart, "Musa Kazim: from *ʿilm* to Polemics," 281–306.

In other journals, İzmirli İsmail Ḥakkı (1868–1946), a prominent figure in revitalizing theology and philosophy, also devoted long sections to al-Ghazālī in series of articles on Islamic philosophical movements in various journals. For instance, he wrote a continuous series of short articles on al-Ghazālī in a non-polemical way in the official journal of the Office of Şeyhulislam, *Ceride-i İlmiyye*, as a first part of a series on "Islamic Scholars and Thinkers."[77] In the fifth part of his later articles in the Journal of Theology Faculty at the *Darülfünun*, he also describes al-Ghazālī's place in the history of Muslim philosophy, and focuses on his criticism of the Peripatetic tradition.[78] Ḥakkı divides al-Ghazālī's intellectual life into three periods: the first when he dealt with theology and philosophy, the second when he focused on mysticism, and the last when he became interested in *hadīth* but could not be an expert because of a limited time before his death.[79] In his late period he studied in Tūs the two famous *ḥadīth* collections by al-Bukhārī and Muslim.[80] Ḥakkı suggests that the reasons for al-Ghazālī's dissatisfaction with the discourse of the theologians in his early career mainly came from their weak methods of argumentation, which did not satisfy those who rely only on necessary and self-evident axiomatic knowledge.[81] He refers to al-Juwayni as the source of Ghazalian theology, and Avicenna as the source of his philosophy. Al-Ghazālī relied on Avicenna in many regards, he says, to a point that he repeated his sentences with no changes. However, al-Ghazālī discussed reason as a faculty in more detail compared to Avicenna, and treated mysticism as a separate field. At the same time, he occasionally used other philosophical sources such as Ikhwān al-ṣafā', Abū Ḥayyān al-Tawḥīdī, and others like them.[82]

Putting al-Ghazālī in the fourth period of Islamic philosophy, Ḥakkı examines his criticism of Muslim philosophers through the *Tahāfut* debate. He argues that al-Ghazālī's efforts were a philosophical demonstration of the inadequacy of the philosophers in accepting previous views of ancient thinkers without full elaboration and discussion. To him, the readers of al-Ghazālī, after a careful examination comparing him with Ibn Rushd, will become aware of the fact that approving any of the philosophers' ideas unquestioningly, as ignorant imitators usually do, was as wrong as rejecting all their opinions, as ardent objectors would recommend. In his *Tahāfut*, al-Ghazālī rejected both

77 Ḥakkı, "İslam Alimleri ve Mütefekkirleri," 5 (1337–8 [1919–20]) 51:1628–33.
78 See Ḥakkı, "İslam'da Felsefe Cereyanları," 16 (1930), 20–45.
79 Ibid, 5 (1337–58 [1919–20]), 51:1629.
80 Ibid, 22 (1341 [1922–23]), 78–79: 2572.
81 Ibid, 5 (1337–58 [1919–20]), 53:1692.
82 Ibid., 56:1795.

tendencies by using a well-founded critical method with logical and dialectical arguments, while discussing the *falāsifa*'s views. It is therefore unfair, Ḥakkı argues, to say that there is no philosophical approach in al-Ghazālī's thought.[83]

Moreover, Ḥakkı suggests, al-Ghazālī proved that it was possible for theologians to compete rationally with philosophers and to employ philosophical methods in their religious discourse. He compares al-Ghazālī to Descartes in his doubt in the search for the truth, to Hume in his denial of a necessary relation between cause and effect, to Kant in his questioning of the authority of reason, and to Bergson in his giving credit to intuition. İzmirli İsmail Ḥakkı was quite sure about al-Ghazālī's influence on some European philosophers, which could be traced in the writings of Thomas Aquinas on God's knowledge of particulars for instance, and then of Pascal on reason and revelation.[84]

Al-Ghazālī's biggest achievement, Ḥakkı affirms, was to take philosophy from representing specific systems of thought, such as the peripatetic school, and turning it into a method of reasoning (*naẓar*) available for various thinkers, such as theologians, political thinkers, moralists, mystics and so on. By following his path, Fakhr al-Dīn al-Rāzī, ʿAḍud al-Dīn al-Ījī, and Saʿd al-Dīn al-Taftāzānī, for instance, were able to focus on the details of arguments in Islamic thought. Despite that achievement, Ḥakkı points out, it is hard to describe al-Ghazālī comprehensively, since he dealt with so many fields; it would be more convenient to discuss him through each of his books, as al-Ghazālī of the *Tahāfut*, of the *Iḥyāʾ*, of the *Mishkāt*, of *Jawāhir al-Qurʾān*. Nevertheless, according to Ḥakkı, there is evidence of a possible rupture of his thought as well as continuity in searching for the truth. For example, contradictions among some of his texts, such as his approaches in *al-Maḍnūn* and *Jawāhir* compared to other books, are signs of al-Ghazālī's inability to disregard philosophy in some issues or in some periods of his life.[85]

These last two figures demonstrate a more academic approach to al-Ghazālī and his relationship with the philosophers. Musa Kazım and İsmail Ḥakkı, in their analysis, tried to question the common acceptance of the presence of a sharp contradiction between al-Ghazālī and Ibn Rushd, and remove the idea of al-Ghazālī's limited understanding of philosophy, which was highlighted by modernist and orientalist discourses. At the same time, they were also critical of some approaches and positions of al-Ghazālī and displayed no romanticism

83 Ḥakkı, "İslam'da Felsefe Cereyanları," 16 (1930), 26–34, 41–2.

84 Ibid, 17 (1930), 9; Cf. Ḥakkı, *İslam Mütefekkirleri ile Garb Mütefekkirleri Arasında Mukayese*, 10, 25–26, 46–47, 52.

85 Ḥakkı, "İslam'da Felsefe Cereyanları," 17 (1930), 11. On more details on Ḥakkı see Özervarlı, "Alternative Approaches to Modernization in the Late Ottoman Period," 77–102.

about his pre-eminence as a thinker. However, being a part of the *madrasa* education and religious circles of the late Ottoman period, they were still reluctant to focus more straightforwardly on Ibn Rushd's contribution to Islamic thought. Nevertheless, they represented a more balanced position between the strict opponents and admirers of both thinkers.

Conclusion

Ottoman intellectual history is quite rich in influences of great thinkers of Islamic thought, especially that of al-Ghazālī. The Ottoman time was a period of the continuation of a Ghazalian legacy that reached the Ottomans via the Anatolian Seljuq intellectual legacy and continued through to the modern age. Scholars such as Fenari, Hocazade, Kemalpaşazade, Ṭaşköprüzade and Birgivi were heavily influenced by him, and represented his position and standard in the Ottoman milieu in a variety of ways. He was, therefore, a main source of Ottoman religious and philosophical thought in various combinations and interpretations.

Al-Ghazālī was understood and presented differently by the late Ottomans of the modernization period during what was thought to be the beginning of a new awakening. Some of the late Ottomans compared their response to modernization and Western philosophy to the historical experience of al-Ghazālī and his criticism of the Muslim *falāsifa* and, indirectly, of Greek thought. Others regarded him and his views as the primary cause of problems in medieval and early Ottoman thought. In this period, the legacy of the *madrasa* learning system was under investigation, and therefore Ottoman modernists were questioning not only al-Ghazālī but also other representatives of Islamic thought. However, due to his essential role in the developments of the post-classical period in general and Ottoman thought in particular, al-Ghazālī had one of the most visible places in their debates.

Among modern Ottomans there were also cases of prejudice without proper examinations of texts, while there were also more scholarly analyses based on questions and comparisons. The main reason for this kind of wide and diverse perception of al-Ghazālī in the modern period was in fact related to the Ottoman search of a way out of their political and intellectual crisis as they approached cultural and technological confrontations with the growing European powers during the 19th century. The more Ottoman thinkers realized their position as a state and society, the more they were interested to find the best example in their past heritage in order to create a new methodology, structure, and objective for their own contemporary thought. Al-Ghazālī, who revitalized religious thought, philosophy, and mysticism in his time, was therefore one of the cornerstones of their scholarship. Since there were many intellectual groups and movements concerning relations between Islamic tradition and Western modernity, it was not surprising to see so many conflicting reactions towards his role and thought.

Bibliography

Akdemir, Abamüslim. *Mehmed Ali Ayni'nin Düşünce Dünyası*. Ankara: Kültür Bakanlığı, 1997.

al-Akiti, Muhammad Afifi. *The Maḍnūn of al-Ghazālī: A Critical Edition of the Unpublished Major Maḍnūn with Discussion of His Restricted, Philosophical Corpus*. 3 vols. PhD dissertation, Worcester College, Oxford University, 2007.

———. "The Good, the Bad, and the Ugly of *Falsafa*: al-Ghazālī's *Maḍnūn, Tahafut*, and *Maqāṣid* with Particular Attention to their *Falsafi* Treatments of God's Knowledge of Temporal Events." In *Avicenna and His Legacy: A Golden Age of Science and Philosophy.* Edited by Y. T. Langermann. Brepols: Turnhout, 2009. 51–100.

al-ʿAydarūs, ʿAbd al-Qādir ibn Shaykh, *Taʿrīf al-aḥyāʾ bi faḍāʾil al-Iḥyāʾ*. Cairo: Maktabat al-Tijāriyya al-Kubra, n. d.

Ayni, Mehmed Ali. *Huccetülislam İmam Gazzali*. Istanbul: Maṭbaʿa-i Amire, 1327 [1909].

Bein, Amit. "Ulama and Activism in the Late Ottoman Empire: The Political Career of Şeyhülislâm Mustafa Sabri Efendi (1869–1954)." In *Guardians of Faith in Modern Times: Ulama in the Middle East*. Edited by Meir Hatina. Leiden: Brill, 2009. 67–90.

Bayezidov, Ataullah. *Redd-i Renan: İslamiyet ve Fünun*. Translated by Gülnar De Lebedev and Ahmed Cevdet. Istanbul: Tercüman-i Ḥaḳiḳat Maṭbaʿası, 1308 [1890–91].

Birgivi (al-Birgī), Meḥmed Efendi. *Sīrat al-rasūl aw al-ṭarīqat al-muhammadiyya*. Edited by M. Ḥ. A. al-Shaybānī. Riyadh: M. Ḥ. A. al-Shaybānī, 1993.

Çağrıcı, Mustafa. "Gazzâlî'nin İhyâ'sı ile Birgivî'nin Tarîkat-i Muhammediyesi'nin Mukayesesi." *İslâmî Araştırmalar* 13 (2000): 473–78.

Çetinkaya, Bayram Ali. *Türkiye'nin Modernleşmesi Sürecinde Şemseddin Günaltay*. Ankara: Araştırma Yayınları, 2003.

Ertan, Veli. *Ahmed Ḥamdi Akseki*. Ankara: Kültür ve Turizm Bakanlığı, 1988.

Frank, Richard M. "Al-Ghazālī on *taqlīd*. Scholars, theologians, and philosophers." *Zeitschrift für Geschichte der Arabisch-Islamischen Wissenschaften* 7 (1991–92): 207–52.

al-Ghazālī, Muḥammad ibn Muḥammad. *Iḥyāʾ ʿulūm al-dīn*. 16 vols. Cairo: Lajnat Nashr al-Thaqāfa al-Islāmiyya, 1356–1357 [1937–1938].

———. *Mishkāt al-anwār wa-miṣfāt al-asrār*. Edited by Abd al-ʿAzīz ʿIzz al-Dīn al-Sayrawān. Beirut: ʿĀlam al-Kutub, 1407/1986.

———. Al-Ghazzālī's Mishkāt al-anwār ("The Niche For Lights"). Translated by W. H. T. Gairdner. London: The Royal Asiatic Society, 1924.

———. *Jawāhir al-Qur'ān wa-duraruhu* [*wa-Kitāb al-Arbaʿīn fī uṣūl al-dīn*]. Edited by Kh. M. Kāmil and ʿI. al-Sharqāwī. Cairo: Maṭbaʿat Dār al-Kutub wa-l-Wathāʾiq al-Qawmiyya, 1432/2011.

———. *al-Maḍnūn bihi ʿalā ghayr ahlih*. Edited by Aḥmad al-Bābī al-Ḥalabī. Cairo: al-Maṭbaʿa al-Maymaniyya, 1309 [1891]. (Published in a volume together with *Iljām al-ʿawāmm*, *al-Munqidh min al-ḍalāl*, and *al-Maḍnūn al-ṣaghīr*.)

———. *al-Maḍnūn al-ṣaghīr wa-huwa al-mawsūm bi-l-Ajwiba al-Ghazāliyya fī l-masāʾil al-ukhrawiyya*. Edited by Aḥmad al-Bābī al-Ḥalabī. Cairo: al-Maṭbaʿa al-Maymaniyya, 1309 [1891]. (Published in a volume together with *Iljām al-ʿawāmm*, *al-Munqidh min al-ḍalāl*, and *al-Maḍnūn al-kabīr*.)

———. *İki Madnun*. Translated into Turkish by Dursun Sabit Ünal. İzmir: İzmir İlahiyat Fakültesi Vakfı Yayınları, 1988.

Günaydın, Yusuf Turan. "Gazâlî Tercümeleri: Osmanlı Devri ve 1928 Sonrası İçin Bir Bibliyografya Denemesi." *Divan. Disiplinlerarası Çalışmalar Dergisi*, 30 (2011): 63–90.

Ḥakkı, İzmirli İsmail. "İslam Alimleri ve Mütefekkirleri." *Ceride-i İlmiyye*, vol. 5 (1337–38 [1919–20]) 51:1628–33; 52:1664–67; 53:1690–92; 54:1724–29; 55:1755–60; 56:1784–96; 57:1821–32; 58:1854–58; 59:1885–92; 60:1911–16; 61:1944–1951–8; 62:1975–81; vol. 6 (1339 [1921]), 63:2007–16; 64:2041–46; 65:2077–82; 66:2100–16; 67:2137–43; 68:2176–80; vol. 7 (1340–41 [1922–23]), 69:2208–14; 70:2255–58; 72:2334–47; 74–75:2437–43; 78–79:2571–78.

———."İslam'da Felsefe Cereyanları: İbni Sina'nın Halefleri." *Darülfünün İlahiyat Fakültesi Mecmuası* 16 (1930): 21–45; 17 (1930): 9–24; 20 (1931): 46–56; 21 (1931): 17–35; 22 (1932): 27–50; 23 (1932): 20–38. See also the collection of these articles and rendering into modern Turkish by N. Ahmet Özalp (ed.), *İslâm'da Felsefe Akımları*. Istanbul: Kitabevi, 1995).

———. *İslam Mütefekkirleri ile Garb Mütefekkirleri Arasında Mukayese*. Edited by S. H. Bolay. Ankara: Diyanet İşleri Başkanlığı, 1973.

Ḥamdi, Aksekili Aḥmed [also: Aḥmed Ḥamdi Aksekil]. "Ṣufiye-i Kiram Ḥadaratının Ruḥ Ḥakkındaki Tarz-ı Telakkileri." *Maḥfil* 3 (1339 [1920–1]): 44–45 and 4 (1339 [1920–1]): 60–62.

———. "Gazzali'nin Ruḥ Ḥakkındaki Telakkiyatı." *Maḥfil* 6 (1339 [1920–21]): 96–99; 7 (1339 [1920–21]): 118–19; 8 (1339 [1920–2]): 133–35,

———. "İmam Gazzali ve el-Mażnun Kitabları." *Maḥfil*, 12 (1339 [1920–21]): 204–10.

Herzog, Christoph. *Geschichte und Ideologie: Mehmed Murad und Celal Nuri über die historischen Ursachen des osmanischen Niedergangs*. Berlin: Klaus Schwarz Verlag, 1996.

Howard, Douglas A. "Genre and Myth in the Ottoman Advice for Kings Literature." In *The Early Modern Ottomans*. Edited by V. H. Aksan and D. Goffman. Cambridge: Cambridge University Press, 2007. 137–66.

Ibn Khallikān, Aḥmad b. Muḥammad. *Wafayāt al-aʿyān wa-anbāʾ abnāʾ al-zamān*. Edited by Iḥsān ʿAbbās. 8 vols. Beirut: Dar Sader, 1968–72.

Ibn Rushd, Muḥammad ibn Aḥmad. *al-Kashf ʿan manāhij al-adillah fī ʿaqāʾid al-milla*. Edited by Muṣṭafā Ḥanafī under the supervision of Muḥammad ʿĀbid al-Jābirī. Beirut: Dirāsāt al-Waḥda al-ʿArabiyya, 1998.

İbnürreşad, Ali Ferruh. *Teshhir-i Ebaṭil*. Istanbul: Mihran Maṭbaʿası, 1306 [1889].

İbrahim, Hafız. "İmam Gazzali ve el-Mażnun Kitabları." *Maḥfil* 10 (1339 [1920–21]): 164–66.

Katib Çelebi. *Kashf al-ẓunūn ʿan asāmī l-kutub wa-l-funūn*. Edited by K. M. Rıfat and S. Yaltkaya. 2 vols. Istanbul: Maarif Vekaleti, 1941–43.

Kazım, Musa. "İbn Rüşd'ün Meslek-i Felsefisi ve İmam Gazzali ile Bazı Mesele Ḥakkında Münaẓarası." In *Külliyat: Dinî İctimaî Makaleler*. Istanbul: Evkaf-i İslamiye Maṭbaʿası, 1918. 139–96.

Kemal, Namık. *Renan Müdafaʿanamesi*. Istanbul: Maḥmud Bey Maṭbaʿası, 1326 [1908].

Kınalızade, ʿAli Çelebi. *Akhlak-i ʿAlaʾi*. Edited by M. Koç. Istanbul: Klasik, 2007.

Lagardère, Vincent. "A propos d'un chapitre du *Nafḫ wal-taswiya* attribué à Ġazālī." *Studia Islamica* 60 (1984): 119–36.

Mardin, Şerif. *The Genesis of Young Ottoman Thought: A Study in the Modernization of Turkish Political Ideas.* Princeton: Princeton University Press, 2000.

Nuri [İleri], Celal. *Tarikh-i İstikbal*. Istanbul: Yeni Os̱manlı Maṭbaʿası, 1331 [1912].

Ömer Ḳastamoni, Muallim. *Taʿyīn al-waẓāʾif fī ḥaqq al-mutashabiḥāt*. Istanbul: Maṭbaʿa-yi Os̱maniyye, 1302 [1885].

———. *Ahiret ḥalleri.* Kastamonu: Ḳastamonu Maṭbaʿasi, 1329 [1911].

Özervarlı, M. Sait. "Arbitrating between al-Ghazālī and the Philosophers: The *Tahāfut* Commentaries in the Ottoman Intellectual Context." *Islam and Rationality: The Impact of al-Ghazālī.* Edited by G. Tamer, Vol. 1. Leiden: Brill, 375–97.

———. "Yanyalı Esad Efendi's Works on Philosophical Texts as Part of the Ottoman Translation Movement in the Early Eighteenth Century." In *Europa und die Türkei im 18. Jahrhundert / Europe and Turkey in the 18th Century*. Edited by B. Schmidt-Haberkamp. Göttingen: V&R Press, 2011. 457–72.

———. "Alternative Approaches to Modernization in the Late Ottoman Period: Izmirli Ismail Hakki's Religious Thought against Materialist Scientism." *International Journal of Middle East Studies* 39 (2007): 77–102.

Pourjavady, Nasrollah (ed.), *Majmūʿah-yi falsafī-yi Marāgha / A Philosophical Anthology from Maragha. Containing Works by Abū Ḥāmid Ghazzālī*, ʿAyn al-Quḍāt al-Hamadānī, Ibn Sīnā, ʿUmar ibn Sahlān Sāvi, Majduddīn Jīlī and others. Facsimile edition with introductions in Persian and English by Nasrollah Pourjavady. Tehran: Markaz-i Nashr-i Dānishgāh, 1380/2002.

Reinhart, A. Kevin. "Musa Kazim: from *ʿilm* to Polemics." *Archivum Ottomanicum* 19 (2001): 281–306.

Ṣabrī, Muṣṭafā. *Mawqif al-ʿaql wa-l-ʿilm wa-l-ʿālam.* Beirut: Dār Iḥya' al-Turāth al-ʿArabī, 1992.

Sakallı, Talat. "Miftahu's-saâde—Ihyau ulumi'd-din Münasebeti." In *Taşköprülü Zâde Ahmet Efendi (1495–1561)*. Edited by A. H. Köker. Kayseri: Erciyes Üniversitesi Gevher Nesibe Tıp Tarihi Enstitüsü, 1992. 65–80.

Sıdkı Mardini, Yūsuf Aḥmed, *Masīr ʿumūm al-muwaḥḥidīn.* MS Istanbul, University Central Library 5851–5859.

———. *Mesîru umûmi l-muvahhidîn şerh u terceme-i Kitâb-i Ihyâu ulûmi d-dîn. Ihyâ tercüme ve şerhi.* 1. Cilt. Edited by M. Koç and E. Tanrıverdi. Istanbul: Türkiye Yazma Eserler Kurumu Başkanliği, 2015.

Şirvani, Meḥmed Emin. *Sharḥ Qawāʿid al-ʿaqā'id li-l-Ghazālī,* MS Istanbul, Süleymaniye Yazma Eser Kütüphanesi, Esad Efendi, 1235, foll. 1–67.

Suavi, Ali. "al-Radd ʿalā man radda ʿalā l-Ghazālī." *ʿUlum Gazetesi* 6 (1286 [1869]): 342–60 and 7 (1286 [1869]): 361–85.

al-Subkī, Tāj al-Dīn ʿAbd al-Wahhāb b. ʿAlī. *Ṭabaqāt al-Shāfiʿiyya al-kubrā.* Edited by ʿAbd al-Fattāḥ M. al-Ḥilw and Maḥmūd M. al-Ṭanāḥī. 10 vols. Cairo: Maṭbaʿat ʿIsā al-Bābī al-Ḥalabī, 1383/1964.

Şemseddin [Günaltay], Meḥmed. *Felsefe-yi Ula: İsbat-ı Vacib ve Ruḥ Naẓariyeleri.* Istanbul: Darülfünun Telifat-i İslamiye Ḥeyeti, 1339 [1920].

———. "İslam Dünyasının İnhitatı Sebebi Selçuk İstilası Mıdır?" *İkinci Türk Tarih Kongresi.* Istanbul: Devlet Basımevi, 1937. 1–15.

Ṭaşköprüzade, Aḥmed ibn Muṣṭafa. *Miftāḥ al-saʿāda wa-miṣbāḥ al-siyāda fi mawdūʿāt al-ʿulūm.* Edited by K. K. Bekri and ʿA. Abū l-Nūr. Cairo: Dār al-Kutub al-Ḥadītha, 1968.

———.*Mawżuʿat al-ʿulūm.* Ottoman Turk translation of *Miftāḥ al-saʿāda* by Kemaleddin Meḥmed Taşköprüzade. Istanbul: Iḳdam Maṭbaʿası, 1313 [1895–96].

Tevfik, Süleyman. *Iḥyā-yi ʿülüm tercümesi.* Istanbul: Artin Asaduryan Maṭbaʿası, 1326 [1910].

Ülken, Hilmi Ziya. "Gazali'nin Bazı Eserlerinin Türkçe Tercümeleri." *Ankara Üniversitesi İlahiyat Fakültesi Dergisi,* 9 (1961): 59–69.

Yazar, Sadık. "Gazzâlî'nin XIII–XIX: Yüzyıllar Arasında Batı Türkçesinde Tercüme Edilen Eserleri." *Divan. Disiplinlerarası Çalışmalar Dergisi,* 31 (2011): 67–156.

Yılmaz, Hüseyin. *The Sultan and the Sultanate: Envisioning Rulership in the Age of Süleyman the Lawgiver, 1520–1566.* PhD diss., Harvard University, 2005.

al-Zabīdī, al-Murtaḍā Muḥammad ibn Muḥammad. *Itḥāf al-sāda al-muttaqīn bi-sharḥ Iḥyā' ʿulūm al-dīn.* 10 vols. Cairo: al-Maṭbaʿa al-Maymaniyya, 1311 [1894].

CHAPTER 11

Al-Ghazālī's "Demarcation of Science"

A Commonplace Apology in the Muslim Reception of Modern Science—and Its Limitations

Martin Riexinger

In Western Islamic studies of the 19th and early 20th century al-Ghazālī was often cast as the villain in the intellectual history of Islam. Al-Ghazālī 's attack on philosophy had allegedly dealt a deadly blow to rational thought, initiating the intellectual stagnation of the Islamic world, if not its decline.[1] Although this image has been considerably revised in Western academic Islamic studies during recent decades,[2] it remains quite common among intellectuals in the Arabic and Islamic worlds who advocate the rediscovery of the rational legacy of Islamic thought, which, they claim, will pave the way for a political and civilizational renewal.[3] Their denigration of al-Ghazālī contrasts strikingly with the role he played for Muslim thinkers who from the 18th century until the early 20th century advocated the reception of modern astronomy.

Al-Ghazālī's importance for these Muslim thinkers stemmed from a position he had taken in an earlier debate about the relationship between scientific knowledge and revelation. In the second introduction to his *Tahāfut al-falāsifa* (*The Incoherence of the Philosophers*), he singles out aspects of philosophy that he is not going to debate because they are either quarrels about terminology or

1 See e.g. Renan, *Averroès et l'averroïsme*, 97: "C'était, on le voit, la negation de toute science. Gazzali fut un des ces esprits bizarre qui n'embrassent la religion que comme une manière de narguer la raison." Cf. also Goldziher, "Stellung der alten islamischen Orthodoxie zu den antiken Wissenschaften," 18–19, 32–34 (Engl. in "The Attitude of Orthodox Islam toward the Ancient Sciences," 194–95, 201–4), and further references in Griffel, *Al-Ghazālī's Philosophical Theology*, 4–5.

2 See e.g. Griffel, *Al-Ghazālī's Philosophical Theology*, 6–7.

3 For a representative example, see the Egyptian philosopher Ḥasan Ḥanafī, in Riexinger, "Nasserism Revitalized: A Critical Reading of Ḥasan Ḥanafī's Projects 'The Islamic Left' and 'Occidentalism' (and Their Uncritical Reading)," 67, 70, 72, 77–79, 93, 95 n. 147, 101; on Muḥammad 'Amāra and the Syrian Marxist Ṭayyib Tīzīnī cf. von Kügelgen, *Averroes und die arabische Moderne*, 184, 243, 254–55; this position appears also in writings on the responses to modern science in the Islamic World, see Hoodbhoy, *Islam and Science: Religious Orthodoxy and the Battle for Rationality*, 104–7 and Huff, *Intellectual Curiosity and the Scientific Revolution. A Global Perspective*, 140–41.

 | DOI 10.1163/9789004307490_012

unproblematic for Islam. In this context he draws a dividing line between astronomy, which has a sound mathematical basis, and speculative types of philosophy. Al-Ghazālī's primary purpose is to define philosophy, and because he declares that investigations based on observation and calculation can deliver indisputable results and are hence legitimate, one can argue that he "demarcates" science without coining a term for it.[4]

Al-Ghazālī declares that one should attempt to refute the philosopher's explanations for celestial phenomena that are based on research with sound methods:

> Whoever thinks that to engage in a disputation for refuting such a theory is a religious duty harms religion and weakens it. For these matters rest on demonstrations—geometrical and arithmetical—that leave no room for doubt.[5]

Such an approach will have devastating consequences for religion, al-Ghazālī continues, because

> [W]hen one who studies these demonstrations and ascertains their proofs, deriving thereby information about the time of the two eclipses [and] their extent and duration, is told that this is contrary to religion, [such an individual] will not suspect this [science, but] only religion. The harm inflicted on religion by those who defend it in a way not proper to it is greater than [the harm caused by] those who attack it in the way proper to it: A rational foe is better than an ignorant friend.[6]

The ritual obligations related to the eclipses are in any case unaffected by the explanations of philosophers and astronomers. Hence even in the case of sound *aḥādīth* the following rule applies:

> Then it would be easier to interpret it metaphorically rather than to reject matters that are conclusively true (*qaṭʿiyya*). For how many apparent [scriptural] meanings have been interpreted metaphorically [on the basis of] rational proof [rejecting their literal sense] that do not attain

4 On the term "demarcation" ("Abgrenzung") with reference to late 19th and early 20th centuries controversies see Popper, *Die beiden Grundprobleme der Erkenntnistheorie*, 341–418 (in English: *The Two Fundamental Problems of the Theory of Knowledge*, 377–424).

5 al-Ghazālī, *Tahāfut al-falāsifa*, 6, Marmura's translation.

6 Ibid.

> the degree of clarity [of the astronomical demonstrations regarding the eclipse]! The greatest thing in which the heretics rejoice is for the defender of religion to declare that these [astronomical demonstrations] and their like are contrary to religion. Thus, the heretics' path for refuting religion becomes easy if the likes [of the above argument for defending religion] are rendered a condition [for its truth].[7]

When it comes to the use of this argument in later discussions, it is important not to overlook that in cases of conflict between astronomy and the wording of revealed texts, al-Ghazālī refers to demonstrative proofs that do not allow any doubt (*barāhīn handasiyya ḥasābiyya lā yabqā maʿahā rība*).

Although the paragraph as a whole belongs in the context of al-Ghazālī's engagement with the *falāsifa*, his words about exegesis are directed against the extremists on the other end of the intellectual spectrum. He defends Ptolemaic astronomy against all who insist that the wording of the revelation is also authoritative with respect to the shape of Earth and the cosmos. Those who advocated the latter idea were referring in particular to the *ḥadīth*, into which many cosmological concepts from Ancient Eastern, Jewish and Christian sources—often apocryphal—had been integrated. Much of this material is found in the canonical collections, for example in the chapter *bud' al-khalq* (*The Beginning of Creation*) in al-Bukhārī's (d. 256/870) collection of sound *ḥadīth* (*al-Ṣaḥīḥ*). This material was used in commentaries on the Qur'an and cosmographies from early on.[8] Because we lack studies of cosmological concepts and their dissemination over the following centuries, it is difficult to assess the impact of al-Ghazālī's argument. The scholar Ibn Kathīr (d. 774/1373), who can be considered a literalist in his approach to exegesis of the Qur'an, did oppose the literal interpretation of *āyāt* and *aḥādīth* when its contradiction by observable astronomical phenomena and geographical facts was too blatant, as in the case of the rivers of paradise or the sun prostrating below the throne or sinking in a muddy well (Q 18:86)—in the latter two cases because they are at odds with the astronomical explanation of eclipses.[9] The most important systematization of this worldview was formulated about four centuries after al-Ghazālī's death, in al-Suyūṭī's (d. 911/1505) *al-Hay'a al-saniyya fī l-hay'a*

7 al-Ghazālī, *Tahāfut al-falāsifa*, 7, Marmura's translation, slightly adapted. A second, shorter version of this whole passage is in al-Ghazālī's later work *al-Munqidh min al-ḍalāl*, 21–22; on the *qānūn al-taʾwīl* in al-Ghazālī's thought in general: Griffel *Al-Ghazālī's Philosophical Theology*, 111–113.

8 Heinen, *Islamic Cosmology*, 24–61.

9 Ibn Kathīr, *al-Bidāya wa-l-nihāya*, 1:34–37, 41–44.

al-sunniyya (*The Radiant Configuration* [*As Seen in*] *the Configuration of the Prophetic Sunna*).[10]

As Anton Heinen demonstrates with reference to the large number of tracts that imitate al-Suyūṭī's treatise, this genre remained popular in the early Ottoman period, and according to Gottfried Hagen, it was particularly popular among Sufis.[11] But this kind of cosmology was also quite popular among Ḥanbalīs, since it fitted well their corporealist image of God.[12] And Al-Ghazālī's argument gained new relevance when Islamic scholars became aware of developments in Western astronomy and geography.

Al-Ghazālī's Argument and the Ottoman Reception of Post-Copernican Astronomy

The first scholar who deserves our attention in this context is the Ottoman Katib Çelebi (d. 1067/1657). Following in the footsteps of his father, Katib Çelebi had entered the army and the imperial administration.[13] A large inheritance allowed him to retire, however, at the age of 27 and to settle in Istanbul in order to pursue his literary and scholarly interests. He studied religious and rational sciences and finally started to teach in a *medrese*.[14] His religious sympathies lay for some time with the puritan movement of Ḳaḍızade Meḥmed Efendi (d. 1044/1635), who campaigned against the Sufi orders and their various "heretical innovations" (*bidaʿ*).[15] The parallels between Ḳaḍızade Meḥmed Efendi's ideas and activities and those of Ibn Taymiyya (d. 728/1328) are obvious, but to date we lack the studies that would enable us to determine the extent to which the former are based on the reception of the latter, which would allow us to determine whether Ḳaḍızade Meḥmed Efendi and his followers were sympathetic to "*sunna*-cosmology."

The Cretan war (1645–1669) drew Katib Çelebi's attention to cartography and geography,[16] two fields that were neither part of the educational canon for *ʿulāmāʾ* nor supported by the government, but rather lay somewhere

10 Heinen, *Islamic Cosmology*, 9–11.
11 Ibid., 7–9; Hagen, *Ein osmanischer Geograph*, 87.
12 See below pp. 295–97.
13 Hagen, *Ein osmanischer Geograph*, 14–21.
14 Ibid., 36–50.
15 Ibid., 22–36, later he distanced himself for political reasons from the Ḳaḍızadeliler movement, 75–77.
16 Ibid., 43–44.

between science and literature.[17] In addition to teaching, Katib Çelebi started writing books, and at a time when the Ottoman Empire was constantly interacting with Western powers, he recognized that in order to understand their policies, European sources would need to be consulted. This activity brought him into contact with European converts in Istanbul, and presumably also with European residents and visitors.[18] As he composed one of his two most famous works, the cosmography *Cihannüma* (*Presentation of the World*), he consulted Gerhard Mercator's (d. 1594) *Atlas Minor*, Abraham Ortelius' (d. 1598) *Theatrum orbis terrarum* (*Theater of the World*), Philipp Cluverius' (d. 1622) *Introductio in universam geographiam, tam veterem quam novam* (*Introduction to Universal Geography, Both Old And New*) and possibly other European works translated from Latin by the French convert Sheykh Muḥammed Efendi.[19]

At that time the Copernican model was far from commonly accepted among educated Europeans, and hence the geographical literature Katib Çelebi consulted was still based on the geocentric paradigm.[20] In the Ottoman context Ptolemaic astronomy had to be defended against the advocates of *sunna*-cosmology. To that end, Katib Çelebi quotes the passage from al-Ghazālī's *Incoherence of the Philosophers* in full, followed by a Turkish translation. He then presents a detailed exposition of geometrical proofs for the sphericity of the earth, supported by diagrams, in particular of the shadows that cause eclipses.[21] In other places he explicitly rejects *sunna*-cosmology and suggests that the whale and the bull, which carry the earth according to an often-cited tradition, should be associated with the respective constellations.[22] Referring to al-Ghazālī's argument in order to justify the Ptolemaic astronomy was common among Ottoman scholars of his time, and in Çelebi's case the most remarkable aspect may be the didactic embedding of that argument.[23]

Sixty-five years after Katib Çelebi's death the *Cihannüma* was among the first books to be printed under the direction of a Muslim. In 1140/1727 Ibrahim Müteferriḳa (d. 1158/1745), a Hungarian convert of Calvinist or—more likely—Unitarian origin from Cluj/ Koloszvár in Transylvania who had made a career in the imperial administration, gained the sultan's permission to start a printing

17 For the concept "Salongeographie," ibid., 79–82, 115–19.

18 Ibid., 65–69.

19 Çelebi, *Cihannüma*, 9–11; Hagen, *Ein osmanischer Geograph*, 160–161, 173, 180–181.

20 Hagen, *Ein osmanischer Geograph*, 370–371.

21 Çelebi, *Cihannüma*, 17, 19–20. The geometrical introduction is based on Cluverius.

22 Hagen, *Ein osmanischer Geograph*, 343–344.

23 Reichmuth, "Bildungskanon und Bildungsreform aus der Sicht eines islamischen Gelehrten der anatolischen Provinz," 507.

press in order to facilitate access to practical knowledge. Religious texts were, however, explicitly excluded from this program.[24]

In his 1143/1730 edition of *Tarihü l-Hindi l-garbi* (*The History of the West-Indies*), an anonymous Ottoman treatise on the Americas, Müteferriḳa had presented the Ptolemaic system alone.[25] When he printed the *Cihanüma* in 1145/1732 he himself revised it in order to bring it into accordance with more recent discoveries. The most important change concerns astronomy. After Çelebi's demonstration of geometrical arguments in favor of the sphericity of the earth, Müteferriḳa inserted a digression in which he explained the two major astronomical concepts current in Europe: the Copernican heliocentric model and Tycho Brahe's (1546–1601) revised geocentric model. Later he also translated the introduction from the *Harmonia macrocosmica* by Andreas Cellarius as *Mecmüʿa-i hey'et-i ḳadīme ve cedīde*, but his text was never printed.[26] His presentation of post-Copernican astronomy was not the first in Ottoman Turkey nor the first in the Islamic world in general, but it did lead the pack in presenting the new concepts as convincing .[27]

Müteferriḳa's insertion immediately follows Katib Çelebi's presentation of the geometrical proofs for the sphericity of earth. The validity of al-Ghazālī's argument is implicitly extended to modern astronomy. The basis for Müteferriḳa's presentation of post-Copernican astronomy in the *Cihannüma* is provided by the encyclopedic *Institutiones philosophicae* by Edmond Pourchot

24 See the article "Ibrahīm Müteferriḳa" by Niyazi Berkes in EI^2, 3:996–98, and idem, *The Development of Secularism in Turkey*, 36–47. See also "Maṭbaʿa 2. In Turkey," by Günay Alpan Kut in EI^2, 4:799–803, and Reichmuth, "Islamic Reformist discourse in the Tulip Period (1718–30): Ibrahim Müteferriḳa and His Arguments for Printing," as well as Sabev, *İbrahim Müteferrika ya da İlk Osmanlı Matbaa Serüveni (1726–1746)*, 78–176; the volume was affordable for high officials. In how far Müteferiḳḳa's *Cihannüma* was taken note of by religious scholars has not yet been investigated into systematically. One *qāḍī* in Serbia dedicated it as the only printed book to his *waqf*-library: Sievert, *Zwischen arabischer Provinz und Hoher Pforte: Beziehungen, Bildung und Politik des osmanischen Bürokraten Rāġıb Meḥmed Paşa (st. 1763)*, 427.

25 Goodrich, *The Ottoman Turks and the New World*, 28–29, 40, 77–81; Kut and Türe, *Yazmadan Basmaya: Müteferrika, Mühendishane*, 42–43.

26 Berkes, *The Development of Secularism*, 147.

27 The first presentation was by Zigetvārlı Köse Ibrāhīm in 1660 and was based on the refutation of the Copernican model by the French Catholic author Nicolas Durret. See İhsanoğlu, "Batı Bilim ve Osmanlı Dünyası: Bir İnceleme Örneği Olarak Modern Astronomi'nin Osmanlıya Girişi," 729–38, and Ben-Zaken, "The Heavens of the Sky and the Heavens of the Heart: the Ottoman Cultural Context for the Introduction of Post-Copernican Astronomy."

(1651–1734, his name is rendered as Porḳuçiyuş by Müteferriḳa), a French Catholic promoter and popularizer of Cartesian philosophy, a book he could have obtained from Venice, where it had been printed two years earlier.[28] That Müteferriḳa presents post-Copernican astronomy in a Cartesian context probably reflects his Hungarian Protestant background, since in the late 17th century Cartesianism had become the dominant philosophy at Hungarian Calvinist colleges as a result of their connections to the Netherlands, with heliocentrism widely accepted at these institutions.[29] Before presenting modern astronomy, however, Müteferriḳa provides a conventional account of the Ptolemaic model.[30] He integrates additional proofs for the spherical nature of the earth, such as the fact that certain astronomical phenomena that can be observed at one point on the earth cannot be observed at points farther east or west, and the fact that the earth had been circumnavigated.[31] He also stresses that according to the Ptolemaic model the spheres of the celestial bodies are compact bodies.[32] Before turning to the Copernican model, he emphasizes that all of this does not concern religiously relevant questions (*umūr-i iʿtiqādiyye*) and that it does not belong among things that are necessarily associated with God's creation (*lewāzim-i halḳiyye*).[33]

Müteferriḳa starts his explanation of geocentrism with the statement that for a long time a number of scholars, for example Aristarchus of Samos (3rd century BC), argued that the earth was moving. They were ridiculed until Cardinal Nicolas of Cues (Ḳujani) spoke out in favor of the concept.[34] The geocentric model was then developed and supported with a number of proofs by Copernicus (Ḳuperniquş) and became commonly accepted in Europe.[35] He then describes the main features of the solar system: the sun is a fixed body at the center of the universe, surrounded by the spheres of the planets; the moon orbits the earth, and similar moons orbit Jupiter and Saturn. Thereafter he presents Descartes' (Ḳartejiyuş, 1596–1650) position that there is no sphere of fixed stars but that the stars are suns similar to our sun, surrounded by planets,

---

28 Müteferriḳa in Çelebi, *Cihannüma* (1145/1730-print), 34–35.

29 Zemplén, "The Reception of Copernicanism in Hungary," 332; Aiton, *The Vortex Theory of Planetary Motions*, 65; Schmutz, "Purchot, Edmond."

30 Müteferriḳa in Çelebi, *Cihannüma*, (1145/1730-print), 20–22.

31 Ibid., 20–21.

32 Ibid., 33.

33 Ibid., 34.

34 Ibid., 35–36.

35 Ibid., 36. His rendering of the Latinized names reflects the pronunciation according to the Hungarian convention.

and that they fill a vast empty space.[36] The moon is the only celestial body to orbit the earth, and the impression that others do so too is created by the rotation of the earth around its axis; the movement of the earth around the sun—with a velocity far exceeding that of a bullet—is responsible for the seasons because the inclination of the earth exposes each hemisphere more strongly to the sun during different times of the year.[37]

After the presentation of the Cartesian-Copernican system, Müteferriḳa addresses criticisms leveled at this model with arguments from Descartes. Regarding religious arguments, he claims that Biblical references to the moon as a lamp/candle have to be interpreted metaphorically.[38] He devotes more space to physical objections, in particular that if the earth rotated, one would be able to perceive that rotation, something thrown in a westward direction would move faster than something thrown towards the east, and bodies would not fall straight down to the earth. He counters these objections with Descartes' argument that the earth is moving in the vortex of sublime matter (*mādde-yi layyine*). Everything on earth moves within that vortex. Furthermore Galileo Galilei (1564–1642)—whom Müteferriḳa does not name when he introduces Jupiter's moons—has demonstrated that everything on earth is moving to its center, even though the earth is not the center of the universe. In this respect, the behavior of a falling object resembles what can be observed when a stone is let down on a moving vessel. Somebody on the ship will see the stone moving straight downward, whereas somebody watching the ship from an external position will see the stone moving down in a curved line (*iğri haṭṭ*).[39]

Although he has stated that the Copernican model is now universally accepted, Müteferriḳa ends by presenting the Tychonian compromise model, according to which Mercury and Venus move around the sun while the sun itself moves around the earth like the planets. He does not explain his inclusion of this model, but as he gives Brahe credit for two important scientific advances—Brahe proved that the comets move on the levels of the spheres (*suṭūḥ-i aflāk*) hence the matter of the heavens is fluid and sublime (*māʿiyye ve layyine*), and he conjectured that Mercury and Venus are "sometimes in a position above or beneath the sun" (*şemsin gah fevḳında gah taḥtında*)—Müteferriḳa

36 Ibid., 36–37; Pourchot (*Institutiones*, 20) attributes *vortices* but not explicitly planets to the fixed stars.

37 Müteferriḳa in Çelebi, *Cihannüma*, (1145/1730-print), 37, 39.

38 Ibid., 43.

39 Ibid., 43–46, 43: "*ve Ḳartejiyuş sugrada dahi tekellüm ederek bu minvāl üzere cevāb etmişdir ki arż bu meẕheb-i cedīde göre dahi ḥadd ẕātinde ḥareket ile muttaṣıf olmayıb haḳīḳaten mutaḥarrik olan kendisini yaʿnī arż iḥāṭe eylen evvel mādde-i layyineden olan girdabidir.*" The passage is translated from Pourchot, *Institutiones*, 32.

may have thought that he should present Brahe's system as a whole. There is also another possible explanation for his inclusion of Brahe's compromise model. Brahe is the only scientist about whom Müteferriḳa provides biographical information, and he focuses in particular on the erection of the observatory at Uraniborg with support of the King of Denmark. Perhaps here is a hint for the Ottoman authorities that scientific knowledge should not only be transferred but also produced with imperial support.[40] Along with their descriptions in words, all three systems are also portrayed in copperplate engravings.

That Müteferriḳa tries to disprove objections to the idea that the earth is in motion by referring to the Cartesian vortex theory even though Newton's *Principia mathematica* had been published in 1696 is not surprising and is not evidence that he was out of touch with contemporary scientific discussion.[41] Pourchot's *Institutiones* had led to the replacement of Aristotelianism and thus also geocentrism at the Sorbonne only two years earlier.[42] In continental Europe Cartesian positions prevailed over Newton's theory on gravity into the 1730s, and persisted well into the mid-18th century.[43] Moreover in Müteferriḳa's days the Eastern European Catholic clergy rejected post-Copernican astronomy (and would continue to do so until the 1750s), a fact of which he was surely aware.[44]

Müteferriḳa's account formed the basis of the first presentation of the geocentric model by a religious scholar, Erżurumlu İbrahim Ḥaḳḳı (d. 1194/1780), a Naqshbandi Sufi from Eastern Anatolia who wrote a large number of books, from presumably conventional Sufi poems and legal treatises[45] to the rhymed syllabus *Tertīb-i ʿülūm*, which contains advice on mnemo-technique, ethics, and what today would be called work-life balance. When it addresses astronomy, this syllabus of the sciences is conventional and follows the Ptolemaic system.[46] Haḳḳı presents modern astronomy in his *Maʿrifetname*, an exposition of various aspects of his Sufi worldview that he wrote in 1169/1756–57, after an earlier stay in the capital (1752–53), during which he had access to the imperial

40 Müteferriḳa in Çelebi, *Cihannüma*, (1145/1730-print), 46–49, esp. 47.

41 Aiton, *Vortex Theory*, 30–64; Slowik, "Descartes' Physics."

42 Brockliss, "The Moment of No Return: The University of Paris and the Death of Aristotelianism."

43 Aiton, *Vortex Theory*, 152–256.

44 Zemplén, "Copernicanism in Hungary," 320–321, 359; Bieńkowska, "From Negation to Acceptance: The Reception of the Heliocentric Theory in Polish Schools in the 17th and 18th Centuries," 85.

45 Altıntaş, *Erzurumlu İbrahim Hakkı*, 19–24, 32–38.

46 Özyılmaz, *Osmanlı Medreselerin Eğitim Programları*, 157–63.

library.[47] In the chapters dealing with astronomy he follows Çelebi and Müteferriḳa almost verbatim.[48] However, the passage is disjointed and presented in two pieces. The quote from al-Ghazālī's *Tahāfut* is immediately followed by the proofs for the sphericity of the earth, yet it is separated from the presentation of the heliocentric model by many chapters on completely different subjects.[49] Furthermore, another central aspect of Müteferriḳa's presentation is missing: Erżurumlu İbrahīm Ḥaḳḳı leaves out any reference to those who made the discoveries, and he passes over the Tychonian model, most probably because it had become obsolete.

Ḥaḳḳı's views on cosmology are far from consistent. In the beginning of the book, he presents the conventional elements of *sunna*-cosmology. He makes only one concession, saying that only a majority of scholars of *ḥadīth* and *tafsīr* say the sun prostrates before the throne (*maʿlūm olsun ki ehl-i tefsīr ve hadīs̱in eks̱eri demişlerdi*), whereas scholars are unanimous with regard to the other aspects (*ittifāq etmishlerdir*).[50] Later in the book he polemicizes against *sunna*-cosmology. With regard to the whale and the bull carrying the earth, he follows Katib Çelebi's reinterpretation of the two animals as the respective constellations.[51]

Whereas Müteferriḳa leaves no doubt that the geocentric model is superior, Ḥaqqı simply concedes that there are no objections to that model from the religious point of view. But his preference for the geocentric model has nothing to do with either the revealed texts or mathematical and physical considerations. The whole *Maʿrifetname*, including its extensive anthropological reflections, is based on the concept of the interaction of the macrocosm and the microcosm, including the sympathetic relationship between the spheres of the celestial bodies and the four substances and humors,[52] a concept that is—to put it

47 Altıntaş, *Erzurumlu İbrahim Hakkı*, 23.

48 Erżurūmlū İbrahīm Ḥaḳḳı, *Maʿrifetname*, 18–19.

49 Ibid., 144–51.

50 Ibid., 3–17.

51 Ibid., 118; this allegorical interpretation was used again in Turkey by Said Nursi (1878–1960), the scholar who produced the most elaborate religious-conservative response to modern science. However, due to the *zeitgeist* of the industrial age he suggested that the two animals might also be symbols for agriculture and industry (whale oil) which both stabilize the world by providing livelihood for mankind. See Nursi, *Muhâkemât*, 62–64; Nursi did not refer to al-Ghazālī's discourse, but anecdotic evidence shows that it was used by scholars who accepted modern astronomy against those who rejected it until the 1940s, see for example the biographical account of one of Said Nursi's followers, Mehmed Kırkıncı, *Hayatım—Hatırlarım*, 30.

52 He explains, for example, the emergence of minerals with the effect of certain planetary constellations on the elements. See Ḥaḳḳı, *Maʿrifetname*, 155.

mildly—hard to reconcile with the Cartesian interpretation found in post-Copernican astronomy.[53] Responses to modern science in the Islamic world cannot always be reduced to a conflict between science and scripture. Intellectual traditions from antiquity that permeated Sufism and dominated medical thought also had their part to play. Denounced as a heretic, in 1777 İbrahim Ḥaḳḳı apparently felt pressed to revoke his views on many issues he had addressed in the *Maʿrifetname*, and in response wrote a *Hayʾat al-Islām* in al-Suyūṭī's style.[54]

Nevertheless, the *Maʿrifetname*, which appears to have been very popular, could have persuaded pious Ottoman Turkish and Turkophone Egyptian readers that the geocentric system did not necessarily conflict with the core doctrines of Islam.[55] Unfortunately, the further reception of modern astronomy beyond the new class of technocrats needs further study. It seems remarkable that geography textbooks based on the geocentric concept were still published as late as 1832.[56]

Al-Ghazālī and the Interpretation of the Qur'an Among a Puritan Islamic Movement

In 1945 a reader of the Indian religious monthly *Ahl-i Ḥadīs̱* asked its editor, S̱anāʾullāh Amritsarī (d. 1367/1948), whether the idea that the earth is moving around the sun was acceptable. S̱anāʾullāh answered in the affirmative and referred to the passage from the *Tahāfut*.[57] S̱anāʾullāh himself had come to accept the heliocentric model very late ,[58] yet this was not the first time that he referred to al-Ghazālī to defend his positions on issues with cosmological implications.[59] The conflict over his two lay-oriented commentaries on the Qur'an (one in Arabic, one in Urdu) is an instructive example of how a traditional scholar might refer to al-Ghazālī in order to come to terms

53 One should be aware, however, that heliocentrist astronomy also arose from the desire to make prognostication more reliable. See Westman, *The Copernican Question.*

54 İhsanoğlu, "Batı Bilim," 755–757.

55 Morrison, "The Reception of Early-Modern European Astronomy by Ottoman Religious Scholars."

56 İhsanoğlu, "Batı Bilim," 757–761.

57 S̱anāʾullāh Amritsarī, *Fatāwā-yi s̱anāʾiyya*, 1:198 (originally *Ahl-i Ḥadīs̱*, July 22, 1945).

58 Riexinger, *S̱anāʾullāh Amritsarī (1868–1948) und die Ahl-i Ḥadīs̱ im Punjab*, 376–78, 382–84.

59 He used the argument from the *Tahāfut* without naming al-Ghazālī in a dispute with conservative scholars of his own movement who claimed that rain pours out of an ocean in the heavens and that the sun sets at a fixed place (*mustaqarr* 36:38). See Riexinger, *S̱anāʾullāh Amritsarī*, 382–385.

with modern scientific findings.[60] This conflict also shows that resentment against al-Ghazālī, "who had climbed down so deep into the intestines/depths of the philosophers that he became unable to find the way out again," was very persistent among puritan Muslims.[61]

Ṣanāʾullāh Amritsarī was a leading scholar of the puritan *ahl-i ḥadīṣ*. The origins of this school of thought can be traced back to Muslims from Delhi and the eastern part of the Ganges plain in the early 19th century who were inspired by the teachings of Shāh Waliyyullāh Dihlawī (d. 1176/1762) and hence rejected Sufi rituals and the *taqlīd* of the *madhāhib*. Known as *ṭarīqa-i muḥammadiyya*, they traveled to the Hijaz in order to perform the *ḥajj* before their military leader, Sayyid Aḥmad Barelwī. Their spiritual head, Sayyid Ismāʿīl Shahīd, the grandson of Waliyyullāh, went to wage *jihād* from the Afghan borderlands against the Sikh Empire in Punjab. At the battle of Balakot in 1246/1831 their forces were routed, and Sayyid Aḥmad Barelwī and Sayyid Ismāʿīl Shahīd were killed.[62] But not all of those who had accompanied them to the Arabian Peninsula returned to India immediately. A number of their followers stayed in Sana'a, in Yemen, where they studied under Muḥammad ibn ʿAlī al-Shawkānī (d. 1250/1834), and after their return to India they spread his teachings, which were based on the concepts of Ibn Ḥazm (d. 456/1064), Ibn Taymiyya, and Ibn Qayyim al-Jawziyya (d. 751/1350).[63] That they thereafter rejected Sufi practices and teachings, and even more the *madhhab* system, set them apart from the majority of Indian Muslims, whose worldview and religious practice were informed by an amalgam of Sufism and Ḥanafism. Inspired by Ibn Taymiyya, the *ahl-i ḥadīṣ* were seen as kindred spirits of the Wahhābīs, to the extent that they were denounced as Wahhābīs by their Indian opponents and also by many British officials. Although a number of Wahhābī scholars had come to India in order to study at *ahl-i ḥadīṣ* schools in the 19th century, systematic contact between the two movements was in fact only established after the Saudi conquest of the Ḥijāz, in 1924.[64]

---

60 As also in Egypt, in India exegesis of the Qur'an had changed from a métier by specialists for specialists into a service for the laymen. See Jansen, *The Interpretation of the Koran in Modern Egypt*, 19.

61 Ibn Taymiyya, *Darʾ taʿāruḍ al-ʿaql wa-l-naql*, 1:5.

62 Preckel, *Islamische Bildungsnetzwerke und Gelehrtenkultur im Indien des 19. Jahrhunderts*, 80–120; Gaborieau, *Le Mahdi incompris: Sayyid Ahmad Barelwî (1786–1831) et le millénarisme en Inde*.

63 Riexinger, *Ṣanāʾullāh Amritsarī*, 142–166; Preckel, *Islamische Bildungsnetzwerke*, 120–138; Haykel, *Revival and Reform in Islam: the Legacy of Muhammad al-Shawkānī*.

64 Riexinger, *Ṣanāʾullāh Amritsarī*, 523–37.

In the Punjab, the province in which Ṣanāʾullāh spent his whole life, the *ahl-i ḥadīs̱* were particularly successful at converting people from the urban middle class, not least people with a secular education (the so-called *taʿlīm yāfte*). This success can in part be explained by the *ahl-i ḥadīs̱*'s source-critical engagement with the religious sciences. Following Ibn Taymiyya and al-Shawkānī, the *ahl-i ḥadīs̱* insisted on proof texts and the explanation of these texts to laymen, rather than simply adopting ideas from earlier scholarly literature. This approach may have appealed to those who, in light of their expertise in engineering, medicine, or secular law, demanded to be treated by the religious scholars on equal footing and expected a detailed explanation of how religious positions are deduced from the primary sources of revelation. But this orientation towards Ibn Taymiyya became a problem for *ahl-i ḥadīs̱* scholars because it implied hostility towards the rational sciences and the adoption of a literalist interpretation of the Qurʾan. Hence the scriptural approach that made the *ahl-i ḥadīs̱* so attractive to members of the new group of the *taʿlīm yāfte* as far as law and criticism of Sufism were concerned, also risked estranging the very same group because of its implications for exegesis. Many interpretations of Qurʾanic verses based on *aḥādīth* were completely at odds with modern scientific findings. In particular, according to the *ahl-i ḥadīs̱* the Taymiyyan concept of God's having a spatial position and spatial borders, as expressed in the corporealist interpretation of the Qurʾanic phrase "then He established Himself on the throne" (*thumma stawā ʿalā l-ʿarsh*, Q 7:57 and elsewhere) depended on the affirmation of *sunna*-cosmology.[65] That these cosmological concepts could be used to ridicule Islam was a real problem in late 19th and early 20th century India: the Āryā Samāj, a Hindu reform movement that called for the "reconversion" of Indian Muslims, aggressively denounced Islam as unscientific and irrational and referred to literal interpretations of statements with cosmological implications in the Qurʾan and the *ḥadīth*, for example, in chapter 14 of the *Satyārth Prakāsh (Radiance of Truth)*, the basic work of the movement, written by its founder, Svamī Dayānand Sarasvatī (1824–1883).[66] Ṣanāʾullāh addressed this problem in his two commentaries on the Qurʾan and in his counterpolemics, in both books and open debates, against the Āryā Samāj. His efforts

---

65   Ibid., 337–38, 410–13; Riexinger, "How Favourable is Puritan Islam to Modernity? A case study on the Ahl-i Hadis in late 19th and early 20th century India;" Idem "Ibn Taymiyya's Worldview and the Challenge of Modernity: A Conflict Among the Ahl-i Ḥadīth in British India."

66   Saraswati, *An English Translation of the Satyarth Prakash*, 527, 537–39, 541–42, 554–556; Riexinger, *Ṣanāʾullāh*, 281–95, 369–75, 414; Jones, *Arya Dharm: Hindu Consciousness in 19th-Century Punjab*.

earned him renown among the Muslim general public as a staunch defender of Islam.

The main characteristic of Ṣanā'ullāh's two commentaries on the Qur'an is the absence of references to exegetical *aḥādīth*. This approach allowed Ṣanā'ullāh to eliminate miracles that are not explicitly mentioned in the Qur'an. In his commentary on verses on eschatology or with cosmological content, he felt free to interpret notions such as *lawḥ maḥfūẓ* ("preserved tablet," Q 85:22), *sidrat al-muntahā* ("the lote-tree of the furthermost boundary," Q 53:14) and the throne and the footstool (*kursī*) allegorically. In particular, he insisted that the *istiwāʾ* ("sitting upright") is only a metaphor for God's exertion of power (*istīlāʾ*), while the interpretation of *istiwāʾ* as physical sitting has a central role for Ibn Taymiyya.[67] All these examples indicate that Ṣanā'ullāh was well aware that the concept of the compact heavens, on which the throne was supposed to rest, had become problematic, a point on which Āryā Samāj polemicists often dwelt in public controversies.[68] He claimed that according to the linguistic conventions of the Arabs, "heaven" is "the height or what is above" (*bulandī yā ūpar kī chīz*), following with this position Sayyid Aḥmad Khān (1817–1898), who had a poor reputation as a "*neycharī*" (a term derived from English "nature") among the religious scholars of his time because he claimed that God's behavior is in keeping with natural laws.[69]

In the conflict with his detractors, Ṣanā'ullāh was careful not to name al-Ghazālī and Fakhr al-Dīn al-Rāzī as his role models. He distinguishes between two types of scholars: first, the majority of scholars who like policemen are responsible for internal security, and second, a small élite who defend the realm of Islam against foreign invaders like an army. That small élite is the real heirs of the prophets.[70] Apparently they were supposed to challenge the opponents of Islam in light of the latter's use of arguments that were not derived from revelation, as, for example, al-Ghazālī had done. Ṣanā'ullāh himself claimed that his arguments were based on *falsafa* and *ʿilm-i sā'ins* (derived

---

67 Riexinger, *Ṣanā'ullāh*, 339–48, 355; Ibn Taymiyya, "al-Fatwā al-ḥamāwiyya al-kubrā," 12–16, 20–21. On p. 9, Ibn Taymiyya polemicizes against the *khalaf* who arrogantly correct the *salaf* and derive the true meaning from the texts through metaphors and by pointing to linguistic oddities. They follow the *taʾwīlāt* of the likes of Bishr al-Marīsī (d. 218/833), who was for Ibn Taymiyya a Murji'ite heretic (p. 23).

68 Riexinger, *Ṣanā'ullāh*, 372.

69 Ibid., 372–373; Sayyid Aḥmad Khān, "Tafsīr al-samawāt," 15.

70 Ṣanā'ullāh Amritsarī, *al-Kalām al-mubīn ba-jawāb al-arbaʿīn*, 129–30; Riexinger, *Ṣanā'ullāh*, 355. Although al-Ghazālī (*Iḥyāʾ*, 1:2, 5, 9) considered the scholars the heirs of the prophets in accordance with the *ḥadīth*, he advised against polemics and debates (*khilāfiyyāt wa-munāẓarāt*), in particular public ones: al-Ghazālī, *Iḥyāʾ*, 1:7081.

from English "science" and referring to modern natural science), which in his eyes were practically the same thing. In a debate they would stand as "external" evidence (*bīrūnī mubāḥaṣa*), that is, as non-scriptural proof.[71]

Ṣanā'ullāh's identification with al-Ghazālī was mirrored by his detractors. ʿAbdu l-Aḥad Khānpūrī, a hardliner among the *ahl-i ḥadīṣ*, wrote a 480-page invective called *Kitābu l-tawḥīd* (*Book of Divine Unity*) in order "to submit Sanā'ullāh to the verdict of Ibn Taymiyya." In addition to affirming *sunna*-cosmology, he denounced al-Ghazālī for having adopted philosophical teachings to such a degree that he denied that God was the willing and omnipotent creator.[72]

Ḥusayn al-Jisr: Saving al-Ghazālī's Argument from Misappropriation

It is difficult to assess how frequently al-Ghazālī's argument was employed in oral debate and how often his strict criteria for the acceptability of allegorical interpretations could be encountered in such discussions. But one of the foundational texts among the Muslim responses to modern science suggests that the use of his argument was quite common, although his standards were only loosely applied.

Although Ḥusayn al-Jisr al-Ṭarābulusī (1845–1909) was one of the most widely read Islamic authors in the late 19th and early 20th centuries, he has hitherto not received the scholarly attention he deserves. His fame among his contemporaries and in the first decades of the 20th century rested on his *al-Risāla al-Ḥamīdiyya fī ḥaqīqat al-diyāna al-Islāmiyya wa-ḥaqiyyat al-sharīʿa al-muḥammadiyya* (*Treatise Dedicated to Sultan ʿAbdü l-Ḥamīd II On the Truth of the Islamic Religion and the Truthfulness of Muḥammad's Law*) of 1888, where many of the arguments that would be current in Islamic apologetics in decades to come were formulated for the first time. The treatise, which was translated into Urdu, Ottoman, and Tatar Turkish, covers both normative questions (gender, punishments) and the relation of science and religion. The strong appeal of this book apparently stemmed from the fact that al-Jisr's experiences in his Levantine environment resembled those of educated Muslims in many other places.

Ḥusayn al-Jisr had been educated as a religious scholar, and his intellectual outlook was quite traditionally Shāfiʿite and Sufi, since ideological currents like

71 Ṣanā'ullāh Amritsarī, *Uṣūl-i Āryā*, 8–9.

72 Riexinger, *Ṣanā'ullāh*, 357–60.

the critique of the *madhhab*-system and Sufism had not yet found followers in Greater Syria. From the 1870s onwards he observed that the educational institutions run by European and American missionaries gave the Christian population of the Levant a considerable edge over the Muslims. This realization motivated him to study Western developments in science and education.[73] To do so had become possible for a wider public not acquainted with Western languages due to *al-Muqtaṭaf* (*The Selection*), a science and technology magazine published by alumni of the Syrian Protestant College. In addition to propagating modern science, the authors of the *Muqtaṭaf* also played a decisive role in the formulation of scientific terminology in Arabic.[74]

Ḥusayn al-Jisr argued that Muslims had to overcome their ignorance of modern science in order to compete with Christians. He advocated reform of the educational system and founded a short-lived school where both secular and traditional religious subjects were taught (its most famous pupil was Muḥammad Rashīd Riḍā).[75] But al-Jisr also held the opinion that not everything called science was both scientifically sound and compatible with religion, and afraid that the disappearance of religion would cause society to disintegrate, he proposed that materialist tendencies be combated. Therefore he set out—not unlike al-Ghazāli—to segregate verifiable concepts from falsehoods.

Only a decade before al-Jisr wrote his *Risāla*, the *Muqtaṭaf* had presented post-Copernican astronomy to a wider public in the Levant and had met with a quite hostile reaction from the Greek-Orthodox clergy.[76] Al-Jisr used what he had learned from the journal, however, to present the findings of modern astronomy as a proof of God: the celestial bodies form an astonishing system (*niẓām gharīb*). The law of general attraction (*nāmūs al-jādhibiyya al-ʿāmma*) means that they move with an exactitude that makes it possible to determine time. Moreover, the celestial bodies bring forth the plants, minerals, and animals and strengthen them according to their respective needs: "The one who brought them forth in this way is the one who knows, who is willing, who is powerful and wise."[77] The celestial bodies thus serve as one group of phenomena that al-Jisr uses as examples to bolster the "argument from design." (The

73 On his biography see Ebert, *Religion und Reform in der arabischen Provinz: Ḥusayn al-Ǧisr aṭ-Ṭarābulusī (1845–1909)*, 73–100.

74 Glaß, *Der Muqtaṭaf und seine Öffentlichkeit*; Elshakry, "Knowledge in Motion: The Cultural Politics of Modern Science Translations in Arabic."

75 Ebert, *Religion und Reform*, 79.

76 Glaß, *Muqtaṭaf*, 391–400.

77 Ḥusayn al-Jisr al-Ṭarābulusī, *al-Risāla al-Ḥamīdiyya fī ḥaqīqat al-diyāna al-Islāmiyya wa-ḥaqīqat al-sharīʿa al-muḥammadiyya*, 180–181; later he addresses aspects of Islamic cosmology. With regard to the seven other earths, he states that this term may refer to

other groupings are geological and meteorological phenomena or come from the world of animals and plants).

The largest single component of the *Risāla* is al-Jisr's attempt to refute the theory of evolution. That theory, too, had been propagated by the authors of the *Muqtaṭaf*, although it was not accepted at the Syrian Protestant College. A peculiar trait of the reception of the theory of evolution among Arabs (as well as Ottoman Turks) is that early presentations were based not on Darwin's writings, which were translated only decades later by Ismāʿīl Maẓhar (1891–1962), but rather on the German publications of Ludwig Büchner (1824–1899), a "vulgar materialist" (*Vulgärmaterialist*) who popularized evolutionist thought in Germany.[78] Büchner considered the theory of evolution a formidable vehicle for furthering his atheistic and materialist *Weltanschauung*. To that end he added issues that Darwin did not address, such as the eternity of matter, the ability of matter to self-organize, and the idea of general progress.[79] Büchner's translator, Shiblī Shumayyil (1850–1917), shared his orientation, and hence it is not surprising that al-Jisr deals with the evolutionists not as supporters of a scientific theory but as ideological foes (he mostly refers to them as *māddiyyūn*, materialists, and sometimes as *ṭabīʿiyyūn*, naturalists), nor is it surprising that his discussion of the theory of evolution is mixed up with discussion of other ideas deemed materialist, like the eternity of matter and its independent self-organization.[80]

In the context of the refutation of the theory of evolution, al-Jisr turns to the question of how far verses from the Qur'an and *aḥādīth* may be interpreted allegorically. With reference to Fakhr al-Dīn al-Rāzī's interpretation of Q 18:86, he acknowledges that the literal interpretation of Qur'anic wordings has to be excluded if it contradicts a definite rational proof (*dalīl ʿaqlī qāṭiʿ*).[81] He even concedes that Muslims had no objections to the nebular theory as an explanation for the origin of the sun, the earth, and the other planets. The revealed texts do not provide details of every aspects of creation, and therefore earlier

---

other planets somewhere in space, whereas he locates the Throne and Paradise beyond the realm of observable astronomy: 261–262.

78 The most important books in this respect were Büchner's *Kraft und Stoff* and his *Sechs Vorlesungen über die Darwin'sche Theorie von der Verwandlung der Arten.*

79 See Meïer, *Al-Muqtataf et le débat sur le darwinisme*; Jeha, *Darwin and the Crisis of 1882*; Glaß, *Muqtaṭaf*, 415–430. On Büchner see Gregory, *Scientific Materialism in Nineteenth Century Germany*, 100–121, 183–188. For the Turkish materialist and evolutionist discourse cf. Hanioğlu, "Blueprints for a Future Society: Late Ottoman Materialists on Science, Religion and Art."

80 al-Jisr, *Risāla*. 218–25, 228–29, 236–41, 258–61.

81 Ibid.. 230–32.

scholars had produced a range of explanations. They would have to accept the nebular theory, should it be supported by definite rational proofs.[82]

But when it comes to the question of original creation versus the evolution of humans from other creatures, al-Jisr first states that the revealed authoritative texts (*al-nuṣūṣ al-sharʿiyya*) describe how God created Adam from earth and clay (Q 6:2; 15:26, 28 and 33; 23:12, 32:7–9; 37:11; 55:14), which al-Rāzī had interpreted in the sense that water and earth are the two basic materials (*aṣlān*) of men. It is also stated that God created Adam with his own hands (Q 38:75). This expression indicates that humans were created in a way distinct from all other beings (*hādhihī l-ʿibāra tadullu ʿalā anna khalqahū kāna bi-ṣūra mumtāza ʿan baqiyat al-ʿawālim*), that God created first Adam and then his wife, Eve, and that He brought forth from them many men and women (Q 4:1). A literal reading of all of these verses makes clear that humans came about as an independent creation—or to use creationist terminology, as a "special creation"—and not through evolution (*Allāh taʿalā khalaqa l-insān nawʿ^an^ mustaqill^an^ lā bi-l-ṭarīq al-nushūʾ*), and that humans do not derive from other species, such as apes. Moreover, al-Jisr records, some prophetic traditions with single transmitters (*baʿḍ al-nuṣūṣ al-aḥādiyya*) state explicitly that humans were created independently, and although that kind of text is not a sufficient basis for articles of faith, such reports in no way confirm the opposite claim. For al-Jisr it is exactly this silence on evolution or derivation in both the Qur'an and the sunna that shows that the verses that do not individually make explicit that Adam was the first man and that he was made from clay, when taken as a whole confirm these origins of Adam with almost absolute certainty. However, if the naturalists should ever be able to prove evolution with a decisive rational proof, their position would then be acceptable, a situation comparable to the issue of whether Eden, where Adam was created, was in the heavens, as the majority claim, or on earth, as a minority of commentators state.[83]

Ḥusayn al-Jisr continues his discussion with an attempt to demonstrate that the materialists' arguments in support of their position are unconvincing. The four laws (*nawāmīs*) with which the materialists try to bolster their claims are speculative and hence unable to override the wording of the texts on the creation of Adam. The laws are (1) the law of inheritance, i.e. that the branch inherits from the root (*anna l-farʿ yarithu min al-aṣl*), (2) the law of intermediate forms (*tabāyunāt*), (3) the law of the struggle for existence (*tanāzuʿ al-biqāʾ*),

82 Ibid., 230–36.

83 al-Jisr, *Risāla*, 241–43. The references to Fakhr al-Dīn al-Rāzī are motivated by the fact that he was the *mufassir* who went furthest in integrating scientific knowledge into his exegesis. He therefore became the most important classical authority for modernists: Riexinger, *Ṣanāʾullāh*, 412–13.

and (4) natural selection.[84] He asserts that their claim that geological discoveries show that lower, and hence earlier, strata contain fossils of more primitive life-forms is speculative and, additionally, does not disprove that these beings were created in accordance with their respective temporal stage.[85] Of course variation can be observed, al-Jisr acknowledges, but variations exist between all individuals of one kind, and therefore it is quite possible that these differences are never so great that they transcend the border of one species.[86] Al-Jisr continues that he can disprove the common origin of men and apes because humans proceed from a state of utter helplessness at birth to sublime intellectual abilities, whereas the young ape is quite self-sufficient from the start but does not make much progress thereafter.[87]

Sayyid Aḥmad Khān: Al-Ghazālī Dismissed as Advocate of "Greek Philosophy"

Unlike Ḥusayn al-Jisr, the Indian Muslim educational reformer and politician Sayyid Aḥmad Khān (1817–1898) has been given the attention he deserves in the study of the modern intellectual history of Islam.[88] Sayyid Aḥmad Khān grew up in an aristocratic household in Delhi, where he was exposed to two different intellectual traditions: Naqshbandī Sufism, on the one hand, and puritan influences from the Waliyyullāh-school, on the other. Apparently he himself was more inclined towards the latter, as his early writings bear witness, and he later continued to pray according to the *ahl-i ḥadīs̱* rite and defended the *ahl-i ḥadīs̱* against the charge of involvement in seditious activities.[89] He was also exposed, however, to new intellectual influences that had followed in the wake of the British occupation of Delhi in 1803. In 1825 the Delhi College had been founded, and under the leadership of Felix Boutros (d. 1864) and later the Austrian Aloys Sprenger (1813–1893) scientific knowledge and Western history were taught in Urdu. Both principals also published translations of English scientific literature.[90] At this early point in his career, Sayyid Aḥmad

84 Ibid., 246–48.

85 Ibid., 249–51.

86 Ibid., 252–55.

87 Ibid., 256–58.

88 Troll, *Sayyid Ahmad Khan: A Reinterpretation of Muslim Theology*; Lelyveld, *Aligarh's First Generation: Muslim Solidarity in British India*.

89 Riexinger, *Ṣanāʾullāh Amritsarī*, 167–70.

90 Troll, *Sayyid Ahmad Khan*, 152; Minault, "The Perils of Cultural Mediation: Master Ram Chandra and Academic Journalism at Delhi College"; eadem, "Aloys Sprenger: German Orientalism's 'Gift' to Delhi College."

Khān was not open to these new ideas: he wrote a tract that ridiculed modern astronomy as taught at Delhi College, which was based on the idea that if the earth was moving all objects on it would remain at their place so that it would slip under them like a carpet.[91]

During the insurrection of 1857–58, Sayyid Aḥmad Khān remained loyal to the British. Nevertheless he was appalled by the reprisals that followed the reinstallation of British supremacy against the many aristocrats who had joined the insurrection. In these new political circumstances he feared that if the Muslim aristocrats bore a permanent grudge against the British, they would soon lose their position to the more upwardly-mobile Hindus. To preserve their status, loyalty alone was not enough according to Sayyid Aḥmad: the Muslims also had to overcome their hostility to modern education. On the practical level, he tried to overcome this perceived gap between Hindus and Muslims by the foundation of educational societies for the advancement of scientific knowledge, the most important of which was the Anglo-Muhammadan College at Aligarh, where the scions of Muslim noble families were to receive a Western education.

Sayyid Aḥmad Khān also saw the necessity of reformulating Islamic creeds in order to bring them into accord with scientific theories and findings. Borrowing a formulation that had originated in deism but had made its way into mainstream theology, he argued that there was no contradiction between the *word of God* and the *work of God*.[92] As a consequence, Sayyid Aḥmad Khān rationalized many miracles in the Qur'an. He rejected the suggestion that the *ḥadīth* is part of revelation and allowed it no religious authority.[93] In contrast to al-Jisr, Sayyid Aḥmad Khān even accepted the theory of evolution,[94] as well as post-Copernican astronomy.

Aḥmad Khān addressed the tension he perceived between the text of the Qur'an and modern scientific findings in a number of articles. In the most extensive of these, *Tafsīru l-samāwāt* (*Explanation of the Heavens*, 1874), he refutes the geocentric spherical model with astronomical arguments but also asserts that the model has nothing to do with Islam as such. Instead, he proposes that the identification of the seven heavens mentioned in the Qur'an with spheres of the planets and the fixed stars was a result of the influx of

---

91 Sayyid Aḥmad Khān, "*al-Qawl al-matīn fī ibṭāl-i ḥarakat-i zamīn*," 485–500; Troll, *Sayyid Ahmad Khan*, 147–149; Bausani, "Sayyid Ahmad Khan (1817–1898) e il moto della terra."

92 Sayyid Aḥmad Khān, "*Imām Ghazālī awr falsafī ḥażrāt*," 76; idem, "*Sūraj kī gardish zamīn kē gird Qur'ān-i majīd sē ṣābit nahīṇ*," 62; Troll, *Sayid Ahmad Khan*, 155–56, 172.

93 Troll, *Sayid Ahmad Khan*, 177–80, 187–88.

94 Riexinger, "Responses of South Asian Muslims to the Theory of Evolution," 217–19.

Greek astronomy during the early Islamic period.[95] After his presentation of the spherical model, he claims that Greek science is built on untenable foundations, because "for we are now clear that it diverges from observations made by telescope, which we hold, along with all who have even a little knowledge and reason, to be undeniable."[96] He then explains that since the discovery of the Jirjīs (*Georgium sidus*, i.e. Uranus), it has become clear that there are more than the six planets that can be observed with the plain eye. The discovery of moons accompanying Jupiter, Saturn, and Uranus shows that the planets do not move in compact spheres, that comets are moving in space and not in close proximity to the earth, that Venus and the other planets have phases like the moon, and that Venus and Mercury are sometimes "above" (*ūpar*) and sometimes "below" (*kē nichē*) the sun. The captions for the sketches of the two systems underline Sayyid Aḥmad Khān's message: "The world system according to the deduction of the Greeks" (*niẓām-i ʿālam yūnānīyoŋ kē qiyās kē muṭābiq*) and "the world system according to observation with the telescope" (*niẓām-i ʿālam muṭābiq-i mushāhida ba-ẕarīʿa-i dūrbīn*).[97]

In this context Sayyid Aḥmad Khān twice makes remarks that allude to al-Ghazālī's discourse: he notes that to oppose something that has been proven definitively would be to suggest that Islam opposes observation,[98] and that to insist on untenable interpretations would undermine Islam by exposing it to ridicule.[99] Sayyid Aḥmad Khān, however, does not plead for, but rather strictly opposes, allegorical interpretation of the relevant verses. He proposes a totally different solution to the problem, claiming that the purpose of the Qur'an is not to provide specific knowledge of astronomy or meteorology; instead it sought to teach Arab Bedouins that God is the creator and therefore its wording reflects the knowledge and linguistic conventions of the Arab Bedouins at the time of Muḥammad. For these Bedouins, heaven simply meant what is up there.[100] Sayyid Aḥmad Khān's abstention from allegorical explanation is more thoroughly explained in two later articles in which he stresses that science is

---

95 Sayyid Aḥmad Khān, "*Tafsīru s-samāwāt*," 1, 8–9, 11.

96 Sayyid Aḥmad Khān, "*Tafsīru s-samāwāt*," 3: "*Ham ko mushāhida sē ba-ẕarīʿa-i dūrbīn kē (jo hamārē nazdīk awr har ēk kē nazdīk jo zirā bʰī wāqifiyyat awr ʿaql rakʰtā hai dalīl qātiʿ hai) bar-khilāf us kē s̱ābit huʾā.*"

97 Sayyid Aḥmad Khān, "*Tafsīru s-samāwāt*," 4–9. It is remarkable that Sayyid Aḥmad Khān scolds others for being out of touch with science but uses himself a dated name for Uranus (finally conventionalized in 1850) and does not mention Neptune, which had been discovered in 1846.

98 Sayyid Aḥmad Khān, "*Tafsīru s-samāwāt*," 12.

99 Ibid., 12–15, 29.

100 Ibid., 27.

constantly subject to revision.[101] He reprimands the author Sayyid Farkhanda ʿAlī from Hyderabad, who claims to have proven the movement of the earth around the sun with the correct interpretation of certain verses. He himself once also believed that astronomy can be derived from scripture, states Sayyid Aḥmad Khān, when he claimed to have refuted the idea that the earth moves.[102] Sayyid Aḥmad Khān's insistence on the permanent progress of science undermines the notion that science can provide the absolute certainty that al-Ghazālī requires as a condition for dismissing the literal meaning of a revealed text.

It is not surprising that Sayyid Aḥmad Khān discards al-Ghazālī's position on exegesis and astronomy. In a critical review of *Munqidh min al-ḍalāl* (*Deliverer from Error*), he attacks al-Ghazālī's claim that the mathematical sciences, among them astronomy, have no relation to religion and hence may be studied. At first glance this position seems strange since Sayyid Aḥmad Khān makes statements similar to those of al-Ghazālī, but Sayyid Aḥmad Khān argues that al-Ghazālī contradicts himself when he opposes those cosmological concepts that were later systematized by al-Suyūṭī and insists that they contradict Greek astronomy. By postulating that the interpretation of the Qur'an had to be adapted to Greek astronomy, al-Ghazālī made Greek astronomy a part of Islam. But who, asks Sayyid Aḥmad Khān, would nowadays deny that Greek astronomy has been refuted?[103]

Conclusion

Whereas Müteferriḳa and S̱anāʾullāh thought that al-Ghazālī's argument against the rejection of demonstrated scientific insights was well suited to easing possible tensions between modern astronomy and the wording of the Qur'an and the *sunna*, Ḥusayn al-Jisr and Sayyid Aḥmad Khān were aware that al-Ghazālī's position was problematic because the character of science had changed entirely in the centuries that had passed. Ḥusayn al-Jisr and Sayyid Aḥmad Khān understood that scientific endeavors were no longer thought able to provide the absolute certainty of demonstration (*burhān*). Now new methods involving telescopes and microscopes led to the gradual progress of scientific observation and an equally gradual advancement of theoretical explanations.

101 Sayyid Aḥmad Khān, "*al-Arż laysat bi-sākina*," 54, 56–57. The epistle was originally published in 1893. Idem, "*Sūraj kī gardish*," 60–61.

102 Sayyid Aḥmad Khān, "*Sūraj kī gardish*," 61.

103 Sayyid Aḥmad Khān, "*Imām Ghazālī*," 71–73.

The conclusions that Ḥusayn al-Jisr and Sayyid Aḥmad Khān drew, however, were diametrically opposed. For Ḥusayn al-Jisr, the fact that evolutionary biology was based not on decisive and demonstrative proofs but on corroborative evidence originating from other fields and disciplines served as a justification to reject it entirely.[104] Accepting that the notions of continuous process and improvement had replaced definite proof as the hallmark of science, Sayyid Aḥmad Khān concluded that science and religion were not in conflict because they dealt with totally different subjects, with nature belonging to the area of responsibility of science.

Bibliography

Aiton, E.J. *The Vortex Theory of Planetary Motions*. New York: Elsevier, 1972.

Altıntaş, Hayrani. *Erzurumlu İbrahim Hakkı*. Istanbul: Millî Eğitim Bakanlığı Yayınları, 1992.

Amritsarī, Ṣanā'ullāh. *Fatāwā-yi ṣanā'iyya*. Sargodha: Maktaba-yi ṣanā'iyya, 1972.

———. *al-Kalām al-mubīn ba-jawābi l-arbaʿīn*. Amritsar: Maṭbaʿ-i Ahl-i Ḥadīṣ, 1904.

———. *Uṣūl-i Āryā*. Amritsar: n.p., 1929.

Bausani, Alessandro. "Sayyid Ahmad Khan (1817–1898) e il moto della terra." *Rivista di studi Orientali* 54 (1980): 303–318.

Ben-Zaken, Avner. "The Heavens of the Sky and the Heavens of the Heart: the Ottoman Cultural Context for the Introduction of Post-Copernican Astronomy." *British Journal for the History of Science* 37 (2004): 1–28.

Berkes, Niyazi. *The Development of Secularism in Turkey*. Montreal: McGill University Press, 1964.

Bieńkowska, Barbara. "From Negation to Acceptance: The Reception of the Heliocentric Theory in Polish Schools in the 17th and 18th Centuries." In *The Reception of Copernicus' Heliocentric Theory: Proceedings of a Symposium Organized by the Nicolas Copernicus Committee of the International Unions of the History and Philosophy of Science, Torún, Poland 1973*. Edited by Jerzy Dobrzycki. Dordrecht: Reidel, 1972. 79–116.

104 One may not forget that for these reasons the status of biology as a science has remained a matter of dispute until present: Mayr, *The Growth of Biological Thought: Diversity, Evolution and Inheritance*, 25–28, 32–45, 51–71, 846–847; Stamos, "Popper, Laws, and the Exclusion of Biology from Genuine Science"; Lienau and DeSalle, "Evidence, Content and Corroboration and the Tree of Life;" Esfeld and Sachse, *Kausale Strukturen: Einheit und Vielfalt in der Natur und den Naturwissenschaften*, 114–54.

Brockliss, Laurence. “The Moment of No Return: The University of Paris and the Death of Aristotelianism.” *Science & Education* 15 (2006): 259–278.

Çelebi, Katib Muṣṭafā. *Kitāb-i Cihannüma*. Istanbul: Dārü l-Ṭibāʿa al-Āmire, 1145/1732–33.

Ebert, Johannes. *Religion und Reform in der arabischen Provinz: Ḥusayn al-Ǧisr aṭ-Ṭarābulusī (1845–1909)—ein islamischer Gelehrter zwischen Tradition und Reform*. Frankfurt: P. Lang, 1991.

Elshakry, Marwa. “Knowledge in Motion: The Cultural Politics of Modern Science Translations in Arabic.” *Isis* 99 (2008): 701–730.

Esfeld, Michael and Christian Sachse. *Kausale Strukturen: Einheit und Vielfalt in der Natur und den Naturwissenschaften*. Frankfurt: Suhrkamp, 2010.

Gaborieau, Marc. *Le Mahdi incompris: Sayyid Ahmad Barelwî (1786–1831) et le millénarisme en Inde*. Paris: CNRS éditions, 2010.

al-Ghazālī, Muḥammad ibn Muḥammad. *The Incoherence of the Philosophers / Tahāfut al-falāsifa*. Edited and transl. by M. E. Marmura. 2nd ed. Provo: Brigham Young University Press, 2000.

———. *al-Munqidh min al-ḍalāl (erreur et deliverance)*. Edited by Farid Jabre. Beyrouth: Commission internationale pour la traduction des chefs-d’œuvre, 1959.

Glaß, Dagmar. *Der Muqtaṭaf und seine Öffentlichkeit: Aufklärung, Räsonnement und Meinungsstreit in der frühen arabischen Zeitschriftenkommunikation*. Würzburg: Ergon, 2004.

Goldziher, Ignaz. “Stellung der alten islamischen Orthodoxie zu den antiken Wissenschaften.” *Abhandlungen der königl. preuss. Akademie der Wissenschaften*. Jahrgang 1915. Philosophisch-historische Klasse, no. 8. 3–36.

———. “The Attitude of Orthodox Islam toward the Ancient Sciences.” In *Studies on Islam*, edited and translated by Merlin Swartz. New York: Oxford University Press, 1981. 185–215.

Goodrich, Thomas D. *The Ottoman Turks and the New World: A Study of the* Tarih-i Hind-i Garbi *and Sixteenth Century Ottoman Americana*. Wiesbaden: Harrassowitz, 1990.

Gregory, Frederick. *Scientific Materialism in Nineteenth Century Germany*. Dordrecht: Reidel, 1977.

Griffel, Frank. *al-Ghazālī’s Philosophical Theology*. Oxford: Oxford University Press, 2009.

Hagen, Gottfried. *Ein osmanischer Geograph bei der Arbeit: Entstehung und Gedankenwelt von Kātib Čelebīs Ǧihānnümā*. Berlin: Klaus Schwarz, 2003.

Ḥaḳḳı, İbrahīm. *Maʿrifetname*. Bulāq, 1245 a.h.

Hanioğlu, Şükrü. “Blueprints for a Future Society: Late Ottoman Materialists on Science, Religion and Art.” In *Late Ottoman Society: The Intellectual Legacy*, edited by Elisabeth Özdalga. London: Routledge Curzon, 2005. 28–116.

Haykel, Bernard. *Revival and Reform in Islam: the Legacy of Muhammad al-Shawkānī*. Cambridge: Cambridge University Press, 2003.

Heinen, Anton M. *Islamic Cosmology: A Study of As-Suyūṭī's* al-Hay'a as-sanīya fī l-hay'a as-sunnīya *with critical edition, translation and commentary.* Wiesbaden: Steiner, 1982.

Hoodbhoy, Pervez. *Islam and Science. Religious Orthodoxy and the Battle for Rationality.* London: Zed Books, 1991.

Huff, Toby E. *Intellectual Curiosity and the Scientific Revolution: A Global Perspective.* Cambridge: Cambridge University Press, 2011.

İhsanoğlu, Ekmeleddin. "Batı Bilim ve Osmanlı Dünyası: Bir İnceleme Örneği Olarak Modern Astronomi'nin Osmanlıya Girişi." *Belleten* 61 (1992): 727–775.

Jansen, Johannes J. G. *The Interpretation of the Koran in Modern Egypt.* Leiden: Brill, 1980.

Jeha, Shafik. *Darwin and the Crisis of 1882 in the Medical Department and the First Student Protest in the Arab World in the Syrian Protestant College.* Beirut: American University of Beirut Press, 2004.

al-Jisr al-Ṭarābulusī, Ḥusayn. *al-Risāla al-ḥamīdiyya fī ḥaqīqat al-diyāna al-Islāmiyya wa-ḥaqqiyyat al-sharī'a al-muḥammadiyya.* Tripoli: Jarrūs, n. d.

Jones, Kenneth W. *Arya Dharm: Hindu Consciousness in 19th-Century Punjab.* Berkeley: University of California Press, 1976.

Ibn Kathīr, Ismā'īl b. 'Umar. *al-Bidāya wal-nihāya.* Edited by Aḥmad Jādd. 14 vols. Cairo: Dār al-ḥadīth, 2006.

Sayyid Aḥmad Khān, "Al-Arż laysat bi-sākina." In *Maqālāt-i Sar Sayyid, 'ilmī wa taḥqīqī mażāmīn.* Edited by Ṣanā'ullāh Panīpattī. Lahore: Majlis-i Taraqqī-yi Adab, 1988. Vol. 4. 51–57.

———. "Imām Ghazālī awr falsafī ḥażrāt." In *Maqālāt-i Sar Sayyid, falsafiyyāna taḥqīqī mażāmīn.* Edited by Ṣanā'ullāh Panīpattī. Lahore: Majlis-i Taraqqī-yi Adab, 1988. Vol. 3. 67–79.

———. "Sūraj kī gardish zamīn kē gird Qur'ān-i majīd sē ṣābit nahīŋ." In *Maqālāt-i Sar Sayyid, 'ilmī wa taḥqīqī mażāmīn.* Edited by Ṣanā'ullāh Panīpattī. Lahore: Majlis-i Taraqqī-yi Adab, 1988. Vol. 4. 58–62.

———. "Tafsīru s-samāwāt." In *Maqālāt-i Sar Sayyid, tafsīrī mażāmīn.* Edited by Ṣanā'ullāh Panīpattī. Lahore: Majlis-i Taraqqī-yi Adab, 1988. Vol. 2. 1–115.

Kırkıncı, Mehmed. *Hayatım—Hatırlarım.* Istanbul: Zafer, 2004.

von Kügelgen, Anke. *Averroes und die arabische Moderne: Ansätze zu einer Neubegründung des Rationalismus im Islam.* Leiden: Brill, 1994.

Kut, Turgut & Türe, Fatma. *Yazmadan Basmaya: Müteferrika, Mühendishane, Üsküdar.* Istanbul: Yapı Kredi Yayınları, 1996.

Lelyveld, David. *Aligarh's First Generation: Muslim Solidarity in British India.* Princeton: Princeton University Press, 1978.

Lienau, E. Kurt and Rob DeSalle. "Evidence, Content and Corroboration and the Tree of Life." *Acta Biotheoretica* 57 (2009): 187–199.

Mayr, Ernst. *The Growth of Biological Thought: Diversity, Evolution and Inheritance.* Cambridge, Mass.: Harvard University Press, 2003.

Meïer, Olivier. *Al-Muqtataf et le débat sur le darwinisme: Beyrouth, 1876–1885*. Cairo: CEDEJ, 1996.

Minault, Gail. "The Perils of Cultural Mediation: Master Ram Chandra and Academic Journalism at Delhi College." In *The Delhi College: Traditional Elites, the Colonial Satet and Education before 1857*, edited by Margrit Pernau. New Delhi: Oxford University Press, 2006.

———. "Aloys Sprenger: German Orientalism's 'Gift' to Delhi College." *South Asia Research* 31 (2011): 7–23.

Morrison, Robert. "The Reception of Early-Modern European Astronomy by Ottoman Religious Scholars." *Archivum Ottomanicum* 21 (2003): 187–196.

Nursi, Said. *Muhâkemât*. Istanbul: Yeni Asya Neşriyat, 2001.

Özyılmaz, Ömer. *Osmanlı Medreselerin Eğitim Programları*. Ankara: T. C. Kültür Bakanlığı, 2002.

Popper, Karl. *Die beiden Grundprobleme der Erkenntnistheorie*. Edited by Troels Eggers Hansen. Tübingen: Mohr, 1979.

———. *The Two Fundamental Problems of the Theory of Knowledge*. Edited by Troels Eggers Hansen and transl. by Andreas Schlick. Abingdon: Routledge, 2009.

Pourchot, Edmond. *Institutiones philosophicae ad faciliorem veterum ac recentiorum philosophorum lectionem comparatae, Tomus tertius, Qui physicam specialem comprehendit*. Venice: Manfrè, 1760.

Preckel, Claudia. "*Islamische Bildungsnetzwerke und Gelehrtenkultur im Indien des 19. Jahrhunderts: Muḥammad Ṣiddīq Ḥasan Ḫān und die Enstehung der* Ahl-e-Ḥadīṯ-*Bewegung in Bhopal*." PhD diss., Ruhr-Universität Bochum, 2008.

Reichmuth, Stefan. "Islamic Reformist discourse in the Tulip Period (1718–30): Ibrahim Müteferriqa and His Arguments for Printing." In *International Congress on Learning and Education in the Ottoman World, Istanbul, 12–15 April 1999*, edited by A. Çaksu. Istanbul: IRCICA, 2001. 149–161.

———. "Bildungskanon und Bildungsreform aus der Sicht eines islamischen Gelehrten der anatolischen Provinz: Muḥammad al-Sājaqlī (Saçaklı-zāde gest. um 1145/1633) und sein Tartīb al-ʿulūm." In: *Words, Texts and Concepts Cruising the Mediterranean Sea: Studies on the sources, contents and influences of Islamic civilization and Arabic philosophy and science*, edited by Rüdiger Arnzen and Jörn Thielmann. Leuven: Peters, 2004. 493–520.

Renan, Ernest. *Averroès et l'averroïsme*. 3rd ed. Paris: Lévy, 1866.

Riexinger, Martin. *Ṣanāʾullāh Amritsarī (1868–1948) und die Ahl-i Ḥadīs̱ im Punjab unter britischer Herrschaft*. Würzburg: Ergon, 2004.

———. "Nasserism Revitalized: A critical reading of Ḥasan Ḥanafī's projects 'The Islamic Left' and 'Occidentalism' (and their uncritical reading)." *Welt des Islams* 47 (2007): 63–118.

———. "How Favourable is Puritan Islam to Modernity? A case study on the Ahl-i Hadis in late 19th and early 20th century India." In *Colonialism, Modernity, and Religious Identities: Religious Reform Movements in South Asia*, edited by Gwilym Beckerlegge. New Delhi: Oxford University Press, 2008. 147–165.

———. "Responses of South Asian Muslims to the Theory of Evolution." *Welt des Islams* 49 (2009): 212–247.

———. "Ibn Taymiyya's Worldview and the Challenge of Modernity: A Conflict Among the Ahl-i Ḥadīth in British India." In *Islamic Theology, Philosophy and Law: Debating Ibn Taymiyya and Ibn Qayyim al-Jawziyya*, edited by Birgit Krawietz and Georges Tamer. Berlin: De Gruyter, 2013. 493–517.

Sabev, Orlin. *İbrahim Müteferrika ya da İlk Osmanlı Matbaa Serüveni (1726–1746): yeniden Değerlendirme.* Istanbul: Yeditepe, 2006.

Sarasvati, Dayananda. *An English Translation of the Satyarth Prakash.* Delhi: Jan Gyan Prakashan, 1978.

Schmutz, Jacob. "Purchot, Edmond" *Index des scolastiques (Scholasticon)*: <http://www.scholasticon.fr/Database/Scholastiques_fr.php?ID=1040> (Accessed October 6 2013).

Sievert, Henning. *Zwischen arabischer Provinz und Hoher Pforte: Beziehungen, Bildung und Politik des osmanischen Bürokraten Rāġıb Meḥmed Paşa (st. 1763)*, Würzburg: Ergon, 2008.

Slowik, Edward. "Descartes' Physics." *Stanford Encyclopedia of Philosophy*: <http://plato.stanford.edu/entries/descartes-physics/> (Accessed October 6 2013).

Stamos, David N. "Popper, Laws, and the Exclusion of Biology from Genuine Science" *Acta Biotheoretica* 55 (2007): 357–375.

Ibn Taymiyya. "al-Fatwā al-ḥamāwiyya al-kubrā." In *Majmūʿ al-fatāwā Shaykh al-Islām Aḥmad ibn Taymiyya*, Edited by ʿAbd al-Raḥmān ibn Muḥammad al-ʿĀṣimī. 37 vols. Riyadh: Matābiʿ al-Riyāḍ, 1381–86/1961–67. Vol 5. 5–121.

———. *Darʾ taʿāruḍ al-ʿaql wa-l-naql*, edited by Muḥammad Rashād Sālim. 11 vols. Beirut: Dār al-Kunūz al-Adabiyya, 1980.

Troll, Christian W. *Sayyid Ahmad Khan: A Reinterpretation of Muslim Theology.* New Delhi: Vikas, 1978.

Westman, Robert S. *The Copernican Question. Prognostication, Skepticism, and Celestial Order.* Berkeley: University of California Press, 2011.

Zemplén, Jolan. "The Reception of Copernicanism in Hungary (A Contribution to the History of National Philosophy and Physics in the 17th and 18th Centuries)." In *The Reception of Copernicus' Heliocentric Theory: Proceedings of a Symposium Organized by the Nicolas Copernicus Committee of the International Unions of the History and Philosophy of Science, Torún, Poland 1973*, edited by Jerzy Dobrzycki. Dordrecht: Reidel, 1972. 311–35.

CHAPTER 12

The Revival of the Religious Sciences in the Twenty-First Century
Suʿād al-Ḥakīm's Adaptation of al-Ghazālī's Revival

Kenneth Garden

There can be no greater testimony to the influence of *Iḥyāʾ ʿulūm al-dīn* (*The Revival of the Religious Sciences*) in the Islamic tradition than the number of epitomes al-Ghazālī's masterpiece has inspired. Al-Ghazālī wrote three of them himself: *Kīmyā-yi saʿādat* (*The Alchemy of Happiness*) in Persian, which he describes as a middle-length (*wasīṭ*) treatment of the "science of the path to the hereafter," the subject of the *Iḥyāʾ*; *al-Arbaʿīn fī uṣūl al-dīn* (*The Book of Forty*), published as a section of *Jawāhir al-Qurʾān* (*Jewels of the Qurʾān*), which he describes as a concise treatment (*wajīz*);[1] and *Lubāb al-Iḥyāʾ* (*The Kernels of the Revival*).[2] Badawī points to 26 other epitomes of the work.[3] Even critics of *Iḥyāʾ ʿulūm al-dīn* saw in it a model for appropriation: al-Ghazālī's Andalusi contemporary Abū Bakr al-Ṭurṭūshī (d. 520/1126), who writes of having met al-Ghazālī personally, detested the book and approved of its being burned in Cordoba in 503/1109. But he himself wrote a version of the *Iḥyāʾ* that, as he put it, corrected its mistakes.[4] The appeal of *Iḥyāʾ ʿulūm al-dīn* extended to the Shiite community, one of whose scholars, al-Muḥsin Fayḍ al-Kāshānī

---

* I would like to thank Frank Griffel for his suggestions that greatly improved this chapter.
1 al-Ghazālī, *al-Mustaṣfā min ʿilm al-uṣūl*, 1:5. Here al-Ghazālī describes *Iḥyāʾ ʿulūm al-dīn* as a "comprehensive" (*basīṭ*) treatment of "the science of the path to the hereafter."
2 Until recently, the *Lubāb* was assumed to be by Aḥmad al-Ghazālī, but Griffel, *Al-Ghazālī's Philosophical Theology*, 62, has argued convincingly that it is by Abū Ḥāmid Muḥammad.
3 Badawī, *Muʾallafāt al-Ghazālī*, 114–18.
4 For extracts of what appears to be a partial manuscript of this work, found in 1983 in a private library in Marrakech see al-Manūnī, "Iḥyāʾ ʿulūm al-dīn fī manẓūr al-gharb al-Islāmī ayyām al-murābiṭīn wa-l-muwaḥḥidīn," 130, and 135–37. On al-Ṭurṭūshī's declaration of intent to write such a book, see his letter to an otherwise unknown and unidentified "Ibn Muẓaffar" in Ghurāb, "Ḥawl iḥrāq al-murābiṭīn li-iḥyāʾ al-Ghazālī," 162, as well as al-Wansharīsī, *al-Miʿyār al-muʿrib wa-jāmiʿ al-mughrib*, 12:187. Ghurāb, "Ḥawl iḥrāq al-murābiṭīn li-iḥyāʾ al-Ghazālī," 162–63, n. 37, reproduces an apparent excerpt of the book found in Ibn al-Khaṭīb's *al-Iḥāṭa fī akhbār Gharnāṭa*, 3:267, which gives its title as *Marāqī l-ʿārifīn*.

© KONINKLIJKE BRILL NV, LEIDEN, 2016 | DOI 10.1163/9789004307490_013

(d. 1090/1679), wrote a Shiite epitome in the 17th century.[5] It even extended beyond the boundaries of the Muslim community: the 7th/13th century Syriac *Ethicon* of Gregory Barhebreus (d. 685/1286) is recognized as being a Christian re-working of *Iḥyāʾ ʿulūm al-dīn*.[6]

This tradition continues to our day. Michael Cook notes two modern epitomes,[7] and this article will consider a further contemporary example: *Iḥyāʾ ʿulūm al-dīn fī-l-qarn al-wāḥid wa-l-ʿishrīn* (*Revival of the Religious Sciences in the 21st Century*), published in 2004 by the Lebanese scholar of Sufism Suʿād al-Ḥakīm (Souad Hakim). Examining this specific instance of an *Iḥyāʾ* adaptation will allow us to explore the phenomenon of epitomizing *Iḥyāʾ ʿulūm al-dīn*, and also raise broader questions of the reception of ideas. We will look at Suʿād al-Ḥakīm's motives for writing an adaptation of the *Iḥyāʾ* rather than simply either referring her audience to al-Ghazālī's original or producing an exposition of her ideas in a wholly original work. We will also look at the kinds of liberties she took with al-Ghazālī's *Iḥyāʾ* in writing her own version to understand her agenda more deeply and to explore the kinds of constraints imposed on an author by adapting an earlier work. We will conclude by asking what is it about the *Iḥyāʾ* in particular that makes it such an appealing source of imitation and adaptation, and how the answer to that question may change through the generations as changing currents in Muslim societies and discourses engender new readings of al-Ghazālī and his *Revival*.

Suʿād al-Ḥakīm and Her Aims in Producing an Epitome of the *Iḥyāʾ*

Suʿād al-Ḥakīm is a professor of Sufism at the Lebanese University in Beirut and is herself a practicing Sufi.[8] Much of her work to date has been on Muḥyī al-Dīn Ibn ʿArabī (d. 638/1240), including *al-Muʿjam al-ṣūfī*, a 1300–page

5 Fayḍ al-Kāshānī, *al-Maḥajja al-bayḍāʾ fī tahdhīb al-Iḥyāʾ*. Fayḍ al-Kāshānī regretted that al-Ghazāli wrote *Iḥyāʾ ʿulūm al-dīn* before what he purports to have been his conversion to Shiism. See Cook, *Commanding Right and Forbidding Wrong in Islamic Thought*, 283, n. 219 and 454, n. 185. See also Griffel, *Al-Ghazālī's Philosophical Theology*, 293, n. 38.

6 Barhebraeus, *Ethicon: Mēmrā I*. On this work and its debt to al-Ghazālī, see Teule, "La vie dans le monde: perspectives chrétiennes et influnces musulmanes." My thanks to Hidemi Takehashi for informing me of Barhebraeus' adaptation of al-Ghazālī and sending me references to these works. See also Cook, *Commanding Right and Forbidding Wrong in Islamic Thought*, appendix 2, pp. 600–3.

7 Cook, *Commanding Right and Forbidding Wrong in Islamic Thought*, 507, n. 8; 57, n. 155. For a discussion of other epitomes, see ibid., 451–52.

8 She implies as much in the book itself. See for example al-Ḥakīm, *Iḥyāʾ ʿulūm al-dīn fī l-qarn al-wāḥid wa-l-ʿishrīn*, 86, 173.

dictionary of 706 technical terms found in his writings,[9] an edition plus parallel Spanish translation—together with Pablo Beneito—of Ibn ʿArabī's *Mashāhid asrār al-qudsiyya wa maṭāliʿ al-anwār al-ilāhiyya* (*Contemplation of the Holy Mysteries and the Rising of the Divine Lights*),[10] as well as numerous articles.

Al-Ḥakīm's *Iḥyāʾ ʿulūm al-dīn fī l-qarn al-wāḥid wa-l-ʿishrīn* is a much briefer work than al-Ghazālī's *Iḥyāʾ*, somewhat shorter than a single one of its quarters. Nonetheless, the book is nearly 700 pages long: demanding, but adapted to the modern attention span. It provides a comprehensive guide to a life informed by al-Ghazālī's great masterpiece as well as al-Ḥakīm's vision of Islam.

The topics covered by the work are largely the same as those covered by the *Iḥyāʾ*. Al-Ḥakīm, however, substantially reorders their treatment to suit her focus and in response to matters on which she disagrees with al-Ghazālī or which have been controversial, as will be discussed below. Al-Ghazālī famously divided *Iḥyāʾ* into four roughly equal quarters of ten "books" each, as follows[11]:

First Quarter: Acts of Worship (*al-ʿibādāt*)	**Second Quarter: Acts of Daily Life (*al-ʿādāt*)**
Knowledge	Manners of Eating
Foundations of Doctrines	Manners of Marriage
Mysteries of Purity	Rules on Earning a Livelihood
Mysteries of Prayer	What is Lawful and What is Prohibited
Mysteries of Almsgiving	Manners of Intimacy, Brotherhood and Friendship
Mysteries of Fasting	Manners of Seclusion
Mysteries of Pilgrimage	Manners of Traveling
Manners of Qurʾānic Recitation	Manners of Music and Singing
Invocations and Supplications	Commanding Right and Forbidding Wrong
Arrangement of Litanies and Divisions of the Night Vigil	Manners of Living and Prophetic Morals

Third Quarter: Qualities Leading to Perdition (*al-muhlikāt*)	**Fourth Quarter: Qualities Leading to Salvation (*al-munjiyyāt*)**
Explanation of the Marvels of the Heart	Repentance
Disciplining the Soul, Refining Morals, and Treating the Diseases of the Heart	Patience and Thankfulness

9 Al-Ḥakīm, *al-Muʿjam al-ṣūfī: al-ḥikma fī ḥudūd al-kalima*.

10 Ibn ʿArabī, *Las contemplaciones de los misterios*.

11 This overview with its translations of the quarters and books of *Iḥyāʾ ʿulūm al-dīn* is taken with very minor modifications from Treiger, *Inspired Knowledge in Islamic Thought*, 38.

Breaking the Two Desires (for Food and Sex)	Fear and Hope
Perils of the Tongue	Poverty and Abstinence
Perils of Anger, Spite, and Envy	Professing Divine Unity and Relying on God
Condemnation of this World	Love, Longing, Affection, and Contentment
Condemnation of Miserliness and Avarice	Intention, Sincerity, and Devotion
Condemnation of Vanity and Ostentation	Self-Inspection and Self-Accounting
Condemnation of Pride and Conceit	Contemplation
Condemnation of Delusion	Remembrance of Death and the Afterlife

In contrast to al-Ghazālī's *Iḥyāʾ*, Suʿād al-Ḥakīm's adaptation is divided into five sections (singl. *bāb*) of unequal length, further divided into chapters (singl. *faṣl*), and in a different order:

Introduction (pp. 7–48)

Section 1: Acts of Worship (*al-ʿibādāt*) (pp. 51–152)
Knowledge and Reason in Islam (*al-ʿilm wa-l-ʿaql fī-l-Islām*)
Islam's Creed (*ʿaqīdat al-Islām*)
Purity (*al-ṭahāra*)
Prayer (*al-ṣalāt*)
Charity (*al-zakāt*)
Fasting (*al-ṣawm*)
Pilgrimage (*al-ḥajj*)

Section 2: The Soul and its Discipline (*al-nafs wa riyāḍatu<u>hā</u>*) (pp. 153–233)
Marvels of the Heart (*ʿajāʾib al-qalb*)
Traits of Character and Ethics (*al-khuluq wa-l-akhlāq*)
Hunger and its Spiritual Role (*al-jūʿ wa dawruhu al-rūḥāniyya*)

Section 3: Qualities Leading to Perdition (*al-muhlikāt*) (pp. 235–346)
The Tongue (*al-lisān*)
Anger (*al-ghaḍab*)
Hatred (*al-ḥiqd*)
Envy (*al-ḥasad*)
Love of the World (*ḥubb al-dunyā*)
Miserliness and Love of Money (*al-bukhl wa-ḥubb al-māl*)
Love of Status and Fame (*ḥubb al-jāh wa-l-shuhra*)
Arrogance (*kibr*)

Vanity (*al-ʿujb*)
Delusions (*al-ghurūr*)

Section 4. Qualities Leading to Salvation (*al-munjiyyāt*) (pp. 347–463)
Repentance (*al-tawba*)
Patience (*al-ṣabr*)
Gratitude (*al-shukr*)
Hope (*al-rajāʾ*)
Fear (*al-khawf*)
Poverty (*al-fuqr*)
Asceticism (*al-zuhd*)
Declaration of Divine Unity (*al-tawḥīd*)
Reliance Upon God (*al-tawakkul*)
Love (*al-maḥabba*)
Longing (*al-shawq*)
Contentment (*al-riḍā*)
Intention (al-*niyya*)
Sincerity and Truthfulness (*al-ikhlāṣ wa-l-ṣidq*)
Self Assessment (*al-muḥāsaba*)
Contemplation (*al-tafakkur*)

Section Five. Etiquette in Islam (*al-ādāb fī-l-Islām*) (pp. 467–684)
The Etiquette of Food and Contemporary Developments (*ādāb al-ṭaʿām wa taṭawwur al-zamān*)
The Etiquette of Marriage (*ādāb al-zawāj*)
The Etiquette of Profit and Earning a Livelihood (*ādāb al-kasb wa-l-rizq*)
The Etiquette of Friendship, Companionship, and Brotherhood (*ādāb al-ṣadāqa wa-l-ṣuḥba wa-l-ukhuwa*)
The Etiquette of Retreat (*ādāb al-ʿuzla*)
The Etiquette of Travel (*ādāb al-safar*)
The Etiquette of Listening to Music and Ecstasy (*ādāb al-samāʿ wa-l-wajd*)
The Etiquette of Commanding Right and Forbidding Wrong (*ādāb al-amr bi-l-maʿrūf wa-l-nahyi ʿan al-munkar*)
The Etiquette of Reciting the Qur'an (*ādāb tilāwat al-Qurʾān*)
Remembrances of God and Prayers upon the Prophet (*al-adhkār wa-l-daʿwāt*)
Supplication (*duʿāʾ*)
Supplications that Have been Handed Down (*adʿiya maʾthūra*)
The Etiquette of Death (*ādāb al-mawt*)
The Etiquette of Life and Prophetic Ethics (*ādāb al-maʿīsha wa akhlāq al-nubuwwa*)

Al-Ghazāli's was very deliberate in creating a book of four equal quarters. Having run out of obligatory ritual matters to cover in the first quarter, he adds books on optional rituals to raise the total to ten. In the fourth quarter, he covers as many as four virtues in a book for the sake of restricting the number of books to ten. Al-Ghazālī's aim in *Iḥyāʾ ʿulūm al-dīn* is to guide his reader to knowledge of God and love of God, which will result in salvation or happiness (*saʿāda*) in the afterlife, the highest purpose for which human beings were created. The four quarters of the book trace this trajectory; rising from performance of the required rituals and observance of the correct creed, to correct conduct in daily life, to purging the soul of vices that distract from God, to cultivating virtues that draw one closer to God. The final of the forty books is *Kitāb Dhikr al-mawt wa-mā baʿdahū*, "The Book on Death and the Afterlife." This teleological progression of four quarters of the *Iḥyāʾ* is reflected in al-Ghazālī's discussions of purity (*ṭahāra*) and professing divine unity (*tawḥīd*), which are likewise divided into four degrees, as will be discussed below. A four-stage progression is a central feature of the book around which it is structured.

Suʿād al-Ḥakīm's rendition of *Iḥyāʾ ʿulūm al-dīn* departs from this structure in telling ways. Her *Revival* has five sections of very unequal length. Its final section is the equivalent of al-Ghazālī's second on the etiquette of daily life, and is twice as long as any other section. The equivalent to al-Ghazālī's *Kitāb Dhikr al-mawt wa-mā baʿdahū* ("Book on Death and the Afterlife") is moved from the quarter on "Qualities that Lead to Salvation" to "the Etiquette of Daily Life" so as to keep it in the final section. But the final book of that section is, as in the second quarter of al-Ghazālī's *Iḥyāʾ*, a book on the moral conduct of daily life and the morals of the Prophet. If the four quarters al-Ghazālī covered and their arrangement reflect the *télos* of his project, so does al-Ḥakīm's structure reflect hers. While not denying the importance of salvation in the afterlife, her aim is to reorient today's Muslims in their worldly life.

She says as much at the beginning of this final chapter:

> If al-Ghazālī, in the fifth century *hijrī*, strove for a revival of the sciences of religion, we today strive for a revival of the human being of that religion.[12]

This speaks as well to a difference in intended audience. In striving to revive the religious sciences (*ʿulūm*), al-Ghazālī addressed mainly the religious scholars (*ʿulamāʾ*). In the modern world of wide-spread literacy and greater piety and scholarly engagement from lay Muslims, al-Ḥakīm is addressing a broader, non-specialist audience.

12 Al-Ḥakīm, *Iḥyāʾ ʿulūm al-dīn fī l-qarn al-wāḥid wa-l-ʿishrīn*, 668.

Re-writing an 6th/11th Century Work to Engage with the 21st Century

Rather than presenting herself as simply channeling al-Ghazālī, Suʿād al-Ḥakīm acknowledges her own role in forging the book at hand. Her 21st century version of *Iḥyāʾ* is "based on" al-Ghazālī's work,[13] and in her introduction, she presents both her own project in writing her book and also her understanding of al-Ghazālī's in writing his. She describes her effort as "simple" and "modest," not rising to the immense scope of al-Ghazālī's undertaking. The circumstances of our day, she writes, differ from those of al-Ghazālī's in that Muslims have become estranged from their religion. Furthermore, as we look at today's Muslims, we rarely perceive in them the grandeur of Islam. Indeed, we are often forced to ask, "does Islam permit this? Is what we see Islam? Are the ethics of Muslims the ethics of Islam?"[14]

Al-Ḥakīm sees many facets of this estrangement from Islam. She writes that she wishes to support tolerance, justice, and peace against fanaticism and extremism, but also to address those Muslims who wish to separate religion from life and to distance it from the undertakings of society. She further insists that the prescriptions of the law must be tied to ethics.[15] These ethics are part of a broader constellation of Islamic etiquette. She sees it as a travesty that the elite have their children instructed in "French manners" or send them to "Swiss institutes of manners" while the highly refined etiquette of the Prophet has been forgotten and Islam's contribution to humanity in the field of etiquette has been obliterated.[16] This partially explains the outsized role the section on customs plays in her *Revival* compared to al-Ghazālī's.

Reacquainting Muslims with Islam must be done in a manner in keeping with the needs of the day and openness to a world of multiple cultures and religious traditions. As a child of the age, she writes, she demands of herself that she be contemporary and participate in the movement of history, that she be open to the Other, adopt a culture of dialogue and peace, and build a philosophy of pluralism. As a Muslim, she sees faith in God and membership in a community of worship as a human necessity for the sake of finding the wisdom of existence in all the facets of human experience.[17] Her aim, then, could be described as a "third way," that is, a mode of Muslim religiosity that

13 Ibid., 47.

14 Ibid., 44.

15 Ibid., 47.

16 Ibid., 41: "*al-qawāʾid al-faransiyya*," and "*maʿāhid al-swīsriyya li-l-ādāb*."

17 Ibid., 7.

shuns both an insular, literalist Salafism, and a secularist approach that divests itself of religion altogether.

Such an attempt to reconsider the Islamic tradition in the contemporary age has many precedents, she notes, and runs the risk of a certain faddishness. These efforts often bear titles coined from "the collected crumbs of the culture of the age," such as "modernization" (*al-taḥdīth*), "evolution" (*al-taṭawwur*), "progress" (*al-taqaddum*), "pluralism" (*al-taʿaddudiyya*), "women's rights" (*ḥuqūq al-marʾa*), and "human civilization" (*ḥadārat al-insān*).[18] She seeks to avoid this, she writes, by presenting Islam as it has been agreed upon among the various disciplines of Islamic religious sciences across the ages. In looking to the heritage of Islamic religious sciences for guidance, she is responding to what she calls "the philosophy of zero" (*falsafat al-ṣifr*), which seeks to sweep away the contributions of one's predecessors and rebuild the edifice of the religion from the ground up, without reference to its rich heritage. Her own effort is a humble recognition of the efforts of her predecessors, a connection to this heritage, and an attempt to preserve it from oblivion.[19]

In addition to these stated aims is a major unstated aim, which is to present a vision of Islam that includes Sufism as an integral part. Sufism has become marginalized over the past century by two trends within Islam: Modernism, which deems it irrational and superstitious, and Salafism, which judges it a blameworthy innovation not present among the venerated first generations of Muslims—*al-salaf al-ṣāliḥ*, from which the movement takes its name. Neither of these two currents are directly named in the book, but they are recognizable in two religious tendencies, between which al-Ḥakīm seeks to navigate. Each, in its own way, can be seen as a manifestation of the "philosophy of zero" she rejects.

The beginnings of Islamic modernism in the Arab world are usually traced to Jamāl al-Dīn al-Afghānī (d. 1897), Muḥammad ʿAbduh (d. 1905), and M. Rashīd Riḍā (d. 1935) at the end of the 19th century and beginning of the 20th. All of these thinkers were attracted to Sufism at some point in their lives, but all were critical of it as well, seeing it as a source of blameworthy innovations and a barrier to the modern scientific agenda they advocated for Muslim societies in their effort to harness the forces that had transformed the West and made possible its world hegemony. This modernist perspective came to regard Sufism as an embarrassing and irrational vestige of the past, a perspective that spread in Muslim societies, leading to the decline of Sufi practice in the 20th

18 Ibid., 7.

19 Ibid., 44.

century and a widespread image of Sufism as an intellectually irrelevant and superstitious custom.[20]

The Salafi/Wahhābī trend has attacked Sufism from a different angle. Rather than presenting Sufism as a barrier to reconciling the Islamic tradition with Modernity and rationalism, Salafis reject Sufism as a blameworthy innovation (*bidʿa*) and corruption of the pristine practice of the Prophet Muhammad and the first three generations of Muslims, known as *al-salaf al-salih* (the Righteous Forebearers). Like the Modernists, they see Sufi practices, such as the veneration of saints (*awliyāʾ*) and the claims of inspired knowledge, to be superstition with no basis in revelation. Unlike the modernists, they seek to limit the role of rationalism, preferring a literal reading of scripture.[21]

Both the modernists and the Salafis could be viewed as practitioners of the "philosophy of zero" that al-Ḥakīm describes. While modernists prefer to return to the sources to reinterpret them in a way in keeping with their modernizing agenda, Salafis view the long centuries of accumulated Islamic learning as little more than a deviation from what they present as the transparent meaning of the scriptural text.

At the end of her chapter on "Knowledge and Reason in Islam" (*al-ʿIlm wa-l-ʿaql fī-l-Islām*), which is the first chapter in her book just as the *Kitāb al-ʿIlm* ("The Book of Knowledge") was in al-Ghazālī's, al-Ḥakīm defends the Sufi notion of divinely inspired knowledge (*ilhām*) against the charge that it is irrational, an accusation often leveled by Muslim modernists. She rejects the charge that acquired (learned) knowledge and inspired knowledge are opposed to one another or that inspired knowledge is irrational. We cannot claim, she asserts, that any knowledge or any human matter is irrational. Human communication and mutual understanding is possible only through reason, and without it, human beings would be as though insane. She follows al-Ghazālī in writing that Sufis acquire knowledge by purifying their hearts of vices and preparing them to receive the lights of inspired knowledge. But such knowledge must be tested against both scripture and reason before it is accepted.[22] She clarifies the distinction between inspired and rational knowledge in her version of the 21st book of *Iḥyāʾ ʿulūm al-dīn*, *Sharḥ ʿAjāʾib al-qalb* ("Explanation

20 Sirriyeh, *Sufis and Anti-Sufis*. On al-Afghānī, see pp. 65–74; on M. ʿAbduh, see pp. 86–98. On M. Rashiḍ Riḍā, see pp. 98–105. On the decline of Sufi *ṭarīqas* in Egypt in the 1950s–60s, see pp. 140–43. Sirriyeh quotes Michael Gilsenan on the growing marginalization of Sufism in Egyptian culture in the 1960s on p. 141. For a similar presentation, though differing in some details, see De Jong, "Opposition to Sufism in Twentieth-Century Egypt."

21 Sirriyeh, *Sufis and Anti-Sufis*, pp. 157–160. On the critique of Sufism by the Muslim Brotherhood, see Mitchell, *Society of the Muslim Brothers*, 214–16.

22 Al-Ḥakīm, *Iḥyāʾ ʿulūm al-dīn fī l-qarn al-wāḥid wa-l-ʿishrīn*, 74.

of the Marvels of the Heart,")[23] as well as explaining how childhood egotism eclipses pristine human nature that is naturally open to inspiration.[24] Nowhere does she mention a specific critic of Sufism and its claim to divinely inspired knowledge, whether a person or a movement or intellectual tendency. Nonetheless, the apologetic element of her discussion is clear, and the rationalist critique to which she is responding is clearly a modernist one.

A clear, though still not overt, response to Salafism is found in the chapter on contemplation (*tafakkur*).[25] In al-Ḥakīm's *Revival*, the chapter on contemplation serves as a summary of the section on virtues or "Qualities Leading to Salvation" (*al-munjiyyāt*), and she begins by asserting that al-Ghazālī's virtue ethics is rooted in scripture and is "in accordance with accounts of the Righteous Ancestors (*al-salaf al-ṣāliḥ*)." She takes pains here and throughout the book to demonstrate that her presentation of the tradition is in accord with the Qur'ān, the Sunna, and the precedent of the *salaf*—much as al-Ghazālī does in the *Iḥyā'*.[26]

This is unremarkable in itself, but shortly thereafter she writes,

> We stand before the *salaf* and before our forefathers, and we do not wish to be cut off from them. But through a certain consciousness and contemplation, it is possible for them to live on in us. For we inherit just as sons inherit from fathers. Their values endure through abiding in us. And rather than returning to the *salaf*, the *salaf* come to us and participate with us in the era with its continuities and changes. Any generation that ceases to carry its past within itself will be like those who bury the past beneath the weight of the present, and will in turn beget sons who abandon them, for he who has no past will have no future.[27]

In this passage we can see both a rejection of modernism and its denial of tradition in its embrace of progress, and also a particular definition of the

23 Ibid., 167–68. Al-Ḥakīm's version bears the title *'Ajā'ib al-qalb*, "The Marvels of the Heart."

24 Ibid., 160–64.

25 In my list of al-Ghazālī's book titles above, I follow Treiger in translating *tafakkur* as "cogitation," which accurately captures al-Ghazālī's use of the term in his *Revival*. "Contemplation" more accurately captures Su'ād al-Ḥakīm's use of the term in her *Iḥyā' 'ulūm al-dīn fī l-qarn al-wāḥid wa-l-'ishrīn*.

26 Anjum, "Cultural Memory of the Pious Ancestors (*Salaf*) in al-Ghazālī," 362, characterizes the *Iḥyā'*s attitude as being, "not a return to the *salaf*, or akin to the Ḥanbalite rejection of post-*salaf* intellectual and spiritual developments, but rather the projection of Sufi spirituality onto the *salaf*, and then the presentation of *salaf* as models for reform."

27 Al-Ḥakīm, *Iḥyā' 'ulūm al-dīn fī l-qarn al-wāḥid wa-l-'ishrīn*, 460–61.

correct relationship to the *salaf*, in which their heritage is preserved not by trying to return to their time—by dressing and grooming as they do, for example—but by inviting them to participate in ours. Nowhere is al-Ḥakīm overtly polemical in her discussion of the correct relation to modernity and the Islamic heritage, but there is no mistaking the trends in contemporary Islam that represent the tendencies she is trying to balance and against which she is trying to justify her Sufi vision of Islam.

Suʿād al-Ḥakīm's Reworkings of al-Ghazālī's Text

As a rule, Suʿād al-Ḥakīm is a careful reader of the *Iḥyāʾ*, and her twenty-first century re-working follows the major themes of its model closely given how much shorter it is than the original. Nonetheless, *Iḥyāʾ ʿulūm al-dīn* contains some prominent discussions and theses that do not fit well with al-Ḥakīm's objectives in re-writing al-Ghazālī's work, and her response is generally to omit or re-cast them, often in ways that shed light on her agenda. As we have already seen, the liberty she takes with the overall structure of the *Iḥyāʾ* makes plainer her goal of re-ordering the worldly lives of Muslims, in sharp contrast to al-Ghazālī's concern with the fate of those Muslims in the afterlife.

Al-Ḥakīm does not draw attention to most of her specific departures from al-Ghazālī's *Revival*, but she ends her introduction with a list of seven kinds of changes she has introduced in her adaptation of the text.[28] Most of these have to do with making *Iḥyāʾ ʿulūm al-dīn* more accessible to a contemporary audience, but her second item is of particular interest: "The removal of flaws that have been criticized before by worthy scholars, or their clarification or comment on them such that the text becomes acceptable to all, jurists and Sufis alike."[29] This is a rule we find her following as she plays down or omits al-Ghazālī's prominent efforts to demote the status of the jurists as well as elements of his book that show a greater debt to philosophy than Sufism, especially such passages as have inspired controversy over the centuries.

The Science of the Hereafter vs. the Sciences of this World

One of the key taxonomies of the sciences presented in *Iḥyāʾ ʿulūm al-dīn* is the contrast between the science of the hereafter (*ʿilm al-ākhira*), which is the subject of the book, with the sciences of this world (*ʿulūm al-dunyā*), by which al-Ghazālī means mainly law and theology. The very revival of the religious

28 Ibid., 45–46.

29 Ibid., 45.

sciences of the book's title is rooted in this distinction. Al-Ghazālī asserts that the science of the hereafter was the original focus of the Companions of the Prophet (*al-ṣaḥāba*) and the founders of the legal schools (*al-aʾimma*), who only practiced the worldly sciences of law and theology reluctantly and secondarily. Later generations, however, found that prestige and money could be won through the law and theology and pursued them as a primary interest, allowing the sciences of this world to eclipse the science of the hereafter, and this brought about the very death of the religious sciences. The "revival" that al-Ghazālī's masterpiece proclaims lies in restoring the primacy of the science of the hereafter over the sciences of this world, especially *fiqh*.[30]

Al-Ḥakīm is certainly aware of this distinction. In her chapter on knowledge, she writes: "The number of times Imam al-Ghazālī categorizes the sciences surprises us. Every time he discusses science (or knowledge: *ʿilm*) in one of his books, we see him divide it into categories."[31] She then illustrates her point by discussing five different taxonomies of science found in *Iḥyāʾ ʿulūm al-dīn*, "by way of example" without once referring to this most central taxonomy. Though she notes some of al-Ghazālī's critiques of *fiqh*, she pairs this observation with the assertion that he also criticized Sufism and theology.[32] This omission must be understood as conscious: though the distinction of the science of the hereafter from the sciences of this world plays a central role in al-Ghazālī's revivalist agenda, it contradicts Suʿād al-Ḥakīm's efforts to present the law and mysticism as equal partners.

Treatment of Ritual Matters

Al-Ghazālī's quarter on rituals (*ʿibādāt*) provides extensive legal details on their correct performance. Al-Ḥakīm's treatment is much shorter and shorn of these detailed instructions. She may assume that instructions on the performance of prayer, for example, would either be commonly known or available elsewhere. A partial exception to this is her chapter on *zakāt*, the "alms tax," for which she provides a chart for calculating the amount due.[33]

In addition to detailed instructions for the performance of rituals, al-Ghazālī includes treatment of the "mysteries" (*asrār*) of several of them. By this he means their role in ethical self-cultivation for the purpose of felicity in the afterlife, which is to say, the way their more profound dimensions fall under

30 Garden, "Coming Down from the Mountaintop: Al-Ghazālī's Autobiographical Writings in Context," 583–84.

31 Al-Ḥakīm, *Iḥyāʾ ʿulūm al-dīn fī l-qarn al-wāḥid wa-l-ʿishrīn*, 66.

32 Ibid., 42.

33 Ibid., 126.

the jurisdiction of the science of the hereafter rather than *fiqh*, a science of this world. For instance, in the book of ritual purity (*ṭahāra*), he asserts that there are, in fact, four degrees of purity. The first is to cleanse the limbs of impurities through washing, as for ablutions before prayer. The second is to cleanse them of wrongdoing. The third is to cleanse the heart of vice. The fourth and highest is to cleanse the heart of everything but God.[34] He prefaces this by writing,

> The insightful understand (…) that the most important of matters is the purification of the inmost essences (*al-asrār*). For it is hardly possible that [Muḥammad] could have meant by his saying, "Cleansing (*al-ṭuhūr*) is half of faith," that the external frame be cleansed by pouring water and plunging into it while destroying the interior and leaving it full of impurities and filth. How preposterous![35]

It is preposterous, in other words, to think that the legal focus on washing before prayer could be anything more than a necessary preamble to the more profound cleansing of the soul of vice, the aim of the science of the hereafter.

In presenting purity in this way, al-Ghazālī weaves his project of ethical purification and drawing oneself near to God into the universally accepted obligation to wash before prayer. On one hand, in doing so, he is advocating the reconciliation between the law and the science of the hereafter that al-Ḥakīm identifies. But this reconciliation is a hierarchical one. In this passage and others like it elsewhere in the *Iḥyāʾ*, al-Ghazālī also insists that only the lowest of these degrees of purity falls within the jurisdiction of the law, a science of this world, while the higher levels fall within the jurisdiction of the science of the hereafter. By wresting jurisdiction over the legal subject of ritual purity away from the law, al-Ghazālī is furthering his agenda of demoting the law and promoting the Science of the Hereafter.

Suʿād al-Ḥakīm's treatment of *ṭahāra* focuses on al-Ghazālī's four levels. Al-Ghazālī, "like every Sufi,"[36] she writes, insists that the inner self be in accordance with the outer self, that bodily purity be matched with ethical conduct, ethical disposition of the heart, and by the attributes of the soul. Just as al-Ghazālī does, she presents a progressively more interior implementation of purity. But there is no sense that *fiqh* has sought to obscure these more essential forms of purity, or that it needs to be demoted for the correct state of affairs to be restored. This is a conscious decision to support her own insistence on *fiqh*

34 Al-Ghazālī, *Iḥyāʾ ʿulūm al-dīn*, 2:222–23.

35 Ibid, 2:222.

36 Al-Ḥakīm, *Iḥyāʾ ʿulūm al-dīn fī l-qarn al-wāḥid wa-l-ʿishrīn*, 89.

and Sufism as mutually dependent equals, despite al-Ghazālī's agenda of subordinating *fiqh* as a science of the world to the one of the hereafter.[37]

Al-Ghazālī's Psychology in *The Marvels of the Heart*

In his *Revival*, al-Ghazālī writes that the first two books of the third quarter, *Sharḥ ʾAjāʾib al-qalb* ("Exposition of the Marvels of the Heart") and *Riyāḍat al-nafs* ("Disciplining the Soul"), serve as an introduction to the entire second half of the book.[38] This being the case, al-Ghazālī's text provides some warrant for al-Ḥakīm's creation of a fifth section out of these two books plus a chapter on "Hunger and its Spiritual Role," the topic, roughly, of half of the book that follows them. The *Sharḥ ʿAjāʾib al-qalb* is important for understanding al-Ghazālī's psychology, particularly how it is that the locus of human knowledge, the heart, comes to know God, and how the heart may be polished and the soul trained so as to make this knowledge possible.

One of the most important issues in the academic study of al-Ghazālī in recent years has been the role of philosophy, especially the writings of Ibn Sīnā, in his thought. While earlier generations of Ghazali-scholars accepted—on the basis of his autobiography *al-Munqidh min al-ḍalāl* (*The Deliverer from Error*)—that he had rejected philosophy and whole-heartedly embraced Sufism, more recent studies, especially over the past two decades, have shown that philosophy had a profound and lasting influence on al-Ghazālī's thought. This influence is plainly on display in these two books of the Revival. Jules Janssens recently offered a study of *Sharḥ ʿAjāʾib al-qalb*, detailing its profound debt to a number of Ibn Sīnā's works, and arguing that it is impossible to determine on the basis of the text alone whether the theory of cognition in the text is ultimately philosophical or mystical.[39] Furthermore, it has long been accepted that the tri-partite soul and virtue ethics al-Ghazālī presents in *Riyāḍat al-nafs* are of Platonic and Aristotelian origin respectively.[40] It seems that the hybridity of al-Ghazālī's thought is what led him to champion the science of the hereafter in the *Iḥyāʾ* rather than Sufism despite what many, including al-Ḥakīm, have claimed.

These are issues of which Suʿād al-Ḥakīm is plainly aware, and her re-writing of *Sharḥ ʿAjāʾib al-qalb* includes a rejection of the possibility of philosophical influence. She opens this chapter with a discussion of four terms that al-Ghazālī

---

37 Ibid., 88–90.

38 Al-Ghazālī, *Iḥyāʾ ʿulūm al-dīn*, 8:1349.

39 Janssens, "Al-Ghazālī between Philosophy (Falsafa) and Sufism (Taṣawwuf): His Complex Attitude in the Marvels of the Heart (*ʿAjāʾib al-Qalb*) of the *Iḥyāʾ ʿUlūm al-Dīn*."

40 Sherif, *Al-Ghazālī's Theory of Virtue*, 24–76.

treats in his corresponding book: the spirit (*al-rūḥ*), the soul (*al-nafs*), the heart (*al-qalb*), and the intellect (*al-ʿaql*). The Philosophers, she notes, claim that all of these terms refer to the same entity. By contrast, in "religious thought" (*al-tafkīr al-dīnī*), each of these plays a different role. She then looks at al-Ghazālī's treatment of these four terms and shows that, while he uses all four terms for the faculty of knowledge, he also finds a distinct meaning in each term and a distinct locus associated with it. The implication, though she does not spell it out plainly, is that al-Ghazālī was therefore not a philosopher.[41] In fact, the ambiguity of his discussion of these four terms suggests the opposite.

Professing Divine Unity (*tawḥīd*)

Al-Ghazālī's treatment of divine unity in the 35th book of *Iḥyāʾ ʿulūm al-dīn*, *Kitāb al-tawḥīd wa-l-tawakkul* (*Professing Divine Unity and Having Trust in God*) is another prominent section of the book that betrays a philosophical content and, in part because of this philosophical content, sparked a controversy in al-Ghazālī's lifetime that continued on and off for eight centuries. It is no surprise, then, to find that Suʿād al-Ḥakīm departs substantially from al-Ghazālī's text in her treatment of the subject.

Much as al-Ghazālī defines four levels of ritual purity, only the most superficial of which are the domain of *fiqh*, so too does he define four levels of professing, or understanding divine unity (*tawḥīd*), the highest of which lies beyond the domain of theology (*ʿilm al-kalām*), being the domain of the science of the hereafter rather than theology, a science of the world. The first level of "professing divine unity" is to declare that there is no god but God with the tongue while being heedless of or denying its meaning, the level of the hypocrites. The second is for the heart to declare sincerely that there is no god but God. The third level is that of "those drawn near" (*al-muqarrabūn*), who see behind the multiplicity of the world the Subduing One (*al-wāḥid al-qahhār*) from which it all stems, the level, al-Ghazālī writes, of the common people and the theologians. The Fourth degree, that of the "sincere ones" (*al-ṣiddiqūn*), is to see in all of reality only One. Al-Ghazālī's aim is not only to make a point about divine unity (*tawḥīd*), but also to carry on his campaign to promote the science of the hereafter by demoting the sciences of this world, in this, case, theology (*ʿilm al-kalām*).[42]

Suʿād al-Ḥakīm reproduces this list with minor changes, but omits his point about the subordination of theology to the science of the hereafter in the field

41 Al-Ḥakīm, *Iḥyāʾ ʿulūm al-dīn fī l-qarn al-wāḥid wa-l-ʿishrīn*, 156–58.

42 Al-Ghazālī, *Iḥyāʾ ʿulūm al-dīn*, 13:2495.

of divine unity.[43] Again, she plainly sees the adversarial and confrontational element of al-Ghazālī's project, but chooses to downplay it in order to portray his agenda as a "project of reconciliation."

She goes on to discuss the highest level of *tawḥīd*, that of "the sincere ones" (*al-ṣiddiqūn*). She writes that al-Ghazālī stops at this point and does not discuss this stage of Sufi insight, and so she turns first to Abū l-Qāsim al-Qushayrī (d. 464/1072) and then to other early Sufi writers for further exposition. It is true that al-Ghazālī does not try to explain the highest understanding of divine unity, declaring, as he does elsewhere, that it is inappropriate to discuss theoretical knowledge of God, a domain he calls the science of unveiling (*ʿilm al-mukāshafa*), a discipline of the science of the hereafter. However, al-Ghazālī does offer a lengthy theoretical discussion of workings of the third level of *tawḥīd* in one of the most controversial passages of *Iḥyāʾ ʿulūm al-dīn*, and al-al-Ḥakīm entirely omits it. In his famous allegory of the pen, al-Ghazālī explains how the physical world of multiplicity and secondary causes can, in fact, be seen as the unitary expression of a single cause, God, who alone can be said to possess true reality: "One of the observers of the niche of God's light" sees a white page blackened and criticizes the page for its blemish. The page refers the observer to the ink the blackened it, the ink to the pen that wrote it, the pen to the hand that moved it. The hand refers this observer to an immaterial, celestial pen, an immaterial celestial hand, and a celestial vision of the one who arranges the causes as causes (*musabbib al-asbāb*), meaning God.[44]

This allegory has been shown to draw on Ibn Sīnā, the pen referring to the active intellect and the hand referring to God's power.[45] The passage provoked a controversy in Nishapur, where al-Ghazālī taught from 500/1106 to 503/1109. He composed his *al-Imlāʾ fī ishkālāt al-Iḥyāʾ* (*Dictation on Difficult Passages in the Revival*) in response to this controversy.[46] Furthermore, his discussion of the allegory and its implications led him to claim that the existing world is the best of all possible ones, a theodicy that was debated over the following 800 years.[47] It is no accident that al-Ḥakīm turns to other Sufi thinkers to reflect on the theory underlying the highest degree of *tawḥīd*, which al-Ghazālī refrained from discussing, rather than engaging with the theoretical examination of the third level of *tawḥīd*, which he discussed at length. Her rehabilitation of Sufism

43 Al-Ḥakīm, *Iḥyāʾ ʿulūm al-dīn fī l-qarn al-wāḥid wa-l-ʿishrīn*, 407–8.

44 Al-Ghazālī, *Iḥyāʾ ʿulūm al-dīn*, 13:2499–507.

45 Treiger, *Inspired Knowledge in Islamic Thought*, 105–7.

46 Garden, "Al-Ghazālī's Contested Revival: Iḥyāʾ ʿulūm al-dīn and its Critics in Khorasan and the Maghrib," 121–26.

47 Ormsby, *Theodicy in Islamic Thought*.

would have been harmed by associating it with the controversial elements of al-Ghazālī's *Iḥyāʾ* and his considered borrowings from philosophy.

As mentioned above, al-Ḥakīm does follow the content of the *Iḥyāʾ* closely. She does aim to revive the religion sciences in much the same way that al-Ghazālī did 900 years ago. But she also has an agenda of her own, and where it diverges from al-Ghazālī's, she does not hesitate to diverge from his text.

Conclusion

What does this brief analysis of Suʿād al-Ḥakīm's 21st century adaptation of *Iḥyāʾ ʿulūm al-dīn* tell us that might be applicable to the widespread phenomenon of *Revival* adaptation more broadly? Each of these acts of adaptation is more than an instance of al-Ghazālī's influence. It is, rather, the confluence of three factors: the text of *Iḥyāʾ*, the context in which it is understood in the adapter's day, and the adapter's agenda in writing his or her own version of *Iḥyāʾ ʿulūm al-dīn*.

There has been a dominant, stable understanding of the significance of *Iḥyāʾ* that has abided over the centuries since its writing. It is seen as a totalizing presentation of Islam, covering law, theology, ethics, and a quest for insight into the nature of God and His creation, taken by most over the years as Sufism, but also seen by many—correctly—as having been philosophically inspired.[48] This unified panorama of the Islamic religious sciences was unprecedented and has never been superseded. The course it charts for the individual Muslim life, from fulfilling fundamental ritual obligations, to comporting one's self in the social world, to overcoming one's vices, to cultivating the virtues that lead to salvation and felicity, is likewise without parallel. This synthesis is, of course, not simply the natural expression of Islam's unquestioned essence, but an assertion that Islam's essence is as *Iḥyāʾ ʿulūm al-dīn* presents it. This presentation has been convincing and compelling to many over the years; its vision of Islam is one many like-minded Muslim scholars over the years have wanted to reiterate.

But the significance of the *Iḥyāʾ* has varied over time as well. In al-Ghazālī's own day, it was burned in Cordoba in 503/1109,[49] and was at the center of a campaign against him and his thought in Nishapur that gave rise to his own

48 Many subsequent Muslim thinkers saw the philosophical influence in al-Ghazālī and continued his efforts. See Treiger, *Inspired Knowledge in Islamic Thought*, 103.

49 Garden, "Al-Ghazālī's Contested Revival: Iḥyāʾ ʿulūm al-dīn and its Critics in Khorasan and the Maghrib," 155–78.

misrepresentation of his life and thought in his *Deliverer from Error*.[50] In the context of this campaign in Nishapur, he was accused of being an Ismaʿīlī, a philosopher, a Zoroastrian, and a follower of the Brethren of Purity (*al-Ikhwān al-Ṣafāʾ*).[51] Later in the same century in the Maghrib, though al-Ghazālī was seen as a philosopher by the likes of Ibn Ṭufayl and Ibn Rushd, *Iḥyāʾ ʿulūm al-dīn* was seen by many Sufis as the very embodiment of Sufism.[52]

In our own time, readings of *Iḥyāʾ* have taken an interesting turn. While there are Wahhābī and Salafi scholars who reject al-Ghazālī as a Sufi inspired by philosophers,[53] he has also found his place in the non-mystical Islamic piety movement over the past few decades. Ḥasan al-Bannāʾ, the founder of the Muslim Brotherhood read and was influenced by al-Ghazālī's great work.[54] Saba Mahmoud notes that excerpts of the *Iḥyāʾ* are sold in pamphlet form in Cairo and are read by adherents of the non-Sufi women's piety movement as guides to their own efforts to refashion themselves as pious subjects.[55] It would seem that the reading of the *Iḥyāʾ* in such circles has associated the book with the piety movement in the mind of the broader culture. ʿAlāʾ al-Aswānī, in his influential contemporary novel *ʿImārat Yaʿqūbiyān* (*The Yacoubian Building*), portrays the induction of a doorman's son into an Islamist terrorist organization, which indoctrinates him by having him read works by Abū Aʿlā Mawdūdī (1903–79), Sayyid Quṭb (1906–66), Yūsuf al-Qaraḍāwī (1926–) and Abū Ḥāmid al-Ghazālī—hardly the intellectual company most Western al-Ghazali-scholars would imagine for him.[56] While meeting with two professors from Cairo's ʿAyn Shams University in a coffee shop in the affluent Zamalek neighborhood in October 2011, I pulled a volume of *Iḥyāʾ ʿulūm al-dīn* out of my bag to cite a passage and was teasingly warned that if anyone saw me with the book, they would take me for a Salafi.

Both the text and its contemporary context, the relatively stable significance of *Iḥyāʾ* and its implications unique to contemporary readings, serve Suʿād

50 Garden, "Al-Māzarī al-Dhakī: Al-Ghazālī's Maghribi Adversary in Nishapur," and Garden, "Coming Down from the Mountaintop: Al-Ghazālī's Autobiographical Writings in Context."

51 Garden, "Coming Down from the Mountaintop: Al-Ghazālī's Autobiographical Writings in Context," 585.

52 For an account of *Iḥyāʾ ʿulūm al-dīn* coming to stand for Sufism as a whole in the Maghrib in the Almohad period, see Rodríguez Mediano, "Biografías Almohades en el *Tašawwuf* de al-Tādilī."

53 Treiger, *Inspired Knowledge in Islamic Thought*, 157, n. 7.

54 Mitchell, *The Society of the Muslim Brothers*, 3.

55 Mahmood, *Politics of Piety*, 137–38.

56 Al-Aswānī, *The Yacoubian Building*, 92.

al-Ḥakīm's purposes. *Iḥyāʾ ʿulūm al-dīn* appeals to her for its comprehensiveness. She writes: "Often people come to me, of every generation, intimates and strangers, Muslims and non-Muslims, pious people and seekers, and ask me for a book that will lay out Islam in its entirety, with neutrality and objectivity. I would usually direct them to read *Iḥyāʾ ʿulūm al-dīn*."[57] As we have seen, she sees in it an effort to unify Islamic culture and reconcile the religious sciences. This comprehensive scope is essential to her effort to reacquaint "estranged" Muslims with their religion in all its facets.

But her aim is to reacquaint them with a particular vision of Islam, namely one in which Sufism is fully integrated. Al-Ghazālī's agenda of weaving his science of the hereafter into the scripture and legal and theological discourses of the Islamic tradition is very much her own. She is aware, as we have seen, that al-Ghazālī's thinking is influenced by philosophy as well as Sufism—or at least that he has been accused of this—and she omits some of his discussions that point in this direction and actively argues that parallels between his thought and philosophical thought are superficial rather than substantial.

If al-Ghazālī felt emboldened to revive the religious sciences by subordinating *fiqh* and theology to the science of the hereafter, Suʿād al-Ḥakīm prefers to present Sufism as the equal and necessary counterpart to the law, a more modest move appropriate to an era suspicious of Sufism. In al-Ghazālī's day, the Sufism that plays a role in *Iḥyāʾ* was already well established by figures like Abū Ṭālib al-Makkī (d. 386/998) and al-Qushayrī. In our day, by contrast, Sufism has been on the defensive for more than a century. Portrayed by modernists as an embarrassing, irrational vestige of the middle ages and by Salafis as a heretical departure from orthodox religion, Sufis in the 21st century must make the case for their practices in the face of widespread skepticism and even hostility. To bolster her efforts to portray Sufism as an orthodox, even essential part of the Islamic tradition, al-Ḥakīm consciously omits the confrontational element of the *Iḥyāʾ*'s "reconciliation" of the religious sciences.

Al-Ghazālī's stature gives her project an authority she would lack if she were simply to write an original work, a fact that certainly motivated many of his adaptors over the centuries. Furthermore, the conservative connotations of the *Iḥyāʾ* in recent decades serve her rhetorically. If al-Ghazālī is read by many today as a thinker in line with the contemporary piety movement, then claiming him for her project of rehabilitating Sufism in the face of its modernist and Salafi critics provides an air of conservative orthodoxy. As a scholar of Ibn ʿArabī, who refers to him in the text of her *Revival* adaptation as *al-Shaykh*

57 Al-Ḥakīm, *Iḥyāʾ ʿulūm al-dīn fī l-qarn al-wāḥid wa-l-ʿishrīn*, 8.

al-Akbār,[58] she might have instead written *The Meccan Openings in the 21st Century*. But doing so would have lent her project the opposite aura.

Suʿād al-Ḥakīm's *Revival of the Religious Sciences in the 21st Century* derives much of its authority from associating itself with an author and a work of the stature of al-Ghazālī and his *Revival of the Religious* Sciences. By so overtly borrowing from the stature of *Iḥyāʾ* and invoking its authority, she and other adaptors also re-inscribe both. The project on whose behalf they invoke that authority cannot, perhaps, diverge entirely from al-Ghazālī's own in writing the original. But because of changing popular understanding of the book's significance and artfully selective adaptation of the text, re-writings of *Iḥyāʾ* also impart al-Ghazālī's masterpiece with new meanings.

Bibliography

Anjum, Ovamir, "Cultural Memory and the Pious Ancestors (*Salaf*) in al-Ghazālī." *Numen* 58 (2011): 344–74.

al-Aswānī, ʿAlāʾ (Alaa Al Aswany). *The Yacoubian Building*. Translated by H. Davies. Cairo: American University in Cairo Press, 2006.

Badawī, ʿAbd al-Raḥmān. *Muʾallafāt al-Ghazālī*. Cairo: al-Majlis al-Aʿlā li-Riʿāyat al-Funūn wa-l-Adab, 1961.

Barhebraeus, Gregory. *Ethicon: Mēmrā I*. Translated by Herman G. B. Teule. Louvain: Peeters Publishers, 1993.

Cook, Michael. *Commanding Right and Forbidding Wrong in Islamic Thought*. Cambridge: Cambridge University Press, 2000.

De Jong, Frederick. "Opposition to Sufism in Twentieth-Century Egypt." *Islamic Mysticism Contested: Thirteen Centuries of Controversies and Polemicsī*. Edited by F. De Jong and B. Radtke. Leiden: Brill, 1999. 310–323.

Fayḍ al-Kāshānī, al-Muḥsin Muḥammad ibn al-Murtaḍā. *al-Maḥajja al-bayḍā fī tahdhīb al-Iḥyāʾ*. Edited by ʿA. A. al-Ghaffārī. 8 vols. Tehran: Maktabat al-Ṣadūq, 1339–42 [1960–64].

Garden, Kenneth. "Al-Ghazālī's Contested Revival: *Iḥyāʾ ʿulūm al-dīn* and its Critics in Khorasan and the Maghrib." Ph.D. diss., University of Chicago, 2005.

———. "Al-Māzarī al-Dhakī: Al-Ghazālī's Maghribi Adversary in Nishapur." *Journal of Islamic Studies* 21 (2010): 89–107.

———. "Coming Down from the Mountaintop: Al-Ghazālī's Autobiographical Writings in Context." *Muslim World* 101 (2011): 581–96.

58 Ibid., 165.

al-Ghazālī, Muḥammad ibn Muḥammad. *Ḥimāqat-i ahl-i ibāḥat*. In *Streitschrift des Ġazālī gegen die Ibāḥīja*. Persian edition and German translation by O. Pretzl. Munich: Bayerische Akademie der Wissenschaften, 1933.

———. *Iḥyāʾ ʿulūm al-dīn*. 16 parts. Cairo: Lajnat Nashr al-Thaqāfa al-Islāmiyya, Cairo 1356–57 [1937–38].

———. *al-Mustaṣfā min ʿilm al-uṣūl*. Edited by Ḥamza ibn Zuhayr Ḥāfiẓ. 4 vols. Medina (Saudi Arabia): al-Jāmiʿa al-Islāmiyya—Kulliyyat al-Sharīʿa, 1413 [1992–93].

Ghurāb, Saʿd (Saâd Ghrab). "Ḥawla iḥrāq al-Murābiṭūn li-Iḥyāʾ al-Ghazālī." *Actas del IV Coloquio Hispano-Tunecino (Palma de Mallorca, 1979)*. Madrid: Instituto Hispano-Arabe de Cultura, 1983. 133–63.

Griffel, Frank. *Al-Ghazālī's Philosophical Theology*. Oxford: Oxford University Press, 2009.

al-Ḥakīm, Suʿād. *Iḥyāʾ ʿulūm al-dīn fī l-qarn al-wāḥid wa-l-ʿishrīn*. 2nd ed. Cairo: Dār al-Shurūq, 2005.

———. *al-Muʿjam al-ṣūfī: al-ḥikma fī ḥudūd al-kalima*. Beirut: Dandara li-l-Ṭibāʿa wa-l-Nashr, 1981.

Ibn ʿArabī, Muḥammad ibn ʿAbdallāh. *Las contemplaciones de los misterios*. Edited and translated by Suad Hakim and Pablo Beneito. Murcia: Consejería de Cultura y Educación, Dirección General de Cultura, 1994.

Ibn al-Khaṭīb, Muḥammad ibn ʿAbdallāh. *al-Iḥāṭa fī akhbār Gharnāṭa*, Edited by M. ʿA. ʿInān. 4 vols. Cairo: Maktabat al-Khānjī: Cairo, 1973–77.

Janssens, Jules. "Al-Ghazālī between Philosophy (Falsafa) and Sufism (Taṣawwuf): His Complex Attitude in the Marvels of the Heart ('Ajā'ib al-Qalb) of the Iḥyāʾ ʿUlūm al-Dīn." *Muslim World* 101 (2011): 614–32.

Mahmood, Saba. *Politics of Piety: The Islamic Revivial and the Feminist Subject*. Princeton: Princeton University Press, 2005.

al-Manūnī, Muḥammad, "Iḥyāʾ ʿulūm al-dīn fī manẓūr al-gharb al-Islāmī ayyām al-murābiṭīn wa-l-muwāḥḥidīn." In: *Abū Ḥāmid al-Ghazālī: dirāsāt fī fikrihi wa ʿaṣrihi wa-ta'thīrihi*. Rabat (Morocco): Jāmiʿat Muḥammad al-Khāmis, Manshūrāt Kulliyyat al-Ādāb wa-l-ʿUlūm al-Insāniyya, 1988. 125–37.

Mitchell, Richard P. *The Society of the Muslim Brothers*. Oxford: Oxford University Press, 1969.

Ormsby, Eric L. *Theodicy in Islamic Thought: The Dispute Over al-Ghazali's "Best of all Possible Worlds."* Princeton: Princeton University Press, 1984.

Rodríguez Mediano, Fernando. "Biografías almohades en el *Tašawwuf* de al-Tādilī." In *Estudios onomásticos-biográficos de Al-Andaluz*. Edited by M. Marín *et al.* 15 vols. Madrid: Consejo Superior de Investigaciones Científicas, 1988–2008. Vol. 10. 167–92.

Sherif, Mohamed A. *Al-Ghazālī's Theory of Virtue*, Albany (N.Y): State University of New York Press, 1975.

Sirriyeh, Elizabeth. *Sufis and Anti-Sufis: The Defense, Rethinking and Rejection of Sufism in the Modern World*. Richmond (UK): Curzon, 1999.

Teule, Herman. "La vie dans le monde: perspectives chrétiennes et influnces musulmanes: Une étude de Memr 6 II de l'Ethicon de Grégoire Abū I-Farag Barhebrreus." *Parole de l'Orient* (Kaslik, Lebanon) 33 (2008): 115–28.

Treiger, Alexander. *Inspired Knowledge in Islamic Thought: Al-Ghazali's Theory of Mystical Cognition and its Avicennian Foundation*. London and New York: Routledge, 2011.

———. "The Science of Divine Disclosure: Al-Ġazālī's Higher Theology and its Philosophical Underpinnings." Ph.D. diss., Yale University, 2008.

al-Wansharīsī, Aḥmad ibn Yaḥyā. *al-Miʿyār al-muʿrib wa-jāmiʿ al-mughrib ʿan fatāwā ʿulamāʾ Ifrīqiyya wa-l-Andalus wa-l-Maghrib*. Edited by M. Ḥajjī. 13 vols. Rabat: Nashr Wizārat al-Awqāf wa-l-Shuʾūn al-Islāmiyya, 1981.

Indices

General Index of Names and Subjects

Abbasid caliphate viii, xii, 259
ʿAbd al-Jabbār, al-Qāḍī 60
ʿAbduh, Muḥammad 317–18
ʿAbdülḥamid II, Ottoman Sultan 256, 258
Abrahamov, Binyamin 23, 221–22
Abū Tammām 155
ad hominem argument 117–19, 125
Adams, Charles 153, 156
Adams, Robert M. 68
al-Afghānī, Jamāl al-Dīn 317–18
ahl-i hadis̱ movement 293–97, 301
Aḥmad Khān, Sayyid vii, xi, xii, 296, 301–5
Aḥmed I, Ottoman Sultan 254
Aḥmed Rushdi 260
al-Akiti, M. Afifi 172n, 267, 273
ʿAlāʾī ibn Muḥibbī al-Shīrāzī 258–59
ʿālam al-mulk (sublunar world) 19
ʿālam al-malakūt (celestial world) 20, 236
Aligargh, Anglo-Oriental College vii, viii, 301–2
ʿAlī ibn Abī Ṭālib 28
Allouche, Adel 178n
ʿAmāra, Muḥammad 283n
al-Āmidī, Sayf al-Dīn 134, 261
al-ʿĀmirī, Abū l-Ḥasan 33, 38–39
Amritsari, S̱anāʾullāh 293–97
Anaxagoras 46
al-Anbārī, Jibrīl ibn Nūḥ 103–104, 106, 107, 108
al-Anbārī, Abū Nūḥ 103–104
anthropomorphists 23, 152
Apaydin, Yasin 178n
ʿaql (intellect), *ʿaqlī* xiii, 3, 5, 13, 21, 24, 39, 193, 203–6, 212, 299, 318, 324
Aristotle 20, 21n, 24, 34, 37, 38, 46, 103, 323
Āryā Samāj movement 295–96
Asad, Talal 148, 154,159, 163
ascetic, asceticism 179, 203, 207–9, 212–14, 218, 220, 225, 314
al-Ashʿarī, Abū l-Ḥasan 37, 41, 62–63, 98, 109, 121
Ashıq Çelebi 259
aṣlaḥ-theory 59–67
al-Aswānī, ʿAlāʾ (Alaa Al Aswany) 327
atheism 103, 145, 162, 243, 299
Averroes (Ibn Rushd) x, 109, 144–45, 262–65, 267, 274–78, 327
Avicenna (Ibn Sīnā) ix, 7, 12, 15, 18, 22, 24, 33, 36, 41, 44, 46, 47, 54–55, 58–60, 74–5. 82, 85, 90, 99, 102, 107, 108, 115, 117–18, 121, 124–26, 135–36, 145, 190, 193–99, 202, 208–16, 219–20, 233–34, 239–40, 247, 261, 274, 276
al-ʿAydarūs, ʿAbd al-Qādir 270
Ayni, Meḥmed Ali 253, 274

al-Bābī al-Ḥalabī, Aḥmad 265
Badawī, ʿAbd al-Raḥmān 94, 273
Baghdādī Aristotelians 38
Baḥya ibn Paqūda 96
al-Balkhī, Abū Zayd 38
Baneth, David Z. 96
al-Bāqillānī, Abū Bakr 98n, 121n
Barhebreus, Gregory 311
Bāṭinites (= Ismāʿīlites) 20, 105, 109, 327
Bayezidov, ʿAtaullah 262
Bedouins 151, 303
Beinecke Rare Book and Manuscript Library 172, 174, 183–86
Benedict XVI, Pope 142, 144, 145, 146, 163
Beneito, Pablo 312
best of all possible worlds 54–61, 64–81, 83–86
bidʿa (innovation) 12, 16, 19, 256, 286, 317–18
Birgivi (al-Birgī), Meḥmed Efendi 256, 278
al-Bīrūnī 150, 154, 160
Boer, Tjitze J. de xi
Bostanzade Meḥmed Efendi 254
Boutros, Felix 301
Bouyges, Maurice 94, 273
Brahe, Tycho 288
Brethren of Purity (*Ikhwān al-safāʾ*) 39, 44, 276, 327
Büchner, Ludwig 264, 299
al-Bukhārī 276, 285
burhān (demonstrative argument) 34, 284, 299, 303–4

Carra de Vaux, Bernard Baron 274
Cartesian physics 290–91, 293

causality 11, 21, 26, 65, 66n, 73, 78n, 100, 114, 124, 245, 325
Chester Beatty Library 169, 171n
Claremont, Council of 261
"clash of civilizations" 143
Cluverius, Philipp 287
Cohen, Daniel 71
comparative religion 154
Cook, Michael 311
Copernican astronomy 286–93, 298, 302
Crusades 144, 261

dahriyyūn (materialists) 37, 100, 243n, 244, 274–75
Dār al Minhāj-edition of *Iḥyā'* 19, 168–72
Dars-i Niẓāmī vii
Darwin, Charles 299
Davānī, Jalāl al-Dīn 259, 264
Decline of Islam and Islamic societies xi, 253, 259, 264, 283
Descartes, René 277, 289–91
Diez, Ernst 173
Diodorus of Tarsus 104, 106, 107
divine command theory 9–10, 54, 60, 77–85, 106–7
Dualists 37, 129, 152
Duns Scotus, John 74

Eller, Jack David 147, 149, 159
Enlightenment 143–44, 148, 149
Ernst, Carl W. 149

Fakhr al-Dīn al-Rāzī x, 47, 85n, 135, 190–225, 229–249, 261, 264, 277, 296, 299–300
falsafa viii, xii, xiii, 164, 221, 229, 264, 268, 274–75, 277–78, 285
al-Fārābī 33–35, 41, 43, 44, 164, 261
Fayḍ al-Kāshānī, al-Muḥsin 310
Fenari, Mullah Shams al-Dīn 278
Ferruh, Ali 262
Firdawsī 173
fiṭra (innate nature) 4–8, 201, 207–8, 210n
Frank, Richard M. ix, 11, 32n, 46n, 55, 58, 74, 78, 82, 83, 116
French Invasion of Egypt 1798 xi

Gabriel (archangel) 233, 237
Gairdner, William H. T. 157n, 161
Gaiser, Adam 155
Galen (of Pergamon) 12, 90, 96, 99–109
Galileo, Galilei 290
Gardet, Louis 149
Gazi Husrev Bey Library, Sarajevo 168n
Gelibolulu Muṣṭafa ʿAli 258
Ghadban, Ralph 162
gharaḍ (aim, purpose) 93
al-Ghazālī, Abū Ḥāmid *passim*
  on error 3–28
  on *kalām* 15, 42, 113–17, 129–39
  on the human soul (psychology) 115–32, 135, 138–39, 265–73
  on Sufism 72, 189, 199n, 232, 240–41
Gibb, Hamilton A. R. 104
Goldziher, Ignaz 283n
Griffel, Frank 18, 22, 64–65, 109, 249
Grover, Stephen 71

Habermas, Jürgen 163
ḥads (intuition) 35, 193–94, 197, 207, 218n, 246n
Hafız İbrahim 268–69, 273
Hagen, Gottfried 286
Hajjaji-Jarrah, Soraya M. 230, 240, 242
al-Ḥakīm, Suʿād (Souad Hakim) 311–329
Ḥakkı, Erżurumlu İbrahim 291–93
Ḥakkı, İzmirli İsmail 253, 276–77
Halevi, Leor 149
Ḥamdi, Aksekili Aḥmed 265–73
Ḥamdi, Elmalılı Muḥammad Yazır 253
Ḥanafī, Ḥasan 283n
al-Ḥaram al-Sharīf, Jerusalem 173
al-Ḥārith al-Muḥāsibī 12
Hārūniyya 173
Heinen, Anton 286
ḥikma (philosophy) xii, 36, 204, 218
al-Ḥillī, Ibn Muṭahhar 135
Hinduism 148, 295, 302
Hobbes, Thomas 161
Hocazade 257, 263, 278
Hodgson, Marshall 146
Hourani, George F. 273
Hume, David 161, 277
Ḥunayn ibn Isḥāq 101, 104, 105

Ibn ʿArabī, Muḥyī l-Dīn 211, 241, 270, 312, 328
Ibn Faḍlān 150

Ibn Hazm 294
Ibn Kathīr 285
Ibn Khallikān 270
Ibn al-Nafīs 109
Ibn Qayyim al-Jawziyya 109–10, 294
Ibn Rushd, see Averroes
Ibn Sīnā, see Avicenna
Ibn Taymiyya 47, 98n, 109, 162, 256, 286, 294–97
Ibn Ṭufayl 16n, 327
İbrahim Giridi 259–60
ijāza (license) 175–181
al-Ījī, Aḍud al-Dīn 259, 264, 277
Ikhwān al-ṣafā' see Brethren of Purity
ilhām (inspiration) 14n, 216, 318
al-ʿilm al-ladunī (inspired knowledge) 200, 205–6, 217
ʿilm-i sāʾins ("science") 296–97
ilzām (forced consequence) 115, 117–18, 127
īmān (belief) 22, 26, 149
ʿirfān (inspired knowledge) 176, 179, 201, 209, 213, 215, 217–20, 240–41
Ismāʿīl Shahīd 294
Isrāfīl (archangel) 237
al-Jāhiẓ 104, 107

Janssens, Jules 46, 323
jawhar (substance) 132–33,
al-Jazā'irī, Hamdān ibn 'Uthmān 69
al-Jīlī, Aḥmad ibn Aḥmad 179–80
al-Jisr al-Ṭarābulsī, Ḥusayn 297–301, 302, 304–5
John Paul II, Pope 142
Julian the Apostate 104
al-Jurjāni, al-Sharīf 259, 261, 277
al-Juwaynī 67, 78, 98n, 132–33, 276

Kadızade Meḥmed Efendi 286
Kadızadeli movement 256, 286
Kant, Immanuel 277
Karrāmites 23, 42n, 152
Katib Çelebi 254, 258, 263, 267–68, 286–92
Kemal, Namık 262
Kemalpaşazade 257, 263, 278
Khānpūrī, 'Abdu l-Aḥad 297
al-Khaṭṭābī, Abū Ismāʿīl 109
khāṭir (stray thought) 11, 14–15
al-Kindī 33, 37–38, 41, 43, 47, 261
Kippenberg, Hans G. 154, 156, 161
al-Kiyā' al-Harrāsī 78
Kınalızade ʿAli 259
Kurds 151

Landolt, Hermann 11, 22, 153, 156–161, 164, 229–30, 243–44, 246
Lazarus-Yafeh, Hava 229, 273
Leibniz, Gottfried Wilhelm 54, 65, 72, 77
logic viii, 18–19, 34, 40–45, 97, 192, 224, 253, 264
Luther, Martin 143

al-Maḥbūbī, Ṣadr al-Sharīʿa 256
Maḥfil (Ottoman Turkish journal) 265–73
al-Makkī, Abū Ṭālib 15n, 328
Mamluk 172, 259
Manchester United 145, 148, 161–62
Manicheans 37, 103, 105, 230
Manuel II Palaiologos, Byzantine Emperor 142, 146
maqāṣid al-sharīʿa (puposes of the law) 90–93, 101, 107
al-Maqdisī, Shams al-Dīn Muḥammad 160
al-Maqqarī 178
Marcionites 37
Mardin, Ebül'ula 256
Mardin, Şerif 256, 265n
al-Marghīnānī, Burhān al-Dīn 256
maṣlaḥa (public benefit) 90–94
al-Masʿūdī 154
al-Māturīdī 37, 41
Mawdūdī, Abū Aʿlā 327
Maymaniyya Press, Cairo 170
Meḥmed II, Ottoman Sultan 260, 263
Meḥmed Reshid 258
Meḥmed Ṭahir 258
Meḥmed Veliyuddin 259
Mercator, Gerhard 287
Menn, Stephen 90
Miskawayh 12, 38, 43, 47
Mohamed, Yasien 12
Moses 103
Mu'allim Ömer Ḳastamoni 260
muʿāmala (transactions) 102
Muḥammad Efendi, Sheikh 287
mukāshafa (disclosure, unveiling) 201, 205, 212, 215n, 325

mulḥida (heretics) 243
Müller, Max 155
Munkar and Nakīr 129
al-Muqtaṭaf (Arabic journal) 298–99
Murad IV, Ottoman Sultan 257
Musa Kazım, Şeyhülislam 274–75
Muslim ibn al-Ḥajjāj 276
Muʿtazilites, Muʿtazilism 37, 42n, 54, 59, 60–67, 81, 85, 91–92, 96, 109, 261
Müteferrika, İbrahim 287–92, 304
Mysticism xi, 96, 144, 153, 189–92, 198–225, 236–37, 240–42, 248–49, 253–54, 261, 271–79, 321–23

Nadwatul Ulamā' vii
Naṣīr al-Dīn al-Ṭūsī 134–35
Naturalists (*aṣḥāb al-ṭabāʾiʿ, ṭabīʿiyyūn*) 37, 106, 229, 236, 243–44, 299
al-Naẓẓām 60–61
Necessary Existent 134
Neo-Platonism 23, 55
Neumark, David 95–96
Newton, Issac 291
neychari ("naturalist") 296
Nicolas of Cues 289
Niẓāmiyya *madrasa* 170
Nuʿmānī, Shiblī vii–xiii
Nuri, Celal 253, 262

Ormsby, Eric 54, 67, 72–79, 81
Ortelius, Abraham 287
Ottomans 253–79

Parmenides 46
Plantinga, Alvin 65
Plato 7, 22, 38, 46, 47n, 323
Plotinus 22
Pourchot, Edmond 289–90
Pourjavady, Nasrollah 229n, 267, 273
predestination 62, 63–64, 67, 79
prophecy 34, 157, 196–98, 209, 215, 219
Ptolemaic astronomy 285, 287–89, 291

al-Qaffāl al-Shāshī, Abū Bakr 91
al-Qaraḍāwī, Yūsuf 327
Qūnawī, Ṣadr al-Dīn 261
al-Qashīshah, Muṣṭafā Muḥammad 265
al-Qushayrī, Abū l-Qāsim 325, 328
Quṭb, Sayyid 327
Quṭṭa al-ʿAdawī, Muḥammad 170

al-Rāghib al-Iṣfahānī 12, 33, 38, 43, 47, 234
Ramadan, Tariq 162
Ramón Llull 144, 160
Rashīd al-Dīn Faẓlallāh 150
Rawls, John 148
Reformation, protestant x, 142
Religionswissenschaft (study of religions) 11, 142, 153, 158–60, 163, 229
Renan, Ernest x, 262, 283n
resurrection 114–17, 121–31, 265
Riḍā, Muḥammad Rashīd 298, 317–18
rubūbiyya (lordliness) 8, 171
rūḥ (spirit) 114, 116, 128–31, 199, 215, 231, 237, 265, 324

Sabra, Abdelhamid I. ix, x
Ṣabri, Muṣṭafa 262
Safavid 259
Ṣafī l-Dīn Abū l-Ḥasan ʿAlī ibn al-Mubārak 258
al-salaf al-ṣāliḥ (the pious forefathers) 317–20
Salafism 256, 296n, 317–18, 327–28
al-Samhūdī 74n, 76, 81
al-Sarakhsī, Aḥmad ibn al-Ṭayyib 38
Sarasvatī, Svamī Dayānand 295
Sayyid Aḥmad Barelwī 294
Sayyid Farkhanda ʿAlī 304
Schreiner, Martin 95–96
securalism 142, 148, 148, 155, 163, 261, 295, 298, 317
Sehabi Husameddin bin Ḥüseyin 257
Seljuq, Seljuqs 174, 259, 278
Şemseddin, Meḥmed Günaltay 253, 260–62
Shāh Waliyyullah Dihlawī 294
al-Shahrastānī 154–55, 160
al-Shahrazūrī, Ibn al-Ṣalāḥ 266–268
sharʿ, *sharīʿa* (revelation, religious law) 36n, 78, 128n, 149, 152, 157, 177, 297, 300
al-Shaʿrānī, ʿAbd al-Wahhāb 270
Sharpe, Eric J. 154, 156, 160, 161
al-Shawkānī, Muḥammad ibn ʿAlī 294
Shihāb al-Dīn Muḥammad ibn al-Marzubān 179–80

Shihadeh, Ayman 190–92, 218, 249
Shumayyil, Shiblī 299
Sıdkı Mardini, Yūsuf Aḥmed 256–57
al-Sijistānī, Abū Sulaymān 38–39, 43–44, 47
al-Simāwī, Badr al-Dīn 261
Şirvani, Ṣadreddinzade Meḥmed Emin 255
skeptic, skepticism x, 3, 37, 66n, 190, 264, 328
Sprenger, Aloys 301
Staatsbibliothek Preussischer Kulturbesitz, Berlin 168n
Suavi, Ali 262–65
al-Subkī, Tāj al-Dīn 266–79, 273
Sufism x, xi, 5–6, 38, 40–42, 44, 72–73, 109, 176, 179, 189–225, 232, 240–41, 246, 256, 261, 264–65, 286, 291, 293–96, 298, 301, 310–329
al-Suhrawardī, Shihāb al-Din Yaḥya 261
al-Suyūṭī 67, 74n, 286, 293, 304
Swinburne, Richard 69, 71
syllogism 19, 34–35, 45, 193–94, 197, 202

Ṭābarān-Ṭūṣ 7, 172–73
al-Ṭabarī 154
al-Taftazānī, Sa'd al-Dīn 259, 261, 277
Tāj al-Dīn ibn Aḥmad al-Ṭūsī 176
taklīf (religious obligation) 15
tanāsukh (metempsychosis) 122–23, 127
taqdīr (postulation) 115, 118–19, 125
Taqī l-Dīn al-Ḥiṣnī 177
taqlīd (emulation) vii, 4, 12, 26, 136, 238, 255, 264, 294
taqrīr (affirmation) 115, 118–19, 125
Ṭaşköprüzade, 'Iṣamaddin Aḥmed 255–56, 278
Ṭaşköprüzade, Meḥmed Kemaleddin 255n
tawḥīd (divine unity) 215, 240–41, 314, 315, 324–25
al-Tawḥidī, Abū Ḥayyān 39n, 276
ta'wīl (allegorical interpretation) 25, 27, 73, 157, 229–30, 247, 264, 285, 295–97, 303–4
teleology 90–93, 105, 108–110
Theodoret of Cyrus 104, 106, 107
Thomas Aquinas 144, 277
Tīzīnī, Ṭayyib 283n
Troll, Christian viii
Turks 152, 157
al-Ṭurṭūshī, Abū Bakr 310
al-Ṭūsī, 'Alā' al-Dīn 257, 263–64
al-Ṭūsī, Naṣīr al-Dīn 99, 134–35, 259
al-Tustarī, Sahl 237

Uranus 303

van Ess, Josef 60–61
Vásquez, Manuel 154
Vüdudi Meḥmed Efendi 258

Waardenburg, Jacques 150, 155, 156, 157, 158, 160, 161
waḥdat al-wujūd (unity of existence) 270
Wahhabism 294, 318, 327
wahm (estimative faculty) 135
al-Wāsiṭī, Abū 'Abdallāh 96
Wasserstrom, Steven 150, 154, 156
Watt, William Montgomery 229–30, 273
Winter, Tim J. 12
Woon, Long Litt 148

Yahuda, Abraham S. 95–96
Yanyavi Esad Efendi 263

al-Zabīdī, al-Murtaḍā 80, 169–71, 269–71
Ẓāhiriyya Collection, Damascus 169
Zeyrekzade Meḥmed Efendi 259
Zolberg, Aristide 148
Zoroastrians 37, 327

Index of Passages in Works by al-Ghazālī

al-Arbaʿīn fī uṣūl al-dīn (ed. M. Ṣabrī al-Kurdī, Cairo: al-Maṭbaʿa al-ʿArabiyya, 1344 [1925]).

24	136

Fayṣal al-tafriqa bayna l-Islām wa-l-zandaqa, (ed. M. Bījū. Damascus: Maḥmūd Bījū, 1993).

49–50	20
50–51	17

al-Ḥikma fī makhlūqāt Allāh (ed. R. F. ʿAbd al-Muṭallib and ʿA. ʿA. Mazīd, Cairo: Maktabat al-Khānjī, 1422/2002).

17–18	108
19	101
36–37	97
43	97
46	101
47	95
51	101
63	105
70	101

Iḥyāʾ ʿulūm al-dīn (16 parts, Cairo: Lajnat Nashr al-Thaqāfa al-Islāmiyya, 1356–57 [1937–38]). In brackets are the page references of the equivalent passages in the new 10-volume edition (introductory volume + 9 numbered vols.), Jeddah: Dār al-Minhāj: 1432/2011. The count of volumes in this edition follows the effective volume division, counting the introductory volume as volume 1 and all following 2–10. Our volume count adds one digit to the volume count on the back of this edition.

1:36–39 (2:79–86)	15
1:57 (2:127–28)	10
1:148 (2:318–19)	5–6, 26
1:157 (2:327)	67
1:162 (2:344)	11, 19
1:167–68 (2:355–56)	28
1:171 (2:361)	15
1:182–183 (2:383–85)	5, 137
1:188–89 (2:395)	59
2:194 (2:407)	63
2:195 (2:408–9)	59, 79, 80, 84
2:196 (2:411–12)	62, 63, 80
2:197 (2:413)	80, 81
2:211–12 (2:441–42)	11
2:222–23 (2:463–65)	322
8:1349 (6:11–12)	323
8:1350 (6:14)	269, 271
8:1359 (6:33–34)	3
8:1363 (6:40)	13
8:1365 (6:44–45)	11
8:1367 (6:49)	14
8:1368 (6:50–51)	17
8:1369 (6:52–53)	5
8:1370 (6:55–56)	6
8:1382 (6:79)	189
8:1390–92 (6:96–99)	14
8:1393 (6:101)	10
8:1450–51 (6:210–11)	6, 9–10
8:1484 (6:272–73)	27
8:1527 (6:326)	10, 13
9:1638–39 (6:578–79)	27
9:1708–58 (7:7–110)	8
11:2096 (8:46)	7
11:2101–02 (8:57–58)	8, 16
11:2108 (8:69–70)	18
12:2187 (8:229)	26
12:2188–89 (8:231–32)	13
12:2215 (8:283)	7
12:2224 (8:299–300)	65
12:2238 (8:323–24)	14
12:2256 (8:357)	12
13:2358 (8:546)	6
13:2371–76 (8:572–81)	19
13:2374 (8:577)	27
13:2377 (8:582)	14
13:2490–577 (9:191–359)	55
13:2495 (9:201)	324
13:2496–97 (9:206–8)	73
13:2499–507 (9:211–25)	325
13:2512–13 (9:234–35)	82
13:2517 (9:243–44)	56, 64, 70, 84
13:2518 (9:245)	79

13:2535 (9:280–81) 67
14:2559 (9:321) 67
14:2611 (9:424) 7
14:2625–27 (9:448–51) 25
14:2627–28 (9:452–53) 14
15:2822–44 (10:268–305) 94
15:2827 (10:276) 95
15:2844 (10:305) 106

al-Imlāʾ fī ishkālāt al-Iḥyāʾ (in: *Iḥyāʾ ʿulūm al-dīn*, 16 parts, Cairo: Lajnat Nashr al-Thaqāfa al-Islāmiyya, 1356–57 [1937–38], part 16, pp. 3035–3095). This is the *textus receptus* which relies on a faulty recension of the text. The correct version can be found in the new 10-volume edition of *Ihyaʾ ʿulūm al-dīn* (introductory volume + 9 numbered vols.), Jeddah: Dār al-Minhāj: 1432/2011, vol. 1, pp. 213–353. Its pagination is added in brackets.

16:3083 (1:343) 56
(1:344) 57
16:3084–85 (1:344) 171

al-Iqtiṣād fī l-iʿtiqād (ed. I. A. Çubukçu and H. Atay, Ankara: Nur Matbaası, 1962).

1 41
11 136
24 132–33
26–34 133
27 41, 137
28 133
81–82 69, 74
82–83 69
84–85 75–76
97–98 65, 68
103 41
104–5 125
129 41
132 41
137 41
174 59
213–15 114–119
250 41

Jawāhir al-Qurʾān (ed. Kh. M. Kāmil and ʿI. al-Sharqāwī, Cairo: Maṭbaʿat Dār al-Kutub wa-l-Wathāʾiq al-Qawmiyya, 1432/2011).

84–85 272
95–96 16–17
81 136

al-Maḍnūn al-ṣaghīr (ed. A. al-Bābī al-Ḥalabī, Cairo: al-Maṭbaʿa al-Maymaniyya, 1309 [1891]. Published in a volume together with *Iljām al-ʿawāmm, al-Munqidh min al-ḍalāl*, and *al-Maḍnūn al-kabīr*.)

4 269

Makātīb-yi fārisī = Makātīb-yi fārisī-yi Ghazzālī be-nām-i Fażāʾil al-anām min rasāʾil Ḥujjat al-Islām (ed. ʿA. Iqbāl, Tehran: Kitābfurūsh-i Ibn Sīnā, 1333 [1954])

12 241

Manuscipt London, British Library, Or. 3126

fol. 238a 99

al-Maqṣad al-asnā fī sharḥ maʿānī asmāʾ Allāh al-ḥusnā (ed. F. Shehadi, Beirut: Imprimerie Catholique, 1982).

44 7
47 56
74 13
107 94
137 238
139 94
147–49 25
152 93
165–71 25

Miḥakk al-naẓar fī l-manṭiq (ed. M. B. al-Naʿsānī and M. al-Qabbānī, Cairo: al-Maṭbaʿa al-Adabiyya, w. d. [1925]).

52–55 18

Mishkāt al-anwār (ed. ʿA. ʿI. al-Sayrawān, Beirut: ʿĀlam al-Kutub, 1407/1986).

116–18	272
121–22	231
123	25
123–27	232
124	16
127–28	25
128–30	236
130–33	236
133–34	237
135	237
136–37	238
137–39	240
141	246
142–44	240
144–45	241
145–46	241
146–47	242
148	25
165	247
172	249
172–73	21, 22
175	243
175–82	151–53
177	243
177–83	21–24
180–83	244, 245
183–85	246
184	245, 246
185	3

Mīzān al-ʿamal (ed. M. Ṣabrī al-Kurdī, Cairo: al-Maṭbaʿa al-ʿArabiyya, 1342 [1923]).

14–15	7
25	234
45–47	234
48–49	12
49–50	20
110	5

al-Munqidh min al-ḍalāl (ed. and French trans. F. Jabre, Beirut: Commission libanaise pour la traduction des chefs-d'œuvre, 1969).

10–11	4
12–14	162
15	vii
16	42
18	42
19	100, 244
21–22	285
22–24	40–41, 137
23	43
25	28, 43
26	43, 44
27	44
33	44
41–44	43
45	138
47–48	15

al-Mustaṣfā min ʿilm al-uṣūl (ed. Ḥ. ibn Z. Ḥāfiẓ, 4 vols., Medina [Saudi Arabia]: al-Jāmiʿa al-Islāmiyya – Kulliyyat al-Sharīʿa, 1413 [1992–93]).

1:5	310
1:153	18
3:479–747	24

al-Qisṭās al-mustaqīm (ed. V. Chelhot, Beirut: Dār al-Mashriq, 1986).

94	61, 63, 65
95	24, 65, 67

Shifāʾ al-ghalīl fī bayān al-shubah wa-l-mukhīl wa-masālik al-taʿlīl (ed. Ḥ. al-Kubaysī, Baghdad: Maṭbaʿat al-Irshād, 1971).

160	92
162–63	92

Tahāfut al-falāsifa = The Incoherence of the Philosophers / Tahāfut al-falāsifa (ed. and English trans. M. E. Marmura, 2nd ed., Provo: Brigham Young University Press, 2000).

1–2	42
4–5	42
5	234

5–7 137, 248
6 284
7 285
22 59
25 125
26–27 125
32–33 18
35–36 18
42 74, 83
56 59
175 68
199 83
201–5 120
215–17 121
217–18 122–13
218–220 117, 120, 122–24, 127, 128
219 75
220 124, 128

Works of al-Ghazālī mentioned without being cited with a page reference:

al-Ajwiba al-Ghazāliyya 268, 270, 271
al-Arbaʿīn fī uṣūl al-dīn 56n, 310
Ayyūhā l-walad 258
al-Basīṭ 255–56
al-Durra al-fākhira 260
Fayṣal al-tafriqa 172n, 271
Iḥyāʾ ʾulūm al-dīn xix, 5, 54, 72, 107, 168–71, 254–58, 259, 260, 269–72, 277, 310–29
Iljām al-ʿawāmm ʿan ʿilm al-kalām 27, 172n, 260
al-Imlāʾ fī ishkālāt al-Iḥyāʾ 170–71, 325
al-Iqtiṣād fī l-iʿtiqād 27, 42, 113, 259
Jawāhir al-Qurʾān 257, 270, 271, 272, 277, 310
Khulāṣat al-mukhtasar 255
Kīmyā-yi saʿādat 241n, 257, 310
Lubāb al-Iḥyāʾ 310
al-Maḍnūn bihī ʿalā ghayr ahlihī 265–73
al-Maḍnūn al-ṣaghīr 265, 267–73
Manuscipt, British Library, Or. 3126 172
Maqāṣid al-falāsifa 56n
al-Maqṣad al-asnā 56n, 107, 240
Miḥakk al-naẓar 45
Mishkāt al-anwār 160, 229, 270–72, 277
Miʿyār al-ʿilm 18, 19, 45
Mīzān al-ʿamal 264
al-Munqidh min al-ḍalāl 3, 10, 33, 90, 108, 172n, 216, 259, 304, 323
al-Nafkh wa-l-rūḥ wa-l-taswiya 269, 271, 273
Naṣīḥat al-mulūk 258–60
al-Qisṭās al-mustaqīm 20, 45
al-Risāla al-laduniyya 205
Tahāfut al-falāsifa xii, 32, 33, 113, 115–16, 263–64, 274–77, 287, 292–93
al-Tibr al-masbūk 258
al-Wajīz 174–77, 180–81
al-Wasīṭ 255

Index of Verses in the Qur'an

1:2 85
2:21–22 221
2:26 107
4:1 300
4:37 244
4:174 236
6:2 300
7:29 114
7:59 295
7:185 94
9:45 244
10:101 106
12:22 204
14:4 64
15:26 300
15:28 300
15:33 300
16:93 64
17:85 265
18:47–49 75
18:65 200, 205, 206
18:86 285, 299
21:23 64
21:104 114
23:12–14 97, 300
24:35 20, 197, 199, 202, 229–249
24:39–40 20
28:88 238, 239
30:29 6
30:30 5
32:7–9 300
32:9 265
33:46 236
36:79 114
36:81 114
37:11 300
38:75 300
38:78 238
41:53 93–94, 99
43:22 12
43:31 12
43:87 5–6
45:23 10, 12
50:15 114
50:22 25
53:14 296
54:24 12
55:14 300
64:8 236
81:21 237
85:22 296
112 215, 221

Printed in the United States
By Bookmasters